THE POLITICAL ECONOMY
OF UNDERDEVELOPMENT

THE POLITICAL ECONOMY
OF UNDERDEVELOPMENT

BY

TAMÁS SZENTES

FOURTH, REVISED AND ENLARGED EDITION

AKADÉMIAI KIADÓ, BUDAPEST 1983

Translated by
I. VÉGES

Translation revised by
A. GARDINER

First edition 1971

Second edition 1973

Third, revised and enlarged edition 1976

Fourth, revised and enlarged edition 1983

ISBN 963 05 2891 6

Printed in Hungary

CONTENTS

PREFACE TO THE FIRST EDITION

The first part of this book is in essence a critical survey of the various explanations of "underdevelopment." The inclusion of this part seemed to be appropriate as it offered the author the opportunity of introducing his own views on the subject in confrontation with those just discussed. It also appeared to him useful and necessary for two further considerations, both of them backed up by his own personal experiences in Tanzania.

The *first* is connected with the fact that certain development and growth theories of Western origin so fashionable in developing countries, and especially the implicit assumptions and orthodox economic principles underlying them, have exercised such a great influence even on the most progressive-minded (and socialist-oriented) people, students, teachers and policy-makers with a training background based on these theories, that a different idea can hardly assert itself unless it is clearly confronted with the former in respect of at least such fundamental questions as these: "What is the historical cause and real nature of underdevelopment?" and "What is the way out of underdevelopment?"

It is only by demanding unambiguous and logical answers to these questions from all those explaining "underdevelopment" and offering their advice on its liquidation that it is possible to see clearly into the various theories and show where the practical advice offered by them would lead to. This seems to be the best way of testing the relevance of the various ideas and also of helping the students to select from among them and reconcile thereby the content of their studies with their own, inherited or gained, experiences of colonialism. The critical investigation of theories may also help to make policy-makers aware of the contradiction between their accepting progressive aims and applying at the same time orthodox economic principles.

When two years ago the author started his teaching activity at the University College, Dar es Salaam, he was surprised and distressed at the same time to experience how much his students using standard Western textbooks of economics were inclined to keep repeating the abstract formulas and sterile definitions of these books when discussing even such economic and social phenomena of their own country as were directly perceptible to them. Many of them gave evidence not only of their incapability of a historical approach but also of having doubts—due to the influence of these textbooks—even about their own empirical experiences or

7

the lingering memories of their parents and the older generations. This was all the more surprising since even at that time, or in fact right from the beginning, a great number of progressive-minded teachers were also teaching at the University College, Dar es Salaam, who made every effort to counteract the spirit of these textbooks and aimed at introducing a historical, empiric and progressive approach to the subject. It seems, however, that in teaching even at the university level, the written word commands a much greater effect than the spoken one.

Almost parallel with this phenomenon there was—and still is—another just as striking as the former: the "peaceful co-existence", in principle as well as in practice, of the sharp condemnation of colonialism and the easy acceptance of a type of economics from which the implicit justification or apology of the latter follows.

The *second* consideration and experience is related to the usefulness of dialogue and argument between colleagues of different outlooks and convictions. The University of Dar es Salaam has ensured, on account of its widely international teaching staff, an exceptional opportunity for the exchange of opinions and for debates often heated enough among teachers and researchers with different training backgrounds, political and theoretical-ideological views and experiences. The author thinks that all who have enjoyed this atmosphere in Dar es Salaam will agree with him that an open confrontation of views helps not only to clear up the positions and promote thereby mutual understanding, but also serves to ensure practical cooperation and overcome preconceived ideas. It is usually not the sharpness of criticism but the "conspiracy of silence" that impedes co-operation.

These considerations encouraged the author to take the risk, and perhaps even incur the charge of immodesty, of starting arguments with otherwise highly distinguished and meritorious authors in the critical survey of the first part of his book, hoping, of course, that the reaction of his readers would be determined by the convincing power, or weakness, of his arguments rather than by their biased attitude to the Marxist view.

As far as the main part of his book is concerned, the author's dilemma is this: to what extent has he succeeded in contributing considerably new or more elements to those of the same idea that have already been outlined in a great many Marxist and other progressive works: e.g. to the "simple" and often proved thesis that present-day underdevelopment is the outcome of the international development of capitalism and thus inseparable from it. Though he could not possibly omit, especially after the critical survey, discussing again this question even ascribing to it a special significance, the author tried, on the one hand, to analyse the external, international and at the same time historical factors in a novel aspect as reflected in recent developments and changes, and, on the other hand, to use the analysis of these basic interrelationships only as a starting point and basis for a more

8

detailed examination of the internal mechanism of the "system of underdevelopment". This very starting point and basis enabled and allowed him to draw, in the analysis of this mechanism and structure, on certain partial results of the theories criticized before.

The examination of this mechanism and the trends arising from it go well beyond the sphere of political economy and open into the field of economic policy, demonstrating that the divergencies in the method and approach of analysis result in essential differences between individual ideas on long-term economic policy.

The chapters dealing with economic policy are of a rather limited size in relation to the total volume of the book and especially to the complex character of the problems involved. In addition, they may give the impression that the author has concentrated too much in the long-run on the historical perspective. He hopes, however, that even by this short summarization of his conclusions he will be able to convince most of his readers that rational economic action aimed at overcoming underdevelopment—together with its "tactical", short-term and micro-elements— presupposes the working out of a long-term "strategy" based on the results of a comprehensive analysis.

On the one hand, the author's prepossession suggests that the organic and comprehensive analysis of the external and internal factors and some of its details, as well as a few of the conclusions for a long-term economic policy, constitute some new contributions to the literature of underdevelopment, on the other hand, the author's fear prompts him to think that this very "new" will justly provide a target for criticism and attack.

The author would also like to take advantage of the Preface to acknowledge gratefully his debt to those who, in one way or another, have made it possible for this book to appear. Thus he is indebted to those in particular who, by their suggestions and critical comments on the manuscript of this book or the previous ones constituting its antecedents, offered him invaluable help: Professor J. Bognár, the late Professor I. Vajda, Professors A. Mátyás, J. Nyilas, M. Simai, G. Göncöl and F. Molnár, and other colleagues in Budapest; and also Professor Svendsen, Dr. Seidman and Dr. Arrighi and all those colleagues in Dar es Salaam, the discussion and debates with whom stimulated him to make corrections of, and additions to, the manuscript.

The author is also grateful to his home university in Budapest and the University of Dar es Salaam in particular for making it possible for him to stay in Tanzania for several years, a benefit which has ensured him not only the completion of his work and the very informative confrontation of its hypotheses with a concrete case but has also offered immeasurable inspiration to his research on the practical questions of development policy.

Dar es Salaam, November 1969   *Tamás Szentes*

PREFACE TO THE FOURTH EDITION

When completing the first version of this book I kept in mind the aim of giving into the hands of my African colleagues and students (at that time I was staying in Tanzania) a comprehensive work, a sort of manual which sheds some light on the fundamental differences between the conventional Western approach to the problems of developing countries and the Marxist one, and which by polemizing with the most typical representatives of the former explains—on the basis of the Marxist literature and my own research—"underdevelopment" as the complex product of a certain historical process. The title of the book also indicates this polemy, the confrontation with the "purely economic" approaches. It points to the purposefully underlined relationship between political economy as a whole and its "chapter" concerning the developing countries, i.e. the indivisibility of political economy and its applicability to the Third World, too. Just like the "underdevelopment" of the periphery of international capitalism cannot be explained *per se*, outside the context of the development of the international system of capitalism, the political economy of underdevelopment cannot exist but only as an organic part of the total body of Marxist political economy.

For various reasons (the date of closing the manuscript of the first edition in 1969, the aim and considerations of the polemy, etc.), the book has focussed much more on the role of colonialism and the dominance of the monopoly capital of the centre in the rise of the "system of underdevelopment" (or more precisely of a peripheral capitalist subsystem), on the type of the international division of labour as embodied in the latter, and the peculiar structure of underdeveloped economies and the mechanism stemming from it, than on the shifts in the investment pattern of international monopolies and the emerging new—I would call neo-colonial—system of the international division of labour.

Even apart from the fact that it would certainly be too early to speak about the operation of a new system of the international division of labour of capitalism, since certain signs show its emergence only, while the developing countries are still functioning mostly as primary producers, a book of this type, intending to reveal the roots and spontaneous tendencies of "underdevelopment" as a subsystem, has obviously to put the emphasis on the former questions.

During the seventies, however, a great many and controversial changes took place in international economic relations, including, besides price explosions and monetary disturbances, a world economic crisis which reflects both the disequilibria stemming from the "colonial" pattern of the international division of labour and the anarchistic nature of the redeployment process run by the transnational corporations. A new idea has also emerged and gained acceptance internationally, namely to establish a New International Economic Order, which, by the various principles, claims, and suggested measures it involves, is certainly challenging not only government representatives, diplomats and UN officers, but also scholars interested in development problems and international economic co-operation.

This is the reason why I added an Appendix to the third edition with the aim of summing up briefly the most important changes and new phenomena as well as my views on them. Since then the scope of new events and issues has, of course, further widened, new documents with new statistical data have appeared, etc. However, to expand the Appendix accordingly did not seem feasible, even apart from the concomitant shortcoming and awkwardness caused by the presentation of a complementary analysis outside the inner structure of the book, separating thereby interrelated issues.

In this fourth edition I have incorporated new chapters in the relevant parts of the book, or filled out the given chapters with new findings and fresh statistics and reinvestigated in the light of new facts, new phenomena, new statistical data and new research results, all the basic relations and trends analysed before as well as the tendencies of the changes. This fourth edition is, therefore, a fully revised and further enlarged edition, without an Appendix.

I have no reason, however, to change my views and main theses on the roots, nature and reproduction mechanism of "underdevelopment". On the contrary. Despite the many recent changes in both the international economy and the economy of developing countries, the basic causes, inherent tendencies, consequences and laws of motion of the "underdevelopment" of the dependent periphery of the world capitalist economy have, unfortunately, remained unaltered.

And so I can only repeat what I said in the Preface to the third edition: I wish I could have put all the statements and conclusions into past tense, that the whole diagnosis given in the book were already outdated and the shameful phenomenon called "underdevelopment" were nothing but a topic of past history!

TAMÁS SZENTES

11

PART ONE

THE THEORIES OF "UNDERDEVELOPMENT"
A CRITICAL APPROACH

INTRODUCTION

There are numerous theories of "economic underdevelopment" available. In non-Marxist economic literature they are often referred to as "theories of development" as distinct from the "theories of growth".

No objection can be raised against this terminological distinction as long as it merely reflects the now general *de facto* practice which "honours" the ex-colonial and semi-colonial, dependent countries by attributing to them the euphemistic or polite epithet "developing". (It is, of course, rather strange to use the phrase "developing countries" when this term refers precisely to *the least developing part* of the world economy. Therefore, it would perhaps be much more appropriate to use the phrase "countries mostly in need of development".) In so far, however, as it is the consequence of the theoretical, or perhaps more exactly, ideological consideration which exempts the advanced capitalist countries from the need for "development" involving structural and organizational changes, it is the implicit manifestation of orthodox apologetics. It is true, nevertheless, that this negation implies an affirmative statement in the other direction, i.e. the acknowledgment of the need for structural-organizational changes in the countries that have not yet developed.[1] On the other hand, this distinction of "development" involving structural changes (in relation to the countries not yet developed) from the "growth" (supposed to be continuous and quantitative) of the countries already developed is, or more exactly would be, a more or less true terminological expression of those theories which postulate as a precondition for the transition to "self-sustained growth" some sort of "big push", "take-off" or "critical minimum effort".[2] It is ironical, however, that it is often the very advocates or even authors of such theories who use another terminology.[3]

---

[1] A. O. Hirschman, among others, has adopted this distinction on the grounds that the structural and organizational changes that turn the traditional economy into a modern one, are no longer necessary in the case of advanced industrial countries.

Similarly, A. Bonné holds the view that economic growth is "a self-induced process of economic expansion" characterized, under given and unchanged institutional conditions, by changes in terms of economic parameters, i.e. by quantitative changes, while "economic development" presupposes a "conscious and active promotion", i.e. institutional changes. (See A. Bonné: *Studies in Economic Development.* London, 1957.)

[2] See below.

[3] The title of Leibenstein's book is *Economic Backwardness and Economic Growth*, and that of Rostow's: *The Stages of Economic Growth*. (Their theories will be dealt with later.)

Professor *Jorgenson* differentiates between the theories of "development" and "growth" on the grounds that "in the theory of development emphasis is laid on the balance between capital accumulation and the growth of population, each adjusting to the other. In the theory of growth the balance between investment and saving is all-important and the growth of population is treated as constant or shunted aside as a qualification to the main argument".[4] This explanation, however, is already based on a definite, clearly outlined theory which connects "underdevelopment" with the problem of "population pressure" and "capital shortage". Although, as we shall see later, this view is shared by many, we cannot regard it as general and even less predominant. On the other hand, the terminological inconsistency can be observed in this case, too.

Any distinction between the theories of "development" and "growth" can at best only be accepted for practical reasons (just like the terms "backward", "less developed", "developing" which are used to designate the ex-colonial and semi-colonial countries), however, by no means, as a scientific distinction.

The terminological distinction on a *semantic* basis is unacceptable, because development always and everywhere involves and presupposes the dialectic of quantitative and qualitative changes, of evolution and revolution. And even if a purely quantitative "growth" can be observed in a given place and at a given time within the framework of the existing structure or system, it is not only the consequence of a previous qualitative change but it also inevitably paves the way for a new one. On the other hand, even if the spheres of quantitative and qualitative changes can be distinguished in *space* within a given period, their separation can be justified only if these spheres represent perfectly separate *closed systems*. If this is not the case, if they are connected with each other, or if they are just parts of a superior, synthetic process, their separation makes it simply impossible to understand them, as the quantitative changes taking place in the one sphere affect the qualitative changes taking place in the other, and *vice versa*.

No doubt, the terminological distinction according to *subject* or sometimes *methodology*—as in the case with Jorgenson—has some practical advantages. The theories related to the "underdeveloped" countries can, in fact, be distinguished to some extent from those related to the advanced capitalist or socialist countries. Political economy or "pure" economics is certainly concerned with different *problems* in the case of the "underdeveloped" countries. Consequently, the methods applied will also

---

[4] Quoted by F. Paukert in The Place of the Traditional Sector in Economic Development. *Lectures on Economic Development.* International Institute for Labour Studies. Geneva, 1962, p. 43.

16

differ. At this point, however, the questions arise: (a) what are these problems, and (b) what is understood by this difference?

The answer to the question depends on the concept, the interpretation of "underdevelopment", and, as we shall see, a uniform opinion can hardly be expected. But the answer to question (b), the assessment of the measure of difference, is based much more on an *a priori* judgement than on empirical experience. Consequently, it might be used equally as an argument in favour of the need to work out a completely new, "custom-tailored" theory for the "underdeveloped" countries, breaking with the theory for the developed countries, and as a justification for merely replacing some bricks in, or adding a new wing to, the building of the theory already in existence. One might infer from the answers either a *complete rejection* of the inherited *methodology* or only a revision or limited application of *certain* methods.

Without doubt, the emphasis on the differences in the methodology to be applied may conceal (as is presumably the case with Joan Robinson) the progressive efforts to get rid of the fetters of orthodox economics. Many suggest returning to the methods of the classical economists, and the view seems to be spreading that the economic theory of "underdeveloped" countries should be a wide-based, socio-political economy built on classical traditions, instead of the narrowed-down and, in our opinion, false "pure" economics.

Here, however, two points have to be made. The *first* is really a question: If "pure" economics and orthodox methodology prove insufficient or inadequate for the "underdeveloped" countries, what justifies their being kept for the advanced capitalist countries? Is it perhaps the negation of qualitative, structural-institutional changes or the naive belief in a mere quantitative growth?!

The *other* point is meant to call attention to a danger. However progressive the return to classical political economy and the revision of orthodox methodology might appear, the theory of "economic underdevelopment" or, if you wish, the theory of "development", may easily lead to a misinterpretation of "underdevelopment", to a sort of apologetics,[5] when separated from the general theory of economic development. The phenomena of the "underdeveloped" world cannot be fully understood without disclosing the phenomena of the "developed" world, and indeed, the interpretation of "underdevelopment" itself is greatly dependent on the evaluation of the development of the advanced countries. The laws of motion of "underdevelopment" are much more widely and deeply rooted than the actual sphere of "underdevelopment" in a given place and at a given time. Therefore, the interpretation of "underdevelopment" must

---

[5] Which does not contradict the fact that it is often the works dealing with the general and universal laws of the development of the whole world, e.g. Rostow's, that represent the highest degree of apologetics.

necessarily include a *historical* and *external* element which is organically inherent not only in "underdevelopment" but also in "development".[6]

Consequently, the political economy of "underdevelopment" cannot be but a single chapter in the whole, i.e. an *organic part* of the general political economy, the basic science of socio-economic development. In order to understand the state of the "underdeveloped" countries, it is necessary to understand the state and historical development of the whole world economy and society as well!

*

As we can see we have strayed a long way from the original problem of terminology. Indeed, the terminological inconsistency even provided us with the opportunity to examine the underlying gnosiological questions that offer a certain framework—however broad it might be—for theoretical interpretations and explanations.

It is time now to start analysing the various interpretations of "underdevelopment" and without attaching a more than practical significance to the matter of terminology,[7] outlining the most important— or at least the most typical—theories.

We do not intend to give an exhaustive account of individual theories and even less the works of individual authors. If the present study were judged on this basis, it would prove highly deficient. But we have not undertaken to write a history of the development of economic thought, or to compile chapters for a small encyclopedia of the history of economic theories. This critical chapter has as its *sole aim* that of clearing the way for an approach to be evolved in the following chapters. Clearing the way in a negative and positive sense.

The preparation will be *negative* in the sense that we shall try to point out just why and to what extent these various theories *cannot* offer a comprehensive and acceptable explanation of "underdevelopment". From this point of view, it is not the question whether the factors and relationships revealed in the theory under discussion play a role or not in the "phylogeny" of "underdevelopment". The answer to this is, of course, related to the conception itself, but at the same time it is also related to *history*. History, after all, is the most important yardstick and test of the validity of the theories of social sciences. All that can and *must* be expected of these

[6] The dialectic relationship of the "part" and the "whole", and within the whole, of the "centre" and the "periphery" is not given perhaps in any underdevelopment theory such a tangible treatment as in Andre Gunder Frank's explanation. (*Capitalism and Underdevelopment in Latin America: Historical Studies of Chile and Brazil*. New York, Monthly Review Press, 1967.)

[7] In the following, the terms "backward", "less-developed", "underdeveloped", "developing", etc. and "development", "progress", etc. respectively, will be given as synonyms, mostly without quotation marks.

18

theories, above and beyond *historical verification*, is only *logical consistency*.[8]

The fact that what we call "underdevelopment" is a historical product is only denied or ignored by those inclined to take everything for granted and to draw conclusions for the laws of the struggle between Man and Nature from the case of Robinson Crusoe (leaving out of account, of course, the origin of Robinson's skills, weapons and tools) rather than from the undoubtedly more strenuous study of the history of human society. They are the types who prefer drawing and analysing preference curves about the behaviour of the African or New Guinean farmer to examining *why* and *how* his behaviour came to be as it is now. They are those who prefer concentrating on the sale of cocoa already produced to questioning *why* people grow cocoa instead of anything else and how they started growing it. Such economists are always led, of course, by practical considerations. It is they who, instead of turning to the "wasteful pleasure of studying the past", are engaged in analysing the "bread-and-butter" tasks of the present. "It is no use", they say "studying the past and the historical causes of underdevelopment when it is before our eyes, and when we can compare it with the state of the developed countries, can see the differences and the problems, and can set about solving them". The "positive pragmatism" of these people assures them a sort of immunity.

There is only one slip in their way of thinking. They forget that it is impossible to bring about a *deliberate and purposeful change in the present without knowing how this present state came about*. We can't successfully fight any phenomenon without knowing its roots! Descriptions, surveys or even preference graphs may be useful in assessing the *measure* of the phenomenon in question, but they don't tell us anything about its causes and so, in consequence, they are unsuitable for any practical policy of change.

Substituting any description of the surface phenomena of underdevelopment for a theory of underdevelopment is totally unacceptable. Only a historical explanation, a historically verifiable theory is good enough. It is just the *most practical policy* of liquidating underdevelopment which needs such a historical explanation! Whether a given policy and the underlying theory is correct or not will finally be decided, of course, only by future events, by the history to come. This is the final historical verification! Any prediction, however, as to whether future history will or will not verify the policy of the present and its underlying theory can be made only on the basis of the knowledge to what extent this policy and theory are based upon the historical lessons of development from the past to the present.

And as for the undoubtedly very pointed question whether the theories to be discussed here provide a historically verifiable explanation of the

[8] It is these two, by the way, which Marxist authors usually call the requirement of "historico-logical unity".

2*

19

emergence of underdevelopment, the question seems to be tautological and undetermined as the answer depends on *what we mean by "underdevelopment"*. Is it merely the relative difference between the developed and underdeveloped countries (and, if so, in terms of what units of measurement); is it an aggregate of certain phenomena deemed characteristic (and, if so, by what principles are these characteristics selected); do we mean a particular form of motion (and, if so, what is the basis of this form of motion, and how does it differ from others); or is it a complex system, a structure (and, if so, what makes it a system and what ensures its persistence)? As we shall see, all these and many other interpretations of underdevelopment do exist. Therefore, the content of the question would also change, depending on the interpretation itself. And if we substituted our own interpretation, any comparison with other theories would become not only subjective and meaningless but also impossible. Answers to questions of different content cannot be compared, after all.[9]

But does the question not have indeed such a common denominator which is independent of the individual interpretation? We think it has. And it is not the acceptance, but rather the rejection of this denominator, which is dependent on arbitrary subjectivism. To be more explicit: underdevelopment as the state of a more or less similarly defined part of the world ought to be interpreted not as a random set of subjectively selected phenomena, i.e. not only as the characteristics of *certain* sectors of the economy and society, but as a *whole*, as a qualifiable entity. Consequently, it is not the existence and development of *certain* heterogeneous phenomena which are to be explained historically, but the heterogeneous whole! Moreover, it is the heterogeneity itself! According to the theory accepted, the explanation, e.g. of the traditional economic elements or the export-oriented monocultural sector, may be different. Both are generally accepted phenomena. But the fact that both of these in their side-by-side existence— together with a number of other phenomena—are to be explained is already an objective requirement that is independent of the theory in question. The existence or lack of this explanation, its historical adequacy or inadequacy provides the possibility for comparing and evaluating the various theories.

The theories to be discussed will often be presented here not in their original individual forms, as worked out by their authors, but, as if receiving an independent life, in their Pygmalion-like forms. On the one hand, they will be made to answer the basic question raised even if one or the other author put the question in a different way. On the other hand, we shall often make logical inferences from the theory under discussion beyond what the author had done in order to better elucidate the answer to the question. This method may seem arbitrary but can be defended on several counts: (1) Most

---

[9] The same problem often crops up, by the way, when e.g. certain theses of Marxist political economy and Western orthodox economics are confronted.

theories, with a few exceptions, cannot be attributed to one single author. (2) Even supposing that the author put the question differently and concentrated on other problems with a different aim in view, however, if his approach claims to be a theory of underdevelopment, or is used by others as an explanation of underdevelopment, then historical verification is justly called for! (3) The logical consistency of a theory can be measured exactly by the logical extending of thought in both directions.

The present chapter is devoted to the critical evaluation of theories intended or used by others, to explain underdevelopment. But it is not meant to be a criticism of the authors or schools unless the author presents it—as he sometimes does—*expressly* so and in no other way as an explanation of underdevelopment.

It is, however, not only in a negative way that this chapter supports the statements of the following chapters but—as has already been mentioned—it does so in a *positive way*, too. Of the theories under discussion quite a few provide partial explanations (and sometimes very good ones too!) for certain partial problems. Hence, while, in our opinion at least, they are on the one hand unacceptable *as* explanations of underdevelopment, they are, on the other, very useful for understanding certain partial phenomena. Consequently, we shall return or refer to some of them in the subsequent chapters, and in this way they will become positive elements of a different explanation.

*

Although an impressive amount of international literature has already been developed on the problems of underdevelopment, this literature is of relatively *recent origin*. This is mainly due to the fact that as long as the colonial system did not collapse and the economic growth of the newly independent countries did not become a problem of the world economy and its solution a "mass demand" of world policy, economics was not induced to carry on research in this sphere.

As regards Western, non-Marxist economics, it had dealt with these questions previously, too, but earlier research was more concerned with backward regions of already developed capitalist countries and/or some less developed European countries, and it failed to produce new ideas or theories of underdevelopment. Indeed, they did not even add any original chapters to the general theory. The colonial and semi-colonial countries as subsidiaries of the "mother" countries did not represent a distinct economic or, more exactly, a national economic problem. If such a problem did crop up at all, it was mostly confined to the question of the exploitation of raw materials—of course, from the aspect of the "mother country's" national economy—or to the question of the efficiency of the exported capital as a problem of micro-economic, business level. The role of the colonies in the international division of labour was dealt with—if at all—as a question of detail within the general theories of international trade.

21

As regards Marxism, it has always considered the colonial system—and capitalism itself—as a transitional historical formation, and analysed it accordingly. Lenin, by further developing Marx's research on colonialism, gave a comprehensive analysis and criticism of imperialism. He threw light on the role of colonial and semi-colonial countries in the international division of labour and pointed out the joint interest of the colonial liberation movements and international labour movements. He also dealt, in practice as well as in theory, with a concrete case: the further development of an economically backward country; he tackled the problem of how to overcome underdevelopment in the young Soviet State liberated by the socialist revolution.

However, the dogmatic-schematic trend which arose in later years and prevailed for a period—mainly in the forties and early fifties—hampered the scientific analysis of the changing world capitalist system, simplified the critique of colonialism by investigating it from a one-sided point of view, and evaluated the problem of colonial liberation merely from the aspect of the "reserves" of the socialist revolution. Moreover, it took proletarian revolutions as *direct* preconditions for the liberation of the colonies and regarded their further post-colonial development as the natural and necessary repetition (i.e. imitation) of the pattern of development of the first socialist countries in all details. Only after this dogmatic-schematic trend had been got rid of could scientific Marxist research resume the analysis of the changes and new phenomena of world capitalism.

Thus scientific analysis lost contact with development and lagged behind the changes of the historical scene just in the critical period, that is at the time of the rapid post-war changes and development. It could not even start to cope with its tasks, either because its sphere of interest lay elsewhere, as in the case of the non-Marxist economics of the West, or because in the hours of the dogmatic disease it temporarily lost its sensitivity and its capacity for quick responses, as in the case of Marxism. So it came about that practical demands that emerged suddenly such as—the working out of the aid policy of international organizations, economic advice to be given to the new states, the re-examination of international trade and credit conditions in the light of the problems of developing countries, etc.—compelled the science of economics to give quick but not sufficiently well-founded answers to the questions of backwardness that were suitable only for immediate purposes and short-term economic decisions. This accounts, at least partly, for the fact that on the one hand the approximate categorization of countries and the determination of "underdevelopment" and its measure and proportion on the basis of statistical indices came to the foreground whilst on the other hand the brakes and impediments to economic development were specified and described.[10] The former aimed at determining the criteria for classifying

[10] François Perroux clearly differentiates between the two in his article: Blocages et freinages de la croissance et du développement. *Tiers Monde*, April–June, 1966.

a country as underdeveloped, the latter at delineating the factors that economic policy has to reckon with. For this purpose statistical measurement and comparisons, as well as the description of phenomena were more or less appropriate methods. (In other branches of science research also begins with describing, measuring and categorizing.) This method, however, must come in for criticism if and when statistical indices and the comparisons made on their basis are supposed to make up a theory of the criteria of underdevelopment, and/or if the description of some surface phenomena or the summing up of even less superficial impediments to development are conceived of as a theory of the causes of under-development.

This trend has become fairly widespread and has left its typical mark upon a substantial part of the literature of underdevelopment.

On the other hand, it could not become dominant in Marxist literature since Marxism has always offered a *historical* explanation for the causes of underdevelopment, though it had its effect on Marxist research, too. This happened perhaps because the historical answer, the criticism of imperialism was a *too historico-philosophical* answer. In addition, it became oversimplified and so irrelevant just at the critical time when concrete solutions were needed for practical situations. In this way the methods of approach and the terminology[11] applied by Western orthodox economics also began to spread in Marxist economic literature. A certain contradiction began to build up[12] between the application of these methods and terminology on the one hand, and the criticism of imperialism on the other. It could (and can) only be resolved by a more thorough theoretical analysis of the practical problems, as well as by critically re-examining and elucidating the methodology and terminology on a theoretical level. The criticism of imperialism must likewise be made more complex, dialectical and realistic, thereby becoming more effective and more faithful to the Marxist-Leninist concept.

[11] As also the terms already mentioned: "less-developed", "backward", "developing country".

[12] In such questions as (a) the summary condemnation of foreign capital when criticizing imperialism in general, while emphasizing at the same time the capital shortage and the necessity of foreign capital imports in the context of practical economic policy; (b) the condemnation of the exploitation of raw materials and agricultural products in the criticism of colonialism, and, at the same time, talking about the difficulties in marketing primary products from the point of view of practical economic policy; (c) a strong criticism of foreign aid and loan policy, together with the demand for increasing them; (d) emphasizing the harmful effects of increased capital inflow through the draining off of capital and the profit repatriation, and the recognition of difficulties arising from the withdrawal of foreign private capital; (e) attacking the influence of colonial officials and experts, and complaining about the crisis caused by their withdrawal, etc.

CHAPTER I

CLASSIFICATION OF UNDERDEVELOPED COUNTRIES ON THE BASIS OF STATISTICAL INDICES

The definition of underdevelopment by *statistical index numbers* is a method of rather universal application even today. It can be met with particularly in works of a less theoretical character, or as a starting point for certain interpretations (e.g. in some vicious circle theories, as we shall see later). It prevails mainly in the documents of international organizations. Nobody can deny the importance of comparisons made on the basis of statistical indices nor that of measuring differences in the level of development of *productive forces* from the aspect of both world and national economy. On the other hand, the determination of a complex socio-economic—and at the same time a world economic—phenomenon by means of statistical indices may lead to very superficial or even false results and does not reveal the real causes of the phenomenon. Hence, if the question is raised from a theoretical aspect rather than from the practical aspect of a short-term economic policy, this starting point is of no avail, and the theories based on it are of even less use.

The first problem to be tackled is what statistical indices or combinations of indices should be chosen? The most usual index applied is the *national income per capita*[1] (or the per capita gross national product).

However, this index is not even appropriate for establishing real differences in the level of development without ambiguity and can only be used to demonstrate a given static situation. The calculations of the American economists, *Myers* and *Harbison*[2] show that the difference in level estimated on the basis of the per capita gross national product of the most developed and the most underdeveloped groups of countries amounts to only about one third of the difference that exists in the development of

[1] It is also very hard to find a valid yardstick. It is much easier to list the countries *generally regarded* or accepted as backward than to specify the order of magnitude of a statistical index number, say, per capita national income, which draws a clear dividing line. Shall it be 100, 200, 300 or 500 dollars? According to Benjamin Higgins: "In general, underdeveloped countries in this sense are those with per capita incomes less than one-quarter those of the United States, or roughly, less than $ 500 per year." But he adds: "The choice of 25 per cent of the United States level as the per capita income dividing advanced from underdeveloped countries is, of course, somewhat arbitrary. It can be justified in terms of policy, but it is harder to defend in terms of pure analysis." (B. Higgins: *Economic Development*. W. W. Norton and Co., New York, 1959, pp. 6, 8.)

[2] F. Harbison and Ch. A. Myers: *Education, Manpower and Economic Growth*. New York, 1964.

"human resources" (i.e. the "production" of skilled personnel). However, in the growth of modern economy "human resources" are of increased importance, and their development is even more significant than that of those investments which are considered "economic" in the strict sense of the word. And what about the scientific capacities of still more striking importance whose distribution between the developed and underdeveloped countries is even far more extreme?! It is true that there is some correlation[3] between the level of national income on the one hand and education, vocational training and scientific capacities on the other, but this balance has always been upset where and when centrally guided large-scale re-allocation and concentrated utilization of the national income was preliminary to, and concomitant with, rapid development.

The index of per capita national income is inconsistent with a dynamic approach. It glosses over the conditions of the production, distribution and utilization of the national income—i.e. the very factors that are of decisive importance from the point of view of the internal possibilities and limitations of development under what production relations and in what social and economic sectors and branches the national income is produced, who gets hold of it, and for what purposes is it utilized.

In addition, the calculation of this index is particularly difficult in the most backward countries as it comes up against almost insuperable difficulties in the assessment and evaluation of the output of the traditional subsistence sector, and often there are only unreliable census data at hand.

As *Myint* points out, "owing to imperfections in basic statistics in calculating both the total national income and the total population, the per capita income figures for many underdeveloped countries are still very crude and liable to wide margins of error... Low income per capita, however important, is only one aspect of the complex problem of underdevelopment and a definition of the underdeveloped countries relying solely on the per capita income criterion is bound to be arbitrary".[4]

Some authors make use of other statistical index numbers instead of or complementarily to the GNP index. For example, S. J. Patel[5] makes comparisons between the per capita production of certain sectors and economic branches and includes besides the growth rate[6] of per capita

---

[3] Tinbergen and Boss have performed such calculations. (J. Tinbergen and H. C. Boss: La demande globale en matière d'enseignement secondaire et supérieur des pays sous-développés en cours de la prochaine décenie. *Conférence de Washington, 16–20 Oct. 1961.* OCDE 1962, Paris IV.)

[4] H. Myint: *The Economics of the Developing Countries.* Hutchinson of London, 1964, p. 10.

[5] S. J. Patel: The Economic Distance between Nations: its Origin, Measurement and Outlook. *The Economic Journal*, No. 293, London, 1964.

[6] Concerning the rate of growth, H. Myint remarks: "The fact that the underdeveloped countries have lower income levels does not necessarily mean that they also have a lower rate of growth in incomes." (H. Myint: Op. cit., p. 11.)

income in the determination of differences. By so doing he tries to illustrate underdevelopment in its dynamics. *Rosenstein-Rodan* works on similar lines in comparing the average rates of income and population growth of developed and underdeveloped countries in the past 150 years.[7]

As comparisons they are very interesting and informative and are doubtless more precise than the previous ones; but they do not bring us much closer to the causes of underdevelopment. The same applies to classifications made on the basis of, or with the help of, indices such as the percentage of the agricultural population, or the structure of employment, or those of the living standard, e.g., per capita calorie consumption.

All these indices connect phenomena of very different origin and motion to one another, and on whatever basis we may choose and combine them, categorization on the strength of them will always rely on *quantitative criteria:* they do not point out qualitative similarities and differences. A classification made on the basis of these indices may put countries with completely different motives and limiting forces of development in the same category. Using the level of per capita national income as the exclusive basis for categorization, some oil-countries e.g. will be classified as belonging to the developed countries' group, while countries in which radical socio-economic changes have taken place may fall into the same category of backward or underdeveloped countries as others with an obsolete, rigid and stagnant social system. These classifications reflect the actual levels of the *productive forces* at a given time but conceal the essential differences in *production and social relations*[8] between developed capitalist and socialist countries just as between developed capitalist and underdeveloped countries, and do not reveal differences in their relation to the world economy either. Therefore, they not only cannot offer any real explanation for underdevelopment or even a substitute for it, but they even take us farther away from the understanding of the true causes of underdevelopment.

[7] P. N. Rosenstein-Rodan: Les besoins des capitaux dans les pays sous-développés. *Économie appliquée*, I–IV, 1954.

[8] Ignacy Sachs writes: "All the averages per head of population conceal sharp differences in class distribution and regional distribution of the income." (I. Sachs: *Patterns of Public Sector in Underdeveloped Economies.* Asia Publishing House, 1964, p. 2, footnote 3.)

CHAPTER II

UNDERDEVELOPMENT AS THE AGGREGATE OF CERTAIN CRITERIA AND LIMITING FACTORS

A rather popular variety of underdevelopment theory offers an explanation of underdevelopment by means of a summary of certain "typical" features or factors hindering or limiting development. This usually specifies the "typical" features and limiting factors by comparing the given "static" state of the most developed capitalist countries—together with a number of surface phenomena—with the similarly "static" state of the underdeveloped countries—also together with a number of surface phenomena.[1] What, as a result of the comparison, appears as a "plus" or "minus" for the underdeveloped countries, constitutes the aggregate of deficiencies or limiting factors that makes up the definition of underdevelopment.

This subtraction approach—or "ideal typical index approach" (as it is called by *A. G. Frank*[2]), or *"gap approach"* (named by *Charles Kindleberger*) is so popular and general, indeed, that it can be found even with such economists who, as *Leibenstein,*[3] go beyond a summarized description and specification of these factors and their superficial interrelationships and demonstrate underdevelopment as a peculiar qualitative "form of motion" or, more exactly, a "system" and not just a relative phenomenon. In other words, this approach is often a starting point also for theories *concentrating* on relationships between the factors.[4] On the other hand, it also offers some support for certain "historical" explanations,[5] and may serve those "historical" conceptions which interpret underdevelopment as an original (or at least earlier) general state from which the natural way of development leads towards the ideal type of the opposite pole. It is also utilized in those theories which, in compliance with or independently of the already

---

[1] This confrontation remains a comparison of "static states" even if it happens to include some dynamic factors (such as the rate of population growth, the rate of accumulation, etc.) as it compares a movement or stagnation observed within a certain period of time with a movement or stagnation again within a certain period of time, i.e. the two states or movements related to each other is a static and not a dynamic relationship. This shows at the same time the unhistorical character of the comparison.

[2] A. G. Frank: Sociology of Development and Underdevelopment of Sociology. *Catalyst*, No. 3, University of Buffalo, 1967.

[3] H. Leibenstein: *Economic Backwardness and Economic Growth.* New York, 1957.

[4] See the critique of the concepts of the "vicious circle", "quasi-stable equilibrium system", etc.

[5] See W. Rostow's theory to be discussed later.

mentioned "historical" approaches, concentrate on the sociological and psychological differences and identify the state of underdevelopment with a closed, stagnant, traditional society.

Thus the "subtraction approach" may gain independence as a separate underdevelopment theory or it may serve as an introduction to other, more complex interpretations. In the former case, like the theory of deficiencies and limiting factors, it is completely false in itself; in the latter case it may turn out false depending on the superimposed theories, though it is originally liable to the possibility of misrepresentation.[6]

Let us examine it first as an independent theory, as a separate interpretation of underdevelopment. It exists in a great number of varieties. It seems that the number of factors considered characteristic or determinant may be added to at will. This is, of course, only the natural result of lifting them out of the real historical context[7] and basic causal relationships.[8] On the other hand, and as a consequence, the characteristics (or limiting factors) of a different number and nature often include very superficial phenomena, or such as would require further explanation. Many of the enumerated characteristics would not prove to be generally common in the underdeveloped world if the latter were classified by qualitative criteria. *Leibenstein*, whose list is perhaps the most comprehensive, considers the following to be the characteristics of underdeveloped countries.[9]

1. Economic

(a) General

(1) A very high proportion of the population in agriculture, usually some 70 to 90 per cent.

(2) "Absolute over-population" in agriculture, that is, it would be possible to reduce the number of workers in agriculture and still obtain the same total output.

(3) Evidence of considerable "disguised unemployment" and lack of employment opportunities outside agriculture.

---

6 It can be regarded—in my opinion—as acceptable only if and in as much as it serves *in concreto* and directly the international comparison of the existence and measure of the factor in question, and not the explanation of underdevelopment as an entity. Moreover, it is acceptable as a prologue, as a preliminary illustration of the phenomenon to be explained for drawing the reader's attention to it and making him aware of the gravity of the problem.

7 H. Leibenstein—though admitting that the explanation of differences in per capita income is as much a historical problem as an analytical one—holds the opinion that "in view of the framework of ignorance" (concerning the economic history of each of the countries under consideration) "within which we are forced to work, it would certainly be convenient if we could frame our problem in such a way as to take the intellectual question out of its historical context". (H. Leibenstein: Op. cit., p. 3.)

8 "It is easy enough to list distinguishing characteristics of underdeveloped countries. Unfortunately, our hopes of isolating causal relationships in this way have not been fulfilled. For each of the characteristics has a hen-and-egg nature that makes it virtually impossible to separate causes from effects," says Benjamin Higgins. In: *Economic Development*. W. W. Norton and Co., New York, 1959, p. 23.

9 H. Leibenstein: Op. cit., pp. 40–41.

(4) Very little capital per head.

(5) Low income per head and, as a consequence, existence near the "subsistence" level.

(6) Practically zero savings for the large mass of the people.

(7) Whatever savings do exist are usually achieved by a landholding class whose values are not conducive to investment in industry or commerce.

(8) The primary industries, that is, agriculture, forestry, and mining, are usually the residual employment categories.

(9) The output in agriculture is made up mostly of cereals and primary raw materials, with relatively low output of protein foods. The reason for this is the conversion ratio between cereals and meat products; that is, if one acre of cereals produces a certain number of calories, it would take between five to seven acres to produce the same number of calories if meat products were produced.

(10) Major proportion of expenditures on food and necessities.

(11) Export of foodstuffs and raw materials.

(12) Low volume of trade per capita.

(13) Poor credit facilities and poor marketing facilities.

(14) Poor housing.

(b) Basic characteristics in agriculture

(1) Although there is low capitalization on the land, there is simultaneously an uneconomic use of whatever capital exists due to the small size of holdings and the existence of exceedingly small plots.

(2) The level of agrarian techniques is exceedingly low, and tools and equipment are limited and primitive in nature.

(3) Even where there are big landowners as, for instance, in certain parts of India, the openings for modernized agricultural production for sale are limited by difficulties of transport and the absence of an efficient demand in the local market. It is significant that in many backward countries a modernized type of agriculture is confined to production for sale in foreign markets.

(4) There is an inability of the small landholders and peasants to weather even a short-term crisis, and, as a consequence, attempts are made to get the highest possible yields from the soil, which leads to soil depletion.

(5) There is a widespread prevalence of high indebtedness relative to assets and income.

(6) The methods of production for the domestic market are generally old-fashioned and inefficient, leaving little surplus for marketing. This is usually true irrespective of whether or not the cultivator owns the land, has tenancy rights, or is a sharecropper.

(7) A most pervasive aspect is a feeling of land hunger due to the exceedingly small size of holdings and small diversified plots. The reason for this is that holdings are continually subdivided as the population on the land increases.

2. Demographic

(1) High fertility rates, usually above 40 per thousand.

(2) High mortality rates and low expectation of life at birth.

(3) Inadequate nutrition and dietary deficiencies.

(4) Rudimentary hygiene, public health, and sanitation.

(5) Rural overcrowding.

3. Cultural and Political

(1) Rudimentary education and usually a high degree of illiteracy among most of the people.

(2) Extensive prevalence of child labour.

(3) General weakness or absence of the middle class.

(4) Inferiority of women's status and position.

(5) Traditionally determined behaviour for the bulk of the populace.

4. Technological and Miscellaneous

(1) Low yields per acre.

(2) No training facilities or inadequate facilities for the training of technicians, engineers, etc.

(3) Inadequate and crude communication and transportation facilities, especially in the rural areas.

(4) Crude technology.

Leibenstein tries to create a logical order in the multitude of characteristics by dividing them into two main categories: into income-determining characteristics (e.g. capital per head, credit facilities, entrepreneurial ability, technical knowledge), and income-determined characteristics (e.g. standard of living, indebtedness, housing, nutrition, etc.). He further distinguishes those characteristics which cannot be explained "in terms of our simple production, consumption, and savings functions". In spite of this, however, the system of his characteristics remains basically arbitrary, unordered, heterogeneous,[10] and even contradictory. Many of the characteristics are already in themselves inexactly formulated and difficult to define (e.g. "poor", "crude", "rudimentary", "exceedingly low", "very little") or they are just overemphasized and exaggerated (e.g. "rural overcrowding", "lack of employment opportunities outside agriculture"). Many characteristics cannot be accepted as general for all or even the majority of the underdeveloped countries. What meaning can be attached e.g. to the aforementioned "rural overcrowding" in a number of sparsely populated regions of Africa, the Near East or Latin America? The interpretation of the terms "absolute overpopulation" and "disguised unemployment" is also debatable on theoretical grounds,[11] and in practice these problems are too complex to be just simply stated. There are several indices among the characteristics whose relative size and trend of change rather than their absolute size, low or high value, must be regarded as crucial. It is true, the high mortality rate is really characteristic and tragic, and therefore demands further effective measures, yet—as Leibenstein himself points out later[12]— it is the divergence of the mortality and fertility rates that constitutes the acute problem, and indeed, to a certain extent, the obstacle to any further decrease in the mortality rate. The low volume of trade per capita is certainly typical of most underdeveloped countries, but at the same time, the comparatively high volume of *foreign* trade per capita in relation to the volume of per capita national income is contradictory and requires

[10] As B. Higgins remarks: "Leibenstein's 'characteristics' are of three different kinds: statistical facts, general observations, and conclusions from analysis." (Op. cit., p. 13.)

[11] See G. Haberler: Critical Observations on Some Current Notions in the Theory of Economic Development. *L'Industria*, No. 2, 1957.—R. Nurkse: Excess Population and Capital Construction. *Malayan Economic Review*, Oct. 1957.

[12] Op. cit., pp. 56–57 and 190–191.

explanation. Similarly, the contradictions inherent in the real essence of underdevelopment are conspicuous even among Leibenstein's characteristics, making the combined list itself contradictory. Thus, no orthodox production, consumption and savings functions can explain the contradiction between the "low volume of trade per capita" and the "major proportion of expenditures on food and necessities" on the one hand, and the "export of foodstuffs and raw materials" on the other. Nor do they explain why the "low capitalization on the land", the "uneconomic use of capital", the "existence of exceedingly small plots", "little surplus for marketing", and *at the same time* "a modernized type of agriculture confined to production for sale in foreign markets" are characteristic of underdevelopment. To explain these obvious and striking contradictions it is not sufficient "to take the intellectual question out of its historical context".

Less detailed but similarly mixed and heterogeneous lists of underdevelopment characteristics are also given by *A. Sauvy* and *É. Gannagé.*

A. Sauvy attributes the following characteristics to underdevelopment: (1) high mortality rate and short life expectancy; (2) high fertility without birth control; (3) poor nutrition; (4) high proportion of illiteracy; (5) lack of full employment owing to insufficient capital supply; (6) strong predominance of agriculture and fishery over the processing industries; (7) low social status of women and child labour; (8) insufficient development of the middle classes; (9) authoritarian political regimes; (10) lack of democratic institutions.[13]

Thus Sauvy lists first among the characteristics of underdeveloped countries the high death and high birth rate. Originally, this was, indeed, characteristic of the traditional, more exactly, precapitalist societies. Today, however, the divergence of the two rates can no longer be explained by the nature and relations of the traditional societies.

As far as Sauvy's other characteristics are concerned, they reveal the justifiable endeavour to account for underdevelopment not only by economic but also social, cultural and political factors, but there is already a certain amount of confusion about the nature and relationships of these factors. Thus factors 3 and 4 and even 7 can be easily explained (just as 1 and 2) on the basis of traditional social relations, while the problems concerning employment and capital supply (5) as well as the structure of the economy (6)—the latter is characterized rather inaccurately without specifying what kind of agriculture is meant by it—already indicate capitalist *commodity-production* relations. Criteria 9 and 10 reflect, at first glance, the peculiarities of traditional societies, but the Arab or Asian feudal relations and the traditional communal system of certain Tropical-African tribes cannot be evaluated on the same basis. On the other hand, the lack of democratic

[13] A. Sauvy: *Théorie générale de la population.* Vol. I. Paris, 1956, pp. 241–242.

institutions may be a characteristic of modern regimes too, and it is not clear either to what extent any evaluation is possible merely on the basis of the formal existence or non-existence of certain institutions.

Thus it seems that Sauvy's criteria, even covering as they do mostly surface phenomena, contain very heterogeneous elements and can hardly be included in a uniform system of causal relationships.

É. Gannagé, too, puts a demographic factor, high birth rate, first among the criteria of underdevelopment.[14] Its consequence, high population growth, is, in his opinion, one of the main obstacles to development. His system of criteria is similar to Sauvy's in that it also involves *both* economic and social factors, and these factors are the elements of highly different rank and nature of different causal relationships. His further criteria are: (2) predominance of agriculture and mining; (3) capital shortage; (4) unbalanced and rigid social structure; (5) insistence on traditions; (6) passive attitude of the population towards necessary changes. Here again certain factors (e.g. 1, 5, and 6) refer to traditional societies, others (e.g. 2 and 3) to capitalist ones. But Gannagé also sheds some light on relationships, investigating the coming into existence of opposite poles, the emergence of a dual structure, various vicious circles (to be discussed later), and also certain international relations.

But instead of going into the lists of characteristics by other authors, let us select the factors considered to be the most characteristic and frequently occurring in the underdevelopment theories and examine to what extent they offer a historically and logically acceptable and consistent explanation for the substance of underdevelopment. Many authors would, presumably, protest against such an isolation of factors, saying that they provide an explanation of underdevelopment only in conjunction with others. But the lists of factors—as we have seen—are rather arbitrary and can be lengthened or shortened at will. If the factors are related at all and are not combined at random, there must be some connection between them. If this relationship is causal, i.e. where one factor determines the other, then it is fully justified to examine them one by one and ask to what extent they can be considered as causes or effects. If, however, the relationship among them is circularly mutual, as supposed by most authors,[15] then in the following we shall treat it as a separate conception.[16]

---

[14] É. Gannagé: *Économie du développement*. Paris, 1962.

[15] "If A, B and C are obstacles that are related in such a way that there is no way of overcoming them one by one, since all of them change as anyone of them is tampered with, there is no way of determining that one is much more important than the others." (H. Leibenstein: Op. cit., p. 55.)

[16] For details, see Part One, Chapter III.

1. THE LESS ADVANTAGEOUS DEMOGRAPHIC POSITION

This is one of the factors most commonly referred to in any explanation of underdevelopment. It is included, as we have seen, in Leibenstein's combined lists, and ranks first among Sauvy's and Gannagé's characteristics, too.

H. W. Singer points out the rapid population growth and unfavourable age distribution as a result of the related motions of birth and death rates. He emphasizes that the unfavourable age distribution (the high proportion of dependents in the total population) is a greater bar to economic development than the high birth rate itself.

François Perroux[17] also refers to demographic factors: the rapid population growth as a result of the decrease in infant mortality with a simultaneous unchanged birth rate, and—relying on Indian data—the unfavourable age distribution and high proportion of dependents. He links the demographic problem very closely with the problems of production and productivity, emphasizing thereby their relative nature.

Jacob Viner[18] also considers the high rate of population growth as one of the main obstacles to economic development. This, in his opinion, becomes especially dangerous when infant mortality—owing to the application of the techniques of modern public health—decreases at a quicker rate than the opportunities of productive employment increase. Thus, Viner connects the question of employment with the problems of population growth and explains the latter mainly by the progress of modern medical science.

Gerald M. Meier and *Robert E. Baldwin*[19] take the same view. "Population pressure" is, in their opinion, one of the characteristics of the underdeveloped countries. It manifests itself in three ways: (a) latent unemployment in agriculture ("rural underemployment"); (b) high proportion of dependents per adult due to the high birth rate; (c) rapid population growth due to the drop in the mortality rate together with a high birth rate. In their view, "population pressure" is responsible for the fact that the labour force is an "abundant factor" in the underdeveloped countries. Since its supply will exceed the demand, the expansion of any sector of the economy (e.g. the export sector) will not bring about an increase in real wages.[20] "Population pressure"—as Viner also emphasized—is primarily caused or increased by the fact that the wider application of modern medical science decreases the mortality rate while the birth rate does not decrease accordingly.

[17] F. Perroux: Blocages et freinages de la croissance et du développement. Loc. cit.

[18] J. Viner: *International Trade and Economic Development.* Oxford, 1963, p. 118.

[19] G. M. Meier and E. Baldwin: *Economic Development. Theory, History, Policy.* New York, 1957, pp. 281–290.

[20] This conception was worked out in more detail by A. Lewis: Economic Development with Unlimited Supplies of Labour. *The Economics of Underdevelopment.* Ed. by A. N. Agarwala and S. P. Singh. Oxford University Press, 1958, pp. 400–449.

There is, in fact, a rapid population growth in the underdeveloped countries, often referred to as "population explosion", and this rapid increase in population and especially the number and proportion of young dependents further deteriorates the economic indices (per capita income, consumption and production). It requires increased efforts to attain a higher level and means serious burdens in the sphere of food supply, public education, health and social services, and also aggravates the employment problem. We wish to mention here only by way of illustration that, according to conservative estimates,[21] by the end of this century the total population of the Third World (and China) will increase by a minimum of 2 billion and will make up approximately 75 to 80 per cent of the world population. (Not counting China, the developing countries will increase their share in the world population from 49 per cent in 1970 to about 58 per cent in 2000).

In 1977, the total labour force of the developing countries numbered about 800 million. Of these about 40 million were unemployed and about 300 million were underemployed. By 2000, the developing countries will need additional productive employment opportunities for about one billion people, and a minimum of 600 million new jobs just to accomodate those entering the labour force.

There is no reason to deny the importance of this factor. However, the space[22] and time aspects of the phenomenon "demographic revolution", the causes of its incidence and particularly its causal relationship with underdevelopment require a more thorough investigation.

On the one hand, the perspective side of the problem of population growth is quite different in the densely populated countries (particularly in those with poor natural resources) from that in the sparsely populated countries. It is true that nearly 50 per cent of the total population of the underdeveloped world (in 1977, 1 billion out of 2093 million) is concentrated in five countries (India, Bangladesh, Pakistan, Indonesia and Nigeria),[23] and most of these countries (or certain regions of them) are very densely populated, but this does not justify us in appraising all underdeveloped countries, including the very sparsely populated ones, in a uniform way, on the basis of high population growth.[24] In a considerable

[21] See the Report of Interfutures: Facing the Future. *The OECD Observer*, No. 100, September 1979, p. 20.

[22] Referring to statistical data Benjamin Higgins emphasizes that the underdeveloped countries in general cannot be said to be densely populated, and he does not even accept high population growth rate as a distinguishing mark since "rates of population growth show a similarly wide range". (B. Higgins: Op. cit., pp. 16–18.)

[23] 1979 Review. Development Co-operation. *OECD*. Nov. 1979, Paris, p. 158.

[24] It seems that underdevelopment theories in general are strongly biassed, due to concentration on the economic problems of the overpopulated Asian countries. This is in many respects understandable and also justifiable, but it often leads to faulty generalizations.

part of the underdeveloped world (mainly in Tropical Africa and in some regions of Latin America) labour shortage is one of the causes of the underutilization of natural resources. The 1951 Africa report of the UNO[25] ascribed the economic backwardness and poverty of the people of the African countries to underpopulation. One need not fully subscribe to this view to realize that rapid population growth does not necessarily prevent, but in the long run (i.e. apart from the temporary problem of age distribution), might, in fact, promote the development of the *sparsely populated* African or Latin-American countries.

On the other hand, the phenomenon itself, namely the rise in the rate of population growth, must be accounted for. It is not enough to compare the motions of the two rates[26] and explain the fall of the mortality rate by improved health service and protection against epidemics. The core of the question is whether or not such a divergence of the two rates is a natural demographic symptom.

If the answer is an affirmative one, then this divergence ought to be discovered also in the history of the present-day developed countries. And this raises the other questions: why did it not bring about economic backwardness in those countries, why did it not prevent their development? *Fritz Baade*[27] points out that the present-day developed countries have also passed through a demographic phase in which the mortality rate began to drop when the birth rate remained virtually unchanged. But it did not prevent economic development, in fact, the two processes coincided until, at a certain stage of economic development, the birth rate, too, began to decrease.

If, however, the divergence of the two rates is not a natural phenomenon, or, if its order of magnitude today is substantially different from what is the case of the developed countries, how can we account for this more or less *new* phenomenon?

Meier and *Baldwin* point out that the fall of the mortality rate in the past of the present-day developed countries was due mainly to economic development itself while in the case of the present underdeveloped countries it is attributable to improved health services, that is to say to a factor more or less independent of economic development. But if this is true, a new question arises again: why does economic development in the underdeveloped countries lag behind the development of sanitary services and population growth? It appears that the high population increase does not account for underdevelopment, and indeed the latter must be explained first to account for the development of the demographic situation. Thus, *Viner's* statement that high population growth involves danger only when

[25] *Review of Economic Conditions in Africa.* UN. New York, 1951.
[26] See H. Leibenstein: Op. cit., pp. 56–57, and 190–191.
[27] F. Baade: *Der Wettlauf zum Jahre 2000.* Unsere Zukunft: Ein Paradies oder Selbstvernichtung der Menschheit. Gerhard Stalling Verlag, Oldenburg, 1964.

employment opportunities do not expand at the same time, is tantamount to saying that a high rate of population growth hinders economic development only if the latter comes up against difficulties in any case, i.e. if the state of underdevelopment exists *de facto*.

The connection—in fact the inverse relationship—between the two rates is clearly demonstrated by *Simon Kuznets*.[28] Pointing out the difference and dissimilar conditions between the demographic patterns of the present-day developed countries prior to their industrial development and of today's underdeveloped countries, he draws the conclusion that the present higher birth rate of the underdeveloped countries is the consequence of their lower level of development, while the fall in the death rate is the result of the economic development, technological and medical progress achieved since *by other*, i.e. by advanced *countries*. The present-day underdeveloped countries cannot resort to emigration which was formerly available to the European countries, and so they have to pay the penalty for "being late", for lagging behind in development.

Whether it is really just a matter of "being late", of "lagging behind", is a question we shall have to discuss later, but even this explanation may have made clear the role of a foreign, external element in the development of population growth.

According to *Ragnar Nurkse*, "the population explosion in Asia, due largely to the fall in death-rates, reflects the *uneven* impact of Western civilization".[29] This, in his interpretation, means that while mortality has decreased due to the adoption of advanced medical techniques—in the consequence of which population has doubled—technology, capital supply and the size of cultivable land too have remained much the same.

"Demographic pressure" as a limiting factor is included, in some way or another, in practically all non-Marxist underdevelopment theories, without being ranked as high, however, in the centre of interpretation, as it was in Malthus' theory of growth. Though *H. Myint* also points to the relationship of overpopulation and underdevelopment, which "mutually aggravate each other in a vicious circle", he adds that the concept of "overpopulation" is not the answer to the problem. Incidentally, it may be the main cause of backwardness, but there are a number of underdeveloped countries which are not under the pressure of overpopulation or became overpopulated only at a later time.[30]

[28] S. Kuznets: Underdeveloped Countries and the Pre-Industrial Phase in Advanced Countries. *The Economics of Underdevelopment*. Ed. by A. N. Agarwala and S. P. Singh. Oxford University Press, 1958, pp. 149–151. — *Six Lectures on Economic Growth*. Frank Cass and Co., 1966, pp. 35–41.

[29] R. Nurkse: Excess Population and Capital Construction. *Malayan Economic Review*, Oct. 1957. Reprinted in *Leading Issues in Development Economics*. Ed. by G. M. Meier. Oxford University Press, 1904, pp. 74–77.

[30] H. Myint: An Interpretation of Economic Backwardness. *The Economics of Underdevelopment*, p. 107.

Gerald M. Meier also remarks that "overpopulation is synonymous with underdevelopment" but "not the answer" to it, and that "the problems of increasing capital per head and raising per capita real income are common to all backward economies, whether overpopulated or not".[31]

In *Leibenstein*'s view the "demographic characteristics of economic backwardness present a dual problem": on the one hand, "they help to explain", and on the other "their existence and persistence have to be explained". On the analogy of induced and autonomous investments he distinguishes "induced changes in population explainable by changes in per capita income" and "autonomous effects" which are independent of the changes in income and consumption. (Such as chemical, bacteriological, medical and public health discoveries by which the central government can decrease the mortality rate without a simultaneous increase in per capita income.[32])

Though *Malthus* is still very often referred to, the problem of "overpopulation"—as might be seen from the above—appears as a much more complex and relative problem[33] in underdevelopment theories. The relative character of "overpopulation" is strongly emphasized, and stress is laid rather on the available technology, modernized production methods and the capital supply.

Colin Clark, for example, when dealing with the problems of population growth and living standards,[34] strongly attacks *Malthus*. In his view the "law of diminishing returns can only be said to be, in any sense of the word, a law if two further conditions are fulfilled: first, that the inhabitants of the more densely settled area do not use any different farming methods from those of the less densely settled area, and secondly, that they do not employ any more capital per head. These two further conditions make the law of very limited application indeed. For the use of improved farming methods and greater quantities of capital per man are precisely the steps taken by progressive countries when they find their population increasing and their area of agricultural land limited".[35] By classifying 26 countries with respect to the relationship between the intensiveness of cultivation and agricultural output per person engaged in cultivation, he proves that there is little relation, if any, between density of settlement and average product per head.

[31] G. M. Meier: The Problem of Limited Economic Development. *The Economics of Underdevelopment*, p. 57.

[32] H. Leibenstein: Op. cit., pp. 55–57.

[33] A. A. Dawson contrasts "the continuous growth of population in the traditional sector" with "the slow or arrested growth of the modern sector". (See: *Lectures on Economic Development*. Delivered to First Study Course: 17 September—7 December 1962. International Institute for Labour Studies. Geneva, 1962, pp. 37, 43.)

[34] C. Clark: Population Growth and Living Standards. *International Labour Review*, August 1953. See also *The Economics of Underdevelopment*, pp. 32–53.

[35] C. Clark: Op. cit. in *The Economics of Underdevelopment*, pp. 35–36.

In Denmark e.g. per capita yield is five times that of Turkey with an identical population density. In Denmark, ten men (working) per square kilometre of land supply 200 people. If "population pressure" is measured by this ratio, i.e. on the standard of Danish agriculture, only Belgium, the Netherlands, Japan and probably Switzerland (none of them is a backward country) can qualify as "overcrowded"; the countries in Latin America, Africa and the Middle East, and even India, Bangladesh and Indonesia cannot be regarded as such. Thus it is obvious that low agricultural output (just as underdevelopment itself) is not caused by overpopulation.

It would, of course, be wrong to underestimate the consequences of rapid population growth and unfavourable age distribution, that is the grave problems of "population pressure" especially in relation to densely populated countries. No doubt, this factor can really be a major *short-run* obstacle, *ceteris paribus*, to development. However, underdevelopment, whether interpreted as a complex socio-economic product or as a mere relative difference, a "lagging behind", cannot be traced back to demographic features. Both refutal by history and logical contradictions and doubts render it unacceptable.

2. UNFAVOURABLE NATURAL ENDOWMENTS. SHORTAGE OR UNDERUTILIZATION OF NATURAL RESOURCES

In addition to the high rate of population growth as a limiting factor, *Jacob Viner* also points to the low level of productivity, which he traces back partly to unfavourable natural endowments (poor-quality soil, virgin forests, lack of mineral resources, and waterpower, unfavourable climatic and precipitation conditions, poor transport facilities, unfavourable geographical situation with respect to its opportunities for profitable foreign trade, etc.), and partly to the poor quality of the working population (in respect of culture and education, health and nutrition).

No doubt, the low level of productivity is a characteristic of the economy of underdeveloped countries, but not even Viner says that low productivity is attributable simply to the lack of natural resources. A case in point is Switzerland whose unfavourable natural conditions have not proved to be a fatal obstacle to development.

As a matter of fact, the natural conditions and resources of underdeveloped countries can hardly be regarded as unfavourable *in general* when it is common knowledge that there are countries in Africa, Latin America and Asia[36] which are very rich in mineral resources. Some of

[36] In 1975, the percentage share of developing countries in the total export of crude oil was 92 per cent (Saudi Arabia and Iran alone made up about 40 per cent), of tin 82 per cent (Malaysia and Thailand supplied 66 per cent), of iron ore 42 per cent (Brazil alone accounted for 17 per cent), of copper 37 per cent (Chile, Zambia and Zaire made up 33 per cent), of non-

them have very high water power potential,[37] and, though the climatic conditions are disadvantageous in a number of countries, they are definitely favourable in others.[38]

The *geographical situation* may, of course, be of primary importance in transport and foreign trade. The backwardness of transport and/or the high cost of its development, as well as the great distance from international trade routes, are indeed considerable obstacles to development. At the same time, the expansion and standard of the transport system itself is dependent on economic development. Its course is determined by the centres of economic growth, and natural obstacles are no longer unsurmountable barriers today. Therefore, the inadequate standard of transport may be an obstacle to a more rapid economic development but it is only a concomitant symptom of underdevelopment, not a determining factor by any means. At the present stage of the development of international trade and transport one must not lay too much importance on the geographical situation as even the remotest parts of the world have already been brought into the blood circulation of international trade, and it is precisely in the economies of the ex-colonial and dependent countries that international trade plays a decisive role.

Meier and *Baldwin* also point to the state of natural resources as one of the factors of underdevelopment.[39] But, as Meier himself asserts in another study, however popular it is to refer to the lack of resources, and however evident it is that the possibilities of development are highly restricted where natural resources are lacking, in 1870 very few countries could have been said to be poor in them. "The present phenomenon of a low amount of resources per head is the result of either the exhaustion of resources or such a rapid growth in population that overpopulation now puts pressure on the available resources."[40]

Thus, Meier only accepts the abundance or shortage of natural resources as a *relative* phenomenon—a standpoint we readily agree with—and he also points out that the position of the developing countries today is more unfavourable in respect of natural resources than it was in 1870. In the end, however, he seems to return to the idea of the scarcity of natural resources.

---

ferrous base metal ore 42 per cent. (See: *Handbook of International Trade and Development Statistics*, UNCTAD 1979, UN, New York, 1979, pp. 266–285.)

The Third World's share in the known resources of tin is about 71 per cent, of zinc 65 per cent, of copper 50 per cent, of nickel 49 per cent, of bauxite 48 per cent, and of iron ore 30 per cent. (See Helge Hveem: *The Political Economy of Third World Producer Associations*. Universitetsforlaget, Oslo, 1977, Appendix, pp. 222–225.)

[37] Africa's water power potential amounts to about 40–50 per cent of the potential hydraulic power of the entire world.

[38] In Latin America there are immense areas of virgin land which could yield three crops annually if they were cultivated.

[39] G. M. Meier and R. E. Baldwin: Op. cit., pp. 291–303.

[40] G. M. Meier: Op. cit., p. 56.

The fact that the resources that had existed earlier were "exhausted" so soon and turned out to be scarce due to a rapid growth of population might prove that they had been considerably limited in an absolute sense, too. If resources did not represent a bottleneck earlier (but only since they became exhausted and scarce in relation to the number of population), the question ought to be answered why they did not promote development to a greater or lesser extent when and where they were still available in abundance? There is convincing evidence that it is no good just pointing to the exhaustion of natural resources without bringing it out clearly: by whom and for what purposes the resources were exploited. Did the given national economy benefit from the exhaustion of its resources or not? And was the exploitation of the resources justified *at that time* and *to such an extent* from the point of view of the development of this economy? It is not necessary to develop this train of thought further. It is obvious that what is needed here too, is a genuinely historical answer and not a type of explanation based on demographic trends or the "natural" exhaustion of resources.

It should be noted that as regards the scarcity or abundance of natural resources it is not scientific to speak of the "drying up" of resources because geological explorations can never be regarded as finished (they are, in fact, still in the initial stage in the underdeveloped countries), and because science and technology are developing continuously.[41] Indeed, the more unfavourable situation which, in fact, exists today as compared with 1870 is due less to the diminishing volume of natural resources than to the impact of changes in world trade and the international division of labour. (Meier and Baldwin also point to the problem of the trends of the terms of trade.)

Thus, it is hardly acceptable to regard the underdeveloped countries as *generally poor* in mineral and power resources. And to talk about the "drying up" of natural resources is not only unjustified but would require answering further questions. As regards the abundance and state of natural resources, the scale of variants is even wider than in respect of the demographic situation, and the differences within the underdeveloped world are considerably larger than between the underdeveloped and developed groups of countries.

There is, no doubt, one natural-geographical endowment which seems to be a more or less common feature: "almost all the newly developing countries are *tropical countries*".[42] In this connection it is usual to refer partly to the unfavourable psychological effect of the hot climate which "does not encourage hard work and makes a primitive way of life bearable

[41] The book by J. Barnett and C. Morse: *Scarcity and Growth. The Economics of Natural Resource Availability* (John Hopkins Press, Baltimore, 1963) sets this problem in its proper perspective.

[42] J. Tinbergen: *Lessons from the Past.* Elsevier Publishing Company, The Hague, 1963, p. 85.

in many respects"[43] and partly to the poor quality of the tropical soil which prevents any considerable agrarian, and thereby also industrial development.

The fact that physical work under tropical conditions is more difficult is realized by everybody. It is also self-evident that the lack of that system of work involving regularly repeated and constant efforts, which is objectively required by agriculture in the temperate zone, and the objectively greater possibility of a mere reliance on the mercy of Nature in the tropical zones: all these may have at least a curbing effect on development. Marx, too, referred to these factors when he called the temperate zone the natural fatherland of capital. At a certain stage of the development of productive forces, natural conditions have an increased importance in social development, and there is no doubt that these and similar factors still largely determine the living conditions and the development of certain tribes inhabiting the depths of the forests. But, on the other hand—as Tinbergen[44] also mentions—it was just in the tropical belt that the great ancient cultures developed, while primitive tribes of that time lived in the temperate zone. Thus, even if in a certain period some zones are more favourable to socio-economic development than others, this does not preclude the possibility of the opposite in another period. And as to the recent historical period, it is in the underdeveloped countries that the most "sweating" methods of exploitation were (and in many places still are) applied, such as a long working day, low wages, various penalties, poor mechanization where hard manual work is done, etc., which are the characteristic phenomena of colonial capitalism.[45]

A realistic assessment of the quality of tropical soil still needs considerable scientific work and research.[46] It seems to be certain, however, that the transplantation of some crops to tropical soil proves unsuccessful, and certain methods of cultivation used in the temperate zone (e.g. deep ploughing) may be definitely harmful in the tropics. It is also an established fact that the qualitative deterioration of the tropical soil (mechanical disintegration and erosion) may be very rapid if it is not protected against the sun which "would burn away the organic matter and kill the micro-organisms" and the heavy rainfall which "would crush the structure of the soil, seal off the underlying soil from the air, and leach out the minerals or carry them so far into the earth that the plant roots cannot reach them".[47]

[43] Ibid.

[44] Ibid.

[45] For further details see J. Woddis: *Africa. The Roots of Revolt.* London, 1961.— *Economic Survey of Africa since 1950.* UN, 1958.—W. A. Hunton: *Decision in Africa.* 1956.—F. Fanon: *Les damnés de la terre.* Maspero, Paris, 1961.

[46] "Little is known about how best to exploit and improve tropical soils." (A. M. Kamarck: *The Economics of African Development.* F. A. Praeger, 1967, p. 92.)

[47] A. M. Kamarck: Op. cit., p. 93.

All this, however, is a long way from the proof that the quality of the soil is a determining factor concerning the state of underdevelopment. A great dependence on weather, a high degree of exposure to natural disasters (flood, drought), uncertainty of the marketable surplus and even the danger of erosion, etc., used to be typical of European agriculture, too. The solution of these problems is to a great extent a social and technical question and is, in this respect, the function of economic development. The considerable share of the underdeveloped countries in the world production of a great number of agricultural products[48] must make us careful in making negative statements about their natural endowments and soil quality. The difficulties in marketing these products call our attention to the fact that the problems of the development of agriculture are not primarily connected with natural factors. It is even less admissible to link up economic development as a whole with the blessings of soil and climate. As *B. Higgins* writes: "The soil and climate of Japan did not suddenly change in the latter part of the nineteenth century when its transformation to an industrialized country began."[49]

According to *H. Leibenstein*, the low agricultural yields of underdeveloped countries can be explained, in principle, by three factors: "(1) some of the capital found in advanced agricultural countries may not be of a kind for which we can substitute labor; (2) advanced countries may utilize superior agricultural techniques; and (3) on the average, the quality of the cultivated land may be superior in the advanced countries." As far as the former two points are concerned, they are obviously the functions of economic development, and not the other way round. About the third factor Leibenstein writes the following: "Certainly, persistently low yields cannot be ascribed to climatic characteristics since these are often more favourable to high yields in the underdeveloped countries than in the developed ones. But the *average quality* of the land may be inferior for two reasons. First, because incomes are low, the margin of cultivation is carried much further in the direction of poorer land... But, second, and more to the point, there may be an inherent dynamic process in the utilization of the land that keeps yields low." And this is because, as a result of certain "counterforces", "an improvement in the quality of the land generates a more intensive utilization of that land". "Increased current yields imply improved nutrition, a diminution of periodic starvation, and consequent diminished mortality

[48] For example, the percentage share of the Third World in the total export of coffee was 91 per cent (Brazil and Colombia supplied 35 per cent), of tea 86 per cent (India and Sri Lanka 59 per cent), of cocoa 83 per cent (Ghana, Nigeria and Brazil more than 50 per cent), of spices 88 per cent, of sugar 75 per cent (Cuba alone nearly 30 per cent), of rubber 61 per cent (Malaysia, Singapore and Indonesia about 50 per cent) and of cotton 53 per cent (Egypt and the Sudan supplied about 17 per cent). (See *Handbook of International Trade and Development Statistics*, UNCTAD 1979, Op. cit., pp. 266–285.)

[49] B. Higgins: Op. cit., p. 273.

rates, resulting in an increased population and necessary further subdivision of holdings ...”; “...there is now little room for quality-maintenance measures that imply a diminution in the current yield.”[50]

Though this explanation is in perfect consonance with Leibenstein's “quasi-stable equilibrium” idea,[51] it is at the same time completely devoid of any genuine historical factor. The fact that the acceleration of population growth in underdeveloped countries is *de facto* not a consequence of improved soil and higher yields is so evident that there is no need to prove it. But the further subdivision of holdings is a fairly general phenomenon, and so is the gradual disuse of the traditional quality-maintenance measures. But is it possible not to see behind these phenomena the spreading of the big monocultural plantations and the growing of export crops?[52]

The question of natural resources is dealt with by several economists, including *H. Myint*, not as an absolute or relative plenty or poverty, but as the measure of the utilization of potentials (which theoretically may mean the utilization of mineral resources as well as soil potentials).[53] Myint indicates “underdevelopment of natural resources” (in connection with “backward people”[54]) as one of the factors of underdevelopment.[55]

The term “underdeveloped resources” means, in fact, the underutilization of potential resources or the non-optimum allocation of the given resources to possible uses, i.e. “a species of deviation from the productive optimum”. Thus the factor “unfavourable natural endowments” is replaced by the factor “underutilization of existing natural resources” (available perhaps in abundance) as a criterion of underdevelopment or obstacle to development. This is, no doubt, more realistic than the generalizing criterion of unfavourable natural endowments though it does not reveal more about the roots, the deep-lying causes of underdevelopment, either. Here, too, quite a

[50] H. Leibenstein: Op. cit., pp. 48–51.

[51] For more details, see p. 55.

[52] Instances of and references to the harmful effects of monocultural plantation farming (depletion of land, increased sensitivity to plant diseases and insects) and its drawbacks, as opposed to traditional cultivation methods can be found in a great number of books, official reports and studies. (See e.g.: B. Higgins: Op. cit., p. 270.—J. Woddis: Op. cit.—K. Brown: *Land in Southern Rhodesia.* Africa Bureau, London, 1959.—*Special Study on Economic Conditions in Non-Self-Governing Territories.* UN, 1958.—T. R. Batten: *Problems of African Development.* London, 1947, p. 54., etc.)

[53] Viner, too, stresses the utilization of potentials when he defines the concept of underdeveloped countries by declaring that an underdeveloped country is one “which has good *potential prospects* for using more capital or more labour or *more available natural resources* to support its present population on a higher level of living or if its per capita income level is already fairly high to support a larger population on a not lower level of living”. (*The Economics of Underdevelopment,* p. 12.)

[54] In this context underdevelopment theories apply an interesting terminological distinction between the concepts “underdeveloped resources” and “backward people”, to which we shall return later, in view of the deriving practical conclusions.

[55] H. Myint: Op. cit., I, pp. 93–96.

number of questions remain unanswered: What is the yardstick by which the inadequate utilization of potential resources can be measured? What are the causes of underutilization? Why did even those colonial countries in which a part of the resources was exploited intensively—according to Meier perhaps even exhaustively—not achieve a higher level of development, i.e. the phase of "self-sustained growth".

3. CAPITAL SHORTAGE OR INSUFFICIENT CAPITAL FORMATION

Capital shortage is usually considered to be one of the most characteristic criteria of underdevelopment, the more so as it also apparently provides a suitable explanation for the low level of productivity, the acute problem of unemployment, and, in general, underemployment, as well as for the underutilization of the natural-resource potential. In addition, the general demand of the underdeveloped countries for increased international financial assistance, their growing budget and balance-of-payments deficits, as well as the rather frequent phenomenon of usurious local credit rates, still further corroborate the assumption that the basic cause—and also the remedy—of underdevelopment must be sought along this line. Therefore, of all limiting factors of development, capital shortage is rated of especial importance by most authors.

It has already been mentioned that *Sauvy*, too, refers to the insufficiency of *capital stock*, in connection with unemployment. *Gannagé* points out the low volume of per capita capital *in production*.

In *Viner*'s view, capital shortage belongs to the second category of obstacles to development (it comes after the quality of natural resources and working population), and he adds that capital shortage should not be measured by the rate of interest. A high rate of interest may be due to economically different causes: high investment risks, high marginal productivity of capital, etc. The measure of capital supply should be related to the available *opportunities for profitable investments*, and it is more appropriate to apply as an index number the amount of capital per capita *in use* within the country than the amount of capital per head *owned* within the country.[56]

This remark of Viner's, touching upon a highly essential problem, needs to be commented upon. It might be really justified to measure the degree of capital supply of a given fiscal year or of a development programme extending over several years by the amount of capital actually used or available. But from the point of view of the present and future position of the country in question, it is far from being immaterial to what extent it can

---

[56] J. Viner: The Economics of Development. *The Economics of Underdevelopment*, pp. 18–19.

44

rely on its own resources and to what extent foreign capital increases within the country, i.e. to what extent it becomes dependent on foreign financial powers. Nor is it permissible, in the search for a correct and historical interpretation of underdevelopment, to overlook differences in the *origin* of the capital *in use*, and differences between foreign and national capital, since it is precisely the activity and predominance of foreign capital that gave rise—deliberately or spontaneously—to factors that can be considered as qualitative criteria of "underdevelopment".

As regards the relative interpretation of insufficient capital supply—i.e. capital shortage related to profitable investment opportunities—the question arises first of all as to whether we should interpret "profitability" on the microeconomic level from the entrepreneur's point of view, or on the macroeconomic level from the long-term view of the national economy. Secondly, this—in my view—basically correct relative interpretation of capital shortage does not offer by any means a general characteristic (even less general than population pressure). As is commonly known, in a number of underdeveloped countries (mainly in Tropical Africa) the increase in capital inflow is also restricted by a limited absorbing capacity. Consequently, in some countries capital abundance rather than capital shortage can be observed in terms of concrete opportunities for profitable investments (of course in an even more relative sense!). *J. M. D. Little*[57] firmly points out that in Tropical Africa it is not capital shortage in general, but rather the lack of skilled labour, the economic fragmentation of the continent and the lack of information on opportunities for profitable capital investment that are the obstacles to development. Man and not money is the limiting factor; that is the final conclusion he reaches.

Capital absorption really does come up against the problem of the availability of skilled labour[58] as a general rule, and is given priority over capital shortage by many economists.

In *Bruno Knall*'s view,[59] too, lack of skill is a greater handicap to development than lack of capital. This opinion is also supported by the above-mentioned American calculations (the analyses of Myers and Harbison) on differences, and their importance, between the development levels of "human resources". *Arthur Lewis* does not share this view, he does, however, accept the shortage of skilled labour as a "very temporary bottleneck". It is in the long-run dynamics of development that he resolves the problem of skilled-labour shortage by transferring it to the sphere of the bottlenecks of capital and natural resources: "If the capital is available for development, the capitalists or their government will soon provide the

57 J. M. D. Little: *Aid to Africa*. Overseas Development Institute, 1964.

58 It is, of course, also connected with several other factors (the state of the infrastructure, external economies, etc.).

59 B. Knall: *Wirtschaftsdienst*, No. 4, 1964.

facilities for training more skilled people"—he says, and adds: "The real bottlenecks to expansion are, therefore, capital and natural resources."[60]

S. P. Schatz, on the basis of the results of surveys and his research carried out in Nigeria, calls attention to the *false appearance of capital shortage*: "Frequently the belief that a capital shortage is the effective or operating impediment to indigenous private investment is mistaken, ...it is an illusion created by a large false demand for capital, ...what really exists is not an immediate shortage of capital at all, but a shortage of viable projects."[61]

Thus it seems justified to say that not only the emergence and chronic character of capital shortage need explanation, but the limitations of investment possibilities, too. *Paul Baran* considers capital insufficiency and the deficiency of investment possibilities as two aspects of one and the same problem.[62]

Ragner Nurkse holds the view that lack of investment incentives rather than the insufficiency of savings constitutes the basic problem. The inducement to invest, however, is limited by the size of the *market*. Nurkse makes this relationship *a circular*[63] and thereby an undetermined one, when determining the expansion of the market by the "reductions in any cost of production", i.e. the rise of the "level of productivity," which, in turn, depends on the use of capital in production. In so far as capital shortage is closely connected with the problem of the narrow market, a new underdevelopment theory might be set up with the factor of the limitedness of the domestic market and market imperfections in its centre. Though this can often be met with, it has developed into an independent theory less than the capital shortage concept, presumably because the determined nature of market relations is more obvious.

Nurkse himself puts the question of domestic market in a circular interdependency, but in *Furtado's*[64] view he even exaggerates its importance. Furtado emphasizes that the investment incentive may also come from the direction of the external market. By this, however, he only widens the question. The basic problem behind the limitedness of the market—whether domestic or foreign—is the problem of the division of labour. It is not simply the rise in productivity and thereby the reduction of

[60] W. A. Lewis: Economic Development with Unlimited Supplies of Labour. *The Economics of Underdevelopment*, p. 406.

[61] S. P. Schatz: The Capital Shortage Illusion: Government Lending in Nigeria. *Readings in the Applied Economics of Africa*. I. Ed. by E. Whetham and J. J. Currie. Cambridge, 1967, p. 93.

[62] P. Baran: *The Political Economy of Growth*. Prometheus, New York, 1960, and On the Political Economy of Backwardness. *The Economics of Underdevelopment*, pp. 75–92.

[63] See the chapter *Underdevelopment as a Specific Form of Motion* of this volume.

[64] C. Furtado: *Capital Formation and Economic Development*. Reprinted in *The Economics of Underdevelopment*. Ed. by A. N. Agarwala and S. P. Singh. Oxford University Press, 1958, pp. 312–313.

production costs which determine the expansion of the market. The latter provides only the *possibility* for an expansion—by increasing the *marketable* surplus. But marketable surpluses build up in vain if there is no adequate organic connection among the individual productive sectors, if the system of complementary sectors has not developed yet. (In addition, the development of the division of labour is the main motive force of the rise in productivity itself!) Thus the question of the economic structure will inevitably arise, the question how and why the "enclave sectors" isolated from and inhibiting the internal division of labour came into being, and why these export-oriented enclaves cannot find an expanding external market either.

Thus the problem of capital shortage (and, for that matter, the market problem, too) needs explanation, rather than being an explanation itself. And as it is a complex problem it can be explained only in its complexity.

Further open questions also arise in connection with the problem of available capital supply.

The available capital supply is evidently equal to the sum of foreign and indigenous, national (government and private) capital. As regards the available *foreign capital*, the question goes far beyond the problem (already discussed) of profitable investment possibilities within the underdeveloped countries and the questions of the government policy concerning foreign capital.[65] It merges into the problems of the *pattern of international capital flow and its changes*. That is to say it becomes part of a problem the understanding of which requires the analysis of processes taking place in advanced capitalist countries and the whole world economy.[66] It raises, in addition, the question of direct and indirect effects of foreign capital on the formation of incomes, the direction and nature of investments, employment, the structure of economy, the structure of foreign trade, the balance of payments and, in general, foreign economic relations, etc.[67]

As regards *local capital formation*, the questions of potential sources of accumulation, income distribution and utilization, and the pattern of consumption, are raised. To quote *Celso Furtado*: "Capital, as is well known, is nothing else but work carried out in the past, the product of which was not consumed."[68] In other words, we are faced with the problem of *surplus*, which has always been emphasized by Marxist economic literature.[69] Thus, investigations must be made as to how and to what extent surplus is produced (what the productivity of social labour is, and how the

[65] This varies considerably, by the way, from country to country.

[66] We shall return to these questions in the subsequent chapters.

[67] This question will be dealt with in more detail in Part Two.

[68] C. Furtado: Op. cit., *The Economics of Underdevelopment*, p. 317.

[69] To mention but one of the present-day Marxists, see P. Baran: *The Political Economy of Growth*.

national labour force is used and allocated among the various economic sectors and activities, i.e. what the *structure of the national economy* is like), who expropriate the surplus *(the class structure of the society)*, and what factors impede the conversion of the surplus into productive investments, or its investment within the country (repatriation and remittance of profits). And, in case the value produced is realized outside the country, on the world market, it is also to be investigated how this affects (just as the purchases made in the world market) the real value of economic surplus.

Consequently, the criteria of underdevelopment must also be sought in this direction of analysis.

As to the proportions and pattern of consumption, it would hardly suffice to refer to the high marginal propensity to consume in the underdeveloped countries and to the elasticity of demand for basic consumer goods. However, a quantitative comparison between the advanced and underdeveloped countries on this basis would perfectly correspond to the "subtraction approach" and it would even simplify the problem of development along the line of an orthodox Keynesianism (high marginal propensity to consume→high value of multiplier→comparatively small increments of investment bringing about high increase in income, etc.[70] But certain qualitative features pointing to deeper relationships are evident enough to rid this sort of orthodoxy[71] and apologetics[72] of its credit. More and more authors regard the proportions and pattern of consumption as being determined by the economic and social structure of the country and influenced by certain external factors.

Hence, capital shortage as a characteristic assumed to be general and as an explanation for underdevelopment has turned out to be very superficial and deficient. Its validity is not only impaired by the wide differences among the individual underdeveloped countries and is rendered unreliable by the problems of profitable investment opportunities and capital-absorptive capacity, but it also raises such further problems as the pattern of international capital flow, the trends in the world market, structural problems connected with the productivity of social labour and the pattern of consumption, the relations of exploitation and questions of class structure, etc.—all problems that must be considered far more fundamental and determining.

Despite all this, a particular importance and priority are attributed to capital shortage by two types of views. The one emphasizes its significance

[70] This set of problems will be touched upon briefly in Chapter III of Part Two.

[71] For a criticism of the application of Keynesianism to underdeveloped economies see e.g. V.K.R.V. Rao: *Essays in Economic Development.* Chapter 2, Asia Publishing House, 1964.

[72] A sort of homogeneous "marginal propensity to consume", reckoned for the society as a whole, is no less apologetic in respect of developed countries as well!

in order to fight for the free inflow of capital from advanced capitalist countries, i.e. it serves capitalist-colonialist interests. The other is intended to support the "comfort policy" of relying exclusively on foreign aid, a policy which has become official particularly in those underdeveloped countries where the reactionary or impotent leading strata wish to divert attention from the necessity of internal social transformation and radical economic reforms.

This criticism of the capital-shortage theory is not, however, aimed at underestimating the seriousness of financial bottlenecks, the acute balance-of-payments problems and the need for international aid.

4. THE LOW PRODUCTIVITY OF LABOUR AND THE POOR QUALITY OF THE WORKING POPULATION

The most striking difference revealed by a comparison between the underdeveloped and advanced countries is in the levels of labour productivity. It is beyond doubt that low productivity is one of the most general and principal obstacles to development, in that it sets narrow—absolute—limits to accumulation.[73] Within the "absolute" limits, however, the possibility of actual accumulation depends on the distribution relations and conditions of consumption.[74] It also stands to reason that the productivity of labour is also dependent on the physical and intellectual capacity of the worker, though not exclusively.[75]

Thus, low productivity appears in some theories not only as one (or in fact the most important and distinguishing) of the general criteria of underdevelopment, but often the poor physical and intellectual efficiency of the worker, the poor quality of the working population is presented as the general explanation of underdevelopment and poverty. Some authors argue that underdeveloped countries are poor because they do not produce enough, because of the deplorably low standard of efficiency of the worker.[76]

[73] The main obstacles in the path of development, . . . are encountered at the lowest levels of productivity." "When productivity is very low, the satisfaction of elementary needs absorbs a high proportion of productive capacity. . ." "When productivity is at such a low level, it is difficult to start a process of capital accumulation within the economy." (C. Furtado: Op. cit., *The Economics of Underdevelopment*, pp. 318–319.)

[74] At this juncture it is worth noting that some authors (Lewis, Prebisch, Myrdal, etc.) do not simply stress the low level of productivity, but also consider how the benefits of a rise in productivity are transferred from underdeveloped to advanced countries. (See later.)

[75] The technological level, the "capital supply" of labour force, is another important factor of productivity. The organization, division and management of labour is also an important factor. To analyse labour productivity without considering these factors is a mere abstraction.

[76] See P. de Briey: The productivity of African labour. *International Labour Review*, August–September 1955, p. 123 or O. Brown: *Labour Conditions in East Africa*. London, 1946, p. 15.

J. Viner,[77] just as other authors not listed here,[78] also mentions the poor quality of the working population, in connection with low labour productivity (as a limiting factor of economic development). This notion comprises, in Viner's view, not only the poor quality and unfavourable composition of industrial and agricultural labour, but also the lack or insufficiency of the entrepreneurial and managerial élite and of engineers and technicians. Differences in this field, when compared with the advanced countries, are attributable, in his opinion, to historical (!) and cultural factors, to environment, quality of health, nutrition and education, as well as to the quality of the leadership provided by government and the social élite. He also adds that where there is a traditional agriculture there is often a strong resistance to technical education, and to any change in the working processes.

Thus the poor physical and intellectual quality and unfavourable composition of labour, and the shortage of skills, etc., though evidently great obstacles to development, are consequences and indicators rather than causes of the present-day state of underdeveloped countries.

As regards the historical factor (referred to by Viner), the question is this: what prevented the quality of the working population from improving even within the *given limits* of economic development; why could the technical and professional skill of manpower not make any appreciable progress, why did its physical and intellectual energy not develop?

We cannot make do with referring to the historical factor in general, or the leadership qualities of governments and the social élite, especially where the last century is concerned. We must ask what *concrete* historical factors prevented the physical[79] and intellectual quality of the working population from improving? And what governments are to be blamed? These are the objective questions.

And, if the efficiency of the labour force and the quality of the working population prove to be related to other phenomena[80] of the economy and society, these *relationships* must be analysed.

---

[77] J. Viner: Op. cit., *The Economics of Underdevelopment*, p. 17.

[78] Due to restrictions imposed by space.

[79] Numerous references and ample evidence can be found in several scientific studies and official reports stating that the physical efficiency of the indigenous labour force is low because *nutrition definitely deteriorated* under colonial economy. See J. de Castro: *Geography of Hunger*. London, 1952, pp. 179–180, 191.—A. Doney and P. Feldheim: Social Implications of Industrialization and Urbanization in Africa, South of the Sahara. *UNESCO paper*, 1956, pp. 680–681.—*Sierra Leone Review of Present Knowledge of Human Nutrition*. Freetown, 1938.—*Summary of Information Regarding Nutrition in the Colonial Empire*. Cmd. 6051, London, 1939.—*WHO report* by J. A. Munoz (quoted by J. Woddis: *Africa. The Roots of Revolt*. London, 1960, pp. 165–167).

[80] Leibenstein writes: "The amount of work that the representative laborer can be expected to perform depends on his energy level, his health, his vitality, etc., which in turn depend on his consumption level (which depends on income level) and, most directly, on the

50

It is true there is not always a close correlation between the level of education, together with social and health services and public food supply, on the one hand, and the level of economic development on the other, as the development of the former is dependent on the character of the society, the distribution and utilization of incomes and in the end even on governmental decisions.[81] Therefore, it seems that investigation can proceed in this direction and reveal a factor that—within certain limits—may be considered as an independent variable. In this case, however, it is questionable, how far these limits extend, as the more backward the economy of a given country, the less the degree of the development of education (and of social and health services) can be called an "independent" variable. On the other hand, we must proceed in our investigation and answer the question: what is the *nature* of the society in question and how does it influence the quality of labour and its development.

Thus the poor quality of the working population, just as with capital shortage, cannot stand on its own as the explanation of underdevelopment. It requires concrete investigation, partly as to its own history, partly as to the causal relationships of which it is itself a part and, consequently, as to its sociological implications.

We shall come across this factor again in the chain of interdependent limiting factors as the element of a particular interpretation (e.g. the vicious circle theory), and again in the theory of a "stagnant, traditional society".[82] Its ideological role, like that of capital shortage, may manifest itself in the support it gives to the policy of a lasting reliance on the increasingly great number of Western experts and of long-run dependence[83] on "technical assistance", by overemphasizing the shortage of educated personnel, managerial élite and technicians. Thus it is the expression of a concept which, together with the former one and, in general, in compliance with the

---

nutritive value of his food intake." "The wage-productivity relationship can best be examined if it is broken up into two parts: (1) the relation between income(= wages) and nutrition, and (2) the relation between nutrition and productivity." To prove this relationship he refers to Lord Boyd Orr: *Food, Health and Income*. 1936, to a FAO report: *The State of Food and Agriculture*. 1948, to V. Ramalingaswami and V. N. Patwardhan: Diet and Health of South Indian Plantation Labor (*Indian Journal of Medical Research*, 1949), to E. R. DeMello and C. J. Modi: A Nutritional Survey Among Factory Workers in Bombay (*Indian Journal of Medical Science*, 1950, 4), to H. C. Sherman: *Chemistry of Food and Nutrition*. 1941, to M. Pyke: *Industrial Nutrition*. 1950, to Kraut and Muller: Calorie Intake and Industrial Output (*Science*, 1946, Vol. 104).

See H. Leibenstein: *Economic Backwardness and Economic Growth*. New York, 1957, pp. 62–65.

[81] This is best proved by the example of several socialist countries where, compared with the level of national income, highly developed systems of education and social and health services have been created.

[82] See subsequent paragraphs.

[83] See Part Two.

"subtraction approach", sees the course of development of the underdeveloped countries in such a way that "the West diffuses knowledge, skills, organization, values, technology and capital to a poor nation, until, over time, its society, culture and personnel become variants of that which made the Atlantic community economically successful".[84]

[84] M. Nash: Introduction, Approaches to the Study of Economic Growth. In: Psycho-Cultural Factors in Asian Economic Growth. (Issue Editors: Manning Nash and Robert Chin), *Journal of Social Issues*, 29, No. 1, January 1963, p. 5.—Quoted by A. G. Frank, (Sociology of Development and Underdevelopment of Sociology. *Catalyst*, No. 3, 1967), who gives an excellent criticism of this sort of "diffusionist approach".

UNDERDEVELOPMENT AS A SPECIFIC FORM OF MOTION. THE ANTIHISTORICAL IDEAS OF THE STATIC "VICIOUS CIRCLE" AND THE DYNAMIC "QUASI-STABLE EQUILIBRIUM"

We have seen that the various inhibiting and limiting factors themselves are links in a chain of relationships, and as such cannot be expected to offer, either separately or in their simple aggregate, a satisfactory explanation of underdevelopment. Let us see now if we can get any farther in understanding underdevelopment by assuming that "underdevelopment" is a particular system of the mutual relationships of the limiting and inhibiting factors, that it is a particular type of motion which, by regularly returning to its starting point, makes any actual progress or development impossible.

1. THE VICIOUS CIRCLE OF LIMITING FACTORS

The substitution of interdependencies for causal relationships has never found such an independent theoretical manifestation, and pure tautology has never reached such a high pedestal as in the vicious circle idea. The explanation of underdevelopment by itself means, of course,—at least seemingly—an escape from the necessity of historical analysis. If, by inserting a few interdependent factors, the direct relationship of underdevelopment to itself can be made indirect, even the appearance of an obvious tautology can be avoided. And the question of the causes of the individual inhibiting and limiting factors can be evaded by reference to another factor, and so on, until we come back to where we started from.

Though it would be possible to set up a number of circular relationships and interdependencies of any advanced country and any historical period, they have become popular and widespread particularly in the various underdevelopment theories so that underdevelopment seems to be, at least in economic literature, the separate world—an independent system of the various vicious circles.

Underdevelopment in these theories is no longer the simple aggregate of individual deficiencies or obstacles, but an interdependent system of their relationships. The explanation of a characteristic deficiency or obstacle is provided by another, and that, in turn, is explained by a third and so on, or vice versa.

By way of example, let us pose the question, what is the cause of capital shortage as one of the obstacles to development?

It is the insufficiency of domestic capital accumulation which, in turn, results from the low rate of savings. And the latter is low because per capital national income is low, which again cannot grow quickly because of capital shortage.

In poor countries—declares *Viner*—the inner accumulation of capital is low. The source of saving is income, and if income per capita is low, the annual rate of saving per capita is low, too.[1] *Gerald Meier* and *Robert E. Baldwin* state that economic backwardness is due to the fact that "... total output is low and after consumption needs are fulfilled, little remains as a surplus for capital accumulation. Because of the low level of real income... the flow of saving is small. The low level of real income is, in turn, primarily due to the lack of an adequate capital stock and secondarily to market imperfections. And the low level of capital stock is, in turn, a result of the low level of real income".[2] (See the schema below.)

What is the cause of poverty of the underdeveloped countries?

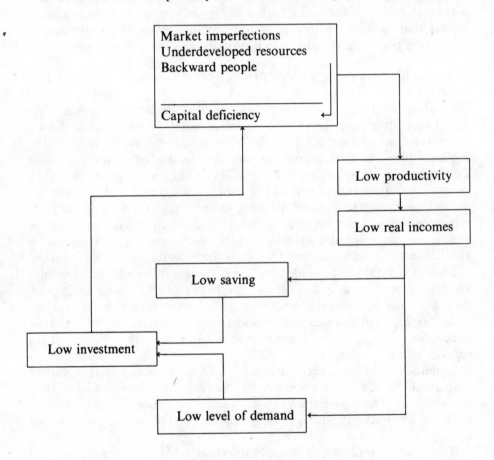

[1] J. Viner: *International Trade and Economic Development.* Oxford, 1953, p. 105.
[2] G. M. Meier and R. E. Baldwin: Op. cit., p. 319.

"A country is poor because it is poor", says *Ragnar Nurkse*.[3] "This seems a trite proposition, but it does express the circular relationships that afflict both the demand and the supply side of the problem of capital formation in economically backward areas... The inducement to invest is limited by the size of the market... The size of the market is determined by the general level of productivity. Capacity to buy means capacity to produce. In its turn, the level of productivity depends—not entirely by any means, but largely— on the use of capital in production. But the use of capital is inhibited, to start with, by the small size of the market."

Gannagé,[4] too, outlines some vicious circles which, however, does not prevent him from referring to factors that go beyond those "magic" circles. He proposes as a vicious circle the relationship between economic development and the rate of population growth and points out the circular connection of the factors: low standard of living → surplus-absorbing consumption → insufficient capital formation → low standard of living.

In his work quoted above *Bruno Knall* describes, in connection with the shortage of skilled labour, another variant: the economy is backward due to low productivity, which is, in turn, the consequence of the shortage of qualified labour, the insufficiency of skills. The latter again is due to the backwardness of public education and vocational training, which, in turn, results from the scarcity of money to expand education, which, in the last resort, is due to the backwardness of the country.

In his textbook for universities *Richard T. Gill*[5] describes the vicious circle theory as one of the general theories of modern economics. He contrasts the vicious circle of poverty with self-sustained growth and attributes the gap between the advanced and backward countries to these two motions of different character and deviating from each other. "Because it is poor, the country does not develop; because it does not develop, it remains poor." But besides this general statement he also illustrates various concrete and more detailed vicious circles. This is one concerning capital accumulation:

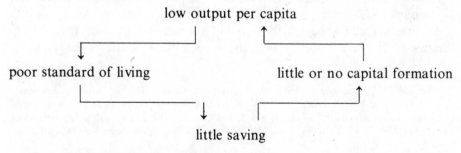

[3] R. Nurkse: Some International Aspects of the Problem of Economic Development. *The American Economic Review*, May 1952. — *The Economics of Underdevelopment*. p. 256. — *Some Aspects of Capital Accumulation in Underdeveloped Countries*. Cairo, 1952, pp. 1–2.
[4] É. Gannagé: *Économie du développement*. Paris, 1962.
[5] R. T. Gill: *Economic Development. Past and Present*. Prentice-Hall, 1963, pp. 28–30.

The author adds that this example is, of course, hypothetical and rather oversimplified, and that, in reality, even in quite poor countries, there are typically some important potential sources of saving and investment. Even in the poorest countries it would be possible to make savings and productive investments from the money spent on ceremonies, celebrations and luxuries. But savings for such purposes are not made not only because of the hindering effect of social attitudes and institutions, but mainly because the market is restricted, because of the vicious circle of a limited market. "Large-scale industry requires a big market. But in a poor country the extent of the market is bound to be small. It will remain small, moreover, until large-scale industry is somehow established."

These and similar circular relationships and "magic" circles could be drawn up in any number, and they really crop up with the followers of the most different schools.[6] As simplified schemas of the results of some partial analyses, these vicious circles undoubtedly reflect actually existing mutual relationships and dialectic contradictions. It is beyond doubt, e.g. that a low national income also limits the volume of accumulation, which, in turn, restricts the growth of national income by means of productive investments. Similarly, a chain of interrelations does indeed exist in many other cases, too. But these chains are never complete. Very often important factors are disregarded and the missing links make the continuity of the chain very doubtful. As regards e.g. the relationship between savings and national income, *Arthur Lewis* is absolutely right when he says that "there is no clear evidence that the proportion of the national income saved increases with national income per head".[7] Arguing with Nurkse, he declares that savings are small not because the people are poor but because the capitalist (or state-capitalist) sector is so small, because the share of capitalist profits in the national income is low. Thus he emphasizes the importance of the distribution of national income. Of course, from the increase in the share of capitalist profits, it does not follow automatically that savings will grow and even less that there will be an increase in those productive investments which are of particular importance for the whole national economy. All this points to the role played by the distribution and *utilization* of national income, i.e. factors which are not involved in the vicious circles outlined above.[8]

[6] See e.g. N. S. Buchanan: Deliberate Industrialization for Higher Incomes. *Economic Journal*, Vol. 56, No. 4, 1946. — H. W. Singer: *Economic Progress in Underdeveloped Countries. Social Research*, Vol. XVI, No. 1, 1949. — S. Enke and V. Salera: *International Economics.* New York, 1951. — A. G. Hirschman: *The Strategy of Economic Development.* New York, 1958, etc.

[7] W. A. Lewis: Op. cit., *The Economics of Underdevelopment*, p. 417.

[8] Richard Gill points to the manner of spending incomes and, in this context, to certain negative features of society (that have already been mentioned earlier). If this only means that another hindering factor has to be included in the vicious circle, which is not only the cause but also the consequence of one of the links, then this interrelation has also to be

But not only can the inaccuracy and deficiency of the chain of relationships be demonstrated—in the case of all vicious circles as well as in the case just discussed—but what is more important is that any factor of the vicious circle can change without the preceding factor being changed, or it can remain unchanged even after the preceding one has changed. Thus the vicious circle, despite the seemingly dialectical character of mutual relationships, is in fact *metaphysical* and *mechanical*. No process, apart from processes under artificial laboratory conditions, can be repeated or repeats itself unchanged in time, especially not the processes of social motion. If there is any circular cause–effect relationship—and such certainly exists—it can only move *spirally* upwards or downwards, and, therefore, has a *starting point*, too (just like a spiral spring but unlike a ring).[9] Now, if it has a starting point, then it is this starting point, i.e. the *fundamental cause* of the circular relationship: the *historical root* of underdevelopment, which must be explored.

Despite their realistic appearance, the main weakness of the vicious circle theories is that they reveal neither the historical circumstances out of which the assumed "magic" circle originated, nor the underlying socio-economic relations and the fundamental, determinant causes.[10]

In trying to explain the vicious circle by itself, the economists see it as a natural, given phenomenon. But, if that is the case, the question is to be answered: how did the present-day developed countries succeed in getting over this natural phenomenon, the vicious circle of poverty? That is, even if they avoid answering the historical question of how the vicious circle came

---

demonstrated in the figure, which most probably will disclose newer gaps and contradictions in it. If, however, the cause of this hindering factor is *outside* the circle, then just this very fundamental cause must be sought for because, maybe, it determines the whole circular motion.

[9] Gunnar Myrdal—to whose views we shall return later—has transcended the static conception of the vicious circle and investigates the interrelation between the factors that promote and those which hinder development in a dialectic way, and describes a cumulative, ascending or descending spiral motion:

"If either of the two factors should change, this is bound to bring a change in the other factor, too, and start a *cumulative process of mutual interaction* in which the change in one factor would continuously be supported by the reaction of the other factor and so on in a circular way.." (The great progress Myrdal made seems to be vitiated by his statement—which, by the way, reveals the influence of the vicious circle idea—that it is absolutely useless to look for one basic, primary factor, "as everything is cause to everything else in an interlocking circular manner".) To illustrate the ascending spiral motion, Myrdal gives the following example: "Quite obviously a circular relationship between less proverty, more food, improved health and higher working capacity would sustain a cumulative process upwards." (G. Myrdal: *Economic Theory and Underdeveloped Regions.* London, 1957, pp. 16–19, and 12.)

[10] Ignacy Sachs is right in saying that without throwing light on the social and historical background, the vicious circle theory assumes "the traits of an apology for the capitalist system". (I. Sachs: Op. cit., p. 11.)

into existence, they must answer the nonetheless historical question of how it was broken.

This question, the historical question proper, of the possible breaking out of the vicious circle is usually answered in one of two ways:

The *first* answer, which is more consistent with the logic of this theory, presupposes the help of an external, exogenous factor, some sort of a "*Deus ex machina*". Such can be the inflow of foreign capital, or technical assistance, the import of skills, knowledge and innovations, or the opening up of foreign markets.[11] Though in full harmony with the "diffusionist approach" mentioned earlier,[12] this assumption is in contradiction, first of all, with the adverse consequences of the "diffusion" of the capital, technology, consumption habits, experts, etc., of the developed countries and the unfavourable effects of the world market.[13] Secondly, it raises the question of why this diffusion and outward orientation have *not* resulted so far in breaking the vicious circle.[14] Thirdly, to regard the diffusion of the superior values of the advanced countries as the prerequisite for breaking the natural vicious circle leads to such a historical and logical absurdity which *ad infinitum* presupposes the existence of a more developed environment, or does not offer any explanation for those very countries which first broke the vicious circle.[15]

According to the *other* answer the breaking of the vicious circle could and can occur by means of a slow, cumulative growth of certain internal factors, or the change of social propensities, independent of the economy, via the emergence of the entrepreneurial class.[16] This answer, however, makes it clear that the vicious circle is *de facto* not vicious but cumulative, and does not determine backwardness, the blockade of development.

[11] The assumption of the unambiguously positive, favourable effects of foreign capital inflow, of technology transfer and of free international trade is in full consonance with the conventional Western theory of international economy. This theory has been built upon two main pillars: (a) *Ricardo*'s conception of free flows between autonomous national economies, of commodities and money establishing or re-establishing equilibrium in the partners' relationship, and his theorem of comparative advantages guiding the specialization of partners and equally shared by them; (b) the *Heckscher-Ohlin* paradigm of factor mobility, which suggests a natural tendency of international capital flow towards the less developed countries with capital shortage, equalizing thereby the national levels of capital supply, factor costs, productivity and income. (For more details and a critique see T. Szentes: *Theories of World Capitalist Economy. A Critical Survey of Conventional, Reformist and Radical Views.* (Forthcoming,) Akadémiai Kiadó, Budapest, 1983.)

[12] See p. 52.

[13] Even the authors adopting the vicious circle idea often admit these adverse effects and consequences. (See the last chapter of Part One.)

[14] The most frequent answer to this question is "resistance to this diffusion" resulting from traditional circumstances. In other words, the inefficiency of the diffusion is explained by the primitive conditions, backwardness, unfavourable propensities and behaviour of people. (See Chapter IV.)

[15] A similar contradiction can be found with Rostow. (See Chapter V.)

[16] See Leibenstein's "critical minimum" thesis and Chapter IV.

2. LEIBENSTEIN'S THEORY OF THE "QUASI-STABLE EQUILIBRIUM SYSTEM"

"If the circle is truly vicious, there would appear to be no way out... But this, of course, does not explain how countries that were once poor are no longer poor, or are not as poor as they were,"[17] writes Leibenstein. In his view the vicious circle idea is worked out somewhat carelessly "in technical economic terms". Though he derives his theory from the vicious circle idea, and acknowledges as his own only its more exact elaboration and the explanation of how the vicious circle can be broken, he, in real fact, substitutes a dynamic, dialectic approach for a static and mechanical one.

Backwardness, in his view, is a self-reproducing state, an equilibrium without development which is re-established through and by permanent changes: through the play of promoting and counteracting forces. "The state of backwardness, as viewed from a day-to-day basis, represents fluctuations of the variables around a low income per capita equilibrium... Periodic stimulants and shocks result in a dance of the values of the actual variables around the equilibrium state. In this way the persistence of general economic backwardness is explained, although the explanation allows for small variations from time to time."[18]

While the advanced countries are characterized by the disequilibrium system (in which there is a continuous secular growth), the backward countries are distinguished by the characteristics of a "quasi-stable subsistence equilibrium system, in which the absolute magnitudes of some of the variables, such as capital and labour force, expand constantly, whereas the relation between the expanding variables is such that their interaction with the other variables in the system manifests itself in a tendency of the resulting per capita income to approach or fluctuate near and about a subsistence level".[19]. The complete stationary state (in which "there is no expansion") is merely a less likely extreme case of this system.

Thus the system is in constant movement; it is dynamic. Unlike the idea of vicious circles, here the quantitative change in the value of the individual variables, or even its constant growth does not contradict the fact that the system returns to its original state, and—or more exactly because—among these factors, there are *dialectic* contradictions instead of harmonious interdependencies.

The system works, in brief, in the following way:

The equilibrium proper is around the subsistence-level value of per capita national income. If this equilibrium is disturbed "the forces or influences that tend to raise per capita income set in motion, directly or indirectly,

---

[17] H. Leibenstein: *Economic Backwardness and Economic Growth*. pp. 95–96.
[18] Ibid.
[19] H. Leibenstein: Op. cit., p. 186.

forces that have the effect of depressing per capita income".[20] Thus, as a result of the direct or indirect effect of an increase in national income (higher living standard, better nutrition, and improved public health, respectively), the mortality rate drops (with the birthrate rising or remaining unchanged), and thus the increased population growth reduces per capita national income. Or likewise, higher agricultural yields improve nutrition, decreasing periodical starvation and, consequently, mortality rates, too, but the increased population growth resulting from it leads in turn to a further subdivision of holdings, which restricts quality-maintenance measures and results in lower yields. Or, the improvement of the quality of soil leads to its more intensive exploitation and eventually to the deterioration of soil fertility. Another example: investments outside agriculture create additional employment opportunities which, in turn, induce a more rapid growth of population and labour force.

And since in the state of disturbed equilibrium "the effects of the income-depressing forces are greater than the effects of the income-raising forces", the system returns to the low, *underdeveloped* equilibrium income.

As we see, it is the *national income per capita* which is put in the centre of Leibenstein's theory, as well as the equilibrium outlined by him. In this respect his theory is in full harmony with the theories that link up backwardness with a certain size of per capita national income. It is also in compliance with the vicious circle idea, in that this size, and with it the whole system, remains unchanged. But this stability reproduces itself through permanent changes, and this is where the *new* feature in Leibenstein's theory comes in. And the variable which restores this stability, the quasi-equilibrium, is connected, in one way or another, with population growth. This is the reason why Leibenstein pays special attention to demographic problems.

The linking up of the problems and laws of economic development with population growth is as old as economics itself. This close symbiosis had its heyday, as is well known, at the time of classical economics. Though working on a different basis and arriving at different conclusions, *Malthus* made the idea the central concept of his theory, a theory concerning the *advanced* countries of his time. *Smith and Ricardo* regarded natural population growth as a factor determining the return of wages to the "natural price of labour", a factor which immediately reacts to the rise in real wages when the expansion of capitalistic production, through the increase in the demand for labour, sends up the market price of labour.[21] But while Malthus assumed a population growth greater (moving at the rate

20 H. Leibenstein: Op. cit., p. 16.

21 "The liberal reward of labour, as it is the effect of increasing wealth, so it is the cause of increasing population," writes A. Smith. (*The Wealth of Nations.* Vol. I. Methuen and Co., 1961, p. 90.)

of geometrical progression) than economic growth (moving in food production at the rate of arithmetical progression), and conceived of it as a quasi-natural fatality (that can be "relieved" only by epidemics, wars, increased self-restraint and the misery of workers), and while *Smith* and *Ricardo* believed in the self-regulating, harmonious and progressive movement of economic development and population growth,[22] *Leibenstein*, by connecting the economic factors (incomes, yields) and the demographic ones (population growth) demonstrates an equilibrium without development. Though he does not regard population growth as an *exclusive*[23] and such a *direct* consequence of the improvement in the economic factor, as Smith[24] and Ricardo do, yet the crucial point on which his hypothesis is built is the same and is similarly false.

The time dimension of the economic and demographic factors—as follows from their very nature—is necessarily *different*, and their coincidence is a mere chance. As it was a naive assumption of Ricardo and Smith to consider the expansion of capitalist production, i.e. capitalist economic development as dependent directly on the absolute increase in population (to interpret it as a dependent variable),[25] nonetheless it is naive and unscientific to assume as a natural matter of course that the interrelated movements of the economic and demographic factors in the whole "Third World" exactly coincide in time and quantity, that is, correspond to each other's size and time-dimension, and so by counteracting each other they determine *economic stagnation*.

What sort of method is it to suppose, on the one hand, that the rise in agricultural yields induces more rapid population growth and leads inevitably, through more intensive exploitation of land and further

---

[22] Apart from the fall in profit rate, which Ricardo attributes not to the absolute natural limits of food production but to *the rise in ground rent*. And though, in his view, this rise in ground rent results from the growing food demand of the increased population, with the consequence that society is obliged to cultivate lands of increasingly inferior quality so that the law of diminishing returns comes more and more into force, in the last analysis, it is the existence of the parasitical landowner class—i.e. a *social* factor—which he defines as the final cause of the fall in profit rate, since this class benefits, on the one hand, from this process accompanied by a steady rise in differential rent, and, on the other, it prevents through legislation (in the England of Ricardo's time) a liberal foreign trade policy, i.e. the import of cheap food.

[23] In addition to the inducing factors, Leibenstein distinguishes in his population theory, as we have seen, autonomous, exogenous factors, too.

[24] "... The demand for men, like that for any other commodity, necessarily regulates the production of men ..." (A. Smith: *The Wealth of Nations*. Vol. I. Methuen and Co., 1961, p. 89.)

[25] It is worthwhile quoting here a critical remark of Marx concerning the "dogma of the economists": "... that would indeed be a beautiful law, which pretends to make the action of capital dependent on the absolute variation of the population, instead of regulating the demand and supply of labour by the alternate expansion and contraction of capital..." (K. Marx: *Capital*. Vol. I. Foreign Languages Publishing House, Moscow, p. 637.)

subdivision of holdings, to a drop in yields, and to disregard, on the other hand, those new opportunities for a further rise in agricultural yields which arise from creating or increasing surplus, particularly when the former is a long-run process while the latter can materialize in the short run?! Would it not be far more reasonable to examine what happens "in the meantime" to the surplus, who gets hold of it, what it is used for, in other words, to analyse the actual social relations of production, and from a historical viewpoint?!

And what sort of explanation is it for the persistent phenomenon of unemployment to say that the expansion of employment opportunities induces a further population increment which, in turn, will offset the former?! How long would it take the labour supply to become overabundant *in this way*? Is it not more realistic to examine[26] how the army of unemployed is filled up from those latent sources which already exist and to analyse the causes of the outflow of labour from one sector to another and the incapability of the latter to keep pace in absorbing more and more?! That is to say, to analyse the character, the growth problems and the relation to each other of the individual sectors of economy!

And is it acceptable at all, to take a *per capita index* (national income per head) as the determinant of a system, of a recurring equilibrium, as the key factor that via its self-reproduction reproduces the whole system as well? Where is that absolutely homogeneous society, without classes and stratification, in which the proportions of the distribution and utilization of incomes are determined solely by the ratios of production and population growth?! Is it permissible to simply average out the figures of income and population growth for such heterogeneous and different societies?!

Finally, the same question has to be answered, as in the case of the vicious circle: How is it possible to break out of this circular movement which, although not static, but dynamic and dialectic, is nonetheless recurring? While the necessity of an external force would follow—in a logical and consistent way—from the vicious circle idea, Leibenstein postulates the necessity of a certain *critical minimum of internal efforts*:

"There is some crucial level of per capita income, and a related level of per capita income growth, above which the economy ceases to be of the equilibrium type and changes into the non-equilibrium type ... a certain minimum per capita income level has to be achieved in order for the economy to generate sustained growth from within."[27]

This thesis is based partly on a tautological hypothesis, and partly on a simple statistical observation (or a logical inference). The *former* states that while "at low per capita income levels the income-depressing forces are more significant than the income-raising ones...", "at high per capita income levels the reverse may be true".[28] And the *latter* asserts that there is,

26 As does Arthur Lewis.
27 H. Leibenstein: Op. cit., p. 187.
28 Ibid.

or at least must be, an absolute limit, a maximum to the rate of population growth.[29]

The changes, within certain magnitudes, in the two factors of the per capita income index neutralize each other. If, however, one of the two factors has an absolute limit, a maximum value, while the other has none, then in case the latter grows *in whatever way* beyond the limit of the former, the value of the index changes. And, subsequently, will there be a sustained growth in the value of the index? Most probably, answers Leibenstein. The advanced countries are in a state of sustained growth, in the system of progressing disequilibrium, *and* the magnitude of their per capita national income is much greater than that of the underdeveloped countries.

Thus, if the state of development of the advanced countries is characterized by sustained growth *and* the per capita income of these countries is much higher, then, Leibenstein concludes, the underdeveloped countries, in order to attain sustained growth, must achieve a per capita income above a certain level.

The question is, first of all, how they can achieve this, if, by the time a backward economy attains this income level, the self-compensating factors are in operation resulting in equilibrium at a lower level. Leibenstein answers by saying that though "an increase in stocks that implies increased income per head" generally results "in roughly compensating increases in other stocks which, in turn, imply decreasing incomes per head", however, "*certain* stocks and forces appear to be *cumulative* in nature",[30] that is, the former mechanism does not always come into operation. (That is why the equilibrium is only a "quasi"-equilibrium!) It would be justified to ask the question: what, then, is the whole idea good for? And then the investigation of underdevelopment should be continued (or even started) *outside* the equilibrium system, concentrating on the problem why "certain stocks and forces" could not grow sufficiently to ensure an escape from a low level equilibrium!

Secondly, the question must be raised: what is the magnitude of the critical minimum effort that makes sustained growth possible? Is it sufficient to achieve an income growth exceeding the maximum rate of population growth of about 3 per cent? Leibenstein does not dare go so far as to state this, as it is easy to find refuting examples. He only says: "*Whatever* we may mean by it, it is clear that the critical minimum effort is *something* that either directly or indirectly has a magnitude of *some sort*, *part* of which can *usually* be stated in terms of money value."[31] Moreover, he adds: "It is probably impossible to define the critical minimum effort in

---

[29] According to Leibenstein, it is around 3 per cent.
[30] H. Leibenstein: Op. cit., p. 36. (My italics.—*T. Sz.*)
[31] H. Leibenstein: Op. cit., p. 105. (My italics.—*T. Sz.*)

such a way that we always, under all conceivable circumstances, mean exactly the same thing by it."[32]

. Consequently, we cannot know what the magnitude of the critical minimum effort is, neither what this effort means at all. We only know that it *must* exist even if it is not the same under all conceivable circumstances and even if its magnitude is indefinable. That it does or did exist can be inferred from the fact that it resulted in sustained growth.[33] It is indeed a delightfully logical explanation from which the peoples of underdeveloped countries will learn *why* their countries are underdeveloped and *how* they can overcome underdevelopment!

*

Thus, as we have seen, despite its dynamic and dialectical approach and vivid mathematical demonstration Leibenstein's theory is of no avail. There is a penalty to be paid for an abstraction from concrete social relations and historical development! No underdevelopment or development theory can do without *social* analysis and *historical* interpretation.

---

[32] Ibid.
[33] As also Rostow's take-off can only be inferred in a similar way—despite its seemingly quantitatively determined character. (See Chapter V.)

CHAPTER IV

THE SOCIOLOGICAL EXPLANATION
OF UNDERDEVELOPMENT

The investigation of the sociological characteristics of underdeveloped countries and the integration of these characteristics into the various underdevelopment or development theories is becoming more and more widespread. One can hardly find any authors today, in fact, who fail to point out, in one way or another, some of the negative phenomena of society and their effects.

"Although a commonplace, it is nevertheless necessary to recognize at the outset that the socio-economic environment within a country may or may not be conducive to development. Certain religious and social attitudes are more favourable to development than are others. . .",[1] says *Meier* when beginning to investigate the obstacles to development. He also points to the socio-political factors in connection with market imperfections, the ignorance of market conditions, the lack of technical know-how, and the immobile nature of the labour force. In his book written together with *Baldwin*, he critizes society's structure and institutions, and its religious and moral set of values.

Viner also emphasizes the importance of the socio-political factors, and *Gannagé*—as mentioned earlier—includes the rigid social structure and the low degree of responsiveness of society among the criteria of "underdevelopment". *Myint* treats the concept of the "backwardness of people" in its wider sense, pointing out the unbalanced relationship between society and changed economic environment, maladjustment of society and its members, the existence of a "plural society" and, in general, the significance of the exogenous, non-economic factors. He interprets the distinction between the economics of "underdeveloped resources" and of "backward people", i.e. between the economic and social sides of underdevelopment, from another aspect as the economics of stagnation or relatively slow rates of growth in total or per capita national income and productivity, and that of social maladjustment and discontent.[2] In another study[3] he emphasizes the importance of the social peculiarities of the underdeveloped countries, and the need for taking them into consideration adequately.

[1] G. M. Meier: The Problem of Limited Economic Development. Loc. cit., p. 55.
[2] H. Myint: Op. cit. *The Economics of Underdevelopment*, p. 119.
[3] H. Myint: Economic Theory and the Underdeveloped Countries. *Journal of Political Economy*, No. 5. Chicago.

5

François Perroux sees the brakes and obstacles to development primarily in social institutions, in the way of thinking and customs of society, i.e. the social and mental structure of the population. In doing so he includes in these factors the system of large estates, the lack or insufficiency of propensity to innovate, poor labour discipline, and the absence of entrepreneurship, as defined by Schumpeter, etc. Of the changes needed for speeding up development he stresses the importance of certain exogenous, non-economic ones: the institutional changes, the transformation of mentality, the changes in the mental structure and social customs. *Perroux* opposes thereby the economistic vision of underdevelopment and the policy of development, which focuses merely on the per-capita GNP level and growth.

A number of other well-known authors could be added to those listed above, authors who in different contexts touch upon the social implications of "economic underdevelopment". This goes to show that factors like social environment, the responsiveness, propensities, customs and institutions of society all rank fairly high in the various underdevelopment theories. However, the sociology of backwardness develops mostly as a theory separate from economics, being concerned with economic theories only at certain marginal points, or the latter include social phenomena only as exogenous factors in the interpretation of underdevelopment, by referring to the results of the "bordering discipline". This rigid dichotomy in the research on economic and social phenomena is the result of the orthodox, and apologetic, isolation of social sciences.[4] The demand frequently made in economic literature, fo. a sociological approach, and, for the necessary and useful cooperation of economics and sociology, as well as the inclusion of sociological factors in the list of criteria determining underdevelopment, are no doubt signs of the turning away to a certain extent from "pure economics" (at least as regards the underdeveloped countries). This is, however, still a long way from accepting a real political economy[5] which, instead of the Robinson-problem of the "distribution and utilization of scarce resources", puts the emphasis on the analysis of the social process of reproduction, the social relations of production and distribution, and examines underdevelopment as a complex socio-economic formation. The sociology of underdevelopment usually disregards the economic determinants, or regards them as secondary, while in the economics of underdevelopment sociological factors appear as exogenous and unexplainable.[6]

4 This is clearly demonstrated by the isolation of "political science", sociology and "pure" economics.

5 As it was not in the case of the reactionary German historical school and institutionalism either.

6 Celso Furtado holds the view that economic development itself is determined by sociological factors not explainable in terms of economics: "The theory of economic

66

Two main types of the sociological interpretation of underdevelopment can be distinguished—even if these two types tend to coalesce in the theory of certain authors. The first regards the society of underdeveloped countries as more or less homogeneous, stagnant, and traditional, and the second emphasizes its heterogeneous, dual or even plural nature.

1. THE IDEA OF A STAGNANT, TRADITIONAL SOCIETY

When *Myint* or *Meier* and *Baldwin* or others speak of the "backwardness of people" as distinct from the economic phenomenon of underdevelopment, they are in fact depicting a *traditional* society, which "has been relatively unsuccessful in solving the economic problem of man's conquest of his superior environment". This failure, they suggest, manifests itself in low labour efficiency, factor immobility, limited specialization in occupations and in trade, lack of entrepreneurship, economic ignorance, lack of individualism, rigid and stratified, caste-like structure, and especially in the institutions and in society's religious and moral scales of value, etc.[7]

This definition of the "backwardness of people" is the obvious outcome of a confrontation with advanced *capitalist* societies, the product of the subtraction approach. This definition, by including the lack of entrepreneurship, an entrepreneurial class and individualism in general among the criteria of backwardness of people, labels, every society not characterized by individualism and *capitalist* private interest as backward.

The lack of capitalist entrepreneurship is usually regarded as the main characteristic of backward societies inhibiting development, and Schumpeter's development theory is now all the rage. Many authors, regarding underdevelopment as an original and stationary state, "invert the problem and ask for the reasons for development rather than for those for underdevelopment".[8] And since, in their view, the development of advanced countries is due to the special qualities of entrepreneurs and "growth agents" who, with a dynamic outlook, constantly tend to disturb the stationary equilibrium by means of innovations[9]—underdevelopment merely means that the idealized entrepreneurial qualities have not yet developed.

In accordance with the subtraction approach, in the relevant literature there is a long list of qualities, propensities, motivations and incentives that,

---

development in its general form does not fall within the categories of economic analysis ... Economic analysis cannot say why any society starts developing and to what social agents this process is due." (C. Furtado: Op. cit., p. 316.)

[7] G. M. Meier and R. E. Baldwin: Op. cit., p. 293.

[8] J. Tinbergen: Op. cit., p. 86.

[9] Schumpeter distinguishes five types of innovations: new goods, new methods of production, new markets, new sources of raw material and new forms of organization. (J. A. Schumpeter: *The Theory of Economic Development.* Harvard, 1951.)

in contrast to the advanced countries, are *missing* in the underdeveloped countries and should be created as an absolute precondition for development.

H. Leibenstein enumerates the following as *desirable attitudes:* (1) Western "market" incentives, that is, a strong profit incentive..., (2) a willingness to accept entrepreneurial risks, (3) an eagerness to be trained for industrial and "dirty" jobs..., (4) an eagerness to engage in and promote scientific and technical progress.[10] While, in his view, developed countries are characterized by *"positive-sum incentives"*, i.e. "those that lead to activities that yield increases in national income" and by such *"growth contributing activities"* as "the creation of entrepreneurship, the expansion of productive skills, and the increase in productive knowledge", the backward societies are marked by *"zero-sum activities* directed toward the maintenance of existing economic privileges through the inhibition and curtailment of potentially expanding economic opportunities; the conservative activities of both organized and unorganized labour directed against change; the resistance to new knowledge and ideas; increases in essentially non-productive conspicuous public or private consumption, etc".[11]

J. Tinbergen is obviously endeavouring not to fashion the list of desirable attitudes exclusively on the model of the Western capitalist entrepreneur— which is presumably in line with his view about the convergency of the development of East and West. He maintains that, at the very least, those who play leading roles in society should "(I) be interested in material wealth, (II) be interested in the future, (III) be willing to take risks, (IV) be interested in technology, (V) show persistency, (VI) be able to work hard, (VII) be able to cooperate with many people, (VIII) be open to new ideas, (IX) be able to make logical analyses of complex phenomena".[12]

The "social behaviour, attitudes and propensities", the "social value system", etc., play a central role in the development theories of *W. Rostow*[13] and *R. Aron*[14] and can also be found in the interpretation of *Buchanan* and *Ellis*[15] and the explanation of *A. Gershenkron*[16] among others. A specific sociological or psychological theory of economic development, or for that

[10] H. Leibenstein: Op. cit., p. 109.

[11] H. Leibenstein: Op. cit., pp. 188–189.

[12] J. Tinbergen: Op. cit., p. 86.

[13] See W. W. Rostow: *The Process of Economic Growth*. Oxford, 1960 and our Chapter V of this book on the stages of development.

[14] R. Aron: *Dix-huit leçons sur la société industrielle*. Gallimard, 1962.

[15] N. S. Buchanan and H. S. Ellis: *Approaches to Economic Development*. New York, The Twentieth Century Fund, 1955.

[16] A. Gershenkron: Economic Progress. Papers presented for a Round Table Conference held by the International Economic Association, Louvain, 1955.

matter, underdevelopment, is represented, however, by the works of *Bert F. Hoselitz, Everett E. Hagen, David McClelland*, and *John H. Kunkel*.[17]

Let us see now—without going into the details of these theories and examining the differences between them or discussing other, similar concepts and their theoretical antecedents—[18] what picture these theories draw of the state of underdevelopment and development.

Hoselitz contrasts the differing nature of social roles and behaviours in advanced and backward countries. While he describes them in the advanced countries, by making use of *Talcott Parsons*'[19] pattern variables, as being characterized by "universalism, achievement orientation and functional specificity", he attributes to the backward countries the opposite characteristics: "particularism, ascription and functional diffuseness". It follows from his view that the backward countries are backward because (a) in their society particularism prevails instead of universalism, particular interests direct the movement and processes of society; (b) recruitment and reward are determined by ascription rather than by achievement and thus achievement motivation is missing in social activities; (c) the social roles are characterized by functional diffuseness rather than by functional specificity.

As far as the scientific value of this comparison is concerned, it will suffice to refer to its criticism by *A. G. Frank*.[20] As regards the *particularism-universalism* contrast, Frank points out that, on the one hand, particularism can be found also in developed capitalist countries where, in fact, particular private interest are the governing factors, and can be discovered even behind the universalist slogans exported to underdeveloped countries (e.g. "freedom", "democracy", "economic liberalism of free trade", "free elections", etc.). On the other hand, the underdeveloped countries also

[17] See B. F. Hoselitz: Social Structure and Economic Growth. *Economia Internazionale*, Vol. 6, No. 3, Aug. 1953. — Economic Growth in Latin America. *Contributions to the First International Conference in Economic History*. Stockholm, 1960. Mouton and Co., The Hague.—Role of Incentives in Industrialization. *Economic Weekly*, Vol. 15, Nos 28, 29, 30 (Special Number, July) Bombay, 1963.—Social Stratification and Economic Development. *International Social Science Journal*, Vol. 16, No. 2, 1964.—*Sociological Factors in Economic Development*. The Free Press, Glencoe, 1960.—E. E. Hagen: *On the Theory of Social Change*. Dorsey Press, Homewood, 1962.—*An Analytical Model of the Transition to Economic Growth*. M.I.T., CIS. Document C/57.12.—The Theory of Economic Development. *EDCC*, Vol. 6, No. 3, April 1957.—D. McClelland: *The Achieving Society*. Van Nostrand, Princeton, 1961.—*The Achievement Motive*. Appleton-Century-Crofts, New York. 1953.— A Psychological Approach to Economic Development. *EDCC*, Vol. 12, N. 3, April 1964.— J. H. Kunkel: Values and Behaviour in Economic Development. *EDCC*, Vol. 13, No. 3, 1965. etc.

[18] For example, Max Weber's theory.

[19] See T. Parsons: *The Social System*. The Free Press, Glencoe, 1951.

[20] See A. G. Frank: Sociology of Development and Underdevelopment of Sociology. *Catalyst*, No. 3. (University of Buffalo, 1967.)—For another Marxist criticism of Hoselitz see A. Mátyás: *A gazdasági fejlődés feltételei. Bevezetés* (The conditions of economic development. Introduction). Közgazdasági és Jogi Könyvkiadó, Budapest, 1963, pp. 60–62.

show—along with false, imported universalism—the signs of true universalism (such as anticolonial movements, militant nationalism, etc.).

To refute the statement that the social, economic and political roles in underdeveloped countries are distributed almost exclusively in terms of *ascriptive norms*, Frank mentions the example of the political leadership produced by the Latin-American coups and that of the emerging African "national" bourgeoisie, and in general the example of those who, having "commercial and financial ties to the developed metropolis", take up top roles. At the same time, he mentions as a striking example of the very ascriptive distribution of roles in advanced countries the position of the Negroes in America.

Not less convincing is the rebuttal Frank gives to another statement of Hoselitz that roles in underdeveloped countries are functionally diffuse rather than specific, in contrast to those in the developed countries. The roles in the lower strata of the underdeveloped countries are really diffuse in that the same person may "practice many professions at a time (such as farmer, trader, peddlar, artisan, odd jobber, thief, etc.)," and such are also the top roles where monopoly control is exercised. But, on the other hand, the same role diffuseness can also be observed in the military-industrial complex of the upper leadership of the USA, while "a whole series of intermediate roles in underdeveloped societies occupied by such members of the middle classes as military officers, government bureaucrats, junior executives, administrators, policemen, and others, are functionally quite specific".[21]

Frank sums up his criticism by saying that Hoselitz, when "confining his attention to the arithmetic sum of social roles in general" forgets "about the social, political and economic structure of a particular society under study"; Hoselitz assumes that even if underdevelopment is connected with a certain structure of social system, "the system's structure can be changed simply by changing some of its parts"—which is "contrary to all empirical reality".[22]

McClelland[23] disregards to an even greater extent than Hoselitz the problem of the social system and structure, and discovers the roots of

[21] A. G. Frank: Op. cit., p. 30.

[22] A. G. Frank: Op. cit., pp. 33–34.

[23] The theories represented by McClelland and Hagen are called by Manning Nash "smaller scale hypotheses" and by Benjamin Higgins "partial theories"—expressing thereby their extraordinarily narrow, limited character. See M. Nash: Psycho-Cultural Factors in Asian Economic Growth. *Journal of Social Issues*, Vol. 29, No. 1, 1963.—B. Higgins: Op. cit., p. 294.

The "small-scale" character, the concentration on merely partial social changes finds a telling expression in J. H. Kunkel's conclusion: "Since usually only a few aspects of the societal environment can be altered, present efforts to create behavioural prerequisites must begin *on a small scale*." (J. H. Kunkel: Values and Behaviour in Economic Development. *EDCC*, Vol. 13, No. 3, 1965, p. 277. My italics.—*T. Sz.*)

underdevelopment (or, in reverse, development) in the differences of individual psychological motivations. *Hagen*'s approach is similar, when in analysing underdevelopment, characterized by him as "peasant society",[24] he concentrates on the different nature of basic motivations and on inter-personal relationships. While *Hoselitz'* arguments allow one at least to draw the conclusion that the liquidation of underdevelopment requires certain changes in social roles and that—although not the whole structure—at least some parts of the social system must be changed, all that follows from McClelland's arguments, however, is the necessity to change the psychological motivations of individuals only.[25]

McClelland also holds the view that the prime mover of economic and social development is entrepreneurial behaviour, i.e. "pioneering service", the "vigorous activities of a number of individuals who behave in an entrepreneurial fashion". However, he characterizes entrepreneurial behaviour not by the profit motive but by the so-called "*n*-Achievement" (a variable for measuring achievement motivation, a factor also used by Hoselitz). What is "new" in his theory as compared to the old apologetics of capitalism is perhaps the greater degree of psychological mystification. Otherwise his line of thought is composed of rather old elements: it is not the way of *action* for profit, which makes the capitalist entrepreneur (and which may undoubtedly include actions *objectively* promoting the development of social productive forces such as innovations, rationalization, etc.), but, instead, it is the inner psychological motives of the "need for achievement", "desiring to do well" and "competing with a standard of excellence". It is these psychological motives that induce individuals to bring in innovations, starting a "pioneering service" for society, and taking risks in the hope of greater results, in other words, to behaving as entrepreneur.[26] (*Profit* is, of course, the product of this idealized activity. Its role in entrepreneurial motivation is no longer the aim but rather "a means of measuring how well one has done one's job".)

McClelland regards these motives as "autonomous forces within individuals", but admits to a certain extent that they are dependent variables, when e.g. he remarks that the motives of individuals can be

---

[24] At the same time, Hagen conceives of peasant society as a dual society. (See in the following subchapter.)

[25] "McClelland is quite explicit in telling his readers that not the social structure as Weber had it, nor even assignment of and reward in social roles based on achievement (as in Hoselitz' view), but only a high degree of individual motivation or need for achievement is the alpha and omega of economic development and cultural change," writes A. G. Frank. (Sociology of Development and Underdevelopment of Sociology. Op. cit., pp. 64–65.)

[26] "... Certain motive combinations predispose individuals to act like the successful business entrepreneurs..." (D. C. McClelland: Community Development and the Nature of Human Motivation: Some Implications of Recent Research. Conference on Community Development and National Change. *MIT. CIS.* Dec. 1957, p. 6.)

changed by "persuasion", "by education", "by early character training", and when he points out that the average n-Achievement varies with children from different "class backgrounds".[27]

Rapid development in advanced countries is due to the fact that the entrepreneur's motivational complex (especially the n-Achievement) has developed in a number of persons, while this motivational complex has been in short supply in underdeveloped countries. McClelland is of the opinion that differences in the average level of certain motives such as n-Achievement, predict differences in the rate of economic growth.

Hagen, who has a somewhat wider outlook, describes[28] the "peasant society" of backward countries in the following way: social mobility through economic success is of a low degree, the middle classes are undeveloped; the physical sciences are backward; the production techniques are primitive. In the sphere of individual motivations, which play such a prominent role in development, rather unfavourable motives: (a) high need-conformity (need to conform, placing high value on conformity), (b) high need-dependency (need to feel inferior to someone), and (c) high need-affiliation (need to please friends)—prevail instead of the characteristics of the advanced capitalist countries: (a) high n-Achievement, (b) high need-dominance (need to be a leader) and (c) high need autonomy (need to be independent of others) which are characteristics of the advanced capitalist societies. The former motivations hamper technological progress.

Though individual motivations also appear autonomous in Hagen's list, it turns out nevertheless that "high need-achievement, aggression and dominance *may* exist among the élite of a peasant society", too. Thus one can draw the conclusion that the difference between advanced and backward countries shows itself less in the mere existence or absence of these motivations than perhaps in the measure of their incidence or intensity. When Hagen speaks, e.g., about the role in the changes that may be played by such factors as social tension among the élite, subordination, imposition of change through physical force such as colonial rule,[29] external threat to

[27] McClelland also makes mention of the fact that it is the middle classes rather than the upper classes, i.e., only the "relatively élite group" that strives upwards, which show a high n-Achievement. Hagen develops it into the "law of the subordinated group", and as McClelland refers to the role of the Jews and Protestants, he mentions the role of Scots in England and of the low-caste samurais in Japan, etc.

[28] E. E. Hagen: An Analytical Model of the Transition to Economic Growth. Loc. cit.

[29] Rostow and other authors, too, refer to the effect of colonialism (and even racial discrimination) eliciting this positive reaction. (See later.)

Sometimes the naive reader may even be led to believe that colonialism had a *doubly positive effect*: in addition to the overpraised transplantation of modern technology and methods of production even its much critized, anti-human, oppressive and humiliating activity had a beneficial role in awakening or setting into motion some positive psychological motivations.

the nation, etc., it appears that what he is talking about really is rather only the setting into motion or the expansion of the latent positive forces already in existence. If, however, this is the case, then the small-scale analysis and the examination of individual psychological motivations will not suffice, and the exploration of the entire social environment is called for.

What can be said finally of the sociological and psychological theories of underdevelopment and development and, in general, about the role of social behaviour, customs, propensities, ideas and individual psychological motivations in socio-economic development?

Two distinct, unmasked hypotheses can be found in the centre or, more exactly, at the basis of both the sociological and the "small-scale", psychological interpretations:

(1) There exist social and individual *qualities generally favourable* and *generally unfavourable* to economic development.

Sociological theories of development tend to emphasize the former, while psychological interpretations usually emphasize the latter. However, insofar as social environment, social behaviour, customs, ideas and roles, and the rise of an entrepreneurial class, etc., are *not* determined by the economic basis, the sociological pattern itself is in the last resort a function of the pattern of individual psychological motivations. Consequently, the sociological qualities seem to be merely an aggregate of individual qualities and so the sociological variant of the development theory is based on the psychological variant. (It is, by the way, not difficult to discover a certain analogy between the starting points of hypothesis No. 1 and of the psychological aptitude tests. As certain adequate and non-adequate qualities, promoting and hindering factors and motivations exist and can be specified for the various activities and professions, in the same way certain favourable and unfavourable qualities must exist and be specified also for economic development *in general*.)

(2) If the international distribution of these generally favourable or generally unfavourable social and individual qualities is such that the *generally favourable qualities* are concentrated in the *developed* and the *generally unfavourable qualities* in the *underdeveloped countries*, then this provides the evidence that economic development is attributable to the

---

It is curious enough that some "purist revolutionaries" use very similar arguments, though with a contrary aim in view, when they say that war, oppression and exploitation (the greater the better)—in spite of the sacrifices involved—are favourable just because they evoke the revolutionary spirit, while peace, democratic reforms or improving standards of living are unfavourable as they endanger it. These "apostles" of revolution forget "only" one thing; *why* and *for whom* a revolution is needed (when it *is* needed). This ideologically reactionary and idealistic view, which gives priority to self-contained psychological values alienated from man and society, is not made any less reactionary by its appearance in works by authors professing themselves to be Marxists. Such elements may also be found in Franz Fanon's "violence dialectics". (See F. Fanon: *Les damnés de la terre*. Maspero, Paris, 1961.)

73

generally favourable individual qualities (or their social aggregate), and economic underdevelopment to the generally unfavourable social and individual qualities. Consequently, the *conditio sine qua non* and determining factor for a society to overcome underdevelopment is a change in the psychological qualities of its individuals.

Nevertheless, the question is raised how and on what basis the generally favourable and unfavourable qualities can be specified. The implicit asnwer is: on the basis of a distinction between those qualities possessed by the developed and the underdeveloped countries. The tautology is evident: economic development is resulting from the favourable social behaviour or its individual psychological components; and those social behaviours can be defined as favourable which have *de facto* resulted in economic development. The advanced countries are advanced because they possess those favourable qualities which *ex definitione* belong to them, and the underdeveloped countries are underdeveloped because they do not possess those favourable qualities which *ex definitione* are not possessed by them.[30]

This tautology is, of course, less evident if a given quality, which is at work in a concrete socio-economic context, is made abstract and idealized, that is, if it is deprived of its concrete content. That is one of the reasons why it is important to substitute in the entrepreneur psychology the general achievement motivation for the profit motive as is suggested by McClelland, and that is the reason for applying such "ideal pattern variables" as Parsons' and Hoselitz' universalism, achievement orientation and functional specificity. In this way even the contradiction inherent in the tautology can be resolved, the contradiction namely that the *concrete* psychological qualities observed in certain societies appeared as qualities *generally* favourable or unfavourable to economic development. If these qualities lose their concrete content and become abstract and idealized, they can already be dealt with, even without the former tautological proof, as *generally* favourable or unfavourable qualities, independently of space and time, from the point of view of an *abstract* economic development, similarly independent of space and time. This sort of idealization, however, will be unmasked as soon as it is confronted with empirical reality. Not only the distribution of Hoselitz' variables prove to be inconsistent with the distribution of development and underdevelopment, as correctly pointed out by *A. G. Frank*, but it turns out that even entrepreneurial behaviour is

---

[30] Higgins points to the same tautological element in Schumpeter's development theory: "Schumpeter's theory of economic growth has a large element of tautology in it, making it difficult to test empirically... Economic growth occurs when the social climate is conducive to the appearance of a sufficient flow of New Men, but the only real way to test whether the social climate is appropriate, is to see whether the New Men are in fact appearing; that is, whether there is economic growth. *If vigorous economic growth cppears, the social climate is appropriate; when there is no vigorous economic growth, the social climate is by definition inimical to it.*" (B. Higgins: Op. cit., pp. 141–142.—My italics.—T. Sz.)

far from being an unambiguous development-promoting factor, in that the profit motive, which determines its content, not only stimulates but may often stifle the idealized achievement motivation and innovation propensity (when, e.g., profit hunger leads to the use of means like speculation, monopoly prices, monopolization or freezing of patents, deliberate quality deterioration, underutilization of capacity, let alone outright destruction by war).

Are we entitled to draw the conclusion from these insufficiencies and contradictions of the sociological-psychological interpretations that there exists no connection or only an inverse one between economic development, on the one hand, and social environment and behaviour, on the other? Not in the least! It would be foolish to deny that social and individual consciousness, customs, propensities, ideas and institutions or even individual psychological qualities play an important part in economic and social development either by furthering or hampering it. Ideas and theories become material forces when they penetrate the masses; outstanding historical personalities may give a boost to the development of their society; increasing the consciousness of the working classes is one of the main preconditions for social revolution and the creation of a new society, etc.— these are the tenets of Marxism based on the *materialistic* philosophy of history.

The question that arises, however, is how outstanding personalities manage to come on the scene of history, how ideas are born and become effective, how a favourable social environment and an appropriate social behaviour are created, how the individual qualities needed for "pioneering service" develop?[31]

It does not help if we refer to such general factors as *Hagen*'s "law of subordinated group", and "social tensions among the élite", to some pressure or other which may threaten the structure of social relationships within the society, or to external factors like attacks and dangers. These may have a stimulating or constraining effect in a given situation and context. They do *not* determine, however, the content of social behaviour itself, the substance of the emerging idea, or the direction of pioneering service. In the course of history they have frequently recurred and in different historical periods helped to give birth to different ideas, propensities and behaviours under different socio-economic conditions.

Moreover, the same sort of behaviour, propensity or psychological motivation, the same type of personality or the same idea, etc. may be found

[31] Celso Furtado also raises this question in connection with Schumpeter's entrepreneurial class: "And what factors make for the existence of such a class in our society? Why do certain individuals have that social function? Indeed, the problem of economic development is but one aspect of the general problem of social change in our society, and cannot be fully understood unless we give it a historical content." (C. Furtado: Capital Formation and Economic Development. *The Economics of Underdevelopment*, p. 315.)

in different historical contexts, amidst different socio-economic relations, and while they may be effective or even dominant in the one case, they may fail to be so in the other; and, what is more, they may prove to be favourable now and unfavourable then, depending on the situation.[32]

In other words, apart from cases bordering on the absurd, there are not *generally* favourable and generally unfavourable behaviours, development-promoting or -hampering ideas, customs, individual qualities and motivations. Their role, impact and value depend on whether they express a *social need* in a given situation. It is indeed this objective social need that gives rise or priority to the adequate ideas and behaviours embodying it. However, the content of this social need is constantly changing and is determined, *in the last analysis*, by the material living conditions of society, by *social existence*, with its main constituent, the *social relations of production*. The primacy of production and production relations over any other social activity and relation follows, both logically and historically, from the primacy of the most fundamental human and social need: physical subsistence. Societies may exist without certain ideas, institutions, customs or propensities, but not without production. However, the ideas, customs and individual qualities of the members of society develop and change under the impact of the social relations of production. The fact that "social roles" cannot manifest themselves *in general* but rather in the context of the social relations of production, and, instead of being independent variables, are determined by these relations, is something Hoselitz fails to realize.

Thus, instead of the investigation of sociological phenomena isolated from the relations of production, and instead of the micro-analysis of the individual psychological motivations, it is, in the first place, the social relations of production (ownership relations with respect to the means of production, distribution relations, the allocation of "roles" in the social organization of production)—in other words, the socio-economic "basis"—that must be analysed in order to get the right answer to the question about the place and role of the above-mentioned sociological and psychological factors, and to assess their favourable or unfavourable nature.

Consequently, *no* pattern of sociological and psychological variables can determine economic development or underdevelopment *in general*. It can, at

---

[32] Many authors attach a particular importance to the *Puritan abstinence* e.g., so much so that they put down the rapid rise of early capitalism in some European countries and in North America either to Puritanism as such, or to its reflection in religion (Protestantism in the first place). They ignore the fact that though Puritanism prevailed in the early Middle Ages, too, it did not produce comparable results. In fact, its direction was altogether different. The squandering age of the Renaissance had to come with capitalistic development in its wake for Puritanism to acquire a new meaning, this time that of serving capitalistic development. *Individualism* and *collectivism* had different roles and meant different things in different periods and under different conditions.

76

best, promote or check it under certain concrete conditions. Since the pattern itself is determined, in the last analysis, by process taking place in the socio-economic "basis", it cannot be the *ultimate* determinant of economic development itself.

These thoughts may appear to the reader as a philosophical problem rather than one directly concerned with the interpretation of economic underdevelopment. In fact, it is a very exact and relevant problem. If it were true that economic growth is determined in the last analysis by people's way of thinking, by social behaviour and individual psychological motivations,[33] furthermore, if we were to assume that the way of thinking and propensities of society are absolutely independent variables, then it would follow from our assumption that some nations live in more advanced economy only because they have more favourable psychological characteristics, better propensities or a more developed way of thinking to begin with, or could take possession of these qualities by their superior consciousness. Just think what consequences this may lead to! Obviously to the conclusion that economic backwardness is due to the *backwardness of the consciousness and propensities of certain nations*. And here we are, within an ace of racial ideology professing the inferiority of certain peoples. That is where a logical inference from our assumption leads to. That, too, is why the explanation of economic growth or of the development of societies by "propensities" and "motivations" is so utterly wrong. That is why it is also wrong to reverse the cause–effect relationships or to substitute vague interdependencies for them. That is why any theory that narrows down the development of societies to the evolution of productive forces, on the one hand, and to changes in consciousness (or to those in socio-political institutions), on the other, is unacceptable! If the development of society is abstracted from the natural geographical environment and, especially, from the *production relations*, then *either* it proves to be completely inexplicable why in one place and in a given historical period the productive forces develop more rapidly than in another place or period, and why the propensities, customs and institutions are different; *or* everything must be ascribed eventually to capacities of intellect and consciousness which is bound to end in differentiating between superior and inferior peoples, i.e. in racial ideology.

The sociological and psychological theories have, as a rule, one more serious shortcoming. Concentrating on the *ideal* pattern variables they forget about the *real* pattern variables, the *heterogeneous* character of behaviours, propensities, motivations, social roles and institutions in underdeveloped countries. They *generalize* certain customs and institutions

---

[33] According to Raymond Aron, the determining factor of growth is the attitude of economic subjects, i.e. certain manner of living and way of thinking of people. (R. Aron: Op. cit., p. 192.)

which were, let us assume, really characteristic of traditional societies, and apply them to the *whole* society of the underdeveloped countries, i.e. they regard these societies in their entirety as traditional (precapitalist) societies.[34]

This deficiency deprives the theories under discussion of validity, even if they regard sociological-psychological factors *not* as *final determinants* but only as interdependent variables. The invalidity of the assumption of a homogeneous traditional society is demonstrated by the *capitalist elements actually present* in economy and society, by the fact of socio-economic dualism.[35] That the basic assumption is false can also often be inferred logically from *the way* some authors assess unfavourable social reactions, behaviours and the backwardness of people. When e.g., they speak of the insufficient knowledge of the peasants of the market, they necessarily, and correctly, presuppose that *de facto* there is some sort of market that they ought to know better. When they speak of the maladjustment of individuals to modern economic relations, they presuppose, of course, the *de facto* existence of these relations. When they speak of the immobility of the labour force from the aspect of employment and wage labour, they implicitly refer to the existence of wage labour itself and its capitalistic conditions, i.e. to the fact that the labour force—or a part of it—can become a commodity, etc. This means that they assess traditional customs, reactions and behaviour in their relation to another (modern) socio-economic element. Then it is not sufficient nor correct just to compare these customs and behaviours or institutions to their "modern" counterparts and explain them in isolation as if they were independent of the latter.

Summing up our conclusions: (1) The sociological-psychological variables are not independent variables and can by no means be regarded as final determinants of economic development or underdevelopment. (2) Their place, role and effect can all be evaluated only in the context of the given socio-economic system. Consequently, the socio-economic system and especially its "basis": the social production and distribution relations, must be given priority in the analysis. (3) The analysis of the socio-economic system, as well as of the sociological-psychological factors themselves, reveals the presence of a "dual" system in underdeveloped countries, the co-existence of alien, imported elements with those of traditional societies.

Let us see how this dualism is reflected in economic theory.

[34] "The folk characteristics which were studied by Robert Redfield, and which Hoselitz seems to associate with the pattern variables of underdeveloped society, do not characterize *any whole society* existing today," writes A.G. Frank. (Sociology of Development and Underdevelopment of Sociology. Loc. cit., p. 32. My italics.—*T. Sz.*)

[35] See the following paragraph and Chapter II of Part Two.

2. THE NARROWED-DOWN INTERPRETATION OF DUALISM: SOCIOLOGICAL AND TECHNOLOGICAL DUALISMS

Instead of the false picture of a homogeneous traditional society,[36] the idea of dualism, of disintegration, is becoming more and more popular and general in the literature of underdevelopment.[37] Though in most underdevelopment theories reference is made, in one way or another, to the existence of the two heterogeneous sectors: the traditional and capitalist or, to put it in more general terms, subsistence and commodity-producing sectors, we can speak of a specific theory of dualism only if dualism constitutes the analytical centre of theory from which the specific problems

[36] Or, perhaps, even together with it, e.g. in Hagen's theory. Hagen describes the traditional "peasant society" itself *as a dual* society. The two poles of dualism: a number of agricultural villages with little migration into or out of each village, on the one hand, and the centre where the élite live, on the other. Contrary to the general interpretation of dualism according to which one pole of dualism, the "modern sector" is in organic contact with foreign countries, Hagen holds the view that this "dual" society as an essentially traditional society has little contact with foreign countries. Thus Higgins has every reason to write, while disregarding Hagen's own terminology, that: "From the analytical point of view the main weakness of Hagen's statement of his thesis is his failure to take account of the dualistic character of most underdeveloped countries." (See E. E. Hagen: An Analytical Model of the Transition to Economic Growth. *M.I.T., CIS.* Document C/57.12.—B. Higgins: *Economic Development.* W. W. Norton and Co., New York, 1959, p. 320.)

[37] See, among others, e.g. J. H. Boeke: *Economics and Economic Policy of Dual Societies.* New York, 1953.— *Three Forms of Disintegration in Dual Societies.* Lecture delivered for the course on Cooperative Education of the ILO, Asian Cooperative Field Mission. October 1953.—Western Influence on the Growth of Eastern Population. *Economia Internazionale,* Vol. VII, No. 2, 1914.—B. Higgins: The Dualistic Theory of Underdeveloped Areas. *Economic Development and Cultural Change,* January 1956.— *Economic Development.* W. W. Norton and Co., New York, 1959.—P. T. Ellsworth: The Dual Economy: A New Approach. *EDCC,* Vol. 10, No. 4, 1962.—H. S. Ellis: Dual Economies and Progress. *Revista de Economica Latino-americana,* 1962.—V. C. Lutz: The Growth Process in a Dual Economic System. Banca Nazionale del Lavoro. *Quarterly Review,* September 1958.—W. Elkan: The Dualistic Economy of the Rhodesias and Nyassaland. *EDCC.* Vol. 11, No. 4, 1963.—A. O. Hirschman: Investment Policies and Dualism in Underdeveloped Countries. *American Economic Review,* September 1957.—H. Leibenstein: Technical Progress. The Production Function and Dualism. Banca Nazionale del Lavoro. *Quarterly Review,* December 1960.— G. Arrighi: *The Political Economy of Rhodesia.* Mouton and Co., The Hague, 1967.— I. Sachs: *Patterns of Public Sector in Underdeveloped Economies.* Asia Publishing House, 1964.—S. Dasgupta: Underdevelopment and Dualism.—A Note. *EDCC,* Vol. 12, No. 2, 1964.—A. Lewis: Economic Development with Unlimited Supplies of Labour. *The Economics of Underdevelopment.*—R. S. Eckaus: The Factor-Proportions Problem in Underdeveloped Areas. *American Economic Review,* September 1965.—A.A. Dawson: The Place of the Traditional Sector in Economic Development. *Lectures on Economic Development.* International Institute for Labour Studies, Geneva, 1962, etc. (And also the paper by the author of the present study: T. Szentes: Economic and Social Disintegration and Some Question of Self-Help in the Developing Countries. *Studies on Developing Countries.* Centre for Afro-Asian Research of the Hungarian Academy of Sciences, No. 9, 1967.)

and laws of motion of underdevelopment are derived. As an independent theory, it appears in two main variants: (a) the theory of *sociological dualism* and (b) the theory of *technological dualism*. More recently, especially in connection with the problems of unemployment and the choice of techniques coming to the forefront, emphasis is usually laid on technological dualism, at least in the economic development theories. The theory of sociological dualism is now being exposed to more attacks and, as we shall see, from various sides. Sociological dualism cannot in fact exist without economic dualism, and *vice versa*, and whether the one or the other is justly criticized is usually due *not* to their different character but rather to their identical or similar shortcomings.

(a) The pioneer of the idea of sociological dualism was *J. H. Boeke*. His theory was given a stormy reception by Western economists, not because of its analysis but rather on account of the unpleasant conclusions that would be drawn from it. Boeke based his work on his experiences in Indonesia and presented it as a theory of "Eastern societies".

His theses may be summed up as follows: "Social dualism is the clashing of an imported social system with an indigenous social system of another style. Most frequently the imported social system is high capitalism." Unlike *temporary social dualism* which, e.g., comes into being "when a late-capitalistic social system is gradually superseded by a socialistic system" (at times by the most violent disturbance, war or revolution), and in which the "society maintains its homogeneous character", a dual social system is a *lasting* formation and always the result of the penetration of an imported, foreign social system. The penetration by Western capitalist societies into Eastern precapitalistic agrarian societies, resulted in "a form of disintegration". Since the two societies are diametrically opposed in character, and "neither of them becomes general and characteristic for that society as a whole", therefore, "as a rule, one policy for the whole country is not possible...and what is more beneficial for one section of society may be harmful for the other".

The radically different character of the two societies manifests itself in many ways. The precapitalistic sector can be characterized by the "limited needs" (in contrast with the "unlimited needs" of a Western society), by the backward-sloping supply curves of effort and risk-taking, by the almost complete absence of profit-seeking (with the exception of speculative profits), by the "aversion to capital" (i.e. by "conscious dislike of investing capital"), lack of business qualities, lack of organization and of discipline, by "fatalism and resignation", lack of mobility of labour, absenteeism of regular labourers, by export being "the great objective", etc—while the capitalistic sector has the opposite characteristics.

As disintegration has caused only disturbances and upset the normal living conditions of precapitalistic society, Boeke concludes that the penetration of Western capitalism has been useless and fruitless. The efforts aimed at the rapid capitalization of Eastern society, at achieving considerable technological progress and a radical change of social reactions have likewise been in vain.[38] They can even enchance the retrogression and decay of this society. "The contrast is too all-inclusive, it goes too deep. We shall have to accept dualism as an irretrievable fact."[39] And as for economics he holds the view that Western economics is totally inapplicable to Eastern economies: "every social system has its own economic theory" and "therefore, the economic theory of a dualistic, heterogeneous society is itself dualistic".[40]

Boeke's theory has been attacked mainly because of this "defeatism". That is which *Higgins* takes Boeke to ask for, saying that his theory generalizing experiences limited in time and space is but the reflection of the Indonesian failure of Dutch "ethical policy". Higgins denies, on the one hand, that the characteristics considered as typical are really characteristic of Eastern societies[41] and points out, on the other, that "many of the specific characteristics of the 'Eastern' society described by Dr. Boeke seem to be attributable to Western societies as well".[42]

Higgins draws the final conclusion that there is no reason to suppose that the Western social theory is inapplicable to dual societies. "If dualism is not

[38] "There is no question of the Eastern producer adapting himself to the Western example technologically, economically and socially." (J. H. Boeke: *Economics and Economic Policy of Dual Societies.* New York, 1953, p. 103.)

[39] J. H. Boeke: Three Forms of Disintegration in Dual Societies. Loc. cit., p. 289.

[40] J. H. Boeke: *Economics and Economic Policy of Dual Societies* p. 5.

[41] Thus he brings into relief, in contrast to the "limited needs", the fact of the high marginal propensity to consume and the high marginal propensity to import, and points to the rise of new needs and through them the applicability of economic incentives. With reference to A. Lewis (*The Theory of Economic Growth.* London, 1955), P. T. Bauer (*Economic Analysis and Policy in Underdeveloped Countries.* N. C., Durham, 1957) and B. S. Yamey (P. T. Bauer and B. S. Yamey: *The Economics of Underdeveloped Countries.* London, 1957) he tries to prove—in disagreement with Boeke—that economic responsiveness may be intensive among the peasant population. The assumption of the immobility of labour contradicts, in his view, the fact of large-scale migration. Moreover, "it may be questioned whether occupational mobility is not greater in underdeveloped areas, where trade unionism is far less widespread than it is in the advanced countries". (See B. Higgins: Op. cit., pp. 281–292.)

[42] "Some degree of *dualism* exists in virtually every economy"—says Higgins. Not only Italy but also the USA and Canada "have areas in which techniques lag behind . . . standards of economic and social welfare are correspondingly low". "The preference for *speculative profits* over long-term investment in productive enterprise appears *wherever* chronic inflation exists or threatens." Western society is not free either from the reluctance of investors to accept risks or illiquidity. Absenteeism is not unknown to it either. As regards the supply curves of effort and risk-taking, they are "normally backward-sloping, in a *static* world . . . In dynamic societies the *illusion* of upward-sloping supply curves has been created by continuous *shifts* to the right of both demand curves and supply curves, in response to population growth, resource discoveries, and technological progress". (B. Higgins: Op. cit., pp. 285–287.)

primarily the product of a clash of two irreconcilable cultures, its existence is not in itself a barrier to the application of Western social theory to underdeveloped areas. Sectoral differences are a challenge to economic theorists, but one that can be met."[43] Instead of socio-cultural dualism, Higgins advocates the sectoral dualism of *economy*. He admits that "some degree of 'dualism' certainly exists in underdeveloped areas" and that "it is possible to discern two major sectors: one which is largely native, in which levels of techniques, and levels of economic and social welfare are relatively low; and another, usually under Western leadership and influence, in which techniques are advanced, and average levels of economic and social welfare are relatively high".[44] The former is "confined mainly to peasant agriculture and handicrafts or very small industry, and the trading activities associated with them"; the latter "consisting of plantations, mines, petroleum fields and refineries, large-scale industries, and the transport and trading activities associated with these operations". In this way, he says, the explanation of dualism must be sought *not* in the nature of society, as Boeke did, but "dualism is more readily explained *in economic and technological terms*".[45]

(b) With Higgins and also other economists the theory of *economico-technological dualism* appears to be the opposite of the idea of Boeke's sociological dualism rather than its complement. Making use of *Higgins*', *Meier*'s and *Eckhaus*'[46] descriptions, the theory may be summed up in brief as follows:

"Technological unemployment" is attributable to "technological dualism" which means the use of different production functions in the advanced and the traditional sector. Productive employment opportunities are limited, not because of the lack of effective demand, but because of limitations on resources and technology in the two sectors.

In the traditional sector the products can be made with a wide range of techniques and alternative combinations of labour and capital (improved land), i.e. this sector has variable technical coefficients of production. Labour is the relatively abundant factor, so the techniques of production are labour-intensive. In the modern, industrial sector they are capital-intensive. Moreover, they are characterized in fact either by relatively fixed technical coefficients (fixed proportions in which factors of production must be combined), or are assumed by entrepreneurs to be so.[47] The former,

43 B. Higgins: Op. cit., p. 288.

44 B. Higgins: The Dualistic Theory of Underdeveloped Areas. *Economic Development and Cultural Change*, January 1956. Reprinted in *Leading Issues in Development Economics*. Ed. by G. M. Meier. New York, 1964, p. 61.

45 B. Higgins: *Economic Development*, p. 281.

46 See B. Higgins: *Economic Development*, pp. 325–344.—G. M. Meier (ed.): *Leading Issues in Development Economics*. pp. 68–71.—R. S. Eckhaus: The Factor-Proportions Problem in Underdeveloped Areas. *The American Economic Review*, September 1965.

47 According to R. Solow's model, the assumption of initially fixed technical coefficients may also be omitted. "The industrial sector, which starts with a relatively high ratio of capital

traditional sector produces as a rule necessities (foodstuffs or handicraft products) for domestic consumption. The latter, the industrial sector usually produces industrial raw materials for export purposes.

The industrial sector was initially developed by an inflow of foreign capital. As foreign enterprises operated under efficient management with modern production techniques, output in this sector expanded. Industrialization, however, generates population explosion. The rate of population increase in some cases considerably exceeded the rate at which capital was accumulated in the advanced sector. And since the production process in this sector was capital-intensive, and fixed technical coefficients were used (or assumed), this sector did not have the capacity to create employment opportunities at a sufficiently fast rate to absorb the greater labour force.

Far from bringing a shift of population from the rural to the industrial sector, industrialization may even have brought a relative decline in the proportion of total employment in the latter sector. Entry into the traditional sector was then the only alternative open to surplus labour. As the labour supply increased in the traditional sector, land eventually became relatively scarce and labour increasingly became the relatively abundant factor. Since technical coefficients were variable, the production process became even more labour-intensive. Finally, the point was reached where all available land was cultivated by highly labour-intensive techniques and the marginal productivity of labour fell to zero, or even below, and disguised unemployment appeared. Under these conditions there was no incentive in the traditional sector to move along the production function toward higher capital–labour ratios, no incentive to introduce labour-saving innovations, no incentive to increase efforts, in order to achieve an increase of output per man.

This "structural" or "technological" unemployment is aggravated if technological progress takes a form favouring the capital-intensive sector, and if wages are kept artificially high by trade-union activity or government policy.

As a result of technological dualism, a strange situation arises which is contradictory to "orthodox theory" that labour does not flow from the rural sector where its marginal productivity is close to zero into the industrial sector because the supply of capital to this sector is limited[48] and technical coefficients are fixed. On the other hand, capital does not flow to the rural sector either where the marginal productivity of capital ought to be

---

to labor, would move toward an equilibrium expansion path with a high ratio of capital to labor, even if *technical coefficients were not fixed*." (See B. Higgins: Op. cit., p. 335. My italics.—*T.Sz.*)

[48] The reason for this is that "each investment project in an underdeveloped country competes against projects the world over in the international capital market". (B. Higgins: Op. cit., pp. 341–342.)

higher (since the ratio of labour to capital is higher). The supply of domestic capital is not directed toward improving techniques, because, although the elasticity of the substitution of labour for capital may be high, the elasticity of the substitution of capital for *land* is low. It may well be then that the marginal productivity of both labour and capital is close to zero in the rural sector.

Thus the theory of technological dualism serves to explain one of the most acute problems of underdeveloped countries, namely the problem of open and disguised unemployment. On the basis of the undoubtedly evident fact of population explosion and the phenomenon of different production functions in the two sectors, it examines why the abundant labour force is not absorbed and how it becomes abundant.

Though the theory reveals numerous important relationships, it is nevertheless open to criticism on several counts.

Although *Meier* accepts it as an answer to the question "why factor endowment and the differences in production functions have resulted *historically* in the rise of underemployment of labour in the traditional sector", he doubts, however, "its *empirical* relevancy".[49] He questions whether the modern sector really works with "fixed coefficients", whether the techniques—even if a capital-intensive one were initially imported—have not been adjusted to the abundant labour supply, and whether technical progress is actually labour-saving in the advanced sector, etc. However, by raising these equally "technological" questions, the criticism itself does not go much farther. The question of the choice of techniques is far from being a simply technological question, and is not a question of factor endowment either, just as the dualism of underdeveloped countries is not identical with the technological dualism of the various production functions.

The main shortcoming of the theory is, however, that by concentrating on the technological problems of the economy, it disregards production and social relations, it ignores the questions of the modes of production. Though its authors point out the precapitalistic character of the traditional sector and the capitalistic nature of the modern sector, and Higgins even refers to certain difficulties arising from the foreign origin and outward orientation of the modern sector,[50] all this appears only on the *surface* and does not

[49] See G. M. Meier: *Leading Issues in Development Economics*, p. 71. It is not completely clear, of course, how something can be true historically and at the same time be irrelevant *empirically*.

[50] "The industrial and rural sectors are not parts of the same 'economy' in the ordinary sense. Geographically, the plantations, mines, and oil fields are in the same country, but economically they may be more closely tied to the metropolitan country providing the capital, technical knowledge, and managerial skill than to the underdeveloped country in which the operation is located." "The demand from the *world* market prevailed in the political as well as the economic sense; achieving the optimal allocation of resources from the

constitute an organic basis of the theory. Yet without this veritable basis the starting assumptions and the conclusions, too, are most unreliable. The theory also offers a narrow and mechanical interpretation of the relation between the two sectors, which again is the source of further weaknesses.

As far as the population explosion is concerned, the statements on its causes, extent and effect are highly debatable. The contention that "industrialization generates a population explosion",[51] is not only an insufficient explanation but *on the whole it is hardly* one at all. (Real and sound industrialization usually has the opposite effect.) And when the extent and effect of the population explosion are discussed, it is impossible *not* to take into account the sparsely populated countries[52] and the time-lag between the actual rise in the number of births and the resulting expansion of labour supply (even if continuity seemingly makes it disappear). Owing to the inaccurate interpretation of the population explosion and the mutual relationship between the two sectors, the labour flow as described by the theory is to some extent just the reverse of the actual one: industrialization brings about a higher population growth in the modern sector, and as this increased population cannot be absorbed because of the technology applied, it "has to seek a livelihood in the other sector",[53] thereby flooding the labour force in the traditional sector, too. In reality, it is the traditional sector, however, which has become the source of a rapid population growth and the expansion of labour supply, and labour force drifts—under the impact of various factors[54]—rather to the modern sector where, owing to several factors, it cannot be absorbed either. *Arthur Lewis* based his theory exactly on this real process of opposite direction and regards the traditional sector as the basis of the unlimited supply of unskilled labour force for the capitalist sector.[55] In Lewis' view, the main source of the abundance of labour is disguised unemployment in rural areas, with the high rate of population growth coming into play only indirectly through the latter.

standpoint of the European entrepreneurs and administrators meant an increasing conflict of that goal with the maintenance of full employment in the rural sector of underdeveloped countries." (B. Higgins: Op. cit., pp. 333, 343.)

[51] B. Higgins: Op. cit., p. 328.

[52] "It is interesting to note that the originators of the idea (Nurkse and Rosenstein-Rodan) are careful to point out that conditions in the sparsely populated countries of Latin America are not the ones where one would expect disguised chronic unemployment." (G. M. Meier: Op. cit., p. 78, in footnote.)

[53] B. Higgins: Op. cit., p. 329.

[54] For more details see Chapter III, 1 (c) in Part Two and the paper by the author of the present study: Migrant Labour System in Black Africa. *Indian Journal of Labour Economics*, Vol. VII, Nos. 1–2, 1964.

[55] For more details see A. Lewis: Economic Development with Unlimited Supplies of Labour. *The Economics of Underdevelopment* (ed. by A. N. Agarwala and S. P. Singh. Oxford University Press, 1958, pp. 400–449) and some comments on his theory in this chapter, and those made by G. M. Meier in *Leading Issues...*, pp. 85–88.

With regard to Lewis' supposition, of course, just the same question may be raised as to the assumption involved in the theory of technological dualism: can the marginal productivity of labour be regarded, indeed, as zero[56] (or close to zero) in the traditional sector or, in other words, can the labour force be drained away from it without an appreciable drop in the aggregate product of the working combination of factors? A number of reports and studies give evidence to the contrary,[57] while *Ragnar Nurkse* examines the question in the context of land use, the problem of the actual ownership relations.[58] A further objection can be raised: Is it true that yields cannot be increased in the traditional sector any more by increased human labour-investments? Economists concentrating on practical possibilities rather than on abstract theoretical models would question this assumption—at least in respect of the majority of underdeveloped countries.

It would likewise be justified to doubt the statement that in the rural sector as a whole labour-intensive cultivation is carried on in the strict sense of the word (and not only with regard to the proportion of the factors of production), i.e. the possibilities of improving the intensity, rational division and organization of labour are already exhausted. As regards capital investment, it is not only the too general questions of the lack of incentives and the obstacles to the inflow of capital from outside, from the advanced sector, which are rightly raised but also the concrete problems of the marketing and actual market relations as well as the formation, distribution and utilization of the economic surplus, and its conversion into productive investments. But a great number of further questions arise in connection with the theory of technological dualism outlined above.

There are such questions concerning the traditional sector as: Why did the process of fragmentation of holdings start and what prevents the type of land use that is burdened by fragmentation from changing? Why did a "continuous shift to the right of both demand curves and supply curves of effort and risk-taking, in response to population growth, resource discoveries, and technological progress" not take place? Why do the incentives to increase efforts, the levels of technique and man-hour productivity not operate, or why did they not operate before the population

---

[56] Which is usually regarded as the criterion for disguised unemployment.

[57] See *Aspects of Economic Development in Africa.* U.N. Document E/2377, 1953, p. 67.—Keiskammahoek: Rural Survey, 1952, pp. 112–113.—W. Elkan: Migrant Labor in Africa: An Economist's Approach. *The American Economic Review*, No. V, 1959, p. 188, etc.—These works point out the harmful effect of labour outflow and migration on the agricultural yields of the traditional economy.

[58] "To that extent that the labour surplus is absorbed—and concealed—through fragmentation (of the individual holdings), it cannot be withdrawn without bad effects on output unless the fragmentation is reversed and the holdings are consolidated." (R. Nurkse: Excess Population and Capital Construction. *Malayan Economic Review*, October 1957, p. 2.)

explosion made itself felt? Why did such subsidiary occupations and employment opportunities not develop in the rural areas so as to have absorbed the labour surplus? And so on...

More questions also present themselves concerning the modern, capitalist sector: Why does industrialization, allegedly proceeding on the path of a capital-intensive technique, preclude the adequate expansion of employment opportunities? This is not natural at all, as capital-intensive technique, when leading to a more rapid expansion of surplus and increased reinvestments may have after all a favourable impact on the expansion of employment opportunities—via the higher rate of growth. If, however, this does not take place, the questions have to be asked: What prevents the increased reinvestment of the surplus; what happens to the surplus; why does industrialization, supposed to be under way, not become cumulative? And is industrialization really capital-intensive at all in the strict sense of the word, and not only in regard to the proportion of labour force employed (or especially in regard to the limited capacity of absorbing unskilled labour)?! And is it true in general that the contradiction of surplus labour and capital-intensive techniques constitute the crucial point of development? Can we speak of labour surplus in general, or, only of the surplus of unskilled labour? Why are there no market incentives of sufficient intensity to raise the output of the modern sector? And so on...

It is obviously impossible to anwer these questions from the limited point of view of technical coefficients and the use of different factors of production. To provide the appropriate answers, it is indispensable to analyse the mode of production, the relations of production and distribution, and the *whole* structure of economy and society.

To explain the fragmentation of holdings, it is necessary to consider e.g. the questions of the alienation of lands and the rigid social system. The lack of incentives is closely connected with the insufficiency of internal market relations and the existence of subsistence economies. Capital formation is hindered not only by the "marginal productivity of labour and capital being close to zero" owing to land shortage, but also by the unproductive utilization of the actual surplus. Not only could the labour-absorbing capacity of the traditional sector not expand sufficiently, but it also dropped owing to the deterioration of its conditions of operation caused precisely by the penetration of the "modern" mode of production. Besides land alienation it was also of importance that "a number of handicraft industries were ruined by competition from cheaper machine-made goods... imported from abroad".[59] Consequently, the growth of the modern sector *per se* created underemployment and reduced the level of income in the traditional sector.

[59] ILO, Employment Objectives in Economic Development. Report of the meeting of experts. Geneva, 1961. Reprinted in *Leading Issues...*, pp. 71–74.

And if the labour-absorbing capacity of even the modern sector did not grow sufficiently, then it is attributable not to the higher rate of population growth but rather to the obstacles of development in this sector: the specific deviating factors of capital accumulation and reinvestment, i.e. profit repatriation and luxury (import) consumption, as well as to the structural diseases of the sector, such as its outward orientation and raw-material producing character.[60] Much more decisive than the allegedly fixed technical coefficients of the modern sector is the internal structure of the sector itself. Its generally capital-intensive character is debatable in any case as some of its typical branches (e.g. some export-oriented monocultures) are based on the abundant supply of cheap unskilled labour (or even on the forced labour of indigenous people) and have not forged ahead on the road of mechanization. It is true that in recent years a certain bias can be observed in favour of capital-intensive techniques, but this is not general in all branches of the sector and is due less to competition on the world market (even less to the belief "that technical coefficients are fixed"), but rather to a number of specific factors.[61] Moreover, from the point of view of the expansion of the sector, its linkage effects and employment opportunities, the bias *against* the capital-goods sector is much more important than the penchant for capital-intensive techniques. The former is at the same time a much less "novel" phenomenon.

Let us not continue the confrontation of the more relevant questions and problems with the narrow and superficial theory of technological dualism. (We shall have to return to the analysis of these problems in Chapters II and III of Part Two.) Let us try to sum up instead the criticism of the theories of sociological and technological dualism!

That the phenomena and problems of dualism have received such a prominent treatment in the theory of underdevelopment is doubtless a significant step towards a better understanding of the real nature and mechanism of underdevelopment. Instead of the superficial, quantitative characteristics, the idea of dualism calls attention to structural diseases, to certain peculiarities of the operation of the system, that is to say, it emphasizes the need for a much more complex analysis.

[60] The above-mentioned ILO report lays emphasis just on these factors in connection with the slow growth and limited absorbing capacity of the modern sector: "A large part of the export earnings returned to the capital exporting countries in the form of withdrawal of profits and other incomes." "... the investment activities hitherto undertaken in the modern sector in a number of less developed countries did not produce on the domestic economy any significant 'linkage' effect...", "the linkage effect mostly leaked abroad." (Op. cit., pp. 71–72.)

[61] For more details, see G. Arrighi: International Corporations, Labour Aristocracies and Economic Development in Tropical Africa. G. Arrighi—J. S. Saul: *Essays on the Political Economy of Africa*. Monthly Review Press, New York, 1973.

The two main variants of the theory of dualism discussed here contain, however, such fundamental weaknesses that finally it seems to be impossible to understand the phenomenon of dualism itself. The one-sided analysis of this complex socio-economic phenomenon, either from an exclusively sociological-cultural or from an exclusively economic-technological point of view doom both variants to failure. Owing to the separation of the *economic* and *social* sides of dualism, sociological dualism becomes unexplainable, while economic dualism is simplified to the problem of technical coefficients and the asymmetry of production functions.

This simplification, in particular, and the overemphasis on the *technological* nature of dualism, in general, are, of course, highly relevant to the final conclusions drawn for economic policy. In this way the question of *social conflict* will be taken off the agenda. (True, in the theory of sociological dualism it appears in a false presentation: as the conflict of different forms of social consciousness, behaviours and cultures.) Technological dualism manifests itself in the last analysis in a vicious circle which—like other vicious circles—can be broken by large-scale foreign aid, by the "infusion" of capital and technical assistance. In this way the qualitative problems are reduced to *quantitative* ones (namely to the questions of the comparative ratios of population growth and of the formation or inflow of capital needed to absorb labour). Consequently, the "efforts to produce a take-off into sustained growth in underdeveloped countries through vigorous development programs supported by technical and capital assistance from the West"[62] cannot be regarded as useless. On the contrary, they provide the key to the solution. Moreover, if the differences between underdeveloped and advanced economies are "of degree rather than of kind",[63] then contemporary Western economic theory—at least its non-orthodox variety—seems to be equally applicable both to the former and the latter.

As we have seen, Higgins' criticism of Boeke's sociological dualism was made just in favour of these very final conclusions. That is, against Boeke's pessimistic conclusions and *in defence* of the policy of the diffusion of Western capital, technology and institutions (and at the same time also in defence of Western theories)! While Boeke lays stress on the resistance of "Eastern" society against which the application of any technical, outside means whatsoever "makes the problem more insoluble than ever", Higgins considers the conquering of backwardness as a process in which transplanted Western capitalism (the modern sector) supported by further transplantations of capital and technical assistance gradually diffuse into the precapitalist, indigenous sector. While Boeke calls for a separate theory,

---

[62] B. Higgins: Op. cit., p. 281.
[63] Reference to P. T. Bauer and B. S. Yamey: *The Economics of Underdeveloped Countries.* Durham, 1957, pp. 8–9. See B. Higgins: Op. cit., p. 293.

Higgins finds that contemporary Western theories provide a proper tool not only for understanding the phenomenon but also for guiding the transformation process.

In spite of these different conclusions, both theories have a *common* and—from the point of view of their evaluation—decisive *basic assumption.* Namely, they assume the traditional social or economic sector as something *given* against which the penetration and spread of the modern, Western, capitalistic sector will be ineffective (as in Boeke's view) or—given above a certain order of magnitude—effective (as in Higgins' view). Insofar as the question of the survival of the traditional sector is raised at all, they seem to explain it merely by the inner essence of the sector itself or by its resistance to the modern sector. Neither variant examines just how the survival and conservation of the traditional sector and thereby dualism as a whole is connected with the specific nature and limits of the operation of the "modern" sector, which is one but the determining part of dualism. Neither variant analyses dualism as a whole, as the product of a specific *historical* development, in which the determining element is the transplanted product of another, *external* development. Neither variant regards dualism as a *particular unity*, the two parts of which not only differ from or contradict one another, or simply react to one another, but in which the differences, contradictions and effects on one another of the two sectors are determined by the specific character of one sector (i.e. "modern").

It is the dialectics of the whole and its parts, of the primary and secondary contradictions and, within the contradiction, of the determining and determined poles that is not grasped.

This is what *Andre Gunder Frank* has in mind when he writes: "They do not deal with, and even deny the existence of, the structure of the whole system through which the parts are related—that is, the structure which determines the duality of wealth and poverty, of one culture and another, and so on... If they see and deal with any structure at all it is at best the structures of the parts." While the two variants of dualism under discussion concentrate on how different the parts (the two sectors) are—in socio-cultural or technological terms—, and how one of them can be (or cannot be) transformed, *A. G. Frank* holds the view that the task proper is "to study what relates the parts to each other in order to be able to explain why they are different or dual" and "to change the relationships that produce these differences: that is, ... the structure of the *entire* social system which gives rise to the relations and, therefore, to the differences of the 'dual' society".[64]

We could completely agree with Frank if, in denying these justly criticized variants of the theory of dualism, he did not go so far as to deny dualism itself by merging it into the "dualism" of the entire capitalist world system,

[64] A. G. Frank: *Sociology of Development...*, p. 61.

90

into the contradiction of the centre and the periphery.[65] Thus his theory loses sight of the existence of dualism and contradictions[66] *within* the socio-economic system of underdeveloped countries and thereby of the actual task of changing *this system* and carrying out the transformation that is possible also *within* the system. Only the "dualism" of and contradiction between the metropolitan centres and backward peripheries are concerned with stressing the task, or the sequence of tasks, that "in order for the underdeveloped parts of the world to develop, the structure of the world social system must change—on the international, national, and local levels".[67] This statement also reveals some sort of failure to understand the dialectic of the parts and the whole. While the former theories failed to understand how the *whole* determines its parts, this latter fails to understand how *the whole* can be changed by changing its parts. It seems that while correctly pointing out that underdevelopment was created by world capitalism and that the socio-economic structure of underdeveloped countries is the product of the forces of world capitalism, Frank forgets that a reverse relationship has also come into existence especially since the system of underdevelopment received a "national" framework with state sovereignty. This very socio-economic structure, this underdevelopment with its internal dualism and structural deformity gives free scope for the operation of those forces. What follows from the recognition of this interaction is a conclusion which stresses the need for and the feasability of actions on *both* "national" and international levels, i.e., a progressive national policy aimed at the *internal* transformation of the local system and structure, and a struggle for structural changes in the *international* economy, for a new policy of international cooperation promoting (instead of inhibiting) the progressive local changes. This dual task is more realistic than the slogan of "world revolution" which can easily be manipulated by the ruling elites as an excuse for not tackling the task of transforming the local system.

[65] "The supposed structural duality is contrary to both historical and contemporary reality: the *entire* social fabric of the underdeveloped countries has long since been penetrated and transformed by, and integrated into, the world embracing system of which it is an integral part." (A. G. Frank: *Sociology of Development*..., p. 60.)

[66] Frank ignores the fact that there are also other interpretations of the dualism within underdeveloped countries than those criticized by him, and that many Marxist authors point out the fact of dualism. (See Ignacy Sachs' two-sector model in his *Patterns of Public Sector in Underdeveloped Economies.* Asia Publishing House, 1964, pp. 37–51.) Frank even goes as far as to refer to J. Woddis' work (*Africa. The Roots of Revolt*) for support of his general denial of dualism, in spite of the fact that it is exactly Woddis who gives an excellent analysis of the dualism of reserves and capitalist plantations, revealing thereby the position of Africans migrating between the traditional and "modern" sectors.

[67] A. G. Frank: Op. cit., p. 63.

CHAPTER V

THE THEORY OF THE STAGES OF GROWTH. ROSTOW'S "HISTORICAL" EXPLANATION

The speeding up of the social development of the world and the striking international aspects of this development (the emergence of new social systems, the collapse of power structures thought to be eternal) gave a new and strong impetus to *historical interpretations* of socio-economic development in Western theories.

It would be an overstatement to declare that the demand for a historical approach to socio-economic phenomena has arisen from the insufficiency of the theories of economic underdevelopment outlined in the preceding chapters. The historical approach had considerable antecedents earlier, too, (as in the German "historical school"). This demand has followed from the fact of the *coexistence* of two systems, of socialism and capitalism, which called for an explanation and prediction as to their future development can no longer be reduced to a merely military issue. But this very explanation and prediction depend very closely on how we answer the question about the prospects of the newly independent countries of the "third" world.

In addition, as the long anticolonialist struggle (lasting decades or even centuries) of these countries provided a favourable psychological atmosphere for them to see colonialism as responsible for their underdevelopment and backward state—a view scientifically confirmed[1] by the Marxist critical analysis of world capitalism—it has become increasingly important for a historical explanation to extend also to the phenomena of economic underdevelopment and include the backward countries in the general picture of socio-economic development by relating their present state to the past of the advanced countries and their future to the present state of the latter.

The historical explanations of socio-economic development are represented in Western social sciences by the *theories of the stages of economic growth.* Among these theories we shall discuss that of *W. W. Rostow,*[2] partly because it is probably the best known and most popular,

---

1 Here we do not wish to touch upon the problem to what extent the oversimplified vulgar Marxist and dogmatic trends have distorted this view by making it one-sided and unhistorical. Nor can we discuss the question here of how the historical responsibility of colonialism has been restricted to the past and how "colonialism" has often been interpreted in a formal sense.

2 For a theory of the stages of growth see also R. Aron: *Dix-huit leçons sur la société industrielle.* Gallimard, 1962.—N. S. B. Gras: Stages in Economic History. *Journal of*

and partly because there is no substantial difference between the various theories as far as their *basic* concept is concerned. Rostow is not specifically concerned with "economic underdevelopment" and merely touches upon it within his theoretical system, but he has exercised considerable influence on underdevelopment theories. In addition, the *general* character of his basic idea in particular justifies that, in discussing the various interpretations of underdevelopment, his views should also be considered.

Rostow purposefully opposes his historical explanation to that of Marxism.[3] He endeavours to present the state and development of all possible societies of the past and present as a certain stage or part of a single, uniform development process. In other words, he wishes to offer a comprehensive historical explanation, just as Marxism does. However, unlike Marxism, he sees in the highest stage of this process not socialism or communism, but the ideal of developed capitalism.

Rostow distinguishes five main stages. These are:

1. *The traditional society.* It is characterized by a lack of systematic understanding of the physical environment which, in turn, hinders the development of technology and productivity. A minimum 75 per cent of the working population is engaged in food production, and national income, apart from consumption, is wasted mostly on unproductive ends. The society is of a hierarchical structure where political power is concentrated in the hands of the landowners or is embodied in a central authority supported by the army and civil servants.

2. *The transitional stage: the preconditions for the take-off.* This stage is characterized by radical changes in three non-industrial sectors, i.e. transport, agriculture and foreign trade. The latter manifests itself in the expansion of imports financed by the more effective exploitation and exports of natural resources or capital imports. The development of transport and communications is often connected with the marketing of raw materials "in which other nations have an economic interest", and is often "financed by foreign capital".[4] Society is characterized by the gradual development of a new mentality, the rise of the propensity to accept new techniques and the emergence and "freedom to operate" of a new class of businessmen. The new mentality, the idea of economic progress usually comes from outside, and spreads within and through the social élite.

Economic and Business History, II, 1930.—B. F. Hoselitz: Theories of Stages of Economic Growth. *Theories of Economic Growth.* Ed. by B. F. Hoselitz. Glencoe, 1960.—C. R. Fay: Stages in Economic History. *English Economic History.* Cambridge, 1940.—H. Giersch: Stages and Spurts of Economic Development. *Economic Progress.* Ed. by L. H. Dupriez. Louvain, 1955, etc.

[3] This is emphasized, among other ways, by the sub-title of his book. (*The Stages of Economic Growth, A Non-Communist Manifesto.* Cambridge, 1960)

[4] See Rostow's study in *The Economics of Underdevelopment*, p. 158.

3. *The "take-off" stage.* This is the crucial stage of growth, a relatively short (one to two decades long) interval in which, under the influence of a "particular sharp stimulus" the rate of investment increases to such an extent that real output per capita rises and the initial increase carries with it radical changes in production techniques. This stage, which in practice involves the industrial revolution, is characterized by a rapid expansion of a small group of sectors (leading sectors), and by such a minimum rate of productive investments over 10 per cent of annual national income which is achieved not only once but has been kept up permanently by society. The take-off witnesses a definitive social, political and cultural victory of those who would modernize the economy over those who would either cling to the traditional society or seek other goals.

4. *Drive to maturity.* Typical of this stage is the spread of growth from the leading sectors to the other sectors and the wider application of modern technology. The structure and quality of the labour force experience a change, shifting towards the urban and skilled categories. Higher consumption demands development. The new labour force makes itself felt in the political life, too. The character of industrial leadership also changes and professional managers (the "nameless comfortable cautious committee-men") with a wider outlook and knowledge come to the force. Society begins to seek objectives which include but transcend the application of modern technology to resources. The extension of industrialization ceases to be acceptable as an overriding goal.

5. *The stage of high mass consumption.* This stage can be reached by a technically and technologically mature society after having attained a certain level of national income if it is able to resist the attractions of world power and chooses the alternative of increased private consumption including automobiles, durable consumer goods, family homes with gardens in suburbs, etc. After a brief and superficial flirtation with the attractions of world power at the turn of the century, the United States— according to Rostow—opted whole-heartedly for this alternative of mass consumption in the twenties and has continued to be in this stage ever since that time.[5] Moreover, while Western Europe and Japan are entering the era of high mass consumption and the Soviet Union "is dallying on its fringes", the USA has already exceeded it to a certain extent in so far that "the march of compound interest" is bringing its society "close to the point where the pursuit of food, shelter, clothing, as well as durable consumer goods and public and private services, may no longer dominate" its life. New horizons have opened up beyond high mass consumption and society is now turning its focus towards new, superior objectives. By referring to the unexpected

---

[5] This needs no comment, indeed, in view of the events of world politics of the last decades (and of reading passages of successive Presidential messages on poverty).

increase of the birthrate and the increase of the proportion of large families in the US, Rostow thinks his statement being proven.

Thus, in Rostow's view, the socialist countries also represent one or another stage or variant of the general development process, and will eventually become similar to the most developed capitalist countries. Rostow no longer considers the socialist countries as a historical absurdity or error, a wilding to be weeded, and this undoubtedly shows a more realistic attitude or only the march of time. What he does, nevertheless, is rather to *blur the basic differences between different social systems*.

The actual possibility of doing so is provided, or he himself tries to have it accepted, by the fact that in a classification according to the achieved level of economic growth, more precisely according to the present level of the productive forces, there is indeed a capitalist country at the top, whereas below it and at the middle and lower grades there can be found both capitalist and socialist countries. The fact is that, contrary to the Marxian expectation, it was not in the most developed capitalist countries but in the underdeveloped or semi-developed countries, that the socialist revolution triumphed first, making the process of socialist transformation start in single countries (instead of the world system as a whole), and these countries have not as yet been able to reach the level of the productive forces of the most developed capitalist countries. This has given the theoreticians of capitalism the opportunity to deny the Marxian theory of the process of historical development drawn up on the basis of the thorough analysis of *production relations* and to replace it by a simple scheme built on differences between the *present* development levels of productive forces.[6]

Thus Rostow—like Raymond Aron, Colin Clark and others—concentrates on the *growth of productive forces*, or on certain manifestations[7] and prerequisites of this growth. Yet, Rostow's theory

[6] It is for the same reason that Richard Gill, too, considers Marx's theory as outdated. He points out that Marx was greatly mistaken, when differentiating the "stages" in social development according to changes brought about by class struggle in the control over the means of production (more precisely: according to changes in the ownership relations), and did not prove a good prophet in that he did not foresee either the considerable improvement in the living standards of the Western countries, or the circumstances of subsequent socialist revolutions.

Although it goes beyond the scope of this study, let it be noted in passing that this sort of refutation of Marx, the assessing of Western capitalism as the highest stage of human development as well as the interpretations of economic backwardness outlined so far, derive from the failure to understand real historical development, i.e. from an approach that continues to analyse the development of individual countries *in themselves* as if colonialism and the worldwide activity of monopoly capital had not made capitalism a *world system*.

[7] Colin Clark, e.g., distinguishes three stages in the general process of growth according to changes in the sectoral structure: (1) In a backward society *agriculture* is the dominant sector. (2) In a developing society the proportion and importance of the *processing industry* increase in relation to agriculture. (3) In a developed society the relative importance of the "tertiary" industries, i.e. *services*, grows. (*Conditions of Economic Progress*. Macmillan, London,

cannot be regarded by any means as a one-sidedly technical-economic approach. In compliance with the traditions of the old "historical school", Rostow, as well, investigates the growth of productive forces from the *aspect of social development*, and by illustrating the historical changes in this growth, he tries—like *W. Roscher*[8]—to present one society, namely capitalism, as the highest stage of social evolution. Of course, by the very nature of the matter, it does not suffice to investigate only the self-movement of productive forces. The real point to be brought out is that the development of productive forces is determined by the *social environment* and that *the most favourable* environment is capitalist society, as it ensures the highest level of growth.

Thus Rostow considers, on the one hand that social environment, i.e. "social relations" (as interpreted by him), determine and are not determined by the evolution of productive forces whilst, on the other hand, he puts societies into an order and specifies the "stages" of historical development according to the level of productive forces.

This is apparently acceptable and convincing as the development of productive forces really does depend on social relations, and, inversely, the superiority of a society is to be proven and demonstrated also by a higher development level of productive forces.

However, Rostow deprives social relations of their economic roots and substance and considers them as economically indeterminate[9] in an absolute sense, explaining them in the last analysis *in se*. He disregards ownership relations, the most important and *determining* element of social relations (blurring thereby the basic differences between societies) and investigates instead the changes in social attitudes, the "propensities" of society.[10] Thus, no matter how strongly he stresses the importance of social

---

1957.)—Clark's theory of stages reminds us of Friedrich List's classification of economic stages. List distinguishes the following 5 stages in economic development: (1) the savage stage, (2) the pastoral stage, (3) the agricultural stage, (4) the agricultural and manufacturing stage, and (5)the agricultural, manufacturing and commercial stage. (See F. List: *Das nationale System der politischen Oekonomie*. Stuttgart, 1841.)

8 Roscher investigates how the relative economic importance of the three factors of production: nature, labour and capital changed in the process of historical development. According to the predominance of each of these factors, he distinguishes three periods in social development: the first, in which the rule of nature was decisive, the second, in which the role of human labour became prominent, and the third, the most developed period, in which capital is the dominant factor. (See *Ansichten der Volkswirtschaft aus dem geschichtlichen Standpunkte*, 1861.) For further particulars and a criticism of the theory of Roscher and the German "historical school", see A. Mátyás: *A polgári közgazdaságtan története* (History of non-Marxian economics). Budapest, 1963, pp. 434–460.

9 "This structure is not economically determinist." (W. W. Rostow: *The Process of Economic Growth*. Oxford, 1960. p. 53.)

10 He distinguishes six fundamental propensities: (1) propensity to develop basic sciences; (2) propensity to apply science to economic ends; (3) propensity to accept innovations; (4)

and political factors and their effect on economic development and no matter how much he emphasizes that the realization of the preconditions for take-off "requires a major change in political and social structure and, even, in effective cultural values",[11]—he does not reveal *how, on what basis and with the agency of what forces* this change takes place in the political and social structure, and in the scale of cultural values. He does not make it clear why the propensities vary from society to society, and even from one class to the other within the same society. It seems that e.g. a capitalist businessman thinks as a businessman not because he is a capitalist but the other way round: he became a capitalist because he began to think as a businessman. And a wage earner, a peasant or even a nomadic tribal herdsman has not yet learnt to think in a business-like way, because his propensities to consume, to innovate, etc., are different.

Thus Rostow tries to define the various stages of economic growth by certain economic *and* social characteristics. However, the economic characteristics appear oversimplified and restricted to quantitative indices or the simple description of the state of productive forces, while the social characteristics are narrowed down to the attitudes, propensities of society or the actual places and roles of individuals, endowed with certain propensities, in society's organization.

As regards the former, it is scarcely possible to distinguish objectively between the different stages and societies on the basis of the *quantitative* evolution of productive forces. Unlike the *qualitative* differences in ownership and distribution relations, i.e. production relations—which provide an objective basis for marking out the individual socio-economic systems or "stages"—distinctions made on the basis of the development level of productive forces are hopelessly arbitrary and artificial.

As to the *latter*, if we conceive social propensities as variables independent of production relations, their very nature and the cause of their change become inexplicable. Since these social propensities, whose nature and change seem to be due to some accident or *Deus ex Machina* (or perhaps some sort of predestination?) constitute the motive forces of growth in Rostow's theory, the sequence of stages remains, as a matter of fact, scientifically undetermined (or just fatalistic?).

---

propensity to seek material advance; (5) propensity to consume; (6) propensity to have children. (Rostow: Ibid.)

According to Raymond Aron these propensities determining economic growth can be reduced to three factors: (1) the capacity for innovations (including theoretical knowledge, the readiness and incentive to apply it: the wish to achieve material improvement); (2) propensity to consume, which is related to the propensity to invest and thus appears, in fact, to have merged with the problem of capital; and finally (3) the demographic factor. (See R. Aron: Op. cit., pp. 200–201.)

[11] W. W. Rostow: The Take-Off into Self-Sustained Growth. *The Economics of Underdevelopment*, p. 157.

Consequently, the individual "stages" do not constitute an organic and qualitative unity either historically or logically; they can hardly be regarded as scientifically defined and the interrelationship between the individual stages is indeterminate, too.

This theory of five stages is practically a theory of the industrial revolution interpreted in a particular way, in which the first two stages are seen as being preparatory to the industrial revolution, and the last two as its result, i.e. self-sustained growth.[12] The fact of the industrial revolution, of the "take-off", however, can only be inferred from its result, from sustained growth.[13] Thus the "take-off" has only *seemingly* a positive definition.

Though according to Rostow "the take-off is defined as requiring all three of the following related conditions: (a) a rise in the *rate of productive investment* from 5 per cent or less to *over 10 per cent of the national income*; (b) the development of one or more substantial manufacturing sectors, with a *high rate of growth*; (c) the existence *or* quick emergence of a political, social and institutional framework which exploits the impulse to expansion...",[14] it turns out that the rate of productive investment cannot alone ensure the take-off,[15] and a "high rate of growth" of the manufacturing sectors can only be considered as defined, "once 'high' is explained",[16] and the passage concerning the "political, social and institutional framework" ... "defines these social phenomena as a complex that produces the effect Professor Rostow wishes to explain; and then he treats this definition as if it were a meaningful identification".[17]

Rostow himself declares that his "definition is also designed to rule out from the take-off the quite substantial economic progress which can occur in an economy before a truly self-reinforcing growth process gets under way".[18]

But as the take-off cannot be unambiguously defined, so it is also impossible to define self-sustained growth either. As *Kuznets* says: "The

[12] "... the sequence of economic development is taken to consist of three periods: a long period, when the preconditions for take-off are established; the take-off itself, defined within two or three decades; and a long period when growth becomes normal and relatively automatic." (Rostow: Ibid.)

[13] This is also pointed out by Habakukk: "The take-offs can only be confidently identified retrospectively; one can only tell if growth is going to be self-sustaining if in fact it has been sustained for a long period." (H. J. Habakukk's review of Rostow's. The Stages of Economic Growth in *Economic Journal*, September 1961.)

[14] W. W. Rostow: Op. cit., p. 164. (My italics.—*T. Sz.*)

[15] W. W. Rostow: Op. cit., p. 170.

[16] S. Kuznets: Notes on the Take-Off. Paper presented at the International Economic Association's Conference at Konstanz in September 1960. Reprinted in *Leading Issues in Development Economics*. (Ed. by G. M. Meier.) p. 28.

[17] Ibid.

[18] W. W. Rostow: Op. cit., p. 165.

concept (and stage) of 'self-sustained' growth is a misleading oversimplification. No growth is purely self-sustaining or purely self-limiting."[19]

The inaccurate and sloppy nature of Rostow's definitions is pointed out by several of his critics. *Simon Kuznets* emphasizes that any division of growth into "stages" sets the minimum requirement that "a given stage must display *empirically testable* characteristics...; ... the characteristics of a given stage must be *distinctive*...; ...the *analytical relation* to the preceding stage...and ...to the succeeding stage must be indicated".[20] But Rostow's classification does not meet this requirement. The characteristics of the individual stages are far from being distinctive. "Yet much of what Professor Rostow would attribute to the take-off has already occurred in the precondition stage." "The line of division between the take-off and the following stage of self-sustained growth or drive to maturity is also blurred...; ...given the distinctiveness only in the statistical level of the rate of productive investment, there is no solid ground upon which to discuss Professor Rostow's view of the analytical relation between the take-off stage and the preceding and succeeding stages."[21]

In connection with the preconditions for the take-off, *Habakukk* points out: "In many cases the increase of agricultural output and the creation of overhead social capital are not conditions *whose pre-existence* explains the acceleration of growth; they are *part of the acceleration* which needs to be explained." Also the definition of the maturity stage is inaccurate in saying that "a society has effectively applied the range of modern technology to the bulk of its resources", as "the bulk of a country's resources has no clear meaning independent of the level of technology".[22]

Cairncross, too, mentions the inaccuracy of the definiton of the various stages and the overlapping of their characteristics. He puts the question: "If the various stages overlap, what is then the meaning of a 'stage'?"[23] He also points out the tautological character of the definiton of "take-off": "a definition in these terms tells us nothing about the factors at work since we can only deduce their existence from the fact of take-off, never the likelihood of take-off from the ascertained fact of their existence."[24]

[19] S. Kuznets: Op. cit., p. 33.

[20] S. Kuznets: Op. cit., pp. 25–33. (My italics.—*T. SZ.)*

[21] S. Kuznets: Op. cit., pp. 26–27.

[22] H. J. Habakukk's review of Rostow's *The Stages of Economic Growth*, reprinted in *Leading Issues...*, p. 37.

[23] A. K. Cairncross: Essays in Bibliography and Criticism, XLV: The Stages of Economic Growth. In *Economic History Review*, April 1961. Reprinted in *Leading Issues...*, pp. 33–36.

[24] For other reviews and critiques of Rostow's doctrine see also S. G. Checkland: Theories of Economic and Social Evolution: the Rostow Challenge. *Scottish Journal of Political Economy*, November 1960.—D. C. North: A Note on Professor Rostow's Take-Off into Self-Sustained Economic Growth. *The Manchester School*, January 1958.—G. L. S. Schackle: The Stages of Economic Growth. *Political Studies*, February 1962.—B. Higgins:

François Perroux also criticizes in general the classification of the stages of development on the basis of quantitative changes in productive forces. In economic history, he writes, the stages of development differ from those periods of growth characterized by the percentual acceleration or slowing down of the growth of production.[25]

Besides the faulty interpretation of the relationship of economy and society, the essence of social development and the superficial or sometimes even tautological definition of the arbitrary stages, there is still a very important and fundamental *methodological* error in Rostow's theory. He outlines the imagined process of social development in such a way that he places societies *existing side by side in space one after the other in time* (or one before the other), as representing different "stages" of a general process of growth (not according to their inner substance and historical content, but simply on the basis of the given level of their productive forces), while the *mutual* relationship of their development, particularly their close intertwining since the emergence of capitalist world economy, finds scarcely any appreciation in the analysis, and if it does, then with prejudice.

There exist the present-day societies, each with its peculiar, variegated face, with its different socio-economic set-up, historical past and natural-geographic environment and, above all, with their interrelationships different in measure and direction. But, despite all these differences and interrelationships the societies can, indeed, be classified at discretion in certain categories according to economic indices representing the levels of their *productive forces.* Thus, irrespective of all differences between them, some countries may be put into the highest, some into the lowest, and many others into the intermediate groups. And then comes the logical "salto mortale": the individual features of the societies already classified reappear, but this time no longer as the indicators—mostly very superficial—of a certain phase of their *own* specific development, but as characteristics of a certain stage of *general* historical development. If a society classified among the highest group has such and such characteristic features, then every society that reaches this stage, owing to the development of its productive forces, will assume the same features. Moreover, in order to reach this higher stage on the strength of its productive forces, it must develop these characteristics. Thus, from groups classified by a very narrow and one-sided criterion, Rostow forms historical "stages": a society in a lower group corresponds to the earlier "stage" of growth of a society in a higher group,

Economic Development, pp. 234–238.—G. Ohlin: Reflections on the Rostow Doctrine. *Economic Development and Cultural Change*, July 1961.—P. Baran and E. Hobsbawm: The Stages of Economic Growth. *Kyklos*, Vol. XIV, No. 2, 1961.—A. G. Frank: Sociology of Development.... Op. cit.—A. Mátyás: *A gazdasági fejlődés feltételei* (Preconditions of Economic Development). Op. cit.

25 F. Perroux: *L'économie du XXième siècle.* Press Univ., Paris, 1961, p. 162.

while a society in a higher group is but a stage to be reached by a lower-ranking society in the further course of its development. After that all that remains to be done is to illustrate this process by historical analogies picked out by sweat, to point out a few phenomena which seem to be really similar in the past of the more developed and the present of the less developed countries—and the logical "somersault" appears justified and acceptable.

By this method not only the socialist countries can be classified, irrespective of their social system, in one or another stage of general development, but even the development of the colonial areas can be treated as "one of the variants" of the general case and allotted to a specific stage of growth.

Of course, all this is not presented by Rostow in such an open, clear way. The individual "stages" are shown to be far more complex and varied, the historical illustrations given are far more numerous (and the number of "or"-s is too many) with the result that it is not easy to find out at first sight the basically unhistorical nature and real sense of this "historical" approach.

Obviously, from the point of view of our study, the first three stages, and particularly the second one, will be of special interest as the picture Rostow draws of the societies in the pre-take-off stage is intended to resemble, in one way or another, most of the present-day underdeveloped countries.[26] Moreover, some of the characteristics of the transitional stage[27] are such that they are far more—or even exclusively—typical of the underdeveloped countries of today than of any earlier historical period in the development of the now advanced countries. Thus it would be useless to seek in history a *general* "stage" which was characterized by a one-sided dependence on trade and foreign capital and, at the same time, by a more rapid development of agriculture than industry. And in any case, having foreign capital to set development in motion, the export of raw materials adjusted to the interests of other countries, together with import sensitivity, and new ideas penetrating from outside—all presuppose a more advanced external environment, that is the existence of more developed countries. And if we presuppose this *ad infinitum*, even for the latter countries, we shall inevitably

---

[26] In his study, published in the book *Economics of Underdevelopment*, Rostow classifies four types of underdeveloped countries on the basis of their economic indices: (a) pretake-off economies (where the apparent savings and investment rates, including limited net capital imports, probably come to under 5 per cent of net national product), (b) economies attempting take-off (where these rates have risen over 5 per cent of net national product), (c) growing economies (where these rates have reached 10 per cent or over), and (d) enclave economies (where the rates have reached 10 per cent or over, but the domestic preconditions for sustained growth have not been achieved). Thus the majority of underdeveloped countries are classified into the transitional stage. (p. 170.)

[27] It is true, Rostow outlines these characteristics far less definitely and also mentions a number of other characteristics, together with various historical examples. Therefore, if we want to grasp the essence of his doctrine, we necessarily have to simplify.

come, in the end, to a *single* country which is an *exception* to the outlined process of general development, which had no recourse to a more developed environment in the transitional stage and whose transition from the traditional stage had to be induced by *other* factors than the typical ones.

Rostow does follow, indeed, this train of thought and considers Great Britain, even within Western Europe, to be such a special case. Great Britain was the first country to outgrow the traditional stage under the influence of a number of mixed factors such as—according to Rostow—the gradual evolution of modern science and the modern scientific attitude (due, among others, to the impetus given by the discovery of new countries and continents), the settling of political and religious issues, increased social mobility, the role of non-comfortists in the process of industrial innovation, on the one hand, and the widening of the external market, the upswing of foreign trade, the increased specialization of production and the extension to *trade* and *colonies* of the old dynastic competition for control over European territories, on the other.

As far as the first group of factors is concerned (progress in scientific thinking, and in social, political and religious fields), the same question must obviously be raised as in the case of "propensities": What determined this change and progress? What real and objective processes were involved? For if this question remains unanswered, we are bound to come to the conclusion that the British people were endowed with specific and superior intellectual qualities differing from those of other peoples. If, however, we consider the factors of the second group as determinant (those that helped Britain to move out of the traditional stage), then the question arises first: How did Britain manage at all, to reach historically (and of course above all economically) the stage of being able to penetrate into external markets, foreign territories and colonies? Then, secondly, we become aware at once that international trade and the "mutual relations" between nations that promoted Britain's and Western Europe's take-off *were by no means* equally advantageous for all parties. If this proves to be true, why do we not look for the causes of the economic underdevelopment of other countries and particularly of the colonies along this line? Do we not come to a logical dead-lock by assuming that the rise out of the traditional stage was furthered by the widening of international economic relations in the case of Britain (and Western Europe), while for the other participants of these relations the precondition for their rise was that Britain (and Western Europe) should have already reached the take-off stage?! (Rostow himself remarks that Britain's take-off set in motion a series of positive and negative demonstration effects which progressively unhinged other traditional societies.)

But apart from the details, what can we think at all of such a theory of growth which makes an *exception* to the law of the general process of growth in the case of the very country which first started on the road of growth?!

102

As far as the present state of the ex-colonial countries is concerned, Rostow considers it as a *natural* stage of growth which every country (except Britain) had or has to undergo. Hence the distorted foreign trade pattern and one-sided dependence are not the harmful consequences of colonialism. Furthermore, colonialism itself must be assessed in the last analysis as favourable. The import of foreign capital and its dominant role in financing, the switching over to raw material production and export, etc. seem to belong to the normal preparatory process of the take-off stage. And the penetration of the ideas of more developed societies into the traditional societies represents the "positive demonstration effect" of colonization, and is likewise an important element of the preparation for take-off.[28] True, Rostow admits that colonization also has its "negative demonstration effect", imposing the will of the more developed society on the less developed one by the use of sheer military force. However, this too is beneficial in the end for "without the affront to human and national dignity caused by the intrusion of more advanced powers, the rate of modernization of traditional societies over the past century and a half would have been much slower than, in fact, it has been . . ."[29]

Rostow's "historical" explanation and similar theories of the present state of the former colonial countries provide the theoretical basis for the use of the terms "economically backward" or "underdeveloped" country. Then, if what these countries pass through—though belatedly, owing to several internal factors—is the *same* natural and general stage of economic growth that the more developed countries also passed through earlier, then their present state is backwardness indeed in the strict sense of the word. If this is true, colonialism cannot be made responsible for that state. On the contrary, it appears as the very accelerator of progress. If the colonized society, even *after the rise* of colonialism, passes through the same stages of growth (only with a certain time lag) as the colonizing one, and if the former colony finds itself even *after the collapse* of colonialism in a stage identical with that which the former colonizing country also passed through in its earlier development, then it seems to be clear that colonialism, itself, whatever negative effect it might display, did *not* fundamentally change the direction and process of development. It did not force the two poles to develop farther away from each other, but rather brought them nearer up to each other.

---

[28] "Characteristic of Rostow's second stage is the penetration of underdeveloped countries by influences created abroad—mostly in the developed countries—and diffused to the underdeveloped ones, where they destroy traditionalism and simultaneously create the preconditions that will lead to the subsequent take-off in the third stage", writes A. G. Frank. And he adds: "Yet these same metropolitan conditions and influences . . . have not brought about economic development or even led to a take-off into development in a single one of the '75 countries'." (A. G. Frank: *Sociology of Development . . .*, p. 39.)

[29] W. W. Rostow: *The Process of Economic Growth*, p. 315.

The interpretation of the present state of "backwardness" as an original, primitive state, or as one of the natural transitional stages of the normal evolution from the original primitive state toward maturity, is explicitly or implicitly the basic idea of most underdevelopment theories.[30] This interpretation gained its proper explicit, theoretical treatment in Rostow's theory. "It is explicit in Rostow, as it is implicit in Hoselitz, that underdevelopment is the original stage of what are *supposedly traditional* societies—that there were no stages prior to the present stage of underdevelopment"—says *A. G. Frank*. "It is further explicit in Rostow that the now developed societies were once underdeveloped. But all this is quite contrary to fact. This entire approach to economic development and cultural change attributes a history to the developed countries but denies all history to the underdeveloped ones."[31] Consequently, this "historical" interpretation of underdevelopment is, in fact, *unhistorical*, denying history to the majority of the world's countries and peoples. But it is also unhistorical from another important point of view: it simply disregards the historical fact, which by the way is truly reflected by the most typical and specific characteristics of underdeveloped countries,[32] that "the economic and political expansion of Europe since the fifteenth century has come to incorporate the now underdeveloped countries into a single stream of world history, which has given rise simultaneously to the present development of some countries and the present underdevelopment of others".[33]

This opinion, which views "the characteristics of development and underdevelopment as *sui generis* to the country concerned",[34] is fairly widespread and is generally spared even by the criticism of those who attack Rostow because of his method of periodization, the economic and non-economic criteria of his classification, the obvious oversimplifications, contradictions, tautologies or the far from precise terminology and definitions.

Most theoreticians of underdevelopment and development, apart from a few exceptions and Marxists, usually accept without reservation this

---

[30] To avoid generalizations, let us take a look at least at one of the non-Marxist exceptions: Celso Furtado says: "Underdevelopment is not a necessary stage in the process of formation of the modern capitalistic economies. It is a special process due to the penetration of modern capitalistic enterprises into archaic structures. The phenomenon of underdevelopment occurs in a number of forms and in various stages." (C. Furtado: *Development and Underdevelopment*. University of California Press, 1964, p. 138.)

[31] A. G. Frank: Op. cit., p. 37.

[32] C. Furtado writes: "The displacement of the European economic frontier almost always resulted in the formation of hybrid economies in which a capitalist nucleus, so to speak, existed in a state of 'peaceful coexistence' with an archaic structure... it would be incorrect to conclude that the hybrid economies we have been discussing have behaved in all circumstances as if they were pre-capitalistic structures." (C. Furtado: Op. cit., pp. 132–133.)

[33] A. G. Frank: Op. cit., p. 37.

[34] A. G. Frank: Op. cit., pp. 43–44.

isolated, undialectical interpretation of backwardness and development, in which they regard backwardness and development as comparable but basically independent. The difference in their views is shown merely in the extent to which they consider the present state of backwardness *identical* with the state the present developed countries found themselves in some time ago.

According to *Leibenstein*, e.g., "the broad characteristics of backward economies today are not different from what they were in advanced economies in a former period".[35] *Simon Kuznets*, on the other hand, when analysing the state of advanced countries prior to industrialization and comparing it with the state of backward countries of today, comes to the conclusion that the latter are in a far worse situation today, both in respect of their income levels and also their demographic conditions (because of the time lag) than the now advanced countries were in earlier periods. "Both the absolute and relative economic position, as well as the general cast of the immediately antecedent history of the now developed countries in their pre-industrial phase were cardinally different from the economic position and the immediate historical heritage of the underdeveloped countries of today."[36]

It is because of the demonstration effect that *Nurkse*[37] sees a considerable difference between the present position of the backward and an earlier state of the advanced countries. The former, seeing the higher consumption levels that exist in the latter, tend to save a smaller percentage of their real per capita income than the now advanced countries did several decades or centuries ago when they had the same real income. *Celso Furtado* agrees in that with Nurske but he is, on the whole, opposed to seeing analogies.[38] When referring to *Kuznets* and *Gerschenkron*[39] *G. M. Meier* also emphasizes, in contradiction to Rostow's analogy, the relatively more unfavourable position of the backward countries of today. Though he does not find this analogy out of place, he maintains that "there are also differences—by way of different kinds of problems now confronting poor countries, and in the manner in which some problems, although similar in

[35] H. Leibenstein: Op. cit., p. 102.

[36] S. Kuznets: Underdeveloped Countries and the Pre-Industrial Phase in the Advanced Countries. *The Economics of Underdevelopment*, p. 151.

[37] See R. Nurkse: *Problems of Capital Formation in Underdeveloped Countries*. Oxford, 1953 and our following chapter.

[38] "The absence of basic information and the resultant ignorance of the real economic facts have given rise, among economists in the underdeveloped countries, to the habit of reasoning by analogy, in the mistaken belief that, up to a certain point, economic phenomena are the same everywhere." (Celso Furtado: Capital Formation and Economic Development. *The Economics of Underdevelopment*, p. 309.)

[39] A. Gerschenkron: *Economic Backwardness in Historical Perspective*. Cambridge, 1962.

kind to those of the past, are now expressed in different degrees of intensity and complexity".[40]

What really matters, however, is not the measure of comparability, neither the degree of identity of states. What is questionable is the sort of approach itself "in all its variations" which ignores that the historical and structural reality of the present underdeveloped countries "is the product of the very same historical process and systemic structure as is the development of the now developed countries".[41]

When discussing theories which explain "economic underdevelopment" by development-inhibiting factors or their vicious circles, we were faced, as we have seen, with the problem *why* these limiting factors were *not* at work in the earlier periods of the now advanced countries, or if they were, why and how these countries managed to break out of these vicious circles. This requires a historical answer. Rostow's answer is to try to find in the history of the now developed countries the stage that corresponds to the present state of underdevelopment. It turns out, however, that he does not succeed, even at the expense of a logical "salto mortale", and is compelled to make the very first country (Britain) that started along the path of growth, exempt from the analogy.

It has also turned out, as evidenced by Kuznets' calculations, that even according to the most superficial economic indices and phenomena, there is a *substantial difference* between the present state of underdeveloped countries and the supposedly analogous state of earlier societies. Therefore, it is obviously impossible to explain this merely by the autonomous and isolated self-evolution of these societies. (Unless we resort to the reactionary ideology of "superior" and "inferior races" by accepting some original, predestinate differences in intellectual capacities.) The autonomous self-evolution of societies proceeds roughly in the same direction and via the same principal stages. The delay, lagging behind, loss of tempo, can be explained by local, internal factors. If, however, the direction and an essential stage of development are different, there must be an *external* cause accounting for this difference. Hence, the present state of "underdevelopment" is also the result of an "external" factor.

This "external" factor, the system of "international" economic relations and colonialism itself did not play only the positive role that Rostow

[40] G. M. Meier: *Leading Issues in Development Economics.* 1964, p. 43.

[41] A. G. Frank: Op. cit., p. 44.—Frank mentions specifically the case of the so-called *tabula rasa* countries, i.e. those Latin-American countries which "had no population at all before they were incorporated into the developing mercantilist and capitalist system", and consequently had never experienced Rostow's first stage, but entered world history by stepping right into Rostow's second stage. And "*the relationship between the mercantilist and capitalist metropolis and these colonies succeeded in implanting* the social, political, and economic structure they now have: that is, *the structure of underdevelopment*". (A. G. Frank: Op. cit., pp. 38, 40.)

assumes, i.e. that it unhinged the traditional societies by its demonstration effects. *The economic colonialism of the world capitalist powers instead diverted the course of development, brought about a different kind of "state" and widened the development gap.*[42] On the basis of what has been said it is rather obvious that economic underdevelopment can neither be satisfactorily explained by internal factors nor can it be seen as a natural stage in the general process of growth.

[42] Kuznets states: "Not only have the relative differences among the developed and underdeveloped countries, judged by per capita income, persisted over the last century, but the disparity has increased." (S. Kuznets: Op. cit., p. 145.)

CHAPTER VI

UNDERDEVELOPMENT IN RELATIONSHIP WITH SOME EXTERNAL, INTERNATIONAL FACTORS

The concept of underdevelopment as an original stage or as a natural stage of transition explicable in itself leads, as we have seen, to an obvious contradiction with both empirical reality and historical facts. The peculiar structural features of underdeveloped countries bear witness to the fact that their present state has been determined by a historical development in which *external forces* have played a prominent part. The practical problems of the economic policy of development also make us aware of the fact that even the most successful "critical minimum (or maximum?) effort" has to face the dangers resulting from the *counteracting forces of international economy*.

As a result, the external, international factors—not only those with a supposedly positive but also those with a negative effect—began to be taken increasingly into consideration in the various theories of development and underdevelopment. In this respect the essential difference between the various theories lies mainly in what sort of concrete relationships these theories discover between the external factors and underdevelopment, what importance they attach to these factors in the explanation of underdevelopment, and how they explain the emergence and operation of these factors themselves.

We can distinguish roughly *three* main trends in the evaluation of the external factors of underdevelopment.

1. *The Marxist approach.* A distinction must be made here between the original, classical dialectic Marxist approach which analyses and adapts the changes on various planes, and the one-sided, vulgar orthodox-dogmatic or purist-idealist trends which are derived from or became attached to the former. Marxism, in its classical form, traces the present state of underdeveloped countries back to colonialism, or, to be more precise, to the international economic system of imperialism (involving the colonial, semi-colonial and dependent countries) and to its changes. It conceives colonialism and imperialism itself as a stage in the development of a specific socio-economic system, i.e. capitalism, following naturally and objectively from its inherent laws and nature. Hence it attaches a *decisive* role to the external, international factors in the formation of the present state and structure of underdeveloped countries.[1]

---

[1] It does not follow from this that he attributes to it an *exclusively negative* role. Nor does it follow that the further development and state of the underdeveloped countries after the collapse of the colonial system are also decided and determined by the above external factors.

2. *The trend of those theoreticians* who, like Myrdal, Prebisch, A. Lewis, Singer, etc., regard the external forces as more or less decisive (sometimes not only retrospectively, i.e. in respect of the emergence of under-development, but even prospectively, i.e. in respect of its liquidation), yet either do not analyse these forces and their effects in the organic system of their relationships, or take the system itself or the individual factors for granted. Thus emphasis on the external factors does not go hand in hand with the analysis of their historical and social origin. The criticism of colonialism, of the capitalist international division of labour and international trade is not accompanied by the criticism of their origin, i.e. capitalist system. As a result of this approach, the specific features of a certain system appear as general.

3. This *trend* points out some unfavourable external factors, too, among the causes and factors of underdevelopment (and analyses them sometimes in detail and even subjects them to strong criticism), but either it does not attach to them a decisive importance, or it regards them as unfavourable only to the extent that they operate under certain internal conditions and together with negative internal factors. In other words, the negative role and effect of the external factors are referred back in the last instance to internal determining factors. Representatives of this trend include H. Myint who, by the way, gives a detailed analysis and criticism of the backwash effects of foreign capital investments and foreign trade, G. M. Meier, R. Baldwin, J. Viner and R. Nurkse. It is, of course, not easy to draw a sharp dividing line either between the former trends and the latter one, or between the latter and those theories which completely disregard the external factors.

Let us examine more closely the 2nd and 3rd trends. In the framework of our critical approach we shall disregard the 1st trend to which this present study also belongs. (As to the pseudo-Marxist trend, we shall offer periodic criticism.) Since this chapter has a *critical* character, we shall evidently have to concentrate our analysis on the 3rd trend and devote most space to it.

1. THE "BACKWASH" EFFECTS OF INTERNATIONAL TRADE, DIVISION OF LABOUR, AND FOREIGN CAPITAL INVESTMENTS

Myrdal's theory

Gunnar Myrdal deduces the present state of the underdeveloped countries basically and primarily from the development of international economic relations, the effects of colonization. Concentrating on the relationship between the mother countries and colonies, he explores the unequalizing

---

(The dialectic unity and contradiction of the negative and positive, of the external and internal, as well as the changes in the determining force within this unity and contradiction are unknown only to the *pseudo*-Marxist trends.)

effects that manifest themselves in this relationship. It sounds like an answer to the theories that look for analogous "stages" of growth and assess present backwardness as a historical transition of general validity, when Myrdal declares: "The now highly developed countries were able to develop as small islands in the large ocean of underdeveloped peoples, they could exploit them as sources of raw materials and markets for cheap industrial goods and could for this purpose even keep them under colonial domination."[2]

Myrdal points out very strongly the economic disadvantage that results for the dependent country from its relations with the mother country. He emphasizes that the development of international trade—owing to the deterioration of the terms of trade for the underdeveloped countries—increases inequalities, i.e. is accompanied by "backwash effects", and elucidates the adverse effect of the economic policy of the colonizing powers on the development of backward countries.

His theory centres on the cumulative process already mentioned, which he describes as the *general* law of the motion of social systems.[3] If the cumulative process is not kept under control, it increases the inequalities in society and the economy. He attributes this cumulative process primarily to *the play of market forces*. In his view "the play of the forces in the market normally tends to increase, rather than to decrease, the inequalities between regions.[4] The increase of inequalities, the backwash effects, can only be compensated by the "spread effect", or by the purposeful intervention and regulation on the part of the state. In a poor country, says Myrdal, "the free play of the market forces will work more powerfully to create regional inequalities and to widen those which already exist", since the centrifugal force of economic expansion, the "spread effect", is weak.[5]

"That there is a tendency inherent in the free play of market forces to create regional inequalities, and that this tendency becomes the more

---

[2] G. Myrdal: *Indian Economic Planning in its Broader Setting.* (Quoted by I. Sachs: *Patterns of Public Sector. . . .* Loc. cit., p. 26.)

[3] " . . . in the normal case there is no such tendency towards automatic self-stabilization in the social system. The system is by itself not moving towards any sort of balance between forces, but is constantly on the move away from such a situation. In the normal case a change does not call forth countervailing changes but, instead, supporting changes, which move the system in the same direction as the first change but much further." (G. Myrdal: *Economic Theory and Underdeveloped Regions.* University Paperbacks. Methuen, London, 1965, p. 13.)

[4] G. Myrdal: Op. cit., p. 26.

[5] " . . . the higher the level of economic development that a country has already attained, the stronger the spread effects will usually be. For a high average level of development is accompanied by improved transportation and communication, higher levels of education, and a more dynamic communion of ideas and values—all of which tends to strengthen the forces for the *centrifugal of economic expansion* or to remove the obstacles for its operation." (G. Myrdal: Op. cit., p. 34.—My italics.—*T. Sz.*)

dominant the poorer a country is *are two of the most important laws of economic underdevelopment and development under laissez-faire.*"[6]

It is worth noting that Myrdal does not mention *which* socio-economic system's laws are reflected by the spontaneity of the market and that the restricts the latter merely to a *laissez-faire* situation. By doing so he gives the impression that these laws of capitalist society were also working in the present-day backward countries from the very outset (or that they cannot work any longer in the advanced capitalist countries under "controlled" and "regulated" capitalism). It seems that the *weakest point* of his analysis is here, the point from which it would be easy to return by logical inference to the interpretation of underdevelopment *per se*, to a new, specific sort of vicious circle.

It seems that the cumulative process, deriving from the free play of market forces and bringing about inequalities, was already at work in all backward countries *prior* to colonialism and the penetration of foreign capital. (Moreover, it seems that the less developed a society was and the farther back we go in history, the more intensive this process.) Hence, what can be witnessed on the *level of international economy* in regard to the increase of inequalities between individual countries seems to be only the *secondary* manifestation of what takes place primarily within the individual countries.[7] Both underdevelopment and its liquidation may appear to be natural phenomena: if the building up of inequalities in a single country is a natural process, independent of the social system, then the rise and growth of international inequalities is just as natural and independent. If it is natural that the poorer and the less developed a single country, the greater the inequalities in its society and economy, then the same is just as natural in the case of the whole world society as well.

And finally: just as the inequalities fade out at a higher level of the development of a single country, so will the relative backwardness of the poor countries of the world fade out, too. But if this is true, then it is *not* the specific laws of the capitalist society of West-European countries which— by expanding their sphere of action over the world economy—penetrated into the backward countries *from outside*, leaving their mark on the whole socio-economic development of the latter, but rather some inherent, *natural* laws being in force in a single backward country, too, which rose to an international level. In other words, underdevelopment can be put down to basically internal causes, not to external ones related to colonialism.

[6] G. Myrdal: Ibid.

[7] Myrdal points out: "The discussion... of the problem of regional inequalities within individual countries is relevant to the... analysis of international inequalities..." (Op. cit., p. 50). At another place he takes an even more negative stand in this matter: "Basically the weak spread effects as between countries are thus for the larger part only a reflection of the weak spread effects within the underdeveloped countries themselves caused by their low level of development attained." (Op. cit., p. 55.—My italics.—*T. Sz.*)

Fortunately, Myrdal does not proceed, or rather return, along this path of reasoning, but, within the limitation of an incorrect generalization of the very particular laws of capitalism, he specifies in a positive way the various factors of the cumulative process responsible for the inequalities that arise, and strongly criticizes colonialism: "Colonialism meant primarily not only a strengthening of all the forces in markets which anyhow were working towards internal and international inequalities. It built itself into, and gave an extra impetus and a peculiar character to, the circular causation of the cumulative process."[8] Above and beyond this spontaneous effect, underdevelopment is also connected with the purposeful policy of colonialism. The present pattern of production[9] in underdeveloped countries is also due to the past policies of the colonial powers, which "took special measures to hamper the growth of indigenous industry". "A metropolitan country had, of course, an interest in using the dependent country as a market for the products of its own manufacturing industry . . . Likewise, the metropolitan country had a clear and obvious interest in procuring primary goods from its dependent territory. . . thereby exploiting in its own interest local natural resources and indigenous cheap labour. . . A metropolitan country had also a self-evident interest in monopolizing the dependent country as far as possible for its own business interest, both as an export and an import market." Myrdal outlines the two features characteristic of underdeveloped countries today: their dependence and exploitation.

Moreover, he also points out that capital exports were directed to the *foreign-controlled economic "enclaves"* producing mainly raw materials for export. These "enclaves" were isolated from the surrounding economy like alien bodies and tied directly to the economy of the metropolitan country. Their economic relations with the indigenous population were restricted to the employment of unskilled labour. The racial and cultural differences and the extremely low level of wages and living conditions brought about as a natural consequence *strict segregation* even within the enclaves themselves. So Myrdal also calls attention to the distortions of the economic and social structure and ascribes the weakness of the "spread effect" and the resulting great intensity of the cumulative process, serving to increase inequalities in backward countries, to this *segregation*, i.e. in the last instance to those distortions which, under colonial rule and as a result of the activity of foreign capital, took place in the economic and social structure of backward countries. "Segregation is one of the main reasons", says Myrdal, "why the

---

[8] G. Myrdal: Op. cit., p. 60.

[9] But this pattern itself is such that it spontaneously limits the strengthening of the spread effects: the rural sector does not produce the raw materials for the expanding industrial sector, nor does the expanding industrial sector demand the products (foodstuffs) of the rural sector.

spread of expansionary momentum was extremely weak or altogether absent".[10] Thus he corroborates—even if, in our view, at the cost of some illogicalities—his positive stand that *under colonialism* a persistent tendency was at work which could "not result in much economic development".[11]

Raul Prebisch's theory

A highly valuable, comprehensive and thorough analysis of the harmful consequences of the development of international trade was carried out in the first place by *Raul Prebisch*. The results and conclusions of his investigation have been summed up—as a consummation of his earlier work—in the famous Prebisch Report submitted to the World Trade Conference.[12] In his view, one of the main obstacles to the economic growth of developing countries is their unfavourable situation in international trade. But he points, especially in his Latin-American studies, to the unsound internal *socio-economic structure* and to the phenomenon of an *income drain-off* (profit repatriation, interest payments and redemption of debts), too.

He considers the deterioration of the terms of trade partly due to the pattern of the international division of labour and the internal structure of the countries participating in it, and to the spontaneous changes that have taken place in this structure mainly as a result of scientific and technological progress, and partly to the deliberately scheming trade and customs policy of the advanced capitalist countries.

Prebisch points out that the backward countries have developed as "the periphery of the world economic system" with the function of providing foodstuffs and raw materials for the centre. He denies that this international division of labour is able to ensure the conventional advantages of international trade and denies the applicability of the thesis of comparative advantages in relation to the periphery. The backward countries could not carry out industrialization, and the advantages of technical progress are unevenly distributed in the world economy. Technical progress seems to have been greater in industry than in the primary production. It is true that if, as a result of the more rapid technical progress, the prices of manufactured goods had dropped in comparison with the prices of primary products—as assumed by the textbook models of pure competition— then the benefits of technical progress would thus have been distributed alike

[10] G. Myrdal: Op. cit., pp. 57—58.
[11] G. Myrdal: Op. cit., p. 57.
[12] R. Prebisch: Towards a New Trade Policy for Development. *Report by the Secretary-General of the United Nations Conference on Trade and Development.* United Nations, New York, 1964.—See his other papers, too: *Essay on the Interpretation of the Process of Economic Development.—Dynamic Economic Policy in Latin America.—The Trade Policy of Developing Countries,* etc.

throughout the world. But it is exactly the opposite tendency that can be observed: not even the benefits of the rise in the productivity of primary production are available for the backward countries, as they are transferred from the periphery to the industrial centres.

Thus Prebisch—like Myrdal, Singer and Lewis—reveals the specific mechanism of income drain-off through international trade and shows how the benefits of the increase of productivity in the export sectors of the underdeveloped countries are systematically transferred to the advanced importing countries. The reason for this is that the wage level in the export sectors is under pressure and so the increase in productivity results in the further expansion of production and consequently a drop in prices instead of an improvement of real wages. This mechanism is closely connected with the higher income elasticity of the demand for industrial products, but an important role is played in it by the "demonstration effect" which increases the demand of the underdeveloped countries for imported industrial products, and also by the considerable difference in the market power of workers (in pressing for higher wages) and of oligopolists (in resting a squeeze on profit) between the industrialized countries and the underdeveloped ones.[13] As a result of this mechanism "in the centre the incomes of entrepreneurs and productive factors increase relatively more than productivity, whereas in the periphery the increase in income is less than that in productivity".[14] All this is unavoidable with unrestricted *market forces*. The market forces and a liberal trade policy allowing them free play are unable to secure the equilibrium and mutual advantages of international trade, the optimum system of the international division of labour.[15]

[13] "The characteristic lack of organization among the workers employed in primary production prevents them from obtaining wage increases comparable to those of the industrial countries..." (Quoted by B. Higgins: Op. cit., pp. 367—368.)

[14] The mechanism of income transfer itself can briefly be described this: Given a "country A which is prevailingly industrial and a country B which is prevailingly primary", and granted that the "income elasticity of demand for industrial products is higher than for primary commodities", and, further, that "B is unable or unwilling to send to A manpower which would increase the latter's rate of industrialization", then B "has no other way out than to decrease the proportion of manpower in primary activities in favour of industry". As in B "manpower is transferred from primary occupations with a favourable productivity ratio to industrial occupations with an unfavourable ratio... consequently, the pressure of the surplus manpower will force employment down on the productivity ratio curve from 1.00 to say 0.80, with the wage ratio falling correspondingly at the new equilibrium point... Export prices will fall, transferring income to country A". (R. Prebisch: Commercial Policy in the Underdeveloped Countries, U.N. Economic Commission for Latin America. International Trade and Payments in the Era of Co-existence. *American Economic Association*, pp. 261—262.)

[15] "... it is not possible to arrive at the optimum solution of this problem if market forces are left unrestricted. The classical mechanism of the free play of market forces, either in its original form of wage adjustments or in its contemporary version of price adjustments through exchange rate movements, does not bring about that optimum solution. On the

114

Prebisch's conception makes it completely clear that present-day "economic underdevelopment" is closely connected with a specific development of world economy. Consequently, no explanation or solution can be found by investigating exclusively or even primarily the internal factors. His interpretation is at the same time a clear answer to all theories which, by referring to the thesis of comparative advantages, try to prove the *mutually* advantageous character of the existing international division of labour between the underdeveloped and advanced capitalist countries.

It is not by mere chance that Prebisch's arguments have become the theoretical weapon of the underdeveloped countries in their fight for a new trade policy and radical reforms in international trade. From these arguments follows the progressive programme of the industrialization of backward countries and the structural change in the international division of labour.

The positive character of his theory is somewhat diminished by the fact that Prebisch, like Myrdal, draws his conclusions from certain generalizing assumptions. He, too, condems colonialism and the role it imposed on underdeveloped countries, but, when analysing the negative factors and effects, he often takes them out of their historical context, disregards their historical origin and the socio-economic system they stem from, and considers them as phenomena of a *general* character. That he explains, e.g., the mechanism of indirect income transfer in the last instance by the general law of income elasticity of demand[16] (Engel's law) makes not only the theory itself vulnerable[17] but also weakens at the same time any comprehensive criticism of the system of the capitalist international division of labour.

---

contrary, the periphery transfers to the outer world a greater part of the fruits of increased productivity than if the market forces had been contained at a certain point, either through customs protection or some other form of interference in the process." (R. Prebisch: Commercial Policy in the Underdeveloped Countries. Loc. cit., pp. 255—256.)

[16] "In the last instance, the pressure upon export prices and the corresponding tendency upwards deterioration in the terms of trade in the peripheral process of growth subject to the unrestricted play of market forces is *the result of disparities in income elasticity of demand* and the uneven form in which technical progress has spread into the world economy." (R. Prebisch: Commercial Policy in the Underdeveloped Countries. Loc. cit., p. 261. (My italics.—*T. Sz.*)

[17] Professor Gottfried Haberler, e.g., denies the Prebisch—Singer thesis on the secular deterioration of the terms of trade for the underdeveloped countries. In his view the Engel's law "cannot bear the heavy burden which is placed on it by the theory under view". For it does not follow from Engel's law that a rising income leads in every case to a relative decline in demand for every kind of food and for industrial raw materials. Haberler also refuses to accept that income transfer takes place, owing to the fact that the monopolistic behaviour of trade unions and oligopolies in the industrial countries increases the gap between the prices of industrial commodities and primary products in favour of the former. (See G. Haberler: Critical Observations on Some Current Notions in the Theory of Economic Development. *L'industria*, No. 2, 1957. See also B. Higgins: Op. cit., pp. 373–374.)

The theses of Hans Singer

Singer's views of the unfavourable position of the non-industrialized countries in international trade are roughly identical with those of Prebisch. He, too, maintains that the benefits from technical progress are unevenly distributed in world economy and that the industrialized countries "have had the best of two worlds, both as consumers of primary commodities and as producers of manufactured articles, whereas the underdeveloped countries had the worst of both worlds, as consumers of manufactures and as producers of raw materials".[18] He claims that "the present structure of comparative advantages and endowments is not such that it should be considered as a permanent basis for a future international division of labour".[19] The over-specialization of underdeveloped countries in the field of food and raw material exports retards their development. It is not only the deterioration of the terms of trade which causes damage, but also their fluctuation is harmful. The income losses resulting from the fall of the food and raw material prices deprive them of capital badly needed for industrialization, while the rise in prices, though enabling them, in principle, to finance the import of capital goods necessary for industrialization, in fact lessens the stimulus to industrialization and structural changes and induces the import of consumer goods and luxury articles.

Singer also points out the enclave character and harmful, structure-distorting effects of foreign investments. These investments "never became a part of the internal economic structure of those underdeveloped countries themselves, except in the purely geographical and physical sense... Economically they were really an outpost of the economies of the more developed investing countries..."[20]

"The specialization of underdeveloped countries on export of food and raw materials to industrialized countries, largely as a result of investment by the latter, has been unfortunate for the underdeveloped countries for two reasons: (1) it removed most of the secondary and cumulative effects of investment from the country in which the investment took place to the investing country; and (2) it diverted the underdeveloped countries into types of activities offering less scope for technical progress, internal and external economies taken by themselves..."

---

[18] H. W. Singer: *International Development: Growth and Change.* McGraw-Hill, 1964, p. 167. We have to note here that later on Singer revised his thesis by putting emphasis on the general weakness of underdeveloped economies and on the harmful effects of the transfer of inappropriate technologies rather than on the type of specialization. For more details and a critique see T. Szentes: *Theories of the World Capitalist Economy. A Critical Survey of Conventional, Reformist and Radical Views.* (Forthcoming) Akadémiai Kiadó, Budapest, 1983.

[19] H. W. Singer: Op. cit., p. 172.

[20] See H. W. Singer: Op. cit., p. 163.

On the other hand, "the capital-exporting countries have received their repayment many times over in the following five forms: (1) possibility of building up exports of manufactures and thus transferring their population from low-productivity occupations to high-productivity occupations; (2) enjoyment of the internal economies of expanded manufacturing industries; (3) enjoyment of the general dynamic impulse radiating from industries on a progressive society; (4) enjoyment of the fruits of technical progress in primary production as main consumers of primary commodities; (5) enjoyment of a contribution from foreign consumers of manufactured articles..."[21]

However, certain unjustified theoretical generalizations which to some extent blunt the edge of Singer's criticism of the colonial international division of labour, can also be found. He is, for example, inclined to interpret the great dependence on foreign trade and the violent effects of international trade fluctuations, which are the results of a very *concrete socio-economic system* and of a *distorted* development,[22] as the *general* and natural consequences of low national income.[23]

The Lewis thesis

Arthur Lewis is also concerned with the inequalities in trade between developed and underdeveloped countries and investigates the specific transfer of income through the channel of foreign trade. "Practically all the benefit of increasing efficiency in export industries goes to the foreign consumer," writes Lewis.[24] But he finds its cause not in differences in the income elasticity of demand, nor does he accept Singer's and Prebisch's thesis of the secular deterioration of the terms of trade.[25] He relates the mechanism of the transfer of gains resulting from the increase in productivity to the unlimited supply of labour of the traditional rural sector of the underdeveloped countries.

[21] H. W. Singer: Op. cit., pp. 165, 168.

[22] This, by the way, follows logically from his own theses, too.

[23] "Foreign trade tends to be proportionately most important when incomes are lowest... fluctuations in the volume and value of foreign trade tend to be proportionately more violent... and therefore a *fortiori* also more important in relation to national income..." (H. W. Singer: Op. cit., p. 161.)

[24] W. A. Lewis: Economic Development with Unlimited Supplies of Labour. *The Economics of Underdevelopment*, p. 449.

[25] After having worked out a statistical relationship between the prices of raw materials and the volume of manufacturing production, and another for prices of foodstuffs as a function of manufacturing production and the volume of food production, he made estimates on the improvement of the prices of primary products. (See W. A. Lewis: World Production Prices and Trade, 1870–1960. *The Manchester School of Economic and Social Studies*, Vol. XX, 1952.)

In countries with unlimited supply of labour—where the marginal productivity of labour is negligible or even zero and the price of labour is adjusted to the subsistence minimum—the wage level of the modern (capitalist) sector is determined by the income relations or, to be more exact, by the living and supply conditions prevailing in the other (traditional) sector. And as this subsistence sector is marked by low productivity (and at the same time by a considerable population growth), its low living standard keeps down the wage level in the modern sector, too.

From all this it might appear (and in fact many economists try to draw their conclusions so as to move in this direction) that it is, in the last analysis, the underdeveloped countries themselves that are responsible for the income transfer through international trade as everything hinges on the low productivity of their traditional sector. But Arthur Lewis also indicates the concrete historical relationships when he writes: "The fact that the wage level in the capitalist sector depends upon earnings in the subsistence sector is sometimes of immense political importance, since its effect is that capitalists have a direct interest in holding down the productivity of the subsistence workers... This is one of the worst features of imperialism. The imperialists invest capital and hire workers, it is to their advantage to keep wages low... In actual fact the record of every imperial power in Africa in modern times is one of impoverishing the subsistence economy, either by taking away the people's land, or by demanding forced labour in the capitalist sector, or by imposing taxes to drive people to work for capitalist employers."[26]

Lewis' thesis also stresses the necessity of *industrialization* as the mechanism can be brought to a stop if the expansion of the industrial sector in the underdeveloped countries is rapid enough to reduce the absolute population in the rural sector, raising the man-hour productivity in that sector. It underlines also the demand for technological progress and raising productivity in the peasant agricultural sector, and consequently, also the need for the transformation of the dual underdeveloped economy.

Lewis' thesis can also be criticized on account of certain generalizing assumptions and simplifications. Thus, e.g., the objection is raised against it that, while assuming the unlimited supply of labour in the traditional sector and the limited absorbing capacity of the modern sector, it disregards the shortage of and the great demand for skilled labour as well as the great pressure of the trade unions in the newly independent countries which compel the governments or employers to raise the wages out of all proportion to the increase in productivity. Thus many reject Lewis' reasoning in respect of the factors determining the wage level of the modern sector. His model, like every model, is no doubt a simplified one. The relationship between the two sectors, too, is far more complex, owing to the

[26] W. A. Lewis: Op. cit., *The Economics of Underdevelopment*, pp. 409–410.

migrant labour system, than it is as actually presented in the model. This is also true for the role and operation of the modern sector. The income transfer is linked up with other factors, too, and the framework of the whole mechanism has much deeper roots than are suggested by the model. Despite all this, Lewis' model is a very valuable contribution as it throws light on many new aspects of the mechanism of dual economies and the international division of labour.

2. THE REDUCTION OF EXTERNAL NEGATIVE FACTORS TO INTERNAL ONES

Besides Myrdal, Prebisch, Singer and Lewis, but, of course, a great many other non-Marxist economists attribute an important or even decisive role to the negative effects of international economy and tie underdevelopment itself, in one or another respect, to the actual relations of the capitalist world economy or even colonialism.[27]

Most of the theories, however, explain underdevelopment in the last instance by itself, and, even if they admit there are some detrimental effects of certain international forces and external factors on backward countries, they regard them as *secondary*, and, what is more, explain their adverse operation by the *internal* relations of the underdeveloped countries.

Let us see how this is done in the theories of those distinguished economists mentioned earlier. We wish to present not only their method in tracing back the harmful external effects to internal ones, but also the positive results of their analysis.

When investigating the limiting factors of economic development, *Jacob Viner* also refers to the unfavourable position of backward countries in world trade. However, unlike Prebisch, Singer and others, he does not accept the assumption that the terms of trade have a *general* and secular deteriorating tendency for the underdeveloped, raw-material exporting countries, and that, consequently, industrialization and the change in the import-export structure would be the way out for them. Neither does he accept the view that trade between the primary producing and the advanced industrial countries necessarily secures one-sided advantages for the latter and that a systematic transfer of income through foreign trade would take place. He, too, admits that the terms of trade are getting worse but regards this tendency as a phenomenon that can be changed and compensated by

---

[27] For example, François Perroux emphasizes the dependence of the underdeveloped countries and points out that a developed nation can force its will on others even in the period of decolonization. The adverse balance of payments of the underdeveloped countries is, according to Perroux, not only the result of the lack of structural equilibrium: the magnitude and nature of the structural disequilibrium greatly depend on the decisions of dominant nations and unions. The consequences of foreign domination aggravate disintegration and the insufficiency of living standards. (F. Perroux: *L'Économie du XXième Siècle*, pp. 156–157.)

other favourable factors (e.g. the growth of the volume of trade, the decrease in the real costs of exports, etc.). He attaches more importance rather to the cyclical fluctuation of the prices of raw materials. The latter can move within a wider range than the prices of manufactured goods and often rise higher in boom periods, which, in his view, can offset the losses sustained in the slump years.

Referring to the comparative advantages Viner holds the view that a policy of agricultural development rather than a policy of subsidized industrialization is the right course for underdeveloped countries to take. If their position in world trade is unfavourable, it is not because they are agrarian countries but because of the obsolete methods used in their agriculture and also because of their "resistance to more efficient procedures".

In this way the unfavourable trend of international trade and the disadvantageous position of the underdeveloped countries in the international division of labour are considered by Viner as transitional and rather relative phenomena, which are attributable to the internal relations of the underdeveloped countries (i.e. to those various growth-inhibiting factors that we have already discussed and evaluated either separately, or included in various vicious circles). And if over and above these unfavourable internal relations there is any further obstacle to a mutually beneficial international division of labour, then it arises from protectionism, from the artificial trade barriers for which the underdeveloped countries are also responsible: "...the underdeveloped countries must acknowledge their great share of responsibility for the failure to achieve more radical progress in removing the barriers to mutually profitable international division of labour."[28]

When dealing with the external factors limiting economic development (the so-called international forces), *Meier* and *Baldwin*—just like Viner— refer to the *cyclical movement of the terms of trade* rather than the trend of general deterioration. In periods of world prosperity, in their opinion, the prices of primary products rise more rapidly than the prices of manufactured commodities. The terms of trade of most of the poor countries then improve, but they spend their foreign exchange proceeds to a large extent on the consumption of imports. Furthermore, during these periods there is usually considerable domestic inflation in the poor countries, leading to the misallocation of domestic investments and severe balance of payments problems. Investment funds tend to be diverted to speculative ventures where profits are high, or to buying real estate in order to get protection against a fall in the purchasing power of money. Another way of seeking protection is to send capital abroad. Moreover, the more rapid rise in domestic prices in comparison with foreign prices discourages

---

[28] J. Viner: The Economics of Development. *The Economics of Underdevelopment*, p. 29.

the import- competing industries. Thus the increased export earnings are quickly dissipated on imports.[29]

Meier and Baldwin are describing here a process which doubtless occurs rather frequently, but they fail to mention that such a dissipation of export earnings and the inflationary process described by them does not necessarily take place when the economy of the country does *not* fall prey to the foreign monopolies, when the government, really concerned with the development of the national economy, pursues a *correct* economic policy. In other words, though the cyclical fluctuation of the terms of trade is *generally* an unfavourable phenomenon, indeed, the improvement of the terms of trade can bring about similarly unfavourable effects *only or mainly if* the cyclical fluctuation is associated with the external factor of economic dependence and defencelessness. The improvement of the terms of trade may be conducive to development even if the export incomes are absorbed by import consumption, for this absorption may involve the increase in imports of capital goods needed for development, or the increase in food imports needed for securing higher standards of living in a monocultural economy, etc.

In periods of depression, however, the world market prices of primary products often fall more rapidly than those of manufactured goods; the terms of trade of the poor countries quickly deteriorate; the inflow of foreign capital tends to fall. All this deprives the poor countries of the funds needed for importing capital goods.

Meier and Baldwin further include among the growth-inhibiting "international forces" the *plantation system*, which requires large supplies of cheap unskilled labour and leads—by its income effects—to the formation of the vicious circle already discussed. By referring to the plantation system as the starting point of a vicious circle, and as an "international factor", Meier and Baldwin tacitly acknowledge that the vicious circle is not merely the spontaneous consequence of internal relations, but the consequence, of the plantation system introduced by the colonizing powers. Even if the plantation economy possesses other natural resources, the domestic development of the country's full potential will come up against limitations set by the lack of adequate market demand based on the highly unequal distribution of income, by the great difficulties in training the uneducated and unskilled plantation workers and by the deficiency of entrepreneurial activity. Instead, these resources are likely to develop as an export sector, and the materials be exported in their raw form.[30]

Among the "international obstacles" to development *Meier* and *Baldwin* also refer to the *detrimental effects of foreign capital investments.* The

[29] G. M. Meier and R. E. Baldwin: Op. cit., pp. 329–330.
[30] G. M. Meier and R. E. Baldwin: Op. cit., p. 331.

discussion of this question is one of the most valuable parts of their analysis. Meier points out that though foreign capital is needed to break the vicious circle, yet "the need for external borrowing does not mean that the development problem is solely a financial one, solved if only foreign investment is forthcoming".[31] Before the First World War, e.g., many countries imported a considerable amount of British capital without scarcely achieving any appreciable progress. Meier admits that foreign capital in itself has not been able to bring about development, and its detrimental effects: the direction of investments, the type of economic organization going with it, and its income effects, have been actually critical.

Foreign capital was concentrated in plantations and mines producing for export, as well as in railways connecting the export-producing areas with the seaports. Thus the export sector developed and gained strength, but growth did not spread to other economic sectors. Demand did not increase in the other sectors owing to the low level of real incomes. The low level of real incomes is connected with the type of economic organization, i.e. also with the plantation system, which is based on a large supply of unskilled labour.

The plantation system not only limits real incomes but usually goes hand in hand with the *outflow of profits abroad* if the plantations are under foreign control. But even where there is no plantation system, the *monopolistic* position of foreign firms, either in the buying up of agrarian produce, in the selling of imported goods or in employing manpower in mining and elsewhere, had as a result that "the native's real income did not rise as much as it would have"[32] under the conditions of free competition.

Because of the limitations on the rise of real incomes and the outflow of profits, interests and dividends to the foreign country "a given amount of investment in the poor country has generated a much smaller amount of income than an equivalent amount of investment would have generated in a less dependent country".[33] Therefore, foreign capitalist companies hinder development—by dint of their monopolistic position—not only by keeping artificially down the wage level and the purchasing prices of agrarian produce and keeping artificially high the selling prices, i.e. by intensively exploiting the population, but also by transferring the larger part of their profits out of the country. By so doing they retard the expansion of investments and the increase in demand for both consumer and capital goods.[34]

---

[31] G. Meier: The Problem of Limited Economic Development. *Economia Internazionale*, Vol. VI, No. 4, 1953.—*The Economics of Underdevelopment*, p. 64.

[32] Op. cit., p. 68.

[33] Op. cit., p. 69.

[34] "The outflow of profits to foreigners has in some cases absorbed a large part of the potential real saving of the poor countries." (G. M. Meier and R. E. Baldwin: *Economic Development*, p. 331.)

Thus Meier and Baldwin are describing here such a vicious circle which is essentially different and leads to opposite conclusions than the one they described earlier and placed in the centre of their theory. This vicious circle is like this: The monopolistic position of foreign capital hinders the expansion of real incomes and leads to the expatriation of a considerable part of the national income. Therefore, domestic saving does not increase and the home market remains limited. Consequently, investments grow only in the export sector, where, induced by foreign demand and owing to the lack of capital, they have to rely on capital imported from abroad.

The relationships outlined clearly by these authors as to the workings of foreign capital take them quite close to an understanding of the real causes and inner mechanism of economic underdevelopment. Yet, they do not follow up this line of analysis conclusions, but *return* to the *original vicious circle idea* and, regardless of the obvious contradictions, eventually explaining away underdevelopment by internal limiting factors. They even readjust that negative role of foreign companies outlined above and declare that they played a basically positive role in development by acquainting the local population with the advantages of market production and by reinvesting "some of their profits within the country". They conclude their discussion of the harmful effects of foreign investments by saying: "The point being made here is not that foreign enterprises have on balance limited development, but simply that *some* of the results have been limiting, and that, even though there have been absolute gains, the relative gains *might have been* greater."[35] Moreover, foreign capital is not even responsible for the "relative losses", because it is the "market imperfections"—e.g. social, geographical immobility of the factors of production, the *insufficient knowledge of the market relations* (i.e. on the part of the indigenous producers), the *rigid social structure*, the lack of specialization and, consequently, the misallocation of resources—which, according to the authors, "have... made it difficult for the full benefits of foreign trade to be diffused throughout the economy. The progress in the export sector has not been able to carry over to the rest of the economy. And to this extent it has been more difficult to break the vicious circles".[36]

Thus the theory of Meier and Baldwin also turns in a vicious circle.

Myint, too, sees clearly that the development problems of backward countries cannot be accounted for merely by the internal factors of the vicious circle and cannot be solved simply by breaking this vicious circle by means of foreign capital import. The "disequalizing factors" that are at work here, says Myint, stem from the very process of international trade or are connected with other *external* factors (foreign capital investments, monopolies), and "instead of being neutralized are cumulatively

[35] Op. cit., p. 332.
[36] Op. cit., p. 333.

123

exaggerated by the free play of economic forces". Wherever foreign capital has been invested to a larger extent, "the result has frequently been too great and rapid an expansion in a few lines of primary production for export, which further aggravated the problem of the adjustment of the indigenous peoples of these countries to outside economic forces".[37]

Myint also points out that "international trade seems to have had very little educative effect on the people of backward countries except in the development of new wants".[38]

He also adds that "the reluctance of European entrepreneurs to make heavy investments of a kind which require a large supply of skilled workers, and their preference for simple labour-intensive techniques... left labour productivity low and afforded few training facilities".[39]

In order to investigate in more detail the detrimental effect of the "disequalizing factors" Myint sets up an abstract model of underdeveloped countries. He attributes three characteristic features to this model: (1) "specialization" for export market, which is connected with the development of the plantation system and with the indigenous peasantry coming under foreign control; (2) the pyramid-like structure of society (with Europeans on top, a stratum of middlemen consisting chiefly of non-European foreign elements in the middle, and the masses of indigenous people at the bottom); (3) the *monopoly power of foreign capital*. Each of these characteristic features, declares Myint, "tends to reduce the relative share of the national incomes of the backward countries accruing to the indigenous peoples".[40]

Myint also points out other characteristics not included in his model, such as, e.g., the prevalence of cheap, *undifferentiated labour* with little vertical mobility into more skilled grades, which, in addition to the monopoly power of the employers, is related to such factors as: (a) the very high rate of turnover of indigenous labour, (b) an official and unofficial colour bar; (c) the additional sources of labour supply (chiefly due to immigrant labourers). Even apart from the monopolistic powers opposed to them, the peasant producers are exposed to *disequalizing effects* that diminish their share in the national income. "The result of the free play of economic forces under conditions of fluctuating export prices is the well-known story of rural indebtedness, land alienation and agrarian unrest."[41]

Myint's analysis goes a long way in revealing the harmful effects of the curious "specialization" for export, the existence of the middlemen strata

[37] H. Myint: Op. cit., p. 106.

[38] H. Myint: The Gains from International Trade and the Backward Countries. *Review of Economic Studies*, Vol. XXII, No. 2, p. 140.

[39] See B. Higgins: Op. cit., p. 347.

[40] H. Myint: An Interpretation of Economic Backwardness. *The Economics of Underdevelopment*, p. 123.

[41] H. Myint: Op. cit., p. 125.

and especially the role the *monopolies* play in impoverishing backward peoples. However, he fails to relate these characteristic features to one another, although by doing so he could lay bare the real background to the objective relationships: the economic dependence of these countries. Instead, like Meier and Baldwin, he puts down the harmful effects of the external factors to internal ones. In his view, specialization for primary export and the lack of manufacturing industries both result in the last instance from the narrowness of the domestic market, i.e. from the limited purchasing power of the indigenous population, while the latter is due to the fact that the backward peoples are unable to adapt themselves in a satisfactory manner to the new economic environment shaped by outside economic forces.[42]

According to Myint, the reason why the plantation system or the foreign control over peasant production came into being is that the newly introduced crop called for a change in the production techniques.[43] In reality, however, plantations were mostly created by external forces or influence, e.g. where and when large estates were placed under foreign private ownership, mainly due to the alienation of tribal lands. As regards foreign control over peasant farming, this was set up as a result of colonization and due to the activity of colonial monopolistic companies even in those regions (e.g. in West Africa) where the introduction of new cash crops did not substantially change the production techniques. Moreover, it was due to the influence of the colonial economic policy itself and the activity of foreign monopolies that peasant farming emerged in a number of countries in Tropical Africa from the disintegration of traditional subsistence agriculture based on the common property of land.

In Myint's view, the *high rate of migration of labour* is due to the fact that "backward peoples are unused to the discipline of the mines and plantations". In reality, however, the migrant labour system as the main source of supply of cheap labour for capitalist plantations and monopolistic firms was—at least primarily—the result of colonial economic policy.

As to the phenomena of *rural indebtedness* and unrest, Myint ascribes them mainly to "the peasants' ignorance of market conditions... their lack of economic strength to hold out against middlemen and speculators".[44]

[42] "One of the most important reasons why the backward countries have been prevented from enjoying the stimulating effect of manufacturing industry is not the wickedness of foreign capitalists and their exclusive concern with raw-material supplies but merely the limitation of the domestic market for manufactured articles." (H. Myint: Op. cit., p. 130.)

[43] "Where a new crop is introduced, the essence of its success as a *peasant* crop depends on the fact that it does not represent a radical departure from the existing techniques of production... If this condition is not fulfilled, the peasant system soon gives way to the plantation system or the peasant is so supervised and controlled that he is reduced to the status of a wage-earner except in name." (See H. Myint: Op. cit., p. 120 and the footnote.)

[44] H. Myint: Op. cit., p. 125.

Though he states that backward peoples as cheap unskilled labour, as peasant producers and also as consumers, are faced with foreign monopolies (which are monopolistic buyers of their labour, monopolistic buyers of their crop and monopolistic sellers or distributors of imported consumer goods), his interpretation suggests that foreign monopolies did *not* force themselves upon backward countries but were lured to them by the backward peoples themselves. According to Myint, the *monopolistic position* has evolved because the process of opening up a new territory for trade is so *risky and costly* that it is only by offering some sort of monopolistic concessions that foreign business concerns can be induced to accept the risks and the heavy initial costs. Myint does not mention that the governments which "induced" foreign companies to embark upon these risky and costly ventures and granted them concessions and privileges were usually nothing else but the local representatives of the state power of the same country these companies came from or its puppets supported by force and money.

The fact that the expansion of foreign trade was unable to induce an over-all economic growth, and that the increasing export activity did not produce the multiplier effects on per capita income, is due, according to Myint's model, to such counteracting factors as "the high turnover of labour, workers' willingness to accept very low wages, the conviction among employers that the supply curve of labour was backward sloping, and the general lack of industrial skills, which made entrepreneurs feel that it was difficult to recruit an adequate labor force".[45]

And as to the one-sided specialization in the international division of labour it has not resulted in adequate economic development only because the backward countries "have not succeeded in building up a labour-intensive export trade to cope with their growing population".[46]

Thus Myint's model, too, represents the harmful effects of the external factors as the consequences of the adverse phenomena of internal development.

The turning inside out of the external growth-inhibiting factors and explaining them by internal factors is particularly striking when Myint speaks of the two *aspects* of underdevelopment, of the objective and the subjective ones.[47] On the objective side we find the well-known vicious circle of the internal limiting forces (low per capita productivity and incomes), while the external factors appear mainly on the *subjective* side as the false forms of consciousness of backward peoples. Getting acquainted with new ways of life imported from the outside world, the backward peoples develop new wants and aspirations that cannot be matched by a corresponding increase in their earning capacity. The result is "a progressive maladjust-

45 B. Higgins: Op. cit., p. 348.
46 Op. cit., p. 349.
47 H. Myint: Op. cit., pp. 115–117.

126

ment between wants and activities, the former outstripping the latter at each round of education and contact with the outside world". This gives rise to "the explosive feeling of *discontent*" which makes slogans about "imperialistic exploitation" all the more credible. But the reason why the earning capacity and economic activity of backward peoples cannot grow accordingly is because "they cannot successfully *adapt* themselves to the new economic environment shaped by outside forces". Thus, in the last analysis, it is not the monopolies, foreign capital, the specialization for export, the activity of the middlemen, racial discrimination, etc., that are responsible for the present state of the underdeveloped countries, but their peoples themselves, as they have been unable to adapt themselves to the new circumstances.

Thus the final conclusion is the old one: underdevelopment is not the consequence of external causes but of internal ones. Myint concludes his comments on monopolies by referring to Schumpeter, according to whom "the growth of monopoly . . . might actually favour technical innovations and economic development". And adds that "monopoly was an essential element in the 'opening-up' process of the backward countries to international trade".[48] Applying *J. K. Galbraith*'s terminology of "countervailing power",[49] Myint declares that "economic backwardness may be described as a phenomenon which arises because the process of 'economic development' has been too rapid (?!) and the initial conditions too unfavourable to give rise to an effective '*countervailing power*' to check the 'foreign economic domination' of the backward peoples".[50]

In other words, the monopolies, foreign economic domination, and the so-called "disequalizing factors" cannot be made responsible, according to Myint, for the present state of backward countries. On the contrary, they are expressly growth-promoting factors. The only trouble is the lack of an adequate *countervailing power*.

Another variant of the explanations tracing the external factors of underdevelopment back to internal or even partly subjective ones can be

[48] H. Myint: Op. cit., p. 128.

[49] Pleading the cause of monopolies in his book *American Capitalism: The Concept of Countervailing Power*, J. K. Galbraith sets forth the following theory: In the developed countries, chiefly in the USA, the growth of monopoly has been accompanied by the growth of "countervailing power" on the opposite side of the market (i.e. that of trade unions, cooperatives, farmers' associations, etc.). Since the growth of monopoly increases the gains from building up the "countervailing power" and induces its growth, this provides a new self-regulatory mechanism which promotes economic development. Thus—according to Galbraith—the automatism of free competition is succeeded by the automatism of monopoly and the corresponding "countervailing power", in order to ensure the harmony of the economy.

[50] H. Myint: Op. cit., pp. 128–129.

found in *Ragnar Nurkse*'s theory.[51] Nurkse also admits that the inflow of foreign capital does not necessarily lead to the breaking of the vicious circle. This is, however, in his view, not because of the very nature of foreign investments and even less due to the domination of foreign capital or colonization, but rather to the circumstances peculiar to underdeveloped countries. Nurkse denies that the so-called colonial type of investment, in mines and plantations producing for export, was generally characteristic of foreign capital investments in the 19th century or later. In support of this statement he draws the line between the investments by foreign private capital and the investments by public authorities from foreign funds, and declares that only the former tended "to shy away from industries working for the domestic market in underdeveloped areas and to concentrate instead on primary production for export to the advanced industrial centres". While the latter, which constituted the major part of total investments, served the development of infrastructure (transport and public services).

Thus, Nurkse sets against each other, as a matter of fact, the *two types* of colonial investments: the investments in primary production, on the one hand, which were *directly* aimed at the exploitation of colonies and the investments, on the other, which served colonial exploitation only *indirectly*, by creating the necessary conditions for it.

But this confrontation is historically unjustified. It is commonly known that the first step in establishing a colonial economy was the construction of transport and communications, i.e. the development of the infrastructure, and it was this very step that provided the basis for starting primary production and for transporting its products to the "mother" country. To be convinced that the construction of transport served the very purpose of colonial exploitation consciously and purposefully, it will suffice to take a look at the railway map of these countries. The railway lines, instead of connecting the various economic areas of the country in question, run between the sources of raw materials and the seaports handling their export to the metropolitan country. Thus, public investments in infrastructure and private investments in primary production were organically complementary, which was only natural as both of them served usually the interests of the same monopolies that penetrated—by the assistance of the colonial government—the economy of the country in question. The only difference was that in the former case it was the taxpayers of the "mother" country and the colony that had to bear the burdens of financing the infrastructural investments to relieve these investing monopolies of the costs of building transport facilities.

[51] R. Nurkse: Op. cit., and Some International Aspects of the Problem of Economic Development. *The Economics of Underdevelopment*. Ed. by A. N. Agarwala and S. P. Singh. 1958, pp. 256–271.

As to the colonial nature and detrimental impact of private investments, Nurkse maintains that the allocation of private business capital in the various sectors of economy is governed simply by the *actual economic conditions* and not by any supposed "sinister conspiracy" or "deliberate policy". Nurkse also applies to international investments the distinction between "induced" and "autonomous" investments. Since the direct investments of foreign private capital belong to the category of induced investments (i.e. investments that have to be induced by tangible market demand), it is natural that these investments were concentrated in the *export sector*. Here "investment was induced by the investing countries' own demand", writes Nurkse.[52]

These statements show that the direction of foreign capital investments is determined simply by *profit considerations* fitting local circumstances. This is indeed so, and it is not necessary at all to presume for every case a predetermined, deliberate "sinister" policy! If certain conditions have already developed, they will so to say reproduce themselves, unless a countervailing force develops. The process of capital investments has, in fact, a certain *automatic, spontaneous mechanism* simply for the reason that capitalistic conditions exist. The only trouble is that Nurkse does not say a word about how these *conditions* came to be established and how the activity of the foreign monopolies preserved the "local circumstances" (narrow domestic market, cheap unskilled labour, low rate of domestic accumulation, etc.). It is not the *aim* or motive of investors but the impact of investments that is debatable from the viewpoint of social and economic development. But Nurkse pleads for the so-called colonial type of investments even from this point of view: "Foreign investment in extractive industries working for export is not to be despised, since it usually carries with it *various direct and indirect benefits* to the country where it is made."[53] He does not concern himself with a thorough analysis of the relationship between economic underdevelopment and the adverse consequences of these investments and their distorting effect on the economic structure.

If, however, public investments in infrastructure, which constitute the larger percentage and are independent of market impulse, i.e. "autonomous", are not of a colonial nature, as Nurkse maintains, and, further, if the private business investments in primary production, which are called "colonial" only by mistake, result in benefits for the poor countries, then the only question that must be answered is this: Why has the inflow of foreign capital not ensured under all circumstances the breaking of the vicious circle? And it is particularly at this point that Nurkse turns the adverse

---

[52] R. Nurkse: Op. cit. *The Economics of Underdevelopment*, p. 261.
[53] Ibid. (My italics. — *T. Sz.*)

effect of the external factors inside out when answering this question by referring to the idea of the so-called "demonstration effect".[54]

The demonstration effect means that backward peoples become familiar, by radio, television, films and personal contacts, etc., with the living conditions of advanced capitalist countries, and this is reflected in their propensities to consume.

Nurkse asserts that it is not only the absolute but also the relative level of real income that determines the capacity to save. Therefore, it is possible and quite usual that with real income growing absolutely—but decreasing relatively, i.e. in relation to advanced countries—the level of savings, instead of growing, decreases because, as a result of the demonstration effect, the general propensity to consume grows. The fact that backward peoples become familiar with the pattern of American consumption and try to copy it[55] brings about the tendency of restricting development funds. The intensity of the attraction exercised by the consumption levels of advanced countries varies depending on the size of the gaps in real income and consumption levels and also *on the extent of people's awareness of them.* This attraction affects not only voluntary personal saving but may also cause political difficulties in using taxation as a means of compulsory saving in that increased taxation burdens may give rise to discontent among the population.

The result of the demonstration effect is the inflationary spiral and the persistent tendency towards disequilibrium in the balance of payments. If the differences in living standards are very large and widely known, then these exert an upward pressure on the consumption propensity. In this sense, the balance of payments deficit means that the population of the country "tries to live beyond its means".[56]

Nurkse's analysis of the operation and consequences of the demonstration effect is in itself a considerable and valuable contribution.[57] The consideration of this effect is indispensable in almost every aspect of the economic policy of developing, ex-colonial countries. The satisfaction of increased consumption demands really means serious problems in the newly independent countries. Familiarity with higher consumption levels induces the leading strata of society, especially where they consist of feudal or semi-feudal elements, to increase their unproductive, luxury expenditures. And as regards the last conclusion he draws from the analysis, it rightly justifies the

[54] About this concept see J. S. Duesenberry: *Income, Saving and the Theory of Consumer Behavior.* Harvard University Press, 1949.

[55] Nurkse adds: "It is always easier to adopt superior consumption habits than improved production methods." (R. Nurkse: Op. cit., p. 264.)

[56] Op. cit., p. 267.

[57] It should be added that Nurkse's scientific results cannot be narrowed down of course to the demonstration effect. Nurkse's idea of "balanced growth" is well worth studying in particular, but it does not pertain, in a strict sense, to the subject of this chapter.

"self-reliance" policy by stressing the necessity of domestic efforts for mobilizing the internal potential resources.[58]

But are we in fact thinking along the right lines if we consider that the backward peoples are themselves responsible for their low consumption levels and the underdevelopment and "open" character of their economies?! And if we keep silent about *other, determinant external causes* which keep their economies in an underdeveloped and "open" state and make no distinction between the *different strata of society*, is it not exactly those who are the poorest of all humanity and live in utmost poverty and under unbearable sanitary conditions that we advise to save and restrict their consumption?!

It is for this very reason that the reference to the demonstration effect cannot be accepted as a sufficient explanation for underdevelopment. It is unacceptable to claim that the negative role of advanced capitalist countries manifests itself only or mainly in demonstrating their higher living and consumption levels and creating thereby "exaggerated" demands in backward peoples.

As far as the economic relations between advanced and backward countries and their effects are concerned, it is, of course, not simply the positive or negative[59] demonstration effects, not even the direction of foreign capital investments or the trend of the terms of trade that constitute the crucial problem. What really matters is the *international production relations*. The crux of the matter is *why* the international division of labour has developed in such a way that the role of primary producers and suppliers has been assigned to backward, former colonial countries, and *how* this international division of labour has functioned, what consequences have resulted from it and what modifications have taken place in it recently. And even if several non-Marxist economists, especially the economists of the underdeveloped countries, realize the harmful consequences and recent disturbances of this division of labour,[60] a considerable number of Western economists[61] find the role assigned to the underdeveloped countries in the international division of labour quite natural, and indicate the direction of

[58] "The upshot is that external resources, even if they become available in the most desirable forms, are not enough. They do not automatically provide a solution to the problem of capital accumulation in underdeveloped areas. No solution is possible without strenuous domestic efforts, particularly in the field of public finance." (R. Nurkse: Op. cit., p. 271.)

[59] We wish to note that several economists deny the exclusively or chiefly negative nature of the demonstration effect and, in disagreement with Nurkse, point out that demonstration may also have a positive, stimulating effect leading to productive efforts to create the conditions for a higher consumption level.

[60] This is also proved, among others, by the Prebisch report to the First UNCTAD Conference.

[61] For example, Viner, Haberler, Benham, Cairncross, Hansen, Chase, Buchanan, Cole— to mention only some of the best-known economists.

further development accordingly. By referring to Ricardo's theory of *comparative advantages*[62] and to the requirements of the *optimum allocation* of the *factors of production* (nature, labour, capital), they declare that the system of international division of labour has developed on the basis of the *natural differences* in production costs—and not as an artificial product of colonization—and, consequently, each country has specialized in the production of those products it can turn out at the lowest comparative cost level. In other words, the kind of division of labour so developed must be regarded as optimum, and it is not expedient to carry out considerable change in it, except, perhaps, on the line of the transfer of some labour-intensive industries to the low-wage-cost countries, according to their comparative advantages. Consequently, the foreign trade relations that represent this optimum international division of labour are favourable for the underdeveloped countries, too.[63]

Thus the orthodox Western economists consider the division of labour between primary producing and industrial countries as the natural consequence of *internal* conditions. And if incidentally any harmful effects or transitional difficulties arise at all from this division of labour, it is, in the last analysis, also due to certain internal circumstances.

Denying the fact of one-sided dependence, they talk about the "mutual interdependence" which has arisen as a result of this natural division of labour between advanced and backward countries. They emphasize that for the latter to achieve rapid economic development it is not necessary to substantially change the pattern of production and to carry out a *real* industrialization which is able to integrate the traditional economy and to serve, by supplying and developing technology, rural development, too. They allow, at best, the *raison d'être* of certain secondhand, technologically

[62] In the debate on the problems of the international division of labour, arranged by UNESCO in Brussels in October 1960, Western economists, almost without exception, discussed the questions of international trade from the—somewhat modernized—position of Ricardo's theory of comparative costs. Professor A. K. Cairncross, of Glasgow University, in particular tried to prove that foreign trade, developed on the basis of comparative costs, was favourable for the underdeveloped countries, too. More recently, a similar argumentation based upon the principle of comparative advantages can often be heard, which urges the developing countries to specialize on some "labour-intensive", export-oriented manufacturing industries, (See, e.g., the documents of the 1976 World Employment Conference.)

[63] Myrdal, as we have seen, is of a completely different opinion. He says: "On the international as on the national level trade does not by itself necessarily work for equality. It may, on the contrary, have strong *backwash effects* on the underdeveloped countries A widening of markets often strengthens in the first instance the rich and progressive countries whose manufacturing industries have the lead . . . while the underdeveloped countries are in continuous danger of seeing even what they have of industry and, in particular, small-scale industry and handicrafts priced out by cheap imports from the industrial countries." (G. Myrdal: Op. cit., pp. 51–52). Similarly, we could also quote the critical articles of Singer, Prebisch and others on the existing international division of labour.

dependent enclave industries, which produce labour-intensive export commodities, i.e. the transfer to the Third World of those industries which no longer ensure comparative advantages to the Western economies. Accordingly, the most rational division of labour requires that the underdeveloped countries utilize their cheap labour by continuing to be suppliers of primary products to the advanced industrialized countries or, at best, by taking over from them certain outworn, labour-intensive (or polluting) industries, while the industrial centre in the metropolitan countries supplies them with sophisticated manufactured goods and technologies. It is only in this way, say some economists, that the optimum allocation of the factors of production, also supported by foreign capital investments, can be ensured.

In their view, the influx of foreign capital should continue to develop in accordance with the consideration of the optimum international allocation of the factors of production and this mechanism should not be interfered with by drastic measures.

Even Myint who has gone a long way in revealing the detrimental effect of the present international division of labour and foreign capital investments on the state of backward countries, and in analysing the "disequalizing effects" stemming from international trade itself, refers to the principles of the "maximization of the total world output" and the "optimum allocation of the world's capital resources" in the context of loans to be extended to underdeveloped countries. In accordance with these principles, "loans should continue to be made strictly on the productivity principle".[64] Myint comes to this conclusion on the basis of a distinction made between "underdeveloped resources" and "backward peoples". The development of the "underdeveloped resources" brings out the "productivity principle", and the improvement of the present state of "backward people" the "principle of needs". It may lead to harmful consequences, says Myint, if these principles are mixed up in the policy of granting loans and aid to backward countries.

It follows from the *productivity principle* that it is expedient to grant loans for productive purposes only to countries (or sectors within a country's economy) where the "social productivity" of the capital supplied is maximized *on a world scale*. This means not only that, given the present structure, conditions and costs of production, the loans would be available for most of the underdeveloped countries only for the development of primary production, but also that it is not reasonable to grant loans for productive purposes to every underdeveloped country. "The social productivity curves of investment must be constructed objectively, and independently of our value judgements concerning needs. This means that

---

[64] H. Myint: An Interpretation of Economic Backwardness. Loc. cit., p. 101.

capital should not be diverted in the form of low interest loans or grants to the poorer countries simply because they are poor."[65]

Conversely, aid for the improvement of the conditions of the backward people should be granted on the basis of the *principle of needs*.[66] Thus, in contrast to loans made in the form of capital goods, "grants should be made in the form of final consumers' goods and services". As "individuals and governments in underdeveloped countries sometimes find themselves with large sums of money which they cannot profitably or safely invest locally", it is more reasonable to distribute the grants as free gifts in the form of consumers' goods and services.[67]

This rigid confrontation of the "principle of productivity" and the "principle of needs", and the subordination to them of the capital export and aid policy may seem perhaps rational from a certain *abstract* point of view of world economy. Provided there is a single integrated, homogeneous world society—together with a system of planned and fair redistribution of the world's incomes—the allocation of the capital investments and the benefits to satisfy local needs could well be rationally separated according to these criteria. However, economic and social processes take place as yet partly within the framework of *national* economies and societies (or even smaller units), and the distribution of economic resources and the allocation of capital investments cannot be made, even within this framework, strictly on the basis of the principle of *economic* efficiency. (A case in point is the government policy aiming at developing the backward regions or minority areas in the advanced countries.)

On the other hand, economic efficiency and the so-called comparative advantages are very *relative* concepts. Even the "static" comparative advantages based upon natural endowments may often appear not static at all. (When, for example, unexpected geological discoveries change the picture of natural endowments that has already been accepted as final, or when new technological processes, scientific and technical inventions make suddenly certain potential resources exploitable.) This is true to an even greater extent of the far more important group of comparative advantages that we might call "dynamic".[68] These "dynamic" advantages which are much more determinant for economic efficiency than the "static" ones, manifest themselves in the economic environment, the existence of external

[65] H. Myint: Op. cit., p. 101.

[66] On the other hand, he admits that "a policy of a more equal redistribution of international incomes based on the pure principle of needs... does not touch the heart of the problem; for fundamentally the problem of the underdeveloped countries is not merely that of low or unequal distribution of final incomes but also that of unequal participation in the processes of economic activity." (H. Myint: Op. cit., p. 103.)

[67] H. Myint: Op. cit., pp. 101–102.

[68] See I. Vajda's study in the May 1963 issue of *Közgazdasági Szemle*. We shall come back to this question in the next chapter.

economies and the actual development level of the productive forces. The "comparative disadvantage" of many underdeveloped countries in the processing industries is far more due to the latter, and concretely to the underdevelopment of these industries themselves, than to their natural endowments.

In addition, let us not forget that the Ricardian theory of international specialization according to (national) comparative costs implicity assumes that capitalist entrepreneurs act (invest, export or import) in consonance with social rationality, i.e. that their comparative cost calculation coincides with that of the nation. It is unnecessary to point out how naive and false this assumption is, and that the fact of private capitalist decision-making and the discrepancy between private and social costs have necessarily prevented the principle of international specialization according to comparative costs from coming into operation even in the case of the advanced capitalist countries. Nor should we forget how far the business considerations and cost calculation of *foreign* monopoly capital must have been from the social rationality and cost calculation of a dependent, economically colonized country!

Myint's views on the distinction between the principles of productivity and needs—though he himself sees "the unsatisfactoriness of trying to apply the *static* rules of the productive optimum to the problem of the underdeveloped countries" and the inadequacy of taking "the productivity curves of international investment on the basis of *existing economic conditions* in the developed and the underdeveloped countries"[69]—provide, independently of his intention, false theoretical arguments for a policy of keeping most of the underdeveloped countries in their primary producing role and in their technological dependence on industrialized countries.

*

In conclusion, let us survey in brief the theories dealt with so far and sum up our comments on them.

1. It has become a fairly widespread practice in conventional Western economics to categorize the "economically underdeveloped countries" on the basis of the *quantitative indices* manifesting the development levels of their productive forces. Even the terms "backward", "less developed" and "underdeveloped" countries are based on the assumption of a simple "lag" in the development of productive forces.

However, a more thorough economic analysis will reveal that these quantitative indices and criteria may cover up qualitative differences. Along with or in spite of the quantitative differences among themselves, the so-called "Third World", i.e. ex-colonial or semi-colonial dependent countries, are *de facto* distinguished from the advanced capitalist and socialist

[69] H. Myint: Op. cit., p. 101.

countries by such *common qualitative criteria* which are related to their specific development and position in the world economy.

2. A number of economists see "economic underdevelopment" as a lagging behind in the development of productive forces due to the effects of certain *growth-inhibiting*, limiting or retarding *factors*. These factors are presented in various combinations, either in a co-existent or successive arrangement.

No doubt, some of these factors really impede and limit development considerably and are also important from the point of view of economic policy. Most of them, however, are symptoms or consequences rather than causes of "backwardness" (e.g. the underutilization of natural resources, low labour productivity, etc.), and, therefore, they require further explanation.

On the other hand, these factors are also closely interrelated, that is, they are links in a series of mutual relationships. Consequently, these relationships and their forms of motion must also be analysed.

3. The combination of the limiting factors in various vicious circles does not solve this problem, nor does it provide an approach to the historical explanation of "economic underdevelopment". It is true, on the other hand, that in this way certain relationships between the limiting factors can be revealed and these relationships can be observed, *ceteris paribus*, in reality, too.

These relationships, however, are indeterminate in the last analysis, as they are interwoven. No account is given of why (after what historical antecedents, under what circumstances) these factors came to be connected in such a way: reproducing themselves on an *identical level*. If, however, this is their natural interconnection, and an abrupt, sudden quantitative change (a critical minimum effort) must take place or an outside effect must come into operation in one of the links of the vicious circle for the circular movement not to be repeated on the same level, then the historical question must be answered: how did the now advanced countries manage to find a way out of the vicious circle?

4. The theories concentrating on the *stages of economic growth*, and demonstrating the general process of the rise of a "mature" or "industrial" society by the example of the most developed capitalist countries, claim to provide a historical explanation. Their approach and outlook are essentially the same as those of the vicious circle theories: some countries are farther ahead than others on the road of the same development process (as shown by certain economic-statistical indices). "Economic underdevelopment" means simply a lag, a lower but natural and inevitable stage of growth. The only difference in outlook is that these theories lay emphasis on the existence or lack of the preconditions for attaining the higher stage ("take-off" or maturity) rather than on the growth-inhibiting factors. Interest is focussed on the explanation of growth rather than that of lagging behind: how did

the present-day advanced countries manage to reach the higher "stages" of growth? Then, if the economic-statistical indices marking the development levels of the productive forces are also indicative of the degree of the societies' maturity, then the present-day underdeveloped countries represent the earlier stages in the social development of the now most advanced capitalist countries which provide thereby a pattern for the development of the backward countries. And since these theories are also intended to idealize capitalism *as society*, and not only its productive forces, therefore the surface phenomena of *capitalist* society, its propensities, customs, the way of thinking, institutions, etc., are markedly expressed and emphasized in the outlined pattern of development.

The confrontation of backward and advanced countries at different stages of growth is also manifested by the *sociological theories of underdevelopment*. They compare the ideal pattern variables of the traditional, supposedly original society with those of the modern advanced society—completely disregarding the real pattern variables, the heterogeneous socio-economic characteristics of underdeveloped countries and those world-economic processes that determine the development of both the underdeveloped and developed countries.

But in order to demonstrate the present state of underdeveloped countries as only an earlier but otherwise general and natural stage of growth, it is necessary to project it back, together with some of its undeniable characteristics, into the past, into the history of the now developed countries. But precisely this projection into the past reveals the deficiency of this "historical" explanation, the unstable basis of the whole theory. For even if certain similar characteristics related to some external, international factors can be demonstrated, with more or less strain, in the earlier historical periods of several developed countries, they certainly cannot be found in the case of the country (or countries) that was first to take off. In other words, the basic difference in the process of growth will inevitably show itself, and precisely in the different character and opposite role of the *external factors*.

It is possible to meditate on and discuss the question what stages of growth a given society passed through, what internal factors accelerated or retarded its development *as long as* this society developed independently. (It would be perhaps not out of place to investigate what development level, what "stage of growth" the West-European and the Tropical-African societies attained respectively before the 15th century, and what internal factors and endowments were responsible for their quicker or slower development,[70] and why exactly Western Europe came to be the colonizer and not the colony.)

---

[70] It was Marx who gave a historical answer to this question when he called Western Europe the first natural fatherland of capital on account of its *natural, geographic and climatic endowments* favourable to the rise of capitalism (i.e. on account of its material

But from the historical moment on when the development of two or more countries became linked up, and particularly if subsequently the development gap between them began to widen, it is no longer sufficient to talk about "lagging behind" and "shooting ahead" but we must also consider what positive and negative consequences this linking-up resulted in for the respective countries. And if it turns out that in some (or even only one, i.e. the very first) of these countries the "take-off", i.e. the rapid economic development, was promoted intensively by the positive effects themselves of this relationship, while the same did not take place in the case of the others, then it also must be revealed what *adverse* effects this relationship had on the latter.

5. Perhaps it is the theoretical problem of exactly these external relationships or rather the practical manifestation of the harmful effects that has induced many economists to include the analysis of certain negative, "disequalizing" *effects* of the *external, international factors* in the explanation of the state of backward countries. Analyses of this sort represent the most valuable part of the underdevelopment theories.

But the majority of theoreticians, even if they admit the existence of certain negative external factors, regard them as relative and transitory, or put down their adverse effects to internal deficiencies.

In reality, however, it is self-evident that *if* the growth-inhibiting internal factors themselves do not provide a sufficient explanation for the fact of "economic underdevelopment", *if* some of these internal factors do not follow at all from the inherent development of a traditional society, and, further, *if* the advanced capitalist countries owe their "take-off", the breaking of the "vicious circle" in a not insignificant measure to the fact that they established international economic relations while the very same relations exert certain negative effects on the development of backward countries—*then* it is precisely these external, international factors and their effects that should be brought into the focus of analysing the causes of present-day "economic underdevelopment". Since the socio-economic development of these countries became linked up with the economies and societies of more advanced countries as a sort of appendix of them, it is the outward orientation rather than the internal brakes and obstacles that has basically determined their development and has diverted it from its original and natural *course*. Therefore, it is not the external negative effects which should be deduced from the internal relations, but quite the contrary is

---

conditions and not of the superior "propensities" of its people). At the same time, he revealed the general trend of development of human society, pointing out that Western Europe's development represented only one concrete form, a variant of this development, and that the same "stage" would have been attained independently and inevitably by other societies as well. On how capitalism has arisen from the crisis of feudalism in Western Europe, see I. Wallerstein: *The Modern World-System. I. Capitalist Agriculture and the Origins of the European World-Economy in the Sixteenth Century.* Academic Press, New York, 1974.

justified both logically and historically, even if the effects work mutually in both ways.

By way of drawing the final conclusion from this polemic chapter and of introducing at the same time the next chapter of our study, let us point out that "economic underdevelopment"—contrary to its literary sense and usual interpretation—does *not* mean simply a lower level in the evolution of productive forces, or merely a falling behind, a loss of tempo or time in economic or social development, *nor* does it represent a lower "stage" in the general and natural process of growth (though this was or might have been the case *prior to* the rise of colonialism and capitalist world economy). It is *the complex socio-economic product of a specific development*, of a development which has been *most closely interrelated with the development of the capitalist world economy* as a whole, and which has been *determined* mainly by the latter, the *external factor*.

PART TWO

THE CAUSES, SUBSTANCE, AND THE LAWS OF MOTION OF UNDERDEVELOPMENT.
A HISTORICAL-ANALYTICAL APPROACH

"UNDERDEVELOPMENT" IN THE CONTEXT OF THE DEVELOPMENT OF THE WORLD CAPITALIST ECONOMY AND ITS RECENT CRISIS

The present economic state (including all the associated problems) of the countries of the "third" world, the so-called underdeveloped or developing countries, is usually called and described in the relevant literature—as we have seen in the preceding chapters—as *economic underdevelopment*. This term refers to the generally less favourable indices marking the lower level of the productive forces of the underdeveloped world, and is connected with the theory according to which these countries have fallen behind in the process of their historical development, have lost time and tempo, and consequently are now at an earlier, lower stage of the general process of growth, i.e. they have been less successful and rapid in their own progress than the more developed countries.

Though there can be no doubt that the countries in question are economically backward (in the strict sense of the word, too) and less developed, and that the rate of economic development has been rather different in the different parts of the world, it is nevertheless not simply economic underdevelopment or backwardness that is characteristic of the present state of the developing countries. We have already tried to prove in Part One, in the polemic and critical survey of the interpretations of economic underdevelopment, the following:

— classifications made on the basis of economic-statistical indices *cannot* disclose the principal economic and social characteristics of the underdeveloped countries (as they fuse essential qualitative differences with quantitative samenesses, or separate qualitative samenesses on the basis of quantitative differences);

— the theories explaining backwardness by various internal obstacles and impediments to development are unhistorical and leave the question unresolved *why* similar hindering factors were not at work in the case of the now developed countries, and *how* factors of such a different nature and origin came together in the case of the now backward countries;

— explanations concerning the earlier, lower "natural" stage of economic growth disregard essential differences between the present state of the underdeveloped countries and the earlier state of the now developed ones, the basically different *external*, international conditions of their internal development, and the diverging and disequalizing effects of the same world-economic process.

The interpretation of "economic underdevelopment" as a simple falling behind may be a more or less correct and acceptable explanation for that historical past which preceded the formation of the world economy, that is, the building up of a system of lasting economic relations and massive interaction of various parts of the world.[1] This interpretation may provide an answer to the question why certain countries rather than others played a leading role in the development of the world economy and how the roles of the colonizer and the colonized were allotted to the various countries. Socio-economic development, owing to its internal laws and self-movement, leads from traditional society (primitive communism) through slavery and feudalism—or their peculiar mixture—to capitalism, which, after reaching a certain development level, produces, in the natural course of its further development and with the emergence of the world market and world economy, the system of colonial and dependent countries, i.e. colonialism. From the "moment", however, that this takes place (when colonialism, which paved the way for the capitalist world economy and became part of it, appears on the scene), it is no longer correct to examine and evaluate the development of the individual countries solely on the basis of internal factors, or to attribute their present state to an independent shooting ahead or lagging behind.

Therefore, the socio-economic state of the developing countries is not merely "economic underdevelopment", not just a sign of their not having participated in development, of their having fallen behind in progress, but it is the product of a *specific development*, which is most closely connected with, moreover derived from the development of capitalist world economy. Therefore, only the analysis of this latter development can provide the key to the understanding of the present state and the growth problems of the developing countries.

To prove this, it will perhaps suffice to refer, by way of introduction, to two indisputable facts:

(1) The measure of economic backwardness in the strict sense of the word, i.e. the difference between the development levels of productive forces—which already existed at the time of the rise of colonialism and determined the roles—has grown even bigger since organic relations became established between the more and the less developed countries.[2]

[1] We consider this more accurate definition to be necessary as, on the one hand, the unfolding of the world economy was preceded and prepared by the colonization of the 15th and 16th centuries, which interrupted the independent development of certain countries, while giving a boost to others, and, on the other hand, because the development of the world economy did not draw all societies at once into the system of mutual effects and interactions.

[2] For example, according to the calculations of S. J. Patel, the share of the underdeveloped countries in the world income was 65 per cent in 1850 and 22 per cent in 1960. (S. J. Patel: The Economic Distance between Nations: Its Origin, Measurement and Outlook. *The Economic Journal*, No. 293, London, 1964, pp. 119–131. For similar

(2) In the economy and society of the colonial or dependent countries such factors, phenomena and alien bodies have developed, and the direction and nature of their external economic relations have been established in such a way that all this not only cannot be derived from the actually attained level of their internal socio-economic development, but it has also come into conflict with this development.[3]

1. THE CAUSAL RELATIONSHIP OF "UNDERDEVELOPMENT" WITH THE DEVELOPMENT OF THE CAPITALIST WORLD ECONOMY

Hence the analysis of the present state of the developing countries must be started both *historically and logically* with the examination and evaluation of colonialism, or more precisely the capitalist world economy and international division of labour.

As far as colonialism is concerned, its evaluation can—and must—be effected from the viewpoint of general human ethics, i.e. of humanism *on the one hand*, and, *on the other*, from the viewpoint of objective historical development, the latter being obviously closer to our subject. As to the former, it is self-evident and unambiguous that only the most severe judgement can be passed on colonialism in view of the immense and almost inconceivable suffering and humiliation it brought upon the subjugated peoples. The indigenous population of America was almost completely wiped out, about 100 million Africans[4] were either dragged away or killed in the slave trade—and all this was only the beginning. And where are the thousands who suffered and fell victims to wars, prisons, concentration camps and racial discrimination?!

Nothing can exonerate from responsibility those who carried out, directed or ideologically defended and supported this colonization! In comparison, the activity of the missionaries, the improvement of public health and education, the introduction of certain positive elements of the European culture, that is, the whole "civilizing mission" can only be regarded at most as an insignificant "attenuating circumstance"—if all this was not intended as a service needed for subjugation. But even when passing this judgement we must not forget that the responsibility rests not with

---

calculations or data see also S. Kuznets: Underdeveloped Countries and the Pre-Industrial Phase in the Advanced Countries. *The Economics of Underdevelopment*. Ed. by A. M. Agarwala and S. P. Singh, Oxford University Press, 1958, p. 145 and R. T. Gill: *Economic Development: Past and Present*. Prentice Hall, 1963, p. 3.)

[3] Again we can also refer to numerous non-Marxist economists (e.g. Perroux, Dawson, Prebisch, Lewis, Myrdal, etc.) who, in one way or another, point out and analyse the lack of internal integration, the dual socio-economic structure, the fact of the "enclaves".

[4] See A. Hunton: *Decision in Africa*. New York, 1956 and W. E. B. du Bois: *The Negro*. New York.

nations or peoples but with *social classes*, the leading strata of certain *societies*. We must bear in mind that their success in reaching their high position, in establishing their power and wealth, was based upon and started with the suffering and exploitation of their *own* people.[5] Colonialism was not simply the conflict of "races", of peoples and nations, but the consequence of the emergence and worldwide development of a certain *social system*. In this sense the moral evaluation cannot be separated from assessment (in respect) of the objective, historical processes.

It would lead to a one-sided value judgement *if* we assessed the role of colonialism without analysing the objective historical process, by simply flying into a passion over the untold suffering and perhaps even conceiving a strong hatred for the people and "race" of the colonizing country;[6] *if*, in addition to the barbaric, inhuman subjugation, we only referred to what colonialism *failed* to do, e.g., to the fact that it did *not* develop the manufacturing industries of the colonized country, did *not* care for the cultural development, education, public health and social security of the subjugated peoples, etc.; *if* we accounted for all these undoubtedly true charges by the *subjective aims* and passions of people who carried out colonization; *if*, in other words, we traced these charges back to the negative

---

[5] Here we can refer not only to the extreme misery and exploitation of the British working class in the period of the emergence of industrial capitalism but also to the cruel suppression of the Scotch and Irish peoples by the British ruling class.

[6] Sometimes even theoreticians professing Marxist views are liable to make this mistake. Franz Fanon, e.g. (*Les damnés de la terre.* Paris, 1961) presents colonialism and the collapse of the colonial system as the dialectics of violence. The first phase of violence is the open violence of colonizers against the colonized. In the second phase the violence develops as a mystic energy in the colonized people, but turns inward for the time being. In the third phase this violence finally finds its real object, its adequate form, and turns against the colonizer. And since, according to Fanon, social stratification in the colonial world was determined basically by racial factors, colonization and the national liberation movements may seem to be the conflict of violence arising from the inner emotions and subconsciousness of the different "races".

Fanon rather misunderstands the essence and inherent laws of colonialism, the capitalist system and world economy. Fanon's trend of thought could also be used as a "foundation" for a new racial ideology and owing to the over-emphasis laid on the supplementary, secondary, surface features of colonialism and on the phenomena of the political sphere, it may exert in addition a demobilizing effect on the struggle for economic liberation and independence. His conclusion that instead of the rather "spoilt" proletariat, the truly revolutionary class of the colonial world can only be the rural working population, i.e. the peasantry (see also Chapter III. 2. about this), which has remained outside the capitalistic relations introduced by foreigners, but which has suffered most from the violence of the colonizers, disregards the inner laws of motion of the dual colonial economy and society. Besides, by neglecting the social laws arising objectively from the development of productive forces, it leads to utopistic, romantic illusions concerning the possible ways of socialism.

For a more detailed criticism see I. Marton's study: Újabb harmadikutas koncepció a Harmadik Világ fejlődéséről (A new third-way concept of the development of the Third World). *Tájékoztató*, No. 3, 1963.

146

qualities of men, peoples and "races", their morbid instincts and cruel, selfish inclinations, or only to the policy of the colonizing powers; *if*, in this way, we conceived colonialism as the conflict of "races" and cultures,[7] and *if* we explained imperialism simply as a policy.

This one-sided view is, in fact, the inverse equivalent of the world outlook which explains away economic underdevelopment by referring to the unfavourable qualities of "inferior" peoples, and regards colonialism and racial discrimination as the mission and self-defence of "superior races".

Whatever direction racial ideology may have, it is not only deeply reactionary and inhuman, but also impedes the understanding of real processes with its prejudiced views.

And as to the interpretation of imperialism as a *policy*, it also leads, even if it does not trace this policy directly back to subjective human qualities, to the same consequence. For as far as a policy in general is independent of the inherent laws and tendencies of a given economic system and the social relations rooted in the latter, it really can only derive from personal qualities being gifts of heaven or hell. Far from intending to underestimate the significance—and, at certain historical moments, even the decisive role—of the personal qualities of those in power, it seems to be rather childish to assume a *whole and long historical period* to be simply the result of the unfortunate coincidence, in a number of countries, of people coming to power with the same propensity to run an imperialist policy. Moreover, such an assumption would lead to an absurd conclusion: it would take only some new elections and the reshuffling of a few cabinets in the countries concerned, rather than the structural transformation of the socio-economic relations to eliminate imperialism as such.

If colonialism were merely the conflict of "races" and cultures, or the manifestation of a certain imperialist policy, then the *formal* liberation of enslaved "races" and cultures, or the withdrawal and disappearance of the colonizing *policy* would seem to radically change the situation. Starting from this assumption, it is equally possible to arrive—without any logical twist—both at the practical acceptance of complete economic submission, of the greatest possible opportunism (only the *open* political forms of

---

[7] It would not be out of place to refer here to President Leopold Senghor's theory. The subjectivist world concept of his work *(Négritude et Humanisme)*, born perhaps from French existentialism and presenting the conflict of colonizers and colonized as the confrontation of certain, vaguely defined, psychocultural communities, takes us a long way from the historical interpretation of the state of the underdeveloped countries, from the understanding of the real *essence* of colonialism, and provides the basis for faulty conclusions concerning the prospects of future development. Senghor's "socialist" view—based on a négritude concept interwoven with the cult of traditions and a subjectivist, moreover, and in the last analysis, *racial* ideology—obscures the real economic relations and the preconditions for a socialist development.

colonial rule should be abolished!), and at a racial ideology proclaiming, and tending to realize by force, a new superiority.

However, such an approach would make it impossible for us to find out what real processes determine or influence the state and development of backward countries.

But even the critique of colonialism becomes weak and ineffective if merely the *negative* features of the colonial system are taken into account. The evaluation of historical phenomena must be done historically, in a historical perspective, with due consideration not only of the sacrifices but also of the lasting achievements. The apologists of colonialism may justly argue by saying that the development of societies in general requires substantial sacrifices, and that we judge the ancient Greek and Roman slave societies not only by the terrible fate of the slaves but also by their achievements. They can justly set against the negative features of colonialism those positive phenomena which are undoubtedly connected with its emergence and development.

Who would deny the existence of the few modern towns, sea- and airports, mines, or modern hotels and hospitals, etc. that were established even in the most backward colonies by the colonial governments and companies?! And who would deny that the systematic contact with the world market, the existence of large export-producing plantations, the expansion of the monetary sector were also due to the mechanism of colonialism?!

It follows from this that we must take colonialism—together with its positive and negative features and consequences—for what it is: the *objective product of capitalism* developed at a certain stage of the historical development of human society.

Historically, it can be assessed first of all as the promoting and accelerating factor of unfolding capitalism and as the *materialization of a peculiar international division of labour*.

And since, from the point of view of its after-effects and the resulting economic phenomena and processes, it was less the "early" colonialism the 15th–16th century conquests, but rather the building up of the colonial *system*, the *economically established colonialism* (i.e. the colonial system of monopoly capitalism as it emerged in the last decades of the 19th century) that played the decisive role, therefore, when exploring the present state of the developing countries, we must also direct our attention to the latter, more precisely to the international division of labour and the changes brought about in it by colonialism. (This does not mean, however, that we want to underestimate the effect of "early" capitalism on, and the role it played in, promoting the development of West-European countries and stopping or hindering the independent development of the colonized countries. It was in "early" colonialism, after all, that the ways parted and the gap began to widen! But the *mechanism* that organically connected these

148

two ways of development and formed the present picture of the developing countries came into being only later, in the *economic system* of colonialism.)

Colonialism is, therefore, primarily and basically an *economic pheno-menon*, an economic cause and effect. Its motive force derives not from subjective emotions, not from a Freudian "violence"-complex, nor from an unselfish disposition undertaking "the mission of civilization" and not even from the conflict of "races" and cultures, nor simply from political tendencies. Its attending phenomena and surface manifestations should not lead us astray as to its inner economic core.

Already "early" colonialism was organically connected with the economic phenomena and laws of motion of unfolding capitalism. West-European society, whose representatives appeared in the remotest parts of the world, on the coasts of Africa and America and in the countries of Asia in the 15th–16th centuries when colonization began, was a society in a *special phase* of its development, a society undergoing its greatest transformation. This was the time of the rise of new social relations already growing within the womb of feudalism, the emergence of *capital*. This then appeared on the scene, still in its ancient form as merchant capital, to break down the old relationships within which it had developed, to disintegrate the feudal mode of production, and give way to the new relations in which it could penetrate into and get possession of the sphere of production.

It was the time of primitive accumulation in which the emerging capital transformed society with merciless speed, according to its own interests, and enslaved foreign peoples with the same cruel greediness with which it created its own social basis; the class of people expropriated, expelled from their land, deprived of their means of production and compelled to work in the hell of capitalist manufacture—the proletariat. This was *the heyday of merchant capital* in West Europe when the instinct of the new society, the hunt for surplus value, began to assert itself in the disintegrating old society. This pursuit of profit, as production was still carried on on a feudal basis, took the form of commercial profit-making, the acquisition of tangible money, of gold. But to get rich in commerce, to get hold of more money, of gold, is possible only if the exchange is unequal if one party always wins while the others constantly lose. But the possibilities of a lasting and repeated unequal exchange are very limited within the society of a given country, so the activity of merchant capital was directed from the beginning to the *outside*, to foreign countries. The ideology of merchant capital, *mercantilism*, points to foreign trade as the source of a country's enrichment and sees the way to increase the nation's wealth in importing as much gold as possible into the country, while exporting as little as possible, preferably nothing, out of it.

These were the economic motives of the open cruelties, robbery and piracy of "early" colonalism, while the subsequent mass slave-trade and slavery institutionalized for centuries was nothing more than the world-wide process and organic part of "primitive accumulation of capital".[8]

The colonial system established in the last third of the 19th and the beginning of the 20th century was but the specific manifestation of the worldwide expansion of the already developed capitalist mode of production, *the form of a peculiar international division of labour in an unfolding capitalist world economy*. The building up of the colonial system, the economic establishment and transformation of the colonies was an important phase in the development of the world economy.

The coming into being of the world economy was a significant step forward in the historical development of human society, proving that capitalism was of a definitely higher and more developed character than any other previous socio-economic system. But it follows from the very *substance* of the capitalist system that this, essentially positive, historical fact has become the source of the sharpest conflicts and most striking inequalities, subjugation and exploitation.

It is true, of course, that the integration into the world economy, the world market, the breaking up of the old, often rigid and stagnant or slowly developing socio-economic systems, the introduction of the elements of a definitely more developed mode of production, the expansion of commodity production and market relations, the abrupt growth of certain branches of production, the adoption of more developed technical, scientific, cultural, sanitary and infrastructural elements which came into being on a higher level of the forces of production, etc.—all these are undoubtedly positive achievements for the development of the colonial and dependent countries as well. Since, however, these results are but parts of a movement wholly governed by the *internal laws of capitalism*, they cannot be evaluated in themselves, but only together with the whole movement. These achievements are the consequences of the penetration of foreign capitalist powers, of the activity of foreign capital, and this very penetration or activity—apart from the violence used—has had, besides the achievements, or just because of them, the gravest consequences. As far as the achievements themselves have turned to detrimental consequences, we are faced with a *specific dialectics of development* in which the steps taken forward give rise to ever newer obstacles to further development, which, in turn, require additional energy to be overcome.

But just what are the grave consequences suffered by the colonial and dependent countries taking part in the international division of labour set up by the emerging world capitalism and which have determined the main,

[8] "The discovery of gold and silver in America, the extirpation, enslavement and entombment in mines of the aboriginal population, the beginning of the conquest and looting of the East Indies, the turning of Africa into a warren for the commercial hunting of black-skins, signalised the rosy dawn of the era of capitalist production." (K. Marx: *Capital*. Vol. I. Foreign Languages Publishing House, Moscow, p. 751.)

essential features of their present state, the so-called "economic underdevelopment"? In other words, what are the consequences of the fact that the achievements mentioned above are connected with the activities of foreign powers and capital? And what are the consequences in general of the participation in the capitalist international division of labour?

As the activities of colonial powers and foreign capital cannot be explained by personal motivations (Nurkse is completely right in saying so),[9] but are determined by the objective relations of the historically given international division of labour of capitalism, let us begin our answer with an examination of this division of labour.

The international division of labour as embodied in the colonial system (also including the semi-colonial and other dependent countries) was the exact expression and result of the historical development of capitalism in a given period of time. We might also say that it was the specific—and in this sense almost "classical"—division of labour of capitalism grown over into imperialism. What determined the concrete structure and operation of this division of labour in the given historical period? It was those internal relations and external power relations which were characteristics of the countries of the developed sector of the capitalist world order and of their positions in the world economy.

In the period of the building up of the colonial system the leading country of world capitalism was Britain, with France, Germany, etc., following behind. In these countries, but especially in Britain, a very rapid industrial development took place, while agriculture, for natural reasons—or rather owing to the survival of obsolete relations of production and productive technology—lagged behind in development. The mineral raw material basis also proved more or less inadequate. Rapid industrial growth, especially in its extensive stage, was accompanied by an increase in the number of the employed (mainly wage workers recruited from the formerly self-supplying rural population) and consequently, by a widening of the demand for foodstuffs, as well as a rapidly expanding demand for mineral and agricultural raw materials for industrial use. It also called for an adequately expanding market for manufactured goods. The rather backward agriculture was not able to ensure a sufficient supply of food, nor was it able to meet—together with the extractive industry—the demand for raw materials. On the other hand, the population being on a very low income level could not provide a large and sufficiently expanding market for the industrial products. The leading capitalist power, Britain, depended heavily on external food and raw material sources as well as on foreign markets for carrying on her industrial development. The more the internal laws of capital accumulation asserted themselves, the more the strange twins of unemployment and the underutilization of part of the accumulated capital

[9] See Part One, Chapter VI.

as concomitants of the new development—along with the falling tendency of the rate of profit—became apparent. Thus, besides the acquisition of external sources of raw materials and foodstuffs and of foreign markets, an outward-oriented *capital drain* (and, through the emigration to the colonies, also a labour drain), as well as the search for investment opportunities promising a higher rate of profit, became natural imperatives.

The increasingly powerful monopolies and the militarily strengthened states succeeded in satisfying these imperative needs. (The fact that the way to it was marked by rivalry, bargaining and cruel wars is relevant to our subject only to the extent that the subjugated territories were "balkanized", cut up and differentiated even in language and culture.[10])

The satisfaction of these needs determined the economic functions of the subjugated territories. Thus the latter, apart from having a strategic role, became:

– the suppliers of mineral and agricultural raw materials to the metropolitan countries;

– the markets for their industrial products;

– the territories of their capital drain and investment activities and thereby their regular source of income.

It was according to this division of labour and these functions that the economies of the colonial and dependent countries were transformed. The present-day developing countries bear the marks of this division of labour. But before analysing these marks and the internal socio-economic consequences of transformation, let us point out right away that this *par excellence* form and system of the capitalist international division of labour has since undergone *substantial changes*, especially after the Second World War, and that, with the emergence of a new kind of division of labour due to the development of productive forces, of science and technology to monopolistic "transnationalization" of capital, and also to changes in political power relations, its operation has come up against increasing difficulties. These changes and their consequences may be summed up briefly in the following way:

The leadership in the developed sector of the capitalist world economy has changed hands from Britain, a traditionally and more or less naturally raw-material and food-importing country, to the USA, a country with rich raw-material resources, the most developed agriculture, a much larger internal market and an economy less sensitive to foreign trade.

The development of the scientific-technical revolution has diminished the significance of certain traditional raw materials, made new sources available, and produced synthetic materials. It has increased the

[10] Which—to be even more detrimental—actually meant that a completely foreign language and culture had been imposed on them without regard to the existing language groups and traditional cultures.

152

productivity of agriculture and gave, for a while, a great impetus—as technical revolutions do in general—to investments, expanding thereby, at least temporarily, the investment opportunities, the internal market and also employment.

State intervention, and the unfolding and advance of state monopoly capitalism in the most developed capitalist countries (partly in connection with the scientific-technical revolution) have widened and ensured the opportunities for profitable private investments also within national boundaries. They promoted the development of agriculture in several countries (as e.g. in France and Germany), by artificial, protectionist means, and have also opened up new ways for the development of the international division of labour by means of the integrational organizations and inter-governmental agreements. The anticyclical policy of state monopoly capitalism, following the Keynesian recipe, operated rather successfully until the early seventies. Private and state monopoly co-operation among the advanced capitalist countries, especially in the framework of the European Economic Community, gave a great impetus to the widening of the division of labour among the developed industrial countries.

As a result of the increasingly oligopolistic structure of the developed capitalist countries, and owing to the shift in the power relations of the world economy and to the progress in decolonization, the structure of capital export to the underdeveloped countries has undergone substantial changes.[11]

The post-colonial development programmes of the underdeveloped countries and the "population explosion" have made the question of their import capacities especially acute and have intensified the marketing and price problems of their exports, whilst the processes of marketing and price formation in the capitalist sector of the world economy have come to be controlled more and more by the oligopolies.

Industrial development and the advance of the scientific-technical revolution have made it possible for the developed countries to mitigate a bit their monopoly on the processing industry and technology as against the developing countries, and so a *certain* industrial development in the latter does not necessarily prejudice their interests. It can even coincide with the interests of the vertically structured oligopolies. (We shall return to this question.)

The rise in the general income level in the developed capitalist countries has brought about a certain shift in the pattern of consumption, especially towards the superior, durable consumer goods, etc.[12]

[11] See in the next chapters.

[12] In this shift in the consumption pattern the well-known Engel's law finds its expression. The rise in income levels results first of all in the relative decrease in the demand for foodstuffs, whose impact makes itself increasingly felt—especially in view of a protectionist

As a result of all these and other changes, the realization of many traditional export products of the developing countries in the world market meets with ever greater difficulties. Owing to synthetic substitutes and to newly discovered resources, the growth in demand on the part of the advanced capitalist countries for a number of primary products, the so-called "colonial commodities", including some raw materials, has considerably slowed (while their reliance on the supply of a few strategic materials, among them crude oil, has rapidly further increased).[13] The development of West-European agriculture and the immense agricultural reserves of the USA and Canada, as well as the shifts in the consumption pattern, have limited the agrarian export possibilities of the underdeveloped countries, and, what is more, a number of backward countries have to rely on agrarian imports from the developed capitalist countries to a greater and greater extent, owing to the extremely rapid population growth and to the lopsided gearing of the economy to export crops ousting foodstuff production for local consumption. The expansion of capital investment opportunities in the advanced sector of the capitalist world economy— owing to state intervention, the scientific-technical revolution and international co-operation and integration—curbed the earlier rapid rise in private capital export to the underdeveloped countries, and, in view of the political risks and the danger of nationalization in the newly independent countries, the interest of foreign private capital (especially private capital independent of the oligopolies) dwindled relatively in the developing countries.[14]

Hence the present state of the developing countries, the so-called "economic underdevelopment", bears not only the marks and conse-quences of the international division of labour which materialized in the colonial system, but it also reflects the detrimental effects of the recent changes in this division of labour. In other words, the developing countries suffer not only from the fact that they have become appendices to a special kind of international division of labour, but, strangely enough, also from

---

trade policy—on food *imports*. According to the data of the UN World Economic Survey (1967) the income elasticity of imports from the developing countries is the following: for agricultural raw materials 0.60; for foodstuffs 0.76; for fuels 1.40; for manufactured goods 1.24.

[13] In this way, the differentiation among the developing countries has also increased.

[14] All these changes and consequences are, of course, far from having absolute validity. Nor are they of equal size or effectivity. By no means do they mean that *all* raw-material resources in the underdeveloped countries have lost importance for the developed countries. They do not mean that the inflow of foreign private capital has slowed down *everywhere*, and especially they don't mean that the significance of earlier capital investments and profit making has diminished. In the late sixties and the early seventies already a certain revival could be observed, though of a different nature and orientation as compared to the colonial investment pattern.

154

the troubles this division of labour is caught up in as a result of its recent changes.[15]

The simple enumeration or confrontation with one another of the peculiar features of the international division of labour and the changes therein may give, however, the impression that we are looking at the unhappy coincidence of certain historical events and circumstances rather than the consequences of a process which progresses according to its own internal laws. The theoretical reflection of this illusion can often be found even in Marxist literature when, e.g., conclusions are drawn from the shift of the "main lines" of the international division of labour to the independent "self-development" of the advanced sector of the capitalist world economy, to a fundamental change in the nature and laws of motion of imperialism, and the attempt is made at a vulgar revision of a loosely interpreted "law".[16]

To arrive at the real understanding of the origin, motion and perspective of "underdevelopment", it is necessary not only to disclose and analyse how this phenomenon is connected with colonialism; how colonialism in its turn is related to a specific type and structure of the international division of labour and, further, how this colonialism and the division of labour embodied thereby follow naturally and objectively from the inherent laws of the motion of capitalism. But it is also necessary to investigate and analyse how the recent changes, shifts and troubles of the international division of labour follow naturally and objectively from the self-development of this capitalist international division of labour. Only if we can succeed in bringing to light all these interconnections can we avoid the usual errors of a short-run approach: overemphasizing the subsidiary trends that deviate either to the right or to the left—and may, of course, lead to false conclusions even in economic policy—instead of sticking to the basic trend. If by way of example an unfavourable economic phenomenon (e.g. the marketing difficulties of primary products or changes in capital movement) follows from the basic trend, then emphasis must be placed not on the symptomatic treatment but on the alteration of this basic trend.

Let us attempt now to look into the background of the mechanism of the international division of labour and its changes.

---

15 See in the next chapters.

16 Namely for the revision of the supposed "law" or "Lenin's thesis" that imperialism cannot do without colonies. The vulgar interpretation of this thesis consists in identifying the essence of colonial *functions* with the *legal* status of the "colony" (excluding thereby from this category such countries, which, in spite of their formal sovereignty, Lenin himself classified among the colonial dependent countries, such as, e.g., the Latin-American countries). The vulgar revision of the thesis consists in interpreting the decolonization, the political independence of the former colonies as the sign and proof that imperialism (or rather advanced capitalism which "has got rid of imperialistic *policy*") no longer needs the periphery of the economically subject, dependent countries (i.e. colonies in the economic sense).

The internal self-movement of capitalism developing within national limits—as already clarified and theoretically proved by Marx in many different ways and as also demonstrated in practice by the systematically recurring crises—has made the *market problem* the aggravated and ever more acute problem of this mode of production. Since simple commodity production was succeeded by capitalist production, the point in question has no longer been simply and merely that the unplanned, anarchistic character of the commodity production of private producers and the separation through money of the two sides of exchange—buying and selling—include the possibility of the crises of *disproportion*. Moreover, the problem points even beyond the fact that this very disproportion has been enhanced, in line with the development of productive forces, by the danger of its manifestation *on a social scale*. From the nature of production, the character of surplus-value production directly follows another contradiction, more basic and determining from the point of view of the market problem, a contradiction which has been created and has become acute, between the way surplus value (profit) is produced and the way it is realized. This is, in other words, a contradiction, on the one hand, between the basic[17] method of *producing* the highest possible profit—i.e. the increase in productivity and unearned incomes, in addition to the simultaneous keeping under pressure of the income share of the working class (i.e. the ratio and the relative wage level of the labour force employed)—and, on the other hand, the precondition for the *realization* of profit—i.e. the adequate expansion of consumption (which presupposes, in the last analysis, the adequate expansion of personal consumption[18] and within that primarily mass consumption,[19] that is the consumption of the proletarians themselves). The increasingly *social* scale and character of *production*

[17] "Basic" in the sense that, unlike the increase in labour intensity and in the number of working hours, it is unlimited in the long run and also because it coincides with the direction of the compulsive force of competition.

[18] The so-called "productive" consumption, i.e. the "consumption" of goods serving productive purposes (machines, raw materials, etc.) becomes, as a matter of fact, senseless and inevitably leads to a crisis unless it can empty itself into the widening flow of real, i.e. personal consumption. "Military consumption" and similar, in every respect unproductive forms of consumption are, of course, closed circuits, but it is just because they constitute the unproductive waste of resources, that they are so detrimental to the rate of economic growth. If, however, as a result of rising "productive consumption" the productive capacity serving personal consumption increases abruptly, the utilization of this capacity, indirectly, or the realization of the marketable mass of consumers goods suddenly increased owing to the utilization of capacity, directly, depends on the development and pattern of effective demand, the purchasing power of population.

[19] Considering that the luxury consumption of the high-income strata has, on the one hand, its physical limit (arising from the relatively small size of these strata) and its social limit (arising from its impact on social tension), and on the other hand, that its luxury-character represents an obstacle as opposed to the nature of mass production.

contradict more and more the *private character of the appropriation*[20] *of the product.*

The manifestation and the growing more acute of the market problem within national limits (with all of its concomitants, e.g. the underutilization of production capacities, the existence of idle capital, the steadily replenishing army of the unemployed, the from time-to-time accumulating, unsold stock of goods, etc.) tend to push toward a solution in the international sphere. Parallel with, although not independently of the latter, technological progress in production increases not only the result (output) of production beyond its national setting but also its very preconditions in that it compels production to use external resources.

The systematic (not accidental and temporary) expansion of the market depends on the expansion of the division of labour, that is of the production linkages. Consequently, the "solution" of the market problem in the international sphere can no longer be built on the system of "accidental" exchange (based on momentary surpluses and shortages) between individual, "national" units. As a suitable means *capital export*, the creator of the international division of labour offers itself. In this way capital export becomes at a given stage of capitalistic development an indispensable means and characteristic feature of a certain phase of capitalism (imperialism). The timing and other characteristic features of this phase naturally follow from the *same process*[21] that makes capital export possible and indispensable.

Capital export has a *double function* (a) "to bridge the gap between the increasing need for industrial raw materials and the need for expanding

[20] The common and chief shortcoming of the various critiques misunderstanding or misinterpreting Marx's crisis theory consists of the very fact that they simply ignore *this* basic contradiction which Marx put in the centre of his crisis theory and they break down his crisis theory into different (or even contradictory) variants (as, e.g., the "consumption shortage" theory, the "disproportion" theory, or the crisis theory based on the fall of the rate of profit, etc.). They do not realize that Marx analysed the same process in several aspects, investigated the parts of the same process from different angles, and that the common basis of these parts and "variants" is the above-mentioned fundamental contradiction.

[21] This process viewed from the aspect of the *market problem* is, on the one hand, the process of the expansion of social production which presupposes ever larger productive units and their ever more organized cooperation, i.e. the concentration of production. On the other hand, it is the process of a permanent increase in the private character of exploitation which finds its expression in the centralization of capital and property. Viewed from the aspect of *capital formation*, it is, on the one hand, the process of the emergence of large enterprises, joint-stock companies with big capital, the intertwining of industrial and bank capital and the increasing separation of capital ownership and capital function making the exportability of capital possible. On the other hand, this process involves the further increase of the minimum size of capital to be invested, and the frequency of capitals being unused ("idle") as well as the tendency (or danger) of the falling rate of profit which exerts a stimulating or even compelling effect on this export of capital. From whatever angle we look at the process, it is the process of the concentration and centralization, the increasing *monopolization* of capital! This is how the monopolistic stage of capitalism is connected with the period of imperialism and with the phenomenon of capital export typical of the latter.

markets for the products of modern large-scale industry" and (b) to be "a safety value of internal over-accumulation... a factor counter-acting the tendency of the depreciation of capital"[22] and of the fall in the rate of profit. The former aims at ensuring the preconditions for undisturbed reproduction, i.e. the marketing condition and raw-material supply; the latter aims at defending capital and ensuring profit-making. There is, however, an antagonistic contradiction between the two functions: the operation of the one is detrimental to the other.

Capital export, besides being a means of financing the export-surplus, also has an independent aim: the acquisition of superprofit. While the former function tends to expand the market and restore at the same time— at least temporarily—the equilibrium of international trade, the latter function has the tendency of restricting the market and upsetting the equilibrium.[23]

As a result of the fact that "in the epoch of imperialism commodity exports are subordinated to capital exports, or more exactly, that commodity exports subserve the purposes of capital exports, the uppermost of which is the acquisition of superprofits",[24] radical changes have taken place in the whole structure and mechanism of international trade and

[22] Gy. Göncöl: On the Transformation of the Capitalist World Economy. *Studies in International Economics.* Hungarian Academy of Sciences, Institute of Economics. Budapest 1966, pp. 15, 16.

[23] Hilferding, who clearly sees this function and effect of capital export, assesses the latter wrongly. He points out that the export of loan capital, in contrast to simple commodity export, raises many times over, depending on the interest rate, the absorbing capacity of the market of the capital-importing country, and he also states that the export of industrial capital is even more advantageous to the exporting country (as "profit is higher than interest" and "in addition the disposal and control of capital is more direct"). In spite of disclosing the exploiting character of capital export, he attributes a more or less harmonious mechanism to the expansion of the market through capital export and assumes that capital export may become independent of the consumption capacity of the capital-importing country. In reality, this "becoming independent" can only take place to the extent that—just as in a single national economy, too,—the market can grow temporarily beyond and over the limits of personal consumption owing to the self-accelerating and cumulative "productive consumption", i.e. the waves of investments. But this "becoming independent" can last only as long (and this is its absolute frontier) as the last wave of investments, the abrupt rise in the production of consumer goods comes into conflict with the limits of that personal consumption from which it became temporarily independent. The production *for* profit and depending *on* profit, which is the "only" factor disturbing and hindering a harmony coming into existence and surviving between the income formation and utilization, on the one hand, and the production and marketing, on the other, clashes at this point with the original and true aim of production, with "physical" consumption, and leads to "overproduction" owing to the *limited* absorbing capacity of actual, effective consumption and the highly underutilized absorbing capacity of "physical" consumption (i.e. consumption abstracted from the existing unfavourable income distribution). (For Hilferding's analyses and the quotations, see R. Hilferding: *Finanzkapital.* Berlin, 1947, pp. 430–433.)

[24] See Gy. Göncöl: Op. cit., p. 12.

world economy. While in the pre-imperialist stage of capitalist international economy the debtor-creditor relationship was basically the consequence and function of the international exchange of goods, in the imperialist stage on the contrary: the international exchange of goods has become more and more the function of the debtor-creditor relationship. With this change of roles, however, the content and the conditions of the mechanism of this relationship have also changed. By this the Ricardian assumption of the unlimited capacity of the world market and of the harmonious equalization between the flows of money and commodity restoring international equilibrium have become totally nonsensical, just as the assumption of a mechanism in which the international specialization of production is governed by the so-called comparative—and consequently, mutual—advantages.[25]

With the debtor-creditor relationship becoming the determinant of the international exchange of goods, the capital of the creditor countries, i.e. the most developed *industrialized* countries, has obtained a determining role in forming or changing the production structure of the debtor (backward) countries, subordinating it to its *own* needs and including it in its own circulation process. This internationalization of the process of circulation and consequently that of production, has brought about the special system of the international division of labour between the industrial-creditor and the agrarian- (and raw-material producing) debtor countries.

In this new world-economic system what ought to be the basic conditions for the harmonious expansion of the world market and for the maintenance of the equilibrium of international payments, that is of the undisturbed mechanism of the trade and debtor-creditor relationships?

It ought to be, first of all "that the industrial sector of the capitalist world economy should serve as a steadily expanding market for the agrarian (and raw-material producing) sector and *vice versa*". This, however, as well as within a single closed national economy, the undisturbed reproduction and the equilibrium of the mutual exchange of the two sectors producing capital and consumption goods (department I and department II), presupposes "a

---

[25] From the point of view of our subject it is of minor importance and is largely irrelevant how these assumptions, or, more precisely, theses of Ricardo are connected, on the one hand, with "certain classical dogmas" (as e.g. with the assumption of the profitable use of any amount of capital in production and of the unlimited expansion of the market, which served as a basis for the former and has got an independent theoretical form in Say's dogma, and, further, with the quantitative theory of money and the assumption of the neutral character of money), and, on the other, with Ricardo's struggle for the liberalization of external trade (in which the practical claim of the contemporary English industrial bourgeoisie and the false explanation by Ricardo of the falling tendency of the rate of profit by the increase in ground rent and the law of diminishing return found its reflection). It is worth noting, however, at least by way of excuse, that these theses and assumptions were made in the pre-imperialist stage!

definite rate of accumulation"[26] in both sectors. Since, however, capital export is necessarily accompanied by the repatriation of profit—and interest—(as naturally follows from the very aim of capital export), this "co-ordinated" rate of accumulation cannot be assured except by "a steady and *steadily increasing flow of capital exports*". This disequilibrium resulting from the latter can only be eliminated if the capital export not only raises "the absorption-capacity of the debtor country producing raw materials as regards the finished goods of the industrially developed creditor country", but "on the other hand, it also enlarges *to a much greater extent* the absorption-capacity of the developed creditor country with regard to raw materials. In this process *the improvement of the terms of trade* is assumed to be necessarily ensured for the exporter of raw materials."[27]

As to the "*steadily increasing flow of capital exports*", it inevitably leads, under the given circumstances, to the cumulative process of over-borrowing and over-lending. Despite the assumption of the neoclassical theories of international equilibrium, "the capacity to export capital and the capacity to import capital are by no manner and means of opposite and equal sign". ... "To the extent that the risk is a determinant of the magnitude of interest and amortization, it becomes in turn one of the chief elements of the utmost risk on the part of the lender, that is bankruptcy and repudiation on the part of the borrower ...; ... the risk involved in international transactions within the framework of creditor-debtor relationship must lead by necessity, if it is to be overcome, to over-borrowing and over-lending: this enhanced risk is discounted by a higher rate of interest and amortization; this in turn, increases the risk of repudiation, and so on and so forth."[28] As the absorption of the same export-surplus requires a larger or smaller capital export according to the interests paid and the rate of amortization, the increasing risks mentioned above will necessarily reduce the market-expanding effect of capital export. The market-expanding effect of accumulation resulting from the operation of imported industrial capital (which accumulation is, by the way, greatly diminished owing to profit repatriation and the disproportionately high unproductive consumption)[29] can only come into full play "if nothing prevents the depreciation of capital" and if "the depreciation of capital ... under the pressure of competition prompts further accumulation". But the *monopoly-capitalist* character of the whole system and process contradicts these latter conditions in that the monopolies, especially the international monopolies with a large capital supply, restrict not only the sphere and efficiency of *competition* (to the extent that they have made whole national economies or industrial branches

[26] Gy. Göncöl: Op. cit., p. 18.
[27] Op. cit., pp. 17, 27–28.
[28] Op. cit., p. 18.
[29] For more details see Chapters II. 2. (a) and III. 1. (b).

160

dependent on them), but they also have effective means (e.g., "withholding their surplus capital from productive investment, i.e. decreasing the rate of accumulation")[30] to prevent the depreciation of their capital—at least within the given time limits.

And as to the *improvement of the terms of trade* for the primary-producing countries *as* the condition of the equilibrium of the mechanism, we can observe a rather opposite tendency, not only incidentally and in a given period but also in the long-run and following from the internal laws of the mechanism of the system. Though in view of the law of diminishing return it would seem justified to assume the relative contraction of the raw-material basis and agricultural food production—and nutrition becoming an international problem seems to corroborate this assumption—but the same process (i.e. the penetration of technology into the raw-material producing and agrarian sector), which anyway cancels out the law of diminishing return in the long run, works along with other processes inherent in capitalist economic development (the strengthening of monopolies, the extension of state-monopolistic intervention, etc.) and the objective tendencies following from economic underdevelopment in the very opposite direction: towards over-supplying primary products.

The development of technology, whose natural starting point and basis was the engineering industry, led in its earlier phase to an extensive growth of the processing industry and thereby to an abrupt increase in the need for raw materials. However, as soon as the progress in science and technology reached a higher stage, which became apparent in the extensive spreading of scientific-technical achievements, in their penetration into other branches of the economy (agriculture, mining, transport), and on the other hand, in the intensive application of science and technology (chemicalization, the utilization of by-products, miniaturization, etc.), this progress produced, at least temporarily and in a relative sense, or tended to produce a double result. On the one hand, it brought about an abrupt rise in productivity in the non-processing branches, that is, an intensive growth of raw material output including the accessibility of new resources and a more effective exploitation of the old ones by means of the new scientific-technological processes. On the other hand, it resulted in a relative decline in the need of the new processing branches for "traditional", natural raw materials and has extended the activities of the processing industries also to the production of synthetic raw materials.

Such a development of science and technology was feasible only in the advanced industrialized countries with a sound R and D basis. Although the achievements of the scientific and technological revolution and their effects, mentioned above, on the demand for traditional raw materials and agricultural imports have of course been limited or countervailed even in

[30] Gy. Göncöl: Op. cit., pp. 21–22.

the advanced capitalist countries, namely by the squandering nature of capitalistic "consumer society" (which gave a temporary and relative character to the above changes), is really important in the context of our topic is the *difference* between the situation in the advanced industrial countries and that prevailing in the underdeveloped countries. The latter lack the natural starting point, the basis for this development: the engineering industry and the related scientific apparatus. Consequently, it is mostly through import and not by a self-generating process that these technical achievements become available for the economy. Therefore, they are not only incapable of adapting themselves to the local endowments and requirements but even their spreading is limited to certain sectors, and they cannot exert a positive effect on the transformation of the economic structure. In primary producing countries, technical development, in the absence of a nationally based engineering industry, normally results in the penetration of advanced (imported) technology into the export enclave, increasing its output or reducing its labour-absorbing capacity and tending thereby to lead to an oversupply of the product (or of labour) and to a relative price fall.

At the same time, along with the processes of a more or less purely technological and scientific development, such socio-economic processes have also made, and are still making progress which further intensify the equilibrium-upsetting effect of the former. In the advanced capitalist countries the expansion of the oligopolism and state interventionalism has made it possible, through monopoly price control and protectionism, to include in production or still keep in operation certain primary producing (mining and agricultural) branches or units which otherwise would not be competitive in the world market. On the other hand, it also prevents the fall due to increased productivity of the price of industrial products[31] and also strives by various artificial means (e.g. by hidden quality deterioration, changes in fashion, the hire-purchase system, and, last but not least, military consumption) to raise the demand for manufactured goods. At the same time, the price level of the primary products of the underdeveloped countries is, owing to the international monopolies as well as for other reasons, under pressure,[32] while their industrial development calls for a

---

[31] What is involved here is not only a monopolistic deviation of prices from value (i.e. from total labour inputs required for reproduction), or an effect of manipultated inflation which keeps high or increases more rapidly the prices of manufactured commodities of the advanced capitalist countries vis-à-vis the primary products of the underdeveloped ones, but also a wide opportunity for product development (i.e. for changing somewhat the use value, for improving or modifying the quality of the manufactured goods and for increasing thereby their value) and, in certain cases, even a kind of unnecessary increase in value, too. (Witness the case of a commodity, say, a motor car produced for the same use, but equipped with a number of extra luxuries irrelevant to its function.)

[32] It is worth pointing here to a further difference even within the category of primary products in Africa due to socio-economic factors: while the overproduction of *mineral* raw

rapid increase in the import of capital goods. This is aggravated by the peculiar character of the investment policy of the foreign oligopolies interested in this industrialization, namely the priority given to the imported capital-intensive technology and the restraint from developing the branches producing capital goods and technologies for the local economy.

Thus the internationalization of the process of capital circulation and production by means of capital export contains such built-in factors which objectively determine not only the world-economic structure born under the sign of this internationalization but also its further transformation. (Against these factors, the importance of such a circumstance that the leading role in capital export passed over to a country rich in raw materials and extremely developed in agriculture too can be regarded as secondary, though this can also be derived from the objective laws of capitalist economic development.)

The tendencies arising from capital exports as an increasingly determining factor from the point of view of international economic relations and the national and international economic equilibrium are summed up by György Göncöl in the following points:[33]

"(1) The depreciation of exported capital takes place more rapidly than that of domestic capital; productive capital invested abroad leads more quickly to a chronic overproduction of raw materials.

(2) Accordingly, the volume of capital exports should be increased at a rate quicker than that of domestic accumulation, in order to be able to maintain or to raise its market-expanding effectiveness.

(3) The acceleration of capital exports, however, would further increase the depreciation of the capital invested abroad.

(4) The monopolies, however, do their best to prevent the depreciation of their capital investments; all the more so, as capital export itself is aimed at the warding off of the depreciation of domestic capital investments.

(5) From the moment when the amount of the outflow of extra profits from the underdeveloped countries producing raw materials regularly exceeds the new capital influx, i.e. when the volume of capital exports decreases and the capital already exported becomes merely a self-perpetuating asset, the international economic balance is upset and the double function of capital exports cannot be accomplished."

So the recent changes and the necessity of a further transformation of the system of the international division of labour are implicitly included in the

---

materials is kept in check by international oligopolies controlling their output in a number of countries, the expansion of *agricultural* raw materials produced by African peasants is in most cases explicitly encouraged by the foreign trade companies or by the foreign economic advisors recommending "diversification" by way of adding another, typically colonial export crop to the former monoculture.

[33] Gy. Göncöl: Op. cit., p. 22.

tendencies and the processes analysed above. Therefore, the simple registration of the recent changes in the world economy and the listing and individual analysis of factors detrimental to the international economic position of the underdeveloped countries cannot be regarded as a sufficient explanation.

We have tried to prove in the foregoing that the present state of the underdeveloped countries basically derives from their external relations, their role in the world economy. It is, on the one hand, primarily the consequence of the colonial system of the international division of labour, and, on the other hand, it is also due to the changes and disturbances this division of labour has undergone.

Let us examine now in a more *concrete* way what consequences have resulted from the fact that the underdeveloped countries as colonies and dependent territories joined in the capitalist international division of labour, and to what extent the inherited situation has changed owing to recent shifts in this division of labour.

2. THE MAIN CONSEQUENCES OF THE MONOPOLY-CAPITALISTIC COLONIAL SYSTEM OF THE INTERNATIONAL DIVISION OF LABOUR

(a) In the colonial system *political power*, exercised by the supporting administrative and military machineries, was concentrated in the hands of the colonial representations of the metropolitan countries or their puppet governments. So the direction of economic development of the dependent countries, their social, political and institutional system, their cultural development including the official language, and in several cases even the country boundaries, etc., could be determined *directly* by foreign powers.

This situation enabled them to develop or suppress in their own interest certain economic sectors, that is to determine the *economic structure*, and by fixing the boundaries of the country, they could even lay down the framework in which, after independence, the development of the national economy, the internal economic process, could start. In consequences, they could determine even the *size* of the "national" economy.

Foreign private capital, flowing into the secured territories and supported by a purposeful economic policy, but also independently of it, by merely relying upon the play of *spontaneous market forces*, developed, according to the given production and market conditions, the primary-producing export sectors in the underdeveloped countries: the agricultural one-crop economy and the mineral raw material production. The limited capacity of the local market, coupled with the then very strong demand induction of the world market justified from the outset the export- orientation of the economy. The inducement of this external demand towards the production of mineral and agricultural primary products, as well as the lack of local skilled labour and

164

the high costs of procuring (from overseas) machines, stimulated at the beginning capital investments in agriculture and mining, i.e. investments of usually low capital-intensity which mainly called for only cheap, unskilled labour. The marketing problem of the industrial products of the metropolitan country as well as the importance of suppressing possible rivalry also worked in the same direction.[34]

Thus foreign capital not only distorted the *economic structure* of the underdeveloped countries with its investments, but within the boundary of its operation it also built into it, at the same time, the *elements of the capitalist mode of production*. It suppressed or at least limited to certain fields the rise and development of the local, "national" capital and occupied the *leading sectors of the economy* and its most important potential sources. At the same time, it put these sources into the service of its activity and made use of them in the process of *profit making*.

In this way, foreign capital created, in conformity with the activity of political power, the foundations and mechanism of direct economic dependence and income drain. It also caused, and in no small measure at that, *socio-economic disintegration*, in addition to the sectoral distortions of the economic structure.

Apart from the dispersion of the internal cohesive forces of natural communities and the eccentric effect of the artificial boundaries, this disintegration manifests itself mainly in the "dual" *structure of the economy and society* and is the result of the fact that capitalist transformation started, or was given a new direction, from outward, in the system of colonialism. Its motive force was foreign capital which, beyond the scope of its own operation, was not interested in the capitalist transformation of the economy and society as a whole, and prevented by its very predominance the development of the local force (national capital) which could have been naturally interested in carrying out such a transformation. Foreign capital, while turning the character of part of the economy and society into a capitalist one—especially where it developed capitalist commodity production in the agricultural plantations, farms, mines, etc., and introduced the new strata of wage workers and paid employees—led to a deterioration of the former conditions of the traditional mode of production and preserved it in remnants as a subordinated "pre-capitalistic" sector of the dependent capitalistic periphery economy. It did not transform the whole traditional economy and society since the survival

[34] "... With the development of large capitalist monopolies in the leading capitalist countries, the capitalists of those countries lost interest in developmental investment in the less developed countries because such investment threatened to cause competition to their established monopolistic position." (O. Lange: Economic Development, Planning and International Cooperation. *Teaching Materials*, Vol. 6. The Advanced Course in National Economic Planning. Warsaw, 1965, pp. 10–11. Reprinted from a pamphlet edited by the Central Bank of Egypt.)

of its remnants neither clashed with its own interests, nor disturbed its own activity, and preserved them as it could make use of them in its own interests. The latter can be observed when, e.g., the labour supply of the capitalist sector (the plantations, farms, mines and urban industries, etc., in the possession of foreign capitalists, and in some countries even the capitalized *African* peasant farms, dominated and controlled, via the control of the export-import trade, by foreign capital) is based organically on the traditional sector as its source, and the low wage level is connected with the high labour-supply capacity of that sector and its role in subsistence. But very often and in many places also the interest in defending foreign (political or only economic) rule induced an alliance with the leadership of the traditional society and thereby the conservation of these strata.[35]

The development and intensification of the bilateral *trade relations* between the metropolitan countries and their colonies touched off, according to the world market situation or, more exactly, according to the needs of the leading capitalist powers of the time, demand and supply inducements towards the colonial economies, and these market effects from outside and the spontaneous market forces channelled, from the outset, economic activity and investments in a direction to which the *local* investors, capitalist entrepreneurs and producers, even independently of the external, foreign aims and of the means used for their influencing, were also compelled to adapt themselves. Thus, along with foreign capital, local capital, where there was any, also *took an active part* in the development of the one-crop export economy and the branches serving it.

The process causing the distortion of the economic structure and the outward orientation of part of the economy, and its isolation from the rest of the economy, made headway as a *cumulative process*. While foreign capital, with its overwhelming predominance and virulence, suppressed and stifled local rival capital, and while the new cumulative economic process suppressed and stifled the local economic activity deviating from or countering its direction (e.g. efforts to create a national industry), there sprang up one after the other, as appendices of foreign capital or in the wake of the spontaneous cumulative process conforming to the activity of foreign capital, those secondary forms of domestic capital and the corresponding strata of the local society (the so-called comprador capital or bourgeoisie) which were directly interested in cooperation with foreign capital and in carrying on the new economic process.

Thus, the *trade relations* established between the advanced industrial countries and their primary-producing colonies or dependent territories

---

[35] "For political reasons the great capitalist powers supported the feudal elements in the underdeveloped countries as an instrument of maintaining their economic and political influence." (O. Lange: Op. cit., p. 11.)

increased in a cumulative way the primary-exporting character of the latter and distorted accordingly their internal economic and social structure. At the same time, the internal composition of the flow of commodities was accompanied not only by a contracted export structure of the colonial countries and the more and more one-crop character of their commodity production, but, owing to the expansion of this one-sided commodity production (and the resulting pushing back of the wide-ranging subsistence production) as well as to the predominance of import articles (privileged against local products), it also brought about increasing and diversified import needs and a strong import sensitivity in these countries.

But the more the whole economic and social structure of the dependent underdeveloped territory adjusted itself to these trade relations and the international division of labour embodied in them, the more it became objectively and *sponte sua* dependent, owing to both its export orientation and import sensitivity, on the country at the opposite end of these trade relations. Thus, the system of political dependence of the colonial rule and the "direct" economic dependence, as manifested in the economic positions taken by the inflowing foreign capital, were increasingly complemented by "*indirect*" *dependence*, as materialized in the direction and structure of external trade relations. (It is justified to call it "indirect" in that it is based on, and becomes effective through, the distorted economic and foreign-trade structure.) If and to the extent that these trade relations of a one-sided and distorted structure are linked to the direct forms of dependence, and if the process of trade relations itself, the transactions and trade conditions are also under the control and pressure of foreign economic powers,[36] then they provide the possibility, by the monopolistic determination of the terms of trade, of an income-drain supplementing the profit repatriation of production capital. This income-drain is based on the *monopolistic* violation of the equality of exchange.

The bilateral capital and commodity flow in the system of the colonial division of labour was organically supplemented—though to a different extent in the various countries—by the *movement of human resources*. This manifested itself, on the one hand, in the "precipitation" to the colonies of part of the labour surplus of the advanced capitalist countries, a surplus created especially in the severe crises of the time and in the post-war period and including small capitalists, farmers and army officers who had lost their existence in the crises and after the war, as well as in the exportation of skilled labour, technicians, foremen and clerical personnel needed for colonial investments (not to speak of the personnel of colonial administration and armies). On the other hand, the movement of human resources to some extent involved also the cheap, unskilled and mainly unorganized

[36] Just as at present, too, the market conditions for a number of countries and commodities are controlled or influenced by the powerful international oligopolies.

labour of the colonies which were transferred into the advanced economies, in a volume varying from country to country and from time to time.[37] Due to the labour inflow (or more exactly the inflow of skilled and administrative personnel) from the metropolitan countries into the colonies, the jobs with higher salaries have become blocked by European expatriates, the demand for developing and expanding the educational system has remained poor, and the indigenous labour force has been "frozen" into unqualified cheap categories.

3. THE COLLAPSE OF THE COLONIAL SYSTEM, CHANGES IN THE WORLD ECONOMY AND THEIR EFFECT ON "UNDERDEVELOPMENT"

The changes in the system of the capitalist international division of labour and the collapse of colonialism have also brought about changes of course in the relations outlined above. It is a peculiar feature of these changes, however, that they are accompanied, at least in several respects, by the further accumulation of the detrimental consequences arising from the division of labour of colonialism. This underlines again the necessity of also considering, when examining the *present* state of the developing countries, the character and direction of the processes begun in the colonial period. This does not mean, however, that the cessation of colonial rule and the gaining of political independence have not brought about *radical changes*, (if not in the character and direction of the economic relations[38] and processes, then at least in the *possibility* of their transformation!) It does not mean either that the changes in the system of the international division of labour, apart from their effect of cumulating negative consequences, do not also contain very important positive elements for the further development of the underdeveloped countries. (As this set of problems belongs already to a logically subsequent topic, the questions relate to the future liquidation of

[37] It is worth remembering the statement made in 1895 by Cecil Rhodes, in which he said that his cherished goal was the solution of the social problem: in order to save forty million inhabitants of the United Kingdom from a destructive civil war, the colonial-minded politicians must conquer new lands in which to accommodate the *surplus population*. (See Y. Pevzner: Developing Countries and Reproduction in Parent-States. *Soviet Economists Discuss: Parent-States and Colonies.* Novosti Press Agency Publishing House, Moscow, p. 26.)

[38] Political independence brought about automatically certain changes in economic relations, too. Thus, for example, "it has led, above all, to a sharp diminution or even to the disappearance of opportunities to wrest resources from oppressed countries *by methods of non-economic compulsion*—all sorts of taxes and extortion, which Marx ironically called payment for 'good colonial administration'. The customs barriers, which the parent-states had erected to ensure their monopoly in exploiting their colonies and spheres of influence, have become weaker..." (E. Khmelnitskaya and A. Mileikovsky: Colonialism, Old and New. *Soviet Economists Discuss...*, pp. 16–17.)

underdevelopment rather than to the analysis of the present state of "economic underdevelopment": let us mention just a few of them *en passant*. The fact that bilateral relations have gradually turned into multilateral ones provides the possibility of loosening the system of dependence to a certain extent. A certain change in the direction of the interest of private capital and the greater role of government loans and grants as against the influx of private capital could give similar opportunities, at least in respect of the restriction of "direct" dependence and undisguised profit transfer. The shift in the sectoral structure of the world economy and the expansion of industrial investments also cause certain changes in the direction of market forces and make a kind of "thaw" possible in the purposeful or spontaneous blockade of the industrial development of backward countries. This makes itself felt, e.g., when foreign capital also turns to the processing branches of industry[39] in the underdeveloped countries.)

The most fundamental change resulting from the collapse of the colonial system is the changed character of the *political power* and with it the disappearance of the most open, most direct form of dependence. (This does not mean, of course, that a more concealed form of political or even military dependence does not survive or replace the other in a number of countries!)

When formerly it was the military-political rule that provided the basis for establishing economic dependence, now it is only a usually hidden form of political (and military) dependence that can be maintained—apart from a few gross exceptions—*where and insofar as* it is based on economic dependence.

The changes in *capital movement* already mentioned (i.e. the shifts in the direction of the export of investment capital and its increased orientation towards the developed countries, due to the new investment possibilities[40]

[39] This latter shift, however, does not mean by any means the promotion of the real process of industrialization, partly because the new orientation itself is limited, and partly because there invariably exists resistance or reluctance to invest in industries manufacturing means of production for the local economy, and to the transfer capacities, also of industrial technology, of R and D.

[40] In the increased orientation of capital towards the developed countries it is not only its *natural* attraction to the less risky and more profitable spheres of investment, that is, the *improvement* for capital of the economic and political conditions in the developed countries—in relation to the conditions in the underdeveloped countries—that finds expression. Over and above this, a less "healthy", but nonetheless natural propensity of capital is also manifest in the re-orientation of capital flow. It is namely the propensity to use in the interest of the "individual" solution of the market problem, such means as lead to the further intensification of the common and general market problem. To be more concrete: the strengthening and increasing competitiveness of the monopolies of the countries integrated into the West European Common Market, together with the customs barriers against outsiders, threatens the markets of US capital whose counter-manoeuvre "consists of the outflanking of the European customs' barrier by means of direct capital investments, of the buying up of foreign firms, of the establishment of foreign subsidiaries... This kind of

169

and the state-monopoly incentives, after the Second World War or to the unsafe "atmosphere" in many underdeveloped countries) made the problem of capital supply in a number of the newly independent colonial countries an acute one. As far as the "atmosphere" in the underdeveloped countries in respect of investments is concerned, the determining factor is not only, and often not even primarily, a change in the *political atmosphere*", as e.g. the pushing into the foreground of a radical nationalism or socialist tendencies endangering *foreign* capital (or capital in general), the expropriations for political reasons, nationalizations, or the regulating of profit reinvestment, etc. (This is, of course, the most direct and the gravest danger to the capital investments of small foreign capital and the expatriate settlers, but much less to the capital-strong international oligopolies, partly because they have at their disposal a whole arsenal of retaliatory measures with which they can enforce at least compensation, and partly because they enjoy the protection and support of those capitalist countries on which the aid and loan supply of the underdeveloped country depends.) But there is also an objective and originally non-political factor which constitutes a cumulatively increasing danger for foreign investors: the *deteriorating balance of payments position* of the country in question. The export of investment capital, owing to the concomitant profit-repatriation and the typical investment pattern of this capital,[41] is in itself one of the principal factors of the deterioration of the balance of payments of the capital-importing underdeveloped country. This, together with other factors listed below, may lead to such a cumulative and acute shortage of foreign exchange that either the repayment of the grants and long-term government loans extended by way of medicine becomes illusory (which prejudices the interests of the metropolitan government that supports the capital-exporting monopolies also with its aid policy), or the freedom to repatriate profits and capital cannot be maintained any longer without the collapse of the whole state budget and the domestic economy. Thus the risks of the expropriation of assets and nationalization without "full"

---

capital export tends to increase superprofits but, at the same time, intensifies abruptly the market problem and international competition, as capital being invested in the very countries and the very industries whose competitiveness on the world market is regarded as the most effective and the most dangerous." (Gy. Göncöl: Op. cit., p. 47.)

[41] Insofar as investments are made in the export-producing "enclave" sector without increasing the linkage effects on the other sectors of economy, particularly on the traditional rural sector [see Chapter III. 1. (a)], they result in an import growth exceeding and overcompensating the accompanying export growth. This follows from the import-intensiveness of the investment itself and the newly established productive units—which is especially high in the case of the adoption of capital-intensive technology—and from the intensive import-orientation of the propensity to consume of those who are engaged in this "modern" sector. Such an investment pattern unfavourably influences, through the balance of trade, the balance of payments.

compensation may increase even independently of changes in the political "àtmosphere", though such economic crises are usually accompanied by political crises, too.

The exodus of settlers' capital following the independence of the colonies (mainly for political or "racial" considerations) and the decreasing inflow of metropolitan private capital, or its refraining from *new* investments in that critical period have caused balance of payments difficulties in several countries and affected the whole of the domestic economy. (It is mainly the export sector that has been directly affected, and with its production and investments being curbed, the balance of trade, the internal incomes and the effective demand have been also indirectly impaired.)

The situation has been aggravated by the abrupt increase in internal and external expenses, due to the establishment of the machinery of the newly independent state (diplomatic representations, army, state apparatus), to the objectives of economic development with its plans and industrialization programmes (often oversized, however, for political reasons), to social and cultural policy, to the large-scale development of public education, etc. The former colonial mechanism of money and capital supply ceased to work (which, of course, can also be regarded as a first step towards economic independence), causing acute financial difficulties.

Where the efforts for economic independence did not prove strong enough, or even came to a halt, or political independence itself remained just a formal, apparent, or sometimes even neo-colonialist act the mechanism of money and capital supply has not changed substantially (if at all) either. A change took place here only to the extent that the increase in expenditure made it even more necessary for the underdeveloped country to draw on the old metropolitan financial sources, and that the more or less general change in the direction of the interest of foreign capital[42] became a greater inducement to grant privileges and guarantees for foreign investors. Thus, an earlier form of financial and "direct" economic dependence embodied in the positions of foreign capital has been strengthened here, thus ensuring the maintenance of the mechanism of income drain (profit-repatriation) and through it the increasing dependence on foreign financial sources.

Where, on the other hand, as a result of independence and the subsequent political changes, or the measures taken in economic policy to achieve economic independence, the earlier (colonial) mechanism of capital supply collapsed abruptly—especially if it coincided with the panick flight of metropolitan private capital—the acute payments difficulties usually created such a *financing vacuum* that its filling up, that is the elimination of the budget and balance of payments deficits, induced a number of countries to draw on other but likewise foreign sources. If in such cases the underdeveloped country committed itself, in the interests of the rapid

[42] Exceptions, such as investments in primary producing sectors, are, of course, not to be underrated.

acquisition of these sources, to another capitalist power and succeeded, through concessions, in winning over other groups of foreign private capital for investments in the country, then a new, neo-colonialist form of financial and "direct" economic dependence (not infrequently even a military-political dependence) usually replaced the earlier dependence.

This picture is perhaps too pessimistic and overdrawn. The collapse of the colonial mechanism of capital supply is, of course, a necessary precondition for progress, and the concomitant difficulties are only temporary and do not necessarily lead to the above-mentioned consequences. This is especially true, if the acquisition of the new foreign capital and money sources is made less urgent by the greater volume and reasonable utilization of the domestic resources, and if the foreign sources are drawn on in a relatively wide sphere—including several capitalist countries at a time, as well as the international organizations and also the socialist and a few capital-rich developing countries (OPEC)—which, no doubt, ensures greater bargaining possibilities and a more independent financial policy.

We also have to be careful in assessing the shifts in the pattern of international capital movement and financial flows, and their impact on the position, of the developing countries, since contradictory tendencies are at work and some of the changes are not only of a very relative nature but also of a more or less temporary character. The relative bias against the less developed countries in the orientation of the international flows of capital and particularly of foreign direct investments is not an entirely new phenomenon of recent decades. As a matter of fact, the bias for the developed economies (or for the relatively more developed regions within the potential external arena which is open and safe for direct investment) has always been—to a greater or lesser extent—characteristic of the orientation of investment capital exports. The exodus of foreign private capital and the drop in new inflows, which contributed a lot to the financial difficulties of the newly independent countries in the late fifties and early sixties, has proved to be a temporary phenomenon in most cases. The escape of colonial (mainly settlers') capital was followed, sooner or later, by the inflow of private capital from new sources and in new forms. While in the fifties and the early sixties the share of private capital (and non-concessional flows in general) in total financial flows to the developing countries considerably declined, as did the share of the Third World in total direct investments of foreign capital, showing indeed a decrease in, or a threat to, the interest of private capital in the developing countries, the proportions re-adjusted again, in the late sixties to a certain extent. This reflected a certain consolidation, based upon neo-colonial solutions, of the "investment climate" in many countries and also the role of the official development assistance of some capitalist countries in serving and defending the business interests of companies, or in opening the door for investments.

The share of private capital in total financial flows to the Third World increased from the rather low level of 34 per cent in 1960–1962 to 48 per cent in 1969–1971.

In the seventies, the share of the "official development assistance" in total financial flows to developing countries continued to decline (from 44 per cent in 1970 down to the level of about 30 per cent in 1978). Though foreign direct investment flows increased faster than ODA, yet within the total amount of private capital flows it was mainly private bank lending and portfolio investments which considerably increased their share.[43] The growth of foreign direct investment flows averaged 15 per cent annually in nominal terms and 4 per cent in real terms in the seventies (between 1970 and 1978). This growth was faster than that of ODA, but slower than non-concessional lending.

The share of the developing countries in total foreign capital investments increased again in the seventies from about 22 per cent in 1970 to about 37 per cent in 1977. More than half of the amount of direct investment capital flows to the Third World originated in the United States, having the highest percentage ratio of private direct investments in total non-concessional flows (58.7 per cent in 1978.)[44] Despite a certain "reorientation" of direct investment capital and a considerable increase in total financial flows[45] to the developing countries since the mid-sixties, their financial position, on the whole, has not improved. This points to the fact that, given the inherited unequal structures and mechanisms of the world capitalist economy and the capitalistic nature of most of these financial transfers, it is "normally" a further widening of the gap between the more developed and the less developed that follows from international capital mobility (just contrary to neo-classical assumptions) and that even changes in the colonial patterns tend, in most cases, to work against the poor, who become poorer while the rich get richer.

Except a few countries in the Third World (primarily the major oil-exporters, which, owing to rapid increases in oil prices in the seventies, improved their financial position) the majority of the developing countries suffered enormous deficits throughout the seventies. While their needs for external financing further increased, the composition of total financial flows shifted towards the less-advantageous non-concessional forms with harder terms, and the share of total resources flows received by the "low-income group" (countries with per-capita incomes below $400 in 1976) considerably declined in the seventies.[46]

[43] See 1979 Review. Development Co-operation. OECD 1979, Paris, Ch. VI.
[44] See Op. cit., pp. 86–92.
[45] According to figures given in the 1979 Review, p. 45, the total "net" receipts of developing countries rose from 8 billion US dollars in 1960 to about 80 billion dollars in 1978 in nominal terms. (In view of the rapid inflation and of the decrease in the value of dollar, these amounts were actually much less in value calculated in real terms).
[46] See below for more details.

Besides shifts in the international flow of capital and financial resources worsening, as a rule, the position of the less developed and poorest countries, there were also changes in the structure and direction of the *flow of commodities*, i.e. in trade relations.

The share of primary products in the total value of world exports has shown a declining tendency. Though this manifested itself most conspicuously in the fifties and sixties, it had been observable, through fluctuations, as early on as the Second World War and even before. According to B. Brown's calculations, the share of primary products in world trade was 62 per cent in 1876–1880, and almost the same, 64 per cent, in 1913; from 1937 to 1970, however, it decreased almost continually: from 55 per cent in 1950, to 50 per cent in 1955, to 45 per cent in 1960, to 39.5 per cent in 1965 and 35 per cent in 1970.[47]

In the early seventies, the "price explosion" marginally pushed up the share of primary products again, but this increase, except in the almost single case of fuels,[48] which, owing to the further price rises of oil managed to increase their share, was a very temporary phenomenon. From 1970 to 1976, the percentage share of all food items in world exports declined from 14.7 to 12.5 per cent, that of agricultural raw materials from 5.8 to 4.3, and that of ores and metals from 12.7 to 8.9 per cent, while the share of fuels increased from 9.2 to 20.1 per cent. By 1979, the combined share of food and agricultural raw materials, which accounted for 30 per cent in 1960, decreased further, down to 16 per cent, while the share of fuels in world exports more than doubled in these two decades.

The share of manufactures in world exports was 53 per cent in 1979, showing again a (slight) increase after its temporary decline in the first part of the seventies.[49]

In the long run, world trade in manufactured goods shows a much faster increase than that of primary products. In the period 1928–1960, the annual growth rate of the former was 3.1 per cent, while that of the latter was 1.4 per cent, and, if crude oil is excluded, only 1 per cent. I. Sachs's computations reveal that, e.g., in the period 1938–1958 the growth rate of the industrial output of the capitalist countries was nearly four times the growth rate of their raw-material and food imports. The average annual growth rate of world trade in manufactured goods exceeded that in all primary products, except fuels, even in the period of 1970–1976 when several raw materials

[47] See B. Brown: *New Trends in Trade and Development*. International Seminar on Imperialism. Paper No. 3, New Delhi, 1972.

[48] Out of the eleven major primary products in the exports of the Third World (namely: crude petroleum, cocoa, coffee, fruit, fresh nuts, copper, nickel, zinc, tea, lead, spices and jute) only two: crude petroleum and zinc achieved an increase in their shares in total world exports (from 4.80 to 12.76 and from 0.13 to 0.15 per cent, respectively).

[49] See *Protectionism and Structural Adjustment. Trends in World Production and Trade*. Study by the UNCTAD secretariat. TD/B/887. January 25, 1982.

enjoyed—temporarily—a relative price increase. Imports by the developed capitalist countries of all primary products, except fuels, decreased in the two decades of the sixties and seventies (from 40 per cent in 1960 to only 24 per cent in 1979), while their imports of manufactures increased (from 40 to nearly 52 per cent).[50]

No doubt, this tendency, which is manifested in diverging growth rates and shifts in the composition of world exports in favour of manufactured commodities, is in general connected with the development of the productive forces and, as regards its intensification after the Second World War, particularly with the effects of the scientific and technological revolution. It also reflects, however, monopolistic market conditions and pricing, and, of course, changes in relative prices, which modify the figures calculated in value terms.

The scientific and technological revolution has brought about substantial and lasting shifts not only in the structure of demand for raw and basic materials, that is, in the producers' demand structure, but also in the pattern of consumers' demand.

The new technology has exerted the most concpicuous impact on the demand for traditional raw materials by expanding the production and range of the utilization of synthetic materials. The postwar years, particularly the fifties and sixties, might as well be called the period of "polymeric revolution" since polymeric substances have been used massively in many fields (in the spheres of production and consumption alike) and in a great variety of applications. Artificial materials (like synthetic rubber, synthetic fibres, synthetic diamonds, metal-substituting synthetic materials, etc.) do not simply replace natural materials, but in many cases even surpass them in quality or technology in that they are specialized products manufactured specifically for certain technologies. With the various synthetic materials coming into prominence, the consumption of a number of traditional raw materials declined considerably. More exactly, their role in satisfying a given volume of raw-material demand, that is, their ratio to total material consumption decreased.[51]

[50] See *Towards a New Trade Policy for Development. UNCTAD I.* Report of the Secretary-General. UN, New York, 1964. J. Sachs: *Foreign Trade and Economic Development of Underdeveloped Countries.* Asia Publishing House, 1965, p. 45.—*Handbook of International Trade and Development Statistics*, p. 22. p. 94.—*Protectionism and Structural Adjustment*, Loc. cit., p. 22.

[51] The consumption of natural rubber in Britain, e.g., fell from 219,700 tons in 1950 to 167,800 tons in 1962. Simultaneously, the consumption of synthetic rubber increased from 2,800 to 139,000 tons. Similar shifts can be observed in the consumption of detergents, vegetable, raw materials, cotton, etc. In 1961, for example, also in Britain, 44 per cent of all detergents bought consisted of synthetic products, and thus the use of palm oil, among others, as a raw material also recorded a sharp fall. In France, the ratio of synthetic chemicals to total consumption rose still higher (reaching 57 per cent in 1961), and the import of

But as regards the role of synthetic materials, particularly their lasting impact on the demand for traditional raw materials, exaggerations, and generalizing over-simplifications are to be avoided. We must not forget that it is the rapid development of the chemical industry producing synthetic materials which increases the demand for its natural basic materials (primarily for mineral oil). (This phenomenon is, by the way, one of the important factors for increasing differentiation in the world-market position of primary producers.) At the same time, the demand for synthetic and natural materials has come not only into a competitive but also into a complementary relationship with one another in several fields of production and consumption (e.g. in the textile industry).

In the developed countries, the shift in the production structure in favour of sophisticated industrial goods and means of production is also becoming manifest in the structural change from industries requiring more imported raw materials towards the less import-sensitive branches, a change which has a certain restricting effect on the raw-material markets of the developing countries.

The improvement of technology, the adoption of modern chemical procedures, the processing of waste materials and defective products, as well as the spread of miniaturization in several fields (primarily in the radio and electronic industries), are all undoubtedly significant contributory factors which cause, by a better utilization of raw materials and a decrease in raw-material inputs per unit of output, a slower rate of increase[52] in the demand for raw materials than in industrial production and also restrict, in this respect, a rise in the demand for traditional raw materials. But it should be noted here that not only the territorial extension (to other countries and to formerly neglected regions) of industrial development and its acceleration should make us wary in evaluating the actual results achieved in economizing on raw materials. We also have to take into account the effects, far more important than the former, of the large-scale squandering stemming mainly from the nature of the capitalist economy (and increasing

vegetable oils also declined more rapidly. On the whole, from 1953 on, the increase in the consumption of synthetic materials accounted for at least 33 per cent of the increment in industrial raw-material consumption. (See A. Shpirt: New Aspects of the Raw Material Problem. *Soviet Economists Discuss: Parent States and Colonies.* Ed. by Boyshov. Novosti Press Agency Publishing House, Moscow, 1968, pp. 79–80.)

[52] "Technical progress promotes a smaller input of raw material per unit of produce. A considerable saving of raw materials has been obtained by the introduction of electrolytic thinning and the resmelting of metals. Thus, parallel with a 50 per cent growth in iron output in Britain, from 1948 to 1962, the consumption of raw materials increased only by 26 per cent, the inputs of imported iron are having been cut by half. The consumption of fuel per ton of iron has been cut by 30 per cent. All this has resulted in the reduction of industrial raw-material imports, particularly those from developing countries.
(Y. Pevzner: Developing Countries and Reproduction in Parent-States. *Soviet Economists Discuss...*, p. 32.)

particularly in the "cheap raw materials" period of the colonial type of the division of labour), as well as the manipulated effects of a "consumer society", the practice of accelerated obsolescence as well as quality deterioration.

It is also to be noted that the development of the productive forces and the rising level and changing pattern of consumption (with shifts towards durable goods, including electric household appliances) are normally accompanied by an increase in energy consumption and in the import of fuels as the main source, for the time being, of energy production, the demand for which is greatly enhanced by the wastefulness of "consumer society". Therefore, world trade in petroleum (which, besides being used in energy production, is also the raw material for one of the most dynamic industries, the chemicals industry) seems to be one of the exceptions to the rule valid for the majority of primary products at least for the time being.

Its exceptional behaviour, however, is manifested in, and to a great extent is a result of, its sudden "price explosion" followed by further price increases in the seventies, which considerably increased the share (in terms of value) of petroleum in world exports. Before the seventies, its share, despite a rapid increase (in terms of volume) in the oil consumption and imports of the advanced countries, could not show an upward trend.[53]

In the seventies, the rising petroleum price has changed the value proportions of world trade so much that even despite the inflating and widely monopolistic prices of the manufactured exports of the metropolitan countries the increasing share of manufactured commodities in world trade was slightly, and rather temporarily, repressed.[54]

In the period 1970–1976, the average annual growth rate of fuel exports was 38.1 per cent (by far the highest), while that of manufactured goods, being the second, accounted for 20.1 per cent.[55]

From the point of view of the non-petroleum exporting countries, however, it is more important that the average growth rates of the developed countries' imports from the latter lagged behind the average growth of total world exports in all primary products except fuels. This shows that the

[53] The percentage share of fuels in world exports actually decreased from 11 to 9.2 per cent between 1955 and 1970, allowing thereby the total share of primary products to decline (from 57.9 to 42.4 per cent). See *Handbook of International Trade and Development Statistics.* Op. cit., Table 3.2 A, p. 94.)

[54] In the early seventies, the share of fuels in world exports increased, however, so much (from 9.2 per cent in 1970 to 20.1 per cent in 1976) that, despite a further decrease in the share of all other primary products (from 46.9 and 33.2 per cent in 1955 and 1970, respectively to 25.7 per cent in 1976), the total share of primary goods, including fuels, showed an increase (from 42.4 to 45.8 per cent). Correspondingly, manufactured commodities suffered a decrease in their share, from 55.5 to 52.6 per cent, in world exports between 1970 and 1976. Ibid.

[55] Ibid.

12

developing countries have a declining share in the world exports of non-petroleum primary products.

The scientific and technological revolution has exerted an effect not only on primary producers in general and has differentiated not just those in the Third World countries, but has also had an impact on the primary producers of the developed capitalist world and has promoted differentiation in their favour. By developing new production and utilization methods and modern technologies, it has made profitable and exploitable those new raw-material and energy sources in the developed capitalist countries that were deemed earlier to be uneconomical or exhausted. By new, more reliable and efficient prospecting and surveying methods, new resources, entirely unknown before, have been discovered.

The scientific and technological revolution has directly influenced not only the production conditions and the producers of minerals but also those of agriculture. By significantly increasing the productivity of agriculture in the developed industrial countries,[56] it has lessened their demand for agrarian imports or has increased their export capacities.

All these circumstances largely account for the fact that, strangely enough, the share in the world export of primary commodities (except petroleum) of the developing countries specialized in primary production has decreased against that of the developed capitalist countries. The share of the latter in world raw-material exports rose from 47 per cent in 1950 to 55 per cent in 1960 (and also remained at the same level in the late 1960s), while that of the developing countries decreased from 41 per cent to 20 per cent over the same period. Between 1960 and 1968, the annual increase in the volume of raw materials exported by the developing countries amounted to only 3 per cent on the average, while the developed capitalist countries increased the quantity of their raw-material exports by an average annual 4.1 per cent. In the same period (1960–1968), the value of the raw-material exports of the developing countries fell by 13 per cent, while that of the developed countries increased by 1 per cent.[57]

[56] The increasing penetration of scientific and technological achievements into agriculture was also connected with the fact that, following the Second World War, the factors or circumstances impeding the technological development of agriculture were pushed into the background in the advanced capitalist countries of the West, while the factors promoting or requiring technical development came to the fore. These circumstances and factors are analysed in detail by A. Sipos. He points to such factors as the expanded domestic market for agricultural products, the role of state-monopoly capitalism, the impact of changes in the labour market, the fall in disguised rural unemployment, the decrease in land rent and the stimulating or compelling effect of sharpening competition of the industrial basis ensuring technical equipment as well as of the massive demand by large-scale manufacturing industries and agricultural productive units. (See A. Sipos: *The Impact of Technical Progress on Agrarian Relations in Developed Capitalist Countries.* A doctoral dissertation, 1972. In Hungarian)

[57] *Review of International Trade and Development.* UN, TD/B/309. New York, 1970, p. 17.

In the period of 1955–1976, we can see a continuous decline in the share of the developing countries in the world exports of all food items, agricultural raw materials, ores and metals.[58] Apart from an increase in the very low share in world manufacture exports, it is only their high and increasing share in fuel exports that slightly compensated for a further and general decline of their overall share in world exports in the seventies. Yet even this countervailing effect proved to be rather weak in the second half of the seventies, when again the Third World share in world exports continued to decline (without reaching its previous lowest level by the end of the decade).

Though in the early seventies the share of the Third World in the total value of world exports increased (up to almost 30 per cent in 1974), this favoured a few countries only, mainly reflecting the price rise of their exports (especially crude oil), and proved to be a rather temporary phenomenon. Since 1975, we have observed a decline again in their share which went down to 22.9 per cent in 1978. (The non-oil exporting countries of the Third World had a share of 11.8 per cent in world exports in 1970, and this level was not surpassed in the seventies. In 1978 their share was 11.3 per cent.) Owing mainly to a further increase of oil prices in 1979, the percentage share of all developing countries in world exports slightly increased again and reached 25 per cent. (Their share in the world exports of manufactures also increased slightly, from 7.7 in 1976 to 9 per cent in 1979.)[59]

The price explosion of crude oil and some other raw materials in the early seventies, to which so many economists attributed the opening of a "new historic era" (the beginning of the period of "interdependence" between

[58]The following data illustrate how the percentage share of the developing countries in the world exports of the main commodity groups changed from the mid-fifties to the mid-seventies:

Percentage shares of developing countries in world exports

Commodity groups	1955	1970	1976
All products	25.4	17.6	25.7
All food items	42.6	31.8	30.9
Agricultural raw materials	40.4	30.3	27.1
Ores and metals	21.0	18.4	15.6
Fuels	57.4	63.3	75.2
Manufactured goods	4.7	5.3	7.7

See *Handbook of International Trade and Development Statistics*, p. 96.

[59] See *Handbook of International Trade and Development Statistics*, p. 25; *Abdellatif Benachenhou: Le Tiers Monde en jeu*, Alger, 1981 p. 99; *Protectionism and Structural Adjustement* loc. cit., p. 22.

more equal economic powers) has actually proved unable to change radically the long-lasting and general tendencies rooted in the centre—periphery relations of the world capitalist economy.

Since the shifts, in general and in the long run, in the production and consumption patterns of the advanced capitalist countries tend to work for an increasing share in world trade of more and more sophisticated manufactured products, new technologies and technological know-hows, there is little chance for the Third World to considerably increase its share in world trade *as long as* the major centres of the production of these commodities and of technological research and development remain the monopoly of the advanced countries, or as long as their pattern of consumption and production dominates the world market.

The shifts in the production and consumption patterns of advanced capitalism are partly connected with the scientific and technological revolution and partly with the inner "instincts" and social contradictions of the system. A general increase in incomes, which comes about amidst the inherent contradictions of capitalist society partly as a result of local economic growth and welfare measures (as happened, e.g. after the Second World War in Western Europe), partly at the cost of increased international exploitation, is usually followed by a shift in consumer demand towards commodities of a "higher order" (in physical, material terms), i.e., durable consumer goods produced with modern technology.

Under the influence of business manipulation, however, such as capitalist advertising, dictated fashion waves, brand wars and status symbols, etc. (that is, owing to the distorted nature and biased operation of the "consumer society") this shift assumes exaggerated, abnormal proportions (deterimental to the satisfaction of other, more important and real human needs, e.g. cultural and educational needs). And since it is this abnormally structured consumption pattern which is still the predominant factor shaping the consumers' demand of the world market, and which is actually radiating from the centre of world capitalism to the countries of the periphery, too, the pattern of demand in the world market also shifts

The percentage share of developing countries in total world exports

	1950	1955	1960	1965	1970	1971	1972	1973	1974	1975	1976	1977	1978
All developing countries	30.8	25.5	21.5	19.6	17.8	17.8	17.9	19.2	26.9	24.2	25.9	25.7	22.9
Major petroleum exporters	6.2	7.1	6.8	6.4	6.0	7.0	6.9	7.7	15.7	13.7	14.7	13.9	11.6
Other developing countries	24.6	18.4	14.9	13.2	11.8	10.8	10.9	11.5	11.2	10.5	11.3	11.8	11.3

Source: Handbook of International Trade and Development Statistics. p. 25.

180

correspondingly. Its effect on the production pattern and on the choice of techniques is complemented and heavily reinforced by the effects of the militarization of state-monopoly capitalism, its increasing expenditures on military investments, on the research on and the production of newer and newer weapons for the arms race.

All these, along with the intensification, after the Second World War, of monopolistic and state-monopolistic cooperation among the developed capitalist countries, as well as the tendency and results of integration in Western Europe, go a long way towards explaining why both the total share of the advanced capitalist countries in world trade and within it the proportion of their intra-trade[60] increased so rapidly in the period of about two and a half decades after the Second World War.

The rise after the Second World War of the dominant position of the United States in the world economy, the fact that the "traditionally" food- and raw-material importing Britain has completely lost her leading position to the latter, has made a direct impact on the trade and financial position of the developing countries, too. It has contributed to the shifts, mentioned above, in the demand structure of the world market, both directly, by the less export-oriented character of the US economy, its rather lasting and rapidly growing export-surplus after the Second World War[61] and its relatively higher degree of self-sufficiency (as compared to Britain) in primary commodities (especially agricultural products and also various

[60] Trade among the developed capitalist countries, which was already at a high level, accounting for 69.7 per cent of their total exports in 1955, increased its share in the exports of these countries to 76.9 per cent by 1970. It was mainly due to the effect of the oil price increases and to the efforts to recycle the oil revenues that the share of intra-trade in their total exports decreased in the seventies (e.g. to 71.3 per cent in 1976). (See *Handbook of International Trade and Development Statistics.* Op. cit., p. 98.)

[61] Contrary to this feature of the US economy after the Second World War, Britain's increasing import needs in the 19th century tended continually to exceed her growing export capacity. "It is precisely for this reason that British capital exports could perform the dual function of securing and enhancing the competitive advantage of British industry on the world market, while at the same time securing the cohesion and efficient functioning of the expanding world market," writes Gy. Göncöl. To this we should add, however, that these were the very features of the British economy and capital export that carried the germs of British economic decline and prepared Britain to fall victim, relatively speaking, to uneven development in the world economy.

To illustrate the case of the USA from the above point of view, let us mention that while her exports trebled between 1936–38 and 1956, her imports increased only by 76 per cent in the same period. (Cahiers de l'Institut de Science Economique Appliquée. Paris, Oct. 1959, p. 163. Quoted by Gy. Göncöl, Op. cit., p. 46).

The share of imports in GNP in the USA is very low as compared with that in Britain and the capitalist countries in Western Europe. In 1958, e.g., the share of imports in GNP was three and a half times greater in Western Europe than in the USA. The volume of trade with the primary-producing countries in 1957 amounted to 5 per cent of GNP in the case of Western Europe, and only 1.5 per cent in the case of the USA. (See Gy. Göncöl: Op. cit., p. 45.).

minerals) and, indirectly, by the influence of American supply and demand on the expansion of the world market for durable consumer goods and new technologies.

We have to note, however, that some of the effects arising from US hegemony worked only temporarily, or in a rather contradictory way. Not only in the sense that this very hegemony was later challenged by integrating Western Europe, but also because the arms race, the increased military production and stock-piling in the USA, as well as unproductive squandering, the behaviour and effect of the American "consumer society", have tended to reduce the degree of US self-sufficiency in natural resources and raw materials.[62]

The changes and shifts in the structure of production and consumption and in the pattern of world trade which have been unfolding since about the Second World War in the context of the scientific and technological revolution, of the rise and expansionary activity of the MNCs and of changes in international political power relations are actually warning signs of the crisis of the colonial-type international division of labour between individual metropolitan countries and their primary-producing peripheries.

The economic implications of this crisis or, in general, the economic consequences of the evolving reallocation process of roles in the capitalist division of labour have led characteristically to a deterioration, mainly in the positions of the developing countries. The crisis led to an accumulation of the detrimental consequences of the colonial division of labour for the majority of the developing countries. This was particularly conspicuous in the period between the late fifties and the early seventies.

After the Korean War, which pushed up raw-material prices, a drastic fall took place in the world-market prices of primary products, and from the mid-fifties to the late sixties a rather general and significant deterioration of the terms of trade had to be suffered by the primary producers in the Third World.

Despite the unfavourable changes in world production and trade and the resulting negative inducements, the economic structure of the developing countries has continued to favour the export of traditional primary products, which, for reasons already discussed, has been faced, apart from a few exceptions,[63] with unfavourable trends in the world market. The so-

---

[62] The reliance of the US economy on the supply of thirteen strategic raw materials (except phosphate) from the Third World ranges from 20 per cent (iron ore) to 98–100 per cent (manganese and natural rubber). The EEC and Japan, however, depend much more on such supplies: the former to the extent of 100 per cent on five out of the thirteen products, the latter on seven, (Ismail-Sabri Abdallah: Heterogeneity and Differentiation—the End of the Third World? *Development Dialogue.* 1978. No. 2, p. 15.)

[63] Among these important exceptions one can find in the first place oil. For example, oil imports by the member countries of the OECD from the underdeveloped countries increased from 56.6 to 167 million tons between 1950 and 1960. Moreover, scientific and technological

182

called "energy-crisis" and the rapid increase in the world-market price of crude oil and some raw materials in 1973–74, with the concomitant "rush" again for raw-material resources preserved for a while the outlined tendencies but not in general. The need of the Western countries to compensate for their increased oil import costs is, no doubt, a factor tending to re-orientate trade and cooperation relations, while the enormous amounts of accumulating oil revenues in the hands of the oil exporters have undoubtedly brought about a new financial power and reshaped some of the conditions in the centre-periphery relations of the world capitalist economy.

The world-trade position of the majority of developing countries has, however, experienced further deterioration.

The import demands of the developing countries have rapidly expanded. The newly independent countries, launching new development programmes, setting up their state apparatuses and armies, making large investments in infrastructure, education, public health, and intending to improve the living conditions of the population, etc., have increased their imports even parallel, in most cases, with their worsening export conditions (relative price falls, marketing difficulties, etc.).

Besides accelerated population growth and the resulting food-supply problem, it is the inherited structure of the economy and society which mostly accounts for the rapid and excessive expansion of their import needs. Dependence on industrial and also on agricultural imports is due to the lop-sided production pattern, to the lack of local industries capable of producing means of production and transport and of meeting the basic needs of mass consumption, as well as to the overwhelmingly monocultural character of agricultural commodity production, etc. It is also due to certain sociological phenomena reflecting the social structure, such as the propensities of luxury and (import) consumption of the local élite and of squandering by prestige investments and unproductive expenditures in many of these countries.

An important role in the increasing import demands has also been played by the new pattern of foreign (MNC) capital investments[64] and the armaments outlays enhanced under the impact of local tensions, regional conflicts and dangers of intervention from the outside.

---

advance may also increase the importance of the underdeveloped countries as the sources of new raw materials (e.g. uranium).

[64] It might be worth referring here again to the impact of the investment pattern on imports. This pattern of foreign investments, which is "characterized by a high capital-intensity of production within each sector and by a sectoral distribution of investment implying a low implicit capital-intensity' (i.e. the low proportion of the labour force employed in the sector producing capital goods) ... restrains the growth of the internal market and is associated with a high income elasticity of import." (G. Arrighi: International Corporations, Labour Aristocracies and Economic Development in Tropical Africa. In: G. Arrighi and J. S. Saul: *Essays on the Political Economy of Africa.* Monthly Review Press, New York, 1973.)

The satisfaction of rapidly increasing import demands needs, of course, additional foreign exchange earnings. This, fact in turn, makes export an even more crucial factor and usually leads to a "forced" export; if this kind of export is done simultaneously by many other countries exporting the same products, and the demand for them is inelastic, and this will result in an oversupply of the primary products in question. Thus, we may note that, paradoxically, even the changes in the "old" colonial structure of the international division of labour often tend to reinforce its harmful consequences and to increase the dependence of the primary-producing developing countries on the major buyers of their products. In other words, the trade dependence of the periphery has survived and strengthened, and even if some of the former opportunities for a monopolistic imposition of the conditions of exchange by the metropolitan countries have disappeared, and certain countervailing forces have begun to work on the side of the periphery, the long-run deterioration of the terms of exchange for the majority of the developing countries and the concomitant income-drain through their international trade relations[65] tend to continue. The acquisition of new markets (e.g. in the socialist countries), the conclusion of international commodity agreements, the organization of producer associations, etc., may all have mitigating effects, but a final solution can be expected only from the transformation of the international division of labour which ensures a more equitable allocation of the structural roles in it.

Besides, the shifts in the pattern of world trade and production changes in the movement of "human resources", associated to a certain extent with the former and primarily with the liberation of colonies, also have, or at least had in a critical period, a detrimental effect in many respects on the economic situation of the developing countries.

The outflow of colonial immigrants, of settlers, businessmen, skilled workers, technicians, self-employed people, doctors, teachers, colonial officials—a process which took place under the influence of independence or the political changes following it—created in several countries a vacuum even greater than the one caused by capital outflow. The reflux of metropolitan manpower made the underdevelopment of "human resources" stand out even more conspiciously and rendered the shortage of skilled labour an acute problem. The construction of the new, young state and the launching of development programmes still further enhanced the shortage and made it necessary for the country to turn to other foreign sources.

In order to attract foreign experts, it became necessary to grant them even more favourable conditions in terms of salary, leave, benefits, etc., which imposed a heavy burden upon the young states. The salary level of skilled

[65] See Chapter II. 2.

labour was determined by the income level of the privileged leading strata of the colonial period and not by the actual potential of the country.

At the same time, the flow of people from the developing to the developed countries for purposes of higher education and vocational training began or increased. These specialists living for a shorter or longer period of time separated from their native environment often become alienated from their own society temporarily or lastingly, and indeed foreign scholarships may often result in their total loss, i.e. "brain drain".[66] The system of granting scholarships for studies abroad has opened another door to the flow of foreign influences and habits. Thus it has a substantial effect both directly on the consumption pattern and through it indirectly on the direction of economic development and on the forming of social and political forces.

In the mid-sixties, the general worsening of the position of the Third World in international trade, capital supply and also in respect of skills and education was so outstanding and cumulative that it induced not only the international organizations to focus on these problems (see the rise of UNCTAD), but also gave birth to the false assumption that the significance for the metropolitan centres of the periphery countries — as suppliers of primary products and sheltered markets and profit sources—was going to end. It appeared temporarily that the metropolitan countries would do without their peripheries, while the latter would increasingly demand the maintenance, or even the expansion, of relations with the developed centres.

Such problems as the marketing of primary products, the need for capital supply, the shortage of skilled personnel as well as the increasing import needs (primarily for foodstuffs) seemed to make former colonies rely to an ever increasing extent on the metropolitan countries.

But this appearance, however succinctly it expressed the gravity of the situation resulting from the restructuring and reallocation processes, proved to be false even in regard to the given period and gave rise to one-sided conclusions.

However, apart from ambiguous phenomena and false assumptions, the obvious signs of the crisis had, already in the mid-sixties given warning that a one-sided specialization of peripheral countries in the world economy could not be maintained for long, that it had become obsolete even to the "centre" countries in regard to a number of primary products.

[66] See Chapter II. 2.

185

4. GROWING DISTURBANCES AND NEO-COLONIAL MODIFICATIONS OF THE INTERNATIONAL DIVISION OF LABOUR AS PAVING THE WAY FOR THE RECENT WORLD ECONOMIC CRISIS

The collapse of the colonial system in the late fifties and early sixties, being first of all the result of the liberation movements and the shifted international power relations, had been already connected to some extent with the changes in the investment policy of international monopoly capital and the shifts and disturbances in the structure and mechanism of the colonial division of labour between industrial centres and underdeveloped peripheries. The declaration of independence in the case of some African countries already involved a kind of neo-colonial action, as well, which reflected not only a transition into the policy of defending by more peaceful and flexible *methods* the unequal economic colonial relations between the metropolitan country and its satellite but also the preparation of certain necessary changes and shifts in the *content* of these economic relations.

As it has been pointed out, the colonial pattern of the international division of labour—with the typical functions of the dependent periphery (as raw material supplier, sheltered market for manufactured commodities and monopolized sphere for highly profitable investments)—has been operating with increasing troubles, difficulties, and disturbances, and has been facing a crisis for a long time, since almost as far back as the Second World War, or particularly since the late fifties. Its crisis manifested itself most obviously in the international economic and political events of the early seventies, first of all in the "energy-crisis"—even if the 1973–74 price increases of raw materials seemed to promise again "comparative advantages" also to the countries specialized for primary production. While the former period, between the mid-fifties and the sixties, of the worsening terms of trade for primary exporters proved "only" that this one-sided specialization with cumulative disadvantages cannot be maintained indefinitely the oil-embargo and the price increases pointed towards the end (or the beginning of the end) of the old terms and conditions of raw-material supply by the periphery even though the colonial production structure remained unchanged.

Colonialism—as has been pointed out in this book—was by no means simply the manifestation of violence, military actions and aggressive government policies: it involved a certain type of international division of labour and has shaped the economic structures. Similarly, the *economic* content of neo-colonialism is reflecting a certain (modified) pattern of international division of labour. The basic means and vehicle of both the colonial and the neo-colonial division of labour have been the export of investment capital, i.e., the direct investments of foreign capital. Therefore, to understand the nature of neo-colonialism, it is necessary to investigate the (shifted) investment activity of foreign monopoly capital, its orientation, motivations and its present or predictable consequences.

The recent shifts in the investment pattern of foreign capital have resulted from both technical and socio-economic changes in the developed capitalist countries, and followed also from changes in the Third World, as well as from the development of the latter's relations with socialist countries. Although it would be premature to speak already about the operation of a new system of international division of labour, particularly in the case of Africa, where the elements of the "classical" pattern of extractive imperialism are still predominant, the increasing difficulties in the operation of the latter and its increasing dilution by new elements seem to be obvious enough to put the question: what sort of international division of labour will come if the observable trends continue, and how can the developing countries benefit from it?

Although the extraction of mineral raw materials, particularly those of a strategic importance, remains one of the most important activities of foreign companies and large international consortiums in the developing countries rich in natural resources,[67] the marked bias of their investment policy against plantation investments[68] and, instead, for investments in certain *manufacturing industries* already refers to a new emerging pattern.[69] A shift in their choice of technique can also be observed. As to their industrial investments, relatively *high capital-intensity* characterizes the new industrial enterprises, which are mostly last-stage assembly and/or processing plants.

The industrial ventures by foreign companies, and the transfer of industrial technology materialized in the former, indicate that the metropolitan countries' monopoly over industry versus the primary-producing periphery is relaxing a bit, or is being rather replaced by another.

[67] Ann Seidman points to the rapid expansion of foreign private investments in Africa's mineral deposits in the post-independence period, and the increasingly multinational character of the new ventures often supported by international financial institutions (Old motives, new methods: foreign enterprise in Africa today. *African Perspectives*. Ed. by C. H. Allen and R. W. Johnson. Cambridge University Press, 1970, pp. 251–272)

[68] Often contrary to the interests of local colonial settlers, and European plantation owners, the international companies trading with African agricultural products have taken the direction towards encouraging the export-oriented cash crop production of African farmers.

[69] Surprisingly, Dr. Arrighi who gives one of the most comprehensive analyses on multinational corporations and the emerging new pattern of investments states in one place of the same paper that "the colonial pattern of capital investment in production for export has basically remained unaltered". I. Shivji repeats the point without defining the limited sphere of the "old" pattern, the changed policy in respect of plantations, the shifts in the composition of capital even within the "old" pattern, etc. (G. Arrighi: International Corporations, Labour Aristocracies and Economic Development in Tropical Africa. In: *Essays on the Political Economy of Africa*, p. 110; Issa G. Shivji: *Class Struggles in Tanzania*. Heinemann, London, 1976.

In addition, considerable changes have taken place also in the origin and character of foreign capital. The monopolistic position of the former colonizers' capital has been increasingly replaced by the—less exclusive—dominance of *multinational corporations*, international monopolies, leaving more opportunities in their service, but less independence, for local entrepreneurs and others. This also reflects the growth of a "collective" neo-colonialism, and behind it the aspirations of the US monopolies to "take over",[70] as well as the need for new methods in the era of national independence, and "East-West competition".

The diversification of the origin of foreign capital owing to the opening, through independence, of the former colonies for capital export from other capitalist countries and the increasing role of the US capital have been accompanied by a shift in the character of foreign capital in favour of the affiliates of large-scale, *vertically integrated industrial corporations.*

The decline in private investments by former colonizers[71] and the outflow (or nationalization), in many countries, of the capital of smaller-scale colonial enterprises, trading houses, transport firms, and particularly of individual settlers, mark the same process.

The apparent tolerance of the new foreign investors and multinational corporations towards certain measures taken by local governments to expand the public sector and increase the national participation and/or the role and control of the State in economy, and in many cases their definite willingness to enter, even with minority ownership, into partnership with the latter and to involve more nationals into their activities and management seem to be elements of a new policy, too. This new policy is, of course, largely induced by the new conditions, but partly reflects also a certain re-orientation of business interests. The same applies to the attitude of the multinational corporations in regard to regional integrations.

Just like all economic phenomena and processes, the crisis and shift in the capitalist international division of labour have been related to both *material-technical* and *socio-political* factors.

In addition to the postwar change in the leadership of world capitalism, the rise and growth of the community of socialist countries, the collapse of colonial empires, the general expansion of state monopoly capitalism and the rise and rapid growth of international monopolies, etc., no doubt, the *scientific and technical revolution* has been one of the decisive factors behind the emerging new pattern of investments, and even behind some of the

[70] For a detailed explanation, see, e.g., Kwame Nkrumah: *Neo-Colonialism. The Last Stage of Imperialism.* Nelson, London, 1963.

[71] For example, British private investments in Sterling Area fell from 30 million pounds in 1960 and 33.4 million in 1961 to 8.8 million in 1962, 2.5 million in 1963 and minus 9 million pounds in 1964. (D. J. Morgan: *British Private Investment in East Africa. Report of a Survey and a Conference.* London, The Overseas Development Institute, 1965. (Quoted by G. Arrighi, op. cit.)

188

above-mentioned phenomena. Its various effects on the colonial-type of international division of labour and the position of the primary-producing countries have already been discussed. However, its effects on the dimensions and patterns of production, the increasing internationalization of the production process and the fronts of competition all need to be stressed in this specific context.

The development of the productive forces with revolutions in science and technology, and leading to the increasing internationalization of the reproduction process, is an objective tendency, independent of—although influenced by and also affecting—the actual socio-economic formations. Under capitalism this tendency has been interrelated with the further concentration and centralization of capital, the rise and strengthening of *multi-* (or *"trans"*-) *national corporations.* The internationalization of production and productive forces takes the form of and has been realized by the internationalization of capital, and been pushed forward by the fundamental problem of the system: marketing, and governed by its main motive force: profit.

In general, the extent to which the international economic relations become, or *de facto* are, the built-in factors of the reproduction process of individual national economies, or rather *vice versa*: to which the latter take part in the internationalized reproduction process, depends on the number and size of the missing links in the "national" system of reproduction process, i.e. horizontally on the absence of entire producing branches to meet local demands, and vertically on the absence of complexity, the discontinuity of the various existing branches. Specialization produces new units as well as new missing links.

Due to the general growth of the productive forces, to the expanding *dimensions* of production and producing units, to the dimensional requirements of up-to-date technology (both in terms of supply and demand), as well as to the rapid expansion of demand under outside demonstration effects, the increasing number of missing links is becoming more and more characteristic for all national economies. The weaker or stronger position in the capitalist system of international cooperation, and the distribution of benefits from it, depend, however, largely on the *location of the missing links.* This explains why the most powerful monopolies strive to—and competition among the most advanced capitalist countries is directed in part towards this end—seize and monopolize the most important, decisive links in the expanding and increasingly internationalized reproduction process—at the expense, if necessary, of leaving or even creating missing links in less important spheres.

The scientific and technical revolution has changed the pattern of leading industries, giving rise to new ones, and creating new centres of technological research and development. It has demonstrated where the decisive links are.

The elements or warning signs of an emerging new international division of capitalist labour appear not only in the shifted pattern and policy of foreign investments in the developing countries, but in other lines as well. If unfolded, the new international division of labour may replace the present and already outdated division of labour between industrial and primary-producing countries. Instead, it will become a division of labour between the *centres* of scientific and technological progress and the *periphery* of *all* those countries relying on the regular imports of the technical achievements and scientific results of the former. Although it may add new features to the economy of developing countries through a certain type and level of industrialization, it may result in an even wider gap between centre and periphery than the present one.

Over and above those more or less temporary effects (like the stimulus for a new, wide wave of investments within the developed sector of world economy, coinciding, however, with other stimuli from the postwar restoration process, from integration and military demand) which biassed the private capital export against investments in the "periphery" countries, the scientific-technical revolution has resulted in far-reaching shifts in the production structure[72] of the "centre"-countries, modifying thereby their input and output patterns, the commodity structure of foreign trade, and also the pattern of demand for products, services, marketing facilities and investment opportunies to be delivered by the periphery. Most of these changes have already been discussed. The capital export to the developing countries also shows accordingly a changing pattern, not only in respect of the composition of the exporters (shifting in favour of MNCs) but also in that of the choice of investment sphere, choice of technique and choice of product orientation, which indicates and realizes the restructuring of the centre—periphery relations on the line of modified functions for the periphery.[73]

The rapidly increasing role in economic competition of the technological research and product development, and the centres of technical progress in general, has induced the most powerful companies to expand or even specialize their activities in this field, requiring thereby expanding markets for the materialized knowledge and technology.

[72] See M. Simai: Structural Changes in the World Economy. In: J. Nyilas (ed.): *Theoretical Problems, Current Structural Changes in the World Economy*. I. Akadémiai Kiadó, Budapest, 1976.

[73] For a more detailed investigation see the papers of the author: Socio-Economic Effects of Two Patterns of Foreign Capital Investments. IDEP Seminar 1972, Dar es·Salaam. IDEP/ET/CS/2367–8. See also in *The Political Economy of Contemporary Africa*. Ed. by Peter O. W. Gutkind and Immanuel Wallerstein. Sage Publ., Beverly Hills, London 1976, pp. 261–290.—A New, Emerging Pattern of International Division of Labour, with Neo-Colonial Dependence. A Possible Strategy to Escape. CAAS Conference, Halifax, 1974. (Reprinted in: *Peace and the Sciences*. International Institute for Peace, Vienna, Series No. 2, May 1975, pp. 72–95.)

The installation of last-stage or processing plants with relatively capital-intensive techniques, relying on the imports of equipment and know-how, the increasing proportion in trade of those export products with a more or less monopolized technical advantage for the producer, the expanding export of licenses, patents, managerial and consultancy services, etc., are all manifestations and different aspects of the same process.

In the case of the vertically integrated corporations expanding their capital goods production at "home", market interests particularly clearly suggest the promotion of the development of consumer-goods-producing industries with capital-intensive techniques abroad. So do these interests also suggest the maintenance of the blockade against the development of the capital-goods-producing sector in the periphery, and particularly of those industries which are the centres of technical progress.

In addition to, and, of course, connected with the market interests (i.e. the orientation of the capital export serving commodity export), and the profit considerations (i.e. the orientation of the capital export as a direct profit source) have also changed. Instead of the "absolute" cheapness of local unskilled labour and natural resources, guaranteed in the past by the colonial (administrative and economic) machineries,[74] it is rather the relative wage differences[75], i.e. related to the productivity differences and the indirect economizing on the metropolitan wage (or other, costs e.g., environment costs) which are getting more and more important in the choice of investments.

What are the actual or predictable effects and consequences which follow from the emerging new pattern of foreign investments? Without going into details,[76] let us sum up some of them:

The new pattern or foreign direct investments, contrary to the expectations concerning their more international character, will hardly widen, but will rather limit the sphere of national decision-making.

The multinational corporations tend to centralize the control over, and impose a hierarchical system upon, national economies. They may play—according to their business interests—by closing down branch plants in one country and moving to another one, by creating parallel capacities in neighbouring countries, by slowing down the expansion of production in one country in favour of another, etc. As they extend over several units of national economies, they can easily escape political regulation of the governments in any one unit. Owing to their great capacity for internal

---

[74] See Chapter III.

[75] This point is strongly stressed by Samir Amin in his *L'échange inégal et la loi de la valeur. La fin du débat.* Anthropos, IDEP 1973, Paris, and his *Unequal Development*, Sussex, 1976.

[76] For more details see the following chapters.

financing, they can free themselves, to a great extent, even from outside financial control.

Instead of bringing about an internal integration of the socio-economic structure, the new pattern of foreign investments seems to reinforce the internal dualism[77] and the partial and "external" integration, i.e. the integration of parts only of the domestic economies with the international capitalist economy.

Both the location of the new plants and their character regarding production linkages work rather for a further disintegration in both a regional and sectoral sense. The income gap between the urban centre and the rural areas tends to increase as a result of the new investments, too.

The orientation of the new investments towards the import-substitutive light industries (particularly those producing relatively luxury items for the high income elite) or the first-stage processing of primary products for export, makes even more serious the absence of the central links in the chain of the vertical structure of production.

The emerging new pattern of investments fails to lead to the changes required for socio-economic development and social justice in respect of human labour and in the field of employment.

Insofar as it tends to reproduce the disintegrated dual structure, instead of integrating the rural "traditional" sector into a new, dynamic modern sector, it does not help in harmonizing the economic and the social-moral-cultural factors behind population growth, and thereby the fertility and mortality rates.[78]

The limited sphere of industrial growth, i.e. the bias against local capital goods production and technology development, the character of the new industries and the techniques applied in them relatively reduce both the expansion of the employment facilities inside, i.e., their own labour-absorptive capacity, as well as their potential employment facilities in ancillary activities, and their ability to promote the expansion of employment outside, in other sectors, as well.

All these show that the emerging new pattern of international division of labour which has still been shaped mainly by the uncontrolled activity and business interests of the international monopoly capital, first of all by the MNCs, is going to become another unequal pattern resulting new tensions, disproportions and increased competition in the world market, and that the former *sectoral imbalance* of the world economy (incorporated by the international division of labour of colonialism) has been completed, rather than eliminated, by the new sectoral disproportions which also set obstacles to the proportional growth of mutual markets.

[77] See Chapter III.
[78] See Chapter III.

5. OTHER CHANGES IN THE BACKGROUND TO THE CRISIS

Besides the shifts in the production structures caused by the scientific and technical revolution, and the related changes in the investment pattern of foreign companies in the developing countries, there are other changes and factors as well, which tend to modify the position of the periphery in international capitalism.

The colonial function of the periphery countries as raw-material suppliers has also been affected in a way by the changes in question. The scientific and technological revolution has as we have seen, made, an impact, particularly by the synthetic substitutes, also on the demand pattern of the "traditional" raw materials imported from the periphery. In the post-Korean-War period, between the mid-fifties and the mid-sixties, this impact seemed to be more or less equally unfavourable for all the primary-producing countries of the Third World.

The decrease of the reliance of the centre as a whole on the periphery's supply of several primary products, which resulted from substitution, chemicalization, by-product processing, miniaturization, new mining and agrarian technologies, etc., may, however, be (over-) compensated by the increase of demand, particularly for some crucial materials, due to the on-going wastage, the manipulated reflexes of the "consumer society", the practice of accelerated amortization and quality deterioration, the expansion of military production, etc. (This has also been stressed in the previous chapters.)

Since the actual role of the various primary products in the technical and scientific progress is widely different (and also changing), the differentiation among the primary-producing countries is a "natural" process (in as much as their one-sided specialization is "natural"). The double function of crude oil as (still) energy source No. 1 and basic material for the dynamic chemical industry is an important factor in the improved position of oil exporters.

In general, however, the effect of the scientific-technological revolution on the relative prices of manufactured and primary products is of a rather opposite direction—even if the monopolistic factors and their different intensity and orientation in different branches are left out of consideration. In the manufacturing industry the effect of the increased productivity achieved in the main process of a certain use value production can hardly be realized in the drop of the value of the product (not to mention its market price, under additional forces). This is because compensating changes may take place in the nature, appearance, and (objective or subjective) quality of the product for basically the same use, which increase the required quality, complexity and secondary supplements of the total input. Or it is because even the use value of the products may change, though designed to meet more or less the same need. In the primary production, however, technical progress is mostly realized simply in the increased output of the same products, due to higher productivity or new resources. This explains, even apart from monopolistic forces, the unfavourable price scissors between manufacturing and primary production. Diminishing returns and an overall exhaustion of the natural resources clearly suggest an opposite trend. It is hardly reasonable, however, to assume a standstill in the technical and scientific progress which normally cancels out the "law" and opens up new resources. It must also be taken into account to what extent the increased prices of raw materials can be built into, and may re-appear also in the increasing prices of the manufactured goods. This question, however, refers, particularly on the international scene, to the power relations of the trade partners.

The shifts in the consumption pattern of the developed capitalist countries, as already pointed out, follow, on the one hand, the natural trend (as expressed, more or less correctly, by the Engel's law), but also those propensities created artificially or increased abnormally by the manipulated system of "consumer" society" with fashion waves, trade-mark wars, quality deterioration, status symbols, credit purchases, etc., which push up the increasing demand for durables and luxury goods so far that they become out of proportion and detrimental to the demand for social values, cultural and educational "products". This also seems to be an important factor behind the "energy crisis" and some raw material problems of the advanced capitalist countries.

The consequences of the shifts in question on the world-market prices and the terms of trade have been widely discussed in international literature. So have the problems of the demand elasticities. One has to stress or add, however, in this context, that the price and/or income elasticities of demand of the typical primary products exported by developing countries do widely differ according to whether the prices (or incomes) are changing in an upward or downward direction. Here again one may refer to the favourable position of, e.g., the oil (the demand for which seems to be highly price-elastic when its relative price falls, but is inelastic enough when the latter increases as a result of successful actions by OPEC), or the unfavourable position of the relatively luxury food products such as cocoa, coffee, tea, etc., which, unlike the luxury durables, neither face a growing demand in the developed countries, nor can meet the expanding need of the Third World masses for basic necessities, but are faced with a demand the elasticity of which seems to behave in almost the opposite fashion to that of crude oil. (This explains, for the most part, the great difficulties in organizing OPEC-like producer associations strong enough to achieve similar success in the case of many other commodities.)

The rise of state monopoly capitalism and the integration processes within the advanced sector of the world capitalist economy play also an important role, as we have seen, in the international reallocation process and in the growing crisis of the colonial type of international division of

194

labour. Over and above the effect (discussed earlier in this book) that the Western European integration with increasing state monopoly co-operation and intertwining business ties has exerted on the development of the intra-regional trade and capital (and also labour) flows, there have been other important effects related to the centre—periphery relations.

State monopoly capitalism, by having developed and experienced the (Keynesian) tools and methods of the intervention into national economy, has become, on the one hand, more capable of influencing the economic processes or economic policies in the periphery via indirect methods (aid, credit and monetary policies, etc.), and of carrying out flexible manoeuvres on the international scene. The transition into neo-colonialism which, of course, has been rather forced upon the metropolitan countries from "outside", by the inevitable liberation of colonies and the changes in international military and political power relations, seems to be connected "from inside" not only with the changes in structure and interests but also with the development of the state monopoly capitalism and its arsenal of economic policy.[79]

On the other hand, however, the very intervention via indirect economic methods into the periphery economies may—and will—meet increasing difficulties or resistance there because of the disintegration of the colonial frameworks and (bilateral) mechanism. This manifests the contradiction between the *national* character and basis of the state monopoly intervention, and, on the other hand, its efforts to exceed the former, to expand its sphere of action *internationally*.

The unfolding integration process has, without doubt, given a stimulus to and strengthened the Western European economies, rebuilding, thereby, the power of the (old) metropolitan centres, to some extent and creating also a certain collective neo-colonial power basis. At the same time, however, it has also considerably contributed to a certain relaxation of the centre—periphery relations, and to the trend of a collective defense of periphery countries.

The changes in the *power relations and leading positions* within the advanced sector of international capitalism have also contributed in various (contradictory) ways to the disintegration of the colonial mechanisms. (Some of these effects are discussed in other chapters of this book.)

The postwar hegemony of the United States in the capitalist world and the rapid penetration of US-based companies (and their political influence) into the spheres formerly monopolized by the "mother" countries, promoted, as a matter of fact, the breaking-up of the colonial bilateralism, even where the liberation movements had left it completely intact. But a

[79] The coincidence of the rise of the Gaullist system of increased state intervention in France with the change-over of the French policy in the overseas territories from colonial to neo-colonial methods shows clearly the point.

complete, military and administrative appropriation of the former British, French, etc., colonies by the US—like that of the German ones, e.g., by Britain after the First World War—would have, on the one hand, proved impossible under the changed international conditions marked by the spread of socialism and successful liberation movements, and, on the other, would have also been unnecessary for, or even contrary to the interests of the US capitalism. Instead of the rigid and fragile system of the bilateralism of Empires, a flexible neo-colonial relation with formally independent countries, based upon the penetration of the US capital, promised, and had actually proved thus in Latin America much before World War II, a far better solution.

The above effects and processes, have however, been able to unfold only within certain limits and with contradictions.

As to the change in the orientation of private capital exports, it has proved to be rather relative and temporary. The rising conflicts and danger areas in the Third World increasingly induced government donations, loans, and assistance funds to be channelled towards developing countries, playing thereby (though not for the same countries) a counteracting role in the period when the inflow of private capital lagged behind.

However, the coming to an end of the postwar "boom" period with favourable investment opportunities in the advanced industrial countries, the sharpening competition between metropolitan companies, and also a certain consolidation of the "investment climate" in the newly independent countries all seem to have induced, as we have already pointed out, a renewed reorientation in private capital export.

The reconstruction of the Western European economy and its rapid growth in the relatively long period of prosperity, supported by the integration process and the scientific-technical revolution, have not only challenged the US hegemony, but also caused shifts in the centre—periphery relations. Contrary to the former post-war or post-crisis periods—when the bilateral mechanism of commodity, capital and labour flows between the centre and the periphery had been rebuilt, destroying all the local results of the temporary breakdown—[80] the reconstruction period following World War II was hardly able to restore the old machinery. The reason—even apart from outside forces—is that the considerable structural changes involved, required not only time for the periphery's readjustment but also a modification in the division of labour.

The changes in the relations between the metropolitan countries and dependent territories have clearly demonstrated the crisis of the colonial structures. The collapse of the colonial power system reflected not only a shift in the political and military power relations but also the need for

---

[80] A number of such cases are presented by A. G. Frank: *Lumpen-Bourgeoisie and Lumpen-Development....*, Monthly Review Press, 1972.

reorganizing the increasingly obsolete colonial division of labour. Typically enough, the negative economic effects and consequences of the colonial crisis and the reallocation process have cumulatively increased the disadvantages of the periphery with its inherited colonial structure, parallel with and contrary to a number of positive *political* changes. The latter (such as the rise of state sovereignty, the shifts in the international forums, etc.) have created, however, only the *possibility* for positive economic changes in the future, while in the short run it was rather the burdens of the crisis and reallocation which came upon the peripheral countries. The contradictory, more or less opposite development of the political and the economic situations appeared, therefore, as a characteristic feature of many developing countries.[81]

Although in a few countries the policy of readjustment to a neo-colonial investment pattern resulted in spectacular growth (without development) and certain advantages in trade and finance, most of the developing countries suffered additional losses due to the disturbances of the colonial division of labour. In some cases the cumulation of the burdens and negative consequences from both the colonial mechanism and its disturbances went so far that the resulting indebtedness, population and food-supply problems, mass unemployment, etc., have produced an almost chronic crisis.

The modifications in the functions of the periphery affect the individual countries rather *unequally*, and contribute thereby to the acceleration of the *differentiation process* within the Third World.

The changes in the centre—periphery relations, the breaking-up or disturbances of the former colonial mechanisms and the unfolding reallocation are all contradictory processes in which the old structures and

[81] This is particularly manifested in the seemingly "paradoxical" phenomenon that a radical change over with a socialist orientation in several developing countries actually led to a deterioration (at least for a while) of the statistical indicators of economic growth, which are assumed (by conventional economism) to express the economic performance and development of a country. This is, however, surprising (and pleasing) only to those who do not understand that a transformation of structures is always and everywhere accompanied, and particularly a radical break with the old ties and mechanisms is necessarily followed, by certain transitional disturbances and difficulties in the operation of the inherited economy even if no external retributions (surprisingly indeed!) and no internal resistance take place. It may also appear as a "paradox" to those who, vulgarizing the Marxist critique of colonialism, assume an absolute "blocking" of the development of the productive forces in colonized economies, and equate "underdevelopment" (i.e. lopsided development) with a lack of development in general.

We also have to note that the deterioration of the statistical indicators of economic growth in the countries or periods in question does not necessarily mean also a real worsening of the living conditions of the working masses, since most of the conventional indicators are biased towards the export enclaves, and conceal the pattern of income distribution and real consumption, which may have changed in favour of the masses even parallel with a declining per capita GDP.

interests are also manifested. That is the main reason why their burdens and costs are—and can be purposefully—transferred to the periphery itself.

Nevertheless, beside the grave burdens and new dangers, no doubt, real *opportunities* also open up, under the changing conditions, for the local political centre, whether it is "old" or newly established by independence, to modify and divert the direction of operation and reorganization of the local economy away from the colonial and neo-colonial interests.

It can hardly be doubted that the shifts in the international power relations, the rise of new political forces, the pressure under which the old ties and mechanisms of the colonial system are broken up and the imperialist powers are forced to modify them, and also the better chances for the developing countries to utilize new economic opportunities—all these have, directly or indirectly, also been connected with the birth of the socialist countries, and the rise and growth of a socialist sector in the world economy.

The recent crisis phenomena in the world capitalist economy reflect not only the disturbances and modifications in the "colonial" pattern of the international division of labour but also the increasing difficulties in the system of state monopoly capitalism and the growing disturbances in the national mechanism of the "Keynesian" regulation policy, which until the early seventies had been operating quite effectively in the postwar period. The commencing breakdown of the latter—though also connected with the processes discussed above—follows in a sense from its very framework and limited character. The "Keynesian" system of state intervention and policies had been devised for a national economy under state sovereignty. (If over and beyond the foreign trade and currency policies of a national economy it had "external" implications at all, it concerned at best the "overseas territories" under the state.) It had practically nothing to do with the international economy as such.[82]

The rise and development of this system has—objectively[83]—resulted from the contradiction between the strengthening of the monopoly capital and the anachronistic operation of the state administration which had been still adjusted to the outworn mechanism of laissez-faire capitalism. This contradiction increased the risk and the harmful consequences of the anarchy under the condition of growing productive forces and the widening amplitudes of the business cycle, and thereby it worked towards the sharpening of the class conflict.

Since both the bourgeoisie, worrying about the excessive fluctuations and political risks, and the working class, frightened by mass unemployment,

[82] On the "shortcomings" of the Keynesian theory in respect of international economy, see among others François Perroux: *Indépendance de l'Économie Nationale et Interdépendance des Nations.* Paris, 1969.

[83] Subjectively: from its recognition.

became increasingly interested in the prevention of economic crises, monopoly capital was inclined to accept (within certain limits), and the labour movement actually demanded (for the improvement of the living conditions and employment security), state intervention into economy. In spite of opposite aims, this actually gave, a narrow, objective basis for a "compromise" ensuring a relatively more balanced operation of the capitalist economy, temporarily less harmful for the working class, and needed by monopoly capital under the pressure of class struggle. The same process of capital accumulation which has produced and strengthened monopoly capital, has also created a metropolitan labour aristocracy, by using the benefits from the colonial exploitation, as well as technical progress, and by differentiating the labour class. This made up a "subjective" basis, too, for a "social contract" with the state in the developed countries.

The above condition seems to explain greatly why the relatively smooth introduction and "harmonious" operation of the state intervention system based upon the "positive Keynesian principles"[84] were characteristic only of those developed capitalist countries where a relatively wide and stable labour aristocracy had already developed and its leadership (like the British Labour Party) had achieved certain positions in the Establishment. In other developed countries, however, where the crisis, the class struggle and the pressure of international capitalist competition forced state-monopoly capitalism to rise in the absence of the above social and political conditions (due to the weakness of the labour aristocracy or the sharpness of the class conflict), the result was a fascist dictatorship, mobilizing, by means of social and chauvinist demagogy, the other extreme side (the lumpen-elements) and applying "negative Keynesian principles" and aggressive imperialist methods. This "original" formula of fascism, reflecting thus a certain social pattern, appears in this context as a by-product (though inherent in the system) of a former transitional period. After its failure and due to the post-war period of prosperity and the changed circumstances internally as well as externally, the conditions for a (temporarily) more "harmonious" and peaceful system of state monopoly capitalism came soon into being also in those countries (West Germany, Italy) where fascism had existed before.

---

[84] As is well known, for the practical policy almost diametrically opposed "recipes" may follow from the Keynesian theory. On the one hand, the "positive principles" (the positive variant of the implication of the Keynesian views) suggest a solution for the saving-investment gap and demand deficiencies via public investments in social welfare, public health, etc., to increase demand for investment goods, and via a shift in the income distribution in favour of the working class with low saving propensity, by higher employment and wages, to increase consumers' demand. On the other, however, for the same purposes the "*negative*" variant may argue for unproductive, squandering expenditures on the state bureaucracy, and armament investments, to increase investment goods demand, and for the reduction of unemployment by military service, to increase consumers' demand.

The "content" or more precisely the actual result of the compromise was an anticyclical policy which safeguarded, for a while, the system against deep crises, and ensured benefits for monopoly capital, on the one hand, by a state market, by public investments, and by regulated inflation, etc., while reducing the size of unemployment, on the other, and giving a little share of the benefits and fruits of the "welfare state" and "consumer' society" to a relatively wide stratum of the working class.

In Western Europe the development after World War II of such a system of state monopoly capitalism actually coincided to some extent with a period of upswing, supported by reconstruction, technical progress and integration. In the case of the USA. it was her worldwide expansion and hegemony efforts which created additional upswing impulses. The relatively mild and short recessions in the United States were not (yet) synchronized with or synchronizing the business cycle of the former. This kept the inherent contradictions concealed, which are involved not only in the very nature of the "compromise" but also by the fact that this period of a relatively smooth and effective operation of state monopoly capitalism unfolding within the *national* framework was, at the same time, a period of rapid *internationalization* of production and capital, the expansion of multinational corporations, and the increasing multilateralization of the centre—periphery relations.

In the case of the US, it seemed to be the (hoped for) hegemony which promised to solve the contradiction (and to create also a "stable" domestic class-peace with the highest mass consumption), by expanding the sphere of action of state intervention, parallel with the expansion of US capital over the world economy as a whole, via direct political influence, leadership in the multilateral institutions and the international monetary and fiscal policies on the basis of the Bretton Woods Agreement.

However, the more the increasing resistance against the hegemony effort of the US has manifested itself and the more its failures appeared, the more the dangers and negative consequences of the foreign activity of the US-based MNCs escaping the state intervention have become obvious from the point of view of the smooth operation of the domestic state monopoly capitalism itself. The runaway industries, the transfer of certain links of the industrial vertical set-up to other economies, the production of former export products abroad, etc., have exerted negative effects on economic equilibrium. By their impact on employment in the USA, and by the concomitant structural changes endangering also the relative stability of the labour aristocracies, they begin to undermine also the very socio-political constellation in which the compromise was affected.

There are, of course, other important factors in operation which also undermine the former constellation and conditions. Beside the internationalization process of capital and the multilateralization of the centre—periphery relations, here again the *scientific and technical revolution* has played a role by modifying the industrial and skill structures and thereby the stratification of the working class, the position and composition of the labour aristocracies. In addition, the concomitant dimensional growth of the productive forces and the new, often unknown dangers and consequences of the scientific-technical progress for human life and mankind, are setting new tasks and dimensions to the state intervention even within a national framework. The increasing pollution and the disrupted ecological equilibrium, the extravagant manifestations of the squandering "consumer' society" in a world still stricken with hunger and misery, have effected not only the economy of the developed countries (by increasing the environmental costs, by exerting a pressure on the natural resources, etc.) but also their social and political life by producing, e.g., the sociological phenomenon of a somewhat new type of unrest, anxiety or disillusion. (The hippy "movement" is only one extreme and impotent variant of the latter.) In addition to the shifts and structural imbalances in the international division of labour and the increasing discrepancy between the actual (internationally expanding) scope of the economic processes and the limited (national) framework of their regulation, no doubt the international *arms race* and militarization have also seriously undermined the conditions of economic stability and development. By cumulatively increasing the unproductive expenditures and diverting investment funds, science and skill away from the sphere of human-needs-oriented production and services, this growing militarization (paradoxically in peace time) of the economy, radiating from the USA where profit interests and political goals induce it, has necessarily caused both a slowing down of economic growth and an acceleration of inflation.

The manifold and contradictory effects and consequences of the crisis of international capitalism, both for single countries and for all of them, clearly show its very complex character and point to the need for an international, peaceful and democratic solution which should serve the interests of the working masses of the world, particularly those in the developing countries, rather than those of international monopoly capital.

6. THE TWO SIDES OF "UNDERDEVELOPMENT" AND ITS MAIN QUALITATIVE FEATURES

Our outline survey has made it clear that the present state of the developing countries derives basically from external factors related to the movement of the capitalist world economy, and that the earlier mechanism of the capitalist world economy and division of labour has resulted for the underdeveloped countries in a tendency of increasing economic dependence and income-drain, which, strangely enough, is reinforced, at least temporarily and in certain aspects, even by the recent disturbances and transformation of this mechanism. At the same time, as a result of the external factors, a peculiarly distorted and disintegrated economic and social structure has come into being which, in turn, has become to a certain extent, independently already of the external factors, the determinant of and the basis for the system of external relations, of the mechanism of dependence and income-drain.

Thus, there are two aspects, two sides of "underdevelopment": the basically external, international aspect, which, from the historical point of view of the emergence of the present state, is the primary aspect; and the internal aspect, which, from the point of view of future development, is increasingly important. A clear distinction between the two, and at the same time the awareness of their close interrelationship are of great importance for the right assessment of the perspectives of development. It is self-evident that the movement of the world economy and of international politics will continue to exert a great influence on the internal life and external relations of the developing countries, but the direction and the intensity of this influence will depend *to a decisive measure* on the progress of the internal changes, on the results of the transformation of the inherited structure.

The main, qualitative features and at the same time the causes of the present state of the developing countries, of the so-called "underdevelopment"—disregarding here the quantitative differences[85]—may be summed up briefly under the following subheadings:

(1) economic dependence on foreign capitalist powers;

(2) systematic income drain by foreign capital and various other forms of regular income losses in external relations;

(3) disintegrated economy with "open", extroverted character, deformed structure and "dualistic"[86] mode of production;

(4) heterogeneous society with "dualistic" features and internal gap.

As we can see, the first two criteria are related to the international aspect, the system of external economic relations, while the other two affect the internal aspect, the structural features within the country. While the first two involve the problems of losses and outward orientation, the other two are concerned with the questions of the immobility of potential energies and the internal tensions. While from the point of view of further development, i.e. for overcoming "underdevelopment", the first two call for changes in the world economy—for the solution of the problems of unequal international structures of ownership, control, division of labour, trade, etc., and external struggles for their attainment, for further changes in

[85] This abstraction is, of course, justified only for the purpose of explaining the historical roots of the present situation and pointing out the most general identical features. It can, however, in no way lead to the underestimation of the quantitative differences and other secondary qualitative characteristics.

[86] As will be clear from the foregoing analysis, our interpretation of "dualism" is diametrically opposed to the Western concept of "sociological" or "technological dualism" (already discussed).

power relations and the building up of new relations—the other two necessitate an internal transformation, structural and institutional changes and democratic reforms.

These are the most general features of the so-called underdeveloped or developing countries and at the same time the main causes of that peculiar phenomenon called "underdevelopment". These criteria and causes do not appear, of course, with the same intensity, nor are they prevalent in relation to each developing country, and there also exist exceptional cases where economic and social development is not hindered primarily by these factors. Thus, for example, in the economic and social life of Afghanistan or Ethiopia foreign capital played a relatively minor role, and we could speak of income-drain and dependence only in a relative sense. Similarly, the distortion of the social structure (and, apart from Ethiopean coffee growing, even of the economic structure) can be referred to in a restricted sense only, since before the revolution modern productive relations could be found only in patches beside the overwhelming predominance of the old, precapitalistic relations. Such and similar exceptions, however, do not refute the general law, for at least two reasons. First, these countries could not develop independently of the world system of imperialism, even if they formed separate islands in the flow of the latter's development. The laws of imperialistic environment also affected their development and gave rise to certain indirect, secondary forms of economic dependence. Even the survival of their obsolete socio-economic system cannot be explained solely by internal factors. On the contrary, it can be interpreted similarly, to a certain extent, as the precapitalistic remnants of a single country where they were preserved but deprived of their vitality by the change of their environment due to foreign capital.

The second and principal reason is that the notion of "underdevelopment" has come to be used for the most general characterization of the present state of the former colonial and semi-colonial countries and expresses, despite its literal meaning, such a phenomenon which is itself the recurrent contradictory result of a specific dialectical development. In this specific, contradictory development, every step forward induces new obstacles to further progress. It is obvious, however, that in the lower, or earlier "stages" of the development in this sense, i.e. of the development of underdevelopment, the above-mentioned characteristics, the new limiting factors, too, are less apparent, whereas the factors that had come into being prior to this specific development have a much greater importance.

There are, of course, many other differences between the individual underdeveloped countries. They differ, e.g., according to:

— the leading branch of the economy (mineral producing vs. agrarian countries, or, recently, also countries with industrial enclaves);

— the size, composition and per-capita level of national income, the rate of economic growth;

— the commodity structure and destination pattern of foreign trade, the balance of payments position, indebtedness;

— the origin, size and position of foreign private capital in the country's economy;

— natural resources and geographical endowments;

— the number, density and composition of population;

— sectoral pattern of economy and society (i.e. what is the content of the traditional and the "modern" sector and how they relate to each other);[87]

— the actual composition of society in respect of classes, nationalities, tribes, religions, etc.;

— the educational and cultural level;

— the economic, political and cultural relations, etc. with the metropolitan countries, the degree of real independence;

— the direction of post-colonial development and economic policy, and so on.

However, in spite of these important and considerable differences, the above-mentioned characteristics are still common and determinant for almost all African, Asian and Latin-American countries, the ex-colonies and semi-colonies (with the rare exception of those countries, on the one hand, which have successfully carried out a socialist transformation of economy and society, and liquidated their dependence on foreign capitalist powers, and those, on the other hand, which have succeeded in building up their own industrial capitalism with their own exploiting classes). It is on the basis of these above-mentioned characteristics that all countries of the "Third World" belong to the same category: the periphery system of world capitalism.

Let us first examine now in more details the substance of the first two criteria, i.e. the international aspect of underdevelopment, and then we shall deal later on with the internal factors and mechanism of underdevelopment.

---

[87] For example, the "dualism" of tribal rural communities and capitalist plantations and mines in a number of Tropical-African countries; semi-feudal land estates controlled by foreign capital in many Latin-American countries; traditional feudalism in rural areas and foreign capital in commerce and industry in most of the Middle East and Asian countries, etc.

THE EXTERNAL FACTORS OF THE SYSTEM OF UNDERDEVELOPMENT: ECONOMIC DEPENDENCE AND INCOME DRAIN

1. THE FORMS OF DEPENDENCE

The most direct, open and basic form of both one-sided economic dependence and international exploitation is the one which is embodied in, or associated with, foreign capital assets, i.e. foreign ownership in the economy concerned.[1] The relations of dependence are rooted in the system of imperialism. They came into being, or became general, on the basis of the early conquests, and were built into a *system* when, in the last third of the 19th century, classical capitalism turned into monopoly capitalism and the finance capital of the advanced capitalist countries divided the whole world into spheres of interest. One-sided dependence gained its most extreme form in the colonial system which meant complete administrative, military, legal, economic and political dependence. But along with the colonies proper and the protectorates and trusteeship territories which hardly differed from them, there came into being the merely formally independent semi-colonial and dependent territories.

The collapse of the colonial system brought about the disappearance of the most extreme forms of dependence: legally independent and sovereign countries have come into existence in the territories liberated from the colonial yoke. But this in itself has not yet put an end to the relations of dependence. On the one hand, the economic and social structure itself, transformed according to the colonial functions, provides now to a certain extent the basis for and the possibilities of maintaining the relations of dependence, and even produces objectively new ties of dependence, while on the other hand the imperialist powers the monopolies, taking advantage of these possibilities, are introducing new forms and methods of reorganizing and strengthening the relations of dependence (neo-colonialism).

(a) "DIRECT" ECONOMIC DEPENDENCE

By "direct" economic dependence, therefore, we mean the situation in which the *key positions of the economy*, the most important economic branches, are in the hands of, or are controlled by, *foreign monopoly capital*.

---

[1] "The basis for ... exploitation and dependency of today's export-economies lies in the ownership and control of mines, plantations, export-import trade, and financial institutions by the colonial monopolists and large corporations." (Jan Annerstedt and Rolf Gustavsson: *Towards a New International Economic Division of Labour*. RVC, Boghandel and Forlag, 1975, pp. 7–8.)

This represents, of course, the most marked form of economic dependence. It ensures, at the same time, the direct exploitation of the population of the underdeveloped country, the systematic appropriation and expatriation of most of the surplus produced by the local labour force as well as part of the surplus realized by the small commodity producers and a certain proportion of the income of the whole population.

This form of dependence has survived partly as *inheritance* in the liberated colonial territories and in those countries which have long ceased to be formal colonies but where it is exactly this intensive form of dependence that has preserved the practically colonial state (Latin America). It has partly come into being as a *result of neo-colonialist penetration.* The two varieties often complement each other or appear in a merged form.

Nowadays, the presence and investment activity of foreign capital have already become part of the everyday practice of the capitalist world and also a characteristic of the most developed capitalist national economies. The intertwining of foreign and local capital, their joint business activity and association in commonly-owned corporations are manifestations of the advancing internationalization process of capital and, at the same time, an essential factor of the expanding interdependence between national economies.

The "internationalization process", or "interdependence" in the system of relations between the advanced metropolitan and the developing countries is, in fact, merely apparent. In fact, this is rather a process of swallowing up or subordinating local capital by the metropolitan one, and the relationship of dependence between national economies is markedly *asymmetric* and not simply *mutual.* This becomes completely evident from the asymmetric character of the international distribution of direct investment capital exported, from the glaring inequalities in the ownership pattern of international capital. It is not (or is only exceptionally) the private capital of the developing countries which penetrates into the economy of the developed metropolitan country and acquires positions there, but just the other way round.

This form of one-sided economic dependence of a given developing country is all the more intensive (i.e. all the more one-sided), the more asymmetric the distribution of capital by "nationalities" (both in the sense that the presence of foreign capital in the economy of the developing country is not compensated for by an equivalent position of the latter's capital in the metropolitan country of foreign capital, and in the sense that the bulk of foreign capital is of the same origin, of the same "nationality").

The intensity of dependence is, of course, a function of whether foreign capital has got hold of the *leading sectors of the economy*, of the so-called "commanding heights". The percentages of ownership participation may often be misleading, of course, with respect to actual control, and it is often

206

extremely difficult to trace the real origin of the capital concerned owing to intertwinings, fictitious names adopted for various reasons, etc. But even the data that have to be handled with reservations as regards their accuracy, unambigously indicate that the dependent, subordinated and vulnerable state of the developing countries is invariably the consequence first of all of the presence and strong positions of foreign capital. Though substantial shifts have often taken place in the percentage ownership composition of capital assets in favour of national (private or public) capital, and this tendency is, for the time being, definitely and promisingly strengthening, yet only a few developing countries have succeeded in shaking the controlling position of foreign capital to its very foundations, or even less in liquidating it.[2] The influence of capital-strong *multinational corporations* has become consolidated in the world capitalist economy as a whole.[3]

The multinational corporations are expanding their sphere of operation and that of their subsidiaries, sub-contractors and other partners in a "putting-out system" over an increasing number of countries. In spite of their "multi-" or "trans-"national sphere of activity and of their mixed, multinational pattern of ownership and management, they are by no means really international business organizations. The pattern of the distribution of ownership rights (equity capital) and of the allocation of roles in decision-making and in effective control is extremely unequal, which means that the relations of dominance and subordination are built into their hierarchical organization with the leadership of certain national capital.

[2] "Many developing countries, in seeking the assistance of transnational corporations in their industrialization and exports, have extended a wide range of fiscal and financial incentives and other types of concessions to attract them. To a certain extent, there would seem to have been competition amongst developing countries in the provision of such incentives. Within such a framework of policies, little or no attention would seem to have been paid to restrictive business practices engaged in by such corporations; the practices were either unnoticed or, if noticed, left unchallenged.

Such policies have tended to reflect the actual or supposed dependence of developing countries on transnational corporations for much of their industrial development, and especially with regard to the supply of technology and managerial skills. At the same time, aspects of their policies may, in certain circumstances, have discouraged or prevented the establishment of indigenously-owned industries, or forced their closure or takeover in particular by transnational corporations." (See UNCTAD IV. Role of Transnational Corporations in the Trade in Manufactures and Semi-manufactures of Developing Countries. Item 9 — *Supporting Paper*. Nairobi, 1976. TD(185) Supp. 2, p. 15.

[3] Multinational corporations, mostly US-based and accounting for less than 1 per cent of all companies, own about 75 per cent of the productive capacities of the world capitalist economy. Helge Hveem estimates that in the early seventies multinational corporations based in the developed capitalist countries controlled directly (through full or majority ownership of production and/or marketing outlets, or indirectly (through joint ventures, minority ownership of outlets) and marketing contracts with local producers) between 75 and 90 per cent of mineral ore and metal, 30 to 40 per cent of agricultural raw materials, and close to 40 per cent of food exports originating in the periphery. (Helge Hveem: *The Political Economy of Third World Producer Associations*. Universitetsforlaget, Oslo, 1978, p. 21.)

It is always in the "centre" that these corporations take their decisions on organizational, technical, financial, investment and marketing policies as well as on questions relating to the composition, quality and quantity of output in the enterprises under their management and control and even in firms of mixed ownership.

Extending simultaneously over several units of national economies, the multinationals can easily escape measures, regulations and restrictions taken by governments in one or another country.

The combination of financial power, technological and information monopoly and managerial skill, as well as a high market-share, at the critical level of the vertical chain of production, in the supply of the commodity in question, etc. ensure the corporations possess strong economic power.

For example, in the case of *Tropical Africa* practically all leading sectors of the economy were under the full control of foreign companies or European settlers on the eve of independence.

Mining and the existing branches of the processing industry were controlled by foreign monopolies; the economic plantations were owned by the European settlers or controlled by foreign purchasing firms; the wholesale trade was completely in the hands of foreign commercial monopolies, while most of the retail trade was also under the control of the latter. Changes in this respect have only occurred to a lesser or greater extent in recent years in a few countries, due to nationalization or to measures restricting the operation of foreign capital as well as a result of the formation of the state sector. On the other hand, increasing changes can be observed in the *character* of foreign capital, in that the share of small-scale, competitive, mainly settler and intermediary capital is decreasing in total capital investments in favour of the international companies; there are also changes in the composition of foreign capital by origin in that the share of the capital of neo-colonial powers (first of all the USA[4]) is increasing at the expense of the former metropolitan countries (England, France and Belgium). This usually takes place in the form of joint investments, mergers and take-overs, i.e. in the framework of the activities of the international monopolies, which means the fusing of foreign capital of a different origin. Besides the new ties of the African countries with the European Economic Community, this also gives dependence and exploitation an increasingly international character and reflects the more and more *collective* nature of neo-colonialism. In spite of changes and shifts, the private capital of the colonizing countries continues to play an important role in African

[4] Of the more than 30,300 million dollars of foreign capital invested in Africa, Latin America, the Near, Middle and Far East, about 50 per cent came from American, 29 per cent from British and 15 per cent from French monopolies. While in 1936 British investments in Africa amounted to seven times the American investments, in the late fifties they came to only 4.5 times as much.

economy. For example, in the sixties, British companies still kept under control more than half of Africa's bauxite production, about 40 per cent of the copper ore, manganese ore and lead reserves, nearly 90 per cent of the chrome ore, 94 per cent of the vanadium reserves and about one third of the cobalt and tin reserves.

Since industrialization (however slowly and unevenly) also started in Africa, certain manufacturing sectors in a few countries creating a "hospitable investment climate" have been particularly attractive for newly penetrating foreign companies. Besides Kenya, Ivory Coast, Senegal, Zaire, etc.—these "traditionally" pro-Western countries with an "open-door policy" for foreign private capital, the oil exporter Nigeria, too, with her large size and strong endeavour to carry on industrialization rapidly, meets with the increasing interest of foreign companies.[5]

Latin America, despite the more than a century-old political independence of most of its countries, has been the "hunting ground" for the monopoly capital of the United States since almost the First and particularly the Second World War. Having ousted most of British and German capitals, US companies gained a nearly unlimited supremacy in the economy of Latin America in the post-Second World War years.

Since the development of productive forces in the Latin-American countries has reached a generally much higher level than in other underdeveloped countries, and the development of capitalism has also considerably advanced to the extent that in certain countries even domestic *monopoly* capital has also appeared, US capital had to make headway or strengthen its position by oppressing or utilizing local capital. Therefore, the penetration of US monopoly capital has taken place in a variety of forms among which we can find the profit-sharing system, the foundation of mixed companies, government agreements, the foundation of banks, the use of bank capital for strengthening exported industrial capital, the control over local capital, and the system of buying up the crops from domestic capitalist farmers and landlords. (The role of the latter has increased recently.) But it has also succeeded in the traditional methods: the buying up of large land estates, the acquisition of concessions, the taking over of companies ruined by merciless competition, etc. The profit-sharing system and the foundation of mixed companies, etc. have made it possible, on the one hand, for US monopoly to expand its influence to an extent much surpassing its actual size,[6] and on the other, to bring about the large-scale merging of foreign and local capital. It has also provided the possibility for

[5] In the mid-seventies, far the biggest share in all new foreign direct investments in Tropical Africa was held by Nigeria, followed by Kenya, Zambia, Zaire, Ivory Coast, Gabon, Senegal, and Niger. (See *Handbook of International Trade and Development Statistics*. pp. 332–360.)

[6] According to the computations of the Brazilian economist, Aristoteles Moura, about 36 per cent of the capital controlled in Latin America by US companies is *not* of US origin.

US capital to gain more or less control over the state sectors greatly expanding since the Second World War in certain Latin-American countries (e.g. in Brazil, Mexico, Uruguay, Argentine, Chile, Peru, Columbia), and to offset thereby some of the independent aspirations of local state capitalism.

US monopoly capital drew under its control first of all the extractive industries but also gained important positions in the processing industries and in the agricultural production of certain Latin-American countries. In the mid-sixties American monopolies controlled about 80 per cent of iron ore production, 94 per cent of manganese, almost 100 per cent of tin, chrome, vanadium, molybdenum production, more than 90 per cent of zinc, lead ore, and bauxite production of Latin America. The American United Fruit Company kept in hand the largest banana, sugar, coffee, cocoa plantations and controlled by the buying-up system also the production of local landlords (e.g. in Columbia, Ecuador, etc.). Nevertheless, a definite shift of US capital investments can be observed in Latin America in favour of certain manufacturing industries. This shift is closely connected with the business policy of US-based multinational corporations, the phenomenon of "run-away industries" and the type of industrialization chosen by several countries. This explains much of the spectacular growth of industrial output (and exports) of countries like Brazil, Argentina, Mexico, etc., but also the expanding, strengthening and increasingly complex influence of the MNCs there.[7]

In recent years British and West German groups of monopoly capital have made efforts to regain their lost positions, by investing in the new industries of the Latin-American countries. West German capital has penetrated mainly into the chemical industry (I.G. Farben in Brazil), the steel industry (DEMAG in the Argentine, Krupp in Mexico), motor-car production (Volkswagen in Brazil), the electrical industry, etc. British capital has strengthened its position in Argentine's food industry, the production of synthetic fibres, the sugar industry, Brazil's energy production and processing industries, and made efforts to retain its position in Venezuela's oil production (Shell, BP).

[7] The total book value of US direct investments in Latin America increased from 3.1 to 10.2 billion US dollars between 1946 and 1967. The share of manufacturing industries in the book value of all US direct investments made in Latin America increased from 13.1 per cent in 1946 to 33.6 per cent in 1968, while the number of US firms with non-manufacturing subsidiaries in Latin America decreased from 19 in 1945 to 11 in 1967, the number of those with manufacturing subsidiaries increased from 74 to 171 in the same period. (See Osvaldo Sunkel: Development, Underdevelopment, Dependence, Marginality and Special Imbalances—Towards a Global Approach. IDEP/Repr. (269. 1971, pp. 49–52.)

In the seventies, the penetration of US and other metropolitan capital has continued mainly into the manufacturing and oil-extracting sectors. In the mid-seventies, Brazil absorbed far the biggest share of all new foreign investments in Latin America, with Mexico, Venezuela, Guatemala and Argentina following her in order of the amounts invested. (See *Handbook of International Trade and Development Statistics.*)

Of the underdeveloped countries in Asia let us take, by way of example, the largest, India. Up to the liberation from colonial rule, foreign (British) capital had controlled almost every branch of the Indian economy, despite the fact that domestic Indian monopoly capital had already developed under colonialism. 90 per cent of the oil, rubber, jute and match industries, over 80 per cent of the tea plantations and two-thirds of the coal mines were controlled by British capital, and in 1948 about one-third of all capital investments were made by foreign (mostly British) capital.

Foreign capital even today has got an important share in certain sectors of the Indian economy (mainly in the processing industries, the oil industry and agricultural plantations, as well as in financial institutions where foreign capital investments have greatly increased), despite the fact that the fairly strong Indian national bourgeoisie has created, partly in its own interests, partly under the pressure of the demand of the masses, a relatively wide state-capitalistic sector (mainly by founding new enterprises rather than by nationalization), and despite the fact that the state economic policy set certain limits to and introduced control over the activity of foreing capital (by the investment licencing system, foreign exchange control, etc.)[8]. In the post-independence period the share of British capital in foreign private investment has decreased in favour of American, Swiss, West-German and Japanese capital,[9] yet even in the early seventies the registered stock value of British investments in India ranked first, slightly exceeding that of US capital.[10]

On the whole, India's economic dependency today is due not primarily to the direct control of foreign capital over the Indian economy, but it has rather a financial (loans) and commercial character. This does not mean, however, that the direct influence of foreign capital on the economy should be understimated. In addition to the former investments and the resulting cumulative re-investments, we also have to take into consideration the fact that foreign capital has been largely intertwined with part of the local private capital, and that there is an increasing penetration of private capital in the form of joint ventures, mixed companies, etc.[11]

[8] See N. K. Sarkar: *Social Structure and Development Strategy in Asia.* People's Publishing House, New Delhi, 1978.

[9] Among the US companies operating in India, we find (in order of their sales value in the late sixties) General Motors, Esso, Ford, General Electric, Mobile Oil, IBM, Standard Oil, Western Electric, ITT, DuPont, etc. Besides them and the "old" British companies, the Japanese Mitsubishi and Hitachi, the West German Siemens, Bayer and Hoeschst, the Swiss Nestle, the Holland-based Philips, etc. are the most typical representatives of foreign capital operating in Indian economy.

[10] See Charan Singh: *India's Economic Policy. The Gandhian Blueprint.* Vikas Publishing House, New Delhi, 1978, p. 69.

[11] The amount of foreign investments rose from 2.600 million rupees in 1948 to 16.118 in 1969, and to 18.163 million in 1973. The Indian government permitted foreign firms to have an equity share of as much as 74 per cent, and to expand their capacities to the extent of 25 per cent. (See op. cit., pp. 68–70.)

As regards the other countries in *South* and *South-East Asia*, Western capital (with a shift in its composition) has increased its penetration in the form of subsidiary investments in primary production, banking, etc., as well as in the form of "run-away industries" of multinational corporations in all countries following an "open-door policy" or creating "free trade zones" for foreign capital investors.[12]

In the underdeveloped countries of the *Middle East*, foreign monopoly capital penetrated primarily into the oil-extracting industry and has kept it, until recently, under full control. Since oil-extraction represents the most important economic sector of the countries concerned, foreign capital had a direct impact on their economy. In the period following World War II, British, French and Dutch capital were ousted to an ever-increasing extent by American capital, which in 1957 already controlled 59.6 per cent of the total oil output of the Middle East, while the share of British capital decreased from 76.8 to 30.6 per cent. Italian, West German and Japanese companies also appeared on the scene as new rivals. In the early sixties, US companies had nevertheless an almost unchallenged control over the oil of Saudi Arabia, Bahrein and the so-called Neutral Belt, and had a share of 50 per cent in Kuwait's oil output, 40 per cent in Iran's and about 24 per cent in Iraq's and Quatar's. The international oil cartel, in which the leading role is taken by the American monopolies, controlled 80 per cent of the proven oil reserves of the Middle East, 60 per cent of its output and 90 per cent of the total oil tanker fleet.[13] Though attempts were made earlier, too by national governments and states (e.g. by the Mosadik government) to take control over oil extraction, considerable changes have taken place only since the early seventies. Following the collective oil embargo measure of the Arab oil-exporting countries against the Western countries supporting Israel, and parallel with the strengthening of the producer association of oil exporters (OPEC) and its dictated price increases, most of the oil-producing countries have made efforts to take their national resources under effective national control. However, despite significant changes in the pattern of ownership and control in the sphere of oil extraction, Western (mainly US-based) monopoly companies still keep in their hands the other links of the vertical chain of oil production: most of the transport, refinery and processing capacities and of the marketing network in international oil business.

---

[12] In the sixties and seventies, this applied particularly to Malaysia, the Philippines, Indonesia, Thailand (South) Korea, Hongkong and Singapore, where the bulk of foreign direct investments concentrated in the area. (See *Handbook of International Trade and Development Statistics*, and N. K. Sarker: Op. cit.)

Frustration over the type of development and the negative consequences of the operation of foreign capital and a rising criticism of dependence on foreign capital can be observed in some of these countries, too, resulting in, or promising, certain changes in policy.

[13] Y. Pevzner: Developing Countries and Reproduction in Parent-States. *Soviet Economists Discuss...*, p. 38.

212

Since by making use of their increased oil revenues some of the oil-exporting countries have launched large-scale domestic investment programmes to develop infrastructure and certain manufacturing industries (e.g. the chemical and steel industries, and including armaments), Western capital has considerably increased its investments in these countries.[14]

The overall picture, as we have seen, of the "direct" economic dependence of the Third World, manifested in foreign ownership and control in the economy, is changing and shows contradictory tendencies. The drive of an increasing number of developing countries for national sovereignty over the economy (and particularly over natural resources) is certainly one of the main forces and tendencies behind the changing picture. The ongoing and expanding internationalization process of capital, linked with the dimensional growth of the objectively unstoppable internationalization of the productive forces as well as with increasing monopolization, capital concentration and centralization, i.e. a hierarchically structured pattern of "international", "multi-" or "trans-national" capital ownership, is another fundamental motive force and tendency. Here again the dialectical contradiction, an inseparable concomitant of capitalism throughout its life-time, between "national" and "international," clearly manifests itself.

Those who do not understand the substance of capital as a social relation of production cannot understand the role and significance of the unequal international ownership structure of capital economy, in the dependence and exploitation of the periphery, in unequal trade relations either.[15] One of the most serious mistakes made by them is the confusion of the export of capital as foreign ownership and the export of a certain amount of money, a financial resource, for investment purposes as it appears in the annual balance of payments.[16]

The role of the export of capital (in the sense of Marxist political economy) can by no means be assessed on the basis of the size of the actually transferred amounts of "direct investment capital" (or its proportion to the size of foreign trade or GDP, etc.). This is not only because the export of

[14] In the mid-seventies, Saudi Arabia, Iran and Kuwait were the main absorbers of all foreign direct investments. See *Handbook of International Trade and Development Statistics*, pp. 332–360.

[15] A typical example is Arghiri Emmanuel's attack upon Lenin's concept of "investment imperialism" and its replacement by his "trade imperialism" theory. (See A. Emmanuel: White-Settler Colonialism and the Myth of Investment Imperialism. *New-Left Review*, 1972, No. 73, and *Unequal Exchange. A Study of the Imperialism of Trade*. NLB, London, 1972.) For a critique see T. Szentes: *Theories of World Capitalist Economy* (forthcoming), and also "A Brief Survey on the Theories of International Trade" in *Studies on Developing Countries*, No. 102, Budapest, 1979.

[16] It is perhaps surprising that sometimes such confusion can be found in the literature of a socialist country, too, namely in the writings of a few Hungarian authors. (See the debate, in the late sixties, in issues of the Hungarian *Economic Review*.) It actually shows that ideological frontiers do not coincide with geographical ones.

"working capital" (in the Marxist sense referring to the separation, internationally, too, of capital ownership from capital function) is not equal to the export of "direct investment capital" (in the conventional sense of Western economics). It is mainly, and primarily, because the local accumulation (from local sources!) of foreign capital, the growth, locally, of foreign ownership and its sphere of control over local producers (labour force, small-commodity producers and local capitalists), normally exceeding the actual size of ownership and expanding via mixed companies, joint ventures, "putting-out" systems, etc., are indeed the most decisive and increasingly important aspect of the internationalization cum monopolization process of capital as ownership relation!

Though the fact that in the seventies the growth of domestically financed investments exceeded the average growth of the flow of foreign direct investments to the developing countries is a positive phenomenon reflecting the expansion of their local accumulation sources (and increased "self-reliance" in this narrow sense), it does not mean at all, however, a weakening of the most direct form of economic dependence. It does not necessarily manifest even a decreasing tendency in the share of foreign ownership in their total capital stock, since the latter may further increase also without new inflows. The very shift in the composition of foreign investors in favour of the giant "multi"- (or "trans"-) national companies makes it actually possible for the metropolitan powers to control a dependent economy, or one of its strategic sectors by an amount and share of equity capital much smaller than before. Therefore, let us stress again, that the data on foreign direct investments are not conclusive either of the actual size of foreign "working capital" in the country concerned or, particularly, of the sphere of economic activities it *de facto* controls.[17] The rapidly expanding activity of foreign resident banks and their increased share in total non-concessional flows[18] to the developing countries reflects anyway the general tendency of the strengthening of *financial imperialism*,

[17] "The TNC's share of production in the periphery (and elsewhere)", stresses Helge Hveem, "is not a function of what they control directly, but of the production capacity at their disposal as *affiliated* (joint ventures) and *associated* (important minority holding) capacity *in addition* to capacity controlled 'as their own'." He also notes that "direct investments are no longer [let us add: have never been—T. Sz.] exclusive as a means of establishing control and securing supply. On the contrary, there is a strong tendency for center interests and TNCs to use other means—long-term loans, minority share-holding (not even joint ventures), or simply management or marketing contracts... In this way, *TNCs may maintain vertical control by new means.*" (Helge Hveem: Op. cit., pp. 73–74.)

[18] While the volume of total non-concessional flows to developing countries quintupled in the period 1970–1978, increasing their share in total financial flows from 56 to 70 per cent, the volume of private bank lending rose sevenfold, and doubled its share from 17 to 32 per cent of the developing countries' net receipts (i.e. exceeding the share of official development assistance). (See *1979 Review*. Development Co-operation, pp. 66–68.)

of the evergrowing role of international bank capital, cooperating or intertwined with multinational industrial corporations and also the "transnationalization" of bank capital itself.

(b) TRADE DEPENDENCE

Trade dependence means, on the one hand, a dependence in trade relations on a few advanced capitalist countries with which most of the trade is transacted (let's call it "relational dependence"), and, on the other hand, the overall dependence and vulnerability of the entire economy on the cyclical changes of the capitalist world market.

How has the trade dependence of the developing countries come about and how has it survived? Let us investigate the two sides of trade dependence first separately, ignoring for the time being how closely interlinked they are.

(1) As regards relational dependence, it is first of all due to the consequence of direct economic dependence and so partly to the heritage of the colonial past, and partly to the result of neo-colonialist penetration. In other words, it basically follows from the dominant position and structural effects of metropolitan capital in the main sectors of the economy. It is as a matter of fact self-evident that a country whose most important economic sectors are controlled by foreign capital will trade primarily or exclusively with the metropolitan country owning that capital[19] and will produce goods that the metropolitan country needs and will buy such products as the firms of the latter wish to sell. Very often foreign trade itself is handled or controlled by foreign monopolies which can determine thereby the direction of foreign trade, too. But even if this is not the case, and, let us suppose, foreign trade happens to be directly controlled by the state or is transacted by state agencies, even then foreign capital, as long as it holds the key positions in the country's economy, will have a great many other possibilities and means to channel foreign trade in the direction it wishes, to prevent the establishment or expansion of trade relations with other countries, in other words, to maintain the country's relational trade dependence. In addition to means such as bribery, retortion, blackmail and extortion, it can also make use of the banks its control and their credit policy in order to promote trade with the metropolitan country or to discourage new trade relations from coming into being. It can ensure relational dependence particularly by profiling the industrial and agricultural sectors under its control, i.e. by determining their production structure and composition according to the needs and market of the metropolitan

[19] Here and also later on, by "mother" (or metropolitan) country we understand, for simplicity's sake, not only the colonizing country, but also the country, *in general*, with which the underdeveloped country in question is in a one-sided, dependent relationship, even if this dependence had never assumed a colonial form.

215

country. It can also ensure the maintenance of relational trade dependence by making investments and introducing the production of commodities for which the necessary machines and equipment can only be purchased or replaced (standardized products!) from firms in the metropolitan country.

From this point of view the recent bias in the pattern of foreign capital investment in favour of capital-intensive techniques (and against the capital-goods sector developing technology) also plays an important role, and results not only in a rapid increase of the import of capital goods but also in a more intensive dependence on bilateral trade relations with the metropolitan countries.

But the metropolitan state itself has various means at its disposal to establish and maintain relational trade dependence. Among those of highest importance are the system of preferences, the financing policy and the monetary relations.

The system of preferences creates, on the one hand, relatively favourable conditions for the exports of the underdeveloped country to the metropolitan centre. On the other hand, it reinforces the bias in its trade for the latter and against the potential partners within the Third World (even the neighbouring developing countries) and discourages the required changes in the production and trade structure.

An important role is played by the European Economic Community (the Common Market) in the strengthening of the relational trade dependence of many developing countries through special contracts (such as the earlier agreement with 18 African countries "associated" to the EEC, and later the *Lome Convention*[20] signed by 45 African, Caribbean and Pacific countries).

The credit-financing of exports, the extension of *loans and aid* and the *monetary relations*, especially the fact that these countries belong to the monetary zone under the control of the metropolitan country, i.e. the mechanism of financial dependence, in general, provide innumerable possibilities for the metropolitan country to strengthen the relational trade dependence of the countries in question, and thereby to ensure its raw material supply and the marketing of its manufactures there.

Dependence on the foreign-trade partner is particularly intensive in the case of countries where the narrowness of the market is coupled with

---

[20] The Lome Convention combined a package of trade, aid and certain technical policy measures. It provided duty-free access to the markets of the nine EEC countries, expanded the aid programme, introduced a special scheme (STABEX) to stabilize (or rather to assure minimum levels of) export earnings of the developing countries, etc. But besides these undoubtedly favourable features (of a rather palliative nature), one has to see its basically unfavourable consequences and long-term effects, too, a discrimination against the other developing countries remaining outside the convention, and the bias reinforced by it against the intra-trade of the Third World countries, a discouragement of fundamental structural changes co-ordinated between themselves, of a policy of "adjustment" to each other's, instead of to the advanced centre's, interests.

extensive one-crop exports. In general, *the smaller the domestic market and the less the number and variety of export goods of a country, on the one hand, and the greater the economic power of the partner, on the other, the stronger and the more dangerous is the form of trade dependence.* The resulting disadvantages and dangers are manifold: the stronger partner country can determine—or at least influence—the terms of exchange (its volume, price relations and point of time) according to her own interests and can use this form of dependence in order to exert pressure upon the dependent country when trying, e.g., to influence the economic policy or even the foreign policy of the country concerned by a sort of trading blackmail.

Owing to the close trade connections and dependence, the economy of the dependent country becomes sensitive to and defenceless against cyclical slumps and crises of the partner country. Moreover, the latter can shift the burden of crisis on to the dependent country.[21] (Remember the effects of the recession of the US economy in 1957/58 on the Latin-American economies!) And, last but not least, this form of dependence strengthens by its very nature the other ties and forms of dependence.

A rather strong trade dependence can be observed between the *Latin-American* countries and the United States, though the past few years have witnessed a decreasing trend owing to a number of factors (as, e.g., the increasing competition of other advanced countries, the shifts in the commodity structure of trade, the increasing endeavour of the Latin American countries to diversify trade relations, etc.). The percentage share of the USA in Latin America's total exports was over 40 in 1955, 32 in 1970 and nearly 36 in 1976.[22] Before the mid-fifties, the US share was around 60 per cent.

There were, and are even today, quite close trade relations between the *African countries* and their former "mother"- country. However, the share of the former colonizing countries[23] in the foreign trade of the liberated African countries has shown a certain decline in the post-independence years,[24] while the share of the other developed capitalist countries, including

[21] It will suffice to recall the effects the recession of the US economy in 1957–1958 exerted on the Latin American economies, and also the harmful consequences of recent crisis phenomena for a great many developing countries.

[22] A continuous and rather sharp decline appeared in the case of food items, ores and metals as well as manufactured goods, while the US share in Latin America's fuel exports increased from less than 32 per cent in 1955 to 57.5 per cent in 1976. (See *Handbook of International Trade and Development Statistics*, p. 118.)

[23] For example, in the late sixties Britain's share in the export and imports of Kenya, Uganda, Tanzania, Ghana and Nigeria was between 27 and 33 per cent and between 23 and 31 per cent, respectively.

[24] A particularly sharp fall or even a stop in the trade between the former colony and the "mother" country took place in a few cases when a major political conflict with the latter accompanied or followed independence (e.g. Guinea). After a few years, however, the trade (and other) relations are usually normalized.

217

the former European rivals and particularly the United States and Japan, is generally increasing. This is considerable especially in the case where a major political conflict broke out between the metropolitan country and her former colony (e.g. in Guinea), while the shares of the United States, West Germany and Japan are generally on the increase. All this may mean a certain easing of relational dependence even if the character of foreign trade relations has remained unchanged. It may, however, also mean an increase in trade dependence if the shift in foreign trade takes place in the direction of the foremost capitalist power (USA), which is ousting the former dominant metropolitan country more and more from the fields of capital export, and financial and technical assistance, or if the shift occurs in favour of a "collective metropolitan empire" such as the EEC, replacing the former single ones.[25]

Similar tendencies can be observed in other Third World regions, the Middle East, South and South-East Asia as well. Along with certain shifts in the orientation of trade relations in favour, as a rule, of the United States, the EEC and Japan, the overall share and role of the metropolitan countries in the international trade of the developing countries have remained decisive,[26] while the intra-trade of the latter and their trade with the socialist countries hardly managed to expand.

(2) The overall dependence of the whole economy of the developing countries on the cyclical changes in the world market—as relational dependence to some extent, too—may be traced back to two factors: (a) the excessively important role of foreign trade in the domestic economy[27], and (b) the distorted structure of foreign trade.

The distorted commodity structure of the foreign trade of developing countries is manifested in the still heavy concentration of exports on a few primary products and in the widely diversified imports, including almost all types of items important for development.

Though the share of manufactured commodities has considerably increased in the total exports of certain regions[28] (or rather of countries

[25] The share of the United States in developing Africa's total exports increased from 10 per cent in 1955 to 23.7 per cent in 1976. The share of EEC was 61.5 per cent in 1970 as against 47.6 per cent in 1976. (*Handbook of International Trade and Development Statistics*, Table 3. 10. A.)

[26] In the seventies, the share of developed capitalist countries in the total exports of the Third World was over 70 per cent.

[27] *Ceteris paribus*, the role and proportion of foreign trade in the national economy is, of course, relatively less significant in the countries whose population is greater and whose internal market therefore is somewhat larger.

[28] The share of manufactured goods increased from 2.8 per cent in 1955 to 12.1 per cent in 1976 in the total exports of Latin America, while it rose from 17 to 49 per cent in the case of South and Southeast Asia. It remained, however, low and even declined from 5.7 per cent in 1955 to 4.3 per cent in 1976 and from 3.9 to 2.4 per cent in Africa and the Middle East, respectively. (See *Handbook of International Trade and Development Statistics*, p. 130.)

within some regions) of the Third World, the predominance of primary products[29] and the low level of export diversification[30] are invariably characteristic of the Third World as a whole, of the majority of developing countries.

Since the most developed economic sectors of the colonial countries (raw material production, agricultural plantations) came into being at the same time as export sectors, and even the new industries are mostly export-oriented or import-sensitive, a substantial proportion of the national income is realized through foreign trade.

For example, about 30–40 per cent of Latin America's total commodity production is exported, but in certain countries the share of exports is as high as 60–70 per cent of the GDP.

The role of foreign trade in the economy of the African countries is a particularly important one. Exports consume here a substantial proportion of the output of the monetary sector.[31] In a number of countries the bulk of

---

The increasing share of manufactured goods in the exports of developing countries is, in general, also connected with the shift of certain stages of the processing of some primary products to these countries (either as a result of transfers by multinational corporations, or owing to the efforts of developing countries themselves to localize the refining and processing of their own raw materials for export purposes). This applies especially to cotton, hard fibres, jute, tin and cooper, of which more than 50 per cent was exported in a processed (refined or semi-processed) form already in the early seventies. In the case of those materials, however, except tin, for which the major part of value added is realized at the higher processing levels (e.g. iron one, bauxite, coffee, cocoa, etc.), the processing stages of production has usually remained in the advanced industrial countries. (See Helge Hveem: Op. cit., pp. 41–44.)

[29] Fuels, for example, made up in the late seventies more than 95 per cent of the total exports of Saudi Arab Emirates and Algeria. The respective shares were over 90 per cent for Kuwait, Venezuela, Nigeria and over 80 per cent for Gabon. The shares of food items and agricultural raw materials in total exports were 80 per cent for Benin, Burma, Burundi, Cameroon, Ethiopia, Gambia, Honduras, Ivory Coast, Laos, Malawi, Mali, Mauritius, Mozambique, Nepal, Paraguay, Reunion, Somalia, Sri Lanka, Sudan, Uganda, Upper Volta. Ore exports accounted for more than 70 per cent of the total exports of Liberia, Mauritania, Zaire and Zambia. (See *Handbook of International Trade and Development Statistics*, pp. 152–173.)

[30] As regards the *diversification* of exports of the Third World in general, there was no considerable progress prior to the late sixties. ("On the average, periphery countries were dependent on one single commodity for 50 per cent of total export incomes in 1965, more or less the same situation as in 1948." During this period, though 34 countries somewhat decreased the monocultural character of exports, owing either to industrialization or rather to a diversification into another primary product, 30 countries became increasingly monocultural and in 22 cases there was no change.) Since the late sixties, diversification has advanced, though very unevenly, in the greater part of the Third World. Between 1965 and 1972, almost twice as many countries diversified their exports as those which became increasingly monocultural. Among the latter, we can find the OPEC countries, too, especially since the oil explosion, but the proportions in value terms do not properly reflect the changes in volume. (See H. Hveem: Op. cit., p. 87.)

[31] For the larger East and Central African states the percentages range from 20 per cent (Kenya, Uganda, Tanzania, Sudan, Ethiopia) to over 50 per cent (Mauritius and Zambia).

rural African money incomes is provided by agricultural exports grown by African farmers, and the bulk of the African wage-earners are employed by the export-producing plantations and farms, agricultural processing plants, mines and in the transport and commercial network serving export-import. A considerable proportion (between 60 and 95 per cent) of the domestic consumption of manufactured goods is supplied by imports. The import-share in the supply of fuels, transport vehicles and certain raw materials is especially high. According to estimates,[32] in the sixties about 95 per cent of the machinery required for the implementation of investment programmes (including transportation and agriculture as well as industry) and up to 50 per cent of the cost of construction (including construction machinery) represented imports. Perhaps 60 per cent of the cost of investment activity in East Africa (and in all probability in the Sudan, Ethiopia and Zambia as well) represented direct import cost in that period. Another 15–25 per cent represented indirect import cost because most of the additional labour and managerial-entrepreneurial incomes generated by investment activity was spent on imported consumer goods.

However, trade dependence, the "excessive role" of foreign trade in the national economy cannot be reduced simply to the ratio of exports-imports to the GNI. It is much more important to examine the role foreign trade plays, together with other factors promoting or limiting development, in the dynamics[33] of the national economy. "A very small share of foreign trade in the national income can go hand in hand with an almost complete dependence of the process of growth on imports of capital goods if the country has no machine-building industry of its own."[34]

The important role of foreign trade in the realization of the national income *cannot be regarded in itself as an unfavourable phenomenon*. In fact, it only leads to a high sensitivity of the economy to world-market trends if it is associated with the *distorted structure* of foreign trade. And this is exactly what is typical of the underdeveloped countries. The overwhelming proportion of their export trade is still accounted for by one or a few agricultural or mineral products.

It is obvious that the biased, distorted structure of exports in itself makes the balance of payments and the general foreign-exchange position of the country concerned defenceless against the cyclical changes of the world market. If, for some reason, the world-market demand for the main or

---

(See R. H. Green: *African Economic Development and the World Economy: Four Essays.* Carnegie Institute in Diplomacy. CID/20/65.)

[32] See R. H. Green: Op. cit.

[33] According to the estimates of R. H. Green, the import requirements of African economies tend to rise more rapidly than the national product, and the 6–8 per cent growth rates are likely to result in 8–12 per cent rates of increase of imports. (See ibid.)

[34] I. Sachs: *Foreign Trade and Economic Development of Underdeveloped Countries,* p. 100.

almost exclusive export commodity drops substantially, the country affected is not, or can hardly be, in a position to find compensation for the loss of her export earnings in an increased export of other products. In addition, in most cases the export commodities in question are still unprocessed primary products or raw materials and, as a rule, the same as exported by many other developing countries, which affects them unfavourably from the point of view of their terms of trade.

Some specialists explain the biased, lopsided structure of exports and the unduly high export ratio simply by the narrowness of the domestic market, and attribute a natural, positive role to foreign trade, which, by its income-generating effect, partly expands the domestic market and leads thereby to the liquidation of its own disproportion, and partly speeds up economic growth by transforming the potential consumption fund into accumulation fund. No doubt, the narrowness and the unfavourable pattern of the domestic market exert a negative inducement towards branches producing for the domestic market and really justify in this respect export-orientation. It is also theoretically undebatable that foreign trade may perform a "transformation function", which "takes the form of an exchange of part of the potential consumption fund into the accumulation fund, by means of trading goods produced in Department II (sectors producing consumer goods) for foreign goods in Department I (sectors producing capital goods)".[35]

But as far as the assumption of this spontaneous, automatic market-expanding effect of foreign trade is concerned, this is not only refuted *in practice* by the decades-old experience of developing countries, but it is even *in theory* the result of a rather one-sided outlook. This is the oulook which reduces the market problem to the question of incomes (and propensities to consume) instead of recognizing its real essence: the commodity metamorphosis built on the *division of labour in production*, the system of linkages between the productive sectors.[36] Yet the market-expanding effect of foreign trade depends on whether the linkage effects come into being and multiply between the export sector and the other sectors of the national economy, and not only indirectly, through incomes, but largely directly, through productive cooperation. And it is exactly in this respect that a peculiar mechanism can be observed in most of the developing countries, a mechanism which, owing partly to the inherited economic (and social) structure, partly to the activity of foreign capital controlling foreign trade

[35] Ibid.

[36] It is a personal experience of mine that when university students fed on Western standard economic textbooks are asked about the reasons for the narrowness of the domestic market and the main ways it can be extended, they, almost invariably, look for an answer in the field of incomes (or the mode of spending incomes, the propensities), usually failing even to mention the problem of production linkages, the division of labour, and the process of reproduction circulation.

and the key positions of the economy, includes the reproduction of the enclave character of the export sector. The expansion of the export sector deprives production for the domestic market of the necessary resources, and the competition of import commodities keeps domestic production under pressure. And even the distribution and spending of incomes and the consumption propensities are such that they induce a growth in import consumption and compel the country to increase export production.[37] Consequently, foreign trade, contrary to the market-expanding effect attributed to it, may limit the expansion of the domestic market by means of its specific structure and exert, therefore, a directly negative effect.[38]

As regards the "transformation function"[39], its validity is limited not only by the deterioration of the terms of trade but if they should improve, even by other factors, too. Part of the export earnings gets lost to the economy through profit repatriation by foreign capitalists transacting foreign trade, or through other channels. And the utilization of export earnings does not usually serve the purposes of a national economic development, but rather non-productive consumption, primarily the luxury consumption of foreigners and the local élite. This is the case even in countries where foreign trade is under state control. Yet, even if this transformation happens to take place, it is usually of such a character and direction that it does not result *sponte sua* in the expansion of the capital-goods producing sector (Department I). Instead, it includes the spontaneous tendency, often reinforced by the conscious business policy of international monopolies,[40] that the maintenance of the results of the transformation makes further transformation necessary, i.e. increases export orientation and import sensitivity.

[37] For more details see Chapter III. 1 (a) and (b).

[38] "The absolute dependence of the export sector (including the railways, power stations and ports necessary for exports) and, via the export sector, that of the whole economy upon the world market, arises from the fact that here the internal market not only cannot get beyond its rudimentary initial stage, but after having been created by the methods of primitive accumulation (above all by the whole-scale dispossession of the peasantry), this internal market begins to contract at once, and this prevents internal accumulation from the outset... the contraction of the internal market is due rather to the pressure exerted by the export sector on the economy as a whole; and the exclusive orientation toward the foreign market is by no means primarily due to the narrow limits of the internal market." (Gy. Göncöl: Op. cit., pp. 36–37.)

[39] This means, of course, in the case of the developing countries, not simply the use of the exports of consumer goods for the purpose of important means of production, but the conversion in general of the export earnings of raw materials (including raw materials that cannot be considered as belonging to the potential consumption fund) into buying machinery and equipment.

[40] This manifests itself in the phenomenon already referred to, namely that their industrial capital investments in underdeveloped countries are also aimed at expanding the imports of capital goods and equipment (or at least they avoid the sphere of substituting for such imports), that is, they work against the creation of a real "Department I".

As also revealed by our investigation, the two sides of trade dependence cannot be separated from one another. Trade dependence and vulnerability (also including the vulnerability of the better-off oil-exporting countries) follow not simply from the high ratio of foreign trade to national income or national product, nor simply from the degree of intensity (related to the size of their "national" economy) of joining in the international division of labour. This dependence is much more a consequence of the disproportion (as related to the actual development level of the productive forces and to the underdevelopment of the internal, national commodity exchange) of their participation in this division of labour as well as of the resulting one-sided production specialization (i.e. of a distorted production structure). Further, this dependence may be traced back to the orientation of trade relations towards the metropolitan economy, which is both larger in size and more advanced in the development level of the productive forces, in the diversification of the production pattern as well as in controlling other factors of dependence, too. Thus one-sided trade dependence and world-market vulnerability are the combined effect of such phenomena as

— a high ratio of foreign-trade turnover (export and import) to national product, more precisely to domestic commodity production;

— a high concentration of the commodity structure of exports[41], that is, a concentration on products representing a low level of the national productive forces (raw materials), or on products of secondary importance for the development of the productive forces (consumption goods, luxuries and products of the "putting-out industry") as well as a low share of export products in domestic consumption and national market;

— a widely diversified import structure, including products of crucial importance for economic development, products which determine the development of the national productive forces;

— a one-sided, distorted pattern of national commodity production as a background to the foregoing;

— a disproportionate and lopsided concentration of foreign-trade turnover on trade with the metropolitan country with its larger, more developed and stronger production structure,

— and, last but not least, a control over or a strong influence on the marketing of the main export products by foreign companies and multinational corporations, either from inside the country (as in the case of

---

[41] *The degree of concentration of the commodity pattern of exports* is usually expressed by the percentage share in the total exports of a country's main export item (e.g. cocoa, tea, cotton, copper, oil, etc.), or in its main commodity groups (e.g. raw materials) as specified by SITC (Standard International Trade Classification) applied in international statistics.

We have to note, however, that there are some more elaborated and meaningful indicators, too, such as the "diversification index of exports" and the "commodity concentration index". (For their formulae and relevant data, see *Handbook of International Trade and Development Statistics*, p. 296.)

"direct economic dependence") or from the outside (through monopoly purchases, marketing contracts, etc.).

The one-sided character of dependence consists, in contrast to mutual trade dependence, partly in the fact that the partners' shares in one another's export and import turnover are extremely unequal. (The share of the metropolitan country in the developing country's foreign trade is large, and conversely, the share of the developing country in that of the metropolitan one is generally small.) One-sidedness manifests itself also— and primarily—in the partner countries' structures differing in power and development. The partners' inequality follows basically from the disparities of their respective production structures. This is the reason why trade dependence cannot become mutual, or even less of an opposite character, even if the advanced countries happen to depend on the export products of countries with a distorted and weak structure (as nowadays in the case of petroleum).

The great sensitivity and vulnerability to world-market effects is connected, first of all, with the fact that the substitutability between the unfavourably affected export products (exposed to marketing difficulties and sustaining losses from price reduction) and other export products is, owing to the one-sided production structure, very limited, while the possibility to contract the diversified import structure and mainly to substitute domestic products for imports needed for the national economy is also restricted.

As is evident from the foregoing, dependence on the capitalist world market has its roots deep in the very structure of the economy. That is why it is so difficult to abolish. It may even happen that the very economic measures taken to liquidate direct economic dependence and also relational trade dependence partly arising from the latter, will temporarily increase dependence on the world market.[42] This may be the case, e.g., when a newly independent country embarks upon the creation of a national industry and the expansion of state investments and is, consequently, compelled substantially to step up machinery imports. And to offset the import growth it has, temporarily, hardly any possibility at its disposal than the enforced export of the traditional product of the one-crop economy.

It should further be noted that the formation of certain industrial enclaves connected with the new investment policy of multinational corporations elicits—through technological dependence and its effect on the consumption pattern—the perpetuation of one-sided trade dependence, or may even lead to its intensification, despite the development of the

[42] On the other hand, it is also feasible that the possible preferences granted in the framework of relational trade dependence provide the opportunity, which, if it arises at all, is usually very limited, for diversifying exports, and in this sense they may decrease, to some extent, the overall dependence on the world market.

industrial exports of developing countries. And not only the export of primary products is biased, namely orientating towards the developed capitalist countries, but also the export of manufactures, despite competition, import duties and other obstacles.[43]

Thus the one-sided foreign-trade dependence of developing countries implies that the development of these countries is determined, to a very great extent, by foreign trade relations, the absorptive capacity of the market of the former metropolitan countries as well as by cyclical changes in the world economy. The domestic economy is really quite defenceless against the detrimental effects of international trade, and so the economic growth achieved by internal efforts may be counteracted by external effects, often connected with conscious neo-colonial interference.

(c) MONETARY AND FINANCIAL DEPENDENCE

(1) The ties of financial dependence are strongest, of course, in countries where the *banking system* and through it the internal money circulation and the *credit system*, too, are under foreign control, where financial dependence is an element and consequence of direct economic dependence. In such a situation foreign capital is free, through the banks under its control, to support or set back by means of its credit policy, any particular economic sector, to promote the development of the industries complying with its own interests, to hinder that of others running counter to them, to influence export trade and to keep the local national capital even in the field of credits in a dependent state. On the other hand, it can, through the regulation of money emission, impose at will inflation (or deflation) on the country, "taxing" thereby the entire population, but especially, by means of the decrease in real wages, the wage workers employed by it. Thus it can also influence the budget position and the balances of trade and payments of the country.

An extreme form of financial and monetary dependence characterized most of the colonial countries, particularly in Tropical Africa. At the eve of independence, none of the countries in Tropical Africa had its own national currency and central bank exclusively authorized for emission. In the British colonies, e.g., the local currency was issued by the so-called currency boards, and the money issued was covered 100 per cent with pound sterling by the Bank of England—ensuring thereby substantial credit sources for the

---

[43] "The international relations of Third World countries as a whole", writes Ismail-Sabri Abdallah, "continue to take place along a North-West/South axis. Three-quarters of Third World exports go to OECD countries. We import from them more than we export, both percentage-wise and in absolute monetary terms, the balance being financed by credit." He refers to the IBRD figures, according to which in 1975 Third World countries' imports from the industrialized countries amounted to 123 billion, while their exports to the latter did not exceed 26 billion US dollars. (Ismail-Sabri Abdallah: Op. cit., p. 18.)

metropolitan country. The British colonies were compelled to keep the exchange reserves (mainly the dollar reserves) earned from foreign trade transactions in the Bank of England, and were deprived of the right of free disposal.

The banking operations were usually handled by the subsidiaries of a major British colonial banks (as, e.g., the Barclays Bank, the Standard Bank of South Africa, the Bank of West Africa). These banks could influence, through the credit-financing of trade, the development of the whole economy of the country in question, could put a check by a discriminative policy (by credit restrictions, by demanding impracticable guarantees, etc.) on the growth of the national capital, and draw out of the country, by transferring a considerable part (30–40 per cent) of their assets to metropolitan banks, a substantial proportion of the national income, diminishing thereby the internal credit sources. The picture was similar in French, Belgian and Portuguese territories where finances were entirely under the control of foreign capital, the currency in circulation was a local variety of the currency of the metropolitan country (as e.g. the French colonial franc), and the banking operations were transacted by the subsidiaries of the metropolitan banks.

Though this extreme form of dependence has mostly disappeared, yet in the majority of developing countries the domestic credit system, banking and insurance activities, especially the banking operation connected with foreign trade, are still under the control or strong influence of foreign banks. The giant international banks with their large capital supply, wide business connections and excellent information are able to influence the entire turnover both in cash and credit, and by granting loans to the state or the state banks of issue, or through the purchases of government bonds, by opening current-account credits to the state, and through their rediscount and interest policy, can control almost the whole financial life. They usually also acquire an interest in the financial institutions established by the national capital or government. In many countries the local, national currency is still tied to the metropolitan one, and the emission policy itself is influenced from the outside. So often is the exchange-rate policy.

(2) Another, perhaps milder, but not less important form of monetary dependence is the one which ties most of the developing countries to one of the leading capitalist countries in matters of foreign exchange. This foreign exchange dependence is the consequence of relational trade dependence and is connected with the distorted structure of foreign trade and, by extension, the whole economy. A country which sells most of its export products or buys most of its imports in the traditional metropolitan market is necessarily also in a dependent relationship in matters of foreign exchange with the latter. (Just as vice versa, foreign exchange dependence strengthens the maintenance of relational trade dependence.)

226

In a sense, we can speak of foreign exchange dependence not only in relation to the developing countries. If there are close trade relations between two countries, then the changes in the foreign exchange position of the one country make themselves also felt in the economy of the other, and vice versa. (This is, of course, mutual dependence.) If, however, one of the two is a country with "hard" and the other with "soft" currency, the latter may find itself in a grave situation if its export sales to the "hard" currency country, for financial or other reasons, come up against difficulties. Unless it succeeds in earning "hard" currency from other, new trade relations, or in finding any other way-out, it will be compelled to restrict those of its purchases on the world market for which hard currency is absolutely necessary.

In the case of the underdeveloped countries, foreign exchange dependence is always such a *one-sided* dependence. It is always the latter that depend for their purchases on the hard currency of the advanced countries. It is only their financial and overall economic situation that reacts most sensitively to the changes in the flow of foreign exchange owing to currency revaluations, import restrictions, tariff modifications, etc. in the advanced capitalist countries, and above all in the metropolitan country itself[44]. In addition, for a developing country which encounters difficulties in the traditional market or finds its foreign exchange balances—for certain, maybe political reasons—frozen, the possibility of earning "hard" currency from another relation or securing the necessary foreign exchange for its imports in some other way is rather limited. Moreover, and this is perhaps the most important factor, the developing countries are, owing to the one-sided, distorted character of their economy, the under- or lopsided development of industry and the monocultural type of agriculture and the distorted pattern of export, increasingly import-sensitive, i.e. their economic development and even their current needs call for a large volume and a wide range of imports (including, of course, "hard" goods, machines and equipment). Therefore, their foreign exchange receipts, usually earned from the export sales of a few agricultural or mineral products, are decisive for their whole economy. Monetary dependence expresses also financial dependence, and vice versa.

The ties of foreign exchange dependence are especially strong in the case of countries which, mainly on account of the foreign exchange problems of their trade relations, are in the monetary zone (sterling or franc zone) to

[44] This applies even to the oil-exporting countries, despite the new financial power they represent now owing to the enormous oil revenues and despite also the "recycling" troubles or the dangers the latter may cause by upsetting the stability of the entire monetary system of the West. Insofar as their oil incomes are directly or indirectly tied to the leading Western currencies, they can hardly avoid (merely compensate for) the consequences and losses arising from the domination of the leading capitalist powers over the international monetary system.

which they belonged prior to their independence and in which the leading role is exercised by the finance capitalists of the metropolitan country. The currency position of the metropolitan country directly affects their finances, and the financial circles of the metropolitan country are able to get an insight into, and in some cases even a control over their foreign exchange policy. (As to the latter, the International Monetary Fund, led by the advanced capitalist powers, plays a particular role in "advising" on exchange-control policies of countries seeking to borrow capital in the case of prolonged balance of payments deficits.)

(3) The most outstanding and form *par excellence* of financial dependence is the heavy *reliance on foreign financial resources* (concessional or non-concessional ones). This form of dependence is the symptom and consequence of both the unequal structure of international economy bringing about a widening "trade gap" and regular losses to the underdeveloped countries and the structural limits of domestic capital accumulation for local, national purposes in the distorted economy of the latter.[45]

Most of the developing countries are faced with an acute shortage of capital and an increasing deficit in balance of payments.[46] They badly need foreign assistance to finance their economic development programmes, the trade deficit caused by unfavourable price changes and increasing import demands, and often even the current budget deficit.

International *financial assistance* is one of the most controversial issues. Not only because the major part of what is actually registered as such can, in a wider context, be doubted, and the way it is measured is subject to various critical remarks and reservations,[47] but also because it is questionable what actual effects and consequences follow from it for the recipient countries and the international economy as a whole.

No massive assistance programme, no planned transfer of financial funds, however enormous, could really solve, even if it happened to be implemented, the basic problems inherent in the structural weaknesses of the world economic position of the underdeveloped countries, which tend to reproduce, in an expanded way, the "gaps" and deficits. Nevertheless, it is beyond doubt that the urgent claim of a great number of developing countries and the fact of poor living conditions, misery, epidemics, illiteracy, hunger and unemployment in the group of countries embracing

[45] See Chapter III.

[46] The current deficit of developing countries, except the major petroleum exporters, increased from 10,758 million US dollars in 1970 to 41,235 in 1975. In 1976 and 1977, it decreased and remained around 28,000 million dollars. (*Handbook of International Trade and Development Statistics*, p. 391.)

[47] One of the most comprehensive critiques is given by Janis Dellagrammatikas: *Monopolkapitalizmus és a harmadik világ* (Monopoly Capitalism and the Third World). Kossuth, Budapest, 1972.

the majority of world population lend the issue of international financial assistance a paramount significance in international economic, political and diplomatic relations. Besides the international flows of private capital, characteristic of the monopolistic stage of capitalism, the practice of extending government loans, credits and grants, bilateral or multilateral financial assistance, of concessional resource transfers, is also an organic constituent of the mechanism of international economy today. Financial assistance policy reacts with great sensitivity to changes in the latter, while it also exercises a considerable influence on the processes and conditions in the world economy. (A debate and the final decisions, e.g., in the United States, the major "donor" country, on the aid programme affect not only a wide sphere of her domestic economy and balance of payments, but, besides the economy of the recipient countries, also the international economy as a whole, owing to a number of indirect consequences in monetary and trade relations.)

Concessional financial flows may serve as palliatives to ease temporarily the disturbances and sharpening contradictions in the mechanism of the world capitalist economy, while they make the latter more defenceless against fluctuations and uncertainties resulting from one-sided manoeuvres.

The contradictory implications of financial assistance both for the donor and the recipient countries warn us to avoid simplifications in its assessment.

Per se, i.e., if taken out of the context of real economic relations in the national and international economy of capitalism, financial assistance to another country means undoubtedly a financial burden, a sacrifice on the part of the *donor* country. Apart from the question of who (which social class or stratum) actually bears this sacrifice, such an assistance certainly reduces, if taxing the consumer incomes, the domestic purchasing power and market, or limits the accumulation fund and investments.

Such a "sterile" case, however, can hardly be applied to any capitalist economy and even less to the dominant powers of international capitalism. First of all, because a capitalist economy, in general and by its very nature, tends to produce (to a varying extent, depending on the business cycle, of course, but regularly) "idle capital",[48] a certain gap between saving and investment,[49] a kind of "overaccumulation". This strange phenomenon, which is just the opposite of what is the concomitant of a socialist economy (where investment opportunities always exceed the available funds of saving) may actually make it economically reasonable and useful to

[48] We have already discussed its implications for the international movement of private capital, the export of working capital in imperialism.

[49] This problem is in the very focus of Keynesian analysis. Since (at least) Keynes, it has been acknowledged by non-Marxist economists, too.

accomplish a financial transfer abroad, even in the form of donations, and reduce there "idle capital" burdening the overall rate of profits. (If, nevertheless, the result is, in most cases, not a reduction of "idle capital", then it is due to the fact that the working masses rather than "over-accumulating" capitalists are taxed to bear the burden of financial assistance.)

Secondly, what is more important and realistic is the role such financial assistance can play in the context of overall economic and political relations between the donor and the recipient countries.

As regards the *political* role of financial aid, which, of course, can hardly be separated from the economic one, it is a common place to refer to the way neo-colonialism makes use of such an "assistance" for its own purposes, and to how the defence of world capitalist interests is served by "sacrifices" made, if necessary, by imperialist powers (more precisely by the working masses in the leading capitalist countries).

One of the most obvious examples is *military aid* given, in whatever form, to puppet regimes to defend them and the dominated area against nationalistic people's forces, or the financial assistance for military and "security" purposes which is supplied for the protection, in general, of the capitalist system, to countries where socialist forces are dangerously growing.

Such an "aid" is, as a rule, not only detrimental to the economy of the recipient country, which is compelled to buy arms in return for a considerable part (often as much as 90 per cent) of the aid, and to incur immense additional military expenses wasting thereby local resources, too,[50] but also means good business for the armaments exporters of the "donor" country.

Political considerations (and military interests) have always played a decisive role in US aid policy. After the Cuban Revolution, in order to prevent further revolutionary changes and to maintain the power *status quo* in Latin America, the US government launched a new aid programme called "Alliance for Progress", which was declared to aim at the promotion of certain (modest) social reforms and at the improvement of the masses' living conditions, social and political circumstances. As a matter of fact, very few of the declared aims have been attained. The foreign policy of the United States has continued to consider the business interests of US companies and the oppression of socialist forces to be much more important than any of the modest reforms in Latin America. Thus the reforms, widely advertised at the beginning, were soon forgotten. The same happened later to the "human

[50] For example in 1957–58, the countries of the Baghdad Pact spent about 1 billion dollars on military investments, in addition to the 332 million dollars received as aid. In the last two decades the military expenditures of the Third World as a whole exceeded about three times the total amount of the official development assistance received.

rights campaign" of the Carter administration, which claimed to aim at cutting the antidemocratic regimes off from any assistance. The leading political and military circles of the United States continue supporting reactionary regimes, even fascist dictatorships, and prefer the status quo to any social reforms with uncertain political results.

Apart from the political (and military) reasons and purposes of financial assistance, the extension of government loans, grants and donations may, indeed, be advantageous *economically*, too, for the donor country if the latter possesses other channels of economic relations with the recipient country. And this is exactly the case with the leading capitalist countries occupying dominant positions in practically all fields of international relations. Their financial assistance usually results in the expansion of their commodity exports and thereby in a boost effect on the national economy. If bringing about such results, the financial sacrifice of a "pure" donation may be (over-)compensated for. This is made possible by the export-multiplier effect, that is, the income-generating chain reaction of expanding production and employment.

In addition, insofar as the expansion of exports takes place in favour of the most dynamic industries, it will further improve the position of the advanced country concerned in the international division of labour, and will make the internal division of social labour more effective by regrouping the productive forces in the interest of the most dynamic industries. And if the expanded export releases the accumulated stock of certain commodities, it may prove of crucial importance for staving off a threatening recession, for preventing a crisis from assuming economy-wide proportions or for diminishing its grave consequences.

In most cases, bilateral government assistance, grants, development lending and other concessional flows are tied either directly (like export credits), or indirectly *to commodity exports* of the donor government.[51] This again applies primarily to the leading capitalist powers.[52]

Over and beyond the marketing interests, namely the expansion of commodity exports to the recipient countries which is, of course, more

[51] According to the Pearson Commission in 1967, for example, more than 5/6 of the government assistance of the OECD countries was "tied" aid, which meant commodity purchases of at least 20 per cent over the world-market prices for the recipient countries. (See *Partners in Development*. Report of the Commission on International Development. New York, 1969, p. 77.) And in the case of commercial credits of a private character, the surplus charge was sometimes over twice the world-market price. (Ibid.)

[52] In 1970, about 98 per cent of the assistance fund of the IDA, the American aid organization, was used for purchases in the United States. (V. Rymalov: Western Aid to the Third World: Statistics and Reality. *International Affairs*, 1972, No. 4, pp. 22–23. For comparison, it is worth noting that in 1978 the share of "untied" flows in the total amount of bilateral official development assistance was only 21.6 per cent in the case of the United States, while it averaged nearly 45 per cent in the total of all DAC countries. (Source: *1979 Review*. Op. cit., p. 231.)

directly served by *export credits*, the extension of financial assistance may involve other economic aims and possible benefits, too. The donors often tie their grants or loans to certain projects conductive to their own interests, or stipulate as a condition their right to supervise the utilization of the financial resources provided. In this way, they may prevent an economic policy contrary to their interests from being pursued, industrial branches competing with their own from developing, and trade relations with non-desired partners from being established by the recipient country.

Prior to offering grants the leading capitalist countries very often send missions to the underdeveloped country, sometimes through the international organizations under their control, to work out recommendations for the size and conditions of the loans and grants, to take part in the detailed working out of the development programme, and of course, to represent in every case the interests of those granting aid. The economic experts of the mission often remain in the country for a considerable time to supervise the implementation of the aid programme, while at the same time, of course, they exert an influence on the government's economic policy.

The government loans and grants of the leading capitalist countries, as well as some of their multilateral concessional contributions, may also be used to strengthen, in general, the *private sector* of the recipient developing country and to improve, in particular, the *operational conditions* for the metropolitan capital there. The leading capitalist countries are reluctant, as a rule, to support the development of the public sector in the productive branches proper, and they give assistance preferably in those areas (such as transport, communication) which improve the profitability of private investors. They often compel the recipient countries, by explicit conditions or implicit expectations, to provide, in return for the loans and grants received, guarantees and certain benefits for the metropolitan capital and staff, and to create a "favourable climate" for foreign investments. Such guarantees and benefits may be: freedom for foreign companies to operate, free repatriation of capital and profits, compensation against expropriation or full indemnity in the case of nationalizations, various tax and customs allowances, free remittances for foreign investors and the technical assistance staff. The easing, by financial aid, of the balance of payments position of the recipient country is itself a factor which objectively alleviates profit and capital repatriation.[53]

[53] "There is a strong possibility that these financial flows, other than those for military purposes, are, for the most part, a dependent factor, i.e. it is likely that they are determined by the flows of direct private investment. In the first place, this financial assistance is increasingly made available on the basis of the 'economic viability' of the projects which it is supposed to support. This, in general, means that private capital must be forthcoming to make use of the overhead capital financed by public capital. In the second place, a large proportion of bilateral assistance aims at easing the balance of payments position of

The economic benefits accruing to the "donor" countries are, of course, much more outstanding and obvious in the case of *non-concessional flows*, such as direct and portfolio investments, export credits, bank lending, etc.

As regards the inflow of financial funds, which, especially in the form of foreign direct investments, but partly also in the case of portfolio investments and resident banks' activity, establish *foreign working capital* with its further growth from local accumulation sources in the recipient developing countries, we have already discussed its basic role in the world economy of monopoly capitalism and in the economic dependence of the latter's periphery. Its consequences far exceed the scope of "financial dependence", since the export of working capital, contrary to conventional economistic assumptions, can by no means be reduced to a transfer of money or to be simplified to the reallocation of a "factor of production". It is exactly by reason of its implications for the unequal pattern of ownership control and the allocation of structural roles in international economy and because of its far-reaching internal effects and socio-economic consequences that we identify and mark it as the most fundamental, direct and *par exellence* capitalistic form of economic dependence.

This does not mean, of course, that reliance in this form on the inflow of foreign financial resources is not a part of financial dependence, too. Moreover, what we have to emphasize in this context is the very *indebtedness* process which follows not only indirectly (via structural effects), but also directly, though implicitly, even from the direct investment form of non-concessional inflows. The growth of capital assets in foreign ownership does imply growing indebtedness, which (though ignored both by the conventional practice of international statistics[54] and by those economists who consider it natural for certain countries to have properties in others' economies without equality and reciprocity) necessarily appears as a debt burden in the balance of payments once this foreign capital is repatriated or nationalized with compensation.

Tropical-African economies in order to make possible either the importation of capital goods or the repatriation of profits and capital." (G. Arrighi: *International Corporations . . . ,* Op. cit., p. 28.)

[54] It would require a separate study, probably a very long one, to survey and critically revise all those statistical methods, measurement norms, indicators and formulae applied in international documents, reports and statistics which, as a growing paradox, contrary to all the results of, and theoretical critiques by, the most prominent scholars also of the West, Marxists and non-Marxists alike and contrary to a number of internationally accepted principles, still reflect and perfectly correspond to the most orthodox, conventional and widely defeated "pure economics". The fault does not lie simply with statisticians. (Just to mention other examples: the application of quantitative indicators of "development", the way of calculating GDP and GNP, the neglect of ecological effects and of non-renewable natural resources in national accounting, etc. (From the great many critiques in international literature of misconcepts and false methods see, e.g., François Perroux: *The Concept of Global, Endogenous and Integrated Development.* Working Document for a UNESCO Expert Group Meeting, Quito, Ecuador, 27–31 August, 1979.)

As to the case of *export credits* (which are mostly, though not exclusively, offered as private credits on commerical, non-concessional terms), they have become, as a matter of fact, general practice in the world' economy, particularly with respect to certain commodity trade (such as capital-goods export). However, owing to the worsening balance-of-payments position of many of the developing countries, the expanded exports to them increasingly presuppose the credit financing of deliveries. Thus the international pattern of export-credit flows is also asymmetric, making this "normal" business practice a component of the indebtedness process and financial dependence of all but a few Third World countries. The same applies also to other non-concessional flows, bank loans, credits, "official capital on market terms", private lending, etc.

In view of the multiple interconnection in the world capitalist economy between most of the financial resource flows, including the concessional ones, and capitalist business, moreover some form of exploitation, it is hardly correct, indeed, to equate all concessional flows with "development assistance" and indiscriminately to assume a financial sacrifice on the part of the "donor", even in the case of grants, donations without any repayment obligation. Since some of the "donors" take advantage of this "assistance" and are the real beneficiaries of the complex system of their economic relations with the recipient countries, maintained by the help of concessional transfers, therefore, the right term to use would be, at best, "financial co-operation" or "business self-financing" rather than "aid" or "assistance".

We should, of course, not generalize and deny or underestimate the cases of real assistance, of unselfish donations motivated by feelings of solidarity and humanitarian considerations.[55] Yet, we can formulate this as a rule or principle: the less a "donor" country is involved in the complex system and machinery of the international exploitation of developing countries, the more her financial (and other) resource tranfers to the latter are to be qualified as assistance. And conversely, the more a "donor" country benefits from this machinery and from the system of economic relations with the developing countries, the less her transfers, including concessional flows, should be considered as assistance, and the more her ODA commitments should be registered as obligations (hardly sufficient) for compensation payments.

---

[55] Such motivations certainly play an important role in the voluntary donations (in money, in kind, or in labour) of the population, individuals and collective social organizations, especially of the labour movement, socialistic and democratic organizations, religious institutions, etc., but are hardly decisive in the policy of most governments. The very influence of the business circles, big companies and military leadership on governments makes it impossible for such motive forces to be primarily considered in their policies even if one or another member or leader of the cabinet should show a certain responsiveness to them.

234

Unfortunately, in UN practice the assessment, the "norms" or targets of the donors' performance do not reflect at all such an obvious rule despite undeniable facts[56] and the principle formulated in the Declaration on the Establishment of a New International Economic Order providing for the right to full compensation for the exploitation and depletion of, and damage to all resources. A re-assessment, therefore, of the donors' performance would certainly shed some light on the "puzzle" of the complete failure of international financial assistance in the Development Decades.

An even more realistic appraisal of financial assistance could be achieved if information were also extended over such questions as *to whom* and *for what purposes* the assistance was given and *how* it was used. Without such information, the public opinion not only of the international community but also of the donor countries themselves is misled (or manipulated).

Looking at the financial transfers, concessional loans, grants and non-concessional foreign funds from the angle of the *recipient countries* in general, we must see, on the one hand, the actual need of the developing countries for foreign financial resources and the potential benefits they draw from them, and, on the other, also the dangers, disadvantages and losses which may, and in most cases do, accompany even the concessional flows (as follows from the above-discussed interests and motivations of the major donors).

External financial resources are, of course, not equally required by all developing countries and can by no means be regarded as an absolute and inevitable precondition for economic development even in the poorest countries. It is obvious and evidenced both by history and logic that it is never scarce financial resources, the so-called capital shortage, that consitutes the basic impediment to socio-economic development and that

---

[56] Statistical figures, despite all their shortcomings (such as incomplete registration of all foreign direct investments and particularly of all incomes from them, concealment of the growth of foreign assets from local resources, of the real size of foreign "working capital" in the developing economies, not to mention its actual sphere of control there, of disguised profit repatriations and of a great many indirect benefits from economic relations and brain drain, etc.) do not leave any doubt about facts, notably about the one *which* country benefits most from economic relations with the Third World and from the international economy in general. For example, the share of the USA in the total direct investment incomes of all developed capitalist countries was around 70 per cent, while its share in total foreign investments was less than 50 per cent only in the mid-seventies. In 1977, the USA had seven times more investment incomes from abroad than what it spent on foreign investments. Nevertheless, the performance of other donors is assessed and compared with the USA's in the same way, by the ratio of total "net" (?!) flows or concessional "official" assistance to GNP. But even a comparison on such an incorrect basis clearly shows that the United States lags far behind a few advanced countries, such as Sweden, the Netherlands, Norway, Denmark, etc., in aid-giving. Ranked according to the ratio of net ODA to GNP, the USA came only thirteenth among the 17 DAC member countries in 1977. (Sources: *Handbook of International Trade and Development Statistics*, pp. 370–376, and *1979 Review*, p. 208.)

this bottleneck itself is the consequence of the social or structural limitations of surplus production and accumulation.[57] Nevertheless, it is also true that the urgent tasks of eliminating mass misery, hunger and unemployment and the pressing need for a more rapid and healthier development make it really imperative for many developing countries, espcially the poorest or least-developed ones, to draw on foreign aid. Also the transformation of internal structures can develop at a higher rate if external resources are made use of temporarily. The financing of growing imports also makes it necessary to rely on external resources.

In this way, the use of foreign financial resources may help to bridge acute difficulties, if only temporarily. Depending on the conditions and the way of utilizing it, foreign aid may be beneficial to the recipient economy in other respects, too, namely by shortening the time of the realization of important projects, by contributing to the expansion of employment, to the improvement of sanitary and socio-cultural services.

The dangers and disadvantages resulting from even concessional loans and grants obviously follow from those motivations and potential advantages already discussed that govern the policy of the leading capitalist powers.

It is self-evident that any country that bases the financing of its economic development programme primarily on foreign resources and is able to maintain the temporary equilibrium of the state budget only by foreign aid and to make good the recurring deficit of its trade balance only by foreign credits will be left to the mercy of the donor countries. This holds true all the more, the fewer the number of donors and creditors. The more the flows of loans and donations originate from one single and the most powerful metropolitan country, and the more these flows accompany the flow of private investment capital from the same country, the greater the danger involved in reliance on financial assistance.

By stopping, for some reason, the flows of financial resources, by withdrawing grant commitments and freezing loans, etc., the major "donor" country may cause unexpected difficulties in the recipient country, may hinder the implementation of its development programme, or even divert the direction of its development policy. Financial assistance, or its withdrawal, may be used for economic, political and military blackmail.

The intensity of the financial dependence of Third World countries is determined, of course, not only by the size of financial inflows, or even by their conditions, including political and economic strings attached to them, but also by the degree of their concentration by origin, i.e. by the more or the less diversified "club" of donors-creditors, by the type and attitude of the latter, and in the post-colonial period increasingly by the size and utilization of domestic accumulation sources, by the bargaining power and repayment

[57] See Chapter III.

236

capacity of the recipient country, by the strength of state control over the country's economy, including especially external relations (foreign trade, monetary transactions, remittances, foreign exchange, etc.) and, last but not least, also by economic cooperation among developing countries, their "collective bargaining power."

In view of all these and the fact that foreign loans, credits and grants, unlike "working capital" in foreign ownership, are of a definite lifetime, financial dependence in this form may actually diminish (even if the amounts received are growing in absolute terms) and lose much of its intensity and one-sidedness according to how the national economy of the recipient country develops, and how, in general, the international economic position of developing countries improves individually and collectively.

If, however, the received loans and grants hamper or discourage the transformation of the distorted economic structure of the recipient country, *if* they contribute to the perpetuation of its unfavourable trade position, losses and deficits, *if* they open the door to foreign monopoly capital and its profit repatriation, i.e. *if* they exert adverse effects on the balance of payments, and *if* they prevent the development of the public sector in profitable industries, depriving thereby the state budget of important sources of revenue—*then* they tend to reinforce and reproduce the country's reliance on new financial inflows from abroad.

Until recently, a self-reinforcing and cumulative tendency has been characteristic of the financial dependence of the greater part of developing countries.

This *increasing indebtedness* of the developing countries is to a certain extent favourable for the leading capitalist powers in that it enables them to force the debtor countries into a more dependent relationship, a consequence fully in line with neo-colonialist aims. But beyond a certain point this cumulative process may threaten actual repayment, and leads to a situation which entails serious economic and political dangers for the capital-exporting countries (e.g. the expropriation of their capital), which may induce these creditor countries rather to write off in the end part of their outstanding claims.

It is partly the danger of such risks and the intention to eliminate competition among themselves, together with the endeavour to conceal neo-colonialist aspirations, that compel the leading capitalist powers to handle the granting of loans and aid to the developing countries through the various international organizations and multinational agencies. It is to be noted, however, that financial assistance from the latter, particularly from UN institutions rather than from individual metropolitan powers, coincides, in general, with the interests of developing countries because it helps to avoid one-sided dependence and also because, and insofar as the operation of these international or multilateral agencies are controlled, or at least influenced, by other than metropolitan countries.

The *volume* of financial flows, both concessional and non-concessional, to the developing countries has considerably though unevenly increased since the fifties. There was an abrupt growth in flows in the second half of the fifties, mainly in official assistance form followed by a certain slow-down or stagnation already in the early sixties. UNCTAD I (1964) gave some impetus to concessional flows, yet in 1968 when UNCTAD II was held, a fall in absolute terms was observed. After 1968, a more or less continuous increase followed again both in concessional and non-concessional flows. In nominal terms, total net flows to the Third World rose from about 8 billion US dollars in 1960 to 18.86 billion in 1970 and to 78.39 billion in 1978. (In real terms, the annual rate of increase was about 7 per cent for the whole period.)[58] Rapid world inflation in the seventies considerably reduced the real value of the resources transferred.[59]

There have also been changes and fluctuations in the pattern of resource flows. While in the sixties concessional flows came in volume close to the non-concessional ones, the latter's growth in the seventies (from 11 billion in 1970 to 56 billion in 1978) far exceeded that of the former (from 8.9 billion US dollars to only 22.5 billion).[60]

Despite the urgent demand of the developing countries and all the efforts made by UN bodies, especially the UNCTAD Secretariat, no essential and lasting improvement has been achieved in the overall conditions, terms and facilities of international financial flows to the countries in the greatest need. The ratio of "tied" aid has continued to be high.[61] Since as early as the late sixties (i.e. prior to the oil-price "explosion") it has become increasingly difficult for the low-income countries to get loans and credits on concessional terms. The situation in this respect showed further and dramatic deterioration when the crisis, with its concomitant domestic problems (such as increased unemployment, accelerated inflation) and the balance-of-payments difficulties caused partly by higher oil-import costs, etc. induced several developed countries to cut their budgets for assistance programmes, moreover to apply protectionist trade policy measures, which plunged their developing partners into additional troubles.

The shift in the pattern of total financial flows in favour of non-concessional finance, the sharp decline in official development assistance as

[58] *1979 Review*, pp. 65, 199.

[59] Between 1970 and 1974, for example, the flow of official development assistance approximately doubled in nominal terms, but practically stagnated in real terms. (World Economic Survey 1975, Ch. II. UN. ECOSOC. E/5790/Add. 1, 1976, p. 34.)

[60] *1979 Review*, p. 199.

[61] According to the 1979 DAC report, approximately 40 per cent of total aid was available only for procurement in the respective donor country in the late seventies. (*1979 Review*, p. 83.)

238

a percentage share of total flows to developing countries,[62] the worsened maturity structure and interest-rate conditions of loan capital supplies (shifting towards relatively short-term and higher interest-rate private resources), parallel with increasing trade problems and deficits caused by the recession, slower growth, protectionism, and inflation in the developed capitalist countries as well as by changes in the structure of world-market prices, etc., harmfully affected the majority of developing countries throughout the seventies, and especially the oil-importing, primary-exporting and low-income countries.[63]

The decrease in the share of concessional resources in total financial flows to the Third World was accompanied by a parallel decline in the share of low-income developing countries in foreign financial resources throughout the seventies. Much of the increase in total financial flows was taken up by a few developing countries with rapidly expanding exports or other attractive conditions for non-concessional financing such as Brazil, Mexico, Venezuela, South Korea, Indonesia, the Philippines, Iran and also Egypt and Algeria.[64]

Owing, besides fundamental structural inequalities in the world capitalist economy, to worsening financial facilities and trade conditions for the major group of low-income countries, on the one hand, and to the relatively higher-income and MNC-dominated industrial exporter countries resorting to foreign resources with shorter maturities and higher interest rates, on the other, the *external indebtedness* of the majority of developing countries increased further and cumulatively in the seventies.

[62] The share in total net resource transfers of official development assistance (including bilateral flows from all resources and multilateral assistance, too) dropped from about 60 per cent in 1960 to 50 per cent in 1970 and then to 30 per cent in 1978. (See op. cit., p. 199.)

[63] "The initial fourfold increase in oil prices between 1973 and 1974 immediately added some 12.5 billion dollars to the total import bill of the non-oil developing countries. The further lo per cent increase agreed by OPEC in September 1975 is estimated to have added another 1–1,5 billion dollars in 1976... A deepening world recession during the first half of 1975 brought about a decline in the real value of their exports which, coupled with a deterioration in their terms of trade, raised their combined deficit on current account ... to the exceptionally high level of some 49 billion dollars". The permanent annual loss of real income of the oil-importer developing countries caused by further oil-price increases (such as the 1979 round) is estimated to amount to about 10 billion dollars, and the annual loss resulting from the recession and inflation in the developed capitalist countries to be a-proximately of the same order of magnitude. (See *1976 Review. Development Cooperation.* Paris, 1976, pp. 35–41 and *1979 Review*, p. 63.)

[64] In 1978, for example, the total share of three countries (South Korea, Indonesia and the Philippines) in the net flow of all foreign financial resources to Far East Asia was over 67 per cent, the share of three countries (Brazil, Mexico and Venezuela) in Latin America's total receipts added up to more than 44 per cent, two countries in Africa (Algeria and Egypt) absorbed around 35 per cent of the total flows to the region, and one country (Iran) alone made up nearly 40 per cent of all resource inflows to the Middle East. (See *1979 Review*, pp. 250—251.)

The total debt of all developing countries (including OPEC members) increased from 75 billion in 1970 to 180 in 1975 and further to 264, 322, 366 and 403 billion US dollars in 1976, 1977, 1978 and 1980, respectively. For non-OPEC countries, the total disbursed debt increased from 63 billion in 1970 to 149, 217, 264 and 303 billion in 1975, 1976, 1977 and 1978, respectively.[65] Despite the oil-price "explosion" and the growth in oil revenues, even the OPEC countries continued to further increase their debts.

Besides the increasing concentration of total debts and especially of debt services in a few countries,[66] the relatively high share in the total debt outstanding of the low-income and large-population countries is a particularly unfavourable phenomenon.[67]

In face of the basic tendencies in the world-capitalist economy with increasing inequalities, development and trade "gaps", and of the self-defeating effects, due to concomitant exploitation and income losses, of most of the resource transfers to the Third World as well as of the lasting structural crisis of the world economy with on-going inflation, etc., there is no hope of halting the cumulative process of indebtedness without fundamental structural changes both in the international division of labour and in the internal economy of the developing countries.

Hence, financial dependence of the developing countries, even in the form of reliance on concessional loans and grants from foreign sources, implies significant dangers, disadvantages and losses to these countries not only as a consequence (though not independently) of the influence that the dominant creditor and donor countries are exerting on their economic policies, nor by providing the possibility, or rather widespread practice, of attaching "strings" to financial assistance and of using it as a political blackmail, etc., but also by bringing about cumulative indebtedness and increasing losses from debt service.

[65] Op. cit., p. 260 and A. Benachenou, op. cit., p. 185. We have to note that the figures, unfortunately, include those of a few non-Third World countries, too (such as Spain, Turkey, Greece, etc.) and that there are slight differences in the figures of different sources.

[66] For example, in 1977, seven countries (Brazil, Mexico, Indonesia, South Korea, Venezuela, Peru and the Philippines) absorbed about 36 per cent of the total disbursed debt of the Third World. In the same year, Brazil and Mexico paid more than 11 billion dollars as debt service, nearly 30 per cent of the total debt service of all developing countries. (This is, by the way, one of the evident signs of the negative consequences of an industrial growth engineered by transnational companies. (See op. cit., pp. 254–258 and our remark in the previous footnote).

[67] The low-income countries with over 1.3 billion population, representing 61 per cent of the total Third World population, had a total debt of 62.5 billion dollars, i.e. a 24 per cent share in the total debt outstanding of the Third World in 1977. India's debt alone was nearly 15 billion dollars. (Ibid.)

(d) DEPENDENCE ON FOREIGN TECHNOLOGY
AND "TECHNICAL" ASSISTANCE

Contrary to what the internationally accepted and applied terminology (stemming from a conventional economistic approach)[68] suggests, this form of dependence involves by no means something like a "technical" or a primarily technological aspect. Its substance is, instead, the human factor of development, i.e. the most decisive factor. Both "technological dependence" and the heavy reliance on "technical assistance", closely interrelated as they are, constitute primarily the manifestation of an asymmetric relationship between the centre (the metropolitan countries) and the periphery (the developing countries) of the world economy in respect of the supply and development of *human resources*. It is perhaps the most serious consequence and symptom of "underdevelopment" that countries with abundant human resources, with what is called an "unlimited supply of labour" or "overpopulation", have to resort to *foreign* human resources and to the imported results of human labour.

This involves dependence on "intellectual" (human skill) imports whether in a materialized form (such as the import of technologies, standardization systems, patents and licences, know-how and research findings) or in a "live" form (as the import of experts, advisers, managers, technicians, teachers, etc., i.e., educated, qualified foreign labour, or as the import of skill and knowledge by those who have been trained and educated abroad on foreign scholarships). No surprise that the metropolitan powers and their monopolies make use of this dependence and tend to bind to themselves the developing countries "intellectually" and "technologically", too. This endeavour of theirs corresponds, no doubt, to the actual needs of the developing countries for assistance in these fields. And, as we shall see, just as "financial assistance" is a phenomenon with two sides, the one being built upon a *real need* for financial resources, and as such exerting, subject to appropriate conditions, a favourable effect, and the other being

---

[68] In conventional Western orthodoxy, labour (i.e. the human "factor") is just one of the equally important factors of production, while capital as technology is another, born independently of the former and substituting it in varying degree. Accordingly, the development of what Marxism calls the productive forces appears as a productivity increase resulting from new, better technology. In this conception, the very source of technology (and capital), of all technological and economic (social and cultural) development, namely *human labour*, is deprived of its central, primary and decisive role. Its relation to technology is merely a question of proportion. Moreover, the qualitative development of human labour and human resources, which (proceeding not only from training and education but also from accumulated practical experience, innovative and research capabilites, etc.) is, in general, the primary determinant, both historically and philosophically, of the development of techniques and technologies, appears itself as a "technical" process making advance if increased inputs are made in schooling. In sofar as these inputs are made or financed from abroad, "technical assistance" is supplied.

accompanied (as pointed out before) by dangers and harmful consequences—so also (and increasingly at that) "technical assistance" and transfers of technologies are controversial phenomena of a mixed character.

This specific form of dependence has come to the fore rather recently, especially in connection with the efforts made by developing countries in industrialization, public education, etc., and also with the technical assistance policy of the leading capitalist countries and the investment policy of their multinational companies.

This does not mean, of course, that the supply of technology and educated people to the underdeveloped countries was not determined by the metropolitan countries and their monopolies even long before.[69] While previously, however, this dependence manifested itself in the general retardation of industrial development and technical education, and thus it could by no means assume—at least in industry—the form of technical assistance, today it appears that the metropolitan countries have relinquished their monopoly over industrial production and technology as well as over technical education and are ready to support industrialization in the developing countries by promoting technical education and sharing their technology. What is really involved here, however, is the fact that the industrial capitalist countries—as compared to the developing ones—have such a strong monopoly position in the production of new technologies and in industrial research and development (R and D) today that it makes not only possible for them to relinquish the monopoly over manufacturing industries, in general, but even necessary because of the required expansion of the market for new capital-goods, technology and know-how. Moreover, we are witnessing today the emergence of a sort of monopoly, which is the more dangerous the more concentrated it is,[70] namely the

[69] "During the course of the historical development of the capitalist system..., the developed countries have always diffused out to their satellite colonial dependencies the technology whose employment in the colonial and now underdeveloped countries has served the interests of the metropolis; and the metropolis has always suppressed the technology in the now underdeveloped countries which conflicted with the interests of the metropolis." (A. G. Frank: Sociology of Development..., Loc. cit., p. 51.)

[70] This monopoly, on account of the economies of scale, the larger capital supply and the accumulated scientific capacities, has been more and more concentrated in the USA. This is the prophecy of Newsweek: "European industries will function more and more under foreign licensing agreements; they will become subsidiaries of U.S. parent companies, which will sell them their know-how and manage Europe's production... Research costs are too high. The transatlantic technological gap is a fact of life." (Quoted by A. G. Frank: Sociology of Development..., Loc. cit., p. 52.) We have to note, however, that US hegemony in R and D has been challenged or limited not only by the progress of the scientific and technological revolution in the socialist countries, first of all in the Soviet Union, but also by the concentrated and more and more collective efforts made by the West European countries within the EEC. (Not to speak of the technological development of Japan.) Hence, the validity for the future of this prophecy is questionable and depends on several unpredictable factors and changing conditions.

monopoly in certain key sectors of industrial development and the scientific and research capacity of the world capitalist economy (such as new electronics, automation, cybernetics, chemicalization, nuclear and space research, etc.). Getting now access to certain manufacturing industries, the Third World is to be excluded, provided the present tendencies survive, from possessing their own local centres of technological research and development, and is doomed to a lasting technological dependence.[71]

For their industrial development, the developing countries need patents and licences, blueprints, standards, technological specifications, machine installations and their component parts, special raw materials and, last but not least, specialists (engineers, geologists, economists, teachers, etc.)

When the leading capitalist powers give these countries "technical assistance" and when the metropolitan companies supply them with technology and know-how, they try to do it in such a way that the realization of the licences, blueprints, standards and technological specifications, etc., as well as the smooth operation of plants installed by them, and the working and repair of the machinery and equipment, should correspond to their technological and business policy and depend on deliveries from metropolitan firms and should remain under their technological control. They see to it that the production of the new plants does not embrace the whole cycle[72] of processing and that the component parts, standard equipment, motors and machines can be supplied from the metropolitan firms only. They arrange things so that the management of

[71] "Over 90 per cent of all living scientists and technologists are at work in the industrialized countries," writes Ismail-Sabri Abdallah. "Over 90 per cent of their activities are concentrated on research for the rich world and on converting their findings into protected technical processes even though a good number of them are relative to Third World nations." (Ismail-Sabri Abdallah: Op. cit., p. 16.) Hans Singer also point out that the present technology is "a technology developed in the rich countries, by the rich countries and for the rich countries." Though the extremely unequal distribution of "technological power" in the world cannot be measured simply by R and D expenditures (i.e. by the money spent on applied research, pilot and experimental development and scientific and technological institutions, etc.), "it is a striking fact that the share of the poor countries in world R and D expenditure is only 2 per cent. (H. W. Singer: The Development Outlook for Poor Countries: Technology is the Key. *Challenge*, May-June 1973, p. 44.) Ch. Moraze stresses that "so long as innovation is virtually the exclusive privilege of the developed countries, there is no hope for the others to make up for the lost ground... Since modern production is conditional upon scientific discovery and technical innovation, the countries where these are concentrated will always control the flow of goods." (Ch. Moraze: Créativité, science et développement: Pour une autre analyse. IDEES. Paris, PUF 1977. Quoted by Moises Ikonicoff: Transfer of Technology and Patterns of Consumption on the Periphery. *Labour and Society*, Vol. 4, No. 3, July 1979, p. 278.)

[72] "The segmentation of the production process which often accompanies multinationalization involves a transfer of technology. But this transfer is only partial, since it results from the separation of the components of the technical process as a whole. This is why, when this phase is reached, the reproduction and mastery of technology in the periphery becomes impossible." (M. Ikonicoff: Op. cit., p. 288.)

production and the technological leadership should remain directly or indirectly controlled by the metropolitan centre, through expatriate specialists sent from there to run the local firms or to advise their managers, and also through local citizens trained in the metropolitan centre and occupying positions in the management.[73] They show very little (if any) interest in local research and technological development. When foreign multinational companies, or the agencies sponsored and influenced by them initiate or support local research, it is focused mainly on the adaptation of metropolitan products and technology to local markets or on the exploration of new natural resources to be exploited by them rather than on developing new production processes and technology. Even if a developing country, owing to the efforts and sponsorship of its national government to establish national research institutions and industrial laboratories, happens to produce practicable research results, some technological innovations or inventions, there is little chance for the latter to be put into practice in local companies or any other firms, industrial and agricultural enterprises which are under their control.[74] Very often plants are only built for the production of the component parts of the main product manufactured in the metropolitan country or for the assembly of parts supplied therefrom. They are nothing but subsidiary units of the metropolitan firm, only appendices, not independent industrial plants. Examples abound in the Latin-American countries. Such cooperation is also a suitable means of tax and customs evasion.

This type of industrial cooperation between metropolitan companies and their local subsidiaries, or other firms under their control, and the concomitant concentration of the decision-making power in company headquarters, and often the leading positions held by their expatriates in the management of local firms, etc. explain why the production in certain industrial branches, the operation of important factories can, depending on foreign interests, be paralyzed overnight in developing countries.

[73] It is worth noting here that while formerly the almost complete blockade of industrial development impeded from the outset the development of education, and especially technical training, this process of "industrialization" which neglects the basic technological centres and relies on imported capital-intensive technology, "not only *restrains* the spreading of the 'learning process' over large sections of the population; in addition, even in the state-owned enterprises, it limits considerably the *range of experiences* that can be undergone in the periphery as crucial economic and technological decisions are made in the industrial countries". (G. Arrighi: *International Corporations* ... op. cit., p. 139.) That is how the materialized form of "intellectual import", that is the import of technology, is connected with "live intellectual import", the increasing demand for borrowing foreign experts, specialists, teachers, etc.

[74] "Even though India is equipped with its own research facilities, financed out of public funds, industry as constituted by subsidiaries of the large multinational firms has made hardly any use of the findings of this national research... As long as undertakings remain nlosely linked with foreign companies, their R and D units can only be an adjunct to the bigger parent company's research complex." (M. Ikonicoff: Op. cit., p. 282.)

This may have grave consequences for employment, the meeting of export commitments, the fulfilment of envisaged plan targets, the satisfaction of the needs of production of other branches, etc. With the unexpected withdrawal of expatriate specialists immense difficulties may be caused in economic management or in any other field of life (in the supply of medical staff, in public education, state administration, public services, etc.).

Through this cooperation the metropolitan monopolies can control the development of the individual industries of the developing countries, and the experts and advisers made available in the framework of "technical" assistance can have a decisive role in determining among other things the direction and spirit of economic policy, public education, etc.

It may become particularly dangerous if foreign experts occupy key positions in the economic and cultural life or in the army, take jobs of crucial importance for state administration in the decision-making or executive sphere. The one-sidedness of dependence and foreign influence may be stronger or weaker depending on whether the source of technical assistance is concentrated or diversified, and on the ratio of experts sent from or educated in the same foreign country, and on the extent to which this dependent relationship coincides—as regards its direction—with the direction of dependence in finances, trade or direct capital investments.

All this implies that "technological" and "technical" dependence, whether in its intellectual or materialized form, i.e. the importation of foreign experts or the training abroad of the local intelligentsia and the importation of foreign technology as embodied in machines, equipment, licences, etc. may constitute, very strong ties to connect the economy (mainly industry) and the intellectual life of the developing country with those of the metropolitan country. Insofar as the technology imported only in its ready-to-use form restricts, depending on its sphere of application, the demand for local research, technological and product development in the given country, and particularly if it does not exert any appreciable positive effect on the productivity and technical level of the supplying or manufacturing branches attached to that industry in a downward or upward direction, then it creates a lasting (not merely temporary) one-sided *technological dependence* and reproduces the need for technological imports.

Education and training on a scholarship basis within the framework of *technical assistance*, and the activity of foreign teachers, consultants and educationalists under such local programmes may bring not only benefits but also harmful consequences to the assisted country.

The direction and spirit of public education is of special importance for economic, social and political development of these countries. The assertion of the demonstration effects via education may result, through increased salary claims, a higher standard of living and greater needs, etc., in serious tensions (see later in Chapter III. 1). And since the development of education in these countries is characterized not by a proportionate widening and increasing of the pyramid of public education but, as in industrial development, by the appearance of "patches" of a superstructure without adequate basis and intermediate elements, the danger of the alienation of the highly qualified cadres from local society is accordingly greater. All this exerts a negative effect on the cohesive forces of society. It is hardly surprising then that the cadres trained in the framework of technical assistance often become also "physically" alienated from their own society, and, yielding to the temptation of better living conditions and a different way of life, and perhaps as a result of marriage, they prefer to settle down in the advanced country.

We also have to point out that in technological relations, in the transfer of technologies and in international educational and scientific cooperation there also finds expression, in general, an objective and therefore inevitable tendency: the internationalization of the development of the productive forces, science and technology. To disregard this process—even in the case of the most developed and largest countries—is tantamount to renouncing the common treasures of the scientific and creative activity of mankind. At the same time, it must also be considered that the inherited technological shortcomings and the scarcity of qualified labour, which are consequences of a foreign-induced and outward-oriented economic growth, compel the developing countries to make use, for the time being, of various forms of "technical" assistance. Consequently, it is not technological transfer and "technical" assistance in general that have to be replaced by other solutions, but rather positive alternatives must be substituted for the concrete negative content and forms of such relations, or their negative effects must be restricted.

What holds true, therefore, of the controversial, two-edged character of financial aid—more precisely, the transfer of foreign financial resources, of their positive and negative effect, depending on the concrete terms, the way and consequences of their utilization and on the given power relations—also applies, perhaps even to greater extent, to "technical" assistance and technology transfer: they may equally be the means of foreign control, intellectual penetration and domination and increase the distortion of structures (of consumption, investment, education, etc.) and even become a device to perpetuate income drain and inequalities just as they may also be the means of a real and successful transfer of intellectual energies and capacities, of free access to the intellectual riches of mankind.

We must not forget that, particularly in the field of "technical" assistance, intellectual sources are far less limited to a few leading capitalist countries than, e.g., capital supply in convertible currencies.

In contrast to "direct" economic dependence (this *par excellence* form of foreign capitalist domination materializing in the presence, the operation and controlling activity of foreign working capital, which reproduces itself and expands by local accumulation) and also contrary to trade dependence rooted in unequal structural roles in the world economy, moreover, in contrast perhaps even to the reliance on foreign concessional finance, insofar as the latter leads to cumulative indebtedness—the form of dependence manifested in reliance on "technical" assistance and technology imports can actually be turned round (though not easily) to gradually liquidate itself. This is the case when, e.g., "technical" assistance is directly used for the training of local cadres to substitute for foreign experts and "technical" assistance staff, or when technology transfer is (made or forced to be) combined with the transfer of R and D capacities to developing countries.

*

The above list and analysis of the forms of asymmetrical economic and "technical" dependence is, of course, far from being complete. Several important aspects and forms of dependence could be added. One of them would certainly be the "*food power*", a potential "food weapon", wielded recently but increasingly by the leading capitalist power, the United States, which, under the conditions of a structural imbalance in world food supply and in view of the grave malnutrition problem of the developing countries in general and of a few densely populated regions in particular, is a rather threatening one.[75]

Since the food-supply problem of the Third World is closely and primarily connected with the structural deformations of its rural

[75] In 1973–1975, the average annual net grain imports of the low-income developing countries amounted to 9–10 million tons. FAO estimated the grain deficit of these countries to reach 42–48 million tons a year by the mid-eighties. According to the estimates of Interfutures, the projected grain deficit of the Third World as a whole for the 1990s may be around 100 million tons. (See *1976 Review. Development Co-operation*. OECD, 1976, p. 30 and *OECD Observer*. Facing the Future. No. 100. Sept. 1979, p. 21.)

As regards US "food power" in the context of the global food supply problem, an excellent analysis of its background and implications is given by *Helena Tuomi*. She points out that the underdeveloped countries, which supplied the developed industrialized countries with an average of 12 million tons of grain a year, have all become net importers of that product. On the other hand, the United States has increased her share in world exportable grain supplies so much that in the seventies, together with Canada, she controlled a larger share in the latter than, e.g., the Middle East in crude-oil supply. During 1973 and 1974, the US share in world wheat exports grew to 53 per cent and in soya-beans and maize exports it was over 90 and around 75 per cent, respectively.

Tuomi calls attention to the serious dangers arising from such a situation by quoting a confidential CIA report, according to which world grain shortages "could give the US a measure of power it never had before—possibly an economic and political dominance greater than that of the immediate post-World War II years.—In bad years, when the US could not meet the demand for food of most would-be importers, Washington would acquire virtual life-and-death power over the fate of millions of the needy." (See Helena Tuomi: *The Food Power: The Position of Main Exporting Countries in World Food Economy*. University of Tampere, Institute of Political Science. Offprint Series 1, 1976. Offprint from Instant Research on Peace and Violence. No. 3, 1975, pp. 120–137.)

development[76] and a "demographic explosion", which is also rooted (as we shall see later) in distorted structures, and also in view of geographic and climatic imbalances, we can hardly expect an easy and rapid liquidation of this form of dependence, a short-run solution to the Third World's food problem even if, since the 1972/73, famine a few seriously affected countries have managed to improve their food production and supply.

Another form of dependence, not an "economic" one, though with certain economic implications as well, is related to Western dominance in *information*[77] *and communication*. The transfer of biased consumption patterns from Western "consumer societies" with all the consequences in import demand, import-substitutive industrialization and capital formation, etc., and a certain cultural dominance retarding, from this side, too, the development of the nation, its language and literature, etc. are but a few of the additional implications and effects arising from such a dependence.[78]

Further, the marked inequalities in the international communication and transport system (as observed, e.g., in the telephone, telex and broadcasting networks, in route maps, world airline and shipping routes, etc. also point to the dependent position of the developing countries in the international capitalist system.

2. INCOME DRAIN AND LOSSES

The systematic income drain from the developing countries (exploitation), and the systematic income losses of these countries manifest themselves (a) in a *direct form*, as a result of the capital export on direct investment account, or of the export of loan capital, and (b) in an *indirect form*, through foreign trade and financial-monetary relations.[79]

---

[76] This structural deformation manifests itself in the fact that—as *Rodolfo Stavenhagen* points out—"cash crops for export have displaced subsistence crops for local consumption, and while monetary incomes may have increased, food consumption has often decreased in the process." This also explains, among other circumstances, the apparent "paradox" why agricultural countries cannot meet their domestic food demand. (Rodolfo Stavenhagen: Basic Needs, Peasants and the Strategy for Rural Development. *Another Development*. The Dag Hammarskjöld Foundation, Uppsala, 1977, p. 40.)

[77] "Four Western news-agencies have a practical monopoly on news dissemination all over the non-socialist world ... Consequently, information within the Third World and about the Third World is inadequate and often biased or misinterpreted." (Ismail-Sabri Abdallah: Op. cit., p. 17.)

[78] "The history of world economy abounds with examples of the classical way of reproducing the dominant culture in a periphery area: *by enforcement*. Other ways, more subtle but not necessarily less important, are by *assimilation or by demonstration*. These are the 'modern' ways of making the various units ... accept the roles and functions assigned them by the centers of decision-making." (Helge Hveem: Op. cit., p. 33.)

[79] We shall disregard here the open forms of colonial exploitation (such as, e.g., the taxation of the local population; customs receipts from trade with a third country; the

(a) DIRECT INCOME DRAIN

Capital export to the underdeveloped countries results in the appropriation of part of the national income produced in these countries. The sums of money appropriated in this way show themselves mainly in the repatriation, the flowing back into the metropolitan country, of profits and interests, and so find their expression also in the balance of payments

The actual loss appears, of course, not only in the sum of repatriated profits and interests, but also in the *local growth of foreign capital assets*. The accumulation affected in this way, by making use of local labour and natural resources, does not constitute a real part of national accumulation, just on the contrary, it is an element of the country's indebtedness to foreign countries. This becomes evident and appears on the list of losses (and in the balance of payments) when foreign capital, together with its increment achieved locally, leaves the country, or when the national government has to pay compensation for the capital expropriated by nationalizations. Of course, not only capital increment, but the "original" capital itself, owing to its multiple reproduction, is, in fact, local production, the product of the labour of the developing country. (Reinvested profits are conducive to the internal accumulation of the national economy, and do not mean increasing indebtedness only if foreign capital is expropriated later without compensation.)

The significance of reinvestment in strengthening the position of foreign capital and in profit-making is much greater than generally assumed. Current capital assets can be regarded as the result of reinvested profits made previously rather than of new capital investments.[80] "Thus the increase of Western assets in the underdeveloped world is only partly due to capital exports in the strict sense of the term; it is primarily the result of the reinvestment abroad of some of the economic surplus secured abroad."[81]

Along with reinvestments, a great role is also played in expanding the profit-making activity of foreign capital by the various additional sources of financing (among them by credits granted by local state funds, banks and

---

maintenance, partly from local sources, of the colonial government, the administration and army, and the payment of foreign personnel employed in them at the expense of the colonial population; reparations imposed in the course of colonial wars; open plunder; requisition; forceful expropriations; forced labour; compulsory production; hired convict labour, and the use of other varieties of slave labour, etc.), as, today, they are, for the majority of the developing countries only the tragic memories of past history.

[80] For example, in the period 1870–1913, when total British investments abroad increased from about 1,000 million to almost 4,000 million pounds sterling, the total amount of *new* investments hardly accounted for 40 per cent of the income from past investments. And in the case of *Brazil*, about 50 per cent of direct US investments derived from the reinvestments of profits. (See Ignacy Sachs: *Foreign Trade and Economic Development of Underdeveloped Countries*. London, 1965, p. 81.)

[81] P. Baran: *The Political Economy of Growth*. New York, 1962, p. 179.

international financial institutions) also creating investment opportunities far in excess of new capital exports.[82]

As is well known, capital export has gained an increased importance since the transitional period from classical capitalism to monopoly capitalism, and it has become one of the principal features of the era of imperialism. The export of investment capital to the underdeveloped countries has, owing to the cheapness of land, raw materials and labour there, secured an immense economic surplus and a higher rate of profit than in the metropolitan country. Thus it has become not only a means of skimming off surplus (idle) capital, but has also counteracted directly the falling tendency of the metropolitan rate of profit. And the export of loan capital has, owing to the *higher* profit rate and the chronic capital shortage in the underdeveloped countries,[83] resulted in high sums of interest, enriching the class of metropolitan creditors.

In addition, capital export has been used as a means of increasing the export trade. The export of investment capital has secured, in the way described above, the relational dependence of the underdeveloped country and thereby a ready market for the metropolitan products. The export of loan capital was either directly associated with compulsory purchases in the metropolitan country, or promoted export trade indirectly, by providing the necessary foreign exchange for the importing country.

Exported *investment capital* enjoyed favourable conditions especially in the colonized territories where the metropolitan country ensured, through getting hold of the state apparatus, complete freedom of operation and the free transfer of profits and other incomes for its monopolies. It provided for these monopolies the necessary lands and the required labour, if necessary by force; it protected them against competitors and granted them various privileges. Where the metropolitan country did not seize the state apparatus, i.e. in the "non-colonized", formally "independent" countries, foreign private capital created these conditions for itself, after a tough struggle, ousting its rivals, gaining control over local capital and the seemingly independent local state apparatus, whilst also making use, if thought to be necessary, of the military and diplomatic support of the metropolitan country.

However, as a result of growing social tension, the evolving liberation movements, the emergence of new independent states in the place of the colonies and the changes in the international political atmosphere in general, the conditions for the export of investment capital, especially small-

[82] Characteristically, in 1969, e.g., only 9 per cent of the total foreign investments of US monopolies came from metropolitan new capital exports. (See Janis Dellagrammatikas: Op. cit., p. 89.)

[83] Both factors worked in the same direction: they pushed up the rate of interest due to the play of demand and supply of capital.

scale competitive capital, *greatly deteriorated* and the risks (owing to dangers like nationalization, restrictions on free profit and income transfer, increased taxation, state control and state regulation of the field of operation, etc.) greatly increased in a number of developing countries in the fifties and sixties. Therefore, the significance and weight of the export of loan capital, especially of *concessional government loans and grants*, grew considerably (at least for a while) in the most endangered domains.

A certain decline in the export of private capital for direct investments was (as we have seen) also connected with the fact that the traditional functions of capital export—the offsetting of the fall of the rate of profit, the acquisition of raw-material sources, the skimming off of capital and production surpluses — lost much of their former significance in the post-World War II period (at least up to the seventies), owing to changes in the economic structure of the advanced capitalist countries, the unfolding of the scientific-technical revolution, the market-expanding effects of integration, the abrupt expansion of state intervention, the emergence of a specific state market, the swelling of the unproductive sphere, etc. It was not, however, justified (not even in the sixties) to conclude from all this that the significance of the profit-making activity of foreign monopoly capital, especially of that already operating in the developing countries, or the importance of markets for the oligopolies have diminished in general, and that the leading capitalist powers only need their former colonies for political (and perhaps military) considerations—i.e. for the worldwide struggle between capitalism and socialism. Loans and grants continued to fulfil important tasks in defending the old positions of the foreign capital exported and invested in the past and preparing new opportunities for the export of investment capital, i.e. in ensuring profit sources and expanding or regaining markets. Loan capital has often been an effective means of securing more favourable conditions for investment capital and played an important role especially in the struggle against local or foreign rival capital,[84] and also in gaining control over the state.

What are the *sources* of the profits and interests that flow continuously as a result of capital export?

Owing to the weakness of the organization of the working class and the almost total lack of a stable and concentrated urban proletariat, and also to the great oversupply of cheap, unqualified labour, and to the fact that labour legislation was in its infancy, etc., *the exploitation of the labour force* was very high in the colonial period. This could be seen not only in the low-wage level, the lack or scarcity of sick benefits, old-age pensions, family allowances, unemployment allowances, and the length and intensity of the working day, but it was often supplemented by the system of various

---

[84] The again increasing role and share of private capital in the total capital inflow into the developing countries since the mid-sixties show the point.

deductions (as for rent, food, travelling expenses, etc.) by which the employers reduced the wages of the workers. In several countries most of the wage-earners were recruited from unskilled migrant workers who were still engaged in subsistence farming and took up wage labour only from time to time when leaving their families behind in the villages. Thus, along with the "absolute" forms of the exploitation of the working class (manifested in the length of working day and labour intensity), certain specific, "extraordinary" forms of relative exploitation (such as the exclusion from the minimum wage of the expenses of education and the maintenance of the family) also played an important role. The abundance of unskilled labour entailed in any case the fall in the price of labour power below its value. The foreign capitalist firms enjoyed monopoly positions as employers. They could often fix the wages arbitrarily and apply various forms of wage discrimination on a "racial" basis or on the basis of such qualities as "reliability", "loyalty", "discipline", etc.

The recent changes in the investment pattern of the foreign monopolies (with the already mentioned bias in favour of capital-intensive techniques) and the strengthening of labour organizations, due partly to the above changes and partly to the political development after independence, have resulted in certain shifts in the position of the working class of developing countries. The position of rural and migrant labour, owing to the limited labour-absorbing capacity of the capital-intensive industrial investments and the preventing or retarding obstacles to rural development and transformation, could not improve substantially. In fact, it has deteriorated even further in many places, as a result of the increasing population pressure in rural areas and the chronic difficulties of marketing the tropical products on the world market and the economic and social differentiation that is also spreading in rural areas. On the other hand, a relatively privileged, better-paid stratum of the wage workers is beginning to develop in the urban centres. Considering its income level and living conditions in relation to those of the rural and migrant workers and the rural population in general, this stratum might be called "labour aristocracy", if the application of this concept to such a specific and above all temporary social product—which, in addition, is not accompanied by any normal stratification of the working class, and whose feeding does not require the increased exploitation of *other* working-class strata or countries—were not to lead to utterly false and deceptive conclusions.[85]

[85] We shall return later to the political implications of the question. As far as the economic and social implications are concerned, it is perhaps worth noting that several economists ascribe the limited growth of employment, with a strange, but from the perspective of orthodox economics a well-known logic, directly to the excessive increase in the wage level of the urban working people. According to H. A. Turner, e.g., the whole benefit of economic development in Africa during the 1950s fell to the wage workers and employees. (Reference in G. Arrighi's paper.)

252

For the profit sources of the foreign monopolies these shifts do not mean any substantial changes. They have not led to any appreciable alteration even in the profit-wage proportions.

Another important source of profit or monopoly extra profit is the systematic appropriation of a part of the new value produced by small-commodity agricultural producers, small and handicraft industries, or the appropriation of part of the profits of the local non-monopoly small capitalists through the mechanism of purchasing and selling prices (as well as by means of usury credit, though the latter belongs rather to the sphere of loan capital). Since in the economic branches occupied by foreign capital monopoly prices prevail, prices in the non-monopolized branches or in the sphere of the small-commodity producers move around a centre much lower than the "prices of production".[86] Foreign firms often force small-commodity producers or smaller local capitalist enterprises into the position of "outside producers" by monopolizing their supply and marketing. They supply them with raw materials, tools, means of transport, etc. at high prices and buy the products at low prices. A similar method is adopted by the big foreign commercial companies in selling manufactured goods to the peasant producers or in buying up their agrarian produce.

The profit source of the foreign-owned commercial companies is not only trade with the small-commodity producers and the appropriation of part of the new value produced by them, but also the appropriation of part of the income of the whole population of the country in general, in that these companies enjoying a monopoly position can sell their goods at prices higher than the "market value" or "the price of production", that is they can share not only in the profit of the industrial capital but also "produce" their own profit.

Foreign capitalist companies often make a profit by selling at high prices to the newly independent state or the national capital the lands formerly received from the colonial government as concessions free of charge or at a nominal price, as well as roads, railways and harbours built by forced labour. They even demand compensation sometimes for the *projected profit*.

Since foreign investment capital is concentrated mainly in the export sectors of the developing countries, the realization of *profit*—as the greater part of the national income, too—comes about through foreign trade and (owing to relational trade dependences, above all in the metropolitan country) by marketing the agricultural or mineral primary products or the metropolitan manufactured goods made from them.

The principal aim of the export of capital on direct investment account was often not to make a profit, but to ensure the supply of the metropolitan industrial branch or company with mineral raw materials, or to seize

[86] "Production price" in the Marxist terminology means (is equal to) costs of production (amortization, cost of materials and wages, etc.) + average profit.

strategic raw materials, or simply to prevent competitors from getting important raw-material bases. The expropriation and exploitation of non-renewable natural resources by foreign capital, though usually fused with those forms of exploitation,[87] already mentioned, can be distinguished as a specific form of exploitation, as a loss of natural resources. The detrimental effects of this will be felt when the growth of the national industry is hampered by the earlier exhaustion of the national resources, the narrowness of the raw-material basis or the deterioration of the conditions of exploitation.

The source of the interests on exported loan capital is different, according to who takes up the loan in the developing country and what he uses it for. If it is the smaller or greater local entrepreneurs who use it for industrial plants, the stepping up of agricultural production, the development of trade, transport or banking business, then the interest income of foreign loan capital stems from the "decimation" of the profit of the local industrial, commercial or bank capital, respectively. If it is landowners who receive the loan (mortgage loans), then part of their ground rent will leave the country, in the form of interest, or, in the extreme case, even their property will come into foreign ownership. If, however, it is the small industrial or agricultural small-commodity producers who take up a loan of foreign origin to ensure the conditions of simple reproduction or to expand production, which is seldom the case, then a further part of the new value of their product (in addition to the part appropriated by trade), or even the disposal of the assets of the bankrupt small-commodity producer constitutes the source of interest income of foreign capital. These various ways foreign capital can be placed exert a more or less detrimental effect on the economy of the developing country as they usually skim off most or the whole of the profit or income surplus realized by the loans, and serve the "harnessing" of local capital and the acquisition, by the means of credit usury, of important economic positions rather than the easing of capital shortage, the artificial expansion of the sources of local accumulation. Private entrepreneurs, and private individuals in general, could very seldom take up foreign loans directly and they usually got them through the local subsidiaries of foreign banks, in which case the interest paid by them left the country as the profit of foreign bank capital, i.e. as the "product" of bank capital.

But the loans advanced in whatever form to the local capitalist entrepreneurs or small-commodity producers proved a very effective means of transforming the economic structure of the underdeveloped country in line with the interests of the foreign capital and the metropolitan country,

[87] One of the most well-founded demands of the developing countries in the context of a New International Economic Order is the claim for full compensation for the exploitation and depletion of their resources.

254

and of artificially developing certain branches that were suitable for the latter. Furthermore, they have been used with great effect for strengthening the local bourgeoisie and especially the local allies of foreign capital, i.e. the comprador strata, especially in recent times when in a number of developing countries the question of power and the question of the way to further socio-economic development have been brought to the fore.

If it is the government of the developing country which receives the foreign loan from the leading capitalist countries—and this is increasingly general practice in the new historical situation, owing to the application of neo-colonialist methods, and the increased risks or simply owing to legislative restrictions in the developing countries—then the source of interest receipts may be the income of state productive investments realized by loans, the taxes levied from the population, the inflationary emission or the foreign exchange surplus achieved by the increase in exports or the decrease in imports. (As a matter of fact, the latter is also true for the former cases as interests have to be paid usually in hard currency.) Insofar as the loans are used for productive purposes, for *profitable investments*, and the interest payment at a reasonable rate and the redemption can be affected from the yield of the investment, i.e. of the new establishment *already in operation* or the foreign exchange saving or surplus achieved by it, they really may be *helpful* for the country and may promote its economic development providing that the investment itself does not further weaken the economic structure of the country.

Very often, however, owing to the conditions of capitalist loans or the faulty economic policy pursued by the government of the developing country, the redemption of loan and the payment of interest are effected from the increased taxation of the population or from inflation—in addition to increasing the traditional export deliveries whose state subsidies are financed from the same sources and which, in the last analysis, further deteriorate the terms of trade. Both solutions affect primarily the working population and, in addition, inflation further deteriorates the country's balance of trade, since it induces increased imports and hampers exports.

In spite of this, such loans may even be useful or necessary for the developing country if they enable really important tasks being already on the agenda to be completed and urgent investments to be made and if the *state control* of commanding heights and the *planned* use of these loans within a strategy to restructure the national economy are guaranteed. The interest charges, at least in terms of quantity, do not usually constitute an important factor in the exploitation of the country by foreign capital. Since, however, these loans (and grants)—as we have seen—are usually tied by the capitalist powers in an open or concealed way to the conditions of guaranteeing free operation for foreign private capital and of raising their exports, they aim at maintaining or increasing exploitation by foreign capital "working" in the country and by exchange inequalities.

Loans spent on infrastructure, e.g., improve the conditions of the realization of foreign private capital (they diminish transportation costs and cut the time of the turnover), increase the rate of profit in the country and as a rule promote the exportation from the country of the mineral and agricultural raw materials. And the loans granted for financing the deficit of the budget or the balance of payments serve only temporarily to bridge the gap arising from the repatriation of profits and the increasing losses in foreign trade, to enable the exploitation of the country through these forms to go on without major difficulties. The credit-financing of *exports* too, which serves mainly the ousting of the competition and the monopolizing of the market or the expansion of export opportunities in general, is profitable above and beyond repayment and interest receipts, or more exactly results in economic surplus in the form of income drain through the channels of foreign trade. (See the next sub-chapter.)

Thus, if we looked at the process in a "pure" sense, and took only partly into account the "disturbing" circumstances, such as, e.g., the definitely anti-colonialist policy of the governments of numerous developing countries, the political pressure of the masses as well as the changes in international political relations, the struggle between socialism and capitalism, in general, which shape political considerations behind aid programmes, then we would arrive at the following mechanism as one of the "pure" manifestations of neo-colonialism,[88] displaying the inherent tendencies of neo-colonialist exploitation in the new international situation.

The government of a leading capitalist country, as the representative of monopoly capital, gives a loan or grant from the tax payments of the population to a developing country. As a result of the utilization of this financial assistance and of the conditions attached to it, on the one hand, the circumstances will improve for the operation and realization of the private capital exported from the metropolitan country, the rate of profit will rise and so more profit will flow back to the metropolitan country (or the withdrawal of capital will be possible owing to the temporary improvement of the balance of payments position of the developing country).[89] On the other hand, the exports to the developing country will increase[90] owing to

[88] The mechanism outlined here is, of course, only one, though a characteristic, manifestation of neo-colonialism, but it by no means exhausts the concept of neo-colonialism.

[89] "... Public capital will in general reinforce whatever tendencies are favoured by the inflow of private capital: in the case of a high propensity to invest in the area, it will provide the financial resources necessary for the materialization of that propensity; in the case of a low propensity it will ease the shortage of foreign exchange to make possible the outflow of capital, thus worsening the situation in the long run." (G. Arrighi: Op. cit., p. 135.)

[90] Talking about the advantages of aid programmes, E. R. Black, a former director of the World Bank, pointed out that they ensure significant and immediate markets for US commodities, stimulate the development of new overseas markets for American companies and orientate the national economies affected towards the free enterprise system in which the

the temporary market-expanding effect of the loan[91] and the income drain will also grow through the channels of foreign trade. Profit repatriation (or especially the withdrawal of private capital) and the deteriorating balance of trade position will unfavourably affect the balance of payments of the • developing country and also diminish the sources of internal accumulation, and so the financing of deficits also has to come from foreign loans. The developing country is compelled to resort to foreign loans in order to fill the gaps arising and constantly recurring from the repatriation of the profit from metropolitan capital and the losses through foreign trade with the metropolitan country while it still pays for it with interest and increased dependence caused by indebtedness.[92] The payment of interest is, in the last analysis, drawn from taxation in the developing countries, too. Thus taxpayers of the latter pay to make it possible for the metropolitan monopoly capital to exploit them and their country more intensively while the taxpayers of the metropolitan country bear the burdens and risks of loans that assure this exploitation in the interest of their own monopoly capital.

This "pure" mechanism provides the explanation for the fact that loans given to the developing countries may be profitable to the monopoly capital of the leading capitalist countries even at a low interest rate and on favourable repayment conditions. Even if they cancel or reduce repayment, these loans as well as the directly or indirectly tied grants may lead to a general increase in exploitation, at the expense of a specific, secondary form of exploitation embodied in interest receipts.

It must be emphasized, however, that the mechanism outlined above only expresses a "tendency" and as such cannot prevail in its "pure" form. Therefore, the question of capitalist loans and grants given to the governments of the developing countries is a complex and contradictory problem, as we have already discussed, which can only be evaluated individually, together with the actual concrete circumstances, and taking into account, of course, the basic tendency.

American firms may prosper. (See H. Magdoff: Economic Aspects of US Imperialism. *Monthly Review Pamphlet*, No. 24, 1966, p. 5.)

[91] As "an ever-increasing share of this income (i.e. the income of the underdeveloped countries derived from their export products sold on the market) is absorbed by the amount spent on the amortization of capital imports and the payment of interests...", therefore "...the market is narrowing down to an extent which can only be compensated for by additional accelerated capital exports (of the advanced countries). In other words, at the given rate of excess-profits the *scope of market creation by capital exports* tends to narrow down." (Gy. Göncöl: Op. cit., p. 23. My italics.—T. Sz.)

[92] J. Kubitchek, a former President of Brazil, stated: "Latin America is ... in the peculiar state of man who is receiving a blood transfusion (i.e. the grants and loans from US) in one arm and donating blood through the other." (*New York Times*, Aug. 20, 1962. Quoted by I. Sachs: Op. cit., p. 82.)

It might be clear from the foregoing that the most direct and "open" form of income transfer from the developing countries is profit repatriation arising from direct capital investment.

It is "open" in the sense that it appears in the balance of payments and can be measured statistically. Since, however, the figures in the balance of payments neither reflect the total investment incomes of foreign capital, nor are they reliable even with respect to the actually repatriated amounts of investment incomes, we can hardly call it "open" in a general sense.

An accurate statistical measurement of actually repatriated profits meets with grave difficulties, which arise from the obvious intention of foreign companies motivated by tax considerations and efforts to improve their local image, or at best to mitigate national resentment against them, to understate the sum of such transfers and disguise profit repatriation in other forms. Besides the intertwinings of capital and, in several countries, the free, still uncontrolled money flows abroad, the loopholes of control, briberies, corruption, etc., also bias downwards the sum registered.

It is especially the "trans" or *multinational" corporations* with their wide international network of operation and a more or less vertically integrated structure crossing national frontiers that have a great many opportunities to disguise their actual profit repatriations. They often enjoy a *monopoly* position in the new industries and a monopoly power or strong influence in market and price relations as well as in local financing, credit and foreign exchange policies, etc., by which they can easily exploit the extra sources of monopoly profits.[93]

The multinational corporations, even under conditions of state control and subordination to parastatals, or of pratnership with the latter, still have various, mostly disguised or indirect opportunities for siphoning their investment incomes out of the country.

Even if a national government in the host country makes serious efforts to check the profit-earning and income repatriation activities of the multinational companies, it is extremely difficult to establish an effective control in a single developing country. Not only because such a control requires anyway an extremely well-trained and politically conscious and reliable staff, but also because of the wide range of business transactions and influences of these companies which manoeuvre between several countries

[93] "Because of the dependence of developing countries on transnational organizations, the latter have frequently been able to obtain *favoured market positions*. This has included assurances of a virtual monopoly position in respect of the local manufacture of particular products. In addition, such a *monopoly position* in respect of manufacture has often been extended to the subsequent sale of products on account of developing countries' wish to conserve foreign exchange by eliminating possible imports of competitive products. The end result of this would seem to have been in many cases *high monopoly profits* for the corporations in question." (UNCTAD IV. Role of Translational Corporations . . ., Op. cit., p. 16.)

as well as between various spheres of activity within the country concerned.[94] "Transfer prices" are one of the most effective ways and means for the vertically structured multinational companies to escape effective control and to siphon off profits in a disguised form.[95]

"The cost of servicing human capital",[96] payments (usually at monopoly prices) for management and technical skill, for patents, licences, feasibility studies, technological specifications, trade marks, expert and consultancy services, etc. may absorb a considerable part of surplus and, in spite of their "cost" appearance, include *de facto* profits.

Close cooperation with, and influence (often very strong) on, the local government may ensure additional advantages and disguised profit opportunities via, e.g., tax concessions, accelerated depreciation allowances, overvalued exchange rates, low interest rates, easy access to public funds, i.e., the use of public financial resources, import duty allowances, etc. Furthermore, the advantage of cooperation with the state may also be realized in government protection against outside competition in the local market and against labour movements (ban on strikes, wage freezes, etc.).

The degree of exploitation by foreign capital is, of course, the highest in countries where the economic position of foreign capital is the strongest and its operative freedom is the greatest, that is, where direct economic dependence is the most intensive.

The profits and dividends foreign capitalist monopolies transfer from the developing countries are usually much more than the capital they export to them. This conclusion can be unambiguously drawn even from the otherwise rather unreliable, always underrated and often contradictory or incomparable figures of various official statistics.

In the mid-fifties—according to GATT data[97]—foreign investors repatriated about 2,500 million US dollars annually from the developing

[94] "If the foreign interests also control patents and licences, they can determine the prices on semi-finished products, the flow of reserve parts and the costs for machines. If it is a vertically-integrated company, they can determine the company's profitability by controling the sale market and various forms of internal price-setting... The MNC also has the possibility of transferring its economic surplus within and between states, which is apparent in regard to currency-speculation. This is connected to the internal trade within the MNC...
...The problem for the national authorities is to find and patch the holes that exist; it is a matter, in other words, of determining the real prices/costs, which is often impossible, and to uncover evidence of manipulation in bookkeeping. There are known cases of MNCs which have made use of two and sometimes three different books." (J. Annerstedt and R. Gustavsson: Op. cit., pp. 40–41, 53–54.)

[95] "Vertically integrated corporations, through their transfer-pricing policies, can avoid taxation"—stresses *Keith Griffin* in his International Transmission of Inequality. (*World Development*. Vol. 2, No. 3, 1974, p. 6.)

[96] See G. Helleiner: New Forms of Foreign Private Investment in Africa. ERB. 1967. No. 12, University Dar es Salaam.

[97] GATT. *International Trade, 1959*. Geneva, 1960.

countries. In 1960—according to estimates made on the basis of UNCTAD figures[98]—the sum total of repatriated profits and interests amounted to about 3,300 million, while in the mid-sixties the profit income alone from direct investments made in the developing countries was estimated[99] to be around 4,500 million dollars, of which more than 90 per cent was repatriated. In the period 1963–1967, the income of foreign capital investors increased by an annual average of 12 per cent, and by 1967 reached 5,800 million dollars.[100] In the late sixties, investment incomes from developing countries surpassed—according to OECD data—7,000 million dollars a year. (The average for 1968–1970 was 7,100 million dollars.)[101] In the early seventies, the outflow of direct investment incomes was around 8 billion dollars. In 1979, as indicated by the same source, about 10 billion dollars were remitted as dividends and repatriated profits to foreign investors from developing countries.[102]

Let us see a few data concerning the profits of British, French and US capital earned in the Third World.

For example, during the fifties 80 per cent of the profits obtained abroad by British monopolies originated from investments in the developing countries, while not more than 52 per cent of their capital export was directed to these territories during the same period. According to official data for 1952–63, the profits coming from the developing countries amounted to 7,600 million pounds sterling and surpassed two and a half times over the sum total of capital exported.[103]

The latter proportion also seemed to be typical of US direct investments in the fifties. It is estimated that the monopolies of the USA repatriated an annual 2.5 dollars' worth of profit on every dollar invested in the developing countries in the period between 1946 and 1959. While only 40 per cent of their capital export was directed to developing countries between 1950 and 1958, nearly 60 per cent of their foreign profits came from there.

In the sixties, though less than one-fifth of American and British private capital investments were made in developing countries, almost half of the total investment incomes of the USA and one-third of Britain's originated in the Third World.[104]

In the period 1950–1965, the total flow of US direct investment capital into Latin America, Asia and Africa (including a few developing countries

[98] V. Rymalov: Western Aid to the Third World: Statistics and Reality. *International Affairs*, 1972. No. 4., pp. 22–23.

[99] *World Bank*. IDA Annual Report. 1970, pp. 47–48. (See V. Rymalov: Op. cit., p. 21.)

[100] *Review of International Trade and Development 1978*. UN, New York, 1970, p. 100.

[101] *1972 Review*. Development Co-operation. OECD, Paris, 1972.

[102] *1979 Review*. Development Co-operation, p. 89.

[103] See E. Khesin's paper in *Soviet Economists Discuss...*, p. 67.

[104] B. Brown: *New Trends in Trade and Development*. Op. cit.

there) amounted to about 9,000 million dollars, while the reflux of investment incomes therefrom registered about 25,600 million dollars.[105]

In 1969, for example, when developing Asia and Africa had only an 11 per cent share in the direct investments of US private capital, 43 per cent of American profits from all foreign investments came from Asian and African developing countries.[106] In the period 1970–1977, the total amount of direct foreign investment incomes earned by the United States and Britain increased 2.4 times and 2.3 times, respectively.[107]

As regards the French companies, in 1963 the Minister for Economic Co-operation emphasized in a discussion in the French National Assembly on the aid policy that the sum of repatriated profits and salaries was almost as high (7,000 million francs in 1962) as the total governmental aid and private capital export.[108]

Besides American, British and French companies, a number of other Western firms (among them West German, Japanese, Dutch, Belgian, Swiss, etc.) are also making huge profits in the Third World.

In the late sixties, all foreign direct investments (in current prices) rose only by 7.25 per cent a year, while the estimated incomes of foreign investors increased by 11.51 per cent, on annual average.[109]

In the seventies, the investment situation showed a somewhat modified picture. For a while, new foreign direct investments, including reinvestments, increased more than total (repatriated and reinvested) investment incomes. Nevertheless, throughout the period 1970–1977, foreign investment incomes each year considerably (about 2–3 times) exceeded total foreign investments in the Third World. The gap between the two was especially wide in the case of developing Africa and the Middle-East (though in both areas the growth rate of foreign investments was faster than that of investment incomes). In South and South-East Asia, even a rapid increase in foreign investments could not keep pace with the growth of investment incomes. The rate of the latter was almost twice the rate of the former from 1970 to 1977. The total amount of the (registered) repatriated profits from the Third World (100.2 billion US dollars) was 2.3 times the sum of all direct foreign investments (42.2 billion) made in the period of 1970–1978. (In the case of Latin America and South and South-East Asia it

[105] H. Magdoff: Economic Aspects of US Imperialism. *Monthly Review*, Vol. 18, No. 6, p. 39.

[106] K. Talbot: *Towards a New Economic Order*. The Budapest Working Group Meeting of the World Development Conference. Feb. 13–15, 1975. Working Document, p. 11.

[107] See *Handbook of International Trade and Development Statistics*, pp. 370–376.

[108] See V. Lyubimova's paper in *Soviet Economists Discuss...*, p. 157.

[109] See Memorandum. Democratic and Popular Republic of Algeria. 1974, Algiers, p. 117.

was 1.2 times the latter, while in the case of Africa and the Middle East it was 3.9 and 51(!) times, respectively.[110]

It is wholly evident from what we have outlined above that here we are dealing with an enormous, systematic and open income drain. Therefore, even if we disregard other detrimental consequences of foreign capital investments such as the distortion of economic structure and the increased import sensitivity, etc., we can hardly say that these investments, in spite of repatriation, have after all been only beneficial to the developing countries as well.

The open form of a "loss" arising from *foreign loans* is the payment of interest. Though, as we have already stressed, the exploitative nature of foreign loans cannot be concluded merely from the fact of interest payments and their rate (moreover, this "cost of servicing" may be negligible in certain cases as compared to the benefits of these loans, depending on their overall conditions and use), yet the cumulative indebtedness of developing countries, reflecting, as a rule, also the nature of most of the loan capital exported to them, is accompanied by a rapid increase in their *debt service*. The latter includes, of course, repayments, too (which, by the way, and contrary to the case of foreign investments, lead to the self-liquidation of at least a given loan). The rising trend of both debt services in general and of interest payments in particular is clearly shown in the statistics.

In the early sixties, the annual debt service of developing countries was between 2,000 and 3,000 million dollars. This grew rapidly during the sixties and reached 9,400 million in 1970, of which 2,800 million served as interest payments. From 1970 to 1977, the total annual debt service of developing countries increased (in nominal terms) to 41,200 million, of which interest payments reached 14,300 million, while total debt burden grew from 74,700 million to 264,400 million (current) dollars. In 1980 the latter reached 403 billion dollars and the annual debt service amounted 59.1 billion.[111]

(b) INDIRECT INCOME DRAINS AND LOSSES

In addition to the direct, mostly open forms of income drain (profit and interest repatriation) dealt with in the foregoing, a whole mechanism of indirect forms of surplus transfer through foreign trade, banking, monetary, technological, etc. relations has been built into the capitalist world economy. These transfers appear mostly in impersonal forms (apart from a few exceptions as marginal cases), owing to their indirect and "natural" character in conformity with the movement of the world economy. While profit-making and repatriation are concerned with

110 See *Handbook of International Trade and Development Statistics*, pp. 364–369, and A. Benachenou; Op. cit., p. 66

111 See *1979 Review*, p. 259, and A. Benachenou: Op. cit., p. 185.

transactions between two or more but always identifiable partners, indirect transfers seem to be simple losses usually sustained by the world economy as a whole (or, in the case of the advanced countries, they seem to be national gains obtained from the world economy as a whole). Among these indirect forms there are some (like the losses due to the deterioration of the terms of trade) which can be grasped and measured more or less easily and there are some which are less or not amenable at all to measurement and appear in disguised and less unambiguous forms (as, e.g., the immanent inequality of exchange between an advanced and an underdeveloped country).

Let us examine a few of those forms of income drain asserting themselves through trade relations, and then those embodied in banking, monetary and other relations. We shall begin with the most hidden, most disguised form: the immanent inequality of exchange[112]. It is all the more justified to start with the latter as the other forms of transfer through trade make it even more concealed and less tangible while at the same time not diminishing but rather strengthening its effect and consequences. Consequently, it is simpler and more logical to proceed from this most abstract form towards the more concrete ones.

(1) *The immanent inequality of exchange*, which in Marxist terminology is usually referred to as the problem of the exchange of unequal quantities of labour, asserts itself *even* in the case of the formal equality of exchange, that is of the observance of the "given" price proportions of the world market, or more exactly (at least in Marxist terminology) in the case of exchange at a certain "international market value" or "price of production".[113] This

---

[112] Since the first edition of this book there has been wide debate in international literature on the so-called "unequal exchange". The debate was sparked off by Arghiri Emmanuel' book, *Unequal Exchange. A Study of the Imperialism of Trade.* (Monthly.Review Press, 1972, NLB, London. First published as *L'Échange inégal* by François Maspero, 1969.)

Though the debate is very relevant, as can be seen from what follows, to our explanation of the "immanent inequality of exchange", we cannot deal with it here in view of the extremely wide scope of the theoretical problems raised by and involved in the debate. My forthcoming *Theories of the World Capitalist Economy*, pays particular attention to the theories of "unequal exchange", critically investigating in detail Emmanuel's work and also the views of the main participants (including Marxists) of the international debate: Charles Bettelheim, Samir Armin, Oscar Braun, Jagdish Saigal and Jan Otto Andersson.

[113] This distinction between exchange at the "given" world-market prices and exchange at the "international value" or "price of production" is worth making, because the former, which includes *monopolistic* relations as can be observed in everyday experience, contradicts from the outset even the *formal* equality of exchange. But even some Marxists would disagree with the application at the world market level of the Marxist technical terms "market value" (the value of a commodity produced by the socially necessary, average amount of total, both "dead" and "live" labour) and "price of production" (the sum total of average profit and the capitalist cost of production the former being the result of the equalization of the rate of profit between different branches of industry), as the monopolistic relations of capitalist world economy make the appearance of such categories impossible from the very outset. No doubt, the *appearance* of such categories, either in the world economy or in individual national economies, presupposes free competition and factor mobility. This does not mean,

immanent inequality can, of course, be pointed out only by way of abstraction, and can be qualified as "income drain" only *under certain conditions.*

As this problem is closely connected with Ricardo's theory of "comparative costs" which does not attribute any significance at all to the lasting disadvantages arising from the inequality of the quantities of labour exchanged and denies the operation of the law of value on the international scene, it seems practical from this point of view to return to the problem we have already often touched upon of the relationship between Ricardo's theory and the reality of capitalist world economy.

Ricardo assumed a "system of unrestricted free trade" (fighting, as a matter of fact, for such a system in the face of the then prevailing feudal restrictions) and laid emphasis only on the differences in "*natural endowments*", on the comparative advantages arising from them. He had in mind such a system of world trade or a system of the international division of labour whose members are equal, with no appreciable developmental differences and unbridgeable gaps between them, each expanding, under the conditions of free competition and liberal external trade, the productive branches most advantageous to it (that is an international division of labour that has never existed nor can ever exist under capitalism).

The question to what extent this theoretical hypothesis of Ricardo was realistic and historically justified *then* (i.e. in the ascending period of capitalism) and *there* (i.e. in England, the country most advanced in capitalist and industrial development) and *from the point of view* of the class he represented, is entirely different from the question whether his theory provides an acceptable explanation for the actual division of labour in the world capitalist system.

The substance of the question concerning the immanent inequality of exchange which denies the Ricardian assumption is the following: if exchange in the trade between the advanced capitalist and the underdeveloped countries is carried on at world-market prices which, let us assume, are *not* monopoly prices, and if the demand for and the supply of these products at the given world-market prices are in equilibrium on the world market, how is it possible that the total values of the products exchanged, or in Marxist terminology, the average quantities of labour ("live" and "dead") that are socially necessary to reproduce those products are still not equal?

It is obvious that we are faced here, as everywhere where the equalization of the natural and social conditions of production is hampered, with a specific form of the operation of the law of value.

---

however, that these categories, which are historically and logically the antecedents of monopoly prices, should not exist under the surface, serving as a basis and, at the same time, as a limit to the movement of monopoly prices. On the other hand, just as perfectly free competition has never existed, so perfect monopolistic relations cannot exist either.

The law of value, as the law regulating the exchange of commodities on the basis of labour socially necessary to reproduce them, asserts itself at the average of price fluctuations following the changes in demand and supply under specific (or rather abstract) conditions[114] through the market value, or, in the general case, through the "price of production".

If looking at the export products of developing countries (and disregarding such commodities as new technologies exclusively produced by the advanced industrial countries, which enjoy thereby a production or technological monopoly), we can distinguish *two groups* of these products. One consists of products (the "colonial articles" proper), which are produced almost exclusively by these countries, while the other group of commodities is produced and marketed also by the developed countries.

Let us take the latter case and examine, with certain simplification, the price formation within a country of a single product, let's say shoes. Disregarding here the differences (in the organic composition and turnover rate of capital) between the individual productive branches and the competition among them, the market value is determined by the individual labour ("live" and "dead") spent on the product of a shoemaker working under average productive conditions. There are, of course, also shoemakers working under better and worse than average conditions. The shoemaker who works under better than average conditions[115] produces his shoes more cheaply. The individual value of his product is lower than its market value, i.e. in the case of selling it at market value, "his labour is considered as a higher-quality labour", and he gets more labour for less labour, i.e. he obtains an "extra income". This, however, lasts only until the other shoemakers have also improved their productive conditions, the productivity of their labour, because as soon as this happens, the individual value of the product produced under average conditions, that is, the market value, will drop to or even below the individual value level of his product and so the "extra income" will disappear (to appear again for other producers).

What would happen, however, if the other shoemakers or some of them were not able to reach the productivity level of the shoemaker working under more favourable conditions? (For reasons, let us suppose, such as the lack of access to up-to-date means of production or technical know-how.) In this case, the latter's "extra income" would obviously be perpetuated and he would even have the opportunity, by expanding production and selling his products below market value, to ruin the other shoemakers.

[114] Namely, when the organic composition and turnover rate of capital invested in the given industry are perfectly identical with the national average.

[115] He possesses, e.g., improved means of production, better technology or organization of production, and more modern technological know-how.

If this happens, the shoemakers working under less favourable conditions will have to give up their industry and disappear from the production and marketing of shoes.

In other words, apart from specific conditions connected with natural factors and from monopolistic dominance over individual producers, competion within the economy of a single country among the free producers of the same industry will either result, if the producers follow each other in improving their production conditions (by acquiring new technologies and know-how from the same—domestic—sources), in a repeated shifting among them of the "extra income" arising from the difference between individual and average (social) value, or it will lead to the ousting, once and for all, of some producers from the given industry and market.

These are, however, not typical cases of the international economy, particularly in the relationship between the metropolitan countries and their underdeveloped peripheries.

A country with a developed industry and skilled personnel, indispensable for achieving a high level of labour productivity, has a *lasting* advantage over the underdeveloped country. The productive conditions of the forces of production in advanced countries are, owing to the higher level of technology and technical know-how, to the more up-to-date production techniques and organization, permanently more favourable than the average.[116] *This is why the "individual" (national) value of their (same) product is lastingly lower than the "international" market value.* In the underdeveloped country, on the other hand, the same product is turned out under conditions lastingly more unfavourable than the average, as a result of which the "individual" ("national") value finds itself above the "international" one.[117]

Owing to the large inequality between the developed industrialized and the underdeveloped countries in the opportunity of, and in the access to, the means of improving their production conditions, the upward and downward deviations of individual (national) values from average (international) values tend to remain on the same sides, ensuring extra income always to the developed partners. The underdeveloped partners, however, do not (or cannot) give up their productive activities and continue to participate as weaker partners in the competition.

Hence, at the international level, when referring to the exchange between the advanced and underdeveloped countries, *the average behind the "international market value" is not the momentary result of alternating*

---

116 It seems justified to disregard here such natural monopolies (as, e.g., in the case of oil), which *may* ensure more favourable production conditions for the underdeveloped countries.

117 Here we may leave out of account both the problem of dispersion and the question in what proportion the developed and the underdeveloped countries are represented in the formation of the average—not only because it varies from commodity to commodity but also because it cannot affect the course of analysis.

266

extremes, as in the non-monopolized industries within a single country, but it is an average with for the most part unchanged positive and negative sides. Therefore, the extra profit of the producers in the advanced countries is not a "fleeting" but a *relatively permanent phenomenon.* The labour of the advanced country with higher productivity will take part in the exchange as "high-quality labour", and thus the developed country will get more in the exchange for less labour. "In this case the richer country is exploiting the poorer country even though the latter is gaining through the exchange."[118]

Here, however, the following objection may be raised while still maintaining the abstraction from monopoly conditions. If it is true that the underdeveloped countries, on account of their lower productivity, regularly lose on the exchange, how can we account for the fact that it is the very capital coming from the advanced countries that has occupied the export sectors of the underdeveloped countries, and how is it possible at all for this foreign capital to draw high profits and repatriate enormous incomes from there. The explanation is this: though the export products of foreign capital, too, are exchanged for less quantity of labour than the total labour embodied by them,[119] the "dead" labour and the *paid* part of the "live" labour within this total labour is considerably less than in the case of the products of the advanced countries. The rate of exploitation of labour cannot be equalized, owing to the natural obstacles to the free flow of labour between countries. Even if we disregard the lower wage level, the individual costs of product for the foreign investor in the underdeveloped countries are generally low (cheap raw materials, low land prices, state subsidies and benefits, etc.). Therefore, although the total labour embodied in the export product is more than the labour he gets in exchange for it, the foreign investor may receive more *unpaid* labour than his colleague in the advanced country (provided the rates of profit are not equalized), merely because of the lower proportion of the costs of the means of production and wages.

Obviously, this phenomenon is not confined to the exchange between the former colonial and semi-colonial countries and the imperialist big powers only, and strictly speaking cannot be regarded as exploitation. The reason for devoting special attention to this phenomenon in relation to the underdeveloped countries and including it among the specific, indirect forms of income drain, is the fact that the conditions for the elimination of this phenomenon, i.e. of the equalization of the social level of labour productivity, have been prevented from coming about by the *colonialist-*

118 See K. Marx: *Theorien über den Mehrwert.* Berlin, 1956. III. p. 280.
119 This again is, for the most part, true only on the basis of the abstractions discussed. If as a matter of fact these export products—or some of them—command monopoly prices, then the opposite may also happen: they are exchanged for *more* labour than actually embodied by them. On the other hand, the disequilibrium of demand and supply may also influence the proportion and may increase or compensate for the former factors.

neo-colonialist economic policy, and the *spontaneous forces set in motion by the penetration of foreign monopolies*. They imposed upon these countries a one-sided specialization in primary production and retarded (in the colonial period) or distorted (as in more recent times) the process of industrialization, preventing thereby the local bases of technological development from arising and the quality of labour from reaching that in the advanced countries. That is, the relative stabilization of this phenomenon is connected, in the last analysis, with the determining external factors of economic underdevelopment. It is in this sense *only* that we can speak here of income drain.

Already two conclusions can be drawn from what has just been said. First, the raising of the level of labour productivity is an especially important task in such export economies as the economies of the developing countries, in general. It is a task that must be observed when choosing the right industrialization policy (the priority of the labour or capital-intensive industries),[120] and must be considered in educational policy, too, etc. Secondly, looking at the problem from its opposite end, it is of special importance, of course, not with a view to economic autarky, to *expand the internal market and introduce protective tariffs* (perhaps in the framework of economic integration with the neighbouring countries) in order to develop the preferred economic sectors and restrict the skimming off abroad of a part of the "national" value.

Let us now discuss the problem of the other group of products—exclusively those produced in the developing countries—and approach the exchange of these products for the products of the developed countries as the commodity exchange between two different industries of a *single capitalist country*.

If the "organic composition" of capital (the value of constant capital compared to the cost of wages, i.e. to the variable capital) in a given industry of a single country is higher than in another industry, then, assuming the same amount of capital investment and the same time of turnover, the surplus value produced in the former (that part of the new value created by labour power which exceeds the value of labour power itself or, to put it in a more simplified way: the cost of wages) will be lower[121] than in the latter with lower "organic composition" of capital. As a result *of the flow of*

[120] This viewpoint may seem to contradict the requirements of increasing employment and decreasing import needs. Without going into details and commenting on the great many ambiguities (both in terminology and content) of the debates about the choice of the technique, let us simply note here that, in general, the bias in favour of capital-intensive techniques can be regarded as unfavourable *insofar as* it is accompanied by a bias against the capital-goods producing sector, which supplies technology to the national economy and induces R and D capacities.

[121] This follows from the labour theory of value, or, in other words, from the assumption that new value can only be produced by labour.

268

capital, the amount of profit *realized* will eventually adjust itself to the total amount of costs and investments and not to the amount of variable capital only, that is to say, an average rate of profit will develop, and the industry working with a lower organic composition will be compelled to sell its products at a "price of production" lower than the market value. This means that part of the surplus value *created* in this sector will flow to the capitalists of other industries with a higher organic composition of capital.

Since this process takes place *within* a single country, what happens is simply the distribution of the profits among the capitalists at a "social" level, just as the value of labour power is set and the rate of exploitation is equalized at a social level, too. (The "pure" operation of this mechanism presupposes, of course, the existence of the conditions of free competition and perfect factor mobility.)

Foreign capital, as we have seen, plays, directly or indirectly, a decisive role in the economy of the developing countries. The reproduction of "underdevelopment" as a sub-system with specific structure, cannot even be understood without an awareness the fact of the penetration of foreign capital. Thus, owing to the emergence of the world economic system of imperialism, the *flow of investment capital* is also a valid and working factor in the relations between the underdeveloped and advanced capitalist countries. Foreign capital penetrating into the economy of the underdeveloped country usually works with a lower "organic composition" than its "colleague" in the developed country.[122] This follows, on the one hand, from the character of the typical investment spheres created under colonialism (agriculture, mineral extraction) and, on the other, from the lack or weakness[123] of capitalist motives to introduce labour-saving techniques (owing, e.g., to cheap unskilled labour), i.e., to increase the organic composition of capital in the given branch of the economy. As a result of international capital flow,[124] this capital cannot realize in full the higher surplus value created in the underdeveloped country when marketing its products on the world market but has to make do with selling them at an

[122] This relative difference applies of course to average capital intensity in the economy as a whole, or more exactly to the capital intensity of *identical* branches.

[123] Even the opposite tendency which can also be observed in recent times, i.e. the bias in favour of capital-intensive techniques, cannot substantially change the picture as the considerable difference of capital intensity in the same industrial branches of the developed and underdeveloped countries will generally remain in favour of the former even in cases when the capital intensity of the latter proves to be relatively high from the point of view of the employment problems. In other words, the point in question is not whether capital intensity is low or high *per se* in a given branch of the underdeveloped country's industry, but whether it is lower than in the *same* branch of the advanced country's industry.

[124] Let us continue to disregard its impediments, caused both by the monopoly position of capital and by the state restriction of capital movement (e.g. in a few independent countries), and not take into account the customs duties and taxes, etc. either.

"international price of production" lower than the "market value".[125] This is true, by the way, not only for this group of products, that is for the economic branches established exclusively in the underdeveloped countries, but also for the former group of products, as competition "within one industry" changes over also at the international level into a competition "between industries".[126]

In other words, assuming international mobility of capital, part of the surplus value created in the underdeveloped countries flows through the channels of foreign trade into the advanced countries and partakes there of the equalization process of the profits, i.e. of the formation of the average rate of profit. The difference between the "transformation" of the market value into price of production at the international level and the corresponding process within a single country lies in the fact that what is taking place in the former is not simply a redistribution among the capitalists of the society concerned but *a redistribution among the different societies, i.e. "nations", in the course of which the value created in one group of countries is appropriated by another group of countries.*

Here, however, two questions or objections may be raised:

The *first* is this: since we are dealing here with the drain of a part of the surplus value(s) of the capital operating in the economy of the underdeveloped countries, why is it necessary to distinguish it from the exploiting activity of foreign capital already discussed, i.e. from the forms of direct exploitation?

A distinction in principle is justified because the skimming off of the surplus value or national income in this form takes place unnoticed as it were, in a *concealed*, indirect way, in the process of *price formation on the world market* while direct exploitation manifests itself in the realized profits of capital operating on the spot and in the repatriation or local consumption (also including "productive consumption") of these profits. Theoretically, the distinction becomes especially evident if we examine it from the point of view of a single country. While the government of the country concerned has relatively effective means at its disposal to restrict direct exploitation by foreign capital, as the profits of this capital—disregarding here other difficulties—can be "seized" by taxation, the government alone is not in a position to take steps against the disguised skimming off[127] outlined above as the world market prices are given magnitudes formed rather independently of the country concerned.

---

[125] "International market value" is assumed to correspond in the case of these products to the "national" value or, in the case of the same product of several underdeveloped countries, to the average of the "national" values.

[126] Let us leave out of account here again the restricted character of this competition.

[127] Unless the country is the exclusive, monopolistic producer of a world market product. (*Substitutability*, however, has even in this case a modifying effect.)

The *second* objection may be this: It is not exclusively foreign but also local capital, feudal landowners and small commodity producers, that take part in the production of the export products of the underdeveloped countries, and, what is more, the production of a great many "colonial wares" is concentrated in the hand of the latter, which goes to show that the process governed by the law of the average rate of profit is greatly limited.

No doubt, this fact really restricts the mechanism under examination in its proportions, since the laws of the capitalist mode of production *generally* operate only to the extent that this mode of production is gaining ground, and the law in question in *particular* is valid only within the scope of capital flow. Here, however, we must take into account a few additional viewpoints—over and above the fact that the present analysis is designed to determine not the *size* of a phenomenon or tendency and the intensity of its operation, but merely to prove its existence.

Though it is true that foreign capital, even where it does take part in producing the product in question, usually makes up only part of the latter, we may extend our conclusions to *local capital*, too (where there is any). This is also proved by the not infrequent flow of local capital to foreign (advanced) countries. Local capital is often satisfied to realize an even lower rate of profit. Incidentally, the same applies to the semi-capitalistic feudal landowners, too.

And, as far as the *small commodity producers* are concerned, even if their number and share in production are large in many countries, two facts must be considered. *First*, that small commodity producers under fully developed capitalist conditions (and the export sectors in backward countries come under this heading) play only a secondary role in price formation even if they happen to produce the bulk of the products concerned.[128] Small commodity producers are compelled to make do with getting prices much below value, prices which ensure, in addition to the replacement of the means of production (c), at least the cost of living, i.e. a minimum wage level (v). (In the underdeveloped countries, owing to specific circumstances, such as, e.g., migrant labour, and the supplementary role in supply of the subsistence economy, they usually go on with the commodity production even if the products are realized at much lower prices.)

Secondly, and partly in connection with the first fact, the products of the small commodity producers in the underdeveloped countries are usually

---

[128] Because even if, say, only 1–2 per cent of the products are turned out in a given industry by the capitalist enterprises and the rest by the small-commodity producers, even then, *assuming free capital movement*, it is the cost of production (c + v) plus the average profit of the *capitalist* firms that determine the price of production of the products. Otherwise, if the higher average value of the small-commodity producers were the determinant, such an influx of capital towards that industry would take place as to put an end to the validity of our initial assumption, i.e. the preponderance of the small commodity producers.

bought up, processed and exported by the big foreign commercial companies. In this way, foreign commercial capital operating in the underdeveloped countries circulates, with a relatively small capital investment, immense commodity capital while it takes part in the prolonged stages of the process of production (packing, storing, transportation) and controls the small commodity producers. Insofar as it purchases the products well below their value, this belongs to the sphere of exploitation already discussed, but insofar as it is forced to share its enormous profits with its "colleagues" in the developed country *via* the selling prices, i.e. through the channels of foreign trade, it already belongs to the subject of our analysis. Foreign commercial capital controlling small commodity producers is of decisive importance for the price formation on the world market of the products of underdeveloped countries and even beyond that extent.

It clearly follows from the foregoing that in the case of the latter group of products the developing countries may fight against this peculiar form of income drain through foreign trade by restricting the *free flow of capital* (which may also have, of course, other negative consequences), or by trying to seize for the state a part of the surplus value above the average profit though *customs duty* (taking into account here too the possible negative consequences) and by liquidating the *power of foreign purchasing companies* over the small commodity producers. If, however, such measures are taken by only one or a few countries—unless they are the monopoly producers of the commodity concerned—they can hardly achieve any appreciable results by influencing price movement from that angle.[129]

Let us now put the question from this aspect, too: Does the mechanism in the sense of Ricardo's theory of comparative costs really work in the system of the capitalist international division of labour? In other words: (1) *Can the underdeveloped countries fully enjoy the "comparative advantages from natural endowments"?* (2) *Have their economic and foreign trade structure really developed according to the "comparative advantages" even if they may not be able to realize all these advantages?*

As far as the first question is concerned, it follows from our analysis that they *cannot* fully enjoy the advantages from their natural endowments, due—among other reasons—to the *international mobility of capital*.

It must be noted that Ricardo disregarded in his assumptions the international flow of capital and the tendency of the international equalization of the rates of profit. Thus his assumption—insofar as it

[129] The organization of producer associations may serve—depending on a number of conditions—as an effective counter-weight to the metropolitan commercial companies dictating the terms and prices of purchases. For the conditions of and the constraints on establishing and effectively operating such associations, see Helge Hveem: *The Political Economy of Third World Producer Associations*. Universitetsforlaget, Oslo, 1978.

272

logically follows from his basic error[130] (the confusion of the market value with the price of production)—can be regarded as "correct" in this respect.

If, however, the international movement of capital were restricted, the underdeveloped countries would be able in principle,[131] assuming again the equilibrium of demand and supply, to realize the full "international market price" of those products which they produce exclusively, and in whose relation they have *monopolistic natural advantages*.

The possibilities of this realization would be rather restricted, of course, by the *substitutability* of products, which is greatly increasing, mainly as a result of the advances in the scientific-technical revolution, and by the modern agricultural technology, the new methods of cultivation which have substantially extended the geographic-climatic frontiers of agricultural production.

Professor Vajda pointed out[132] that the significance of comparative advantages based on natural endowments, the *static* advantages as he called them, is strongly decreasing as against the *dynamic* advantages (manifested in the higher level of organization, efficiency and dynamics of social labour, and in the social relations), particularly in the advanced countries.

But apart from this, the "static comparative advantages", based themselves on natural endowments, cannot be evaluated independently of the "dynamic" advantages in respect of the underdeveloped countries

[130] Ricardo identified the rate of profit with the rate of surplus value and therefore denied, or played down, the role of foreign trade in the domestic rate of profit.

And, though well aware of the differences in capital intensity and turnover rates, between the various branches of the economy, he did not attach to them, for the same reasons, any importance in regard to the distortions of the price structure, namely to the deviation of relative prices from the proportions of "natural prices" (i.e. values).

Consequently, he held that the comparative costs in the export branch of the economy perfectly reflected (in a free-competition economy without interventions) the proportions of "natural prices" (values). Moreover, Ricardo, who believed that capitalism was the natural order of economy and society, in which the spontaneous activity of private capitalists, motivated by individual self-interests and rationality, necessarily expressed and corresponded to social rationality, completely neglected the divergence between "comparative costs" for private capitalists and those for society as a whole.

These errors, though historically understandable in his case, have also been taken into account when the validity of the comparative cost theory is put to test. For in the light of these errors it becomes obvious that in an international capitalist economy, *even if* all countries were free, sovereign and autonomous, and capital internationally immobile, the division of labour shaped by private capitalists' decisions according to their own comparative-cost calculus in the individual countries cannot manifest a rational pattern of specialization for the partner countries, i.e., a specialization according to the comparative costs of their national society as a whole. (Needless to say, such a division of labour can correspond to social rationality on a worldwide scale.)

[131] See the limiting errors explained in footnote 130.

[132] I. Vajda: A komparativ költségek elmélete és a szocialista világgazdaság (The theory of comparative costs and the socialist world economy). *Közgazdasági Szemle*, May, 1963.

either. There is an exact dialectical relationship between the two, and this provides the answer to the second question.

The general developmental level is of decisive importance from the point of view of "*comparative natural advantages*"—even beyond the problems analysed here. If we assume that in the underdeveloped countries labour productivity is relatively higher in the production of primary products owing to more favourable natural conditions, than in the industrial production, in terms of the relative productivities of the same branches in the advanced countries where the level of average productivity is on the whole and, further, that this advantage could be realized in foreign trade, indeed (i.e. if both problems discussed in our analysis were dismissed), then too, the "comparative advantages" would have a different aspect in relation to the advanced and to the underdeveloped countries, owing to differences in the level of development (dynamic factors).

It is as a matter of fact true, on the one hand, that according to the theory of comparative costs, the advanced country, if it were to produce itself the product in question instead of buying it in international exchange, would have to spend much more labour on its production than on the exchange product, owing to the more unfavourable *natural* conditions. (This means that the developed country gains on the exchange not only because, owing to the general difference between the levels of labour productivity, it gets more labour for less labour, but also because of the fact that it need not spend a part of social labour on the production of such products for which the conditions are relatively less favourable than in other production branches.)

On the other hand, if the underdeveloped countries, at the given level of the development of productive forces, were really to spend more labour on the local production of manufactured goods imported from the advanced countries than on the exchange products, this would not necessarily be the consequence of the less favourable natural conditions for manufactured goods but it would have *historical and social reasons*. (Above all there is the fact that open or disguised colonialism has prevented their industrialization, the development of the sectors producing capital goods, having frozen thereby the majority of the labour force into the cheap, unqualified categories, and that even the proceeding modification of the colonial pattern of the international division of labour, with the recent growth of manufacturing industries in these countries, does not allow a *real industrialization* of, and for their national economy as a whole.)

Who would claim that the present-day *advanced capitalist countries* have, in general, relatively more favourable natural conditions for industrial development than the underdeveloped countries, separately or taken as a whole, as the former have (or had) to import from the underdeveloped countries most of the raw materials needed for the supply of their industries and most of the energy sources, too (oil!). It is quite possible that once the *present-day underdeveloped countries* have developed their own basic industries with the external and internal economies, and particularly with R and D capacities serving the national economy as a whole, they will be able, just owing to the favourable natural conditions,[133] to attain an even higher level of labour productivity in producing those manufactured goods and technologies they are compelled to import today, than in primary production, as compared to the productivity differences in the present industrial countries. Today, however, they are unable, as we have seen, to realize (except a few countries which have organized strong producer associations) the advantage from their more favourable natural conditions even at the world market price of those products with which they supply the advanced capitalist countries.

Consequently, while, on the one side, for the present advanced countries the *real* advantage of exchange would derive from the difference in *natural* endowments, on the other side, for the underdeveloped countries, the *supposed* advantage, practically disadvantage, would be related to the differences in *economic* and *social* conditions subject to radical changes.

Thus we cannot say by any means that the production and foreign trade structure of countries has in general developed according to the comparative natural advantages. The operation and the effect itself of the "static" comparative natural advantages are also dependent on the "dynamic" comparative advantages based on differences in development level, and "the comparative advantages based on differences in development level perpetuate and increase in their effect these very differences".[134]

For this reason we must regard those views as harmful and detrimental to the interests of the developing countries which, by referring to the theory of comparative costs, defend the maintenance of the present international division of labour (which, by the way, is in a state of transformation) and suggest that the developing countries, instead of creating their own industries, should continue to produce mineral and agricultural raw materials for the advanced capitalist countries or they should, at best, develop certain secondary industries (already outgrown by the advanced countries) with labour-intensive technologies, to enjoy the "comparative advantages" of abundant cheap, low-wage unskilled labour. It is obvious and has been historically proved true that the higher productivity of labour in the countries is connected with the existence of a widely based developed manufacturing industry supplying all sectors of the national economy with

[133] We are, of course, discussing here the underdeveloped countries *in general* and disregard, therefore, those countries whose development is decisively hampered by unfavourable natural endowments, and whose industrialization is also impeded by the lack of natural resources. This seems to be justified not only because most of the underdeveloped countries do not belong to this category but also because the exploration of natural resources is for the most part still in its initial stage in these countries.

[134] See I. Vajda: Op. cit., p. 542.

machinery and modern technology, and raising the qualitative and professional level of labour. Where and when such an industry has developed, it substantially changes the pattern of comparative costs.

But even in the advanced countries labour productivity and the level of technical supply are, as a rule, higher in the processing industries than in other branches, such as, e.g., in agriculture or mining. Those countries in which there are no basic industries, in which the majority of the working population are engaged in agriculture or mining, and which can only get hold of the machines and equipment needed for raising the technical and productivity through imports, fall not only into a dependent relationship with the suppliers of manufactured goods but continually lag behind in the raising of labour productivity and allow thereby their main trading partners, the advanced capitalist countries, to regularly come by extra profit. The same applies to the countries which, though complementing the primary-producing export sector by certain manufacturing branches, remain in a technologically dependent position owing to the perpetuated lack, in all main sectors of the economy, of the local bases of technological R and D.

(2) A specific form of disguised income drain, often only of a relative loss, can be distinguished in the *transfer or the unequal distribution of the benefits resulting from the specialization of production* adjusted to foreign trade and from *the increase of productivity in the export sectors.* Not unlike the form discussed earlier, this form cannot be isolated and measured in itself as its consequences manifest themselves in the joint, common effect of several other factors. While, however, the manifestation of the immanent inequality of exchange in the exchange of non-equal quantities of labour, presupposing as its theoretical basis the acceptance of the labour theory of value, is acknowledged only in Marxist literature (even there not generally and without reservation), the latter thesis has gained rather widespread publicity by the studies of authors who subjected the mechanism of the international division of labour to sharp criticism from the point of view of the developing countries.

Since these are the theses which we became acquainted with when discussing the theories of *Prebisch, Myrdal, Lewis,* and *Singer*[135] in Part One, it seems sufficient to summarize them here briefly.

As far as the benefits resulting from the increase of productivity in the export sectors and from technical progress in general are concerned, we are faced with the "strange" situation that though technical progress and productivity increase are generally greater and more rapid in the manufacturing sectors than in primary production, from which the

---

[135] For similar explanations see also I. Sachs: *Foreign Trade and Economic Development of Underdeveloped Countries.* Chapter III.—A. K. Cairncross: International Trade and Economic Development. *Economica,* No. 8, 1961.

textbook conclusion could be drawn that the relative prices of manufactured goods should decrease compared with the prices of primary products, in fact the very opposite occurs and in the industrial centres the incomes of entrepreneurs and of productive factors often increase relatively more than productivity, whereas in the primary producing periphery the increase in income is less than that in productivity. In other words, not only technical progress itself is very uneven at the expense of primary producing countries, but even the benefits of the advancing technical progress in the latter are being realized mainly elsewhere, i.e. in the industrial countries. This transfer of benefits resulting from technical progress is realized through foreign trade prices (and fuses to this extent with the problem of the terms of trade). Its cause, however, must be sought in factors determining the incomes and the way incomes are spent. *A. Lewis*, as we have already seen, traces it back to the dual structure of the underdeveloped economy. The cause of the transfer of benefits is, in his opinion, the fact that the traditional rural sector (serving as a source of the unlimited supply of labour force for the modern export producing sector) exerts a permanent pressure on the wage level of the modern sector by creating labour abundance and by adjusting the wage level of the latter to the low level of its own productivity. Thus the productivity increase of the export sector is for the most part realized only in the growth of output and, owing to a more or less regular oversupply on the world market of the same product also exported by other underdeveloped countries, it tends to lead to a relative decline in its price (or, if it results first in an increase in profits, it tends to increase the demand for imports and thereby also the prices of metropolitan products imported by other underdeveloped countries, too). This means that the benefits from a productivity increase in the export sector of underdeveloped countries are reaped for the most part by the developed countries.

Prebisch explains it in a similar way but instead of putting emphasis on the specific mechanism of the dual economies he stresses the differences of the strength of trade unions, i.e. the bargaining power of workers, in pressing for higher wages, and of entrepreneurs in resisting a squeeze on profit, between the advanced and underdeveloped countries. He also points to the "demonstration effect" of the consumption of the metropolitan industrialized countries, which induces increasing import demands in the periphery and to the impressive disparity in the income elasticity of demand for the manufactured commodities exported by the metropolitan countries and for the products of the underdeveloped periphery.

The inequality in the distribution of benefits resulting from foreign trade and the subsequent specialization consists in the fact that the *secondary and cumulative effects of investments* made in the export sector (either in the export sector of the industrial, advanced economy or in that of the primary producing, underdeveloped economy) will be concentrated mostly in the industrial country, while in the underdeveloped country the character of specialization itself offers less scope for technical progress, and for the internal and external economies.

By their very nature the primary producing sectors are accompanied by considerably fewer and weaker linkage effects[136] than the manufacturing sectors. Consequently, they do not require and induce such an expansion of economic activity and, moreover, cannot become, unlike the heavy industries manufacturing machines, tools, instruments and chemicals, etc. for the other branches in the country, the dynamic motive force of technical progress embracing the whole of the national economy. They cannot become the active generators and transmitters, but merely the passive beneficiaries of technical development. (The same also applies to those manufacturing industries established as import-substitutive branches to produce, from foreign inputs other than labour, luxury consumer goods for the local élite, or as export-oriented links in the transnational network of vertically integrated foreign companies' "putting-out system", which are able only to take over the results of scientific and technical progress from abroad but unable to produce and develop new technologies for local use.) These disadvantages in respect of the external and internal economies and the generation and spread of technical progress manifest themselves— *ceteris paribus*—in the higher costs of investments and operation, and in the—*ceteris paribus*—lower level of productivity, together with the tendency of widening this gap, and consequently narrowing down "vertically" the potential sources of accumulation. In addition, the fact that the spontaneous expansion of the scope of economic activity is less demanded and induced, i.e. it has been rather retarded, also narrows down "horizontally" the potential sources of accumulation in that the creation of profit, or more exactly surplus, is confined to a few branches only. Insofar as the intermediary and/or final processing of primary products are allocated to the advanced industrial countries (as it was certainly the rule in the colonial period and is still characteristic in most cases even today) and the transport and marketing of these products too are in the hands of the latter, the potential sources of income formation and accumulation *for which* the individual primary products provide a material basis, are considerably reduced for the underdeveloped producer countries and transferred to the advanced industrial centre.

A further and, from this aspect, indirect consequence of all that is the relatively limited scope for profitable investment possibilities and state revenue sources.

In contrast to all this, the advanced industrial countries enjoy fully (not just in a reduced way as the primary producing countries) not only the benefits[137] resulting from their *own* specialization, but also a considerable

[136] See Chapter II. 1. (a).

[137] Among others, W. Singer spells out these benefits in detail. (See H. W. Singer: *International Development: Growth and Change.* McGraw-Hill, 1964, p. 168.)

278

proportion of the benefits resulting from the specialization of the other countries, the primary producing underdeveloped economies in that a part of the economic activities based on or complementing primary production also belongs to them. In this way they have access to sources of income and accumulation which lie outside the "original" potentials of their own. This expansion of their own sphere of activity beyond its "original" limit means at the same time the expansion of profitable investment possibilities and the potential extension of the revenue sources of the state.[138]

We may distinguish, perhaps as an additional manifestation of the unequal distribution of the benefits from international trade, the relative loss to the underdeveloped countries, which results from their difficulties, owing to the rather immobile nature of their available resources, in the reallocation of

---

[138] "The economically stronger partner can register proceeds from a larger number of sources and on more occasions than can the weaker partner if we transfer the exchange between the enterprises to the level of the national economies. Thus the stronger partner can make profit *by transportation, by the various forms processing and also by marketing* the finished goods at home or abroad. Thereby many enterprises obtain high profits in the different sectors of the economy, and the investment activities can thus enhanced, i.e. expanded. As a result of these economic activities, the *State also benefits* from further incomes (customs duties, purchase taxes, etc.). And one more thing: in present-day capitalist economy, profit increases toward the production and sale of finished goods and decreases in the opposite direction. The economically weaker countries are far from having similar possibilities, as the production or export of raw materials does not prompt such an extended economic activity as does production and sale of finished goods. Hence the possibilities of accumulation in weaker countries are more restricted." (J. Bognár: The Future Place and Role of the Developing Countries in the World Economy. *Studies on Developing Countries.* Centre for Afro-Asian Research of the Hungarian Academy of Sciences. Budapest, 1965.) To illustrate this point, we may refer to official US estimates, according to which the value of basic mineral materials (including metals, non-metallics and fuels, too) is multiplied five-fold at the processing stages, or to the RIO Report, which estimates that the value of primary products exported by the developing countries increased from 30 billion US dollars paid to them for unprocessed exports to approximately 200 billion paid by the final consumers for processed commodities. (See Helge Hveem: Op. cit., p. 44.)

The extremely low share of primary producers in the total income generated throughout the whole process of reproduction, including transport, processing and marketing, up to the final consumer can be clearly demonstrated by such different products as bananas and crude oil. In 1971, for example, the average world retail price formation of bananas allowed only 11.5 per cent gross return to the growers (which, in view of the participation of foreign companies in the production, was, of course, much higher than what was actually returned to the nation) while the rest accrued to foreign enterprises (ripeners, wholesalers, retailers, insurance firms, etc.). In 1967, e.g., the OPEC countries realized only about 8 per cent of the total oil revenues from their natural resource. (This also reflected, of course, the effect of the former posted-price system of crude oil, which before its collapse in the early seventies had caused a loss of about 215 billion US dollars to the producing countries in twenty years.) (See Frederick F. Clairmonte: *The Banana Empire.* CERES. No. 43, FAO Review on Development. January-February 1975, pp. 33–34. Memorandum. Democratic and Popular Republic of Algeria. Op. cit.)

productive activities[139] towards the most dynamic spheres corresponding to their long-term comparative advantages in the context of natural and human endowments as well as of scientific and technical progress.

Furthermore, the very fact that, owing to their close linkage to the industrial centre, where production and consumption patterns radiate from, and also to their reduced capability of a dynamic resource reallocation as well as of technological and product innovations, they always have to follow in their "adjustment policy" (if they have such a policy at all) the changes taking place in the advanced industrial countries and to readjust their economy over and over again to the latter. The costs of this readjustment also constitute asymmetrical burdens and relative losses to them.[140]

(3) Another form of indirect and disguised income drain is connected with the *mechanism of "internal" price formation and accounting techniques or bookkeeping manipulation* of the usually vertically structured *international companies* and oligopolies. The most typical example of this form is the *transfer-pricing* of multinational companies, which is widely practiced nowadays in the vertical structure of their integrated activity crossing the frontiers of several national economies. Bookkeeping manipulations include the over-invoicing of imports from foreign subsidiaries and the under-invoicing of exports to the latter from the local ones in a developing country as well as the practice of double accounting (one for the local tax authorities and another for company headquarters, etc.).

The system of "*internal price formation*," however, was not unknown in the past either. One of the most illustrative examples[141] was the former

---

[139] "If ... resources are immobile, both the static and dynamic gains from trade will be greatly reduced, because the gains from trade arise in large part from the ability of an economy to reallocate resources towards those sectors which experience a comparative advantage. If reallocation is impossible ..., many of the advantages of free international trade disappear." (Keith Griffin: The International Transmission of Inequality. *World Development*, Vol. 2, No. 3, 1974, p. 7.)

[140] The International Transmission of Inequality. *World Development*. Vol. 2, No. 3, 1974, p. 7. For more on this problem, see Thomas Balogh: *Unequal Partners*, I, Oxford, Basil Blackwell, 1963.

[141] Another example refers to the American copper mines in Chile, such as Kennecot and Anaconda. "Their first action is to fake their sheets, showing high allotments for depreciations, and thus pay taxes to the Chileans on smaller declared profits. Secondly and chiefly, copper is exported from Chile not to external market to be sold at world prices, but is delivered by the Anaconda from its own enterprises in Chile to its own enteprises in the USA—at prices that are understated for the same purpose of paying less in taxes." (P. Khvoinik: Borrowed Prosperity. *Soviet Economists Discuss...*, p. 123.)

An interesting study on fifteen pharmaceutical subsidiary enterprises revealed an enormous gap between the profit rate (less than 7 per cent) declared by foreign companies for local taxation purposes and their actual profit rate (more than 136 per cent). (See Constantine Vaitsos: *Inter-Country Income Distribution and Multinational Enterprise*. Oxford University Press, 1974.)

"posted-price" system, imposed by the international monopolies on the oil-producing countries of the Middle East. Though since the early seventies radical changes have taken place in international oil business relations (including ownership relations) and also in the pricing system, implying practically the explosion of the former posted-price system, which had been in operation for a long time, it is worthwhile to investigate the mechanism of the latter in its original form not only for illustration purposes, but also for a better understanding of the changes themselves. Since the "price explosion" posted prices have been not much more than mere figures on a blackboard, because increasingly large quantities of crude oil are sold under other arrangements by the producers (sold by auction in the open market, sold back to the companies or directly to the consumer countries' governments). The former posted-price system was an artifical accounting price system calculated on the basis of the higher extracting costs of American oil wells and the costs of the transportation of oil to the American market. It skimmed off unnoticed the differential rent of the oil fields in the Middle East and kept down the basis for calculating the share of the local states. In addition, part of the profit from extraction passed over, often by a simple bookkeeping manipulation, to the profits of the transportation, processing and marketing which was made possible by the fact that these operations, overstepping the boundaries of the national economy of the countries in question, were mostly in the hands of the same monopolistic organization.

(This opportunity is, by the way, not yet fully excluded in so far as foreign companies still retain important positions in the buying, transporting, processing and marketing of Middle East oil.)

An excellent analysis of the operation of the former international oil-price mechanism and the exploitation disguised in the posted-price system was given in the dissertation of *F. A. Hasab* (Hungarian Academy of Sciences, 1966), the relevant parts of which were summarized in his study published in *Acta Oeconomica*.[142]

Hasab pointed out that the International Oil Cartel which comprised the greatest international monopolies, controlled through its subsidiaries and holding companies more than 60 per cent of the world's oil extraction, transportation, processing and marketing. This fact gave the Oil Cartel the possibility of maintaining a special accounting and price system.

The uniform posted-price system adjusted itself to the costs of crude oil extraction in the USA. To be more exact: "The posted prices are practically based on the FOB Gulf Mexico price which is at present $ 2.91 per barrel (gravity degree: API 34). To this the freight from the Gulf of Mexico to New York ($ 0.26) is added. These two factors together give the posted price of crude oil in New York, i.e. $ 3.17 per barrel, CIF New York. It is on this

---

142 F. A. Hasab: The International Oil Price Mechanism. *Acta Oeconomica Academiae Scientiarum Hungaricae*. Tomus 3, Facs. 1. Budapest, 1968, pp. 91–107.

basis that the posted prices for oil from Venezuela, the Middle East and the Far East are calculated. In the case of Kuwait, e.g., from this price ($ 3.17), the cost of freight between Kuwait and CIF New York ($ 1.19) and the tax on oil established by the government of the United States ($ 0.11 per barrel) are deducted. This is how the posted price of $ 1.87 per barrel in Kuwait is worked out."[143]

What was the effect of this special crude-oil price system and its special advantage for the international cartel or the advanced capitalist countries?

The accounting basis was not only artificial, but also false. The principal market of the Middle East crude oil was not the USA[144] but Europe. Consequently, the deduction of the cost of freight to the USA and of the tax imposed by the American government radically cut the accounting price which served as a basis for the profit sharing.

It is true that the international monopoly also paid royalties[145] to the oil-producing countries, but the differences between the extraction costs of oil in the United States and in the Middle East were so enormous that even if the costs of freight to the actual markets had been discounted, the oil-producing countries of the Middle East would have been able to obtain a differential rent far exceeding the amount of royalties and profit sharing. For example, the extraction costs in Algeria amounted to only 45 per cent of the average costs of the American oil extraction in the sixties. The percentages for Iraq, Iran and Kuwait were 12, 10 and 7 per cent, respectively. The relatively high discrepancy between the oil-extracting costs in the developing countries and the relating posted price (e.g., in the case of Kuwait the former amounted to $ 0.14, the latter to $ 1.87 in the early sixties) enabled the vertically integrated monopolies to introduce a system of rebates,[146] with the subsidiaries granted a rebate of up to 30 per cent on their oil purchases from the mother company. The producing countries receiving royalties in the form of oil were inclined to re-sell the oil thus obtained to the companies rather than market it themselves.[147]

[143] Op. cit., p. 93.

[144] "The protectionism of the monopolies excludes in practice Venezuelan and Middle-Eastern oil from the competition in the American domestic market... Ever since 1959, the import of crude oil into the USA is regulated by official quotas fixed by the administration." (Op. cit., p. 94.)

[145] "The system of *royalty* means that the oil companies hand over a fixed amount of oil to the state granting the concession which disposes of this oil at liberty. The *profit share* means the sharing of the owner state in the profits realized in oil extraction. In the calculation of the share the value of the royalty is generally also included." (Op. cit., p. 101.)

[146] "The secret rebates... are a practical proof that a considerable part of crude oil is never traded in the international market at the posted prices." (Op. cit., p. 100.)

[147] Op. cit., pp. 99–100. We have to note here that in most cases the "buying back" of the crude oil by the same foreign companies mostly on a contract basis has remained characteristic of the bulk of the oil sold by the producing countries even where and after the oil production was nationalized in the seventies.

The differential advantages of the Middle East oil fields from the point of view of capital lie not only in higher productivity (the oil deposits lie less deep. their yields are higher,[148] the crust pressure is more favourable, etc.) but they are also manifest in the more rapid realization cycle (turnover) of capital and the lower wage level.

For a better understanding of the true value relations, let us assume a "classical" mechanism—confined for the time being only to the sphere of crude-oil *extraction*. We shall try to outline how the incomes would be formed and distributed *if*, as in the Marxian model, competition could freely develop for the capital, and a monopoly position were only enjoyed by the owners of natural resources (oil fields, in our case) with limited availability. This case is almost the opposite of that in the past when foreign capital enjoyed a monopoly position, the monopoly price of crude oil was dictated by the international cartel, and the rent (in the form of royalties) was not a decisive factor in price formation but only a dependent variable.

As is well known, the formation of rent (whether ground or mine rent) can be attributed in the "classical" mechanism to the fact that the individual rate of profit, which is, for some reason,[149] higher than the average, is reduced to an average rate of profit, *not* at the level of the national economy, and *not* through the price mechanism, but within the sector and through the mechanism of income distribution, so that the difference will pass, owing to the monopolized state of the natural resource, into the possession of the latter. In other words, that part of the surplus value produced which exceeds the average profit does *not* disappear in the price mechanism,[150] but is

[148] The average daily yield in the Arab East was 6.783 barrels, in Venezuela 318, in the USA altogether 12.3 barrels in the sixties (op. cit., p. 99).

[149] In the case of absolute rent it is the lower organic composition of capital in agriculture and usually in mining as compared to that in other branches.

In the case of differential rent No. I, it is the difference in labour productivity. The productivity of labour performed on the land, or in the mine in question is higher than that determining the market value, i.e. the productivity of labour performed on the "marginal" land (the less fertile land being still cultivated) or in the "marginal" mine. (In the case of differential rent No. II, it is the lower costs of marketing due to the more favourable location.)

[150] The difference arising from the lower organic composition of capital disappears with the commodities being exchanged at "price of production" (cost of production + average profit), that is it moves from the branches with a lower organic composition to branches with a higher composition. The obstacle to this equalization, to the value getting reduced to "price of production", gives rise to the formation of absolute rent.

The difference, however, arising from different productivity, that is between the individual and the social (average) value, which is by the way the source of extra profit, disappears from time to time for one capitalist unit and appears for another as a result of the competition in the improvement of technology and labour organization. Where, on the other hand, the equalization of productivity is hampered by *natural* factors, a lasting difference appears in the return—instead of, or beyond the temporary extra profit—which provides the basis for differential rent.

realized, and will be later lost as profit the capitalist tenant, only to appear as rent to the landowner.

Rent, just as the price which includes it, is by its very nature of a monopolistic character. Its distinction from other monopolistic incomes and monopoly prices can be made, in our opinion, not only on the grounds of who determines the magnitude of the monopoly price and rent and who enjoys the latter as income, but also on the basis of *how it relates to the value actually created*. The question is *whether*—as in the case of the monopoly prices and incomes in general—a monopolistic organization, owing to its influence on price formation, realizes a higher price than the value created in its sphere (or, the "normal" price of production according to its costs), i.e. appropriates part of the surplus value (or average profit) of other, non-monopolist producers, *or* the monopoly based on the scarcity of the natural resources prevents other, non-monopolist producers from also sharing the (higher) surplus value created in this monopolized sphere of production.

This distinction seems, of course, too abstract and theoretical for its own sake as it is hardly feasible to disclose the real value relations "purely", i.e. independently of prices, owing to the vertical relationships, the wide range of simple and complex labour and the existence of various kinds of monopolies. Thus we must make do with the distorted reflection of value relations through prices.[151] But this abstract distinction has the *practical* significance of clearing up the problems under discussion, and making the origin and distribution of oil incomes understood. It helps also to understand some of the reasons and effects of the necessary explosion of the *former* oil-price mechanism and to answer the question why the revenues of the oil-producing countries of the Middle East would have increased (though to a lesser extent, especially in nominal terms, than they actually did) even if this "explosion" had been accompanied by the elimination of the monopoly position of the companies not only in production, but also in transport, processing and marketing, and if it had allowed free play to competition either among foreign capitalist firms taking part as "tenants" in nationalized oil production or among the producer countries themselves. It is obvious that in this case—according to the "classical" mechanism—the

[151] From this it does not follow in the least that the tautological "price theories" explaining prices from themselves, i.e. completely disregarding value, should be also acceptable scientifically—apart from certain practical purposes. They are unable to provide either a historically verifiable or a logically consistent answer to the question of what eventually determines prices, over and above the short-run price fluctuation. At the same time, the labour theory of value gives a historically and logically consistent explanation of how the prices have come into existence and are moving (around what) in the long run.

On the other hand, the assessment of value relations independently of prices (in labour units) is, despite its very complexity, by no means insoluble as the reduction of "dead labour" (capital) to "living labour", and of "complex" labour to "simple" labour (e.g. by means of electronic computers) could be quite practicable.

differential rent arising from the more favourable productivity (and concealed, as in the past, in the posted-price) could have been fully appropriated by the owners, i.e., the oil-producing countries themselves. Moreover, it would have been possible for them to realize even the difference which, as a result of the lower wage level (and, in value terms, also independently of it) and of a presumably lower organic composition[152] would have appeared in the profit rate. A national *state* ownership of extraction would have immediately changed all this difference, together with the average profit, into the direct revenue of the state (instead of into the direct form of profit share and rent) provided, of course, that the producing countries had been free to take over a decisive part of transportation, processing and marketing, too, or at least to do without monopolistic partners in the above fields. The changes in the final market price of crude oil, however, would have been subject in this case, too, not only to the above conditions, but also to the price formation of the processed derivatives, and particularly of the substitutes of crude oil, as well as to the impact of other (including institutional) factors.

F. A. Hasab not only pointed out that the margin between the local posted price and the international price of crude oil[153] was substantially wider than the actual costs of transportation (to the West European markets), which meant that the extra profit arising from the higher productivity of the Middle East oil fields was largely expropriated by the international oil cartel. He also referred to the disproportionately wide gap between the prices of crude oil and the processed derivatives, a gap also artificially created and maintained by the monopolies that time. The extracting costs accounted only for a relatively small part of the retail price of the processed products.[154] This extremely wide margin between the prices of crude oil and the final products was due to the vertical structure and the monopolistic situation in the entire oil industry, i.e., to the fact that the international oil cartel controlled through its subsidiaries and holding

[152] The capital-intensive character of oil extraction is evident insofar as compared with the other productive branches of the oil-producing countries themselves. What really matters from the point of view of the rate of profit, however, is the organic composition of the more or less freely flowing capital in the productive branches turning out commodities for the *same* market (i.e., not for the internal market of the oil producing countries, but the international market). We have every reason to suppose that the organic composition of capital invested in oil extraction—which, being calculated in value terms, also reflects the lower wage costs in the oil-producing countries—was lower than the average organic composition of capital in the immense and largely automatized large-scale industry of the capital-exporting countries and the main oil-consuming economies.

[153] He referred to the computations of Abdullah Tariki, former minister of the oil industry in Saudi Arabia, according to which American companies made a profit of 880 million dollars in 1962 instead of one of 300 million dollars, due to the difference between the two prices. (F. A. Hasab: Op. cit., p. 94.)

[154] A barrel of crude oil costed $3.17 CIF New York, while the average retail price of processed derivatives (gasoline, fuel oil, etc.) amounted to about $11.00. (Op. cit., p. 100.)

companies the major part of oil exploration, extraction, transportation, processing and marketing. The oil cartel had thereby an opportunity "to conceal the extra profit in the accounts of the purchasing and processing companies instead of showing it in the books of the subsidiaries engaged in the extraction of oil".[155]

Consequently, the concealed income drain was based not only on the false calculation of the posted price of crude oil but also on the artificially low level of this posted price related to the monopolistic prices of the final products. The relatively low prime costs made it possible for the advanced capitalist countries to impose an unusually high consumer tax or import duty. In this way, not only the oil monopolies and their crude oil consuming (processing) subsidiaries but also the state budgets of the capitalist countries had a share in the oil incomes created in the Middle East.[156]

The heavy taxes on the Arab crude oil and the adjustment of its posted price to the extraction costs of the American oil fields made it possible to operate those Texan oil fields the productivity of which is much lower than that of the "would-be marginal" field.[157] The institutional factors (such as taxation) affecting the price of exported oil were also connected with the pricing of the oil substitutes (coal, natural gas). For example in Britain, the competitiveness of coal and the operation of coal mines, which would have been uneconomical under the conditions of the cheap oil of that time, were ensured by the import-consumption tax imposed on heavy fuel oil and by state subsidies (e.g. tax reductions, special freight rates, etc.) given to the coal mines and covered largely from those taxes.[158]

From all these follow that (1) a mere explosion of the former posted price system, of this artificial, monopolistic pricing, which ensured all major benefits to the international oil cartel (the "Seven Sisters") and the breaking of the latter's monopoly position in oil production would not have

[155] Op. cit., pp. 93–94.

[156] Here again it seems advisable, in order to avoid the charge of a biased attitude, to note that we use the terms of "share" or "skimming off" in this case (in contrast to other import commodities, similarly subject to taxes and duties) only insofar as, and because, the ratable price before taxes and duties was determined artificially by the monopolies of the *same* advanced capitalist countries whose governments imposed the taxes and customs duties.

[157] A mine (or land) of the poorest productivity can be called "would-be marginal" (or "otherwise marginal") if its products can still be sold in such a way, assuming the free play of demand and supply, that the selling price just ensures the average profit above the production costs.

[158] It was characteristic of the proportions that while, e.g., the price of a ton of coal was about 95 sh at the mine in England, the price of heavy fuel oil of the caloric value of one ton of coal was made up of the following components: production price 78/1 sh plus consumption tax: 21/1 sh, i.e., it amounted to 99/2 sh. (F. A. Hasab: Op. cit., p. 97.) As we know, the oil-price explosion in the seventies has also solved the problem of the lower-productivity oil fields in the United States and of the coal mines with high production costs in many countries. This is another instance which shows that certain capitalist interests of the West actually converge with the price increases of crude oil.

286

necessarily led to a drop in crude oil prices. Besides the dominance (if left unchanged) of the same oil companies also in transport, processing and marketing, the actually much higher cost level of the production of substitutes, compensated for by artificial means to ensure their competitiveness, the disproportionately high rates of taxes and duties imposed on crude-oil imports in the main consumer countries and also the gap made and kept artificially wide between the market prices of crude oil and its final products (oil derivatives), etc. could have, probably, prevented crude-oil prices from declining even under the assumed conditions. Instead, a collapse of the posted price system could have, at best, only narrowed the scope of application of the above artificial means. (2) If the collapse of the monopolistic posted price system could have nevertheless led to a drop in crude-oil prices, it would, on the one hand, have had a detrimental effect—assuming unchanged taxes and import duty rates—mainly on American oil extraction (and also British and other coal mining), by making the operation of a great many enterprises impossible, and, on the other hand, it would have been in all probability a transitory phenomenon only, as the increased demand for oil, due to the substitutability of fuels and the expansion of the oil-based industries stimulated by lower oil prices, would have led, in turn, to a strengthening of prices. (3) The nationalization of oil extraction—leaving out of account here the problems of retaliatory measures and the sabotage actions of the companies monopolizing transportation, processing and marketing—would have ensured in this case, too additional incomes for the oil-producing countries and enabled them to realize a greater proportion of the relative advantages arising from the higher productivity of the oil fields and from the lower wage level. Nationalization would not have ensured, however, all the benefits from specialization and from its local cost conditions to the oil-producing countries, nor would have ensured a "classical" price formation on the international market of crude oil and its end products unless the dominant position of foreign monopolies had been broken in the spheres of transportation, processing and marketing, too. To make the other forms of concealed income drain from the international oil-price mechanism disappear and the price formation of crude oil and its end products correspond to a "classical" mechanism, it would have also been necessary for the oil-producing countries to develop their processing industries and transport capacities as well as free marketing channels to the consumers. (4) We may assume that if all these conditions had been fulfilled and a really competitive international oil market had evolved, then not only the oil-producing countries could have enjoyed benefits greater than before, but, owing to a likely relative drop in the final consumer prices of oil and oil products, the consumers would have also gained advantages.

As we all know, what has actually happened is quite different from, if not the very opposite to, what has been outlined above. The breaking of the monopoly position of the international cartel consisting of foreign companies was restricted to oil production rather[159] than to the entire vertical structure of international oil business, and, as a matter of fact, was preceded and introduced by price increases dictated this time by the governments of the oil-producing countries forming a (counter-)monopoly organization, the OPEC. It is to be stressed that under the conditions of the international market of *monopoly* capitalism there is, indeed, *no other way* to break the power of *foreign* monopoly but by the creation of an opposite monopoly to represent the national interests of the producing countries.

The consequence of the price increases of crude oil (from which the foreign oil companies have also drawn substantial benefits[160]) and of the successful steps taken by the oil-exporting countries to control their own production without changing, however, the monopolistic pattern of the oil business, has been, under the given conditions of the world economy, a further and even greater increase in final consumer prices, a perpetuation or rather a widening of the gap between crude-oil and end-product prices. Thus, instead of narrowing the spheres of artificial, institutional methods affecting price relations, they have resulted in a shift caused by the latter and the powerful capitalist firms the burden of increased import costs of crude oil onto the shoulders of the consumers, i.e. in a further "cost push" to the inflation in the West.

This explains why the results of the first successful action of the periphery countries *within* international capitalism against its centre (however important it is from a great many aspects of the centre-periphery relations[161], and for the development of these countries themselves) have proved to be harmful not only to the countries of the capitalist centre (and within it not primarily—if at all—to the exploiting classes), but also to other countries, especially to the oil-exporting Third World countries. It further

[159] This is true even if some progress has been achieved since the early seventies also with respect to developing local processing industries and to organizing an own (or joint) transport system in the Middle East.

[160] ". . . Most corporations have benefited as much or more from the so-called 'oil crisis' and from the 'resource boom' of 1972–1974 as have the producing-exporting countries"— says H. Hveem, and for illustration he refers to the 82 and 62 per cent increases in profits for US firms engaged in petroleum and petroleum products and in gasoline distribution, resp. within the US economy in three months time, from January to April, 1974." (See Helge Hveem: Op. cit., pp. 30–171.)

[161] Besides the effects on international politics we may mention the strong impulse the OPEC countries have given to other developing countries to make similar efforts, and the rise, within the Third World, of a new financial power which may not only widen, but also add new features to, the practice of international assistance to the low-income developing countries. Since 1973, the OPEC countries have considerably contributed to development aid, and largely in a untied form. Their total concessional assistance flows increased from 1.3 billion US dollars in 1973 (corresponding to 1.42 per cent of their total GNP) to 5.8 billion in 1977 (1.96 per cent of GNP). (See *1979 Review*. Development Co-operation. Op. cit., p. 269.)

explains why even the OPEC countries have actually lost a considerable part of their increased oil revenues.[162] The big corporations, both in the oil business and other dynamic industries, have been able to compensate, or rather overcompensate themselves for the increased crude-oil costs. And since the fundamental antagonism in the world capitalist economy does not lie between geographical areas (such as the "North" and the "South") but between the monopoly capital of the centre and the working masses of the world, there is no reason for us to be surprised if actions by countries, or a group of countries (in this case by OPEC), cannot lead *per se* to a socially just and desired distribution of the costs and benefits arising from such actions. (Not to mention the necessarily but none the less markedly monopolistic character of the group's organized actions, with rather different political regimes and socio-economic structures behind them, which also accounts for the uneven internal distribution of the benefits among the social strata of the individual countries.)

(4) Manipulated prices and accounting systems can, of course, be employed not only by and within the international monopoly companies. Similar arrangements with the resulting income drain can also be observed in the country-to-country relations of trade, particularly in the colonial period. Therefore, we may distinguish as a separate form of losses the *manipulated system of administered prices*, "contracted" or forced to be applied in the trade between a metropolitan country and its periphery. It is obviously based on the unequal economic power and unequal position of the partners concerned. It implies a more or less *open* violation of the formal equality of exchange. This income drain can be "legalized" by including in the treaties and agreements imposed on the underdeveloped countries certain privileges enjoyed by the developed capitalist countries or by certain institutions also imposed by them on the former.

The essence of income drain through manipulated administered prices is this: the advanced country diverts the prices of the commodities sold to or bought from the underdeveloped country from the world-market prices, by means of the institution set up by the colonial government or by a specific accounting system laid down in a treaty based on "equal rights", so that the deviations in the price levels should result in a net surplus for it. (The simplest way of doing this is, of course, to push the prices of the products sold above and those of the products bought below the world-market prices, but the same result may also be attained by diverting the prices of both the goods sold and the goods bought in the same direction, but to *different* extent.)

[162] According to the speech made by Minister Pronk of the Netherlands at the SID Conference in 1976, by that time "the oil prices had already lost more than 30 per cent of their overall purchasing power, while prices of equipment imported by OPEC countries had doubled." (Quoted by Ismail-Sabri Abdallah: Op. cit., p. 13.)

There was an especially great possibility for introducing such manipulated prices under the colonial system. The marketing boards set up in the *British African colonies*, which enjoyed practically a monopoly position in buying up the agricultural export products, bought them at half or one third of the world-market price, and the considerable margins were transferred to the so-called stabilization fund in London. This pound sterling reserve fund, formed in the metropolitan country, served in principle the aim of keeping up the level of purchasing prices even if the world-market prices drop. Since, however, such transfers back to the colony seldom occurred, it was merely a forced loan to the metropolitan country.

Within the franc area another price mechanism came into being, but also involving an obvious inequality of exchange. The purchasing prices of the export commodities produced in the African underdeveloped countries were driven above the world market prices, but the prices of the French manufactured goods were raised higher. This not only enabled the French monopolies to gain extra profit from the differences in price levels,[163] but also to gain nearly unlimited control over the markets of the countries in the franc area and to prevent the African exporters from selling their products on the world market independently, i.e. by by-passing France.

The proportions of the income drain through manipulated and administered prices are best shown by the fact that, owing to the special purchasing and export-price systems prevailing under colonialism, the producers in the British colonies received only 37–55 per cent of the commercial price of their products, and in the French colonies only 15–20 per cent, while the rest flowed to the metropolitan country.[164]

(5) The best-known and in the literature the most widely debated form of income loss through foreign trade is that arising from the *deterioration of the terms of trade*.

As we have already pointed out, in the colonial era the leading capitalist powers made the underdeveloped, colonial or dependent countries of the

---

[163] "The extra increment on the prices of French goods surpasses that on African goods. Thus, for instance, from 1956 to 1962 the prices of the French goods imported to Senegal rose by 35 points, while those of Senegalese goods exported to France rose by only 3 points. The whole burden of the extra-price policy is shouldered by the African ex-colonies. Moreover, while the African countries overpay France by some 15–20 per cent above world prices on the average, for some goods, such as textiles, motor cars and machinery this surplus payment rises to 30 per cent and even 60 per cent (refined sugar)." (L. Krasavina: Changes in the Franc Area. *Soviet Economists Discuss . . .*, pp. 85–86.) In 1962 the prices of French products going to West Africa were 120 per cent above world prices for sugar, 100 per cent for beef, etc. Admittedly, France also paid more for the primary products of West Africa, but: "Excess prices paid by the West African countries were 58,300 million; excess prices paid by France were 31,200 million, loss to the African countries was 27,100 million francs." (*The Nationalist*, May 17, 1968.)

[164] J. C. de Graft-Johnson: *An Introduction to the African Economy*. Bombay, 1959, p. 63.
— Surét-Canale: Les rapports économiques franco-africains. *Économie et Politique*. IX–X, 1958, p. 62.

290

world the sources of their raw-material and food supply, and geared the economies of these countries to the production of one or a few agricultural products or minerals. The rapidly growing industry of the leading capitalist countries absorbed in large quantities the primary products of the underdeveloped countries, giving thereby new impetus for stepping up their production. Since the development of agriculture in the advanced countries lagged for a long time behind the rapid industrial growth they had also to rely on food imports from the underdeveloped countries of that time, in order to meet the food supply of the population.

In this international division of labour the industry of the advanced capitalist countries found a relatively wide market in the underdeveloped countries, while the development of industry in the latter was impeded not only by the competition of the imported industrial goods, not to speak of the colonial economic policy, capital shortage and labour problems, but also by the fact that only the production of industrial raw materials and foodstuffs for export was stimulated by demand. The demand of the metropolitan industrial centres for primary products seemed to grow and expand so rapidly as to meet the growing import capacities of the primary-producing periphery, though at the expense, even in the past, of wide fluctuations in both demand and supply. Later, however, a discrepancy has become more and more apparent, but always to a very different extent, in respect of the individual primary products. By and large, since the Second World War (for various reasons already discussed, such as the effects of the scientific-technological revolution, of the postwar hegemonic position of the US economy, etc.), the rate of increase in the import demand for primary products in general in the advanced countries has shown, behind the fluctuations also including "peak" periods, and except a few privileged primary commodities (such as, first of all, crude oil and also some strategic raw materials), an unfavourable trend, particularly as compared to the growth of the export capacities in the Third World. At the same time, the demand of the developing countries for manufactured commodities, technologies and also for food products has rapidly increased.[165]

The growing discrepancy in the size and structure of mutual demand, which reflects the very unequal pattern of the world capitalist division of labour, is the main factor behind the tendency of the deterioration of the terms of trade for the (majority of) developing countries. This tendency is

[165] Sachs writes: "... before World War II (excluding the years 1876–80), the share of primary producers in world exports exceeded their share in world imports. Thus primary producers had a favourable balance of trade which enabled them to cover the deficit on the remaining portion of the balance of payments. In the years 1953–55 the share of imports equalled that of exports. It, however, exceeded the latter considerably in 1958. *It has become a rule*, in recent years, for exports to lag behind import requirements, and one should expect this trend to continue..." (I. Sachs: *Foreign Trade and Economic Development...*, p. 42.)

also connected with the "one-sided policy of the concentrated economic powers (monopolies supported by the leading capitalist countries)".[166]

As far as the policy and activity of the "concentrated economic powers" are concerned, the state monopolistic, or sometimes suprastate-monopolistic associations and the organizations of economic integration interfere in the economy, and the system of trade relations in such a way that the measures taken by them (e.g. in the spheres of import duties, export subsidies and import restrictions, etc.[167]) considerably hamper or directly prevent the adequate expansion of the export of the developing countries. On the other hand, the big international monopolies also hinder, through their influence on the formation of world-market prices, the operation of that opposite—and otherwise natural—tendency which, owing to the more rapid rate of productivity growth in the manufacturing industries, would push the price of manufactured goods *downwards* in relation to raw materials. Instead, by applying high monopolistic prices to their manufactured commodities, especially to technologies,[168] they contribute directly to an increase in the price level of the metropolitan countries and of the exports of the latter in addition to the inflation process also related to their interests. Besides influencing prices directly,[169] they also exert an indirect effect on the prices of manufactures in that the same monopolies, or their sisters in the metropolitan country, further increase, by their investment policy pursued in the developing countries (see the already discussed bias in favour of capital-intensive techniques) the import needs of the latter. At the same time, the growth of manufactured exports of the

[166] J. Bognár: Gazdasági kapcsolataink távlatai a fejlődő országokkal (The perspectives of our economic relations with developing countries). *Közgazdasági Szemle*, May 1963, p. 515

[167] This still applies, first of all, to the processed products exported by the developing countries. As Helge Hveem points out and also proves by illustrating it by data for 1973: "the discriminating tariff structures maintained by the major importing countries´... favour continued production of unprocessed materials in the periphery as in the "classical" division of labour. The more imports take place at higher processing levels, the higher tariffs are imposed..." (Helge Hveem: Op. cit., pp. 141–142.)

[168] "The concentration of technical change in a few countries, industries and firms constantly re-creates a monopolistic organization of industry and enables innovating enterprises to price their products in such a way as to include a substantial element of rent. The rent element in prices, in turn, ensures that value exchanged through trade will favour the rich countries (where innovation occurs) and prejudice the development of poor countries (whose exports frequently but not always are sold on competitive markets".) (Keith Griffin: Op. cit., p. 9.)

[169] This applies, in a characteristic way, not only to manufactured goods. The concentrated economic powers prove strong enough, even in the face of a general decrease in the prices of *primary products*. While, e.g., the average price of the primary products exported from the developing countries fell by 7 per cent, that of the primary products exported from the developed countries rose by 10 per cent. (*Review of International Trade and Development*, Part I, TD/15, 1967, pp. 1–2.)

developing countries is also retarded, besides the discriminating customs regulations and the oppressive competition of the cheaper and better products of the monopolies, by the fact that they are handicapped in respect of the "extra-price factors" (e.g. trade marks, models, the network of servicing stations).

In addition, most of the developing countries, when facing the rapid growth of import needs,[170] have no other choice but to increase the output of the "traditional" export products in which they are competing with each other on the world market.

But the developing countries are harmfully affected not only by the deterioration but also by the frequent fluctuations of the terms of trade. The world-market prices of industrial raw materials are, as a rule, highly sensitive to the business cycles of the economies of the advanced capitalist countries. The prices of these products generally increase rapidly in boom periods, due partly to the speculative stockpiling trade policy which encourages a fictive demand divorced from actual industrial demands, and drops faster and further than any other goods in the times of recession. Price fluctuations are particularly intensive in the case of those raw materials exported by the economically weak dependent periphery.[171]

This means, as we have already seen, that the whole economy of the developing country depends, through its export sector, on the fluctuations of the economy of other countries, and that the uncertainties of the foreign currency receipts from exports cause great difficulties in long-range planning and the implementation of the development plans already worked out. A further consequence is that the advanced countries, through the terms of trade, can transfer most of the burdens of the crisis onto the developing countries or can manage to extricate themselves from the depression somewhat earlier and at the expense of the developing countries.

[170] In this way most of the "export economies" have become "*import-sensitive*" economies. An important part has also been played, of course, by the population explosion in this, which turned former grain exporting countries into grain importing countries. (In the late thirties the underdeveloped countries exported about 11 million tons of grain a year, but from the late forties they started to import, and the amount of their imports attained 25 million tons by 1964.) Considerable impact on import-sensitivity has been exerted also by the double bias in the investment pattern, already referred to, which has increased the expansion of the capital-intensive techniques, with the simultaneous retarding of the development of basic industries producing capital goods and developing technologies for the national economy. The import sensitivity is also enhanced by the fact that "as the demand for food, fuel and materials is inelastic, any drop in foreign incomes affects first of all the imports of capital goods", on which the rate of economic development depends. (I. Sachs: *Foreign Trade and Economic Development of Underdeveloped Countries*, p. 85.)

[171] By referring to an analysis by *Paul Bairoch*, H. Hveem states that "price fluctuations are greater for raw materials typically originating in periphery areas than for those from center areas." (See H. Hveem: Op. cit., p. 48, and Paul Bairoch: *Diagnostic de l'évolution économique du Tiers Monde 1900–1968*. Paris, Gauthier-Villars, 1969.)

The world-market position of industrial raw materials, especially the strategic materials (e.g. non-ferrous metals), strongly reflects the changes in world politics and in the arms race, too. The increase in international tension and the large-scale stockpiling in the time of a concrete danger of war máy lead to a steep rise in prices, followed by an abrupt drop if, owing to the easing of tension or some structural changes in military technology, the purchases are restricted or even stopped. (This was the effect, e.g., of the outbreak of the Korean war and, later, of the signing of the armistice.)

The statistical measurement of *losses* from the change in relative world-market prices, from the deterioration of the terms of trade is not free from problems. The magnitude of these losses pointed out statistically depends not only on the chosen variant of the terms-of-trade indices, but also on the choice of the base year, i.e., of the basis of comparison, and on the shifts in the commodity structure of exports and imports. The circle of beneficiaries is also difficult to determine, owing to the intricate transmissions in world trade.

Though the deterioration of the terms of trade was especially conspicuous in the second half of the 1950s and in the early 1960s, the tendency towards deterioration on the whole can already be observed from the end of the last century.

From as early as the eighteen-seventies, taking the average of the years 1876–1880 to be 100, the quantities of manufactures obtainable for the given quantity of primary products were until the First World War, expressed in five-year averages, as follows: 102, 96, 90, 87, 85, 86; from 1921 until the beginning of the Second World War: 87, 73, 62, 64; and, finally, as the average of the years 1946–1947: 69.[172]

In the mid-sixties, the terms of trade for the Third World as a whole showed greater stability up to the sudden price increases in 1972–1974. But behind the averages considerable differences can be found in the terms of trade for the individual countries or groups of countries exporting different products.

Between the mid-fifties and 1970, due to the rather stagnant or declining prices of the export products (except, e.g., oil) of the developing countries versus the increasing prices of the (both primary and manufactured) export products of the developed capitalist countries, the terms of trade (1963 = 100) for the non-oil exporting developing countries deteriorated by 12 per cent and for the oil exporters by 10 per cent.[173]

In the early seventies, there was some improvement in the terms of trade also for the non-oil mineral exporters, owing to an increase in their export

---

[172] See E. de Figuerca's paper on the deterioration of the terms of trade for developing countries. (Mimeographed translation, Documentation Service of the Institute for World Economics, Budapest.)

[173] See *1972 Review*. Development Co-operation. OECD, p. 91.

prices,[174] but the unfolding recession in the advanced capitalist countries, together with other unfavourable conditions (such as the protectionist measures of the latter and also the increased oil-import prices) resulted soon in their deterioration again. The export prices of the major petroleum exporters, which suddenly and considerably improved their terms of trade in 1973–1974, continued to remain high, or to increase further, in relation to their import prices also in the mid- and the late seventies. In 1979, the terms of trade for the Third World as a whole deteriorated (it was 96 only, if the 1975 level = 100, while in 1977 and 1978 it was 106 and 97, respectively). It improved only for the major oil exporters. The corresponding figures for the latter were 114 in 1979, and 107 and 94 in 1977 and 1978, respectively, while for the non-oil producing countries they were 90 in 1979, and 105 and 98 in 1977 and 1978, respectively.[175]

However different the figures of this simple terms-of-trade indicator[176] may be, depending on the chosen base year, and however divergent the trend of the terms of trade for the oil exporters may appear in the seventies, the general tendency of deterioration in a historical perspective and for the Third World as a whole is obvious enough.

The *losses* of the developing countries from the deterioration of the terms of trade can, of course, be measured only relatively (and even then rather inaccurately). In any case, according to official statistics, these losses amounted to 16,700 million dollars in the period 1951–1962. In the mid-sixties, the annual losses were around 2,500 million dollars. (There are estimates indicating the losses sustained in commodity exchange as considerably higher than that, owing to the choice of the base year and for other reasons.)[177]

[174] According to the UNCTAD Secretariat, the 1972–1974 price increases of minerals in markets, where CIF prices are quoted, might have partly resulted from increased freight rates. (UNCTAD Monthly Commodity Price Bulletin. Jan./Febr. 1974.—See H. Hveem: Op. cit., p. 176.)

[175] See *Protectionism and Structural Adjustment.* Loc. cit., Annex III. p. 11. Taking the terms of trade to be 100 for 1970, they were 123, 335(!), 341, 362, 361, 324, for the years 1973, 1974, 1975, 1976, 1977 and 1978, respectively, for the major oil-exporting countries. In the same period, the terms of trade for other developing countries were: 96, 93, 87, 88, 91, 86. (See *Handbook of International Trade and Development Statistics*, p. 62.)

[176] We have no comparable data available on the double factoral terms of trade. Their deteriorating trend, however, is even more obvious in the light of the widening productivity gap. (See, e.g., the industrial productivity indices in the *Handbook of International Trade and Development Statistics*, p. 532.) We fully agree to *Keith Griffin*'s statement that "... the double factoral terms of trade tend to move persistently in favour of the rich countries", because "exports from rich countries, and especially the rapidly expanding exporting sectors are intensive in knowledge and advanced technology." (Op. cit., p. 8.)

[177] According to *Ch. Bettelheim*, in the period 1950–1960, e.g., the foreign-trade loss sustained by the developing countries was 6,000 million dollars a year. (Ch. Bettelheim: *Planification et croissance accelerée.* Paris, 1967.) (See J. Dellagrammatikas: Op. cit., p. 29.)

(5) Another indirect form of income losses, which is also connected with foreign trade and export orientation resulting from the colonial division of labour, manifests itself in the *net balance of shipping freights, insurance and other services.*

Besides its abnormal and distorted structure, production for exports that is geared to foreign interests also has the harmful consequence that it means mostly overseas deliveries for which foreign merchant shipping must be used.[178] The net balance of sums paid as shipping charges alone amounted to around 4,000 million dollars in the mid-sixties. During the same period, the developing countries paid as a net deficit for other services a further 4,000 million dollars to the developed capitalist countries. The shipping and insurance costs constitute an evergrowing burden particularly for the "land-locked" and the least developed countries. In the years 1964–1967, the net payments by the least developed countries amounted to 200 million dollars a year on average, and this sum increased more than threefold by the end of the sixties, and was 700 million as the average of the years 1968–1970.[179]

During the seventies, the deficit of the developing countries in the balance of freight and insurance payments showed a further rapid growth and by 1971 reached more than 33,000 million dollars (in current prices), out of which nearly 18,000 million dollars represented the deficit of the oil-exporting countries. While the total receipts of all developing countries for such services increased only 3.7 times from 1970 to 1977, their payments rose almost 4.5 times (in constant dollar prices) during the same period. Their net deficit was equivalent to approximately 43 per cent of the total financial inflows in 1970, and about 69 per cent of that in 1977. The net payments deficit on account of services of all developing countries reached about 80 billion US dollars in 1980. Its annual average rate of increase was 25 per cent in the period 1972–1980.[180]

Though what is involved here is really payments for actual services, i.e., apparently "fair" business transactions, yet what we are, in fact, faced with is a form of income drain, at least for two reasons. First and foremost, because these services, or more exactly the greater part of them, have

[178] The share of developing countries (excluding Liberia and Panama) in world merchant fleet was only 8.1 per cent in 1964 and even less in the late sixties (7.6 per cent in 1969). This sharply contrasts with their high share in world sea-born trade, which exceeded 60 per cent for goods loaded and reached almost 20 per cent for goods unloaded in the sixties. (Review of Maritime Transport, 1969, and Review of International Trade and Development 1970. Op. cit., p. 103.) Though there has been some progress also in the development of the merchant fleet of developing countries, owing especially to joint efforts to establish own shipping companies (see, e.g., the Arab Shipping Transport Company, a Saudi Arabian-Brazilian joint venture, and NAMUCAR, a joint Caribian company, etc.), this progress cannot keep pace with the increased needs.

[179] *1972 Review.* Development Co-operation, p. 196.

[180] See *Handbook of International Trade and Development Statistics*, pp. 364–365 and *Protectionism and Structural Adjustment.* Op. cit., p. 37.

become necessary on account of their performing functions gained in the system of the colonial division of labour, i.e., primarily in the interest of the metropolitan countries and foreign capital, or, since the importance of these functions has decreased, owing to the colonial heritage of the economic and foreign-trade structure. In case the development of the economies of the countries concerned were sound and normal, most of these services would hardly be necessary, at least not in overseas relations and at the given level of their economic development. If the external economic relations developed in a sound proportion to, and in harmony with, internal economic development, there would be a sort of more balanced state between the need for these external services and the material conditions satisfying them (own transportation facilities, etc.) or between the use and the provision of these services. By no means is it possible that there should develop by itself, without any external force, influence or intervention, such a disproportionate, abnormal situation in which a national economy directs the overwhelming proportion of its *export products to far-away overseas markets*, while it is unable to provide the necessary minimum of transportation facilities—not only in the case of overseas deliveries, but even of deliveries within the country. Secondly, the service charges and the terms of payments are determined mostly by Western capitalist firms enjoying monopoly positions.

We could further lengthen the list of losses (e.g. by postal and communication services, banking operations, insurance, experts' and managerial fees, etc.) which appear in the constant deficit of the "balance" of services and result from the striking disproportion between the internal development and external relations of the economy.

(6) There are further income losses and drains *through monetary relations and the banking systems.*

The links between the internal financial and monetary system, including the national currency, of many developing countries and those of the metropolitan powers (in most cases of the former mother country), the central pool of currency zones with a concentration of the foreign-exchange reserves of the member countries in the central bank of the leading metropolitan country, the high proportion of the international reserves of developing countries kept in metropolitan currencies, the weaker position and various disadvantages of their banks vis-à-vis the metropolitan ones, etc., can be the sources of additional grave losses to the developing countries and of further unilateral benefits and extra incomes accruing to metropolitan finance capital.

The links with the metropolitan currency and banking are realized not only through international channels, that is, by the intertwining of the banking system, of the local agencies of metropolitan banks, but also in matters of foreign exchange in general, through the (already discussed) foreign-exchange dependence in the spheres of money supply and reserve formation. In this way, changes or even minor fluctuations in the metropolitan country's financial and foreign-exchange position can exert an intensive impact on the economy of the developing country, irrespective of its financial results actually achieved, and also cause serious losses.

The inequality of foreign-exchange positions also reflects the inequality of structures. The national currencies of the developing countries are in a weaker and subordinate position in relation to those of the developed capitalist countries. Since the former need for the "normal" conduct of their foreign purchases a large quantity of the currency of the stronger (developed capitalist) partner—which does not apply to the opposite case—,they are compelled to accumulate significant reserves of that currency. On the other hand, it is exactly because of this inequality, of the weaker, more unstable or at least dependent position of the developing country's currency (which also finds expression in the administrative and economic limitations of convertibility and may be reflected in multiple and black-market exchange rates) that a usually strong tendency of outward-oriented *speculative capital flow* makes itself felt, which counteracts the endeavour of the developing countries to accumulate reserves and may further weaken their currencies.

The most apparent and best-known variety of income losses sustained in foreign-exchange relations is the detrimental effect of the devaluation of the metropolitan country's currency on the value of reserves.[181] This does a relatively greater damage to the weaker economy, which is in a more unfavourable position also in respect of the reserves being divided into gold and convertible currencies.

The central pool of the currency areas means, in fact, constant credits to the metropolitan country, enabling it to meet deficites in other currencies by surpluses received from the member countries. For example, it was prescribed for the members of the franc area to transfer their entire foreign-currency recepts to a central pool controlled by the French treasury. In 1964, the former colonial countries transferred over 1,000 million francs in foreign currency to the pool.[182]

It was, e.g., thanks to the dollar pool of the sterling area that Britain was able to ease her dollar shortage with the help of the dollar receipts of her colonies. Between 1947 and 1957 Britain's dollar deficit amounted to about 1,500 million dollars while her colonies netted an annual average of 100 million pound worth of dollar receipts. Between 1954 and 1956 Britain's dollar deficit was 334 million while the net dollar receipts of the colonies rose to 356 million pounds.[183] From 1952 to 1957 the currency pool

[181] It will suffice here to refer again to the losses suffered by the sterling-area countries owing to the devaluation of the pound sterling, or to the loss of about 1 billion dollars of the developing countries as a result of the first dollar devaluation.

[182] L. Krasavina: Changes in the Franc Area. *Soviet Economists Discuss...*, p. 86.

[183] R. P. Dutt: Contemporary British Colonial Policy. *International Affairs*, No. 2, 1959, pp. 54–55.

operations enabled Britain to appropriate some 500 million dollars' worth of foreign currency. The figure for 1958–63 was still 420 million dollars.[184]

Systematic losses are also sustained by the developing countries through various *banking operations* (deposits in the metropolitan banks at low, often negative[185] interest rates, the unequal distribution of reserves for purposes of inter-bank settlements, etc.). At the same time, this opens up additional credit and interest sources for the stronger metropolitan banks.

The national banks of the countries with strongly export-orientated economy, which for this as well as for other reasons (as, e.g., the presence and role of foreign capital and expatriates) must maintain wide-ranging international payments relations quite out of proportion to the real capacity of their national economy, are at a disadvantage relative to the banks of the advanced countries in international reputation and capital supply. (This can be accounted for by their insignificant financial reserves, their less qualified and experienced clerks and the shortage of internationally known managers, etc.) Thus they are less attractive because foreign depositors consider them less credit-worthy. While they attract less foreign deposits, they are bound—because of their wide range of payments relations—to keep considerable amounts of money in foreign banks on non-interest-bearing current accounts, i.e. "in a non-earning form". These amounts serving the aims of interbank accounts are, because of slow and expensive communication, difficult to keep at an optimum level and can hardly be reduced, without jeopardizing reliability. "They money received from foreign banks (loro accounts) will be small compared to the money deposited with them (nostro accounts). The difference between the two represents a continuous loss of interest, reflected in the balance payments."[186]

It also follows from the generally lower reputation and capital strength of the national banks of developing countries that foreign exporters usually turn to their own banks for the confirmation of letters of credit for which the latter make a service charge, raising thereby the cost of imports for the developing countries.

Similar additional charges also arise for the developing country from the practice of foreign exporters often wanting payments to be made in the currency of a third country, in which case the charge for the conversion from one currency to another usually has to be borne by the soft-currency

[184] S. Borisov: The Sterling Area and British Neocolonialism. *Soviet Economists Discuss...*, pp. 98–99.

[185] As in the case of the bank deposits of those local, reactionary elements facing an uncertain political future in some developing countries who prefer the security of their wealth and the secrecy of their deposits to incomes from interests.

[186] M. J. H. Yaffey: Foreign Exchange Loss through Banking Operations: The Case of Tanzania. *Economic Research Bureau Paper*, 1967, 3, University College, Dar es Salaam, 1967.

developing country. Another source of losses may be the fact that "for technical reasons" the currency of the developing country "must be rigidly valued",[187] and the rate of exchange cannot adjust itself flexibly to the real economic relationships without incurring substantial expenses of communication.

These losses are the consequences of the structural disproportion which has evolved between the development level and capacity of the national economies of the developing countries, on the one hand, and their participation in the world-economic processes, the international economic relations, on the other, owing to the mechanism of the international division of labour (discussed in this chapter) and the internal distortions resulting from it (to be discussed in more detail in the following chapter). At the same time, however, we can also observe with regard to these losses and their causes that even the steps—at least the initial ones—taken to change the situation may induce newer losses or the causes to produce them. (Which can *by no means* justify the policy of *not* taking these positive and necessary steps!) What we must conclude from the foregoing is not only that these losses sustained through banking operations may follow also from the creation of an independent banking system, i.e. an important step taken towards economic independence, but we must also take into account that the more the developing countries, in the interest of loosening their one-sided trade and financial dependence, widen their trade and financial relations, the more such and similar losses (e.g. expenses from the maintenance of diplomatic representations) are liable to appear.

(7) An increasing role in the regular income drain and resource losses is played by *the costs of transferred technology* and of international manpower flows such as the *brain drain*.

The UNCTAD Secretariat has given[188] a more or less comprehensive list[189] of the main costs paid by the developing countries for transferred technologies. These costs are as follows:

— for the right to use patents, licences, know-how and trade marks;[190]
— for technical knowledge and know-how needed both at the pre-investment and investment stage and at the operation stage;

[187] Ibid.

[188] See *Transfer of Technology*. Report by the UNCTAD Secretariat. TD/106. 1971. New York, p. 9.

[189] It does not include, of course, all possible *social* costs (particularly those indirect costs which arise from the consumption pattern affected, or from the inappropriate quality of foreign technology. Such indirect losses (not calculable, of course) are strongly stressed by several prominent economists (e.g. Celso Furtado, Hans Singer, François Perroux, etc.).

[190] "The direct cost of technology—writes Ikonicoff—is particularly high in the case of the sale of patents and licences... Royalty payments for the use of patents and brand names are related to net sales or turnover of technology-importing units. Under this formula, the higher the price of the product, the higher the value of the royalty payment. Yet general policy decisions (on price fixing in particular) never adequately reflect the value of

300

— through over-pricing of imports of intermediate products and equipment ("hidden" costs or "price mark-ups");
— through profits on the capitalization of know-how (acquisition of equity participation in place of other means of payment for the transfer of technology); profits on these equity holdings are therefore to be regarded in part as payments for the transfer of technology;
— through a portion of repatriated profits of the wholly-owned subsidiaries and joint ventures which do not make specific provision for payments for technology transfer;
— through imports of capital and other technical equipment, the price of which usually allows for the exporter's valuation of the cost of technology.

In the case of 15 countries only the first two items of the above list accounted for about 1,500 million dollars a year in the late sixties, which represented about 56 per cent of the annual inflows of foreign direct investments.[191]

In one single year, 1970, Latin America paid 321 million dollars to the USA for technological transfer, which usually contained "purchases" by American subsidiaries from their American parent companies.[192]

The United States' net income from technology payments made only on account of the first two headings of the UNCTAD list were 575 million dollars in 1960 and 2,275 million in 1971.[193]

To the losses included in the costs mentioned above we must also add— though their consequences can hardly be measured statistically—the losses resulting from monopolistic exchange, price and information conditions[194], or from the relative obsolesence of "technological commodities" bought, as well as the losses arising from the more or less inferior productivity of transferred technology[195] as compared to the one developed in the metropolitan country and, further, from the fact that the technology transferred is usually not adjusted to local conditions (geographic, climatic,

---

technology. In addition to these direct costs, there are induced costs deriving from certain commitments imposed on the purchaser, such as an undertaking to buy spare parts from the firm selling the licence or to finance periodic inspections by technicians supervising production." (M. Ikonicoff: Op. cit., p. 283.)

[191] J. Annerstedt and R. Gustavsson: Op. cit., p. 59.

[192] C. Brundenius: The Anatomy of Imperialism. The Case of the Multinational Mining Corporations in Peru..., *Journal of Peace Research*, 1972, No. 3, p. 202.

[193] J. Annerstedt and R. Gustavsson: Op. cit., p. 60.

[194] On this point see C. V. Vaitsos: *Bargaining and the Distribution of Returns in the Purchase of Technology by Developing Countries.* IDEP/283. Repr. Dakar, 1971.

[195] A. G. Frank illustrates and proves by concrete examples that the metropolitan companies often deliberately transfer technologies of an inferior productivity (and therefore of a lesser competitiveness) to industrial plants, even to their own subsidiaries, in developing countries. (See A. G. Frank: *Lumpen-Bourgeoisie and Lumpen-Development*, pp. 108–109.)

or to those relating to the local labour and cost patterns), or is not used in plants of the appropriate size and on the right scale for serial production.[196]

One of the most serious losses with the gravest consequences from the point of view of development is the loss in human resources by *brain drain*. It means the emigration of qualified labour (in most cases from among those trained under the technical assistance programme in the developed capitalist countries) for various reasons such as better living conditions and research opportunities, the adoption of the "Western way of living", marriage, etc.

The danger of emigration is the greatest in the professionally most talented and best qualified people as they find it relatively easy to find rewarding jobs in the advanced countries, where the possibilities of further development (research institutes, experimental laboratories, scientific societies and the atmosphere of scientific life in general, etc.) represent great attraction for them. Such brain drain, that is, the withdrawal of human resources, constitutes a much greater loss than the number of the emigrant specialists or the costs of their training would suggest.[197]

It is simply impossible to measure or even to estimate what direct and mainly indirect positive spread effects and benefits would have stemmed from the life-long activity of the trained, qualified labour in their own country for the national economy and society. Similarly, it is impossible to estimate the indirect losses to the nation's development arising from the negative spread effects of the absence of educated people in respect of income level and distribution, of cultural life, social cohesion and national integration, etc.[198]

---

[196] R. Prebisch stresses the uneconomical character of the many small passenger-car plants set up in Latin America and the duplicated capacities of industrial plants producing or assembling identical products often not only in the neigbouring countries but also within the same country. (Integracion de America Latina. Mexico-Fondo de Cultura Economica. 1964, p. 143.)

[197] According the estimates, the brain drain from developing countries to the most advanced economies involved about 40,000 people a year in the 1960s, which was more than the technical assistance personnel received by them. The number of qualified labour that emigrated to the USA alone from the Third World rose from 2,200 in 1955–1956 to 10,250 in 1966–1967. Among them there were 4,200 engineers, 4,300 medical doctors and other persons trained in health service, and 1,500 persons educated in the natural sciences. (A. K. Sen: A quantitative study of the flow of trained personnel from the developing countries to the United States of America. *Journal of Development Planning*. UN, New York, 1971, No. 3, p. 107.)

The estimated extra income generated by immigrant qualified labour in the United States was about 3.5 billion dollars a year (!) in 1970. (See information from the documents of international organizations. *MTI Bulletin*, 1975, No. 4. Budapest.)

[198] *Keith Griffin* points out that besides the reduction of economic surplus and income, i.e., the distributable sum, a no less serious consequence of brain drain is the reinforced tendency of increasing income inequalities within the society left by the emigrating professionals, inequalities in favour of the remaining scarce staff of highly qualified labour,

But even if no actual emigration takes place, many of those educated abroad often get alienated in their way of thinking and habits, that is, they become "intellectual emigrants". They find it usually hard to readjust themselves to the domestic environment. They tend to orientate themselves towards the "western" world of cities and university campuses and wish by no means to return to the earlier environment of their mother country. Though, owing to their experiences and knowledge, they might be the vanguards of enlightenment against traditional superstition and of the new technology and organization, of the transformation of the obsolete order in general, but in many cases they look at their environment rather with passive dissatisfaction and regard uncritically the scene of their studies abroad as a "model" country. The greater the contrast between the living standard enjoyed abroad and experienced at home, the greater the danger of alienation.

Other unquantifiable losses are those that find expression in the additional import needs and negative saving incentives induced by the presence, the way of living and consumption habits, also extending over local strata, of the large number of *foreign experts*. Such losses belong to the actual social costs of the services rendered by foreign skilled personnel—just as to the costs of taking advantage of foreign scholarships. In other words, besides the salaries and various fringe benefits (generally much higher than those enjoyed by local labour), even if they are financed from foreign grants, account must also be taken of the consequences of the demonstration effects on the pattern of consumption, not to speak of the positive or negative "balance" of the socio-political effects as factors influencing the development of the national intelligentsia.

It would not be difficult to lengthen at will the list of the forms of concealed, indirect income drains or income losses.[199] But, without going into further details, let us make a simple comparison, just for the sake of a partial illustration, between the amounts of total inflows of financial resources to the Third World and the measured (mostly underrated and obviously incomplete) outflows from it:

For example, in the mid-sixties—according to official statistical data— the total flows of concessional and non-concessional financial resources (direct private investments, credits, government loans, etc.) to the developing countries made up 10 billion US dollars a year, and the annual outflows (only those shown in the balance of payments or relatively easily

---

and at the expense of the non- or less educated masses, which may undermine the social cohesion of the nation. (See Keith Griffin: Op. cit., p. 10.)

[199] Such might be, e.g., the disguised drains via overpaid management services and advisory fees, the illegal exports of national values or the pension and commutation payments and compensations that a number of newly independent countries are compelled to pay their ex-colonial expatriate officers, etc.

calculable from statistical data) amounted to more than 15 billion (out of which about 3 billion was the bill of declared profit repatriation, 2.5 billion represented the average loss from deteriorated terms of trade, 4 billion the net balance of shipping charges and another 4 billion the net payments for other services and 2 billion the annual debt service).

Though since the mid-sixties the total inflows of financial resources from developed capitalist countries have considerably increased (in nominal terms), the outflows have tended to rise even more rapidly. (For example, by the early seventies the total amount of financial inflows almost doubled, while that of the declared profit repatriations doubled, and the increase in debt services was more than fivefold. By 1976, the total annual inflows, in nominal terms, surpassed the mid-sixties' level about 5 times, while the annual debt services increased more than 11 times and the total outflows continued to exceed the total inflows.[200]

This illustrative comparison will hopefully dispel first of all the illusion that the gap between the advanced and the developing countries can be narrowed down substantially by simply increasing (or even multiplying) the amount of aid and/or by easing for the developing countries' exports the access to the market of the advanced economies. As long as the influx of financial, technological and intellectual resources to the developing countries is connected with an increasing outflow of development resources, with direct and indirect losses exceeding the inflows, and also with resource misutilization induced by structural deformations, which all follow from the spontaneous mechanism of the world capitalist economy and the structural characteristics of "underdevelopment", and as long as the fundamental inequalities in the international relations of ownership, control and distribution of the dynamic "factors" of development (qualified labour, science, research and development capacities, technologies and the related industries capable of creating and/or promoting them) are perpetuated and increasingly reproduced, there is no hope of narrowing the "development gap" in the world, nor even of preventing its further widening.

It would be easy to advise the developing countries to prevent the skimming off of their resources by simply expropriating the expropriators overnight, i.e. by immediately nationalizing foreign capital, or to suggest that they should trade with, and receive aid and credits from, the socialist countries instead of the capitalist ones. Such a simplification underestimates not only the economic and technical conditions of nationalization (let alone social and political ones) and the actual needs to cooperate, in one way or another, with foreign capital and to continue to trade with metropolitan countries, as well as the structural and monetary difficulties of trading with

[200] Estimates and calculations were made on the basis of data in the *1972, 1973* and *1974 Reviews.* Development Co-operation, and *Handbook of International Trade and Development Statistics.*

304

the socialist countries, but fails to take into full account the actual state of the international economic power relations. There are no immediate and one-sided solutions for the whole Third World at once, but there do exist possibilities for short-cuts, for accelerated development on the basis of internal and international concerted efforts.

Where the mechanism of exploitation is a spontaneous mechanism built on the internal structure of the exploited countries on the one hand, and is part and consequence of the whole mechanism of the world economy itself, on the other, the *internal* solution can only be a *structural*, consequently also a political one, and the *international* solution only a *political*, consequently also a structural one.

CHAPTER III

THE INTERNAL FACTORS AND MECHANISM
OF THE SYSTEM OF UNDERDEVELOPMENT

In the preceding chapters we have often touched upon the internal socio-economic state of developing countries and the characteristics of this state. As we have seen in Part One the typical variant of the conveniontal "underdevelopment" theories concentrates on these internal factors and characteristics. When criticizing these theories, it was not our intention to underestimate the significance of the internal factors. What we aimed at was first of all to point out that the internal factors do not provide a satisfactory, logically consistent and historically verifiable explanation of underdevelopment, and that the most typical of the large number of various factors are the very ones that can only be derived from the effect of the external, international forces. Such a factor is above all the *lack of economic and social integration, the dual, distorted socio-economic structure.*

Since the relevant international literature treats extensively and with rich illustrating statistical data the role and effect of the individual internal factors and the way they work, it seems unnecessary to give them the same detailed analysis as is given to the much more neglected subject of the negative role of external, international factors. Beyond the criticism given in Part One of the *isolated* treatment of the internal factors and their use for the *explanation* of underdevelopment, it appears sufficient and more expedient to confine ourselves to the investigation of the disintegrated structure and, within that, to the relationship of the main internal factors to each other and to some external factors.

This investigation aims not only at adding further arguments to our statements in the critical chapters, but also sets out to prove the *complex* nature of underdevelopment. While the existence of the disintegrated, dual structure refers to the historical causes and the international roots of underdevelopment, the mechanism of that structure and the complexity of the resulting effects and tendencies already show the *relative independence and self-reproducing spontaneity* of underdevelopment as a historical product. Thus we shall be in a position to shed some light not only on the historically and logically primary and determining relationship between the two aspects, the external and internal aspects of underdevelopment, but also on the complex system of mutual interdependencies. In this way, perhaps, we shall also be able to assess more realistically the strategic possibilities of overcoming underdevelopment. It will not only turn out, as it did in the preceding chapter, viz. that given the unchanged international mechanism of dependence and income-drain, *no* substantial progress in surmounting underdevelopment *can* be attained (even if the dream of aid programmes satifying the most ambitious expectations should become a reality), but it will also be proved that the survival of dependence and income-drain mechanism is to a great extent a function of the internal structures as well. In other words, that the internal structure of the developing countries is not only the product of the penetration of external, international forces, but that this structure, once it has become established, will itself provide a basis for maintaining this penetration.

1. THE DISINTEGRATION OF THE MODE OF PRODUCTION AND THE DISTORTIONS OF THE ECONOMIC STRUCTURE

The disintegration of the mode of production is due to the fact that it was not the internal evolution of their own economy which led the underdeveloped countries to become organic parts of world economy but, on the contrary, it is their linking to world economy that has set the wheels of certain sectors of their economy in motion. Consequently, the elements of a more modern form of production (and a more modern society) were imposed on traditional economy (and society) *from outside*, as a strange and isolated element, generally within the framework of colonialism and by sheer force. These well-known "enclaves" were, from the beginning, outwardly orientated and also remained so subsequently, partly because their establishment and functioning were attached to alien interests, to those of the colonial powers and foreign capital in general, and partly because they were under the influence of spontaneous economic forces which stimulated even the national investors—if there were any—to engage in economic branches producing for exports.

It is obvious that these *enclaves* could not become the driving forces of the inner economic development, *first of all* because they embodied the sort of international division of labour which has brought about, even at its height, a number of negative consequences for the countries in question (e.g. a biassed economic structure, different ways of skimming off incomes, etc.). Moreover, as a consequence of scientific and technical progress and the shifts in the production and consumption patterns and in the international division of labour, the enclave sectors of primary products lost even their initial dynamism. *On the other hand*, these export sectors could not become the driving forces of economy because they were scarcely ever in direct contact with their environment, with other sectors of the economy (and society) of the given country. Thus the traditional forms of economy (and society) have not disappeared but, instead, have survived alongside, and subordinated to, those "modern", capitalistic sectors induced from outside.

The internally non-integrated character of the economy (and society) of the developing countries manifests itself in:

(a) the "dualism" of the dominant, capitalistic (so-called "modern") and the subordinated capitalistic, "traditional" socio-economic sectors;

(b) the co-existence of export economy and subsistence economy; and

(c) the distorted sectoral structure and the inadequacy of the relations between different branches of the economy.

Thus this distorted, disintegrated structure means that alongside a more or less modern capitalist sector there also exists a considerable precapitalist sector, that the economy consists of two, diametrically opposed sectors, and the individual branches of economy did not develop simultaneously, by being connected with and complemented by each other, but in a strikingly disproportionate way, so that some, usually similar, economic branches began to grow rapidly like "alien bodies", isolated from the development of other economic branches and mostly even hindering or preventing their development. It is common knowledge that these "alien bodies" developed in the fields of raw-material extraction and agricultural export production, according to the interests of the advanced capitalist countries and as a result of their purposeful intervention.

But it would not be correct to make a fetish of the purposeful intervention of the capitalist powers and imagine that the investment activity of foreign capitalists or the loan and aid policy of the advanced capitalist countries have always been aimed at distorting the economic structure or maintaining it by preventing industrialization. The awareness of distant interests has, of course, a certain significance. If, however, we interpret the one-sided development of the extraction industries and the monocultural economy exclusively as the consequence of activities in line with the long-term objectives of colonial policy, we can hardly explain the fact that national capital, where there was any, tended to engage in the same branches, too, and that these very branches are being developed also in a number of those underdeveloped countries where otherwise a decolonizing economic policy is being pursued. It is obvious that, in addition to the purposeful activities, the *spontaneous movement of economic forces* has worked in the direction of distorting the economic structure of the underdeveloped countries, and some sort of cumulative process has developed, but these spontaneous economic forces were originally set in motion either directly by advanced capitalism penetrating from outside or indirectly by its various effects.[1]

Prior to the penetration of colonial or semi-colonial capitalism, the fairly narrow market relations in the present-day underdeveloped countries corresponded to the development level of the productive forces of that time, and they expanded slowly according to the rise in the latter, exerting at the same time a stimulating effect on the further widening of the inner social

[1] It is important to add this, because, as we have seen, many theoreticians fail to mention this very fact while emphasizing at the same time that the investment decisions of foreign private capital are justified from a business point of view

308

division of labour and the development of all economic branches taking part in it. All this did not go, however, beyond the limits of simple reproduction. If it did, it was a temporary and irregular phenomenon. But when western capitalism penetrated into this slow but more or less harmonious process, it exported its own "natural laws". The metropolitan investor who exported investment capital to the colonial or semi-colonial country, acted according to the economic considerations to which he had been conditioned in his own country. He did not necessarily think of what investment policy the long-term interests of colonialism expected him to pursue, or of the consequences a given economic decision may have had for the future of the country in question. He was only interested in how he could make the best use of his capital, i.e. he was led by "daily" business considerations.[2]

The market demand of the low-income population which, because of the predominantly subsistence character of production, had hardly joined yet in the sphere of monetary economy, was confined to a few essentials, while the demand of the narrow "top" stratum only to some imported luxuries. The economic mechanism to meet the requirements of the realization of capital had not yet developed. There had not yet come into being at the level of the national economy those "external" conditions (as, e.g., in the field of material and labour supply, marketing, transportation, etc.) that are required by the metamorphosis of capital. In the underdeveloped areas a new industrial undertaking usually breaks up a virgin territory—writes Paul Baran.[3] There is no *operating* economic system. It has to organize from its own resources not only the production process within its boundaries but also all external conditions for its operation. It does not enjoy the benefits of "*external* economies". Therefore, it was bound to choose for its field of activity a branch of production which was not limited by the local market with its narrow and unfavourably structured demand, which did not require large investment in machinery—considering the problems of purchase, transportation, delivery, replacement, repair and, consequently, the expensiveness and handling of the machines in general. It chose a branch for which the available (often forcibly available) low-quality manpower seemed suitable.

Such branches of production are raw-material extraction and agriculture with their relatively low need for fixed-capital investments, their preference for unskilled manual labour and the ability to adjust themselves to the external markets. And what was originally a starting point, became later a

[2] Many of the authors of theories "only" make the mistake that they take the presence of foreign capitalists in the underdeveloped countries for granted and regard therefore these business considerations as natural. Thus it appears as if the "*homo oeconomicus*" of the Robinsonades, the "born" capitalist had arrived anyway, independently of space and time, under the same considerations.

[3] P. Baran: Op. cit., *The Economics of Underdevelopment*, p. 83.

result and at the same time a new starting point. If the extractive industries and agriculture were preferred in the early investment schemes because e.g. they scarcely needed any investment in machinery, then they did not induce the development of the local machine industry even later when they had already reached a certain degree of expansion. Therefore, the original economic consideration (low need for machinery, investment of a low organic composition)[4] reproduced itself even in the later enterprises. If at the beginning it was necessary to adjust any particular investment to the availability of cheap, unskilled labour and to the priority of manual labour, then later, the economic mechanism set in motion reproduced this cheap, unskilled labour in ever-increasing numbers, and the investors of the new enterprises were also faced with the same labour-market relations. And while capitalist production in the extractive industries and agriculture originally adjusted itself—owing to the limited internal market—to the external market, this adjustment to export considerations was even more compelling for it later on,[5] when increasing import needs for manufactured goods and foodstuffs had to be met. Consequently, increasing pressure has been exerted on stifling or restricting the development of the processing industries and food production.

In this way, "purely", i.e. even exclusively as a result of the free play of economic forces, a *cumulative process* began to evolve spontaneously, which, even without the conscious, purposeful assertion of colonial interests but objectively in conformity with them, proceeded in the direction of the *increasing distortion of the economic structure*. This process, however, cannot be explained by itself[6] as it was originally started by a penetration from *outside*, by the intrusion of the "ready-made" forms of the developed capitalist mode of production into an economy at a lower development level of productive forces and relations.

In outlining this spontaneous cumulative process here we had to temporarily disregard a number of otherwise important factors, e.g. that dependence had already existed at the start, as well as the consequences of the general development of the capitalist international division of labour. We also left out of account such factors as, e.g., the monopolistic position of foreign capitalists and the consequences of the restricted competition that follows, the subsidies granted by the colonial governments, the role of

[4] In this respect, the investment policy already discussed of the vertically structured foreign monopolies constitutes a certain change of exception in that it has established, especially since independence, subsidiary or mixed companies with capital-intensive techniques in certain branches in order to create a market for its machine-manufacturing plants in the metropolitan country.

[5] The growth of employment expanded the local market, whose supply, however, owing to the backwardness of the processing industries and the contraction of food production for the satisfaction of internal needs, demanded increasing imports.

[6] That is, *not* a vicious circle!

metropolitan commodity exporters, the various aspects of banking and crediting, etc.

Thus the distortion of the economic structure of the underdeveloped countries manifested in the one-sided, disproportionate development of mining and a monocultural agriculture, as well as in the underdevelopment of other economic sectors in general. It is also reflected, of course, in the structural pattern of foreign trade.

A rapid development started only in a few economic sectors of the colonial and semi-colonial countries, but these sectors sprang up as "alien bodies", adjusting themselves to, and serving directly, the economy of the advanced capitalist countries while they remained isolated from the other sectors of domestic economy.

Since these sectors constituted islands within the economy, they did not only fail to stimulate but even hampered the development of the other sectors. The growth of export production did not increase the accumulation and investment sources of the other sectors, even if they yielded considerable foreign exchange receipts, but they led rather to increasing import of manufactures which, in turn, held back even further the development of the local industry. The separation of the developing export sectors from the rest of the economy resulted at the same time in the survival and preservation of the remnants of the primitive mode of production, of subsistence economy. In this way the most advanced form of commodity production, *production for the world market, became intermingled in a peculiar way with the subsistence economy*. This strange symbiosis could not have come into existence if capitalist development in these countries had not been started from outside.

Thus the developing countries have inherited from colonialism an economy of a distorted structure reflecting their structural role and subordinated position in the world capitalist division of labour. Despite some modification of the latter, resulting from the rise of certain dependent "enclave industries" in the Third World, it is still characteristic that while the developing countries supply the greater part of world exports in a number of agricultural and mineral primary commodities (e.g. 75–92 per cent of the sugar, cocoa, tea, spices, coffee, sisal, etc. exports more than half of the cotton, rubber and over 90 per cent of the crude-oil exports of the world), their total manufactured production and exports remain—as has been shown—at a low level (representing only a 8–9 per cent share in world manufactured exports). And what is even more characteristic of the distorted structure is that while their agriculture yields the bulk of the world output of several commodities, a grave nutrition problem is threatening millions with death by starvation, and these countries rely to an increasing extent on agricultural food and raw-material imports from the industrialized countries (constituting a growing share in their world imports).

The economic structure of the developing countries is still characterized on the whole by the *dominant role of agriculture*[7] and the *underdevelopment of industry*. But agriculture itself is of a distorted, monocultural structure and, as regards industry, the most important branches of the manufacturing industry, namely those producing and developing an appropriate technology for the local economy, are completely lacking or hardly developed, while the development of the extractive industries shows a one-sided pattern. The processing industry is mostly confined to getting raw materials ready for export, to food processing and the textile industries. The factories producing and/or assembling spare parts and components mostly belong to the corporate network of transnational companies. There are, of course, considerable differences in this respect between individual countries and regions.

This distorted structure of the economy is also reflected in *the commodity pattern of foreign trade*. While on the export side there are only one or a few agricultural or mineral raw materials, the imports have a wide range, generally including agricultural produce and foodstuffs in addition to the manufactured products.

This pattern of foreign trade renders their economy as a whole sensitive to external, world-market movements, and cyclical changes, since their import needs, as a rule, far exceed their actual purchasing capacity, while their exports, owing to the rigid pattern, do not even make it possible for them to resort, in the case of an unfavourable world-market position, to substitutes. Consequently, the deterioration of their foreign-trade position is one of the most acute problems they have to face, and the upward trend of their trade deficit makes it imperative for them to reshape their production pattern and modify their role in the international division of labour.

Having looked into the problems of economic dependence, income drain and the distorted economic structure, we may have also shed some light on the question of the *low per-capita national income*. The point is that, owing to the skimming off of profits by foreign capital and to the role the developing countries play, or rather are in fact compelled to play, in the international division of labour, part of their national income gets absorbed in their external economic relations while this peculiar role, together with the economic structure adjusted to it, deteriorates also the very conditions for the production of national income, and hampers the growth of the productive forces, too. It hinders them not only by blocking the development of the most dynamic productive branches of the key sectors

[7] Agriculture provides employment for 80–95 per cent of the population in Tropical Africa, 60 per cent in Latin America, and about 70 per cent in the Arab East, in India and Indonesia. It is in this economic sector that most of the gross national product, and the bulk of the national income and export returns are produced in the majority of developing countries.

312

and technological centres, but also by isolating the export sectors from their environment and preserving the remnants of the primitive mode of production in other sectors, moreover even within the one-sidedly developed export sectors.

The low level of the productive forces is undoubtedly connected with the remnants of the primitive, ancient mode of production. But the conservations of these remnants cannot be accounted for today without the analysis of the peculiar historical development which these countries as constituents of *world capitalism* have undergone. The disclosure of this historical relationship, however, does not diminish the development-impeding role of the precapitalistic remnants themselves and does not free the traditional modes of production and the related social structures from their responsibility for the low level of productive forces.

It will suffice here to refer to the obsolete form of subsistence economy that is incapable of any progress, and is the organic consequence of the traditional land tenure system and various precapitalistic relations. Furthermore, we scarcely need to point out the fact that the surviving land tenure, ownership and distribution relations, and the forms of labour organization do not make the producers and even their expropriators keen on adopting modern productive methods or interested in commodity production and restrict the expansion of the internal market. They prevent not only the free sale of land, and the labour force from becoming "free", i.e. deprived of the means of production (which are the preconditions of a proper capitalist mechanism) but also their rational social utilization in any other (e.g. socialist) way. They set a limit, by the unproductive squandering of resources, to the growth of productive accumulation. In addition, they are also responsible for maintaining the low quality of the labour force. These feudal, or prefeudal remnants are the veritable hotbeds of superstitious habits, ingrained conservatism, and an aversion to all that is new. They maintain a social isolation, a stratification according to tribes, religions, nationalities and castes.

The growth-limiting effect of the precapitalistic remnants and of the traditional economic sector preserving them is best shown by the fact that this sector is incapable of a systematic *expanded reproduction*. And it is precisely here, in the diverging and contrastive characters of simple and expanded reproduction that the difference between the traditional sector, producing merely for consumption, and the new sector, emerging under colonialism and producing for the (world) market, manifests itself in the most conspicuous way.

Thus the distorted economic structure of the developing countries also includes these precapitalistic remnants, and without their liquidation neither the sound transformation of this structure nor the speeding up of the development of the productive forces is imaginable.

313

In the following, we shall examine the consequences of the disintegrated, dual structure in the principal spheres of the process of economic development, and its impact on market relations, as well as on the process of capital accumulation and the employment situation.

(a) THE CONSEQUENCES OF INTERNAL DISINTEGRATION IN MARKET RELATIONS

A common and well-known problem of the developing countries is the narrowness of the domestic market. This fact is due not only to the generally low income level and to the unfavourable distribution of incomes but also to the heterogeneous and distorted structure of the economy.

Both the outwardly orientated, modern sector and, particularly, the traditional sector, due to its inherent nature, set limits to the development of internal commodity relations.

(A) The capitalistic, "modern sector", originally restricted to, and including even today only or mainly, the production of agricultural primary commodities for export purposes and/or—if such resources are available— an export-oriented mining sector, hardly generates any induction effect on the development of the internal division of labour and on the expansion, thereby, of the domestic market.

"*Downward (or forward) linkage effects*", which work from the producer towards the consumer, appear only in some of the sidelines of industry, e.g., in the processing of raw materials for export (cleaning, packing); these, however, contribute at best to the expansion of the export sector but scarcely modify commodity relations directed towards inland trade. This is due to the fact that raw materials are processed abroad and, therefore, the positive effects act on the processing industries of other countries.

The "*upward (or backward) linkage effects*"—ranging from the consumer to the producer of raw materials and means of production—are also negligible, because of the raw material producing character of these export sectors. They do not require further raw and basic materials, only fuels, lubricants, means of transport and machines, though the latter ones are confined to a small scale because of the large amount of cheap and unskilled labour available. However, the demand induction in the majority of cases is also outward-bound and tends towards foreign industries producing capital goods, because

– no appropriate capital goods producing industry has yet developed within the given economy, or

– without protectionism the products of such an industry are not competitive even on the home market, or

– exporters, if having at their exclusive disposal the currency acquired abroad, can get the capital goods under more favourable conditions there, or

– simply because the export sector is in several cases under the control or in the hands of foreign firms which are interested in the import of capital goods or have got used to the processing technology that is suitable in their own country.

Neither does the raw-material producing sector exert a notable demand induction on the home production of consumption goods. This means that its *secondary, or indirect linkage effect* (with an upward trend from the consumer to the producer through the personal income of those taking part in the production sector) is also considerably limited. The reasons are the following:

(a) In the *agricultural* export sector the personal utilization of income is embodied:

– by the consumption of big landowners and owners of plantations who chiefly demand imported goods out of habit or on account of a better quality or because of pretentiousness; (if the proprietors are foreign capitalists, consumption is transferred to foreign countries)

– and by the consumption by peasants and agricultural wage workers, the market effect of which is, however, limited not only by their low income but by the traditional subsistence economy of the family and by the low level of demand for manufactured goods.

(b) *In the mining sector*, the personal consumption of the capitalists and the employees in a higher income bracket makes a demand also on imported commodities. (The demand of foreign capitalists and employees in this branch of the economy is also transferred abroad.) The market effect of the consumption of the wage labourers is limited by their meagre income and the low level of employment and, in the case of migrant labourers, by the role of the subsistence economy in the supply of their families.[8]

(B) The *"traditional" sector* as a subsistence economy is, in the main, a vast "island" within the national economy, which hardly generates or receives any induction effects except those arising from contacts with state administration and with the neighbouring commodity-producing sectors (e.g. taxation, communal development in the district, migrant labourers, etc.). However, "purely" subsistence economic units are rather rare today,[9]

---

[8] Let us disregard here the other, less typical branches or elements of the modern sector, which are of a different origin or have come about as a result of recent changes. It is, however, worth noting that the growth of the urban élite usually means a shift in favour of import consumption, and that the demand of those in the public sector is characterized both by the absolute limitation of the demand, for local commodities, of those in the low-income brackets, and by the import orientation of the demand of those in the high-income brackets.

[9] According to Winter's scheme, the transformation of traditional agriculture involves the following stages:

"(1) pure subsistence (no cash crops, no taxes, no import or export of labour);

(2) subsistence with taxes (some cash crops, labour seeking employment primarily to pay taxes);

315

and a certain degree of market production and other additional income sources (e.g. in the form of migrant labour) are nearly always tied, mostly as a result of tax payments or certain "target" purchases, to the economy producing basically for its own consumption. But the growth of income or the decreasing effect of the outside factors inducing marketing (e.g. taxation) leads as a rule to the expansion of self-consumption, i.e. it decreases the marketable surplus.[10] This follows from the nature of subsistence economy.

The lack of a division of labour between the *agricultural* and *non-agricultural* activities within the traditional sector (or merely its expression in the division of labour *within* the family by sex and age) sets a limit to the development of market relations.

But the negative effect of the traditional sector on the market relations also manifests itself indirectly:

(a) The traditional sector as an "inexhaustible" source of cheap and unskilled labour exerts a pressure on the income level and purchasing power of the wage workers of the modern sector.

(b) In many places the families of wage workers of the modern sector live within the traditional sector and are provided for by subsistence economy.

(c) The traditional sector influences the consumer demand and the way of spending incomes, through its ancient social customs, particularly in the case of migrant labourers leading a "double life".

The export orientation of the modern sector and its structure, as well as the isolation of the traditional sector and its indirect negative effects, restrict the development of internal commodity relations and spread effects. It is obvious that in the last resort only the dissolution of the dual structure and

---

(3) subsistence and cash crops (cash crops grown primarily for own cash needs, not primarily for taxes; no labour export);

(4) subsistence and cash (cash crops grown primarily for own cash needs, not primarily for taxes; labour export important);

(5) agricultural plantations (most agricultural labour working for wages);

(6) industrial economy."

(Quoted and referred to by B. W. Hodder: *Economic Development in the Tropics*. Methuen, London, 1968, p. 106.)

Though the sequence in time of these "stages" was either different in reality (as, e.g., the 2nd and 5th stages appeared at the same time in such settlers' colonies as Kenya, Rhodesia, etc.), or is attributable to specific circumstances, and is therefore not the result of a natural self-evolution, these "stages", or more exactly, forms really exist and indicate the transformation process of the traditional agrarian economy.

[10] "In the case of an underdeveloped economy"—says Rao—"however, household enterprises predominate, and production is much more for self-consumption than for the market, with the result that when there is an increase in income, the marginal propensity to consume leads to an increase in the demand for self-consumption rather than for purchases in the market." (V.K.R.V. Rao: *Essays in Economic Development*. Asia Publishing House, London, 1964, p. 46.)

modification of the sectoral pattern will bring about the intensification of internal market relations.

No doubt, some steps in this direction have already been taken, especially recently, even in such African countries whose economy is of a particularly distorted and dual character. Some of these steps are, e.g., the creation of some manufacturing industries based either on domestic raw materials or the domestic market, the launching of various rural settlement programmes, the infrastructural investments in those rural areas which also include the traditional sector, the direction towards the home market of the consumption of those enjoying higher incomes in the modern sector by employing foreign-exchange restrictions and customs regulations, etc., while the increasing flow of the labour force into the towns, and the migrant-labour system itself lead to a loosening of the ties and isolation of the traditional sector. But as long as the most important, central links are missing in the chain of the vertical structure of national production, these steps are bound to produce only minor quantitative changes.

The missing central links in the chain of the vertical structure of social production provide the explanation why the system of the inter-sectoral relations and linkage effects has *not* changed and cannot essentially change in spite of the fact that the *originally predominant labour-intensive techniques*, preferred by private capital because of the abundance of cheap and unskilled labour and the nature of the primary-producing sectors, was replaced in certain newly established branches of light industry (mainly as a result of the business policy of foreign vertical oligopolies) *by capital-intensive techniques*. Where there is a lack of domestic industries manufacturing capital goods, machines, tools and equipment, and a lack, particularly, of local technological R & D facilities, the adoption of capital-intensive techniques leads to an intensification of import orientation. And since the imported capital-intensive technology with a relatively high technical level (relative to the general level of education in the country) means the exclusion of the local labour force from the training process, or at least the restriction of this process to a narrow workers' élite, it leaves, strangely enough, the old mechanism, which ensures the predominance of the labour-intensive sectors and techniques with hardly any linkage effects, unchanged in the rest of the economy.

Moreover, this method of industrialization which, instead of creating the central links in the process of industrial (and agricultural) development— i.e. of the capital-goods producing industries with technological development facilities, determining the technical and productivity level, and expanding both the productive and future labour-absorbing capacity as well as the market of the national economy—implants in the national economy only the superstructural elements of industry (almost just as "alien" bodies as the "enclave" sectors), hinders the process of socio-economic

317

integration[11] and has, as one of the results, the tendency to reduce the market relations and linkage effects among sectors. This tendency manifests itself in the impact of this type of industrialization on
- the import sensitivity of the national economy,
- the volume and composition of the labour force employed,
- the traditional rural sector and
- the other branches and economic units of the urban sector.

The increase in import sensitivity resulting from the fact that the operation of the capital-intensive technique depends on the importing of machines, equipment, means of transport and sometimes even of raw materials and fuels,[12] aggravates the export dependence of the national economy and results in the cumulative strengthening of the enclave character of the export sectors.

As a result of the shift towards the capital-intensive techniques, the employment of the labour force, in other words the absorbing capacity of the modern sector, decreases in relative terms, while there is a change in the composition of labourers employed in favour of the highly paid employees and élite workers. This leads to a decrease in exactly that sort of purchasing power, i.e. the purchasing power of those in the lower income brackets (as a result of the relative shrinking of their employment and the freezing or fall of real wages), which would induce the demand for local products and thereby the development of industries producing for the domestic market and would also induce the transformation of the traditional economy. On the other hand, the purchasing power interested in imported goods, i.e. the purchasing power of expatriates directing or teaching the advanced techniques and of the local élite employees imitating the consumption habits of the latter, tends to increase.[13]

The process of the transformation and integration of the traditional sector is strongly impeded by the relative contraction of the employment opportunities of the unskilled labour moving out of that sector, and by the structural shift of purchasing power and demand (at the expense of the potential market of the products of the traditional sector). Even those contacts and relations between the traditional and modern sector which were formerly realized by the migrant-labour system and the sale of the occasional surplus products and simple handicraft products of the

---

[11] This question, especially its socio-political implications, is dealt with in G. Arrighi: *International Corporations, Labour Aristocracies and Economic Development in Tropical Africa*.

[12] It is in this sense that this sort of import substitution is called self-defeating.

[13] It is worth pointing to a phenomenon which appears to be a special manifestation of Engel's law. The rise in wages and salaries, or the shift towards the higher income brackets among the employed brings about a shift in the demand structure not simply from the lower-grade goods to the higher-grade ones, from basic food and clothing articles towards durable consumer goods, but very often from local products to import goods even within the commodity category of the same or similar grade.

318

traditional sector to the urban low-income strata, among them the migrant workers, are liable to reduction.

This type of "industrialization" on the line of capital-intensive light industries (or other industries unable to produce and develop technologies for the domestic economy) also makes its influence felt in the other spheres of the urban sector. Thus the domain of the local small and handicraft industries continues to contract and the small or medium capital belonging to a few indigenous entrepreneurs or rather to the local racial minorities engaged in the processing or marketing of local products, is either ousted from its activity or compelled to turn elsewhere. As a rule, the labour force of the new light-industrial plants is recruited not from among the self-employed artisans or handicraft workers engaged in the same trade—even if they do exist as in the case of the textile, clothing and shoe industries, etc.—, and so not only the periods of guilds and manufactories are missing (very understandably, by the way) in the development process, but also the phase of the labour-intensive handicraft cooperatives and small-scale plants of the light industry. (This means that the previously established forms of specialization become not only obsolete and incapable of development but they turn out to be completely abortive, too.) As a consequence, products are ousted from the market and their producers dropped from among those having their own purchasing power. This process is a negative one not because it is painful (other societies also had to undergo similar painful processes) but because, instead of promoting the expansion of the internal social division of labour it works rather in the direction of its contraction.

The self-employed artisans, handicraft workers as well as migrant labourers who have lost their jobs are usually re-employed *not* by those emerging productive branches which ousted them from their former activities (this is made impossible by the peculiar structure of the modern sector) but they either return to the sphere of the traditional sector or seek employment in the non-productive sectors (usually in domestic services).

Due partly to the shift of demand towards imported goods, and partly to its decreasing competitiveness vis-à-vis large-scale enterprises with a longer time horizon, with capital-intensive techniques and the capability of paying higher wages and taking greater risks, small and medium capital engaged in producing local products is compelled either to retreat to other branches (mainly to the service industries or the retail trade of imported goods) or usually comes under the control of foreign big capital. The result is again *not* the expansion of production linkages and market relations between the sectors and branches, a concomitant of the apparently similar process of concentration, but their contraction.

All this only goes to show that it is not just *any* change is capable of starting a positive chain-reaction which can dissolve the dualism of the disintegrated economy by setting in motion the dynamism generating the linkage effects.

On the preceding pages, we have examined the effects and consequences of this peculiar "industrialization" rather "purely" of course, disregarding the modifying role of such "subsidiary" and "external" factors as, e.g., the measure and form of the participation of the state (on the basis of ownership and shares or taxation) in the profit of light-industry enterprises with capital-intensive techniques, as well as the offsetting or easing effects of the economic policy and intervention of the state (import restrictions, employment, educational and wage policy, price control, etc.).

But the model of the dual economy outlined in this chapter is a fairly abstract model, and in analysing from different angles its partial mechanisms and the effects and interaction arising from the two sectors, we necessarily leave out of account a number of secondary and incidental factors. Thus it is obvious, e.g. that the contours of the two sectors cannot be drawn that sharply; that the character and compositions of either the traditional or modern sector are not that homogeneous; that there exist within and between these two sectors several other transitional, mixed or intermediate "sub-sectors"; that the urban sector cannot simply be identified with the modern, nor the rural with the traditional sector; that the existing and generally expanding public sector cannot simply be regarded as part of the modern sector having the described characteristics, etc. Yet, the abstraction is justified as it is possible only in this way to separate the tendencies arising from the *nature* of the phenomenon under examination from effects of a different origin.

(b) THE IMPACT OF INTERNAL DISINTEGRATION ON ACCUMULATION

Another well-known problem of most of the developing countries is related to the lack of capital and the insufficiency of accumulation. In addition to the low level of the national income,[14] the unfavourable distribution of incomes and the outflow and loss of a considerable part of national income through international economic relations, the lack of capital is directly related to the heterogeneous, dual structure and to the lack of internal integration.

(A) In the *modern* (export) commodity-producing *sector*, saving and accumulation for reinvestment purposes are restricted by the following factors: the unfavourable trend, in most cases and in the long run, of changes in the relative prices of the main export products on the world market, i.e. a deterioration of the terms of trade, which indirectly has a negative induction effect and directly shows itself in the form of a decreasing profit margin;

[14] Which results, in general, from the poor *utilization* of the potential labour force of society, the inadequate *organization* and *division* of social labour and its low *productivity*. (These deficiencies, however, are analysed here in their concrete manifestations and relationship with the structure of economy.)

— the profit repatriation of the foreign capital engaged in the modern sector;

— the weakness and lack of specialization of the domestic capital;[15]

— the limits of profitable investment possibilities due to the low level of the capital-absorptive capacity[16] of the national economy and the lack of stimulus for reinvestments[17] in the given (export) branch (owing to the earlier mentioned external factors and the latter internal factors);

— the income level of the local labour force employed in the modern sector,[18] and

— the *consumption habits* of persons belonging to the modern sector.

Consumer habits do not adjust themselves to the average level of development (including that of both sectors) of the given national economy but are under the influence of effects which come from different directions

[15] "Lack of specialization generally characterizes African petty capitalism: wage-employment, trade, farming, and artisanal activities are often combined. This lack of specialization favours the dispersal of capital, labour and managerial resources and in consequence it hampers the growth of productivity and credit-worthiness in each line." (G. Arrighi: *International Corporations*... Op. cit., p. 21.)

[16] It is common knowledge that this is connected with the backwardness of the infra-structure, the lack of external economies, the limited supply of managerial élite and skilled workers, etc. In this respect, too, there are substantial differences between the individual areas and countries.

[17] Here, too, a distinction must be made according to the actual composition of the modern sector (as to what particular branches and products it comprises), the character of capital operating in it (vertical foreign monopolies, "independent" foreign private capitals, "settler" capitals, or national capital, etc.), the political environment influencing investments, etc. The (re)investment propensity of foreign private and settlers' capital independent of the vertical monopolies, e.g., has fallen back especially where the risk of nationalization or the foreign currency difficulties, due to the adverse balance of payments, have increased.

As for the originally untypical, new branches of the modern sector, which are not included in the model, such as the import-substituting (usually capital-intensive) branches, the expansion of accumulation in them is usually impeded by the high import share of the costs of production, the outflow of profits and dividends in the case of foreign investments, and in many places by obstacles to the utilization of capacity due to the narrowness of the market, the deficiencies of management and organization, and the difficulties of raw-material supply and transportation.

[18] It is again appropriate to refer to those changes that have taken place in many countries in the pattern of the modern sector owing to the creation of new processing industries and, as a result of this, and also of the pressure of the unions, in the individual wage categories. If, however, we also take into account the whole urban sector with its mixed composition, including the non-productive branches of the public sector and the state bureaucracy, then it is even more justified to distinguish between the invariably low wage level of the masses of unskilled workers and the income level of the élite of skilled workers, employees and officials. Since this élite imitates, as a rule, the way of life and consumption habits of the colonial personnel it replaces and, in general, the expatriates it is in contact with, its personal savings are fairly limited or immobilized. Apart from a few countries, where progressive taxation has been introduced, the higher income level of this élite usually does not contribute to any extent to the expansion of accumulation either by voluntary or enforced saving.

but likewise stimulate *"over-consumption"* in a cumulative way. Of course, this *"tendency to over-consumption"* manifests itself in a different way in the case of persons with high incomes belonging to the leading class of the modern sector (foreign and local capitalists, landowners, bureaucrats, etc.) and in the case of small employees with low salaries.

The effects and their cumulation which act as a spur to "over-consumption" are derived, characteristically, from the nature and co-existence of the two sectors.[19]

The modern sector represents, primarily, the open door to the so-called *demonstration effect*[20] related to the higher consumption level of more developed countries and inducing employees in a higher income bracket, local capitalist entrepreneurs, owners of plantations, farmers, merchants, etc., to imitate the higher consumption pattern of more developed countries. The "demonstration effect" and the "imitative propensity" following in its wake are particularly strongly marked in cases where foreigners are engaged in the modern sector (capitalist entrepreneurs, employees and skilled labourers with high wages) who try to follow the consumer habits of the metropolitan country.

The existence and influence of the traditional sector and the social habits from the past produce the *"propensity to conspicuous consumption"*, which also spreads to the modern sector and leads to unproductive expenditure on luxuries. It is rooted in the authoritarian system of the traditional society where the rung on the social ladder was and still is determined by the relative degree of luxury and splendour a person can afford in order to rise above the others. The "propensity to conspicuous consumption" manifests itself within the traditional sector in the following way: the rich upper strata of this sector (reigning princes, maharajahs, chiefs of tribes, sheiks, etc.) waste their incomes on the ancient symbols of wealth, in addition to the new ones which came into fashion as a result of the demonstration effect (hoarding of gold and silver treasures, luxurious palaces, servants, luxury cars, pleasure yachts, etc.).[21] Similar symptoms can also be observed among the poorer

[19] As a subsidiary and more or less new factor may be mentioned the fairly general practice of that type of "localization" of the colonial civil service in which, with the structure and mechanism of state administration left intact, the posts of the colonial officials are gradually filled up by local cadres who inherit not only the payments and service scales but also the way of life and consumption habits of their predecessors.

[20] This question is dealt with in more detail by R. Nurkse: *Some Aspects of Capital Accumulation in Underdeveloped Countries.*

[21] As an example of gold and silver hoarding, we can mention the data quoted by B. Datta, according to which about 105 million ounces of gold and 4.235 million ounces of silver, the equivalent of almost half the total investments of the 3rd five-year plan, were hoarded by private people in India. According to M. Poniatowski, a sum corresponding to about 10 per cent of the national income was hoarded in the Arab countries before the oil-price explosion." (Quoted by I. Sachs: *Patterns of Public Sector in Underdeveloped Economies.* p. 40.)

population of this sector: they squander their relatively trifling "surpluses" on the lavish entertainment of guests and on other outward signs of wealth in order to enhance their prestige and social status within the community. (This may have, of course, some faint traces of an economic aim, e.g. a suitable marriage, or to obtain some public post.)

The wealthy stratum of the modern society is not immune either from the "propensity to conspicuous consumption", being members of the *same* but non-homogeneous society, where the aim is to become well established within one and the same social hierarchy. The "propensity to conspicuous consumption" in the modern sector is particularly noticeable if the leading strata of the two sectors are anxious to outdo each other, and if the "propensity to conspicuous consumption" is also intensified by the strong demonstration effect.[22]

The stratum of the modern sector including small employees and wage workers cannot avoid the influence of the traditional sector either, especially if most of them are "migrant workers" from the traditional sector. A part of their income acquired by toil is wasted in a similar way instead of being used to satisfy more important needs.

The saving possibilities of the members of the modern sector are also restricted by the customs taken over from the traditional sector that force people to waste a considerable part of their income on religious ceremonies and the celebration of certain social events (e.g. marriages, funerals, communal feasts). These practices are not only in accordance with but surpass the "propensity to conspicuous consumption" and stem from social and religious habits rooted in traditional society.

Thus the result is that the capitalists of the modern sector: industrialists, businessmen, farmers, merchants etc. spend as a consequence of the "propensity to conspicuous consumption" and the demonstration effect, excessive sums on consumption and unproductive expenses[23] which are out of all proportion to their actual economic position, instead of saving money for productive purposes. Minor employees often prefer to spend money on "luxuries" instead of satisfying basic needs in the order of their importance.

This propensity to "overconsumption" does not contribute to the expansion of the internal market either, and goes hand in hand with the increase of import requirements.

However, the accumulation-restricting effect of the traditional sector exerts yet another influence on the modern sector: *extended families* are the norm in the traditional sector, and this applies more or less to the modern

[22] This is typically the case where the élite of state bureaucracy has been recruited from the leading stratum of the traditional sector and has become assimilated to the group of colonial expatriates or inherited their position.

[23] As, e.g., on the purchase of uncultivated lands to demonstrate their wealth or just to "freeze in" their assets. These unproductive purchases of land by the urban population are especially frequent in the Middle East and Latin-American countries.

sector, too. The basic unit of society is, to a greater or lesser extent, the clan, that is large families which include all the relatives. The consequence is the *frittering away of incomes*, which works against on the possibilities of capitalists to accumulate capital and of employees with low incomes to meet higher consumption requirements and to save money.

(B) The expansion of saving and productive accumulation *within the traditional sector* is limited by the *low and stagnant level of production*. This is the consequence in general of

— the underdevelopment of the division of labour, and its organization;
— the low level of techniques and productive methods applied;
— the domination of a short "time horizon" in economic decisions, and the consequence, in particular of
— the effects resulting from the transplantation of the modern sector from outside, and its operation; these effects, instead of transforming the traditional economy, bring about only its decline.

The *underdevelopment of the division of labour* impedes not only the growth of productivity and the surplus-producing capacity but also the unfolding of *exchange*. As a consequence, there is no possibility for that *incentive* to develop which manifests itself in the rationality of surplus production, i.e. in the fact that production in excess of one's own needs becomes rational in the sense that it makes possible to satisfy one's needs at a higher level. As long as everybody produces for his own needs[24] and is able to produce the same products as others, production beyond one's own consumption is totally irrational.

The low level of the techniques and productive methods employed is already due, of course, to the lack of the division of labour as it is primarily this which provides both the subjective preconditions of technical development (the accumulation of professional experiences of specialized labour force which enables it to produce technical innovations) and its objective preconditions (the breaking down of the productive processes which makes it possible to introduce specialized, that is, more developed means of labour). If the productive methods and techniques do not develop, the growth of labour productivity is also hampered. Under such circumstances the necessity of increasing output due to certain "endogenous" factors (e.g. the growth of population to be supplied)[25] or "exogenous" factors (e.g. new

[24] Here we must distinguish, of course, between traditional tribal communities and semifeudal social structures. In the latter, in spite of the backwardness of exchange, there are systematic surplus production and appropriation. Since, however, this appropriation is based on violence and not on exchange, the incentive referred to is missing just as it is in a primitive communal society.

[25] The increase in the rate of population growth cannot be regarded as an endogenous factor as it is usually closely related to changes stemming from the existence of the modern sector. The fact that the "demographic explosion" and the so-called "population pressure" are *not* a natural phenomenon but the consequence of a distorted development which must be

324

demands resulting from the existence of the modern sector, taxation, etc.) induces the *extensive* utilization of the factors of production. This extensive utilization of the factors of production takes place with constant and later dimishing returns, and leads sooner or later to a shortage of the factors of production (primarily of land) and results in "over-population" (a relative and in many respects an ostensible phenomenon) even where originally the abundance of unutilized lands and natural resources was typical. As a consequence, the surplus-producing capacity of the traditional economy is not only incapable of any expansion but it is bound to contract.

The *short time horizon* of economic decisions is generally unfavourable for productive accumulation. The more direct the relationship and interconnection between the investment decisions and the personal consumption of those taking these decisions is, the shorter the time horizon and the more the investment of saving appears as "sacrifices" and "abstinence". Thus the time horizon depends basically on the system of income distribution, i.e. on the relations of production and distribution.[26]

---

explained mainly from the interaction of the two sectors, is sufficiently emphasized by the relevant critical notes in Part One and the statements in the subsequent sub-chapter (c)

[26] When the authors of fairly orthodox studies or textbooks complain about the short time horizon of the peasant producers of the underdeveloped countries, comparing it usually to the long time horizon of Schumpeter's capitalist entrepreneur endowed with exceptional abilities, they fail to mention this very relationship, the objective and material basis of the time horizon.

The reason for the fact that the long-time horizon in the capitalist economy could play a role at all in economic decisions—we must add: only from the point of view of the individual capitalist (or group capitalist, the monopoly company) and not of the whole national economy—is not the exceptional foresight of the entrepreneur but partly the emergence of the capitalist form of commodity metamorphosis and partly, but in connection with the former, the capitalist mechanism of price and income formation. The *former* means in brief that the metamorphosis typical of simple commodity production: Commodity—Money—Commodity (C—M—C) is replaced by the metamorphosis typical of capitalist commodity production: Money—Commodity—Money' (M—C—M'), in which, at the end point the metamorphosis there is not a concrete kind of commodity aimed at the satisfaction of a certain, clearly defined and therefore *limited* personal need but the endlessly multipliable *money* which may also serve as the starting point for another metamorphosis. But for this metamorphosis to have a sense at all, M' must be greater than M ($M' = M + \Delta M$), which "miracle" materializes in the process of production by the appropriation of the labour product of *others*. The repetition of this "miracle", the reproduction of ΔM (at the same or higher level) presupposes, however, reinvestment, and therefore this "sacrifice" to be made by the capitalist is the very precondition for him to be able to remain a capitalist, to live on *other* people's work. The relationship between his personal consumption and investment decision is in this respect *indirect*. (It appears direct only on the basis of such an irreal, lunatic assumption that the capitalist, contrary to his real character, to his *capitalist existence*, would think in a *non*-capitalist way, that, in the interest of the intemperate satisfaction of this momentary needs, he would renounce his claim to remain a capitalist, to satisfy intemperately his needs at the expense of other people's work in the future, as well.) Investment made by the capitalist, just as the preceding accumulation, is, in fact, no "sacrifice", *no deduction* from his personal consumption fund (by no means in the dynamics

325

Under the circumstances of the traditional community, where production *directly* serves the consumption of the producers and is *directly*[27] under the "authority" of the producing individuals,[28] or to put it more exactly, is confined to the economy of the producing individuals, the time horizon is necessarily very short. Long-term accumulations and investments mean the drastic renunciation of the satisfaction of urgent present needs, or at best, as in the case of exceptionally good harvests, of a permissible degree of "comfort", which, in addition, cannot even be justified directly by the necessity to build up the security of the distant future, due to the system of the security of subsistence prevailing in the societies of a primitive communistic character. In these societies it is the fact of belonging to the community which provides for the individual, beyond and rather independently of the sphere of his own economic decisions, the security of subsistence, ensuring him the right to a share in the institutionalized distribution or redistribution of the means of production (land) and, as a

---

of the repeated process) since the reinvestment of part of the surplus wrested out of other people's work reproduces or even increases in the last analysis his own personal consumption fund. Hence Marx's ironical remark: if the capitalist makes such a "sacrifice", philanthropy requires us to rid him of this "burdensome sacrifice" by socializing his capital.

The fact itself, however, that in this way the relationship between investment decision and personal consumption has become indirect, cannot eliminate the absolute advantage of investments with short-term realization and quick returns. It does not explain concretely why *long-term* investments with slow returns do not even mean a relative "sacrifice". The explanation is provided by the mechanism of price formation. The formation of "*prices of production*", i.e. the redistribution of surplus value among the capitalists through the mechanism of price formation resulting in *average profit*, eliminates the relative disadvantages of long-term investments with slow returns and renders the time horizon virtually equal. And in the case of *monopoly prices* the undertaking of long-term, slow returns, of the long time horizon is even overcompensated.

[27] The direction and supervision of social production in a socialist economy cannot be atomized! Instead of being reduced to the spheres of activity of the producing individuals or groups, it must be a *social* direction and supervision exercised by central organs representing the society *as a whole*. The increased role of the market, and the decentralization of a considerable proportion of economic decisions to ensure a more flexible adjustment of production to the concrete consumption demands, which is a characteristic of recent economic reforms in Eastern Europe, do not affect the fact and necessity of the centralization of the long-term development decisions. In this way, the long-time horizon is ensured at a social level, at the level of the national economy. We have to note, however, that in view of the increasing internationalization of production and the anarchistic nature of the still predominantly capitalistic world market in which the socialist countries are also participating, this long-time horizon applied within the national economies may conflict with the large-scale uncertainties of the global processes of the world economy. All this points to the need for long-term planning on a *world*-level, i.e., the application of a long-time horizon to the decisions affecting world development.

[28] This is virtually the case in spite of the common ownership of land and the common performance of certain productive activities or operations preparing them (forest and bush burning, irrigation, etc.).

326

last resort, even in the redistribution of the consumer goods—according to the traditional customs—in the form of gifts or in the support by relatives.

The *transplantation* from outside of the *modern sector* and the outward orientation of its operation has in general caused a deterioration in the operating conditions and the surplus-generating capacity of the traditional sector. The most direct and most unconcealed of these detrimental effects was *land alienation* widely practised in many countries (especially in South-Middle- and East Africa), which coincided with the establishment of the colonial commodity-producing economies (plantations, mines) and compelled the traditional economies to make do with smaller areas of usually much inferior land. The consequence of all this is the disruption of the normal rate of crop rotation, the excessive exploitation of the fertility of lands and pastures, soil erosion, the diminishing return of crop production and animal husbandry, the appearance of "population pressure" on rural areas, etc.[29] *Taxation* (imposed by the colonial government representing the modern sector) and the *demonstration effects* coming from the changed economic environment and the new demands and needs arising in their wake have created, on the one hand, the necessity of making cash incomes, i.e. of transforming the subsistence economy, while, on the other hand, the way of carrying it out has been limited and distorted by the character of the modern sector. Instead of the final secession of the surplus labour force from the traditional sector and instead of the transformation of the subsistence economy, the migrant-labour system, built upon the subsistence economy and, supplemented by partial and incidental market production has evolved. Instead of fulfilling its only possible rational function,[30] namely the mobilization of under-employed manpower, the migrant-labour system, owing to the large-scale absenteeism of the young male manpower, has led to a decreasing intensity of economic activity in the traditional sector, to the deterioration of its productivity and, consequently, to the increase of relative population pressure there. Thereby it has also reproduced the necessity of maintaining itself as an additional source of income or subsistence. While land alienation, taxation, migrant labour, diminishing returns and increasing population pressure, etc. have reduced the sector's capacity of producing marketable surplus and while the need for production for market and cash-making and the unproductive absorption of surplus have increased, the greater *competitiveness* of the economies of the modern sector (owing to the better quality of their lands, the state subsidy they enjoy, the more favourable transport facilities, greater credit-worthiness,

[29] See in more detail in T. Szentes: Introduction to the Economy of Tropical Africa. *Studies on Developing Countries.* Centre for Afro-Asian Research of the Hungarian Academy of Sciences. No. 12, 1968.

[30] Its real function was, of course, the supply of cheap labour for the colonial capitalist economies.

the economies of scale, the higher quality of their products, etc.) has reduced for the traditional sector the very possibilities of marketing. The *general decline of the handicraft industries* resulting from the same factors but particularly from the competition of goods produced in the modern sector or imported from abroad, has further narrowed the sphere of economic activity and the internal division of labour, and limited the possibility of the internal mobilization of the seasonally under-employed, and is therefore one further additional factor in decreasing the surplus-producing capacity.

Thus the accumulation possibilities in the traditional sector are limited by the obstacles to creating and expanding surplus. However, even in the case of regular or occasional surplus formation (depending, e.g., on weather conditions), there are "built-in diverting factors" which prevent the surplus from being accumulated for production purposes. Such factors include:

— "*the propensity to total consumption*", i.e. the propensity to turn the surplus production into surplus consumption. This again is the consequence of the low *consumption and nourishment level* of the rural population that mostly meets the level of minimum needs only by entirely consuming the surplus produce that arises occasionally;

— *the markedly subsistence character of the economy*, the lack of knowledge of market conditions, the technical and economic difficulties in transporting products to the market (distance, lack of the means of transport; non-competitiveness)—in general, circumstances which hinder surplus products from being converted into cash earmarked for accumulation, and

— the lack of appropriate producers' goods (e.g. simple agricultural implements) needed for the realization of productive accumulation as well as the difficulties of acquiring these goods (distant markets).

Other diverting factors which impede surplus production being used for productive accumulation purposes are:

— "*The propensity to conspicuous consumption*" which is particularly noticeable in the traditional ruling class.[31] Since the income of the latter chiefly originates from poor rural farmers, the satisfaction of this propensity induces an ever-increasing expropriation of the economic surplus and also strengthens thereby the motive already mentioned of the "propensity to total consumption".

— *Compulsory propensity to ritual and traditional expenses* (related to religious ceremonies and certain social habits).[32]

---

[31] We can find an exquisite psychological description of the propensity to conspicuous consumption of feudal landowners in the young Marx's manuscript. (See *Economic and Philosophical Manuscripts of 1844.*)

[32] We may mention, by way of example that, according to the estimate made by V. Desai, Indian peasants spend about 4,400 million rupees on wedding and funeral ceremonies, a sum which amounted to 27 per cent of their expenditures in the fifties. This, of course, is partly due to the "conspicuous propensity" as well.

328

(The influence of the latter two propensities was discussed earlier but here they are mentioned as "built-in" factors because they pertain, originally, to the traditional society.)

— *Weak demand for the meeting of the higher-grade needs* that stimulate savings and productive accumulation particularly among the poorer rural population. This is also the consequence of unsatisfied basic needs, i.e. of the low income level which goes together with the still elastic demand for foodstuffs, though in many places it simply means that higher-grade commodities are unknown, so that there is no wish to acquire them.

— *Insufficient knowledge* of how to turn the surplus into productive *investments* and of the usefulness of the latter. This insufficiency is closely connected with the backwardness of the way of economic thinking, generally characteristic of traditional societies, though it is also indirectly connected with the quantitative and qualitative deficiencies of public education, and the underdevelopment of the communication and information services, i.e. with the weakness of the positive spread effects of the modern sector.

— *Some negative circumstances related to the transfer of potential investment factors* in the case of marketing
— of land,
— of surplus production and
— of the labour force.

The transfer ensues partly within the traditional sector and partly between, or on the contact line of, the two sectors. Theoretically, the conversion into money or the utilization of all three items,—land, surplus production and an underutilized labour force[33]—means potential investment possibilities. However, the specific trend and manner of the transfer mostly stops or reduces these possibilities.

The *sale of land*, e.g.—where it is not customarily prohibited—usually aims at satisfying the seller's "propensity to conspicuous consumption" and meeting the needs determined by ritual habits or the cost of living, though it may also serve to pay off debts (usurious loans) made on account of the above reasons. In this case, it indirectly serves consumption purposes. On the part of the buyer, too, it serves to satisfy his "propensity to conspicuous consumption" or to "immobilize" his fortune (in a more secure form) or to expand the source for his unproductive consumption.

The *sale of surplus production* is often carried out through *intermediaries and usurers* who skim off a considerable part of the surplus and, in addition, eliminate it from the productive accumulation process and use it for their own "overconsumption" or usurious businesses.

---

[33] Nurkse writes: "... the state of disguised unemployment implies at least to some extent a disguised saving potential as well." (R. Nurkse: *Problems of Capital Formation in Underdeveloped Countries.* Basil Blackwell, Oxford, 1962, p. 37.)

The marketing of labour force comes up against the limitations of the absorptive capacity of the modern sector. Thus, even if workers are "physically" transferred to the modern sector—which often only means a temporary shift because of the migration of the workers—it is, strictly speaking, not really "labour investment", i.e. the utilization to a greater extent of the traditional sector's underutilized labour force.

While in Western Europe, at the time of the emergence of capitalism, both the commercialization of land (after the abolition of feudal law) and the marketing of the surplus product (as a result of the careful separation of even the slightest amount of surplus from the product necessary for reproduction and the bare subsistence of the agrarian producers) as well as the marketing of the labour power moving, or rather ousted, from the rural economies, fitted into the single integral process of *primitive accumulation*, and the transfer of these potential accumulation factors served the complete transformation of traditional agriculture and the development of a truly viable urban industry—similar phenomena in the underdeveloped countries have not resulted in genuine primitive accumulation.

Land alienation prior to the establishment of foreign-owned plantations cannot be compared to enclosures in England which prepared the creation of a domestic agricultural capitalist class, on the one hand, and a proletariat, finally "freed", i.e. deprived of its means of production and rural basis, on the other. But even where the commodity-producing large estates developed under indigenous ownership and, consequently, the transfer of land from the subsistence economy into market economy opened up real sources of accumulation, even there these sources of accumulation remained for the most part unutilized, owing to the lack of other conditions required for a complete socio-economic transformation.

The conditions for either the "English" or the "American" or the "Prussian type" of agrarian capitalist development could not be created in the colonial or dependent countries. Not even the development of Latin-American agriculture, in many respects exceptional and the most capitalized among others, can be regarded as a real "Prussian type" development. This is not only because the transformation was induced from outside and served primarily foreign interests with foreign capital playing a predominant role in it, but because here the "feudal" forms of the appropriation of surplus product must be evaluated less as transitory remnants but rather as the specific results of a mixed process which were transplanted from abroad and became the factors of stagnation and immobility instead of the forcible accumulation of national agrarian capital.

Thus the transfer of land from one economic form ensuring less accumulation possibility to another, more developed one, has remained, on the one hand, partial, that is the primitive forms of the economic utilization of land have widely survived (largely accounting for the "population pressure" on land), and, on the other, it has not attained its real aim: the expansion of productive national accumulation. This transfer served, on the part of the buyers or expropriators, *either* the accumulation of foreign capital, *or*, instead of the growth of productive accumulation, the unproductive consumption or hoarding of certain indigenous strata, *or* it led, as in the case of the export enclaves, to the halting of accumulation, due to their international price mechanism. And as to the sellers, the typical motive for them was not the productive use of the means acquired by the sale of land (or the more rational exploitation of the remaining land) but rather the maintenance or expansion of their consumption.

The same is more or less true of the realization of surplus, too. The greedy and mercilessly rational endeavour in the early phase of European capitalist development not only to concentrate every available surplus but also to convert it into *productive* accumulation did not unfold in the underdeveloped countries, except for certain spheres of the operation of foreign capital. Instead, that type of surplus transfer which aims at consumption has remained typical both of the—mostly "occasional"—sellers of the traditional sector and the exploiting intermediaries.

The transfer of labour (in many places a forceful one at the beginning) from the traditional to the modern sector may be a form of the productive mobilization of disguised unemployment, or even a starting point for rural social transformation. In other words, the transfer of this factor of production may fit into the process of productive accumulation. The specific circumstances of this transfer in the developing countries, however, usually render a real mobilization impossible. The transfer itself has mostly remained temporary or periodical (migrant labour) and could therefore not become the driving force of the transformation of the traditional sector and could not produce an independent urban proletariat free from traditional ties. Since the exodus of the male labour force has been—in spite of rural "overpopulation"—often detrimental to the production results of traditional agriculture, the accumulation potential of this sector continues to deteriorate in spite of the decrease in the number of consumers. At the same time, owing to the limited and slowly increasing absorptive capacity of the productive branches of the modern sector, in many cases disguised rural unemployment has changed into open urban unemployment (i.e. an even more unfavourable form both socially and also from the point of view of the accumulation potential). And if the labour force that cannot be absorbed by the productive branches of the modern sector finds employment in the non-productive branches (usually in the domestic service), then this again does not mean the realization of the investment potential.

In the foregoing we have summarized the obstacles to the expansion of productive accumulation caused partly by the modern and partly by the traditional sector or a combination of the two working together. Now it would be worthwhile adding also *the problems of the necessary transforma-*

tion function[34] *of foreign trade.* Foreign trade has to take over this transformation function because of the lack of "department I", and has to keep it until the capital-goods producing industries can develop. In other words, this function is the result of the distorted sectoral structure. The difficulties in going through with this function, however, are also connected, in addition to the unfavourable trend of the terms of trade, with the earlier mentioned tendency of import-orientated personal consumption and the growth of other non-productive imports (e.g. arms purchases).

(c) THE EFFECTS OF INTERNAL DISINTEGRATION ON POPULATION GROWTH AND LABOUR SUPPLY

"Population pressure" is a well-known phenomenon in the developing countries: it manifests itself in the fact that the results of the growth of production and income become futile due to the more rapid increase in population. Consequently, there is a permanent tension in the field of foodstuff supply and employment. On the labour market of the developing countries an odd situation has developed: on the one hand, there is a considerable surplus of cheap unskilled labour and, on the other, an acute shortage of skilled labour.[35]

This time again let us try to examine the aspects of the phenomenon that can be traced back to the coexistence of the two sectors, to the lack of internal integration.

"Population pressure" as well as the unutilized excess manpower are definitely relative phenomena since they depend not only on the high rate of population growth but also on the relatively lagging production growth which cannot keep up with the rapid increase in population, as well as on the insufficient labour-absorptive capacity of the modern sector.[36] This relativity and its background are particularly striking when the mutual effects of the traditional and modern sectors are examined.

(1) It is common knowledge that the rapid increase in population is due to a decreasing death rate and an unchanged high birthrate. The decline of the mortality rate is the result of the positive effect of the modern sector and of the new improvement in the health services the traditional sector receives from outside which is, by the way, far from satisfactory. On the other hand, the birth rate is still decisively influenced by moral laws and ancient customs deeply rooted in the traditional sector as well as, indirectly, by the actual or assumed future need for labour supply.

[34] See Chapter II. 1.

[35] In a number of countries the—quite recently—arising employment difficulties for the school leavers (and even the university graduates) by no means cancel out this acute shortage, since the problem of school leavers is rather the manifestation and consequence of the disproportions and "missing links" in both the employment and educational patterns.

[36] That it is not an "absolute" phenomenon, is proved by the fact that it may be accompanied by a very low population density just as well as by a very high one.

It is obvious that the only acceptable human solution, in the interests of a more favourable rate of population growth, should aim at a further decrease in the mortality rate and a vigorous increase in the health services as well as an unlimited freedom in terminating pregnancy, with the elimination of the very influences that restrict that freedom.

Let us mention a few of the factors that restrict the freedom of parents in family planning and make for a high population growth:

— first of all, child labour which still plays a role in the organization and division of labour of the traditional sector;

— "compulsory propensities" which develop in parents due to the influence of religion, ancient customs, moral laws and under the psychological "pressure" of the extended family comprising a large number of relatives;

— the institution of the extended family as a basic unit of society (instead of the nuclear family) which restricts in general the authority of the individual small family and, sharing with it the burden of maintaining the children, relieves the parents not only of some of their subsistence expenses (and by so doing makes the parents' decision rather independent of any consideration for these expenses) but also of their freedom of family planning;

— the lack of knowledge of those methods of birth control which are acceptable from both a medical and a human point of view;

— the insufficiency of the supply of medical means needed for birth control (difficulties in purchase and distribution, price and other problems), etc.

It should be emphasized again that the high birthrate (population growth) is but one of the factors of "population pressure". It is not an unfavourable symptom in itself, though it can be detrimental when taken together with the lagging rate of the growth of production and the labour-absorbing capacity of the modern sector. Moreover, if it is detrimental, this is so because of the latter! But while the increase in population is determined in the last analysis by influences deriving from the traditional sector, the rate of economic growth is basically dependent on the development and expansion possibilities of the modern sector. Due to the lack of internal integration the movements of the two sectors are out of gear. This also accounts, in the last analysis, for the development of excess labour.

(2) The *quantitative* aspect of the labour problem, i.e. the overabundance of an unskilled labour force is likewise connected with the dualism of an underdeveloped economy: the coexistence of the traditional sector as an abundant and rapidly expanding source of labour and the modern sector which absorbs that labour far more slowly.

The volume and rhythm of the labour outflow of the traditional sector depend upon:

— the development of the demographic situation outlined above;

— the "space" and "time" limitations of the absorptive capacity within the sector, i.e. the volume of cultivable land and other available means of production on the one hand, and seasonal changes in labour requirements, on the other;

— the effect of the alienating factors of an economic and non-economic character in the traditional sector (insufficiency of the means of subsistence,[37] debts, escape from primitive living conditions and customs as well as from feudal dependence and ties of kindred);

— the suction effect of the modern sector (conveniences of urban life, prospects of higher consumption and higher living standards, etc.);

— the extent and structure of education in the traditional sector (generally enhancing the effect of the former two factors);

— the volume and regularity of reflux, etc.

The latter is due to the insufficient labour-absorbing capacity of the modern sector, to the low wage level kept under pressure by unemployment and the predominance of unskilled labour, to the necessity of ensuring additional incomes (i.e. in addition to the wage earned in the modern sector) for the supply of families which the traditional sector can provide under the given circumstances of land tenure and traditional customs, and to the resulting separation of the families of migrant workers, etc.

Insofar as the repeated reflux, together with the systematic outflow, forms one and the same system (the migrant-labour system[38]), it basically determined the structure of labour force (predominance of unskilled, temporary, migrant workers), the wage level of the unskilled workers (on the basis of the "minimum subsistence level" of a male worker living separated from, and providing only partly for his family) and prevents them from becoming skilled or even semi-skilled workers. At the same time, it also hinders the development of a wide-based and stable urban proletariat.

The total effect of the previously outlined factors, as well as the mutual effect of the traditional sector supplying labour, and the modern sector destined to absorb it, add up to the *cumulative tendency of labour over-supply*. The development of labour abundance depends not only on the outflow from the traditional sector but also on the absorbing capacity of the modern sector. The expansion of the latter, however, is hindered by the well-

[37] We have already seen how this is connected, like the demographic situation and the restricted absorptive capacity, too, with the destructive effect of the modern sector.

[38] See: T. Szentes: Migrant-Labour System in Black Africa. *ILO Conference on Problems of Employment in Economic Development*. Geneva, 12–18 December 1963, CEMP. 12. Reprinted in *Indian Journal of Labour Economics*. Vol. VII, 1964. — G. Arrighi: *Labour Supplies in Historical Perspective: The Rhodesian Case*. Univ. College, Dar es Salaam, 1967. — J. C. Mitchell: Labour Migration in Africa South of the Sahara: The Causes of Labour Migration. *Bulletin of the Inter-African Labour Institute*. Vol. VI, No. 1. — W. Elkan: Migrant Labour in Africa: An Economist's Approach. *The American Economic Review*, Vol. V, 1959. — J. Woddis: *Africa. The Roots of Revolt*. London, 1960.

known difficulties of the growth of the constituent branches of this sector and the limitations of accumulation and unfavourable market relations or, in the case of the newly established (mostly import-substituting light) industries, of the capital-intensive techniques. In addition, the growth of the modern sector elicits the increase of its suction effect.

Owing to the over-supply of manpower, the increase in productivity in the modern sector does not generally result in rising wages, at least not for the unskilled workers—and if it does, it increases the suction effect and the over-supply. It leads instead to the expansion of production which usually means the growth of enclaves struggling with unfavourable world-market conditions or to the increased import-orientated luxury consumption of entrepreneurs and proprietors, or, even of the workers' and employees' élite.

(3) The *unfavourable qualitative structure* of the labour force, the acute shortage of skilled and semi-skilled workmen is the consequence, first of all, of the backwardness of public education, though it is also related to the quantitative development of manpower, the characteristics of its movement and turnover. The nature and effects of the two sectors are reflected not only in the above-mentioned features but also to a large extent in the state and structure of education.

The appropriate quantitative and qualitative development of education and vocational training, i.e. expansion of an appropriate rate, structure and direction, is limited and adversely affected by:

— the low level of the national income and budgetary revenues (which, in turn, is also connected with the brakes on internal accumulation already discussed);

— the insufficiency of the positive incentive effects of the modern sector and the infiltration of negative effects from abroad through this sector;

— the "resistance" or the negative effect of the traditional sector;

— the consequences of the coexistence of the two sectors, etc.

(A) Most of the guiding and leading personnel in the *modern sector* were foreigners in the colonial period and are still so today in many places. Owing to this and to the low technical level of the main and originally characteristic branches of this sector (agricultural and mining enclaves) there has been a *limited demand*—at least by the latter—for local skilled labour, and production in these main branches has been based on cheap, unskilled manpower. Consequently, it has not induced the development of public education and vocational training.

In addition, this sector itself, as the externally orientated part of the economy, opened up the way for the *transplantation of the West European educational systems* (primarily, as a result of the policy of the colonial governments). This school system, however, not only corresponded to an economic and social environment of an entirely *different* structure and development, but was already outdated even in its original environment, in view of the new demands of economic development. With its highly unpractical orientation towards the humanities and with its obsolete degree and course structure, this school system cannot prove suitable for adoption in the developing countries.

The complementing of the modern sector by some new branches different from the primary producing export enclaves (e.g. import-substituting plants based on capital-intensive techniques) as well as the policy of replacing foreign personnel in general and substituting local cadres for colonial expatriates in the civil service in particular, have brought about *changes* in the pattern of the labour demand even in those (mainly African) countries where formerly the employment of the local labour force remained almost exclusively restricted to the uneducated, mostly migrant, workers, and where the backwardness of public education was *extreme*, too. But a certain shift in the demand for labour[39] towards the qualified categories has not yet resulted in a sound demand pattern which could stimulate the building up of a system of public education and vocational training adjusted to the needs of a dynamic economic development. The "*missing links*" are characteristic features not only in the industrial structure but also in the pattern of labour force. In the former they prevent the "economic linkage effects" from coming into operation and strengthen outward orientation, while in the latter they disrupt the "social linkage effects" and hinder the natural supply of skilled labour and the general and simultaneous upgrading of the entire labour force.

Besides semi-skilled but unqualified workers experienced only in simple technical operations, the new industries demand a labour force of a *small number* of highly qualified and *specialized* workmen rather than a core of mobile and versatile skilled workers with wide, complex professional knowledge and practice, which is able to supplement its own ranks by training the less-qualified and less-experienced workers and promote the supply of the higher cadres of the labour force (technicians, foremen, workshop managers) partly by its own further education.

The increasing replacement of expatriates by local cadres in the civil service, together, unfortunately in many places, with the further expansion of state bureaucracy, has brought about abrupt and disproportionately increasing demands for administrators. This, in turn, has stimulated, together with the income-expectations attached to such posts, the overproduction of non-specialized bureaucrats.

While changes of this nature give new scope for social differentiation and induce among the workers the increasing separation of a narrow élite from the uneducated masses, and increase, on the other hand, the danger of the state bureaucracy becoming alienated from society, they do *not* stimulate the large development of public education and the formation of a widely

---

[39] This does not affect, or scarcely affects the invariably dominant primary-producing branches, and even less the domestic service that still plays an important role in employment.

based pattern of vocational training comprising interlocking vertical grades.[40]

But the spontaneous forces exert a poor or even negative inducement not only for the transformation and a sound development of public education but also for *on-the-job training*. On-the-job vocational training does not make for satisfactory progress because it is held back, among other reasons, by the fear that the worker, after having been educated and trained, will leave his job, and the expenses of his training will be lost. (In an internally non-integrated economy including enclaves this is all the more important as one can find there no or scarcely any possibility of replacing a trained worker who leaves his job by a worker trained elsewhere. Moreover, a trained worker returning to the traditional sector may be lost for good to the labour market or at least to the trade in question.[41])

(B) The "resistance" of the *traditional sector* to the development of education may manifest itself:

— in *the subjective aversion* of part of the leading traditional strata or even of some heads of families to a body of knowledge endangering old-established institutions, as well as, in general, to the education of young people who may want to outdo and eventually oust them from their positions;

— above all in the *objective obstacle* that *child labour* in this sector is fairly widespread and almost indispensable as an important part of the productive forces of the family or community;

— further in the similarly objective obstacle that this sector is characterized in general by the *territorial dispersion* of families and communities and by the backwardness of transport and communication.

The traditional sector exerts a negative impact on the development trend of public education by the fact that, owing to

---

[40] It is worth noting, in passing that in a few countries there is progress, following *not* from, but rather achieved in spite of the mechanism of actions and interactions described. This progress follows from government measures contrary to, offsetting or counteracting, these tendencies, as, e.g., measures taken for the expansion of general education, the transformation of the structure of public education, the priority of technical and vocational training, the formation of sounder wage and income proportions, the curb on bureaucracy, the prevention of the emergence or strengthening and enrichment of a new élite, etc. The results and, of course, the attending conflicts, too, can be observed in several socialist-oriented developing countries where progressive state intervention is especially well developed. The clash of state intervention and the various spontaneous mechanisms, and the interference of consequences and effects arising from them would deserve a special study, but the present work dealing with the general laws of motion of underdevelopment is hardly appropriate to investigate this topic in detail.

[41] This danger is, of course, less apparent in the case of the highly specialized (and well-paid) élite workers. This is, by the way, one of the subsidiary reasons and incentives for applying capital-intensive techniques where the other extreme, the combination of the wide masses of unskilled labour with a small staff of expatriate guiding personnel (as in the primary-producing export enclaves), does not seem to be suitable.

— its primitive production methods, the limitations of specialization and its division of labour,

— the backwardness of economic thinking,

— the predominance of historical, legal and religious institutions, etc., it takes a greater interest—of course, within the limitations mentioned earlier and only in relation to the children of the wealthier upper strata—in philosophic, legal, religious, i.e. *liberal education* than in the teaching of sciences and vocational training.

(C) From the point of view of education and vocational training the *coexistence and interaction of the two sectors* manifest themselves in the following, negative consequences and effects which have already been touched upon to some extent:

— increased labour migration and fluctuation as a result of the combined effect of the attracting and repelling forces, which leads to the loss of skills acquired in practice and makes on-the-job training difficult;

— a rather "open" labour market in the sense that the volume of inflow and outflow is uncertain, which makes the outlays on education and training rather risky and expensive for employers in general, but especially for the individual employer;

— the intensive and interconnected fluctuation of the labour market and the internal labour demand of the traditional sector, which makes enrolment unstable and the rate of drop-outs considerable;

— the extremely uneven character and different levels of basic education of the labour force due to migration and school drop-outs, which make further education and on-the-job training difficult;

— the "liberal" orientation and the highly unpractical and non-descript character of public education, adjusted to migration, inherited from colonialism and influenced by the imitative propensity prevailing in the modern sector and by the religious, political and historical affinities of the traditional sector,[42] etc.;

— as a result of all these, the considerable role and share of import (and technical assistance) in satisfying the demand for qualified labour, which, apart from the danger of neo-colonialist influences, leads to wage gaps between expatriates and local cadres at first, and later strengthens the tendency of the formation of a local élite and of the creation of income gaps and tensions within the local society;

— the resort to foreign scholarships in higher education which, besides enhancing dependence on grants, brings out alien ways of thinking, makes the formation of a homogeneous national intelligentsia difficult, and may even lead to "brain drain" caused by those offering the grants.

---

[42] The tendency of bureaucratization itself acts against the shift in public education in favour of practical, technical training.

338

(d) SOME OTHER MANIFESTATIONS AND CONSEQUENCES OF INTERNAL DISINTEGRATION

The two-sector character, the lack of internal integration of the economy, makes itself felt not only in the spheres of market relations, accumulation, the labour force and education, but in other fields as well. Some of these are for example the building up of the transport and communication network; the applicability of mathematical methods in macro-economics and planning; the interdependent system of economic incentives and social reactions; the efficiency of foreign aid, etc. It will suffice to refer in brief to a few of them.

The transport network is characterized not only by a high degree of centralization and the predominance of outward directed transport lines (closely connected with the export orientation of the modern sector) but also by the extreme contrasts of the means and methods of transport. Between the up-to-date and largely long-range means of conveyance of the modern sector and the primitive, mainly "human" means of conveyance of the traditional sector intermediate methods (such as horse- or oxen-drawn vehicles and even pack animals) which played such an important part, e.g., in the development of the European short-haul trade, and which could also be made available at a relatively low cost to the rural producers of the underdeveloped economies, are not usually to be found. The demonstration effect manifesting itself through the modern sector and the imitative propensities following in its wake, as well as the "prestige propensity" of the young states, induce them to adopt a costly transport development policy (a network of first-class roads, expensive air- and seaports, etc.).

There is a striking disproportion and contrast in *communications*, too. Along with developed networks of radio, television (in some places even colour television) and telephones in the towns, communications in rural areas are still often based on personal contacts and primitive signalling (drumbeats, smoke signals, etc.). It is obvious that modern telecommunication and verbal information services as methods of out-of-school mass education, especially in countries with a high rate of illiteracy, are indispensable in mobilizing public support for the implementation of economic objectives.

The application of mathematical methods in macroeconomics and planning is hindered not only by the insufficiency of the supply of statistical data (especially in regard to the traditional sector) but also by the high degree of "asymmetry of the production functions", as the ratio of the factors of production in the two sectors is very different and, in addition, the labour force is highly unstable.

(We wish to mention only parenthetically that in an underdeveloped economy of specific structure the free and full operation of the Keynesian multiplier principle comes up against such barriers and disturbing factors as large-scale, disguised unemployment, the highly inelastic supply curve of

22*

agriculture which is the main branch of the economy, the specific reaction of agricultural producers and consumers, the lack of free capacities and the backwardness or technological dependence of the processing industries, the inelasticity of supply and acute shortage of skilled labour etc. Thus the increase in employment and incomes through investments will not necessarily bring about an increase in the production of consumer goods by its demand effect, partly because the agricultural producer may react to a higher income due to higher prices by increasing his "self-consumption" and by decreasing his marketable produce, and partly because the expansion of the production of consumer-goods industries—if such industries do exist at all—may prove quite impossible, owing to the lack of free capacity and qualified labour and the comparatively inelastic supply of operating capital needed for increasing production.[43])

As a result of the interference of the effects of customs and propensities rooted in the traditional sector (as e.g. the afore-mentioned religious-ritual "compulsory propensities", the propensity to conspicuous consumption, the propensity to hoaring up and the propensity to full consumption, etc.) and of the effects operating through the modern sector (as, e.g., the demonstration and imitation effects, etc.), the *social reactions* to economic decisions are of a very heterogeneous character within the society as a whole and, in addition, highly deviating in the two sectors, too. Therefore, the *incentives* applied for the implementation of the economic development programme cannot be identical in the two sectors, nor can the incentives applied in the modern sector be the mere replica of those proved effective in the advanced countries. (It is well known, e.g. that in many places wage incentives were not only ineffective but often had a contrary effect and led to a setback in work, or that price incentives applied in agricultural production likewise proved a failure.)

Economic disintegration and the coexistence of the two heterogeneous sectors may come into unfavourable interaction with the *direction and utilization of foreign aid.* Here we are faced with the well-known fact that those offering foreign aid and loans prefer the modern sector and within it the already established enclave-branches and/or those capital-intensive dependent industries which have hardly any contact with the traditional sector and the other branches of the economy either. By so doing, they enhance economic disintegration and export orientation and/or the import-sensitive character of the whole economy, together with the other unfavourable effects already mentioned. The modern sector is given preference partly to strengthen either old capitalist interests inherited from colonialism or the new ones, and partly to safeguard the trading interests of

---

[43] See in more detail, V. K. R. V. Rao: *Essays in Economic Development.* Asia Publishing House, London, 1964, Chapter 2, pp. 35–49.

the creditor countries as well as for the sake of investments which promise spectacular results, require lower costs and involve lesser risks.

On the other hand, from the fact of disintegration and from the interaction of the two sectors a tendency ensues which shifts the utilization of foreign aid to the line of least resistance and follows the beaten track towards the modern sector and its already existing branches. This tendency is brought about by both objective and subjective effects.

In the modern sector, the easier realization of investments, the lesser need for complementary investments, the more or less existing communal services, the transport and communication networks, the better known and developed marketing opportunities and labour supply, fewer organizational difficulties, better-known and tested technologies, the easier way of assessing the profitability and feasibility of investments and their undoubtedly more favourable indices (if we disregard the less easily assessable indirect effects), etc. may appear as predominantly objective reasons for giving preference to the modern sector when taking decisions on investments and the utilization of foreign aid.[44] The pressure of unemployment in the modern sector with all its threats of social and even political tension also urges the increase of investments in this sector. To all this must be added motives of a mainly subjective nature. Such are, e.g., the personal economic interests of some political leaders in investments made in the modern sector or in the development of one or another branch or enterprise in it, and in the cooperation with foreign capital working in this sector. Such are, further, the party political considerations in governmental decisions on aid utilization which derive from political movements concentrated in towns and from the pressure of urban demands (either of the urban bourgeoisie or the workers united in the trade unions). Such is also the well-known propensity to prestige investments aimed at enhancing one's personal reputation, or that of the party or the nation, and at giving the impression of rapid development. The frequently encountered resistance of the traditional sector to everything that is new as well as the danger of conflicts over questions of authority and ownership in the course of the implementation of development programme and the realization of investments also shift the utilization of foreign aid towards the modern sector.

As a result of all this, the differences between the two sectors, i.e. disintegration with all its consequences, become more pronounced, and greatly weaken the aggregate social and economic efficiency of aid even if the individual efficiency of the projects themselves increases.

[44] "The already established enterprises attract new investments, thus creating a cumulative process of uneven development in the 'ocean' of pre-capitalistic economy, causing the emergence of 'islands' of capitalistic industry." (I. Sachs: *Foreign Trade and Economic Development...*, p. 101.)

2. THE HETEROGENEOUS SOCIAL STRUCTURE

In accordance with the disintegrated and distorted character of the mode of production and economic structure of the developing countries, their class structure is distorted and disintegrated, too. Along with the elements of a capitalist society the remnants of precapitalistic formations still widely survive in these countries. The penetration of foreign Western capitalism has interrupted the natural course of their socio-economic development and made it impossible for them to proceed along the way and at the rate determined by the internal laws of their previous development.

The breaking up of the old mode of production and the traditional structure of society, the penetration of the capitalist production and social relations into the old forms of economy and society undoubtedly coincided with the general trend of development. In general, the capitalist mode of production is far superior to any previous mode of production, and the capitalist form of society ensures not only greater mobility for the internal forces of society but also witnesses the emergence and strengthening of the basic social factor of the future socialist society.

These internal changes, the breaking up of the old system, however, took place under specific circumstances, under colonial or semi-colonial conditions. Thus the conditions, course and results of these changes were not determined by the internal laws of the development of the traditional economy but by external factors: the interests of foreign monopoly-capitalism. The transformation therefore was not only more painful and forcible for the societies concerned but it also resulted in a misbirth: the old did not completely disappear, and the new was built not on the ruins but among the remnants of the old. In addition, the penetration and strengthening of the new did not occur evenly everywhere, and even where the old was ousted by the new, it still retained its influence. Thus modern relations became associated with primitive traditional conditions. Just as the breaking up of the old forms of economy failed to be followed by a completely new and full economic formation, in fact, the old and new forms remained side by side, so, in the same way, substantial remnants of the old structure of society have survived.

Owing to the export orientation of the new, capitalistic sector as well as to the repatriation of profits and their spending mainly in the metropolitan country, foreign capital came into conflict with the precapitalistic socio-economic remnants (feudal and pre-feudal land tenure, slave and serf labour, communal subsistence economy, the political and military hierarchy of old societies) *only insofar as* they happened to fall directly within the sphere of its own activity. In that case, however, it mercilessly destroyed these remnants or put them into its service,[45] often with the help

---

[45] As, e.g., it made use of the quasi-feudal immobility of the plantation workers bound to the soil, and the African squatter and the Latin-American peon systems, as well as quasi-

of the state administration, the colonial or puppet governments. Otherwise foreign capital was not interested in the complete liquidation of the precapitalist formations as its growth was determined by laws *independent* of these formations.

This externally induced and foreign-controlled *capitalist* development, however, impeded or restricted the emergence of the very class, the indigenous bourgeoisie, which *otherwise* would have been naturally interested in the consistent carrying out of the process of capitalist transformation and development in every sector of the economy and society.

The national bourgeoisie, whose existence and development require the capitalist transformation of the whole economy and society, and whose character *otherwise* coincides with the equally capitalist character of the externally induced process, was able to develop and strengthen, strangely enough, only despite and against the most important forces determining this process. (Let us disregard here the impotent parasitic, mainly intermediary bourgeois and semi-bourgeois elements, which sprang up usually as appendices of foreign capital.) In the struggle to control the natural resources, the national labour force and the domestic market, the domestic bourgeoisie had to combat not only, and not in the first place, with the obsolete precapitalist forces of local society, but also the foreign capital that was setting this capitalist development in motion. This local bourgeoisie which, to a certain extent, lagged behind the development of the domestic proletariat (of a peculiar character) that grew parallel with the expansion of capitalist enterprises of not only local but mostly foreign origin, had to face even at that stage a plebeian movement of considerable strength that was directed against exploitation in general and foreign exploitation in particular.

Under these circumstances the national bourgeoisie did not regard the struggle against the precapitalistic social remnants as its main task, since it really had to be a struggle against foreign capital and foreign oppressors. On the other hand, faced with quite a strong popular-national movement, it was inclined to put a certain restraint on the intensity of this fight. (Partly because in some countries even the feudal leaders took part in the anti-imperialist national movement, and partly because the democratic and radical trend of the people's movement threatened all property-owning and exploiting strata.)

Thus neither the basic external forces of this development, nor the internal forces succeeded or were interested in the final and complete getting rid of the precapitalistic formations. The objective contradiction itself between *foreign* monopoly capitalism, which started and has to some extent

---

slavery in the form of colonial forced labour. In many areas traditional tribal economies were also utilized by it as inexhaustible sources of cheap migrant labour.

realized this *capitalist* development, and the *national* bourgeoisie, the only possible social basis and internal force for this capitalist development, accounted for the preservation of certain remnants of precapitalistic formations.

The preservation of precapitalistic elements was further promoted by the fact that in many countries the colonial administration or the puppet governments of foreign monopoly capital, trying to find allies in the reactionary feudal leaders and tribal chiefs, supported their obsolete power and helped them in amassing great riches.[46]

This is the explanation for the specific coexistence of foreign monopoly capital and the precapitalistic formations which are of a *diametrically opposed nature*, and for the formation of a distorted, heterogeneous social structure.

The distortion of the social structure, the extent of the survival of precapitalistic formations and their location, function and role in the social structure may vary from one developing country to another, depending on *what historical periods these remnants can be traced back to*, i.e. at what level of their historical development these societies were originally affected by the penetration of foreign capitalism, and, on the other hand, *what changes these remnants have undergone* as a result of external influences and the adjustment to a changed, heterogeneous environment. Thus it is due also to the original, i.e. the precolonial, differences in their development that the remnants of the most different periods of primitive communistic, slave and feudal, or "Asiatic", society can be found in the countries of Africa, Asia and Latin America.

The capitalist element, which, through the penetration of foreign monopoly capital, became predominant in the heterogeneous structure, affected and restricted only *horizontally* the economic "breeding ground" of the precapitalistic elements (the traditional tribal subsistence economy, village communities, and feudal economies), and even then only insofar as it accorded with its interests. It also exercised, of course, a certain *vertical* effect: "at the bottom" mainly through the migrant workers, that is male labour leaving the traditional economy for temporary wage employment, and "at the top" through feudal landowners and chiefs, etc., who, in order to get rich, started trading in goods, land, labour and money. This effect, however, proved too weak to induce a genuine social transformation, partly because the economic sphere of such a transformation became, from the outset, a very "difficult terrain", owing to the nature of the modern sector and partly because the effect itself, which "at the top" involved the appearance of an alien way of life, and "at the bottom" meant employment

---

[46] In certain areas of Tropical Africa, for example, the tribal chiefs had a share in the taxes collected for the colonial government, and in certain Arab countries the feudal monarch shared in the profits with the oil monopolies, etc.

and exploitation by foreigners, was greatly offset by the bonds and the cohesive forces of the old society often becoming stronger and tighter when on the defensive.

Even in countries such as India where already prior to independence the capitalist element had been considerably expanded by local, "national" components derived from the traditional element, these components have either remained in the bonds of the traditional society,[47] i.e. have not really become capitalist elements, or they have themselves become estranged, coming into conflict with the rules, customs and religion of the indigenous society.[48]

Thus the changes in the structure of the heterogenous society were rather confined only to the periphery of the traditional element, the part connected with the capitalist one, and all that they amounted to was the—rather partial—breaking away of this periphery, but they never achieved a real internal transformation. Despite this fact, not a single traditional community has survived intact and untouched by the impact of colonialism and the capital operating in the modern sector; not a single community has been able to preserve the original conditions of its existence and independent evolution. There are no real primitive communal or feudal societies in the "Third World", only fragmentary, mutilated remnants blocked in their growth, remnants which have become the subservient, though alien and contradictory accessories of the predominant system of capitalism.[49] Whatever resistance these precapitalistic communities may have put up in some places against the penetration of *foreign* capitalism, and the spread of colonialism, this resistance, though a definitely positive phenomenon from the point of view of preserving and strengthening the *idea* of independence, could not be successful and can hardly represent a positive force in the perspective of social progress *beyond* the aim of regaining national independence.

Though in many countries the new national governments are making efforts to resuscitate the traditional customs, the resistance against and isolation from the capitalist element and the defensive strengthening of traditions have slackened with the disappearance of the *overt* signs of foreign rule, of colonialism, and with the progress in the economic and cultural development of the traditional sector within the national development programmes. Nevertheless, the effects of the traditional social

[47] A good example for this is the case of the Indian capitalists who support the whole extended family (the whole kinship).

[48] There are authors in the West who complain that capitalist activity is a socially condemned occupation in India even today, which is partly due to the effect of Ghandism.

[49] The real nature of "feudalism" in Latin America and its role *within* the capitalist system are illuminated by Andre Gunder Frank in his article in the December 1963 issue of *Monthly Review*.

behaviour and rules will make themselves felt for a long time yet and will influence the social processes.

The distorted, heterogeneous social structure, the coexistence and preservation of the inherently different and contradictory elements have, of course, hindered and are still hindering the progress of social processes. This accounts in no small measure for the fact that the dividing lines between the social classes and strata are less distinct in these countries than in Europe. They are less distinct not only between the capitalist and non-capitalist elements (because of the *partial* changes already referred to) but also within the non-capitalist element (between wage workers and peasant farmers, between the community and tribal chiefs and feudal landlords, etc.). This accounts, moreover, for the fact that at the points of contact of the heterogeneous structure relatively broad *intermediate strata* were able to come into being which can play an important part even in politics.

On the other hand, as a result of the effect of the traditional social elements, class consciousness can be strongly influenced and offset by such *forms of social consciousness* as traditional religion, tribalism, clan, caste and sect interests, nationalism, etc.

This peculiar character of the social structure and processes explains the reason why the path of the *political changes and shifts* in these countries may deviate so much from the boundary-lines of social classes. The political groups in power may shift to the right or the left, in a reactionary or a progressive direction, not only on the surface of their "own" class, within the limits of the class interests, but over a much wider area. Without losing their social basis, and with the help of the intermediate strata or with the assistance of other forms of social consciousness, they may turn to a political direction leading beyond or even counter to the interests of the class serving previously as their social basis.

The problem of *class formation* and of the *character* of the existing or emerging *classes* is one of the most hotly debated questions of the literature on underdeveloped countries, especially in the light of the post-colonial development. The divided views here are not simply the manifestations of the *usual* differences deriving from the different ways of defining classes and of determining class criteria but they also stem from the objective fact that social stratification proceeds both horizontally and vertically under the inducement of processes of various origin which to a great extent overlap or cross each other. This is why it often happens that even authors professing the same social ideology assess the phenomena of class formation rather differently, depending on the particular process or the particular result of the interfering processes they concentrate on. And since it is easier to seize hold of the concrete result of a given, usually short period than to separate the intertwined tendencies, it is no wonder that we often come across *generalizing* evaluations made on the basis of simplified and short-term phenomena. These evaluations show the emergence of new, specific classes,

346

or attribute a new, specific character to classes also existing and well known elsewhere.

There is a wide range of theories which appraise the formations of classes or the change of their characteristics by generalizing certain superficial phenomena, or by projecting short-run statements into the long run. A distinction must be made between them not only according to the form in which they appear (whether primitive and vulgar, or at the high level of theoretical explanations), but also according to the aims and interests they serve. No doubt, many of the authors or followers of such theories are led by the positive endeavour partly to get rid of the dogmatic, rigid evaluation and treatment of class categories which simply ignore the phenomena that do not fit into the "classical" categories, and partly to disclose by an empirical approach to the new phenomena where the revolutionary energies of a given historical period can be found and mobilized. A positive endeavour, however, does not necessarily guarantee a positive result.

What are the main phenomena which provide the ground for the new approaches and concepts of class formation?

Such is, e.g., the phenomenon to be found in the countries of Tropical Africa especially under colonialism, namely that the dividing line between the rich and the poor, or more exactly, between the exploiter and the exploited coincided with the *"racial" dividing line* between Europeans and Africans. This is a special phenomenon arising from the *African characteristics* of the precolonial and colonial development which can be observed, indeed. Its theoretical generalization, however, has led to the illusion of an "undifferentiated African society", to the slogan of the "preservation of intact classless society",[50] and by raising generalizations to an international level, to the identification of the international class struggle with the struggle between "white" and "coloured" peoples. While the demonstration of this phenomenon in a given place and period of time may have served the African anti-colonial movement, and may still do so, its generalization *beyond* that given space and time serves the *apologetic* covering up of an actual social differentiation and class formation, or the apologetic protection of obsolete social remnants and the "indigenous" reactionary exploiting strata.

Another phenomenon which also induces theoretical generalizations and simplifications is the *property and income* "pyramid", the stratification of the poor and the rich in developing countries.[51] It corresponds much less to the relative position in the "normal" social scale of the basic classes and the various strata within them than in European countries (though the

50 This illusion has found its—rather diversified—theoretical expression in the concept of the "special", "extraordinary", "African" socialism.

51 For example, the living standard of the Arab workers employed in the oil fields of the Middle East may even surpass that of the landowners with relatively large areas of land, while the lowest strata of urban merchants live at the standard of the fellahs.

assumption of a "coincidence" for the latter, too, is but the result of a gross simplification!). Differences within the otherwise identical class category are often not only greater than between two subsequent categories but they are sometimes of the opposite sign, and certain strata belonging to a higher class category may be at a much lower income level than the upper strata of a lower class category. These *overlappings*, which are on a much larger scale than those in Europe, are again the temporary results of a number of tendencies of different origin and time of validity.[52] The registration of this phenomenon induces some people to substitute the distinction between the rich and the poor, the "haves" and the "have-nots" for real class boundaries. And when this view is associated with the vulgar-Marxist interpretation of class consciousness, it often leads to the conclusion that the truly revolutionary forces are those with the least incomes, and the measure of poverty is in close correlation with the measure of revolutionary attitude.[53] This view, projected on to the international plane, appears in the confrontation of the "poor" and the "rich" countries as the new concept of the international "class struggle". Despite its seemingly "anti-imperialist revolutionary" character, it not only conceals the historical causes of "poverty" and "wealth", the laws of development of the capitalist world economy and the role of colonialism, but in addition,—if logically

[52] A source of overlapping may be, e.g., the racial discrimination introduced under colonialism or its aftermath, or in general, the relative isolation of "racial", national or religious communities, which, though they have their own internal vertical structure, appear temporarily as horizontal units in the vertical structure of society as a whole.

A similar source may be the abrupt and "autonomous" development of the educational system, if it takes in and turns out the young people *largely* independently of social stratification, and creates temporarily thereby an occasionally wide social gap between the young and older generations.

The fact of socio-economic disintegration; the external influences which, because of the "open" character of economy and society, affect certain sectors very strongly (others hardly at all); the fact that interactions, because of the "missing links", scarcely make themselves felt (or only in a circuitous way) among the various sectors of economy and society; the concentration of state intervention on certain spheres, etc.—these provide the answer to the question of why it takes *relatively so long* for such "closed" units or strata brought up in a social sphere different from or exceeding their own spheres of activity, to dissolve or adjust themselves to the "normal" pattern (i.e. corresponding to the dominant *production relations*) of social class allocation.

[53] It would be perhaps superfluous, had it not been for the frequent misinterpretation of the Marxian views, to refer here to the fact that Marx accounted for the necessary collapse of capitalism not by the "poverty" and a sort of "absolute pauperization" coming to a head, nor by the rioting of the poorest lumpenproletarians or beggars, but by the *development* of productive forces assuming social dimensions and requiring, therefore, *social control*, as well as by the *organized struggle* of the workers engaged in large-scale production; the workers whose numbers and social role but also their social consciousness are steadily growing, who are able not only to distribute more justly the wealth produced by them, but also to manage without capitalists and landowners, the process of the whole social reproduction much more rationally than ever.

consistent—it also offers the newly independent countries a strange alternative. *Either* they do not do anything about liquidating poverty and exploitation, thereby preserving their revolutionary spirit, *or*, if they succeed, by mobilizing their own resources and abolishing foreign exploitation, in achieving certain results, and if they allow the people whose struggle and work produced these results, to have a share in them—then their former revolutionary drive will inevitably turn into petty bourgeois opportunism.[54]

There is a view that is similar to but much more substantial than the concept substituting the distinction between the rich and the poor for class boundaries *within* the developing countries. This draws a line of social distinction between those who "benefit from imperialism" and those who "suffer from it". Such a distinction is fully justifiable if the aim is to assess the social forces either fighting for, or indifferent, or even hostile to national (political or economic) independence, and if the distinction is based on the analysis of the production relations and the structure of the whole society. Very often, however, the aim is to illustrate in this way the formation of the class structure, and the basis for a distinction is simply the income position. In *one* social category the wealthy people are aligned: businessmen, kulaks, operators of export-import firms, lawyers and accountants working for mines and other establishments, personnel managers, storekeepers selling foreign goods, sometimes even the industrial skilled workers, who, just *because* they draw somewhat higher incomes, are supposed to derive their wealth and power from imperialism. In the *other* category the poorer individuals are classified, who *because* they are poorer or honest, do not enjoy the favours of imperialism: subsistence farmers, unskilled labourers, artisans, the lower echelons of the civil service and "honest politicians". Such a distinction which separates strata of the same social and economic roots, and merges utterly different ones into the same category, may easily be misleading when one wants to be informed about the real tendencies of social class formation. In order to assess the relative position and movement of the individual social strata the relations of income distribution *alone* are a highly important but by no means sufficient factor, and, in addition, the income relations themselves may vary, according to laws operating in the depth of the production relations.

It is true that the relations of income distribution may enjoy a great measure of "independence" where the production relations themselves are mixed, unestablished and transitory, and here they may have an increasingly important role in the unfolding of the new production relations. But just as it would not be right to ignore this and conceal the

---

[54] If this new interpretation of the international class struggle has gained a relatively great popularity, then it is obviously due *not* to such logical absurdity, nor to its unhistorical approach, but to the fact that real material forces and interests make use of it as an ideological camouflage.

empirically justified facts under some abstract model of general tendencies, it would be equally wrong to deny the also empirically justified and historically verified general tendencies by referring to a model constructed on the basis of a few facts contradicting these tendencies. It would, of course, be unwise to ignore the gap that exists today *de facto* between a subsistence farmer and a kulak, or between a self-employed artisan or small shopkeeper and a capitalist businessman, or between an unskilled wage labourer and a well-paid skilled worker in respect of their income position, way of life and thinking. But it would be equally and even more unwise to ignore the identities or similarities that exist between them in their relation to the means of production and in their role in the social organization of labour, and to disregard whether the tendencies arising from their social existence interpreted in a more widely and deeply (in other words, in a more exact) way are convergent or not. It would be a mistake not to see, e.g. that the spontaneous process of the transformation of subsistence economies also includes the tendency to develop kulak economies; that some of the artisans and small merchants become real capitalist businessmen employing wage labour; that the gap between unskilled and skilled workers will be bridged sooner or later by the educational and training process and the wage and employment mechanism; that the "honest politician" may turn into a corrupted hypocrite, or an "honestly" reactionary (or even poor) politician, etc. It is not the fact of making distinctions, nor is it the statement of the income gap or different attitudes to imperialism and foreign capital that is objectionable in this categorization. It is *only* the fact that these distinctions are made not within the basic class categories but *instead* of and concealing them.

The rather conspicuous phenomenon, namely that the gap of incomes and living standards is rapidly widening between the *urban* and *rural* areas in the newly independent countries, also gives an opportunity to draw far-reaching theoretical conclusions about class relations and revolutionary forces.

This is not simply the repetition of the process that has also taken place in the advanced capitalist countries on account of the unequal development of industry and agriculture, but it is partly a more drastic process, and partly a different one as it is determined by special factors.[55] Such special factors are, e.g. the agrarian crisis unfolding in the developing countries as a result of the changes and troubles[56] in the international division of labour, and because

---

[55] A *real* industrialization process creates, by the way, not only the gap (by the faster development of the urban industries, the imposing on agriculture of the burdens of accumulation for industrialization, the urban concentration of the use of resources, etc.) but also the possibilities of bridging that gap (by the growth of industries serving the development of agriculture, the reallocation of the resources of accumulation, which have grown as a result of industrialization, etc.).

[56] See Part Two, Chapter I. 1.

of their disintegrated economic structure. This agrarian crisis is manifested by the agricultural export enclaves coming to a deadlock, and by the slowness of, and the internal obstacles to, the transformation of the traditional agrarian sector. A further special but related factor is the increasing overpopulation of the rural areas and, in many places, the shift in foreign investments and sometimes in foreign aid programmes, too, in favour of the urban light industries and urban infrastructure and services at the expense of agriculture.[57] The political "prestige investments" and the accelerated political and cultural life in towns following liberation, the build-up of the new state and party apparatus, the proliferation of central institutions, the rapidly expanding international relations, etc. are further special factors.

As in such a way the distribution and utilization of the national income undergo in many countries a conspicuous shift towards the urban areas, many ideologists tend to discover therein the deep process of a new social set-up coming into being in which "the town exploits the village". In the class structure of society they claim to see the outlines of two basic categories evolving: the *urban* and *rural population*.

And since this distinction, applied to the basic economic sectors and the social strata *working* in them, may also imply, by and large, the distinction between industry and agriculture, or industrial workers and peasantry, the simplification and generalization amount to the confrontation of *urban labour aristocracy* and *rural workers* as two basic classes.

As a result of the greater role of the trade unions, and the shift of employment towards the skilled categories, in a number of countries there has been a substantial increase in the level of urban wages. Lagging behind this is not only the rural wage level but also the growth rate of national income and productivity and the expansion of employment.[58] This phenomenon is worth looking at not only from the point of view of economic policy (the growth opportunities of accumulation, the more even distribution of the burdens of accumulation, the regulation of the extent and structure of consumption, etc.), but also from the angle of social stratification. The above-outlined demonstration, by simplification and generalization, of class formation—and not stratification *within* the basic classes!—leads, however, to false conclusions as it ignores, in the interests of transitory and superficial phenomena (as the differentiation between rural

[57] The mineral-producing enclaves, which continue to be favoured as sources of raw materials, are invariably insignificant as a factor generating rural development.

[58] See G. Arrighi: Labour Supplies in Historical Perspective: The Rhodesian Case, and also: International Corporations, Labour Aristocracies and Economic Development...— R. H. Green: *Wage Levels, Employment, Productivity and Consumption*... University College, Nairobi.—H. A. Turner: Wage Trends, Wage Policies, and Collective Bargaining: The Problems of Underdeveloped Countries. University of Cambridge, Occassional Paper. No. 6, Cambridge University Press, 1965.

and urban areas), the lasting and deep-rooted tendencies (as the differentiation going on in both urban and rural areas alike), not taking into account the transitory nature of certain special factors responsible for the phenomenon in question, and disregarding the *mixed* character and composition of both the urban and the rural sector.

Such a simplified class analysis leads then to catastrophic ideological conclusions like the statements that the real social conflict, the clash of interests, lies between the urban labour aristocracy and the semi-proletarianized peasantry, and that the workers settled in towns have become a sort of exploiting and privileged élite who, having certain interests in common with foreign capital or the local state and party bureaucracy favouring them against the rural farmers and migrant workers, have lost their revolutionary role. Consequently, the revolutionary forces have shifted to the rural areas,[59] and the core of the army fighting against imperialism and capitalist exploitation is made up now of rural workers (subsistence farmers, small-commodity producing farmers and migrant workers). This is a new variant of narodnikism, populism,[60] which sets the ideal of romantic peasant revolutionarism against "urban conformism" and petty bourgeois opportunism,[61] and opposes rural messianism to "proletarian messianism".[62] And since the rural masses, unlike the urban

[59] This thesis when raised to an international level and often intertwined with the idea of confrontation of the "rich" and "poor" and/or the "white" and "coloured" countries, appears as a concept of the antagonism between "industrial" and "agrarian" countries, in general, and professes the concentration of the revolutionary forces of the world and their leadership in the agrarian countries.

[60] See P. Worsley: *The Third World*. London, 1964 and F. Fanon: Op. cit.

[61] Here again we are faced with the usual simplified interpretation of class consciousness which regards the latter as merely the function of the size of income. What is, however, far more important for generating the workers' class consciousness and solidarity than their similarly low living standards, is their sense of community which arises and develops particularly in the big industrial enterprises, i.e. the sense of belonging to and relying on each other, and being exploited by and depending on the same capitalists. It is not accidental that, in spite of their much lower incomes, the workers of small-scale enterprises are much more inclined to have petty bourgeois and individualistic propensities.

[62] Marx did not look upon the historical role and revolutionary mission of the working class as a sort of "messianism" at all, nor did he explain it by the specific qualities of the workers or the measure of their poverty, even less by their staying out of the process of economic development. Just the contrary: he deduced it from the natural growth of the social role and weight of the working class which completely coincides with the inevitable trend of the process of economic development, and from the increasing contradiction between that role and its adequate social recognition. Instead of "messianism" he pointed out the "simple" historical tendency and the fact that this is the class whose *social existence*, and role in the economic basis of society, whose class *consciousness* (more exactly the *social* character of its consciousness), as well as its *organization* come into force, grow and develop together with the *general* and *objective* tendency of the historical development of productive forces and the expansion of industry and technology.

To deny this historical role means the denial of history and, in relation to the underdeveloped countries, the implicit assumption that the process of their industrialization

working class, are difficult to organize and the propensity to individualism is much stronger in them, the logical conclusion is the *idealization of guerilla warfare* and the practice of adventurous coups rather than an organized class struggle.

A specific, more or less African variant of the above theory is the one which refers in its reasoning not only to the great inequality of income distribution between town and country, and accordingly to the poverty and exploitation of the rural population making up the majority of society, on the one hand, and to the privileged position and bourgeois-mindedness of the urban population including the élite of the working class, on the other, but it also contains the assumption that rural society is not yet contaminated by capitalism, that the ancient communistic traditions still survive, that society is still undifferentiated. Consequently, the preservation or restoration of the ancient rural way of life opens up the direct road to socialism.

The communistic traditions and organizational forms, the common property of land, the high degree of solidarity within the community, etc. really constitute great values and powerful reserves in the case of a socialist short cut. The theory in question includes, however, not only the acknowledgement of this value but also the unawareness of the consequences and effects of colonial capitalism, the operation of the dual economy and the developmental tendencies of rural economy as well as an ignorance of the differentiation which has in reality clearly got under way.[63] Thus, despite all good intentions, it is an irremediably naive theory.[64] Nevertheless, as an ideological theory directed against bourgeois or middle-class individualism and as a political tendency demanding the improvement of the living conditions of the masses of African society and a more equal income distribution, African "populism" based on this theory may fulfil a

---

and agrarian transformation is blocked *permanently*, and this blockade, at least according to this logic, can only be raised by the worldwide revolt of rural revolutionaries.

[63] The differences between the individual African countries are, of course, considerable in this respect, too. (For particulars, see R. Barbé: *Social Classes in Black Africa*, or I. Cox: *Socialist Ideas in Africa*. Lawrence and Wishart, London, 1966.)

[64] Similar, or perhaps even more unfounded illusions were nourished by the Russian narodniks about the rural society supposed to be still untouched by capitalism and the communal system of "mir" still surviving in its remnants in tzarist Russia, which, they thought, could therefore provide the foundations of socialism. Lenin is again worth quoting: "We have just mentioned the bad counsellors... who are fond of saying that the peasants already have such a union. That union is the *mir*, the village community... This is not true. It is a fairy tale. A fairy tale invented by kind hearted people... If we listen to fairy tales we shall only wreck our cause, the cause of uniting the rural poor with the urban workers." (English translation quoted by I. Cox: *Socialist Ideas in Africa*. Lawrence and Wishart, London, 1966, p. 49.—The original in Russian: The Alliance of the Working Class and Peasantry. *The Two Tactics of Social Democracy...*)

positive *practical* role, provided that it is not "manipulative populism" serving the concealment of real interests and processes.[65]

One of the most crucial phenomena which deserves particular attention when analysing class formation and provides an opportunity and a tool not only for efforts like those mentioned before to blur over the basic class boundaries but also for a better understanding of real processes, is the rapid growth of an *"élite"* of civil servants, managers, administrators, bureaucratic, intellectual and military elements—especially in the newly independent African countries.

The growth of this "élite" is closely connected with the complex structure of administration inherited from colonial period and the disproportionate increase in the state apparatus (and army) in the rather balkanized African countries, as well as with a number of other factors as, e.g., the way of Africanization of the state administration and army without changes in patterns; the "Africanization" policy of foreign firms adopted in order to feel secure and achieve a better reputation (by putting token Africans in managerial and senior positions); greater possibilities for Africans in professional careers (as a result of the abolition of racial discrimination, a certain withdrawal of racial minorities and extended educational opportunities); the increased demand for leading personnel of African origin, i.e. for managers, administrators, accountants, engineers, technicians, and other educated staff, etc. (as a result of the nationalizations in a number of countries and/or the establishment of mixed state companies and para-statal organizations). The privileged position and high income of this élite is due above all to the great shortage of adequately qualified and trained personnel. It also arises from the fact, however, that the *gradual* replacement of expatriates by nationals leaves the scale of salaries, which was adjusted to metropolitan income relations, practically unchanged (according to the principle "equal pay for equal work"), which is often revised even upwards by the *corruptive* policy of foreign firms and states. The increased political role of this élite follows from the fact that as a result of the mixed and transitory nature of production relations and the rather unformed character of class relations there are hardly any politically organized class forces available, and the leaders of the political parties are recruited mostly from this social group. (This group, smaller by far in number and material power, enjoyed even under colonialism a privileged position when compared with the great masses of the population. At the same time, they could increasingly feel the drawbacks of racial discrimination, the humiliating subordination and the colonial relations blocking the way to get to the top in their career. This provides the explanation for the *dual* position and dual behaviour of this élite which

[65] For a short but comprehensive summary and critique of African populism see J. S. Saul: *On African Populism*. University College, Dar es Salaam, March, 1967.

354

supplied both loyal servants of colonialism and leaders for the national liberation movements.)

No doubt, we are faced here with an important source of *class formation*, or, since the "classical" ways of class formation are *relatively* impeded,[66] probably even with its most important source at present. The real *question*, however, is not whether the emergence of the élite is or is not a source of class formation, but rather: *what* class it is a source for and whether it is for a new, independent one.

A social stratum of a composition similar to this élite (the so-called 'middle class" and intelligentsia) also exists in the developed (European) class societies. Its social position and role and its relation to the basic classes, however, are fairly clear and well defined; its character is determined by the prevailing class relations. It is merely a supplementary appendix to the basic classes. It may constitute a communication channel between them and even a source of supply for them, but cannot develop into an independent class.

The question is whether this stratum, under the mixed, heterogeneous and transitory socio-economic relations prevailing in the underdeveloped countries, can develop into an independent, ruling class of society.

Social classes cannot exist without the characteristic production relations giving birth to them. However, the formation of this élite is not connected with the change of the character of production relations but only with some modifications in them and a few transitory, temporarily effective factors. In the possession of state power, this élite can undoubtedly influence the development of production relations, too, but the way it does also determines its own fate. Since the predominant relations of production in an underdeveloped economy inherited from colonialism are *de facto* capitalist relations which make even the surviving forms of precapitalist relations carry in them the tendency of capitalization, this élite will *either* fight against these relations *or* serve their expansion and further development. In the latter case its fate and role is clear and unambiguous enough: the élite itself will become part of the capitalist class, i.e. instead of an independent class, a source of the formation of the bourgeoisie.

[66] The transformation of *the rural sector* is impeded, as we have seen, by external and internal factors, and the formation of an African agrarian bourgeoisie, the kulak stratum— just like that of a real agrarian proletariat—can only proceed very slowly, though the differentiation process has already got under way. The spontaneous rise of a local *urban industrial and merchant bourgeoisie* from the further evolution and dissociation-transformation of the urban small-scale industry and petty trade also comes up against innumerable obstacles and difficulties though it also has already made some progress. In addition to the obstacles already discussed (e.g. the overwhelming competition of foreign capital, lack of specialization, dispersal of capital, accumulation and marketing difficulties, etc.), we must also take into account the fact that it is precisely this petty and intermediary trade, small and service industries, etc., that are usually handled by the "racial" minorities (Asians, Arabs), whose business expansion is also impeded by objective and subjective factors arising from their peculiar position.

In the former case, however, the question—as the question of socialist development in general, too,[67]—is more complicated, in view of the lack of one of the essential conditions of anti-capitalist development, a well-developed industrial working class. Is it possible for this élite—if supported by various internal and external forces—to bring about, on the one hand, a broad state (more exactly state-capitalist) sector by ousting foreign capital and preventing the creation of, or appropriating the local private capital, and to develop, on the other, into a self-reproducing class and ensure permanently its privileged position and parasitical existence based on the sharp inequalities of income distribution? In other words, shall we witness the coming into being of a social system similar to the "Asiatic mode of production" embodying a specific form of coexistence of communistic and exploiting relations in which the communal ownership as the basic production relation and the horizontally effective communistic relations are supplemented by and subordinated to the vertical relations of exploitation operating through and by state power?

Like all analogies, the comparison with the Asiatic mode of production is, of course, rather shaky, yet it helps to illuminate certain crucial points. After all, the Asiatic mode of production, though it lasted for centuries, was also transitional, and the state élite constituted a veritable exploiting "class". But the lasting character of this "transitory" period was ensured by the *external* isolation of the society as a whole, and within the society by the *internal* isolation of the state aristocracy and the great socio-economic *immobility* and *stagnation* stemming from the primitive communistic relations coupled with the undeveloped forces of production. The reproduction of the ruling élite was realized as the *natural reproduction of a hereditary aristocracy* whose stability and basis were provided by the determined sequence of ruling personalities.

It is obvious that in the developing countries today, however large the backwardness of their productive forces and the alienation of their élite from the masses of society may be, such a transitory formation cannot be maintained for long even by open military force. This is not only because the precondition of external isolation cannot be ensured (in view of the open character of 'the economy and the modern means of international communication, etc.) but mainly because *social mobility* will necessarily assume such proportions, owing to the inevitable development of industry and education, that the very preconditions for the formation and isolation of an élite will gradually cease to exist.

A social stratum, which is *not the owner* of the means of production and cannot ensure its privileged material position but only by regulating the distribution relations by *non-economic (political)*, exogenous means contradicting the actual production relations, which is unable to maintain

---

[67] We shall return to this question for a brief discussion in the final chapter.

356

its own isolation and reproduction, and whose objective social function does prescribe, after all, to develop the productive forces and to increase social mobility, this social stratum is bound to lose sooner or later the *political power* which could maintain, beyond the effect of the temporary factors, the inequalities of income distribution.

Consequently, it is impossible for the élite to become a new, independent social class. The alienation from society of the bureaucratic élite may retard the process of socialist development but cannot determine by itself, without changes in ownership relations, a new direction for the basic cause of development. The élite, as it exists today, will either merge with the bourgeoisie of an unfolding capitalist society,[68] or will dissolve, losing its élite character, in the process of socialist development.

Since, however, not only the fate of the élite depends on the direction of socio-economic development but the élite, itself is, under the conditions of a *mixed* economy and a *transitory* society, one of the most important social factors influencing the choice between the alternative directions of development, therefore the investigation into its formation, character and changes constitutes an indispensable part of class analysis.

At this juncture, let us sum up in brief the *main characteristics* of the *basic social classes*.

(1) The *proletariat* has strong links with the village, the peasantry. The bulk of wage workers are semi-proletarians engaged in *agriculture*, and their separation from the basic means of production, of land, is in most cases only partial, especially in territories where the precapitalistic forms of exploitation have survived to a large extent (as in Southeast Asia), or where the primtive communistic relations are still existent in the traditional agriculture (Tropical Africa). A considerable number of wage workers still have lands of their own which are cultivated by their families and to which they themselves return for seasonal work from time to time. Consequently, the dividing line between peasantry and proletariat is a rather blurred one.

The number of the *urban industrial* proletariat is relatively low. The majority of the urban wage workers are employed not in industry, but either in households (domestic servants), or in trade and the services, and as auxiliary labour in civil service, or they do all kinds of odd jobs. As to the ratio of industrial workers there are, of course, considerable differences between the individual underdeveloped areas, depending on the achieved level of industrial development, the direction of industrialization, the techniques employed, etc. The degree of the *concentration* of the industrial proletariat is generally low, with most of the wage workers being employed in small plants. The degree of concentration is higher in the extractive

---

[68] This can be observed, e.g., when the members of state bureaucracy are increasingly merged into the management of capitalist companies, become their shareholders, or embark upon business ventures of their own.

industries and certain light industries[69] owned by the big foreign monopolies and/or in the large state enterprises newly established under the development programmes. It also varies to a considerable extent, of course, from country to country, and, e.g. in the large cities of the more developed Latin-American countries and a few Asian cities a fairly concentrated proletariat of the large-scale industry has already developed.

The composition of the working class is extremely *heterogeneous*, and its internal stratification is great. This follows, first of all, from the *different measure of proletarianization*, that is the different degree of dependence on wage labour. In this respect two main categories can be distinguished: the proletariat proper (who have been completely "freed" from the means of production and the traditional precapitalist bonds restricting their mobility) and the semi-proletarianized peasants and artisans who carry out, in the possession of their own means of production, independent production, too, in addition to wage labour. The greatly heterogeneous character is further manifest in "*racial*" *stratification*,[70] in the relatively great dispersion of *skills* and *wages* and the different character and conditions of the *employment spheres*. There is usually a big disproportionate gap between the wage levels of the skilled and unskilled, the settled and migrant workers in general, and between the more concentrated and organized workers of industry, mining, the docks and railways, on the one hand, the dispersed, unorganized workers of agriculture, the building industry, trade and especially the domestic workers, on the other. This gap is also connected with the fact of the "missing links" in the sectoral structure of the economy (particularly of industry) and even in the educational pyramid, i.e. with the lack of socio-economic integration in general. This justifies indeed—at least temporarily—to make an approximate distinction between a small group of settled workers skilled in a higher (foreign) technology, of a quasi-"labour aristocracy" with wages usually adjusted to an imported income level, on the one hand, and the broad masses of unstable, unskilled, badly paid and only semi-proletarianized and migrant workers, on the other. The intermediate strata and mainly the socio-politically decisive and well-organized and class-conscious army of workers from large-scale industry are lacking or hardly developed.

[69] The degree of concentration, however, is greatly reduced here by the light industry character itself of the production which gives greater scope to the putting-out system involving small plants, cottage industries and homecraft artisans as outworkers and, on the other hand, by the preference given, recently, to the capital-intensive techniques in many places.

[70] In Tropical Africa, e.g., the following main categories were formed in the colonial period: the best-paid (and usually skilled) European élite workers, the intermediate strata of workers belonging to the (Asian or Arab) minorities and the African "subproletariat". Since independence considerable shifts have, of course, taken place, due especially to a—narrow—group of African workers rising into the upper categories.

(2) The *peasantry* of the developing countries is a social group of very specific composition which cannot by any means be compared with its equivalent in West European countries. This group is the most important constituent in the class structure of the developing countries. Since, on the one hand, this peasantry is the inexhaustible source of the urban proletariat, which, in turn, is attached *permanently* by thousands of links to the rural population (migrant workers!), and since, on the other, the precapitalistic social remnants have naturally been preserved in the rural areas, while the export enclaves have also developed there, the peasantry of the developing countries includes very different and contradictory elements, and takes on very different influences.

It was first in agriculture that violent colonial penetration and the beginning of the economic establishment of the colonizers made themselves felt (expropriations of land, forced production, the emergence of the plantation economies, recruiting of manpower, forced labour, etc.) and had the gravest consequences: decline of the nutrition level due to the introduction of the one-crop production and the subsequent drop in food production; overpopulation relative to the available land and cultivation techniques (in countries where the unequal distribution of land was caused by colonial land alienations); general indebtedness of the peasantry, etc.

At the same time, it is the peasantry that has to bear most of the burdens of the precapitalistic remnants and forms of exploitation (produce deliveries, labour service, share farming, usury credits, etc.). And in many countries where these forms have been widely preserved, unequal land distribution, the indebtedness of the peasantry, rural overpopulation and the low nutrition level are, last but not least, the consequence of these precapitalistic forms, too.

The composition of the peasantry varies in the underdeveloped world not only from continent to continent but virtually from country to country. The majority of the peasantry consist everywhere of smallholders and farmers working on their plots, even if the large-scale concentration of lands is characteristic in some countries, and the relation of these small-plot farmers to the land, and the forms of their exploitation are rather different. We can equally find the small plot, based on the communal ownership of land and cultivated by the equal right of use, holdings ceded by the feudal landlords as a reward for feudal services (perhaps as part of the land divided by the village community), the independent, individually owned small holdings and the various forms of land tenure, etc., associated with the diverse varieties of feudal, semi-feudal and capitalistic exploitation.

The agrarian proletariat, or more exactly the semi-proletarianized peasants, the subsistence farmers, and the cash cropper smallholders are difficult to separate from one another, and the possession of small holdings is, as a rule, just as typical of the agricultural wage workers as of the independent farmers.

Small farmers who make up the majority of the peasantry, whether peasants living in tribal communities, or serf-peasants in the yoke of feudal landlords, or small farmers "competing" with capitalist plantations and suffering from the exploitation of capitalist purchasing companies, are alike social groups filled with immense tension. They see the possibility of their rise either in a radical land reform and a large-scale agrarian programme, or in the increasing labour-absorbing capacity of the urban industry. Double exploitation, both from the parasitic activity of the feudal and semi-feudal ruling strata of the obsolete traditional society and from the cunning exploitation by the foreign companies, settlers, commercial purchasing firms, as well as the keen competition of the big plantations, bring about great *revolutionary energies* in the peasantry of the developing countries.

The fact that these revolutionary energies really exist, and that the degree of the differentiation within the small-farm peasantry is still relatively low, while the experience of quite a large number of them has gained experience in wage labour via the migrant-labour system, etc. provide the basis for the afore-mentioned concepts which look upon this poor rural population as the potential or actual leading forces of social revolution and the anti-imperialist movement. The political attitude of this peasantry is doubtless strongly influenced by the pressure and exploitation from above and from outside. In many places this influence is even stronger than that caused by the new tensions and conflicts arising from inner differentiation. At the same time, however, the development in consciousness of this social stratum is held back to a great extent by the ancient ritual customs, tribal and religious prejudices. In addition, the large dispersion of the producing units prevents them from being easily organized. On the other hand, with capitalist development making progress in agriculture, even when or rather especially when this process is introduced by the abolition of feudal land ownership and the dividing up of big land estates and even foreign-owned plantations, too, this social stratum is subject to a rapid *differentiation* in the course of which the more well-to-do peasants, who have succeeded in making use of the new opportunities to get rich, turn into capitalist farmers. As a result, they break away from the other strata of peasantry and come to terms with other exploiting elements.

(3) Owing to economic dependence, to the activity of foreign monopoly capital and to the existence of the remnants of precapitalistic social formations, the *bourgeoisie* of the developing countries occupies a *special place* in society. As an exploiting class it is, on the one hand, opposed to the working people of society just as the feudal exploiters and foreign monopoly capital are, and, on the other hand, as a class retarded and crippled in its development by the external (imperialist) and internal (feudal and prefeudal) factors of "underdevelopment" it may also have anti-imperialist and anti-feudal features *as well*.

360

Depending on which of the two opposing features is *dominant* with one or the other part of the bourgeoisie, which of the different influences determines its behaviour in the *given* historical period, a distinction must be made between the so-called *national bourgeoisie* which supports the national and democratic (anti-imperialist and anti-feudal) tendencies, on the one hand, and the so-called *comprador bourgeoisie*, which is opposed to them.

It is obvious that a distinction can only be made on the basis of *objective* and primarily *economic criteria*. This means that we must first find out to what extent and under what conditions the concrete economic interests of the various strata of the bourgeoisie require cooperation with or struggle against foreign monopoly capital, and how the various strata of the bourgeoisie are related to the sound development of the national economy, to economic decolonization and industrialization.

In this connection, it is of great importance to know what position these bourgeois strata occupy in the various sectors of the national economy, in what branches their capital is concentrated and how the interests of these strata differ and also change in the process of economic development. This investigation alone, however, is not sufficient and is informative only if it also points out the role and policy[71] of foreign capital with regard to the individual economic sectors and its relation within the sectors with indigenous capital, or with other sectors controlled by local capital.[72]

The development of a peripheral, dependent capitalism with an abortive process of primitive accumulation has hindered the rise and the strengthening of a genuine national bourgeoisie (just like the growth of a real proletariat) and distorted the pattern of its emergence and development.[73] In many countries, the bourgeoisie as a conscious class has

[71] From this point of view it appears important to examine the weight, sphere of activity and the relation to international capital of the *colonial settler bourgeoisie*, where there is any, and, further, how the interests and investment policies of the international monopolies change (e.g. by shifting towards the import-substituting, capital-intensive light industries).

For a thorough analysis of the changes in the positions and relationship of local settlers capital and foreign monopoly capital, see G. Arrighi: *The Political Economy of Rhodesia.* Mouton, The Hague, 1967.

[72] In the countries where the local petty and middle bourgeoisie are made up mainly of the "racial" minorities, their social and political behaviour has been determined to a great extent by their *foreign* exploiting character and their activity often serving, or collaborating with capital. To avoid any unjust generalization, we must admit the existence of a few bourgeois elements belonging to the racial minorities who, because of their conflicting economic interests or from political (or economic) foresight, are opposed to imperialism.

[73] The following description of the Indian bourgeoisie illustrates the point. "The national bourgeoisie was ... very weak. Its capital stock was small, its power of taking risk very limited. Moreover, it could obtain a very high rate of return for its capital from trade, usury and rack-renting. Very few industries could yield such a high rate of return. The domestic market was small; the peasants had very little to spare to buy industrial goods. The foreign market was dominated by foreign multinational corporations. The national bourgeoisie did not come forward to enter any area in which a high and safe return was not ensured. The state

361

hardly developed, the national bourgeoisie is a weak, mixed social stratum doomed to a secondary role and peripheral activity.

The lasting co-existence of the capitalistic and precapitalistic modes of production has created a wide margin providing an appropriate sphere for "antedeluvian" *merchant capital*, i.e., for capital getting rich by cheating (unequal exchange) and usury. The discrepancy which has evolved between the higher concentration of foreign capital (territorially: in towns and the enclaves, organizationally: in the monopoly-capitalistic forms of developed capitalism), on the one hand, and the structurally and organizationally loose character of the economy as a whole (dispersion of the objective and subjective elements of production, the scarcity of linkages), i.e. the economic environment contradicting the organizational forms of foreign capital, on the other, provides a relatively wide room for *intermediary economic activities*. The typical zone of the rise of the urban bourgeois strata has become, or remained, the *intermediary, trading and service industries* attached and subordinated to the activities of public administration and foreign capital.

The commercial bourgeoisie is usually the most important group of the bourgeoisie in the developing countries. It comprises the broad masses of small merchants and middlemen with a small capital supply and just a few employees, as well as the wholesale merchants who in a few countries have already seized hold of a considerable part of the local market and also carry out foreign-trade activity. In many countries, this group is in direct contact with foreign commercial monopolies, often acting as its mediators and satellites. As a considerable proportion of this commercial bourgeoisie and especially the small-merchant groups are of alien origin in a number of countries, stemming in most cases not even from the colonizing country but as "racial" minorities from other countries (e.g. Indians and Arabs in East Africa, Chinese in Southeast Asia, etc.), wide differences show up accordingly between the individual countries in social stratification and the character of the bourgeoisie. With foreign and distributive wholesale trade coming under the control of the public sector, the sphere of activity and the growth potential of merchant bourgeoisie have been reduced in several countries.

In the sphere of production it was only *agriculture* (in the colonial period) which opened up wider horizons for the rise of the national bourgeoisie, namely by the differentiation process taking place in rural economy as a consequence of the introduction of (export) cash crop production. In countries where agricultural commodity production developed on the lands of local farmers, the upper stratum of the peasantry or the local feudal-capitalist landowners (such as, e.g., in Latin America) make up a certain

had to take the initiative..." (N. K. Sarkar: *Social Structure and Development in Asia.* Peoples's Publishing House, New Delhi, 1978, p. 179.

362

agrarian bourgeoisie, which may also be complemented by the bureaucratic élite who, as absentee owners, invest their capital in land estates. This stratum of the bourgeoisie, even if it is a rich and politically powerful group, is again a somewhat deformed and abnormally developed stratum.

It usually comes into contact with foreign monopolies through the marketing of its agrarian produce and above all in export business. Its growth and strengthening are hindered partly by the unfavourable world-market trend of the agrarian exports and the competition of foreign-owned plantations and partly by the narrowness of the domestic market and the underdevelopment of the industries processing agricultural raw materials. As a matter of fact, due to the dominant position of foreign companies in the market (or even in the production) of the main cash crops and to the disintegrated economic structure, together with the lack of linkages between agriculture and industry, neither the "American", nor the "Prussian" type of development of agrarian capitalism could unfold.

The *industrial bourgeoisie* is usually a very narrow and less developed group, which is concentrated mostly in the light and food industries and the smaller or larger plants of the repair industry. It consists mostly of small and medium capitalists. This is the group which was most exposed to the detrimental effects of colonialism, the activity and competition of colonial monopolies, the narrowness of the domestic market, the general deficiency of capital, the shortage of qualified labour and the import-sensitivity of the economy. Owing to its capital shortage and poor competitiveness, this group, unless it receives effective support by the state, and given the existing open and disintegrated structure of the economy is hardly able to become the leading stratum of the national bourgeoisie, the motor of a national capitalist development.

Since it was this stratum whose development was particularly blocked by the colonial system and its economic mechanism, industrial bourgeoisie (or more precisely: all those interested in the industrial development of the country), could be considered—almost by definition—as national bourgeoisie, as part or an ally of the national liberation movements.

In the postcolonial period, however, either as a consequence of the internal class struggle in the newly independent countries sharpening under the conditions of internal economic difficulties and world-economic crisis, and of a political choice between development alternatives, or, and in general, because of changes in the pattern of foreign investments and of the rise of neo-colonialism, the face and behaviour of *industrial bourgeoisie* have also changed.[74]

[74] "As the capitalist crisis deepens, the national bourgeoisie becomes more and more dependent on foreign capitalists and multinational corporations and compromises the independence of the country..." (Op. cit., p. 183.)

Since the investment pattern and policy of multinational corporations have actually opened up relatively broad perspectives for cooperation and "putting-out" activities in the sphere of the manufacturing industries, the industrial bourgeoisie is more inclined to collaborate with foreign companies, or to prepare with its investments the ground for the multinational corporations.

In view of these modified relations between this stratum and foreign capital, and of the strengthening business and political ties of the former with various neo-colonial forces in general, it would be a great mistake today to identify "national" (anti-imperialist) bourgeoisie with industrial bourgeoisie versus the comprador strata. Nevertheless, the anti-imperialist features and interests of this stratum have not necessarily disappeared everywhere and totally, for a real leadership of the national economy and a real industrialization presuppose, indeed, not only minor improvements in its bargaining position vis-à-vis the multinational companies, but also a real struggle against economic dependence.

The *financial* or *banking bourgeoisie* is engaged in supplying credit for industry, agriculture, trade and transport, or is involved in usury credits granted to peasants or landowners, and the related speculative land operations. Since the banking and credit business has developed almost everywhere under the control of foreign monopolies, a strong local banking bourgeoisie could develop only in a few countries in the past (e.g. in Egypt) where the local industrial, agricultural and merchant bourgeoisie was strong enough to occupy independent positions in the banking and credit business, in the face of foreign capital. Where this took place, the strengthening of the whole of the national bourgeoisie was given a boost. The *usury bourgeoisie*, on the other hand, which is a parasitic stratum, taking advantage of the backward relations, the insufficiency of the internal resources of accumulation, and the existence of precapitalist remnants, does not usually come into direct contact or conflict with foreign capital. Owing to the nationalization of the banking and credit institution in a number of countries, this stratum has slipped back.

These strata of the bourgeoisie cannot be found, at least not in the same proportion and of the same weight, in every developing country. In some countries, the national bourgeoisie has not come into being at all, while in others a relatively strong big bourgeoisie and even groups of monopoly capital have already emerged. The more backward the economy and society of a country is and the more they bear the stamp of the colonial system, the more the rise and activity of the local bourgeoisie are confined to the fields of trade and agriculture. And the more the new investment pattern of the multinational companies have evolved, the more a *neo-comprador industrial bourgeoisie* appear, together with a semi-capitalist bureaucratic stratum playing an intermediary role as board members of the companies between the latter and the state administration. The latter, by acquiring shares in equity capital may easily become a real, though parasitic bourgeoisie, or, by its leading positions in civil service, can turn the operation of the public sector to the advantage of foreign companies.

Besides these tendencies, the bourgeoisie, e.g., in several countries of Tropical Africa, is still represented only by the relatively well-to-do agrarian "kulak" stratum employing wage labour (often only temporarily), and the stratum engaged and employing wage labour in the retail trade or the service industries. The latter's subordinate role and usually direct dependence on foreign monopolies make it a sort of "lumpen-bourgeoisie" while the living standards of the poorest strata of small merchants and artisans (mainly peddlers and vendors) are even lower than those of the permanently employed urban wage workers.

(4) *The position of "feudal" landlords and other leading strata of the traditional sector* has, as a rule, substantially weakened of late in the developing countries. This is due partly to the agrarian reforms which, though carried out mostly as a compromise in an inconsistent way, pushed back the precapitalist, feudal and semi-feudal relations in the villages, and partly to the fact that the struggles for national liberation and against imperialism-colonialism revealed a considerable proportion of these strata as openly supporting imperialism and resulted in their being ousted from the political leadership.

This applies mainly to the feudal leadership of some countries in the Middle East and Asia as well as to some tribal chiefs collaborating with the colonizers in some countries of Tropical Africa. Here again, it would be a mistake to make general statements about the political behaviour of this precapitalist social group as some of the feudal landlords in a few countries also took part in the liberation struggles, and in other countries the orientation in foreign policy of the traditional leadership shows positive features, true, mainly for historical or international motivations. And many a tribal chief in Tropical Africa was martyred in the liberation movements.

It would also be wrong to grant equal treatment to both the upper strata of "feudal" landlords and the church, on the one hand, and also the tribal leadership of the communal society, as the former, apart from their affiliation with foreign monopoly capital and colonial rule, are the representatives of feudal bonds and exploitation, while the latter are the depositaries of the political and religious authority of the ancient communal society and the custodians of tribal affinity and ancient customs. The breaking up of the political and economic power of the former is just as much a precondition for development as the liquidation of economic dependence. But tribalism is also an outdated system and the power of the tribal chief may also be an obstacle to social integration.

These strata still have considerable economic and political power even today in many countries. However, beyond or along with the changes referred to, a certain *transformation* process can be observed, in the course

365

of which the "feudal" landlords increasingly adjust themselves to the new relations, embrace the capitalist economy and gradually merge with the bourgeoisie. At the same time, the rural development programmes, the differentiation process already started and the administrative reforms shake the very foundations of the position of tribal chiefs and the whole system of tribal leadership in general.

CHAPTER IV

PROSPECTS FOR THE OVERCOMING
OF UNDERDEVELOPMENT.
SUMMARY AND CONCLUSIONS

The analysis of the true nature, causes, inner mechanism and the two interrelated, external and internal, aspects of underdevelopment, and the investigation into the objective tendencies arising from the movement of this complex socio-economic phenomenon, are not aimed at supporting an abstract philosophical-ideological concept. They are rather intended to serve practical action, to draw the type of conclusions and work out the sort of directives for putting into practice an economic policy, which concern and concentrate on the causes and the elimination of the disease itself, instead of its merely accessory, superficial symptoms producing illusions and misleading as to the right treatment.

An uninitiated patient usually tends to believe in his own ideas dictated by his momentary pains or relief rather than the physician's diagnosis. His illusions, however, are soon dispelled when the hidden nature of his real illness comes' to light. It may, of course, also happen that the physician himself fosters these illusions and, instead of treating the illness or even stating exactly its diagnosis, he merely prescribes some palliatives. The real value and "science" of such a physician is also soon disclosed. The duration of individual human illnesses and recoveries, as a matter of course, falls within the life of the patient (and mostly the physician, too).

The duration of the diseases of the society and economy, and the time needed for the curing of such diseases, however, may spread over the life of a long series of subsequent human generations, that is over a whole historical period. Consequently, it may fall beyond the time horizon of the living generations (or part of them). The diagnosis and treatment itself can only be stated after the long-run tendencies have been revealed. Though the accumulated experience of human history and the scientific methods make it possible for everybody to get to know these tendencies, the length of the time horizon needed makes many people lose interest in such investigations. "In the long run we are all dead" teaches the "revolution-maker" of economics (J. M. Keynes). Though the sense of responsibility and care of parents for the fate of their children (and even grandchildren) are undoubted, this is not usually so for the fate of other peoples's children. In the case of the diseases of society one generation may be given palliatives but the subsequent generation may suffer from the protraction or worsening of the disease. And since society is not a single homogeneous organism but consists of classes, and world society is made up even of nations and peoples, the disease may not affect equally the individual parts of this society, moreover, the very overgrowth of one part may cause the atrophy of the other.

Thus it is no wonder that a specific type of the "physician" of the sick society and economy has evolved who—even if he is not *personally* interested in the defence of the overgrown parts—acts as a proponent of symptomatic treatment, of palliatives, as an apostle of the "short run". We have witnessed the appearance of the "coffeehouse"-theoretician of underdevelopment,[1] of the advocate of "mini-research" and "mini-programmes".[2] For him the questions of long-run dynamism, i.e. *historical* perspective and the whole socio-economic complex, i.e. the *dialectic* unity belong to the world of "political belief", "political religion" and not to the sphere of "exact" economics. It is obviously in this fashion that he will evaluate the following conclusions too, merely because, instead of searching for new coffee markets and hunting for new creditors and donors, we emphasize the necessity of perspective and structural solutions and also comprises the socio-political aspects of further development.

The investigations in the preceding chapters intended not only to shed some light on the causes of the present state of the developing countries but also to reveal the tendencies which arise from the existence of the complex socio-economic formation called "underdevelopment" and from the changes in world-economic relations constituting the external aspect and a determining factor of this phenomenon. These are the *tendencies of the spontaneous reproduction of underdevelopment.*

The dialectic interrelationship of the individual factors of this complex formation also comprises—as we have seen—a certain exchange of the causes and effects. The movement of the formation gains thereby a *relative independence* compared with, or rather corresponding to, the original *external* factor, i.e. colonial penetration. Thus, e.g., the distorted nature of the economy itself provides the basis for maintaining or re-establishing dependence.

The relative independence of the movement of the formation is strengthened partly by the coming to the fore of the *indirect forms* of dependence and exploitation, which are closely connected with the economic structure as a whole, and partly by the causal connection of the

---

[1] Who, instead of raising the question of the sense and function of the one-crop production, e.g. the coffee-monoculture, or of the economic structure in general, reduces the issue of the causes and the way out of underdevelopment to the marketing problems of "coffee".

[2] Who, instead of investigating the structural problems of the whole national economy, restricts research to elementary particles, to minor, narrowly defined fields, often referring to the "economicalness" of research or "more direct practical applicability", and prefers development programmes with minor patching-up and tinkering tasks to those with structural transformation.

distortion and dualism of the economic and social structures and the lack of internal integration, which are also connected with the *spontaneous* forces working in the economy and society. *Internally*: the effects and interactions stemming from the two sectors strengthen one another cumulatively, increase disintegration[3] and restrict the development of factors and forces needed for the transformation of the structure. *Externally*: the survival of the mechanism of dependence and income drains and thereby—and also by the preservation of the inner structure—the *reproduction of "underdevelopment" as a system*, on the one hand, and the increasing concentration of the dynamic factors of growth in the most advanced countries[4] (R and D capacities, highly qualified labour[5] and industries applying and developing the most advanced techniques) on the other, lead to the expanded reproduction of *relative backwardness*, i.e. to the increase of the international gap between the development levels of productive forces.

This reproduction of underdevelopment is, by no means, a sort of vicious circle. It is the reproduction of a *qualitative* state: of internal socio-economic relations and structures, and specific external economic relations, which does not exclude, on the contrary, includes and presupposes the *quantitative* changes.

Therefore, from the point of view of the liquidation of underde-velopment, the question is not whether there are or are not quantitative changes, and whether these quantitative changes may lead sooner or later to qualitative changes or not. (A positive answer to this question has already been *de facto* provided by history, and is provided day by day by the *general* laws of the dialectics of development which are equally valid in both nature and society!) Nor is the question raised in the form whether it is possible at all to break the magic circle of the recurrence of the invariable (or hardly variable) quantities (the vicious circle) and, consequently, what quantitative change, at what point of the circle, is necessary to ensure the induced change of the other quantities—instead of their unchanged reproduction. The concepts of "big push", "take-off", "critical minimum effort", etc. are, at least from this point of view, inapplicable not for the reason that they call

---

[3] See, e.g., the spontaneous gravitation of investments towards the existing enclave sectors. Strangely (but understandably) enough, this is often the consequence of steps taken consciously and deliberately to *transform* the structure as, e.g., where and when the imports, greatly stepped up in the interest of industrialization or rural development, necessitate the increasing production of the export enclave and/or where and when the machine and material supply of the new import-substituting industries is based for a while on imports.

[4] Due not only to the more advanced and generally more dynamic educational system but also to the "brain drain" which came about under the attractive effect of higher living standards (and often as a result of organized actions and manipulations for enticing qualified people).

[5] For a comprehensive analysis and good illustration of this process see Gy. Ádám: *Új technika, új struktúra* (New Technology, New Structure). Közgazdasági és Jogi Könyvkiadó, Budapest, 1966.

attention to the necessity for quantitative cummulation. (It is, in fact, their virtue!) They are inapplicable because *without* the proper analysis of the present qualitative state and the determination of that state in the future which, historically, can be and must be achieved, and which will accelerate by itself the further quantitative changes, the place, direction and extent of the necessary quantitative changes remain *undetermined or arbitrarily determined.*[6] (In this respect it does not make but negligible difference if the qualitative state is determined but this determination denies—as with Rostow—the actual process of historical development, or the assumed new qualitative state and the quantitative changes assumed to be necessary to attain it contradict one another.[7])

Thus this is how the question has to be put: which is the qualitative state which not only differs from underdevelopment as the present *qualitative* state but also denies it; and consequently and accordingly which are the quantitative changes that are necessary to attain this qualitative state in the *shortest* possible time?

No doubt, the quantitative changes (and so the preparation of the qualitative change, too) take place in the short-run processes of daily practice and their sequence. Therefore the significance of everyday practice, and of short-run concepts and economic policy is extremely great. The reason, therefore, why this last chapter concentrates not on the acute and tactical questions of short-term economic policy, is *by no means* an underestimation of the importance of a short-run economic policy inducing quantitative changes and aiming at overcoming the immediate "daily" problems. The reasons are different: on the one hand, there are a great number of scientific studies dealing with such questions of economic policy as industrialization, agrarian development, foreign trade and financing, employment and wages, etc. illuminating these problems from various angles and revealing various relationships. Insofar as these questions appear as *tactical* questions, as questions of the concrete *priorities* of development and of the *methods* to be adopted, the conclusions of these studies, even if they are contradictory, are hardly open to criticism, unless

---

[6] If the abstraction, the theoretical generalization of the conditions necessary for the liquidation of underdevelopment, is merely a logical act devoid of any historical verification, then the result is *either* a model which can be applied even to a small number of developing countries only arbitrarily and with contradictions, producing a one-sidedly distorted recipe of economic policy, *or* an empty and tautological formula from which no concept of economic policy can be derived, as e.g. the proposition that *somewhere* the vicious circle must be broken, that *a sort* of minimum concentration of efforts, *some sort of* magnitude of accumulation must be achieved.

[7] In addition, it turns out—as we have seen in Part One—that the only quantitative criterion which can also be measured empirically: the 10 per cent margin of net investments as a precondition for "take-off", is, itself, inadequate as its attainment or even prolonged existence cannot provide a guarantee for take-off, and it is usually only from the *actual* occurrence of the latter that we can infer the *previous* existence of its preconditions.

we question their applicability to a given country. Who would deny that there are countries where the priority of agrarian development—at least for the preparation of industrialization—is fully justified, or that in another country the development of the light industries ensures the most favourable start? The choice of technique, the sectoral priority, the priority of export orientation or of import substitution, etc. as tactical questions can be debated only if time and place, that is, the concrete relations, are indicated, i.e. if these questions are put in the framework of case studies. In a work, however, dealing with the general laws of movement of underdevelopment and the prospects of overcoming it, they should be discussed only if they appear as strategic, long-run questions or if the answers to them claim to apply to all developing countries. Therefore, it is justified in this respect, too to concentrate here on the general prospects of further development, on the strategic long-run problems. On the other hand, the raising of long-run, strategic questions makes it easier to evaluate the tactical questions of a short-term economic policy too, and enables us to determine the right direction of the necessary short-run quantitative changes.

The political economy of underdevelopment proves that there are *two aspects* of this historical product of which originally, i.e. from the point of view of the determination of the origin and nature of the product, the *external* aspect was the dominant one. Today, however, owing to the complex character and relative independence of this product, the external and internal factors *mutually* presuppose and determine each other.

Consequently, the liquidation of underdevelopment also embraces *two* interrelated *aspects:* the *external* and *internal* ones.

Insofar as we are examining the external aspect not from the angle of a single developing country, that is not as the aspect of the dependence and exploitation of a single country, but in relation to the entire underdeveloped world, the Third World, then we are, as a matter of fact, faced with the question of the *international* solution, of the international liquidation of underdevelopment. Thus it is not the questions of a national economic policy, not even of a national foreign policy but the problems of the transformation of international economic and political relations which come to the fore in the analysis. It is anyway justified to deal with these questions first: if the international factor played a determining role in the *emergence* of underdevelopment, then it may seem logical that the liquidation of underdevelopment too requires an *international* solution.

1. THE PROSPECTS OF THE INTERNATIONAL LIQUIDATION OF UNDERDEVELOPMENT

What kind of international solution[8] can be expected?

Underdevelopment as an international problem appears not only in the way the socio-economic development of certain countries is blocked by and within the complex phenomenon called "underdevelopment", and that this phenomenon and its external factors must be eliminated in order to clear the way for development, but it is manifest also as *relative underdevelopment*, as a gap between wealth and poverty. This dual aspect of the problem can also be found in the case of class antagonism within a single society: the worker is not only prevented by his exploited and oppressed position from achieving an adequate improvement in his living standard and cultural-educational level and from evolving freely all his qualities, but he also feels the burden of his relative poverty. According to which of the two aspects is emphasized the suggested solution is either the redistribution of goods or the liquidation of exploitation and dependence.

If the *redistribution* of goods or, more exactly, *incomes* at the international level (as well as within a single society, too) is not accompanied by (or rather results not from) the transformation of the bases of the system or formation, i.e. by the liquidation of the relations of exploitation and dependence, a final solution, no matter how radical the change in income distribution, cannot be brought about. Just as much as it demonstrates the misunderstánding of the essence of capitalist society to assume that the social problem and the revolutionary trend stem simply from the poverty of the workers, it also shows the failure to understand the nature of international capitalism and underdevelopment if we cherish *illusions* about an income-redistribution through aid, concessional loans, grants or other forms of assistance.[9]

The supposition that a *world state*, a supra-national government, that is independent of national interests, might soon develop out of the international organizations, perhaps from the United Nations Organization, which could control and govern the redistribution of incomes as well as the allocation of the factors of production, is also unfounded and just as chimerical (or even more) as the belief in the possibility of a state above classes and free of class interests.

[8] Let us disregard here those minor quantitative changes that are opposed to the tendency of the international reproduction of underdevelopment or at least tend to ease the effect of the unfavourable international factors.

[9] Our position against such illusion *does not mean* on any account that we intend to underestimate the efforts (or the concrete partial results they may yield) made to intensify the aiding activity of the international organizations, to improve the structure and effectiveness of loans, to extend grants increasingly on a multilateral basis, to reallocate, in favour of the developing countries, the intellectual and material resources released through the reduction of the costs of armament, to solve the nutrition problem by international actions, etc.

If this is so, then nothing seems to be left but the revolutionary overthrow of the international system, a world revolution by the peoples of developing countries. If the solution within the society of a single country is provided by the revolution and takeover by the exploited, then the solution at the international level seems to be revolution and the seizure of power by the exploited *nations*. This analogy is highly tempting, but nevertheless misleading, not only because the boundaries of exploitation *do not coincide* with the national boundaries (though this is the main reason!), but also because the conditions for such a "revolution" are entirely different from those for a social revolution (and also self-contradictory). While the conditions for the social revolution[10] of the proletariat are created and its success assured by the objective process of economic development in which the social significance, force and organization of this class are continually increasing, the international revolution, or rather the war of the developing countries *as such* is hopeless from the very start, because their uprising, unlike that of the proletariat, could hardly paralyse the total life mechanism of the enemy, and so its success would presuppose such a concentration of forces which the underdeveloped economies are incapable of producing. To suppose the availability of the military and material force necessary for the faintest hope of success simply contradicts the primary condition, i.e. the existence of underdevelopment.

As a counter-argument one could perhaps refer to the victory of revolutionary Russia, though an underdeveloped country, over the intervention of 14 countries. The argument, however, is a false one. This is partly (and less significantly for us now) because Russia's revolution was *not* a *world* revolution but the transformation of the social system of one single country,[11] and partly because it was above all not the revolution of "underdevelopment" or "poverty" against "development" or "affluence", but a social, a *class* revolution. And as such it did enjoy also the support of the exploited classes of the advanced countries. The front lines ran not along the national boundaries of underdevelopment and development but along the international lines of social classes. Soviet Russia was not only the first underdeveloped country to come into conflict with international capitalism and to start building socialism, but she was, at the same time, also the *product* of international socialism, in the sense that it was *also* owing to the international forces of socialism (existing in the advanced countries as well), that she could start the liquidation of her underdevelopment.

[10] By which we should not necessarily understand a violent revolution but a revolutionary, that is a radical, *qualitative*, social transformation, either (if unavoidable) in a violent or (preferably) in a peaceful way.

[11] True, parallel with some attempts also made in other countries. But without the revolution in the advanced capitalist countries it could not lead to a world revolution. "World revolution" on the basis of underdevelopment can only be an illusion, or adventure and tragic attempt.

Isn't it possible then to overcome underdevelopment by such a world revolution in which the developing countries would enjoy the support of certain advanced countries or of certain social forces in the advanced countries?

Such a revolution is, of course, possible but then it would be *no longer* the world revolution of "underdevelopment", the war of the "underdeveloped" nations against the "developed" ones, but a *social* revolution and as such the only possible one: the revolution of the *international working class*. The real "front lines" of such a revolution would cross—in a similar but much more decisive way than in the case of the revolution of the Russian proletariat—the national frontiers of not only the developed capitalist but also developing countries, in other words it would be for both of them a revolution against both the local just as well as the international exploiting *class*.

But the conditions for such a revolution do not come into being so easily. It would also be necessary for the maturation of revolutionary conditions in the various countries to be synchronized in time. Such a synchronization could, however, be created only by a common, worldwide event. Apart from a natural catastrophe necessitating the rapid transformation of world society and the control by it of the economic resources, or from the attack by the inhabitants of another planet—for the time being only the subject matter of science fiction, comics and primitive films—, such an event could be, e.g., a world war sparked off by the imperialist powers, or an international economic crisis. As to the former, the imperialist powers themselves are becoming increasingly aware not only of the military risks (in view of the cessation of the nuclear hegemony), but also of the *social dangers*, especially the internal ones, arising from an imperialist war.

Though in the late seventies, East—West relations changed for the worse again and the spirit of cold war threatened to return, yet the recognition, not only by the wide masses but also by responsible politicians, of the fact that .*détente* with peaceful cooperation is a matter of survival for humanity, seems to be strong enough to prevent a brinkmanship policy from unfolding.

As regards a world-economic crisis, it certainly came in the early seventies and has remained with us ever since. However, the crisis by no means affects the working classes of all countries with equal force, and though the roots of the crisis lie—as has been shown—in the very structure and mechanism of the system, monopoly capital and its state policy seem to succeed not only in unequally distributing and shifting the burdens of the crisis both within the country and internationally, but also in appealing to the nationalistic emotions of considerable strata of the working class to turn them against other countries.

World revolution is impossible without the participation or support of the working class in the advanced capitalist countries, or at least its

374

majority. An *export* of the revolution or a world war started *not* by the imperialist powers would immediately transform the intended social revolution into a war between nations (or even "races"), regrouping thereby the real front lines of the opposing forces in such a way that this war would *no longer* be a war between the exploiters and the exploited.

A worldwide revolutionary solution for the liquidation of the basic external factors of underdevelopment, that is one which would equally and simultaneously affect all developing countries, could only be provided by the collapse of capitalism in the advanced countries, i.e. by a *social* revolution, which *as* and insofar as an international revolution spreading over the entire capitalist world should necessarily and primarily include the action of the working class of the developed countries, too.

Neither the palliating actions of the international organizations, and the measures aiming only at a certain income and benefit redistribution, nor a war between the "poor" and "rich" countries (or, as they are sometimes called the "primary producing" and industrial countries) and not even the proclamation of such a war as "world revolution" by an ideology falsifying the real class relations, can bring about a solution. The former prove necessarily abortive because they leave the basic relations unchanged, and the latter is also foredoomed to failure, because its essence is utterly false.

If, however, the victory of a social world revolution presupposes a revolution within the advanced countries, too, the question arises whether it is only the proletariat or also other social strata that can carry out such a revolution. And whether the working class of the most advanced countries can be supposed to start a revolutionary action at all? To answer these questions, it is necessary to understand the essence of capitalism and the nature of classes. As long as anyone tries to understand the necessity of the historical fall of capitalism simply from the angle of growing poverty— instead of the increasing antagonism between the private ownership of the means of production and the increasingly social character of the rapidly developing productive forces—, and regards the forces of a revolutionary transformation as a messianic force born out of poverty and not as a class belonging to and growing and concentrating with the development of the productive forces of an increasingly social character, a class separated from the productive forces "only" by capitalist private ownership, he will answer these questions by statements about the proletariat of the industrial countries getting poisoned by "general corruptness", "bourgeois-mentality" and merging increasingly into the middle class, and consequently, by searching for the new Messiahs and apostles of the revolution.[12]

---

[12] Consequently and logically, the proponents of this theory are bound to make a stand against the steps taken to raise the living standards of the workers in any country, in the socialist as well as in the developing countries alike, since each of these steps decreases, in their opinion, the revolutionary energies and increases opportunism. In other words, the

It is true that with the unfolding of imperialism, and the colonial system, the actual sphere of overthrowing capitalism has shifted towards the less developed countries. It is equally true that this shift is partly and quite considerably due to the formation within the Western working class of a labour aristocracy also benefitting from international exploitation, and also the considerable rise in the living standards of the employed workers, in general, after the Second World War.[13]

On the one hand, however, this shift is not simply and generally a shift from the rich, industrial countries towards the poor, primary-producing countries but a shift, resulting from the *concrete* relations of international capitalism, towards less developed countries where the contradiction between *labour* and *capital*, owing to the *dual* exploitation by foreign capital, has assumed an especially sharp form. On the other hand, this shift does not testify by any means to a drying up of the revolutionary energies in the Western working class. The advent of a new and successful revolutionary wave is no far-fetched illusion nor is it just a remote possibility. Whether it would be confined to a few countries or would embrace simultaneously the entire advanced capitalist world is, of course, another question.

Thus the way to liquidate underdevelopment in a revolutionary way on a world-wide scale is not a blocked road, but a road fit for traffic only if the coexistence of certain conditions is secured. Otherwise, it inevitably leads either to a blind alley or an abyss. From this it follows at the same time that the historical-logical succession of the causes of underdevelopment does not necessarily determine in the same order the course of its liquidation. In other words, it does not necessarily follow from the fact that underdevelopment is the product of international capitalism, that *without and before* collapse of international capitalism as a whole *nothing* can be done about its liquidation. The philosophy of dialectics, based upon the laws of nature and social history, teaches us that the *whole* can be changed by changes in its *parts*, and revolutions, qualitative transformations, may involve, and be prepared by, long processes, gradual evolutions. To overcome underdevelopment and to change international relations, national and international changes alike are needed and possible even under present-day conditions. They will not result yet in a final and hundred-per-cent solution, but if properly designed, coordinated and implemented, they will certainly bring us nearer to it.

---

success of "world revolution" aimed at liquidating underdevelopment seem to require the preservation and intensification of poverty, if necessary, in an artificial way.

[13] Of course, alongside and in connection with a number of other factors, e.g. the intensification of state intervention to prevent major economic and social conclusions, the boom effect of the scientific-technological revolution, and, on the other hand, the errors and splits in the leadership of the labour movement and, last but not least, the negative effect of *Stalinism* on the international workers' movement.

Let us first investigate what prospects are open within the individual countries for a national policy aimed at the liquidation of underdevelopment, and proceed, subsequently, to discussing briefly the possible international actions, assistance and cooperation policies required to gradually eliminate the international "gap" (more precisely: the disequalizing mechanism).

2. DEVELOPMENT STRATEGY WITHIN THE FRAMEWORK OF A SINGLE NATIONAL ECONOMY

The external aspect of underdevelopment appears, from the point of view of *a single developing country*, as dependence on, and income loss through, foreign capital and the capitalist world market. A radical change in this situation raises the alternative of either a complete isolationism, the policy of "delinking" and autarchy, or of joining the community of socialist countries.

Though it undoubtedly also includes considerable advantages[14] and may become, under certain conditions, a necessary, enforced solution,[15] *isolationism* alone, apart from the various external (and internal) forces against its implementation, cannot ensure the elimination of underdevelopment and may even be the source of obstacles and losses to it. Autarchy not only makes it impossible for even the positive effects arising from international specialization, trade, the "demonstration effects" of production and techniques, etc., to unfold and may also deprive the country of the accessory resources which may prove necessary, but its "success" even in the past presupposed substantial and easily mobilizable internal resources, in other words a potentially rich and large country. The liquidation of underdevelopment would fully depend in this case on the way of internal mobilization, that is the *internal socio-economic transformation*. Leaving out of account here what effect isolationism may have on the very process of socio-economic transformation in an underdeveloped country embracing heterogeneous, mixed socio-economic sectors, it seems at least *unjustified to suppose isolationism* as a policy to be followed by a society which is still *before* the socio-economic transformation determining its way of development.

The joining of the community of socialist countries and their system of international division of labour as an alternative also presupposes a preceding socio-economic transformation either already fulfilled or started.

---

[14] As, e.g., the abolition of profit and income repatriation, the elimination of unfavourable world market and "demonstration" effects, the more energetic concentration of internal resources, etc.

[15] As it became an economic necessity in the Soviet Union for a time, under the pressure of the hostile environment.

As long as the current tasks are confined to the questions of establishing and expanding trade relations, hunting up new sources of finance and technology, and particularly selling the unsaleable surpluses of export crops, a developing country may achieve, perhaps, more favourable conditions of cooperation, and may use these relations (and she is wise if doing so) to strengthen her position on the capitalist world market and improve her bargaining position with foreign capital, but the socialist countries can hardly disregard in these relations the laws of movement and effects of the capitalist world economy nor are they themselves fully exempted from the latter. Without (or before) the socio-economic transformation of a developing country, these relations mean essentially— even if partly by transmission—relations between *de facto* capitalist and socialist actors on the world market. The more favourable prices, credit conditions and grants may only mean assuming part of the burdens and losses the capitalist world economy imposed on the developing country. That is why, apart from the problem of structures and resources of the socialist countries and the potential conflict between the international and national aspects of policy, such an alternative *per se* does not change the substance of the matter.[16]

Let us examine now if there exists a strategy for the liquidation of underdevelopment which, in spite of obviously external, international factors of the emergence of underdevelopment, can be implemented even *within the national economies.* If there exists such a strategy, let us examine what aims, means and processes it necessarily includes, and in what *direction* it is likely to develop.

When examining the outlines of this strategy, let us disregard the tactical questions of economic policy varying from country to country. And let us also disregard those general problems which appear, in the course of the practical implementation of economic policy subordinated to strategy, as the complex of social reactions within or across the class boundaries, and which show certain regularities apt to make generalizations from. However, the latter abstraction is less justified as such reactions also limit the possibilities of rational economic action at the level of the national economy especially in societies with transitory or less-defined class boundaries. In addition, disregarding these reactions when taking political decisions, may bring about such shifts or even a vacuum in the political power relations as may endanger the implementation of the strategy.[17] If we nevertheless

---

[16] When we point to these problems, we do not intend by any means to underestimate the socialist countries' commitments deriving from *international solidarity* and their common interests in the progress achieved by the developing countries.

[17] The "national-economic optimum" in a transitory economy with its mixed sectors, comprising heterogeneous social elements, does not coincide with the "social optimum" by a long way. Economic decisions give rise to new clashes of interests and social conflicts which, if driven to the extreme, may doom the otherwise economically "optimum" decisions to

dispense here with the discussion of the dialectics of political decisions and social reactions, we do it partly because we are able to refer to a monograph written with exceptional insight and experience in the subject,[18] and partly because the questions touched upon in this chapter are concerned with the *main* processes and criteria promoting the liquidation of underdevelopment, and not so much with the more or less regular difficulties of these processes, nor with the ways and means of avoiding or easing them. Besides these abstractions, let us suppose a developing country which, *when* implementing the strategy under examination, does not break away from the capitalist world economy and is not isolated internationally.

The liquidation of underdevelopment within a single national economy is a very complex task. It follows from the dialectical relationships between its individual factors that it can only be eliminated in a *complex* way because with one single factor remaining unchanged, the progress achieved in the liquidation of the other factors may be jeopardized. It is impossible to achieve lasting results in the transformation of the economic structure and the development of productive forces if economic dependence and exploitation survive. And conversely: economic dependence cannot be eliminated without the transformation of the distorted economic structure. And the transformation of the ancient social remnants is also the precondition for all progress.

(1) *The breaking of the monopolistic position of foreign capital*, its ousting from the key positions of the economy and the restriction of its exploiting activities, is in itself a very difficult task. It is especially difficult if one or a few monopoly groups control the whole of the economy. It will suffice to recall how the nationalization by the Mossadik government in Iran in 1952 was answered by the international oil cartel, and remember in what way Britain reacted to the nationalization by Egypt of the Suez Canal, etc.

It is quite obvious that a weak national capital, if it exists at all, is unable to stand up to the big foreign monopolies. It must make concentrated efforts, by resorting to state power, if it wants to get rid of their dominance and "leading strings". The use of state intervention to break the power of foreign capital may very well coincide with the interests of the national bourgeoisie as the state is expected to provide protection for the domestic

---

failure. Therefore, the reaction of the agents of economic life to the decisions of economic policy and the possible means of influencing this reaction require a thorough study. It is by no means a matter of indifference, e.g., for the future and efficiency of the otherwise progressive political trend and economic strategy what the position and reaction of the dynamic political institutions, the executive power, the army, the regional power factors, the groups, organizations and personalities embodying the power of the modern economic sectors are like and how they change, what shifts take place within and between the factors of political power as a result of economic policy decisions and the implementation process.

[18] J. Bognár: *Economic Policy and Planning in Developing Countries*. Akadémiai Kiadó, Budapest, 1968.

industry, to ensure more favourable export prices and cheaper import possibilities, financial stability and the creation of an independent credit system, and to guarantee the right for this bourgeoisie to control the national market and national manpower. All this requires, in one or another respect, a struggle against the monopolistic position of foreign capital. On the other hand, owing to capital shortage or because of its international trade relations, transportation facilities, business routine or complementary investments, foreign capital is often needed by local capital and bourgeoisie, in addition to the fact that these countries *in general* are in need of foreign loans and aid which are often very difficult to obtain without strings to ensure the free operation of foreign private capital. In addition, under the changed conditions (already discussed), the local bourgeoisie, particularly its state representatives, members of the bureaucratic élite, may find attractive opportunities to cooperate with foreign companies and seek for an alliance with them against the working masses. Yet, in the question of leadership and so in the question of economic independence, too, a strong contradiction may develop between foreign and local capital.

If the interests of the national bourgeoisie require the breaking of the hegemony of foreign capital, it is far more true for the working people of the society, above all for the working class and the peasantry exploited and oppressed in various ways.[19] But even those "feudal" strata relying for their power and incomes on foreign monopoly capital, e.g. some of the "oil princes" of the Middle East, may happen to turn against foreign monopoly capital and try to restrict its operation, partly to wrest from it a greater share of profit, and partly acting under the pressure of the masses and public sentiment.

But neither the national bourgeoisie nor the other classes of society have at their disposal *any other*, more effective means in their fight against foreign capital and for the creation of an independent national economy than *state intervention* in the economy.

For the breaking of the power of foreign monopoly capital a whole *array of state-intervention methods* has developed in the former colonial and semi-colonial countries. No doubt, the most suitable and most radical means is full appropriation by nationalization, but only where and when the socio-political and the economic and technical conditions have matured. In a number of smaller countries, however, where foreign monopoly capital keeps its hand on a rather narrow national economy and controls not only production but also marketing, transportation and the supply of qualified

---

[19] When emphasizing the *basically* conflicting interests in respect of *economic independence* we must not, however, disregard the existence of common short-term interests between foreign capital and certain *groups or elements* of nearly all classes of society (e.g. local intellectuals and businessmen involved in the management of foreign corporations, or merchants and even peasant producers cooperating with foreign capital, or privileged élite workers, etc.).

380

labour, these conditions usually are not yet ripe. Although in a crucial situation a lot of difficulties can be bridged over by getting help from outside (from socialist countries or from other developing countries, and from the international organizations) or by establishing closer cooperation with the neighbour countries), these conditions must not be left out of account. Not to mention that nationalization *per se*, even a hundred-per-cent state ownership in itself, cannot guarantee the elimination of foreign control over the national economy. Foreign capital, particularly multinational corporations, can have, even if losing or giving up local ownership, several other means and channels at their disposal to exert influence, including corruption and paid agents inside the public sector. Nationalization and state ownership promise a solution only if accompanied by the operation of the nationalized sector for the interest of the people.

There are many other means of state intervention which may also be of great importance in the struggle against foreign capital. Such are: partial nationalization (usually with compensation), taxes, customs duties, legal regulation of the re-investment ratio of profits, restriction of profit repatriation, state supervision of foreign companies, mixed enterprises and joint ventures, legal regulation of state plans or plan targets, etc.

The actual content and efficiency of these means depend on whether they are aimed at, and working gradually towards, a complete liquidation of the dominance and control of foreign monopoly capital. Otherwise, some of these forms (e.g. mixed companies) may also serve to promote the influence of foreign capital.

Such means of state intervention aimed at restricting the monopoly position, or influencing the activity of foreign capital, can be found in a number of developing countries, and sometimes even states which cannot be said to be progressive strive to defend, by various means and to some extent, the interests of the national economy as opposed to foreign capital. (On the other hand, even the most progressive countries, including those which have chosen the socialist alternative of development, often apply the policy of inviting foreign capital, whilst limiting the field and conditions of its activity.)

(2) *The transformation of the distorted structure of the economy and society* is an even more complicated and long-term task. While the liquidation of economic dependence and exploitation, i.e. the gaining of economic sovereignty and the completion thereby of the liberation from colonial rule is an almost self-evident task for every movement consistently representing the *national* interests, this latter task must be equally evident for those concerned with the problems of the acceleration of economic growth and the development of productive forces. The changes in the world economy and the trend of world-market prices in the Last few decades have conclusively proved the disadvantages of the one-crop economies. And the slow development of the internal division of labour and the market, the

obstacles to attaining higher productivity and introducing better and more up-to-date methods of production, cultivation and technology, have all unambiguously demonstrated the limiting and hindering role of the "dual" economy and within it the traditional sector in particular.

As far as social transformation is concerned, the local bourgeoisie and even foreign capital may be interested in it but *as long as* its aim is to oust he *non*-capitalist elements, i.e. the precapitalistic remnants and to introduce democratic reforms in the sense of bourgeois transformation. Though the representatives of the bourgeoisie have different views about the method, implementation and above all the orientation of this transformation, as well as about the role of the masses involved in it, and although they are even inclined to give up any bourgeois-democratic reform when being afraid of the danger of a socialist way, yet they cannot deny the necessity of transformation, and the democratic forces of the liberation movement usually press for this transformation as without it they cannot enjoy the fruits of independence.

Resistance to the implementation of these tasks is usually experienced either *where* the expected transformation involves the danger of the collapse of the whole political system, a risk not tolerated by the interests of imperialist forces or the ruling classes, or *where* the opposition to imperialism has developed a specific traditionalism, an insistence on the forms and customs of ancient society.

Both sorts of resistance, however, are opposed to the very interests of those putting it up to such an extent that it can be neither lasting nor consistent. This is so, because in the first case it hinders capitalist development, which would give them far greater security from the point of view of the world-capitalist system and better chances also for the "feudal" leaders to get rich; in the second case, because the anti-imperialist movement becomes formal and senseless unless it finds its continuation in the upswing of the national economy and the raising of the living standard of the masses, which, however, is not feasible in the framework of ancient forms.

Hence, both the transformation of the economic structure and the removal of the obsolete forms of society appear more or less intensely as *general* requirements in the developing countries.

Let us now examine what concrete tasks are involved in these requirements, and how they can be fulfilled!

(a) The transformation of the economic and social structures requires first of all the elimination of "dualism", *the merging* of the different socio-economic sectors and *the integration* of the more or less separately developing branches into an organic and dynamic mechanism. It follows from the criterion of development that this integration cannot be anything else but the integration of the traditional sector into the modern one, however, with the simultaneous transformation of the modern sector itself.

382

The fact that the spontaneous mechanism of a disintegrated, "dual" economy works against such a transformation, that neither the spontaneous play of economic forces, nor, particularly, the purposeful policy of international monopoly capital can bring about the rapid development of organic, integrated national economies, is something we have tried to demonstrate from various angles in the preceding chapter. Consequently, it is only the *state intervention*, the purposeful state development policy taking action against spontaneous mechanism (and foreign monopoly capital), that can ensure appropriate progress in this respect. In other words, the allocation of investments, the determination of their direction, nature and extent cannot be left to the spontaneous activity of private economies but require a *centrally coordinated development programme*. But this development policy and its realization in development programmes and long-range plans cannot be confined merely to the allocation of investments among sectors and regions, on the basis of an assessment of the individual profitability of the various projects. It must also include the tasks and viewpoints following from the requirement of socio-economic integration. Moreover, the selection of the projects themselves and the assessment of their profitability and efficiency must also take into account this requirement.

But before an answer can be given at all to these questions of development policy, the questions of choosing the right projects which will best promote integration, two fundamental problems must be faced: *(a) of what type should the modern sector be* towards which the traditional sector should orientate, according to which it should be transformed; and *(b) in what form should the trnasformation of the traditional sector take place?* The *first* question refers not only to the social character of the modern sector, i.e. to the question of ownership relations and the mode of the appropriation of surplus, but also to the structural pattern of the modern sector, the problems of the individual sectors included and the techniques applied by the modern sector as well as the utilization of surplus. The *second (b)* question is related to the individual or collective forms of the transformation and further development of the traditional sector. (On the following pages we shall return to some extent to these questions.)

As to the structural pattern of the modern sector and the problems of the choice of techniques and the surplus utilization, let us discuss these questions in connection with a comprehensive paper[20] written on this topic and seize the good opportunities offered by it to concentrate on the crucial points. The authors of the study in question outline *three* main patterns of the utilization of surplus and thereby the character of the modern and the orientation of the traditional sector.

[20] G. Arrighi and J. Saul: Socialism and Economic Development in Tropical Africa. In: *Essays on the Political Economy of Africa.*

The first model (Pattern A) is characterized by a relatively high share in the surplus actually produced (SAP), of the surplus transferred abroad (ST), and the surplus absorbed by the discretionary or conspicuous consumption of the bourgeoisie and working class of the modern sector (SC), and the productive investments in the sector producing consumer goods suited to the requirements of the modern sector (SPCM) as well as by the relatively high share, in total productive investments, of investments for "capital-deepening" (SPD), that is the share of investments in sectors operating with capital-intensive techniques, with high "organic composition".

The second model (Pattern B) is characterized by the high share of the surplus actually produced (SAP), of the discretionary and conspicuous consumption (SC) of the modern sector, and those productive investments made in the sectors producing capital goods and consumer goods suited to the modern sector (SPM = SPKM + SPCM, where SPKM means productive investments in the sector producing capital goods suited to the requirements of the modern sector and SPCM means investments in the sector producing consumer goods suited to the requirements of the modern sector), as well as by the low proportion of "capital-deepening" investments to productive investments (SPD).

The third model (Pattern C) is characterized partly by the high share in the surplus actually produced (SAP) of productive investments made both in the sectors producing capital goods and those producing consumer goods, suited in each case to the requirements of both the modern and the traditional sector (SPM + SPT, where SPT means investments in the sectors producing capital goods—SPKT—and consumer goods—SPCT—suited to the requirements of the traditional sector) and partly by the relatively low proportion of "capital-deepening" investments in relation to productive investments.

According to the authors, Pattern A—characterized by a relatively high $\frac{ST + SC + SPCM}{SAP}$ ratio and a relatively high $\frac{SPD}{SAP}$ ratio—may ensure a more rapid growth than the other two patterns during the so-called "phase of easy import substitution", when the inflow of foreign capital may offset the outflow of investment income (ST). In the long run, however, it increases the dependence on the external supply of capital for further expansion, and also restrains the growth of the internal market by hampering the "widening" of the modern economy. This "perverse growth" is therefore severely limited by its contradictory nature since it is only the fast expansion of the internal market that can favour the growing inflow of new foreign capital made necessary by the greater dependence on outside finance.

In the case of Pattern B—characterized by a relatively high $\frac{SC + SPM}{SAP}$ ratio and a relatively low $\frac{SPD}{SAP}$ ratio—the development of capital goods production suited to the requirements of the modern sector (high $\frac{SPKM}{SAP}$ ratio) is advantageous due to the endogenous increase in internal demand and the decrease in the dependence on outside finance for the supply of capital goods. The low $\frac{SPD}{SAP}$ ratio, that is the low share of capital-intensive investments is also favourable in that it leads to a steady increase in the demand for the labour and the produce of the traditional economies. Owing, however, to the slow, inadequate growth of the sectors producing capital goods and consumer goods suited to the requirements of the traditional sector (low $\frac{SPT}{SAP}$ ratio), the expansion of the supply of these goods will tend to fall short of the growth of the monetary incomes of the traditional sector. As a consequence, the growth of the supply of labour and produce to the modern sector will, sooner or later, slow down, hampering the further widening of the modern sector itself.

The third model, Pattern C, characterized by a relatively high $\frac{SPM+SPT}{SAP}$ ratio and a relatively low $\frac{SPD}{SAP}$ ratio is, according to the authors, the most favourable one—at least for the African economies. The sacrificing of the "discretionary consumption" of the modern sector and the high proportion of productive investments will enable the modern sector to absorb an increasing proportion of the labour force. The Priority of the labour-intensive techniques, i.e. the relatively low $\frac{SPD}{SAP}$ ratio, will ensure the steady growth of demand for the labour and the produce of the traditional sector while the expansion of the production of capital and consumer goods suited to the requirements of the traditional sector (a high $\frac{SPT}{SAP}$ ratio) will ensure the adequate supply of this sector which is the precondition of its transformation.

The models outlined above point out the importance of some *basic relationships* which, by the way, find a plastic demonstration in *Marx*'s reproduction schemes. Such are, first of all, that the expansion of reproduction, it other words growth, depends on the amount of reinvested surplus and, further, that the rate of economic growth and the expansion of the domestic market are—*ceteris paribus*—the function of the rate of surplus reinvested for the expansion of the sector (I) producing capital goods, and finally, that the equilibrium between the mutual demand and supply of the individual sectors, i.e. the right proportions among the various branches must be ensured *both in physical and monetary terms*. These basic relationships themselves reveal the general deficiency of Pattern A, at least as far as the unproductive squandering of surplus is concerned. The high $\frac{SPD}{SAP}$ ratio means, however, a relative disadvantage only under the *specific* circumstances of unemployment and the need to import capital goods. It is also quite obvious that Pattern B is inadequate, too, owing to the lack of equilibrium between the production and consumption, and mutual supply and demand of the sectors. On the other hand, Pattern C seems to be favourable, indeed, at least in regard to the high ratio of productive investments and the more favourable equilibrium relations between the two sectors in general, and to the labour-intensive techniques enabling, under certain conditions, the faster absorption of unemployment, in particular.

It appears, however, that by including in a general model of growth some special requirements, valid for a given time and in the given circumstances, the authors overestimate the advantages of Pattern C, even if they only recommend it for certain African countries. On the one hand, they put the emphasis only on the reduction of overconsumption of the modern sector, whereas conspicuous consumption can also be found in the African traditional sector in spite of its low living standard. Therefore, the productive mobilization of the potential (perhaps only seasonal) surplus would be possible in this sector, too. On the other hand, (apart from the general ambiguity in the interpretation of the employment effect of labour-intensive *vs.* capital-intensive technology if the choice of technique is made at the enterprise level, i.e. on a micro-level), they fail to point out the growth limitations of Pattern C, following just from the "labour-intensive" techniques, the low $\dfrac{SPD}{SAP}$ ratio. Yet, as appears from both Marx's schemes and the preceding relationships, the acceleration of expanded reproduction presupposes the faster growth of the sector producing the means of production and thereby a general increase in the "organic composition of capital", that is an increasing rate of "capital-deepening" investments, too. The rise in technical level, and so in the productivity level of the national economy, too, depends, in the last analysis, on the development of the capital-goods producing sectors applying modern technology, that is using "capital-intensive" techniques. But beyond this general objection it is also worth considering, even in relation to the concrete African circumstances, that on the one hand, the *labour emission capacity* of the traditional sector has certain absolute limits, which, taking into account the actual figures of population density, is relatively easy to reach *if* the industrial growth is fast enough and particularly if it is accompanied by rural transformation and development. On the other hand, owing to the absolute and relative limitations of the internal market, a "sound" *export-orientation*, in other words, not the abnormal export-orientation of the primary producing enclaves but the export-orientation of industries exceeding, by their mass production, the needs of the national economy, may become necessary in a relatively short time. In the case of manufactured goods, and because of the keen competition on the world market, such an export-orientation will be possible only if high quality requirements and a high technical level are met.

386

Therefore, it seems to be more realistic and more appropriate to choose, instead of Pattern C, a *combined* development model which, along with the *wide* use of labour-intensive techniques, introduces right from the outset capital-intensive techniques into the sectors on whose development the technical level of the entire national economy depends and whose products have to compete on the international markets with the corresponding products of the advanced countries. (Since the actual employment effect depends on the input and output linkages with other branches of the economy much more than on "labour-intensity" within the gates of a firm or of an industrial branch, therefore modern, capital-intensive technology, if applied in a proper place and at a proper time, may be advantageous even from the point of view of employment.)

As far as the question of *selection*, both the selection of the sectors having priority and that of the techniques to be applied, is concerned in development policy, there are, *in principle and in general*, two main criteria:

– to ensure a sound structural transformation and fastest possible development of the national economy;

– to achieve, within the system of the international division of labour, a favourable role, favourable in the long run, too, and adequate to the natural and geographical endowments also in the dynamics of economic development.

The neglect of either of these criteria may lead the development policy astray. The neglect of the adjustment to the future pattern of the international division of labour may give, e.g., a one-sided import-substituting character and direction to development. In this case, by reinforcing the autarchic tendencies and by using the temporary means of protectionism as a permanent method, it may even counteract the requirement of the fastest possible development.[21] On the other hand, without the rapid development and structural transformation of the economy there is no hope of ensuring a more equal and favourable structural role in the changing system of the international division of labour.

These general criteria, however, need, primarily in the light of the acute need for mobilizing the potential resources and the urgent necessity for integration, certain qualifying additions and some corrections, too.

The fastest development of the national economy and the more favourable position in the international division of labour are likely to be ensured by the most dynamic industries applying modern technology and having the widest linkage effects, industries which, by means of their high and rapidly growing productivity, permit a vigorous increase in the national per capita income to come about and, by their effect on the internal division

---

[21] A critique of such policies can be found in the works of several Latin American economists, especially those by Raul Prebisch.

of labour, also expand the internal market. Such are primarily the industries producing means of production for the national economy and the modern, completely vertically complete industries based on local natural resources and incorporating local R and D centres.

It is common knowledge, however, that the development of such up-to-date, dynamic industries permitting the fastest expansion and structural transformation of the national economy may, owing to the application of a capital-intensive technology?, come into conflict with the chronic quantitative and acute qualitative problems of the labour market. During the investment period, i.e. for a considerable time, they not only fail to increase the export capacity but also require increased imports and add by the concomitant large-scale and lasting demand on assets, to the sharpening of sectoral—and also regional—differences. In addition, the development of these industries may also be accompanied by the tendency of a disproportionately rapid rise in wages (in connection with the structural change in the pattern of the employed labour force and also with other special factors such as, e.g., the increased influence of the trade unions or the possibility for the employers to shift the effect of pay rises, etc.), which hampers the expansion of the surplus-producing capacity or leads to the unproductive absorption of the surplus produced.

In other words, we are faced with the problem that, in order to *utilize* the existing *limited resources* in the most rational way and therefore to concentrate them, we must select the dynamic *leading industries*, on the one hand, and must also solve the problem of mobilizing the *un(der)utilized potential resources* (not to speak of the great social problem of unemployment), which presupposes the elimination of the sectoral—and usually regional—differences and heterogeneities, i.e. the internal integration of economy and society.

This problem, i.e. that of the increasing sectoral and regional differences as a result of the more rapid growth of the leading industries, seems to be less pronounced and lasting in a more advanced and more homogeneous economy and society because, apart from other factors, the linkage and spread effects of the leading industries and sectors are much stronger, owing to the more developed intersectoral and institutional "channels", mainly of communication and transport. In the developing countries, however, the intensification of the spread effects itself requires substantial expenditure and investments.

Under these circumstances, the most rational utilization of the available limited resources, as related to direct economic results, and the mobilization of other potential resources appear in the investment policy as two more or less opposed requirements.

The joint observation and reconciliation of these two requirements, i.e. the need to concentrate the limited resources on the most dynamic industries or projects, and the necessity to make the potential resources accessible by

388

building "channels" for the linkage and spread effects, is only possible in the case of a *"development pole"*—to use a term of François Perroux—which is able not only to develop itself rapidly but is at the same time the generator of economic activity. That is, in the case of a unit which can exert its influence on the environment, on other units by means of

– regional coherence (horizontally);

– vertical (sectoral, professional, technical, etc.) relationships, or more concretely: by means of

– investment complexity (complementary investments);

– cost reduction or profit increase, also affecting other units, and

– the labour force employed, etc.

But even in such cases it is often necessary to build "channels", "media" for the spread effects.

Thus the two main, general criteria of the selection must be complemented or corrected in a way which ensures that the following viewpoints are considered:

– internal integration and restructuring of the economy, with due regard to the indirect effects;

– international division of labour;

– "direct" profitability;

– the mobilization of potential resources, and within it especially (and because of its social implications, primarily):

– the adequate expansion of employment, and

– the impact on social, political and regional relations and on the institutional structure.

The relatively most favourable removal of the contradictions involved can only be ensured by a *combined* solution in which, along with the *concentration* of a considerable part of the available resources on the "leading" industries, i.e. on the "development poles" selected by their direct and indirect economic effects, the mobilization of *hidden*, potential resources as a "self-help" is directed mainly towards the *transformation* of the environment of the former, to the building of channels for the spread effect.

This *"canalization"*, the building of media for the "spread effect", requires the *state* to make the kind of economic investments, or grant the kind of subsidies and incur other expenses (e.g. the development of public transport and communication for the expansion of the market relations of the traditional sector, the support of the small, cottage and handicraft industries to expand employment and the internal market, the financing of communal development programmes, investments in the infrastructure within the traditional sector, etc.) which, temporarily or permanently, also draw on existing resources in order to open up new ones. On the other hand, it needs a purposeful *activity* in *organization*, information and propaganda which are not or are only partly accompanied by additional financial outlays but which may also make new resources accessible.

It is evident that all these tasks aimed at the integration of the socio-economic sectors and the restructuring of the national economy emphasize *the necessity for the state to regulate* and *influence the economy*.

(b) In getting rid of underdevelopment, *the development of agriculture* has a specific role to play. The agriculture of the developing countries has, as we have seen, two inherent diseases: the precapitalist remnants as concomitants of the subsistence economy and the one-crop economy.

The *precapitalist remnants* themselves vary from one country to another. They may appear either in the form of big semi-feudal estates (e.g. the South-American latifundia, the large estates in the countries of the Arab East, the "zamindar" land estates in India), or in the tribal subsistence economies based on the common property of land (in many countries of Tropical Africa) or subordinated to or as an appendix of the former, in the form of the village communities (village communities in India, in Latin America, etc.).

The existence of big land estates makes *land reform* a burning question in many of the developing countries. The "Prussian" type of agricultural development, that is the capitalistic transformation of the feudal estates, has not been successful as the example of the Latin-American countries shows. The capitalization of the economy has been very slow and incomplete; the productive forces of agriculture, which at the beginning of the last century were more developed here than those of agriculture in North America, have hardly developed and the economy has continued to remain of an *extensive* type. The primitive mode of production, the miserable living conditions of the agricultural working population, and the extravagant way of life of the landowners who have got rich by exploiting the labourers with methods still of a semi-feudal or slave character, create such tension as foredooms the "Prussian" type of development to failure from the very outset. And in those Asian countries where there is large-scale rural overpopulation (e.g. in India), this type of development is even more hopeless.

However, land reform *in itself* cannot bring about a final solution. Even if it is carried out in the most radical way, it can do nothing more than allot land to the rural population. The parcelling out of the large estates may constitute another obstacle to the development of commodity production. Most of the peasants who have been given land are unable to stand on their own feet without help, as they lack the necessary means of production and skills. In addition, where there is rural overpopulation on a large scale, only dwarf holdings can be allotted. Under such circumstances, agrarian reform, if carried out *without* further social reforms, will start a process of *differentiation* among the peasantry leading to even more disastrous consequences, namely to the indebtedness of most of the rural population, the forced sale of lands allotted, the formation of a wide stratum of agrarian

390

proletariat deprived for ever of its means of production, and the growth of open unemployment. Thus the "American" way of the capitalist transformation of agriculture is not appropriate to the developing countries either: it is a too long and painful road and does not lead out of underdevelopment.

Thus the agrarian reform raises the problem of choosing the most appropriate form of organization and production, the problem of the further development of the newly established peasant economies. It is not accidental that the programme of the agrarian reform in the developing countries is usually *connected* with that of the development of the *co-operative movement*, even in the countries where the representatives of the national bourgeoisie are in power. The distribution of plots to peasants can only be reconciled with the task of developing large-scale commodity producing economies in this form of organization. Not only that, it also provides a firm basis for the support of farmers by the state, without which the rapid development of productive forces is unimaginable.

At the same time, the cooperative form has also proved to be the most suitable form in those African countries where the precapitalistic remnants have survived, not in "feudal" land estates, but rather in communal land ownership. Though in some areas, attempts were and are being made, at the initiative or suggestion of the colonizers or foreign advisors to solve the problems of traditional agriculture and to introduce more up-to-date ways of production by commercializing the tribal lands and forming thereby small private peasant holdings or "kulak" farms, while in other areas there has started a *spontaneous* breaking up of the traditional economies, the concomitant process of differentiation, however, is accompanied by the same disastrous consequences which we have spoken about in the foregoing. In addition, owing to the deep-rooted tradition of communal ownership, the private ownership of land is for the most part an alien concept to the population. At the same time, the increase in agricultural productivity in many places makes it necessary to carry out the type of tasks (such as the removal of forests and bushes, the construction of irrigation canals and roads, etc.) which can be easily performed by joint efforts, that is by cooperative self-help (even without major investments in machinery and without wage labour). The cooperatives and the communal villages are also the best means for eliminating the large dispersion of families and producing units and for mobilizing the hidden potential resources by rationally organizing and dividing the united labour of the associated families.

We could lengthen the list of the concrete advantages of cooperative economy in relation to the developing countries even further, but the fact remains that the transformation of precapitalist remnants in agriculture, i.e. the fulfilment of a task following from the need to overcome economic, underdevelopment, itself, brings to the fore the cooperative movement. Though it may assume different forms and may even have very *different character* in different places, the cooperative movement in the developing countries is noted for its reliance on effective *state support*.

Contrary to the cooperatives of the advanced capitalist countries, it is usually extremely difficult for the cooperatives of the developing countries to start their activity without state support because of the small capital supply of their members. The establishment, organization and capital supply of the cooperatives has become largely a state function. But beyond financial aid and organization, state support also extends to help given in education, information about new methods of cultivation, the training of specialists, human and veterinary public health service, etc. State support usually ensures an increased possibility for the state to exercise its influence and control over the cooperatives.

Thus the wide organizational activity of the state is required not only by the land reform itself but by the agrarian development after the land reform, too. The transformation of the precapitalistic remnants in the quickest and most effective way also requires *intensive state intervention* in the economy—mainly through the cooperative movement.

It is even less possible to change the *one-crop structure*, to diversify the agricultural commodity production without state intervention. As we have already mentioned, this one-crop structure has evolved, like the lopsided growth of extractive industries, not only under the influence of a deliberate colonial economic policy but also as a result of spontaneous economic forces. These spontaneous forces, especially in the form of external demand induction, or rather through the acute import needs, are still at work in spite of the changes and disturbances on the world market, and for lack of other export products, induce the further expansion of this type of export production. In other words, although the world market shows for these one-crop exports as we have seen, an unfavourable tendency but, owing to the narrow and unorganized character of the internal market and as a result of the difficulty of earning foreign exchange in any other way, the spontaneous diversification, i.e. the introduction of other crops *without* state intervention, is practically impossible. Moreover, to prevent the necessary contraction of the one-crop economy and the urgent diversification of agricultural production from leading to a disastrous drop in export revenues and thereby to a further curb on machine imports equally needed for the development of agrarian productive forces and industrialization, it is necessary to take a number of centrally planned comprehensive measures which can counteract the effect of the spontaneous market mechanism and ensure the gradual transformation of the production structure. This, however, also presupposes a *whole system of state intervention* in agriculture.

(c) The principal way and guarantee for changing the distorted economic structure and developing rapidly the productive forces is, of course, *industrialization.* No country has ever reached a high level of productive forces without industrialization.

Industrialization has developed in different ways and forms. In the advanced countries of Western Europe it usually began with the development of the light industries, and experienced later a major boost from the unfolding machine manufacturing. It was revolutionized later on by electricity, and more recently by the chemical and plastic industries, atomic energy and electronics. All this has taken about 150–200 years.

Industrialization in the socialist countries has required a much shorter time, usually a few 5-year periods. They started with and gave priority to the development of the heavy industries, and primarily machine manufacturing. It was on this basis that the most advanced socialist countries began to apply the achievements of the modern scientific and technological revolution.

It is a debatable subject to decide which branches the present-day developing countries have to develop first in their industrialization programmes. The individual phases of industrialization will obviously vary from country to country as there are already great differences between them in the industrial level reached. It is, however, beyond any doubt that the road to industrialization taken by the most advanced capitalist countries is not suitable for them either, and not only for the reason that it is too long.

In the industrialization of the most advanced capitalist countries, a decisive part was played by the *external resources* connected with economic colonization (cheap raw materials, cheap labour, a monopolized market, etc.), the plundering of other countries, wars and reparations, etc.

For the developing countries similar external sources used by *capitalist* industrialization are no longer available as under the new international circumstances the conquest of new colonies, the subjugation and plundering of new countries, are hardly practicable methods. It might be suggested that besides the oil revenues in the case of a few oil-exporting countries the aid to be given by the advanced countries would, in an opposite direction, now be the external resources which could ensure the rapid industrialization of the developing countries. It is likely that there will be some "model countries" where foreign capital will bring about rapid industrialization on an up-to-date basis,[22] either in the form of private investments or state loans and grants. The intention of such a development can only be the protection of the world capitalist system, and the "model countries" would have to pay a

---

[22] Foreign capital may be interested in the development of a few modern branches of industry, even on the basis of the most up-to-date, capital-intensive techniques, especially in the case of light industry plants which produce for the internal market but import their machines, equipment, and perhaps even raw materials form the metropolitan enterprises of the same foreign capital. The same applies to the assembly and component plants. But foreign capital is hardly willing to support the building up of a completely vertical industry unless it is, either wholly or partly, owned or controlled by that capital.

heavy price for it, namely their independence. It is highly unlikely that the capitalist countries themselves would industrialize the *whole* developing world and pay them back all that they had gained from them. Foreign capitalist loans and grants may, of course, play an important role in the industrialization of other countries but only if they are subordinated to a correct internal industrialization policy.

There is no other way for the developing countries to carry out their industrialization programmes than to fully use their *internal* resources and concentrate their efforts. But the national private capital is too weak to perform this task, the task of making those enormous capital investments needed by industrialization. Its activity adjusts itself in any case to the spontaneous economic mechanism discussed above and does not concentrate on the branches ensuring rapid development for the national economy. (As for foreign capital, apart from the above consideration, it is also its own interests which prevent it from carrying out a genuine industrialization of the developing countries, i.e. the one which includes the basic, leading industries with R and D capacities and supplying technology to the national economy.)

Industrialization needs enormous sources of accumulation. The private, capitalist way of accumulation cannot ensure them. What is needed is concentrated social accumulation, *state accumulation*. In addition to foreign loans, for which, in the interests of independence, the cover, in the form of the expansion of production, must also be provided by the *state*, only state accumulation can bridge the gap caused by the lack of capital.

The limited availability of accumulation resources makes it necessary for them to be utilized to the utmost, and in an optimum way in the sense that they should ensure the fastest possible development of the entire national economy. This is possible again only under a *centrally planned economy*, which restricts the spontaneity of the economy and is based directly on the state productive sector but also makes use of the activity, under strict control and guidance of the state, of foreign capital, *if* it is necessary and reasonable, and also of national private capital, *if* it is possible at all.

Industrialization also presupposes the adequate development of the infrastructure, i.e. transport, telecommunications, education, public health, public utilities, social services, etc. Private capital is usually not willing to participate in such investments as they are not profitable and their time of realization is too long. On the other hand, the state can fulfil these tasks, without the danger of a budget bankruptcy, only if it obtains adequate revenues, preferably by way of its *own productive investments*, and if it also mobilizes for this purpose the resources outside the public sector that can be withdrawn from the other sectors without a drop in the growth of production. This presupposes again the concentration and planned distribution of resources, in other words, a large-scale economic intervention on the part of the state.

(d) An especially serious problem of economic development is that of *employment and labour supply.* As we have seen, owing to the distorted structure of the economy and the low level of productive forces, there is an increasing urban unemployment and an immense rural disguised unemployment in the developing countries. In addition, there is a chronic shortage of skilled workers and specialists, which is a major handicap in the raising of the technical level and industrialization itself, too.

Disguised rural unemployment is especially marked in the densely populated Asian countries, but exists even in those countries of Latin America and Africa where otherwise there are still large uncultivated land reserves with the possibility to increase agricultural production in an extensive way. The slightest growth of the urban industries exerts a tremendous suction effect on the rural underdeveloped labour, and leads, consequently, to an even larger urban unemployment.

It is obvious then that only measures covering the *entire* economy, agriculture and industry alike, can bring about an improvement in this situation.

In the densely populated countries, it is extremely difficult to realize in the near future such a continuous industrialization that is extensive and fast enough to absorb the army of unemployed labour being permanently and increasingly replenished from the rural areas. In the sparsely populated (e.g. African) countries, on the other hand, but to some extent even in the densely populated territories, the urban suction effect that accompanies industrialization may have disastrous consequences for agriculture unless radical and fast changes take place in it simultaneously. In many countries of Tropical Africa the regular, though mostly seasonal, and massive exodus of male labourers causes the further decline of the traditional agriculture, linking a specific overpopulation with labour shortage (the former being related to the actual level of land utilization, while the latter to the possible level of utilization).

All this renders labour supply very unstable, and even the slightest changes (a new industrial establishment, construction work, etc.) may bring about large-scale shifts and reverse movements, causing alternately labour shortage or labour surplus.

Because of its effect on the entire economy, spontaneity in labour supply is even less permissible here than elsewhere if the liquidation of underdevelopment is on the agenda. Not only troubles in the supply of the adequate quantity and quality of labour but also other difficulties related to labour supply can paralyse the growth of one or another economic sector. What grave socio-political consequences and tensions may arise from the unsolved manpower problems (employment, wages etc.), it is unnecessary to emphasize again. It will suffice to recall that in many countries the leadership of the national liberation movement, after having taken over power, often came into conflict with the trade unions. (Whether these conflicts were provoked from outside or not is another question.)

Central measures and planned intervention are needed here, too. Since compulsory regulations for the movement of the labour force cannot be applied, the state must have control over wages rates and labour conditions, etc. for the interest of the society as a whole.

The state has also to assume responsibility for the task of providing trained cadres for the economy. This presupposes the long-term build-up and programme of vocational training as part of the general educational system which must adjust itself to the long-run objectives and demands of economic development. Today, secondary and higher education in most of the developing countries are inadequate not only in respect of their output but also as regards their internal structures. Most of students are engaged in studies of secondary importance and not in those which are the most important from the point of view of economic development.

Even in those countries where the concept of central manpower planning is generally accepted, a real (long-term) plan for the expansion and pattern of public education adjusted to economic strategy is usually still lacking.

How big the gap is between the advanced and underdeveloped countries in respect of education and vocational training, and, consequently, what immense tasks the latter have to perform can best be illustrated by the calculations made by the American economists Harbison and Myers.[23]

(e) All this makes it understandable why the practice of *state planning* is rapidly spreading in the developing countries. There is hardly any country where medium- and long-term plans of economic development are not being prepared. It is true that there are great differences between the individual countries with regard to the character, scope and content of these plans, and planning in a number of developing countries does not go beyond the economic "prognoses" like those in the advanced capitalist countries, and contains mainly the estimates of the state budget for a few years.

It can, however, be observed as a general *tendency* that the role and importance of the central plans are rapidly increasing. Their scope is also widening and the system of the means for their implementation is also improving. Though without the socialist ownership of the means of production, this sort of planning, even in its most advanced form, does not mean socialist *planned economy*, and furthermore without going down, below the surface of financial-commercial aspects, to the basic processes overall proportions and sectoral linkages of production, it does not mean planned production, nevertheless, it goes far beyond the planning principles and practice of the capitalist countries in its tendency, and may be regarded as a stepping stone of the former.

[23] See F. Harbison and Ch. A. Myers: *Education, Manpower and Economic Growth.* New York, 1964.

396

Thus the liquidation of underdevelopment in the framework of the national economy raises, as we have seen, the sort of requirements that call for the increased role of the state in the economy. Neither the liquidation of economic dependence and exploitation nor the elimination of the precapitalistic economic and social remnants is feasible without the effective participation and the intensive economic intervention of the state. State intervention is made especially necessary by the play of the spontaneous economic forces which, when left alone, reproduce the distortions of the economic structure and divert private investments in a wrong direction. The transformation of the subsistence economy and the diversification of the one-crop economy, which usually also give rise to the forms of economic organization typical of the agriculture of the socialist countries, require comprehensive measures to be taken by the state. Industrialization requires the same, otherwise it cannot be realized within a historically short period of time and from internal resources. The unfavourable and unstable manpower situation and the immense tasks of training cadres and organizing appropriate national research centres also necessitate that the guiding and stimulating activity of the state be extended over the *whole* economy. Hence, one of the *preconditions* for liquidating economic underdevelopment, for eliminating the obstacles to development, is *increased state intervention in the economy.*

3. PECULIARITIES AND PROSPECTS OF STATE CAPITALISM IN DEVELOPING COUNTRIES

From the motion and interaction of the various factors of underdevelopment there follows the reproduction of this complex phenomenon, while the necessity to liquidate underdevelopment gives rise, as we have seen, to the tendency of expanding state intervention.

The economic intervention of the state assumes the form of *state capitalism.*

State capitalism, under whatever conditions it may come to life, is nothing else but the restriction and regulation of economic spontaneity stemming from the existence of private capital. It embodies the peculiar relationship of state and private capital which, depending on the socio-economic system of the country in question, may be of a varying nature.

The state capitalist sector can also be met with in certain phases of the development of various *socialist* countries, e.g. in Soviet Russia, where in the early period of socialist construction, they also made use of foreign capital (by giving concessions to it) under the direct guidance and control of the socialist state. This state capitalism, however, as the similar ones in other socialist countries, was merely a secondary, complementary element in the whole of the socialist economic system. It embodied the peculiar relationship of private capital and the socialist state, with the latter being the absolute determinant of this relationship, i.e. the one which is part of the superstructure built on an economic basis diametrically *opposed* to the nature of private capital. The methods and means of guiding and controlling the activity of private capital used by this state capitalism were different from the methods and means used by the state in guiding and controlling the economy *in general.*

Almost a whole system of state capitalism has developed in the most advanced capitalist countries as *state monopoly capitalism.* Here the relationship of state and private capital is characterized by the fact that private capital, or its most powerful groups, the monopolies, control or strongly influence the state. State intervention takes place mostly in their interests and for the protection of the whole capitalist system of the economy, in order to curb the spontaneous tendencies and effects. This intervention is made necessary by the fact that, owing to the spontaneous mechanism arising from the private capitalist basis of the economy the highly developed productive forces brought about periodically grave crises which threatened the existence of the whole capitalist order, or by the fact that their further growth has been partly paralysed by the spontaneous mechanism. Though state intervention may extend to the whole economy, it usually adopts secondary, indirect methods only. These methods are *general* in the whole economy and at most only the methods of running the public sector are special and even they are not always so. The direct state-control applied in the public sector cannot extend over the whole economy, it cannot become general and decisive. Since state intervention is subject to private capital, the existence of which gives rise to *spontaneity,* consequently, the sphere and effectivity of this state intervention is rather limited.

State intervention in the developing countries is, as we have seen, a necessary requisite and tool in the process of overcoming "underdevelopment", i.e., of restructuring the economy and of achieving economic sovereignty and eliminating thereby the main obstacles to an endogenous, self-determined, integrated national development.

State intervention and a kind of state capitalism may, of course, develop contrary to the above requirements, too, and, as it has happened, indeed, in several countries, may also function as a neo-colonial set-up, as a factor of protecting and serving the reproduction of the dependent, peripheral capitalism in the interest of metropolitan monopoly capital, of MNCs and their local allies. Such a system often resorts to fascist methods to oppress popular forces, particularly the labour movement, to ban political organizations, wage demands and strikes, etc., and to offer thereby "security" for foreign companies to exploit cheap local labour. Except a narrow leading stratum, the privileged group of the dictatorship, the local society is almost totally excluded from the benefits of economic growth,

398

which, however spectacular in some cases, tends to be limited to a few enclaves, thereby perpetuating structural disintegration.

The concomitant economic imbalances, heavy and cumulative indebtedness, intensive exploitation by foreign companies and the special allowances, privileges and protection given to them, the high rate of inflation and serious balance-of-payments problems, etc., along with a widening internal income gap, increasing social and political tensions, tend to lead to a grave crisis and either to the collapse of the regime, or to the military intervention of some imperialist power to prevent a radical change.

Thus, such a system carries in itself the seeds of its own decay, cannot survive without external assistance and by no means corresponds to the historical task of overcoming underdevelopment.

In the following we shall discuss, instead, the type of state capitalism which stems from the objective tendency and requirements of the struggle to eliminate underdevelopment.[24]

State capitalism in the underdeveloped countries differs from state monopoly capitalism in the advanced countries primarily because of its different function: instead of regulating—within certain limits—the spontaneous mechanism of the already highly developed productive forces, it must rather aim at *creating the conditions for the rapid growth of the hardly developed productive forces.*[25] In other words, it comes into being at a low developmental level of the productive forces. It is also the expression of the relationship of state and private capital, but in most cases this relationship is *not yet determined* in itself. Contrary to state capitalism in both the advanced capitalist and socialist countries, this state capitalism may have a *different and changing class content*, depending on the character and change in character of the state.

State capitalism here usually means intervention extending over the whole of the economy, but since the latter is composed of very

[24] We shall also disregard the colonial type of state intervention exercised by the colonial administration or the puppet governments of the colonial empires, which is therefore a sort of "subsidiary" of state monopoly capitalism in the metropolitan country, of course in a very different environment. We disregard it as it appeared this "pure" form only exceptionally, usually in war times or states of emergency. Otherwise private capital, beyond ensuring the general conditions for capitalist economy, which meant the interference of the colonial or puppet governments with *non*-capitalist elements, that is *not* state capitalism, did not need state intervention in the spontaneous movement of the economy coinciding with its own interests.

[25] "The functions of State capitalism in underdeveloped countries are also of a special type. In a developed economy, State intervention is directed towards market regulation, i.e. anticyclical—as in America—or towards stepping up production—in Western Europe— while in underdeveloped countries intervention is primarily meant to expand capital accumulation. In developed countries State monopoly capitalism develops in conditions characterized by an excess of private capital, in underdeveloped countries State capitalism substitutes for the non-existing capitalists, performing actually the function of 'collective capitalism'." (I. Sachs: *Patterns of Public Sector in Underdeveloped Economies*, pp. 68–69.)

heterogeneous elements, it applies different methods and means. It extends, besides the capitalist elements, to the precapitalistic elements as well, but it is also heterogeneous in relation to foreign and national capital. This system of state intervention is a state capitalism in the sense that the decisive, determining elements in it are also the relationship of state and private capital—which may equally include both the policy of supporting and the policy of restricting this capital—and *state* control over the spontaneity arising from the existence of *capital*.

Judged by the tendencies giving rise to its existence, the character of this state capitalism in itself is determined only to the extent that, in fulfilling its *function*, it must also include among its measures steps to be taken both against foreign capital and "feudal" interests. This gives a *progressive* feature to state capitalism just as the task of developing the productive forces is progressive, too.[26] Since, however, underdevelopment is a complex phenomenon, and its liquidation raises manifold and often contradictory requirements, the anti-imperialist or anti-feudal character of state capitalism is not equally pronounced in the individual countries and periods. It may even be suppressed for a relatively long time.

Thus, apart from its negative relation to foreign capital and the precapitalistic elements, this state capitalism in itself has *no definite character*.[27] While state capitalism in the socialist countries means a control over the restricted activity of capital in general, i.e. a defence against capitalist tendencies, and in the capitalist countries it aims at defending the capitalist system of production against crises and socialist transformation, state capitalism in the developing countries means only attack, or defence, against the *pre*-capitalist forms and *foreign* capitalism. This explains why wide strata of society, the national bourgeoisie and the working classes alike, may be interested in its development.

The national bourgeoisie is also interested in the creation of an independent national economy and the abolition of the precapitalist relations. It also needs direct support and protection by the government. It is for this reason that it often takes the lead in developing state capitalism.

However, the relationship between state and national capital within state capitalism in the developing countries is *contradictory*. State capitalism in

[26] Oscar Lange writes: "The creation through public investment of a State capitalist sector means a certain degree of industrialization and general economic development which otherwise would not be forthcoming. It also implies a diminution of the dependence of the native capitalists on foreign monopoly capital and thus a corresponding measure of liberation of the country, to a certain extent, from the domination of imperialism. For this reason the development of State capitalism in an underdeveloped country is on the whole a progressive phenomenon." (Quoted by I. Sachs: Op. cit.)

[27] "The very term 'State capitalism' suggests that the impact of each State capitalistic venture depends on the nature of the State and on the concrete policy pursued by it." (Op. cit., p. 58.)

400

these countries, unlike that in the advanced capitalist countries came into being when capitalism had not yet been completed and firmly established in the whole economy and society.[28] Therefore, laws different from those of capitalism also assert themselves and have an influence on the system of state intervention.

The motion and growth of state capitalism take place on the basis of several contradictory tendencies, and therefore several transitory and mixed formations may come into being. Not only the national and the comprador strata of the local bourgeoisie, but also the various elements within the *national* bourgeoisie may have different attitudes towards state capitalism, and the relationship may be even more differentiated regarding the other classes and strata of society.

Since state capitalism here has basically *national* tasks to perform aimed at creating an independent national economy, and is, sooner or later, necessarily directed against foreign capital (except, of course, the case mentioned before, when a neo-colonial alliance between the state bureaucratic élite and foreign companies lies behind state capitalism), it may be well supported by all the social factors belonging to the national independence movement as long as *these* tasks have to be fulfilled. The comprador strata of the local bourgeoisie are, of course, opposed to it (except again the above case, which may involve the participation and interest in state capitalism, of the neo-comprador stratum of the local industrial bourgeoisie, too).

In this respect, state capitalism may include *different relationships* between state and capital at the same time. There may be, *on the one hand*, a clash of interests, i.e. an antagonistic relationship between state and the *foreign* and local *comprador* capital, which relationship is quite similar to that of the state capitalism in the socialist countries, with the vital difference that the state is *not* a socialist, proletarian one, moreover it is perhaps under the guidance, control or influence of the national bourgeoisie. *On the other hand*, there may be a sort of identity of interests, a harmonious relationship between state and the *national* capital, which is similar to that of the state monopoly capitalism in the advanced capitalist countries, with the essential difference that the state itself is much less in control of this capital.

With the anti-feudal tasks coming to the foreground, the picture changes to the extent that the attitude to state capitalism of the "feudal" (semi-feudal) strata, some of which might have happened to be active participants or supporters of the national liberation movements in one or another country, turns into hostility, while the support of the system of state

---

[28] "Historically, the basic difference arises from the fact that in the underdeveloped countries, State capitalism enters the stage when the capitalist structure is still weak and the domestic monopoly pressure groups have not acquired as yet a durable control over the newly born State apparatus: while in developed countries State capitalism emerges as the offspring of monopoly capitalism." (Op. cit., p. 68.)

26

intervention by the popular forces increases and widens. On the other hand, private capital and state capitalism may come to terms in this respect.

It may come to terms, but not always and not necessarily. Though, in principle, all kinds of capital, local or foreign, may be interested in the liquidation of the precapitalistic remnants as the precondition for capitalist development, but foreign capital in many countries has entered into alliance with the leading "feudal" strata to ensure its rule and monopoly position, while in other countries the various strata of the national bourgeoisie have merged with the "feudal" landowning aristocracy, tribal chiefs, etc., or have themselves emerged from their ranks.

Thus another area may appear in one country or another on which state capitalism, destined to liquidate underdevelopment, may come into conflict with the interests of part of the private capital, this time not, or not primarily, with foreign and comprador capital but also with national capital. In addition, this conflict of interests may also take place under circumstances when the state performing anti-feudal tasks is just under the decisive influence of the national bourgeoisie (its more progressive part), which illustrates again very conspicuously the contradictory relationship between state capitalism and private capital.

An important task of state capitalism is the development of productive forces and, in connection with it, the transformation of the distorted economic structure and the creation of an organic and integrated national economy. Apart from foreign capital and, under certain circumstances, comprador private capital too, *national* capital is interested in the fulfillment of these tasks. The question is how these tasks are to be fulfilled, and how state intervention affects the activity of national capital, whether it promotes or hinders the operation and growth of the latter. But even if state intervention prejudices the interests of national capital in certain spheres, in one or another sector of the economy, this may happen even under a national-bourgeois leadership of the state and in conformity with the interests of the majority of the national bourgeoisie. Therefore, here too, various and different relationships may evolve in the course of the operation of state capitalism.

Before having a look at the various social and political factors determining the class content of state capitalism and the direction of the further development of the developing countries, let us raise this general question which is one of principle: What are *the alternative prospects of state capitalism* after, or rather in the course of, performing its original function: the liquidation of underdevelopment, the creation of an independent, integrated and advanced national economy?

There are, in principle, *various possibilities* for the further development or historical fate of state capitalism in the developing countries.

One possibility is that after liquidating the monopoly position of foreign capital, creating the conditions for an independent capitalist development, transforming the economic structure and ensuring a new role in the international division of labour, winding up the remnants of precapitalistic social formations, and developing productive forces, state capitalism gradually declines, loses its strength, and lets *national private capitalism* take over. The strengthened national capital does not need the system of state intervention any longer. The spontaneous play of economic forces itself ensures favourable conditions for its growth.

The probability, however, of this possibility being realized is negligible. Though state capitalism in the developing countries emerges from the internal tendencies outlined above, it must also be taken into consideration that state capitalism has become a *general phenomenon* in the whole capitalist world.

Not only in the course of winding up underdevelopment do the respective countries come into conflict with foreign capital supported by the state capitalism of the metropolitan countries, but also after the liquidation of underdevelopment in the system of the "normal" commercial, financial and other relations of the capitalist world market and world economy. Therefore, it will hardly be possible for the national capital of any country to hold its own, however developed productive forces it may have in the future, unless it enjoys the support of its own state capitalism. We must not forget that it was the rather high development level of the productive forces that made it necessary to evolve the system of state intervention in the advanced capitalist countries. A country may either reach this development level, and then the same need will inevitably emerge for it too, or it fails to reach it, or before reaching that level it winds up its state capitalism, and then its backwardness will be preserved and foreign capital will triumph over the country.

The *second possibility* is that after performing its original function: the development of productive forces and the creation of an independent, integrated economy, it gives way to *state monopoly capitalism* based on highly developed productive forces. Though there are some signs of such a tendency in a few countries, where local, national monopoly capitalist elements have come into existence and gained influential positions (e.g., in India, Brazil, etc.), however, the unfolding of an independent and fully developed national monopoly capitalism with its state intervention comes up against serious obstacles, which may divert its development from the path of economic independence, or prevent the monopoly capitalistic group from seizing or keeping power. Thus such a road of further development can hardly become a general or typical alternative.[29]

[29] An example of this type of development of state capitalism is provided by the "Japanese pattern" though the underdevelopment that Japanese state capitalism came into being to liquidate was different on many counts from the present systems labelled by the term "underdevelopment" (due to the relatively insignificant penetration of foreign capital, the less distorted structure of agricultural production, the much more favourable state of public

For this we must take into account the fact that the emergence and activity of the biggest monopolies of the most advanced capitalist countries presupposed, almost from the very beginning, the exploitation of other countries too, not only the working classes of their own country. And though the exploitation of foreign countries may assume, as we have seen, many forms, some of which are disguised, or indirect, the changed international political and world economic situation makes it highly unlikely for the newly born monopoly capital of other countries to also get a foothold in international exploitation, the territory of which has anyway contracted. On the other hand, if the growth and power of such a new monopoly capital relied on exclusively internal sources of exploitation, it would be at the cost of immense inner tensions and would have an extremely unstable social basis. As a consequence, national monopoly capital, particularly if collaborating with foreign companies, would compromise with the latter at the expense of independence and resort to a neo-colonial variant of state capitalism and to fascist methods.

But we must also take into consideration the fact that even the activity of state capitalism aimed at winding up underdevelopment brings about, as we have seen, contradictions in the relationship between state and private capital, and these very contradictions restrict, if not prevent, the unreserved cooperation of the national bourgeoisie with state capitalism.

From these contradictions it follows that in the period of the liquidation of underdevelopment, the national bourgeoisie is but one, though occasionally the main, supporting force behind state capitalism, and the other social forces, the working classes and the "intermediate" social strata, above all the stratum of intellectuals, military officers and civil servants also play an important role in giving rise and strength to it. Under such circumstances the national capital often shrinks back from developing state capitalism before it could have performed its task, and tends to come to terms with foreign monopoly capital on the basis of underdevelopment and dependence. This may provide some security for the system based upon private ownership and help prevent a radical social transformation, but it

---

nutrition, and foreign trade not being a "bottleneck", etc. in the Japanese economy). The chances for the Japanese model to be repeated historically are very limited, not only because in the Japanese "take-off" there were also such factors at work as the failure of crops of raw silk in France and Italy at the crucial time, providing an exceptionally good opportunity for the rapid development and expansion on the world market of the Japanese silk industry, but because the military adventurism and colonial conquest that was an organic part of Japanese development and constituted the motor of the rapid development of the leading branches, the munitions and export industries, are unlikely to be successful under the new international circumstances. In addition, the allocation of accumulation resources to industrialization at the expense of agriculture and the consumption of the working classes in general (through taxation and inflation) while maintaining and increasing income inequalities to such an extent as it happened in Japan, and which is necessary for the formation of a monopoly capitalist group, is now socially much less tolerable than it was at that time.

does not show a way out of underdevelopment nor does it bring about the unrestricted rule of national capital over the national economy, it does not create an independent state monopoly capitalism.

Thus both the external and internal factors set limits to the realization of this possibility.

There is a *third possibility* when state capitalism, while (or even before) performing the tasks of liquidating underdevelopment, leads on to the socialist *system of planned economy* that is, when it *follows a non-capitalist, socialist-oriented way of development*. This possibility follows from the consistent pursuit of getting rid of underdevelopment, that is, also from the internal tendency of state capitalism performing this task.

Sometimes even a *fourth possibility* also appears: the prospect of the emergence of *bureaucratic state capitalism*,[30] i.e. *étatism*. This would be characterized by the state ownership of the means of production, the "quasi-social" appropriation of economic surplus by the state, on the one hand, and the privileged position of a narrow state bureaucratic élite and an income distribution system in which the income share would be determined not by capital, that is property, nor by work, that is the socialist principle of distribution, but by the relative proximity to political power. Though the tendency for the development of this sort of structure can be observed, in a *temporary and elementary* form, in several developing countries, it does *not* seem appropriate to consider it among the long-term alternatives as a general prospect, in view of the obstacles to the élite becoming a separate class,[31] that is, in view of the transitional character of such a structure. Instead, it is justified to evaluate the development and strengthening of the privileged position of the élite as one of the potential sources of the formation of the *capitalist* class, that is, as part of the first, capitalist alternatives (including the neo-colonial variant with an alliance between the bureaucratic élite and multinational companies), or as the significant but temporary obstacle to socialist orientation and a final socialist transformation.

Which of the possibilities outlined above becomes reality, whether the liquidation of underdevelopment is achieved at all, and if it is, whether the further development of state capitalism is finally connected with the *socialist or capitalist* alternative—this depends first of all on the internal socio-political development and on the class power relations of the individual countries, within the framework set by the international political and world economic relations.

[30] According to Bettelheim, besides the strengthening of private capitalism, the main danger for the further progressive development of state capitalism in Africa is bureaucratic degeneration. (See Ch. Bettelheim: Planification économique en Afrique Noire. *Cahiers Internationaux*, I–II, Paris 1961, p. 70.)

[31] See Chapter III. 2.

What is, however, specific in the dialectics of the development of state capitalism in the developing countries is the fact that the further development of state capitalism and the way of socio-political development are rather *mutually* determined by each other since also the internal socio-political development, and class relations themselves depend on the direction, scope and content of the activity of state capitalism. State capitalism in the developing countries is not simply the means of strengthening and preserving an already established social system but it is also a determinant—to a great extent—for the type of social system to come. Consequently, the inner logic of its development is much less tied to the actual state of the social forces. Thus it may occur that a relatively slight shift in the political power relations—even within the same political group, e.g. owing to the emergence of unexpected economic difficulties or international political problems and consequently to the actual necessity of revising the economic or foreign policy—which otherwise would have hardly any direct effect on the class relations, brings about such quantitative changes in the mechanism of state capitalism as lead directly to a *qualitative* change determining more or less the direction of further social development.

One can come across this *metamorphosis* of state capitalism when economic intervention by the state, without being preceded or accompanied by a social revolution or a radical regrouping of social class forces, "outgrows" the limits of its original function (that is, the tasks of supplanting foreign capital and transforming the precapitalistic remnants) and also sets limits to the formation and growth of local, national private capital. Since this precludes the way of the natural[32] formation and coming to power of the bourgeoisie, it may become the *overture* to socialist development without, or more exactly before, a socialist revolutionary transformation.

Of course, not all over-expansion of state capitalism means socialist oriented development even if it happens to impede the development of local and foreign capital. A *bureaucratic* over-expansion of the system of state intervention which impedes not only the activity of private capital but also social-economic development in general and, consequently, does not serve the interests of the masses, is only a wild offshoot, but not a socialist path of development.

The metamorphosis of state capitalism as the criterion and basis of a socialist oriented development is usually realized in the *expansion of the state sector of the economy.* But nationalizations or the predominance of plants built in state ownership in the main economic sectors are *not*

[32] The process of the élite changing into a real bourgeoisie as a result of its acquiring a shareholder position (and board-of-director membership) in private capitalist companies allowed to operate, or in the reprivatized state capitalist sector, cannot be conceived of as a natural, normal way of class formation. Instead, it is a rather specific, exceptional kind of formation of a bourgeois class and power.

indispensable and exclusive, not even unambiguous indicators of such a development. State capitalism comprises, on the one hand, a wide range of diversified forms of intervention, besides nationalization and state investments and, on the other hand, the expansion of the state sector may also take place foɪ the lack of or owing to the counteracting effect of, other factors, in conformity with, or subordinated to, the interests of local (or foreign) private capital. From this it follows that the existence of this criterion of a socialist-oriented development can only be analysed and assessed "*in concreto*" in the thorough knowledge of the economic relations and structure of the country concerned.[33]

As far as this metamorphosis or "over-expansion" of state capitalism starting a socialist oriented development is concerned, we can distinguish, according to the relative development of class relations, *two main types* (with several combinations of intermediate variants):

(a) Characteristic of the first type is that at the time of the rise of state capitalism no substantial local capital is yet available, the national bourgeoisie is either undeveloped or lacking altogether, and even the subsequent development of local capital *lags behind* the development of state capitalism.

Thus the expansion and strengthening of the system of state capitalism means not so much the restriction of the already acquired position of local capital—as such hardly exists at all—but rather the limitation of its coming into being. State capitalism of this type is therefore directed partly against foreign capital, and partly the local capitalist elements that may arise from the transformation of the precapitalistic forms of society and economy. Thus it expresses in this respect a specific economic relationship between state and private capital in which private capital (i.e. local private capital) is virtually non-existent, but the danger of its coming into existence is imminent. This danger arises from the wide survival of the precapitalistic remnants, the direction of whose further development and transformation, by the way, points to capitalism via commodity production.

It is, of course, not a matter of no concern at all, what character these precapitalist remnants have. Wherever precapitalism means predominantly primitive communal relations, there the traditions of communal ownership and the traditional community spirit contradict the tendency of private ecoɾiomy, however different the mode of production is from that of a socialist economy. It makes it at least easier for the state to solve the problem of introducing modern forms of economy under the exclusion or

---

[33] "A distinction should be made between several types of nationalization, according to the specific aim underlying it and the political climate in which it occurs... *negative* nationalization aimed at saving from bankruptcy private capitalist firms... *functional* nationalization of public services, and *progressive* nationalization, undertaken under the pressure of a powerful left-wing movement." (I. Sachs: *Patterns of Public Sector in Underdeveloped Economies*, p. 64.)

restriction of capitalist development. It is not accidental that this type of socialist-oriented development has found its historical application in those African countries where the precapitalist remnants include strong elements of primitive communal relations.

(b) Typical of the *second type* of socialist-oriented development is the fact that the formation of state capitalism starts under the conditions or even under the rule of an already existing local capital and thus of a *relatively significant local bourgeoisie.* The process of the strengthening of state capitalism gains, however, such a momentum in performing the tasks arising from the necessary liquidation of underdevelopment and under the pressure of social forces as local capital is unable to keep it under control.

This usually occurs when an obstacle to development is removed in an explosive way (e.g. the conquest of the strategic positions of foreign capital), or when radical measures are taken against the speculative and growth-impeding activity of a part of the local bourgeoisie. This usually sudden extension of the sphere of state capitalism is, as a rule, accompanied by the wresting of important positions from local capital.

This type of development is naturally much closer to the transformation that has taken place in the socialist countries, as both types of transformation mean challenges to the already existing local capital, and involve a deviation from the *capitalist* road *already* taken, after which any turn in the direction of capitalist development would be equivalent to a bourgeois restoration or at least some of its elements. This is especially the case when the national bourgeoisie has already previously played a leading role in running the state machinery.

But along with the usually much higher proportion of the precapitalistic remnants and the less significant power and rather secondary role of local capital, the main difference between them is shown in the fact that the anticapitalist changeover in these countries is not ushered in by a socialist revolution. The working class has not yet been able to rise to power, and the activity of local private capital, though restricted, does not cease to exist, and continues to play a—sometimes important—role in economic develop-ment.

Consequently, the danger of a bourgeois take-over, the possibility of a return to the capitalist way of development is much greater, and this danger stems not only from the tendencies of private ownership that may arise from the liquidation of the precapitalistic remnants, but mainly from the activity of existing private capital.

The situation may, of course, be very different here, too, from country to country, depending on whether national capital has acquired positions only at the periphery of the economy, in the shadow of foreign capital, or has become significant also as industrial and bank capital, and whether foreign capital has given rise to a proletariat much exceeding the development level and range of the activity of local private capital, or, concentrating mainly in the fields of trade and finance, has left the "production" of the proletariat to local capital.

Hence, the expansion of state capitalism, or even the predominance of state and community ownership, differs from the socialist transformation not only by preceding the latter, that is, by its being established without a socialist revolution, but also by the fact that the social forces supporting it are fairly undeveloped and changeable.

4. FACTORS INFLUENCING THE DIRECTION OF FURTHER DEVELOPMENT

The fate of state capitalism, the realization of a socialist transformation or a capitalist way of development, depends primarily on those internal economic processes which have an effect on social stratification and the position of the various classes.

The question is usually raised in this form: is it possible, under the *specific international* and/or *specific internal conditions*, to develop a socialist socio-economic system when its social basis "par excellence", the industrial working class, has not yet developed.

As far as the "international social basis" of a socialist transformation is concerned, it is true that the existence and support of the socialist countries may mean some protection against interventions on behalf of capitalist restoration. The significance of this factor is hard to *overestimate*, but it cannot supersede the internal social basis. As long as the liquidation of underdevelopment takes place within the framework of the national economy, i.e. *not* in the wake of a radical social transformation of the whole world, the socio-economic processes too take place mostly at the level of the national economy. Thus the analogy, or even theory, which projects the role of the urban basis of socialism (industry and industrial proletariat) in determining the socialist transformation of the rural areas to the international plane, and denies the necessity of the industrial and proletarian basis of socialism in relation to the developing countries, the "village" of the world, proves to be a deceptive illusion.

No doubt, one of the most conspicuous characteristics of the existing internal class relations is the wide gap between the living conditions of the rural and urban working people, the extremely low income level and great exploitation of the agrarian strata, and their way of life that call for radical changes. But can these strata constitute the basis of a socialist development—*for lack* of the urban working class or *instead of* the urban workers' élite living in much more favourable conditions than the rural strata? Can rural socialist transformation carried out in the framework of a comprehensive cooperative movement and/or the ancient traditional communities really provide a sufficient and stable basis for the socialist development of the *whole* economy and society?

The question has not only social and political implications but also economic ones, too. If the answer is in the affirmative, then the *absolute*, not only the relative and temporary, priority of rural development in the programme of economic development follows from it. In this case state capitalism must ensure an absorption and utilization of surplus which leads, over and above the reduction of urban discretionary and conspicuous consumption and the correction of the existing income inequalities, to the fastest possible development of the agrarian sector, with the other sectors and branches serving that development.

Agriculture, however, is unable to play the role of the leading sector in a modern, developed economy. The *general* direction of the development of the productive forces leads from the agrarian and agrarian-industrial economies to the industrial-agrarian and industrial economies. And if socialism is destined to accelerate (and not paralyse) this development, then rural development may be the transitory phase and means of the rational preparation of industrialization (and as such the most important one), but by no means the final objective of economic policy. Consequently, the stable social basis of socialist development must be built, if only for *economic* reasons, in the industry.

At the same time, the processes going on in the rural sectors of the developing countries and the development of agriculture itself make it dubious whether the rural basis of socialism could be sufficient and lasting.

If agriculture was for a long time a source of *capitalist* tendencies in the European socialist countries too, it is even more true in the developing countries where it is even more difficult to raise industry to a leading sector. In many developing countries, especially in Africa, unlike in Europe after the agrarian reforms, no strong spirit of private ownership has developed. But, whether the agrarian reform here is directed against foreign plantations, or "feudal" estates or even the primitive prefeudal forms of land tenure only, it necessarily raises not only the question of what the economic and organizational forms most appropriate for the liquidation of underdevelopment are, but it also poses the problem of the future of the private sector of agriculture as well.

The formation and spread of the *cooperative form* is a fairly general phenomenon. It can, however, have very *different contents*, depending on the dominant factor determining socio-economic development. The cooperative form itself may include a variety of forms, some of which (e.g. the marketing-purchasing cooperatives or the cooperatives) are also suitable for pooling capitalist economies and accelerating their development, but even producers' cooperatives with the common ownership of the means of production may become capitalist enterprises based on capitalist group ownership and operating as kinds of "joint stock companies".

410

The transition to commodity production within the traditional communities and the increase of external influence may be accompanied by the tendency of strengthening individualism, including the danger of the spontaneous disintegration of such communities.

It is the "economic environment", the effect of the leading sector of the economy on production relations and, for the lack or weakness of that sector, state intervention itself, which determines the social content of the cooperatives and the fate of the traditional communities.

Even in the case of the predominance of cooperatives (and communes), that is, of the economic and organizational forms characteristic of a socialist agriculture, the system of state capitalism extending over the whole economy and restricting capitalist tendencies, cannot be dispensed with. It is even more indispensable where the consistent implementation of the agrarian reform has not been concluded, which anyway hinders the liquidation of underdevelopment, or where, after the land reform, the small peasant holding has become the basic form of agriculture.

Small commodity production, which came into being perhaps as a result of the transformation of subsistence economies by means of state intervention, may become the source of capitalist tendencies and the natural law of its development is the *class differentiation* of the peasantry. Considering that the restriction of the working of this law is no easy task in the socialist countries either, even under the conditions of a socialist industry, trade and finances, then it is definitely much more difficult in the developing countries where these conditions are almost entirely absent. And the working of this law may have disastrous consequences not only for the labour market, the development of the rural productive forces and the social state of the rural population, but it may even block the road to further socialist development.

The dominant role of agriculture in the production of national income in general and in the export production in particular, makes it a real danger in most countries that even in the case of industrial nationalizations and state control over foreign trade and finances, and with the simultaneous anti-capitalist development in the other branches of the economy, there may develop and strengthen, for lack of an intensive and appropriately orientated state intervention, a strong national capital in this sector that may stop or hold up socialist-oriented development.

From this it follows that the rural basis of socialist transformation in a not yet industrialized society can perform only a *temporary function*. (This *temporary* character means not the subsequent termination of this basis but its complementation with something more important.)

Whether it really performs this function or not, depends on (1) whether, economically, it succeeds in creating, by the expansion of its surplus productive capacity, the accumulation sources of industrialization; (2) whether, *socially*, rural development is not accompanied by a process of differentiation leading to the formation of a rural bourgeois stratum; and in connection with the latter conditions; (3) whether the communal forms of the appropriation of the surplus produced become (or remain) dominant against the individual forms of appropriation, and whether the utilization of surplus takes place in keeping with the interests of the working classes of society and in compliance with the requirements of the acceleration of economic development (including the task of industrialization). The realization of these conditions requires not only the increased controlling and guiding-influencing role of the state but also the intensive activity of the social and political organizations. If this involves the danger of a possible growth of state bureaucracy and of the strengthening of the power and privileged material position of the ruling élite, then this indicates only the difficulty, but does not reduce the real possibility and extraordinary importance of such a transition. And if in the countries starting from the basis of a not yet industrialized, predominantly agricultural and extremely backward economy the *process of building socialism* is longer and progresses by trial and error, involving perhaps more mistakes and "infantile disorders" than would be in an industrialized, advanced society, this again indicates only the difficulties of such a development but *by no means* the wrong direction of it.

Even if the rural working population and the rural economy are unable to perform the function of a *real* social and economic basis of socialist development, the former despite its however revolutionary character, the latter despite its development to whatever extent, they may serve to a certain extent and *temporarily* as substitutes for it, making it easier for this basis to develop.

The special importance of this transition is duly emphasized by the fact that the improvement of the situation of the rural working population and rural development in general have become, *on the one hand*, a central issue of economic policy, in view of such problems as the expansion of the internal market, the mobilization of the sources of accumulation, the budget and foreign exchange revenues of the state, public nutrition, the easing of import-dependence, open and disguised unemployment, the levelling of striking income inequalities, etc., that is, they coincide with the general trend of the acute development needs. *On the other hand*, the transition itself means the utilization of the available and mobilizable social forces for a socialist-orientated development, instead of waiting idly for the formation of a more appropriate social basis.

In addition to, but of course *not* independently of, the economic and the attending social processes—such as rural development, industrialization, and the appropriation and utilization of surplus in general—further development is influenced by a number of other, social and political processes, among them several factors related to certain *specific circumstances*. When analysing the distorted, heterogeneous social

412

structure of the developing countries we emphasized that the boundaries between the social classes and groups are much more blurred in these countries than in Europe, and that relatively wide *intermediate strata* may develop along these boundaries, in the marginal spheres of the heterogeneous structures, which may also play an important role in politics. We have also pointed out that class consciousness may be strongly influenced and offset, as a result of the intensive effect of the traditional social elements, by other forms of social consciousness such as traditional religion, the sense of belonging to a tribe, kinship, sect loyalty, the sense of nationalism, etc. This specific character of the social structure and processes provides the explanation for the fact that the political changes and shifts quite rarely take place along a more or less clear line of class boundaries.[34]

Let us enumerate a few of the specific factors and circumstances affecting the political processes.

(a) *The inherited forms of political organization.* The liberated countries inherited more or less *ready-made* organizational forms from the colonizers. They were usually the replica of Western parliamentary and party systems which have developed on the basis of an entirely different historical and social reality. These forms do not correspond to the requirements of a system of representation built on real communities. They are either gradually abolished (and this in itself involves great political shifts and regrouping), or they strengthen further the isolation and alienation from society, of the group of functionaries raised above fictitious communities. In this connection, we may refer again to the analogy of the Asian mode of production where "the group of public functionaries ceased to perform real public functions and developed into a ruling *class* when the communities, whose representatives these chiefs and officials originally had been, broke up or were transformed".[35] The only difference is that the group of public functionaries of the developing countries was already an alienated group in the colonial period and was in contact—e.g. under the British type of colonial administration—only at the lower end with a real community, the tribe. (In this case, however, the transformation of the tribal chiefs into paid

---

[34] It is common knowledge that after the seizure of power and also in the subsequent process of development *internal shifts and regroupings* may occur among the progressive forces which fought for political power. Part of the revolutionary forces fighting against colonialism, e.g., may regard their struggle as completed after gaining independence and demand a greater share in its benefits as their just deserts. This gives rise to a real danger that the posts and roles in state administration which have become vacant with the removal of the former oppressors and privileged persons, only "change hands". Therefore, the progressive political power, if it is to remain as such, must also be prepared to face a sort of resistance or negative striving on the part of its former followers, too. Such political and economic decisions may then create additional political tensions—*within the framework of power.*

[35] F. Tőkei: Az ázsiai termelési mód (The Asiatic mode of production). *Valóság*, No. 6, 1962.

civil servants destroyed the real, political and religious-authoritarian, non-economic foundations of the inner representation system of this community.) Though this alienation of the group of public functionaries eases after independence—as a result, e.g., of the replacement of expatriate officials by local ones—,yet its tendency stays unchanged and it is, as we have seen, usually along this line that we can look for the tendencies of the formation of a new bourgeois class.

(b) *The tendency of the formation of the one-party system* resulted from the inadequacy of the inherited political forms and the blurred character of the boundaries of social classes. It emerges, as a rule, from the national resistance against foreign oppression, that is, from an independence movement embracing the broad masses of society. It is usually *not after* a differentiation process, *not* on the basis of the identity of interest, concerning the direction of internal development of the working classes already in power, that it comes into being. In other words, it is not built upon the process of social integration already under way. This accounts for its special character and the instability of the formation itself.

The one-party system may, of course, be filled with very different contents. It cannot, however, abolish the internal social contradictions which unfold more and more with the outlines of the social classes becoming more distinct. Its existence, however, and consequently the fact that these contradictions tend to manifest themselves within its own organization, give new characteristics to political development, too. The fact that the one-party system merges at its top with state administration, provides the means of state power to oppress or solve the contradictions within the party, and makes, on the other hand, the direction of economic state intervention directly dependent on the power relations *within* the one-party system.

(c) *Tribal and caste systems.* Their existence and intensity exert an effect on the political processes, and even on the forms of organization, not only indirectly, through the formation of consciousness, but also directly.

(d) *Religion.* In addition to its cohesive or divisive effects which cross the social class boundaries, it influences the way of political thinking, too. Much depends on which particular religion is dominant as there are substantial differences in this respect between the Muslim, Buddhist and Christian religions. It is also important which strata this particular religion is primarily tied to, and what parts of its teaching are most pronounced. (There are considerable differences here too, even between the individual Muslim countries.)

(e) *The progress in nation formation.* Much depends on whether this process exceeds in its tendency the given state boundaries of the country concerned (in which case it is already an external factor), or conforms to the state boundaries, or lies well within them. In the latter case new bases and boundaries appear, beyond those already mentioned, for the political groupings and shifts.

414

If the process of the creation of a new nation exceeds the inherited artificial boundaries, or if one or another factor of this process (e.g. language or culture) gives rise to the tendency of forming larger communities, this may as an external effect influence the development of the countries concerned. There will be equalizing effects at work between the economic, social and political processes of these countries, which may promote or hinder development.

The tendency of the large communities developing into a nation exerts a *preserving* effect on all those forms of traditional social consciousness and customs which are common also beyond the existing country boundaries (e.g. Arab culture and customs, the Muslim religion, etc.). It also gives a new impulse to the integration movements. At the same time, it may modify the grouping and distribution of social forces and provide greater scope for political "landslides".

(f) In addition to promoting the development of productive forces and the transformation of distorted economic structures and to providing a kind of protection against external economic impacts, *integration* and its various forms and degrees also affect the integrated countries by demanding increasing state economic intervention and the development of state capitalism, and by strengthening the mutual socio-political effects between the individual member countries.

(g) Such *mutual effects* may, of course, develop not only between the integrating countries but also between the developing countries in general, especially if they are neighbouring countries. The successful implementation of an economic task or social reform in one country exerts a stimulating effect on another to solve the same problems in a similar and the fastest possible way.

It is obvious, and, therefore, perhaps needless to add, that the direction and course of the further development of developing countries are strongly influenced, besides the enumerated and other specific factors (but usually in connection with them), by the development of the whole world economy and international politics.

The dialectical relationship between national and international aspects, processes and factors of development in general, and the discussed external causes, historical roots and still effective conditions of underdevelopment clearly suggest that even before a complete and radical transformation of the world economic system a lot can and should be done not only inside the individual countries, but also internationally.

The forces which are interested in gradual but purposeful changes of international relations are, indeed, considerable and strong enough, embracing not only the poor masses of developing countries, their progressive movements and governments, but also the socialist countries and all those democratic forces and social strata which oppose or suffer from the dominance of monopolistic companies and the anarchistic operation, due to the monopoly-capitalistic rules of game, of the world economy.

This explains why the demand to change the existing international economic "order" has become so popular and pressing, and consequently, why even those interested in, and benefiting from, the present "order" do not oppose frankly, but pay instead lip-service to the idea of establishing a New International Economic Order.

5. THE IDEA OF A
NEW INTERNATIONAL ECONOMIC ORDER

Though the idea of a new international economic order can be traced back many years[36], it has gained general acceptance and increasing popularity only quite recently, since about the Sixth Special Session of the General Assembly on Raw Materials and National Resources in April-May 1974, which adopted the "Declaration" and the "Programme of Action on the Establishment of a New International Economic Order" followed by the "Charter of Economic Rights and Duties of States" adopted by the General Assembly in December 1974.

These UN documents represent, no doubt, a historical milestone in the approach to the development problem of the world even if they are necessarily compromises only, still involving a great many controversies, ambiguities, inconsistencies and remnants of the old approach, and have not been adopted without strong reservations and resistance (particularly by the leading capitalist countries).[37] As a matter of fact, this is the first time that the international economic relations in their structural and institutional complexity have been placed under a critical re-appraisal not only by Marxism or a few other progressive theories and by the representatives of a few countries committed to socialism, but by a wide range of international politicians, economists, diplomats from all over the world and by the absolute majority of the UN family.

The need for a change has been almost generally accepted.[38] But, of course, the ways, means, and the objectives of change have been interpreted

[36] A UN document notes that the measures taken with this idea in view "culminate in more than 25 years of steadily growing UN efforts to solve the problems of an inequitable, poorly balanced and increasingly inefficient world economy". (*Decisions for development.*) In chronicling the evolution of the concept within the UN, one should certainly refer to the first UNCTAD in 1964 and to the words of U Thant about the way towards "a more just and rational economic order".

[37] "Nevertheless", as B.T.G. Chidzero correctly points out, "it is clear that the key elements, however controversial, relate essentially to the questions of equity and the sovereign equality and democratic independence of nations..." (B. T. G. Chidzero: An Agenda for Negotiations. *Development Dialogue.* 1976, No. 1, Uppsala, p. 28.)

[38] Expressing the same views as Henry Kissinger, the then US State Secretary, William E. Simon, the US Treasury Secretary stressed that "the answer to the problems of development

in a very different manner—according to ideological as well as practical considerations, to individual, national, class and group interests, etc.

The most positive elements in the general demand for, and in the implementation concept of, the NIEO seem to be the following:

(a) strong emphasis on economic independence and sovereignty of all countries, including their free choice of the socio-economic system, the principle of national sovereignty over natural resources and all economic activities, as well as the right to nationalization according to national laws;

(b) the right of countries to full compensation for exploitation, damages and losses caused by colonialism and neo-colonial practices, etc.;

(c) deep concern about the activity of transnational (multinational) corporations, the need for regulating, re-orientating and controlling their operations, for measures against their restrictive business practices, the idea of an international code of conduct;[39]

(d) demand for a radical improvement of the international supply of appropriate technologies, a stand against technological monopolies and dependence, revision of the industrial property system, emphasis on the building up of the technological capabilities of developing countries, the development of their own technological (and research) bases, the idea of an international code of conduct on the transfer of technologies;[40]

(e) the (UNCTAD) concept of an integrated programme of commodities, breaking (unfortunately still only in a limited field) with the traditional piece-meal "commodity-by-commodity approach", raising the complex problem of regulating the world market for the benefits of all nations interested in greater stability and, especially, for those of disadvantaged countries;

(f) a markedly increased attention to the promotion of economic co-operation amongst developing countries, the idea of a collective self-reliance (if it is not interpreted as autarchy and isolationism);[41]

(g) growing concern about internal inequalities, social gaps and tensions within countries, the increasingly emphasized linkage between the necessary change in international and national order;[42]

---

lies in strengthening the current international economic system rather than in a radical restructuring of it." (See B. T. G. Chidzero: Op. cit., p. 29.)

[39] The idea of a compulsory code of conduct legally binding on the multinational corporations meets, of course, with their resistance.

[40] Here again, the debated question is whether the code of conduct should be a legally binding instrument or an optional one.

[41] "Self-reliance" is often interpreted as a more or less complete isolation from the developed world. Such an isolation, however, is hardly feasible in the short run because of their inherited structural ties with the metropolitan countries. On the other hand, it would be hardly advantageous either since the developing countries would deprive themselves of the very achievements of humanity's science and technology, which they have also contributed to, and which should be the common treasure of mankind.

[42] "The growing disparity between the incomes of different countries (developed and developing), resulting from the conditions in which material goods are produced and the

(h) a call for certain institutional reforms in multinational and international organizations in the spirit of full, non-discriminating representation and democratization.

In addition to the above issues, which are not necessarily new in all respects and details or free from ambiguities and controversial interpretations either, we have to refer to some other important or partial issues which, as already agreed measures or still debated proposals only, also belong to the "basket" now:

(i) in respect of commodity trade and prices:

— setting up of international commodity stocking (stock-piling) arrangements;

— harmonization of stocking (stock-piling) policies and the setting up of co-ordinated national stocks;

— establishment of pricing arrangements, in particular negotiated price ranges, which would be periodically reviewed and appropriately revised, taking into account, *inter alia*, movements in the prices of imported manufactured goods, exchange rates, production costs and world inflation and levels of production and consumption;

— internationally agreed supply management measures, including export quotas and production policies and, where appropriate, multilateral long-term supply and purchasing commitments;

— improvements and enlargement of compensatory financing facilities for the stabilization, along a growing trend, of the export earnings of developing countries;

— improvement of the market access for the primary and processed products of developing countries through multilateral trade measures in multilateral trade negotiations, improvement of schemes of generalized preferences and their extension beyond the period originally envisaged, trade promotion measures, etc.;

— the creation of a Common Fund to be supported by both exporting and importing countries in order to finance international stocks;

— establishment of producers' associations for a wide range of important commodities of export interest to developing countries;

— concrete effective measures against those transnational corporations which dominate many commodity markets as monopolistic buyers from developing countries;

— the concept of industrial cooperation arrangements at governmental and other levels taking various forms, such as coproduction and

---

present system of international trade, is paralleled within each nation by inequality of distribution among the various social categories and frequently, too, by a discrepancy between town and country. The demarcation line between poverty and wealth does not, therefore, only separate countries into two groups, but is found again within individual countries and between geographical areas." (Moving Towards Change. UNESCO, Paris, 1976, pp. 13–14.)

418

specialization agreements, joint ventures, licencing and sub-contracting agreements, joint tendering and marketing;

— expansion, by various methods, of the absorptive capacity of developed countries for manufactured products from developing countries;

— the idea of working out a set of guidelines on restrictive business practices and measures to control the activity of transnational corporations in manufacture trade;

— an appropriate re-orientation of the industrial policies of developing countries for faster growing and more broadly-based industrialization to meet the basic needs of their population and to reduce dependence on transnational corporations;

(j) in regard to monetary and financial issues:

— *a reform of the international monetary system* to suit the needs of the development and long-term capital movement to developing countries;

— an early and general attainment of the 0.7 per cent target for official development assistance;

— a link between SDR (special drawing rights) creation and additional development finance in the International Monetary Fund;

— the proposal to use part of ODA funds to subsidize the interest costs on loans to developing countries in order to increase the amount of concessional loans without increasing budgetary outlays;

— the idea of a special "development tax" on incomes in developed countries to finance bilateral and/or multilateral interest-subsidy schemes;

— the proposal of granting moratoria on the official debts of the most heavily affected countries;

— the idea of an international fund for the refinancing of service payments on the commercial debts of middle-income developing countries, etc.

In addition to the above issues, several other important ones, which are on the agenda of various UN bodies and international forums, also belong to the general concept of NIEO (such as, e.g., a special programme for the least-developed countries), not to mention some other related ideas of a "new order" (such as in the sphere of science and technology, information and communications, etc.).

Such and similar ideas, principles and measures under the umbrella of the New International Economic Order clearly manifest the increasing awareness of a crisis situation in the international economy and of the need for urgent changes. They also reflect *controversies and differences in approach and interests*.

Without going into the details of the great many ambiguities and inconsistencies or controversies, which can be observed in the total set of principles, recommended measures and implementation methods of

NIEO[43], and particularly in the debates and negotiations on it, we have to note that one of the greatest shortcomings of the NIEO "basket" and negotiations is the mixing up of certain relevant strategic issues with short-run palliative measures, of sound, well-based principles and demands with naive illusions or contradictory recommendations. This gives room for manipulations aimed to present palliatives as real remedies and to make use of the conflict of interests in the short-term reforms of trade and aid with a "zero-sum-game" for dividing the forces which are interested in and support more fundamental changes.

It is regrettable, though by no means accidental, that since the first NIEO documents and debates there has been an obvious shift in international negotiations and conferences away from the most positive, strategic issues (those mainfested mainly in the Declaration and the Charter about economic sovereignty, national control, compensation for exploitation, structural changes, etc.) towards some minor pragmatic measures, palliatives and short-term issues.

The most crucial question which can be raised in respect of almost all proposed short-term measures on trade and finance is the following: *who* will actually benefit from them and who will pay the costs? The privileges, monopoly positions, appropriated incomes are not allocated according to geographical frontiers in the world. The historical and present responsibility for the perpetuation of underdevelopment in the Third World lies not simply upon the "North" as a whole, nor even upon the peoples of the colonizing countries, but on certain classes and business groups within the leading capitalist countries. On the other hand, the burdens of international disadvantages and of exploitation from both outside and inside rest upon

[43] Besides a few unambiguously positive, substantial and basic principles of NIEO, which, following from a thorough critical analysis of the world capitalist economy, point to the aim and means of national sovereignty, to changes in production structures, relations of ownership and control, to rules, etc., some of the elements of NIEO are still related to the conventional orthodox ideas of Western economies on international trade and factor mobility (such as reflecting the illusions about the free flows of commodities, the promotion of foreign investments, the further expansion of the existing division of labour, etc.). Other components and actually most of the negotiated issues of the Action Programme stem from the new school of international economics, which not only criticizes the market mechanism for its imperfections and monopolistic business practice, the unequal distribution of benefits from trade and technological development, call for reforms in international trade and finance, but creates also illusions about a possible solution by market reforms, income redistribution and the connection of the TNCs' behaviour, about the aim of "just prices", "equal exchange", etc. For a critical appraisal of the conception of NIEO, see T. Szentes: The Strategic Issues of NIEO and Global Negotiations. *Second Congress of the Associations of Third World Economists*, April 26–30, 1981, Havana. The New International Economic Order: Redistribution or Restructuring? In C. T. Saunders (ed.): *East—West—South. Economic Interactions between Three Worlds*. The Macmillan Press, London, 1981. The conception of a New International Order: is it a fashionable slogan or a feasible strategy? *IPSA Tokyo Round Table Conference*. March 29—April 1, 1982, Tokyo.

the working masses of developing countries. Measures aimed at helping the poor and at disadvantaging the rich countries do not necessarily help the poor and tax the rich. Moreover, taking into account the inside position of foreign capital, particularly the MNCs in developing countries, it is easy to visualize cases when some measures, though made or suggested with good intentions, such as the general preference system, the promotion of manufacture exports of developing countries, or financing international stocks, etc., may actually benefit foreign companies rather than the poor countries themselves.

As regards the strategic issues and principles (the implementation of which does not necessarily mean a "zero-sum-game", at least not for the working masses of all countries, but instead can result in benefits for all), let us point to some of the possible implications and related practical steps and measures which could bring us nearer to the final solution, together with a few thoughts of ours concerning possible progress in various fields.

(1) The present "order" of the international capitalist economy involves, as we have seen, unequal power structures and dominance. The new, alternative international economic order must be built on, and promote, the *equality of partners*, excluding the opportunity for one to curtail the legitimate sovereignty of others.

It is no accident that the developing countries demand respect for their *national sovereignty* also in the economic sense, including the right to nationalization, full control over their natural resources and the economy as a whole. And it is not accidental either that the more the national leadership of a developing country is committed to self-reliance, development and social justice, the more it is concerned about the liquidation of foreign dominance and influence in the economy. The nationalization of foreign assets in the key sectors of the economy finds itself necessarily on the agenda of development policy. Such measures of national development policy, infringing the business interests of foreign enterprises, however, have often to face the danger of retaliation by the foreign capital concerned even if the national takeover of foreign assets is in consonance with the "international norms" or customs of nationalization.

The developing countries, particularly those with weak bargaining power vis-à-vis the giant foreign firms, obviously need international protection and assistance against retaliation and for reparations for the damage caused by them.

In view of the absolute importance of complete national sovereignty over the economy as a precondition for working out and implementing appropriate national development strategies, and for establishing mutually dependent relations based on sovereign equality among nations, it would be reasonable and necessary to establish an *international economic security system* to defend all states exercising their sovereign rights from retaliatory measures. This system could be based on multilateral interstate agreements

421

which would include commitments by each state to refrain from interfering in the economic affairs of other states and to take full responsibility for the activity of their enterprises and citizens abroad.

(2) Unequal power structures in the international economy, however, are also related to the inequalities of the *production structures and division of labour*.

The strategic objective in eliminating the international development gap is obvious. Instead of developing and perpetuating the primary-producing and/or manufacturing enclaves, efforts must be made to ensure that developing countries establish—in consonance with their natural and human endowments—those basic industries which, given their sectoral linkages, may become the engines for developing their national economy, and within it primarily agriculture, and for creating appropriate centres of scientific and technological research and product development. Accordingly, progress should be made in developing international economic cooperation gradually but increasingly towards an *intra-industrial* division of labour and towards extending it to research and development. This would encourage the elimination of the monopoly over scientific and technological achievements and knowledge.

But in order to attain these long-term strategic aims, a kind of international cooperation is needed, even in the short run, which makes commodity exchange, on the basis of the existing complementarities, the planned means of developing new complementarities.

The aim of restructuring the international division of labour and making it more equal and balanced requires in particular an overall integration of all relevant issues, which are rather fragmented and isolated from each other in negotiations and action programmes (undoubtedly for practical reasons). First of all, the issue of primary commodities and of manufactures could and should be much more closely connected with the aim of working out and implementing patterns and programmes of international cooperation, in which the countries importing primary commodities give direct assistance to producers to build up their processing industry based on local primary production. Consequently, both the importers and the producers would shift the composition of their exports and imports gradually and in a mutually planned way towards more balanced and equal structures. This reflects progress towards the inter- and intra-industrial division of labour.

In other words, in certain fields new cooperation schemes could be put into practice which link, in a long-term planned programme, the import of primary products from developing countries with the support of development of their manufacturing industries (e.g. by exporting related machinery and gradually increasing imports of new manufacturing products) built on the given local raw materials. It could also link the supply of technologies for new industries with the support aimed at making them increasingly capable not only of adopting but also researching, developing and producing technologies locally. Such long-term cooperation schemes could resolve the contradiction between the strategic aim of developing a more equitable system for the international division of labour and the existing complementarities of unequal production structures. Such schemes could also take the sharp edge off the debates on "just" or "equity" prices of primary commodities versus manufacture prices. Furthermore, they could mitigate the conflicts of interest between producers and consumers at least insofar as, by implementing such a restructuring of trade through building adequate structural adjustments into the *national plans* of the partners, these long-term cooperation agreements can compensate present losses or gains by future losses or gains.

(3) International cooperation and the progressive integration of national economies into the international economy should not be accompanied—as has been the case of developing countries up to now—by the disintegration of the former. Instead, it should promote *internal (and regional) integration*, the elimination of "dualistic" socio-economic structures and rural-urban gaps.

The requirement of internal socio-economic integration should be one of the most fundamental criteria of investment choices, project selection and cooperation policy. Accordingly, a much greater emphasis than placed before on production and trade *for* rural development is required in development assistance.

(4) The required alternative pattern of the international division of labour may develop, of course, in various ways and different *forms of co-operation*. Ample evidence suggests, however, that the form of international economic relations which has characterized both the "colonial" and the emerging new patterns, namely the one-way transfer of private investment capital by foreign companies, can hardly be appropriate for the development of a (really) New International Economic Order. This form has been accompanied by the opposite transfer of investment incomes, and has one-sidedly resulted in cumulatively growing and unterminated foreign property in the economy of developing countries as well as in foreign control over important parts of their national economy.

Though *foreign investments* by private capital export may act as an effective vehicle of the transfer of financial and managerial resources, provided that their negative consequences and effects are prevented or counteracted by government regulations, there is sufficient reason to suggest that this form of transfer should increasingly be replaced by alternative forms of economic cooperation, or be modified according to the requirements of national sovereignty over the national economy.

Developing countries may need to cooperate with foreign companies not only for financial reasons, but primarily to acquire new technologies to foreign markets or to share with these countries the risk involved in launching and developing economic ventures and new productive branches.

Realistic solutions must be found on *how* to reconcile the need for cooperation with the requirements of national sovereignty.

There are great many forms of cooperation which already exist or have been recommended by scholars, and seem to be suitable for avoiding or gradually eliminating the most harmful consequences of cooperation with foreign companies. One example is the type of production and/or market cooperation which is widely practiced in East—West relations. Such cooperation does not involve foreign ownership and control. Another example is the schemes which terminate foreign ownership by contract or programme, a gradual "fading-out" of foreign capital ownership participation by converting direct investment into a kind of loan capital to be repaid from the rising revenues of the established productive enterprise. Mention should also be made of the type of joint ventures which are established and operated on a truly reciprocal basis. These ventures entail a symmetrical pattern of distribution of ownership, operation and incomes, and effective control by each partner state over the part of its activity which affects the national economy.

(5) The grave problem of the cumulative indebtedness of many developing countries certainly deserves special attention. Besides immediate measures (such as those suggested at UNCTAD) to release the countries in the most serious situation from their debt burden (the costs of which should be borne primarily by those who have profited from these countries' economies through exploitation), there is a need for new loan policies, new patterns of debtor–creditor cooperation. These should include improvements in the repayment capacities and financial self-reliance of the recipient country. These improvements could be made by adjusting debt servicing in size and time to the increase, resulting from the use of the loan, in production and export capacities, and by channelling repayments, if possible in kind, that is, through the export of newly created production capacities. The strategic issue is, however, the gradual liquidation of structural inequalities which reproduce the need for financial transfers.

Let us recall the principle, stated in the Declaration on the Establishment of the New International Economic Order, of the right of the countries concerned "to full compensation . . . for . . . exploitation." This should be a substantial source of *financial transfers* to developing countries. Let us also stress the need for increased international financial assistance to poor countries, based upon solidarity throughout the world. We believe that international assistance may be considerably and directly increased if the arms race is stopped for good and measures are taken to curb military and other inhuman and wasteful, unproductive expenditures.

(6) The problem of *international cooperation in science and technology* is highly relevant not only to the issue of private capital flows, foreign investments and the participation of MNCs, but also to problems in foreign trade, industrialization and finance in the world economy, East—West

relations and perspectives for peaceful cooperation between countries with different socio-economic systems. Moreover, it is important to the question of war or peace, too.

The prevailing anomalies, unfavourable conditions and harmful effects in the fields of industrial technology transfers and cooperation cannot be conclusive arguments for an isolation policy, for stopping international cooperation in science and technology. These problems do not even comprise good arguments for a general attack on the application of modern technologies as such in underdeveloped countries. Instead, they point to the need to give all nations easy access to the common treasure of human knowledge, to prevent science and technology from being misused for military purposes and to urge the arrangement of only those forms and terms of cooperation which do not involve technological monopolies, dependence and the transfer and use of inappropriate technologies. For all countries striving for sovereign equality and independent development, the establishment of their own technological basis and R and D capacities is a long-term imperative need. On the other hand, none of the countries (not even the most advanced) can afford to develop their own R and D bases in all fields, thus making their technological development completely independent of, and isolated from, those of others. International cooperation has become a natural need for all nations; it is also reinforced by the well-known ecological problems and the need for a more rational (and peaceful) utilization and management of the resources of the Earth.

The task is to reconcile national and international interests, to defend the developing countries from technological dependence, monopolistic subordination, unfair business practices, restrictions, brain drain and losses caused by pricing policy and inappropriate technology. It is also necessary to develop and put into practice the most proper (preferably complex but flexible) long-term and mutually planned forms of cooperation by collecting and spreading available information on such cooperation and improving its terms.

For this purpose it would be desirable to establish, wherever possible, a link between the transfer of ready-made technologies and assistance to developing local production and research capacities. (This could be done in such a way that foreign technical experts and advisors associate their activities, wherever possible, with the training of their local replacements.)

There is an urgent need for measures to reduce the harmful consequences of international *brain drain*, including the establishment of a bilateral, or preferably of a multilateral mechanism, and the need for compensatory payments for losses suffered by those developing countries which are short of qualified manpower. The general principle stated by the Declaration on the Establishment of a New International Economic Order, of the right to full compensation for all exploited, depleted and damaged resources, would implicitly apply here.

(7) Efforts on the part of developing countries, such as *internal, national development strategies* aimed at satisfying the *material and cultural needs of the masses* constitute an indispensable prerequisite for eliminating social inequalities and for overcoming mass misery and unemployment within developing countries. In other words, the creation of a new democratic international economic order implies the construction of a new, socially more equitable and economically viable democratic national order, the transformation of the distorted economic structure and the elimination of glaring social inequalities. This is a development strategy with a democratic content and representing national interests. It requires the mobilization and active participation of the working masses and their political struggle against anti-democratic forces and a new colonial influence.

Such a development strategy is, of course, much easier to implement if manifestations of anti-social behaviour, conspicuous luxury consumption and squandering in general (also experienced in developed countries and manipulated by business interests) are prevented from playing a role. From this follows the need to eliminate social inequalities and to give priority to the interests of the working masses all over the world.